NORMAN DOUGLAS

NORMAN DOUGLAS

A Biography

———◦———

Mark Holloway

SECKER & WARBURG
LONDON

First published in England 1976 by
Martin Secker & Warburg Limited
14 Carlisle Street, London W1V 6NN

Copyright © Mark Holloway 1976

SBN 436 20075 9

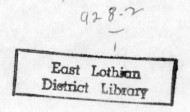

Printed in Great Britain by
Cox & Wyman Limited
London, Fakenham and Reading

To the memory
of many happy hours
too long ago
in the company of
KENNETH FYFE
MERVYN SAVILL
&
GEORGE THOMPSON
when the subject of this book
was often discussed

"The business of life is to enjoy oneself; everything else is a mockery": this does not necessarily mean the hedonist's oysters and champagne, as the reviewer of an earlier book of mine seemed to think. It means, for me at least, that one should always be able to do what one wants to do. That is the way to enjoy oneself . . . I, for example, seldom enjoyed myself more than while writing with infinite trouble a series of dull monographs. They who find these pamphlets unreadable, as well they may do, can look for something else. I pleasured my *Daimon* . . .

Late Harvest (1947)

Self-indulgence is what the ancients blithely called "indulging one's genius" . . . How all the glad warmth and innocence have faded out of that phrase!

Alone

The fact is, when a temptation becomes too great, I simply yield. What is the good, I say, of wrestling with the inevitable? At the same time, I take full responsibility for all my actions. I do not lay the blame on others.

The diarist of *Nerinda*

Always do what you please, and send every body to Hell, and take the consequences. Damned Good Rule of Life.

Inscription by ND in a
friend's copy of *Old Calabria*

I can conceive the subtlest and profoundest sage desiring nothing better than to retain, ever undiminished, a childlike capacity for [these] simple pleasures.

Fountains in the Sand

*

He is remarkable among the important writers of our time for a certain coherent simplicity . . . Douglas was sanguine and choleric, and above all, boyish. He had the hearty appetites and the objective curiosity of a healthy schoolboy. He often grumbled, but he never brooded. He looked out, not in . . . He was a very naughty old boy, rather than a very wicked old man.

Review of Nancy Cunard's *Grand Man*
in the Times Literary Supplement,
27 August 1954

Contents

List of Illustrations

Acknowledgments

My greatest debt is to the late Mr Kenneth Macpherson, Douglas' literary executor, who gave me access to his large collection of Douglas manuscripts, diaries, letters and other documents, allowed me to quote from his own reminiscences as well as from the whole body of Douglas' work, published and unpublished, protected my interest while I was working on the book, and good-humouredly endured and replied to a great many questions.

I am also deeply indebted to Mr Archie Douglas for replying to countless questions about his father, for lending me letters and his mother's diary, and for permission to quote freely from correspondence; and to Major J. S. Douglas of Tilquhillie, for reminiscences of his father and uncle, for other information about the family, for photographs, letters, other documents, and permission to quote from a letter.

Special thanks are due to Mr Alan Anderson, whose help has been extensive and whose continuing interest has been sustaining; to Mr Cecil Woolf, for help, interest, and his indispensable bibliography of Douglas' work; and to Mr A. S. Frere, for painstaking courtesy in answering an entire book annotated with questions. For information about the Douglasses in Austria I am much indebted to Mr Walter Fairholme; to Dr-Ingenieur Ernst Mahle, and to Frau Doris Kissenberth, who drew my attention to the novel *Violet*, and gave me numerous photographs; and to Dr Otto Wolf of St Anton, for facts I could never have obtained without his help.

For reading the original manuscript, for patience, generosity of time, and advice, grateful thanks to the late Professor Norman Holmes Pearson of Yale, and to Mr Michael Holroyd.

I am also deeply grateful to the following for all kinds of help and advice, and for permission to quote from interviews and correspondence: Sir Harold Acton, Mrs Ellen Aveline, the late Miss Natalie Barney, Professor Angus Bellairs, Mr T. B. Belk, Mrs Clare Bergqvist, Frau Eva Bornemann, the late Mrs Romaine Brooks, Bryher, Signor G. Carrozza, Mr David Carr, Mrs Ianthe Carswell, Mr Borys Conrad, Mr Edward Crankshaw, Mr Adam Curle, Mrs Valerie Cuthbert, Mrs Elizabeth David, Mr David Davies, the late Mr Tom Driberg MP (Lord Bradwell), Mr Geoffrey Ehlers, the late Mrs Emily Feild, Miss Gracie Fields, Mr Constantine FitzGibbon, the

late Mr E. M. Forster, Mr Donald Gallup, Mrs L. T. M. Gray, Mr Graham
Greene, Mr Ian Greenlees, Frau Dagny Gulbransson, Mr Clifford Har-
greaves, Sir Rupert Hart-Davis, Mrs Wyn Henderson, Mr Anthony
Hobson, the Hon Neil Hogg, the late Mrs Alice Honn, Mrs Madeleine
Hummel, the Revd John Hurst, the late Mr Edward Hutton, Mr Peter
Hutton, Mr Robin Jasper, Mrs Viola Johnson and Mr John Jukes Johnson,
Mr W. R. P. Johnstone, Mr Frederick R. Karl, Mrs Viva King, Mrs
Margaret Langdown, Mr Walter Leuba, Mr Walter Lowenfels, Mr D. M.
Low, Mr Mark Lutz, Mr Islay Lyons, Mr Andrew McKenna, the late Sir
Compton Mackenzie, Mr Ernest Martin, the late Professor John Mavro-
gordato, Dr Michael Mavrogordato, the late Mr Andrew Monypenny,
Dottoressa Moor, Mr Raymond Mortimer, the Hon Arnold Palmer, Mr
Ian Parsons, HRH Prince Paul of Yugoslavia, Monsieur Roger Peyrefitte,
Frau Prantl, Mr Maurice Richardson, Mr and Mrs Rissik, Mrs Maud
Rosenthal, Mr J. C. G. Rouse, the Hon Mrs Nancy Sandilands, Mr Alan
Searle, Mr Edwin Seaver, Mr and Mrs Martin Secker, Dr Anthony Storr,
the late Mr James Strachey, Mr John Symonds, Mrs Lola Szladits, Mrs
Myfanwy Thomas, Madame Yvonne Vismara, Mr Alec Waugh, Dame
Rebecca West, Mr Eric Whelpton, Mr Angus Wilson, Mrs Hetta Wolton,
Mr Percy John Wolton, Miss Marjorie Wynne, Il Colonello Alfredo
Zanchino, and Signor Carlo Zanotti.

To the following institutions, for permission to study their collections,
for help in such research, and for permission to quote from letters and
manuscripts in their possession, I am greatly indebted: The Beinecke Rare
Book and Manuscript Library, Yale University; The Berg Collection, New
York Public Library; The Department of Special Collections, University
of California, Los Angeles; The Academic Center Library, University of
Texas; The Rare Book Department, Baker Memorial Library, Dartmouth
College; The Rare Books and Special Collections Department, University
of California, Berkeley; The Houghton Library, Harvard University; The
Morris Library, Southern Illinois University; The University Library,
Princeton; Bryn Mawr College Library; The University of Virginia; and
The Rosenbach Foundation Museum, Philadelphia. To Miss Elspeth Yeo
and The National Library of Scotland; to Mr D. W. Evans, Rare Book
Librarian, University Library, Birmingham; to Mr A. J. P. Taylor and
The Beaverbrook Library; to Her Majesty's Librarian, Windsor Castle;
and, as ever, to the constant services of the British Library Reading Room
staff, and to the staff of the Department of Manuscripts; to the Public
Record Office; to the London Library; and to Miss Munro-Kerr and the
Society of Authors, I am deeply grateful. I must also thank the Deutsche
Bibliothek, Frankfurt am Main; the Bayerische Staatsbibliothek, Munich;

both Douglas and Orioli, its twin subjects; but it was the work of a man suffering from one of the saddest complaints that anyone can be afflicted with – a combination of envy, jealousy and feelings of persecution. Aldington came not to praise Douglas but to bury him with sanctimonious suggestions and insinuations which whenever possible are of the nastiest kind. He over-reached himself by admitting that he did not even know whether some of the accusations he made were founded on fact.

Loyal friends of Douglas charged into *Pinorman* with sabres whirling, intent on letting out the sawdust. This object they undoubtedly achieved; but they refused to see, or admit, that some parts of the book are as real and solid as was the flesh of Douglas and Orioli. Merely to state this fact, in certain circles, is tantamount to treason; and the idolatrous, having read it, will be after my blood. So be it. They must enjoy themselves as they may, as I have enjoyed myself by trying to look the facts in the face and make truthful judgments.

This is a difficult task even in the case of a subject who himself helps the biographer by revealing his thoughts and feelings in letters or diaries. Douglas wrote many letters, but on the whole revealed little in them about his thoughts and feelings. He kept no diary after his school-days except one in which he noted engagements, change of address, and names of correspondents. And in the whole range of his writing, published and unpublished, the more intimately a matter touched him emotionally, the more taciturn his comments, if any. There are a few exceptions to this practice, but usually his deeper feelings have to be deduced. It would be a mistake to assume, as some people have done, that because he seldom revealed them, he had no feelings of this kind: evidence points in the opposite direction.

Whether or not Douglas, if alive, would approve of an attempt to tell the truth about him, it is almost certain that he would disapprove of my attempt to reveal what he refrained from revealing or actually took steps to conceal; but I would defend myself on two grounds. Firstly, the truth about a man's life, ideally, is indivisible; only by knowing all, or, for practical purposes, as much as possible, can any complete likeness be arrived at. Social curiosity may be vulgar, as Ouida and Douglas and others have professed it to be; but if it is, we are all avid vulgarians when it comes to reading Pepys or Boswell or Montaigne or Léautaud. Secondly, Douglas himself provokes such enquiries. With that extraordinary combination of opposites which is one of the distinguishing marks of his character, he carried both frankness and reticence to extremes. This is a habit that could not be better calculated to whet the appetite for more and more biographical information. Both Hugh Walpole and Lytton Strachey remarked, unknown to each other, that it was what Douglas

the Biblioteca Nazionale, Naples; the Cerio Institute, Capri; and the Landesarchiv, Bregenz, Vorarlberg, for valuable assistance.

For permission to quote from copyright material my thanks are due to: Sir Harold Acton and David Higham Associates Ltd for extracts from *Memoirs of an Aesthete* and *More Memoirs of an Aesthete*, published by Methuen Ltd; to Rosica Colin Ltd for passages from Richard Aldington's *Pinorman*, published by William Heinemann Ltd; to Laurence Pollinger Ltd and the Estate of the late Mrs Frieda Lawrence for extracts from books by D. H. Lawrence; to Signor Carlo Zanotti and Chatto and Windus Ltd for extracts from Pino Orioli's *Moving Along*; to Chatto and Windus Ltd for the many extracts from *Looking Back*; to the Society of Authors as agents for the Douglas estate; and finally, and in abundance, grateful thanks to Mr Islay Lyons, Mr Kenneth Macpherson's successor as Douglas' literary executor, for renewal of permission to quote all the numerous extracts from Douglas' work, published and unpublished.

Introduction

The subject of this biography made two comments which I have tried to bear in mind while writing it. The first remark was made to Constantine FitzGibbon as soon as he arrived on Capri in 1948 with the intention of writing Douglas' life: "You can write anything you like about me so long as it's true." It is a relief to me to be able to believe that if Douglas were still alive he might not be offended, on this point, by what I have written. I have tried throughout to discover and tell the truth, and to discard rumour and legend unsupported by fact. If I have slipped into error, I shall be grateful for correction.

Secondly, Douglas was fond of repeating the saying "no man is ever written down except by himself" – a conveniently ambiguous statement: but if one takes it to mean that a man, particularly a writer, will reveal himself, consciously or unconsciously, better than anyone else can, I believe he would find that he is as well served in this particular as he could be except in an actual anthology of extracts from his work and letters. I have taken as many opportunities as possible of letting him speak for himself.

Telling the truth is not merely a matter of sticking to the facts, when one can find them: these facts have to be selected, and in the selection the biographer is likely to reveal partialities even when he makes a conscious effort not to. This would be particularly easy in the case of Douglas, in whom certain characteristics are greatly exaggerated, and whose life has been the subject of much gossip and speculation. If there were no reliable documents to correct these impressions, it would be impossible to write a biography that was more than half convincing.

Such a book has already been written, excellently, by Nancy Cunard. Douglas steps out of that book alive, recognisable, and loved. One sees him more closely and more familiarly than one would if one had casually met or known him. Yet the book deals only with his later years, ignores his private life so blandly, and is occasionally so undiscriminating in its starry-eyed approval of his sillier moments that one has finally to recognise the book for what it is: a tribute. It is a fine one – warm-hearted, loyal, vivid, and engagingly written.

In the year in which this laudatory account of Douglas was published, a book of the opposite kind also appeared: *Pinorman*, by Richard Aldington. This book too was vivid, and written from first-hand knowledge of did not say in his books as much as what he did say that intrigued them. Many others, myself included, have been impressed in the same way. Here, indeed, lay the motive for writing this biography: a desire to find answers to a hundred questions suggested by reading his books, and an insistent curiosity concerning all the lacunae – sometimes coalescing into a length of years – in his scattered autobiographical writings.

This ambition took hold during the last years of Douglas' life, largely as a means of settling once and for all various doubts concerning a man whose work I enjoyed almost without reservation, and much of whose attitude to life I thought I admired. Yet it was difficult to be sure – there was so much exaggeration, so much sarcasm, together with a particular kind of zestful, malicious high spirits and an apparent ruthlessness of a truly radical sort. Were these characteristics a part of his everyday life, or were they part of a *persona*, a writer's mask to be worn in public? Was his life, which appeared to be such an easy combination of rational sagacity with zestful hedonism, a happy one? I remember praising what I at that time supposed his philosophy of life to be to someone who had known him well. "But would you like to have *lived* like Norman Douglas?" he finally said, and took his hat and departed, leaving my rather querulous reply – "I don't *know* how he lived" – hanging in air. That was in 1948 or thereabouts, when John Davenport had just been commissioned to write Douglas' life. Not until Davenport's death, more than eighteen years later, with no biography written, was I able to begin to realise my ambition to learn the truth about Douglas.

Author's Note

In this biography there are frequent references to Douglas' books. Apart from his first book *Unprofessional Tales*, 1901, written under the pseudonym "Normyx" in collaboration with his wife, the titles and subjects are as follows: *Siren Land* (on the Sorrentine Peninsula in Italy), 1911; *Fountains in the Sand* (Tunisia), 1912; *Old Calabria*, 1915; *London Street Games*, 1916; *South Wind* (novel), 1917; *They Went* (novel), 1920; *Alone* (Central Italy), 1921; *Together* (Austria), 1923; *D. H. Lawrence & Maurice Magnus, A Plea for Better Manners* (polemical pamphlet), 1925; *Birds & Beasts of the Greek Anthology*, 1927; *In the Beginning* (novel), 1927; *Some Limericks*, 1928; *How About Europe?* (the American edition was called *Good-bye to Western Culture*), 1929; *Paneros* (on aphrodisiacs), 1930; *Summer Islands* (Ischia & Ponza), 1931; *Looking Back* (autobiography), 1933; *An Almanac* (an aphorism for every day of the year chosen from his books), 1941; *Late Harvest* (autobiographical and bibliographical comments on his books), 1946; *Footnote on Capri*, 1952; and *Venus in the Kitchen* (aphrodisiacal recipes), 1952.

In addition to the above there were a few reprints in book form of earlier work: *Experiments*, 1925, contains essays, book reviews, and stories. *Three of Them*, 1930, includes the short story *Nerinda*; the essay *One Day* on Greece, otherwise only found in a limited edition; and one of the early papers on natural history, the *Herpetology of the Grand Duchy of Baden*. *Capri: Materials for a Description of the Island*, 1930, a scarce book, is nevertheless not quite so scarce as some of the ten pamphlets from which it was composed.

In the four or five years after 1942, when William King was Douglas' literary executor, he and Douglas went through most of the non-fiction books page by page, King asking questions and Douglas supplying answers which King (usually, but Douglas sometimes) wrote in the margins. The copy of *Looking Back* that was thus annotated is of particular interest, containing information which can be found nowhere else: it is now in The Berg Collection, New York Public Library, and is referred to hereafter in this book as "the Berg copy", "Berg annotation", or "Berg *Looking Back*".

PART 1

*Ancestors and Childhood
Up to 1883*

CHAPTER ONE

―――――――――――――

Grandparents and Parents:
Up to 1864

i

Everyone who is familiar with the map of Europe knows Lake Constance, where Germany, Austria, and Switzerland meet, but not many people seem to know that the part of Austria which verges on this lake is called the Vorarlberg. This is the westernmost province of Austria, about the same size as the English county of Dorset, and smaller than the American State of Rhode Island. It is an extremely mountainous region, containing a single valley system, that of the river Ill and its tributaries. Only in the north-west is there a small corner of the province on low-lying land around Lake Constance. Here, near the Bavarian border, and climbing a short way up the hills behind it from the lake's edge, is Bregenz, the little capital city of the Vorarlberg.

Until the first road over the Arlberg Pass was made in 1824, the province was cut off from the rest of the world for about six months of the year, except for the north-west access through Feldkirch. It was almost as isolated as it had been when the Romans had entered it centuries earlier: a land of sturdy peasants living in the villages and small towns scattered up and down the Walgau (the main valley of the Ill) and its side valleys: independent, diligent people with a strong regional patriotism.

During the second half of the nineteenth century several families of Scottish origin were settled in the province: two daughters and five granddaughters of Lord Forbes, for instance; the Fairholmes of Lugate and William Cotesworth of Cowdenknowes: they were all living at Bregenz. About eighteen miles further south, at Feldkirch, were Kennedys from Kirkcudbrightshire and Manchester; and six or seven miles further up the valley, at Thüringen, were Douglasses from Kincardine-shire. It was here that Norman Douglas was born – three quarters Scottish and one quarter German – at about midnight between 8th–9th December 1868. He maintained that he had been born early on the 9th, but that the Catholic midwife so much wished him to be born on the 8th, that she insisted he had been. This was because the 8th was an important feast day,

3

the Immaculate Conception of the Blessed Virgin Mary: he seldom failed
to point out how appropriate he considered the day to be for the debut
of someone as pure and irreproachable in thought and deed as himself. . . .

December 8th, at any rate, was his registered and accepted birthday,
and George Norman Douglass his registered name.

ii

His paternal grandfather's family, the Douglasses or Douglases (the
spelling varies[1]) of Tilquhillie, were Scottish lairds and professional men
related to the nobility. They were a branch, including a sprinkling of
knights, of that enormous tree which has included the Dukes of Hamilton,
the Marquises of Queensberry, and the Earls of Douglas, Mar, Angus
and Morton – Border Douglasses with histories as bloody as any Border-
ers', Black Douglas, Red Douglas, Douglasses good, bad and average;
ecclesiastical, military, scholarly, and forensic Douglasses.

His other, maternal grandfather, Freiherr von Poellnitz, was of a
German aristocratic family with a branch in the Ur-Adela, the upper-
most layer so to speak of the Almanach de Gotha. Von Poellnitz's wife,
Norman Douglas' maternal grandmother, was the daughter of Lord
Forbes, premier baron of Scotland.

Douglas' paternal grandmother, Jane Kennedy, of whom he was to
write at some length, came from a Scottish family which played a prominent part in the industrial revolution in England and was the link in the
chain of circumstances through which the Douglasses of Tilquhillie
found themselves in a remote Austrian valley.

iii

Tilquhillie Castle near Banchory on Deeside was built in 1567 by the
fourth laird, a descendant of Sir Henry Douglas of Lochleven and also of
Janet Ogstoun of Fettercairn who brought the Tilquhillie lands into the
Douglas family. The castle, modest in size, still stands, rather forlorn
among tall trees and arable fields, a representative example of the semi-
fortified type commonly built in the sixteenth century. It has not been
inhabited by the Douglasses, to whom it still belongs, for more than a
hundred years, and for most of that time, not by anyone. The present
laird, seventeenth of Tilquhillie and Norman Douglas' nephew, lives
nearby. He owes possession of his ancestral lands particularly to the
enterprise of his great-grandfather (Norman Douglas' grandfather), John
Douglass, fourteenth of Tilquhillie. During this laird's minority, in the
early years of the nineteenth century, the hereditary Douglas lands –

Tilquhillie, Inchmarlo and Kincardine O'Neil – were sold. John Douglass determined if he could to make enough money to buy them back.

It seems that John Douglass was connected by marriage with the Kennedy family of Manchester before his own marriage. He was born in 1804, but nothing is heard of him until 1837 when he began working as manager of a cotton mill in Austria. It is likely that he would have spent at least part of the intervening period acquiring experience of the cotton business in Manchester where the Kennedys were already a household name by the time Douglass was a young man.

Jane Kennedy, whom Douglass eventually married, was the third daughter of James, younger brother and partner of John Kennedy,[2] a well-known and respected figure in the cotton industry. In 1783 John had arrived from Scotland as apprentice to a neighbouring Kirkcudbright-shire man who had already migrated south: William Cannan of Chowbent in Derbyshire, the machine-maker. About eight years later, Kennedy joined the firm of Sandford and McConnel (the latter was also a Scot from the same neighbourhood). This firm was for years the only manu-facturer of Samuel Crompton's spinning mule, which John Kennedy greatly improved with additional inventions. The machine was unrivalled in the trade, and established the fortunes of McConnel and the Kennedys (for John was soon joined by his brother James). By skill, ingenuity, inventiveness, hard work and determination, and also, no doubt, by Scottish canniness and clannishness, they had won their way to the top of the cotton business, just as others, sometimes closely connected, like Adam and George Murray and William Fairbairn,[3] became famous in the iron industry. All these men worked long hours but they did not neglect intellectual pursuits; largely self-educated, they had wide inter-ests, and liked to exchange ideas. John Kennedy was a friend of James Watt, George Stephenson, and many other scientific men of his time. Like many of his associates, he was a railway enthusiast and was one of the three men chosen to judge the famous Rainhill locomotive trials in 1829, won by Stephenson's "Rocket".

William Fairbairn and his partner James Lillie's firm of millwrights played its part in the Douglas story. It had begun its industrial career with a contract from the brothers Murray. The Murrays, pleased with the result, recommended Fairbairn and Lillie to McConnel and Kennedy, for whom they fitted up a completely new cotton mill in 1818. This was such an improvement on anything which had preceded it that the Fair-bairn success (which was to culminate in ironclad battleships and knight-hoods) was founded on it. By 1826 Fairbairns were supplying the best hydraulic machines in the world, not only to the British Isles, but abroad; and at about this time they made all the mill-gearing and water-machinery for Messrs Escher and Company's works at Zurich, one of the largest cotton mills on the continent. Peter Kennedy, Jane's cousin, went out there, perhaps to help install the machinery, or on a visit; and with him, or to visit him, went John Douglass of Tilquhillie.

iv

In 1828 the firm of Escher built its first cotton factory outside Switzerland, at Feldkirch in the Vorarlberg. It was apparently financed by Peter Kennedy. It would not have taken either him or John Douglass long to discover at Thüringen, five or six miles to the south, the long cataract that fell 255 feet, and could be recognised from a distance by any prospective factory owner as a powerful and not too inaccessible source of energy. By 1837 they had, in fact, built a new factory there. Again, it seems to have been financed by Peter Kennedy; Douglass was installed as manager. It became the finest factory in the Vorarlberg, and one of the best-equipped on the continent. Its fame, with its 9,300 spindles and 1,800 looms, spread even to Vienna: it was visited by the Archdukes Rainier and Johann who were connoisseurs of engineering. They said they had seen nothing better of its kind in the Monarchy.

In 1837, the year in which the factory was completed, John Douglass married Jane Kennedy and built for himself on the same shelf of land above the village that the factory stands on, but at a convenient distance from it, a modest-sized well-proportioned Georgian-type house. Although it cannot be more than a hundred and fifty feet above the floor of the valley, it was called Falkenhorst – Falcon's Nest. The name is saved from pretentiousness by the fact that the whole panorama of the Walgau is spread out beneath the house, while across this broadest part of the valley rise the formidable foothills and peaks of the Rhaetikon Alps, over which, had one the wings of a falcon, one would certainly be tempted to soar, so airy and commanding does this comparatively low perch seem. Falkenhorst – it was hardly believable! – was fitted when built with central heating; later, steam heating was even fitted in greenhouses in the garden. And the garden, simply but pleasantly laid out, was filled with all kinds of exotic trees and shrubs and flowers, many brought as seedlings from Britain. The house, as much as the factory, was a source of wonder in the neighbourhood, an attraction even to the citizens of Bludenz who would drive or walk the four or five miles to see it on a Sunday afternoon. There was always something new to be seen, such, for instance, as the huge factory workers' barracks that was built, in which a hundred and fifty single men and women were segregated and housed. It was a structure typical of its kind, that might have been dropped down out of New

Lanark or from one of half a dozen cotton processing establishments in Lancashire.

John Douglass showed that he was made of the same stuff as his wife's father and uncle and those other Mancunian Scotsmen. They were all tough practical self-reliant men who believed that hard work and observation of Christian principle (as interpreted by Protestant industrialists) would win through in the end. Above all, they were builders – builders of new sources of power, new means of communication, new tools and tool-making machines, new social principles. They had a strong sense of duty and mission: the world was still of immense extent, and only waiting, many of them thought, to be filled with the benefits of a mercantile civilisation. They belonged to what Norman Douglas in a sour but heartfelt phrase was to call "the biliously moral middle classes".[4] Their biliousness, undoubtedly, lay in the fact that they were very near to him.

John Douglass succeeded. It was not easy, for the cotton market was never stable: there were constant impediments to be overcome – wars, tariffs, competitors – yet the market was still expanding sufficiently to give him a reasonable profit. Eighteen years after the opening of the factory, he had long since bought out his partners, and was able to repay the loan with which the business had been started. This was a matter of £36,000. He was also able to put down £24,000 towards buying back his ancestral estates. And that was not all; during this period he had built up a fund of goodwill in the neighbourhood: the name of Douglass was honoured and respected; the foreign mill-owners were regarded as good employers.

John Douglass had achieved much. His son, in one particular at least, was to achieve more. He became an almost legendary figure in the Vorarlberg during his own lifetime and seems to have inspired affection as well as awe and respect.

v

This son, John Sholto, fifteenth of Tilquhillie, Norman Douglas' father, was born in 1838. As the second generation usually does, he took to his environment and grew up like a native Vorarlberger, although actually born in Scotland. He seems to have been endowed with most of the gifts a man could desire. He was strong and healthy; by local standards at least, he was rich and his family was influential. He was physically courageous. He possessed a lively and enquiring mind. In addition, his demeanour seems to have been impeccable: as a "Lutheran" or Evangelical (actually Church of Scotland) among Catholics, as an employer among employees, as a young man among hordes of elderly relations during his visits to England and Scotland, he seems never to have put a foot wrong and everywhere to have been greeted with affectionate respect. He was tall, slim and bearded, pleasing to look at, and energetic. He was educated at a Gymnasium at Augsburg, and at Geneva, and spoke and wrote fluently in English, German and French. Judging by his writings, published and unpublished, and by letters written to his parents as a young man, everything seems to have interested him and to have provided matter for thought and comment. He could also sketch and paint tolerably well. He seems to have been capable and conscientious in all that concerned his family, even the more remote of cousins and relations by marriage, and in his family business affairs. So much of a paragon does he sound that one suspects the presence somewhere of a less desirable characteristic that has been omitted. It is hard to find one, unless perhaps there was a certain coldness or aloofness in his nature. His passion was for the mountains, and it was this that was to make him a somewhat awesome figure in Vorarlberg folklore. The mountains, apparently, came first, before everything and everyone, including his wife, though perhaps at the time of their marriage Vanda von Poellnitz did not know that this would be so.

vi

Vanda von Poellnitz was the granddaughter of the seventeenth Lord Forbes, a rather typical rich nobleman of the late eighteenth century, born in 1765. He had several sons and five daughters and was one of those travelling *milords* who criss-crossed Europe in style in his own chaise. He was mildly eccentric, was always in a hurry, wore steel-rimmed spectacles, and lost his temper rather easily with innkeepers. On one of his journeys, with two daughters, he happened to be visiting Ludwig I of Bavaria at Wurzburg. There, waiting on the famous Louis Seize staircase of the Residenz to receive them, was a young red-haired lieutenant in a superb sky-blue uniform. Apart from his decorative coloration, he happened to be slim and handsome in the romantic-melancholic manner, the Wertherian or Byronic type that was then so fashionable; and was also an ADC to the King. Isabella, the younger of the two Forbes girls present, fell in love with him at once. Her love seems to have been returned, and the King to have aided and abetted the young couple, unknown to Lord Forbes. When his lordship found out what was going on, he was furious, and whisked his daughters off home across Europe at top speed.

No doubt Isabella was furious too, as well as heartbroken; but there was little a girl in such a situation could do about it in those days except appeal to her father's clemency by "going into a decline". This Isabella did, until her father became alarmed for her health. Eventually his anxiety culminated in the consoling thought that the von Poellnitzes were in the best part of the Almanach de Gotha. He wrote to Ludwig, who gave Ernst leave to visit Scotland – leave that was continually renewed for the rest of his life. Once he had agreed to the marriage, Lord Forbes, who did nothing by halves, arranged for Ernst to become ADC to Prince Albert, and provided Isabella with a handsome dowry. They lived for a while at Windsor Castle, and there, according to their granddaughter,* their eldest child Vanda was born. She is said to have occupied a golden cradle; and Queen Victoria apparently consented to be her godmother.[5]

Vanda was born on 6th June 1840. A year or two later, Lord Forbes and his daughters and son-in-law, on tour together, visited Bregenz. They liked it so much, they could not bear to leave it. Lord Forbes, in fact, never did leave it: he died there in 1843. His son-in-law, meanwhile, had bought Schloss Riedenburg, in which he was to live with his growing family of daughters for ten years. He had his father-in-law's remains buried in a plot of land on which he then built a Protestant church; and in 1854 he bought and almost completely rebuilt the dilapidated Schloss Babenwohl.

Babenwohl, like Riedenburg, was built on a height above Bregenz, and from it, at that time, five countries could be seen – Baden, Württemberg, Bavaria, Austria and Switzerland. The Baron managed to rebuild in mediaeval style: there were bleak stone passages as cold as dungeons, hung with ancient weapons – "sombre panelling, relieved by armorial designs, covered the walls and ceilings and made the rooms uncommonly dusky" and the furnishings consisted of "a haphazard collection of Persian carpets, harmoniums, lacquer tables, Tiepolo portraits, glittering chandeliers, marbles". It all looked, wrote his grandson, like loot pillaged from the rich burghers of Bregenz. Up there on his perch above the town the young Wertherian lieutenant gradually turned into "the old cock on his dunghill, crowing and gobbling" and ruling his wife, his sister-in-law Elizabeth (always known as "Cis") and his five daughters like a despot. The daughters escaped as soon as they could into marriage. For the others there was no escape: he lived on their money and never did a day's work in his life. Let the women do it! – and leave him in peace, looking twenty years younger than his age, fresh and rosy-cheeked as a baby. Let the women do the work, while he smoked the Latakia cigarettes they made

---

*This was Grete Gulbransson, Norman Douglas' half-sister, whose book of family reminiscences, *Geliebte Schatten* (1934; new edition, 1959), is the source of much of the information in the first part of this biography.

for him and bragged endlessly about his exploits as a young man in
Hungary, Greece, Wurzburg and Windsor.

This boasting one might have enjoyed, apparently, for "his voice was
the best part of him at all times; his very curses sounded like a ripple of
celestial laughter. He also painted sunny landscapes in oil, and composed
an amusing valse or two. Such things went well with his exterior childlike
equipment. Primaeval ferocity was lurking underneath."

So wrote his grandson. And his granddaughter Grete also has something to say about Babenwohl voices – not von Poellnitz's, but the cello-
like voices of the women, unmistakable even in the third generation. She
writes of the old man as a house-tyrant, and describes how his long-
suffering wife had to listen every night to his thundering grumbles about
all the petty blemishes of the day. Nevertheless, Isabella lived to be
eighty-one, and Cis, seventy-eight; and life at Babenwohl, in spite of
Papa – perhaps partly because of him, because of his style and his delight
in singing and story-telling and painting – was warm and human and by
no means devoid of tenderness and love. Indeed, the girls lived in a
dream-world, innocent, protected, rich in fantasy and artistic preoccupations. Only occasionally had they to face the reality of a world in
which most people struggle, more or less, for what they want. They
lacked practice in this craft, and one of them, at least, was to be destroyed
by her inability to free herself from conflicting allegiances arising from
this unreal, sentimental background. Vanda, the eldest, was the most
capable of dealing with life on its own terms.

vii

Vanda's mother was Scottish, and the Babenwohlers were, like the
Douglasses, Protestant in a Catholic country; and both families were
well known in the neighbourhood, so it is not surprising that they met.
Vanda had been told by a gipsy that she would marry a man who had the
same number of letters in his name as she had in hers. When he first left
his card at Babenwohl before she had even seen him, she noted that
there are fourteen letters in "Sholto Douglass" as there are in "Vanda
Poellnitz" and knew, according to her daughter, that destiny was at hand
and that she would undoubtedly marry this man.

Presumably for the sake of the young couple the families visited one
another frequently. The Douglasses could not have failed to be attracted
by Babenwohl, in which Isabella and Cis had done all they could to keep
alive the Scottish way of life; but the Poellnitzes may not have cared
much for Sholto's parents. Vanda certainly did not, and old Ernst,
though perhaps pleased that his daughter had found a handsome com-

fortably-off husband, would have considered that Vanda had stepped down a rung in the social ladder in order to do so.

In due course, in 1864, Sholto and Vanda were married. They went on a touring honeymoon to Vienna, Graz, Trieste, Venice and Florence. Sholto is described as shy; Vanda, in making up her mind to marry him, may have made up his mind too. On returning from their honeymoon they set up house at Falkenhorst with the older Douglasses still in residence: a bad beginning, which Vanda did not like. After about a year John Douglass and his wife left for Scotland, having handed over control of the business to Sholto. Vanda is said to have lit a bonfire in the garden to celebrate the event and to have danced round it singing songs of victory. Such rejoicings may have been a little premature, for old Mrs Douglass returned from time to time to spend part of the year at Falkenhorst, which belonged to her after the death of her husband in 1870. She survived him by twenty-one years.

CHAPTER TWO

Sholto, Vanda, and their Children
1865–1875

i

The new young proprietor of the cotton factory no doubt did his duty
by the business – he was a conscientious man – but he also found plenty
of time for chamois-hunting and mountaineering. His young wife pleaded
with him not to take risks up there in the heights, and was suddenly made
alarmingly aware of what the mountains really meant to him. He turned to
her, so her daughter wrote, as though to a stranger and warned her that
she must never again interfere in these matters, or she would ruin his
happiness. She would have to choose: "Either you leave me the mountains, or I leave you!"

This was a hard condition for a newly married man to impose upon
his wife, even by Victorian standards. Quite often he was away for several
days on end, and Vanda, as much probably from the implied rejection as
from lack of company, felt deep loneliness, as well as anxiety. She would
often go to Babenwohl for consolation, or send the Falkenhorst coach
to bring the Babenwohlers to her. Near to tears, or actually weeping,
she would come out to greet them with one or more of her children.
The Babenwohlers would pour out of the coach and envelop her in
hugs and kisses. The baby would be handed round from arm to arm.
The cello voices would resound from every corner of house and garden;
merriment, and pranks, songs and laughter, music and recitations, "dressing
up", walks, explorations, bathing – these kinds of activity followed the
arrival of the Babenwohlers, who brought with them some of the
enchantment of their dream world. Sholto would come back sometimes
while they were still there, and move about among them unobtrusively.
Often he would be off again early next morning. He seemed to live more
with the Vorarlberg than with his family.

As his son has shown, Sholto's interests were by no means confined to
mountains. Apart from his writings for the Alpine Club, he also had
printed two archaeological monographs on local subjects, full of original
speculations and scholarly references. He also left forty or fifty manuscript

12

essays on a variety of themes which display a widespread intellectual curiosity.[6]

In the mountains he led what his son called "an enchanted life" among the rocks and ice. A mountaineering friend spoke of his contempt for danger, of how he seemed to tread on air, and could not be made to understand what was meant by giddiness. In writing of his own climbs, either in letters to his wife, or in accounts printed in the Journal of the Alpine Club, the tone is calm, buoyant, and optimistic. A typical phrase used to describe the crossing of a glacier which no one had traversed before, was that it presented "no difficulty" – *keine Schwierigkeit*. One has the impression of a man not only obsessed and devoted, but also perhaps dangerously convinced that he was favoured by fate and could take risks with impunity, even in the high mountains on which snow and ice lie throughout the year. This *Urwelt*, or upper world, was a feared and mysterious region into which even the most enthusiastic huntsman pursuing a chamois (or in former days, a wolf or bear) seldom penetrated. Sholto Douglass and a few kindred spirits (such as the old Brunnen-macher of Bludenz, Anton Neyer or "Bühel-Toni") liberated this Urwelt and opened it to other men. Amongst these pioneers Douglass was pre-eminent in the Vorarlberg, and it is not surprising that he was endowed by the wondering and superstitious natives with the attributes of a hero.

One has only to look up almost anywhere in the western half of the province to be reminded of him—there is scarcely a peak of any eminence that he did not climb, and the "Douglashütte" at the edge of the Lünersee is a replacement of the first alpine hut ever built, and built by him, in the Vorarlberg – for the convenience of climbers who were headed for or returning from the Scesaplana. His name is still well known, and spoken of with pride and respect in a world which has brought so many formerly inaccessible places within reach of all of us.

ii

To be a wife to such a man can never be easy; and if, like Vanda, one has lived a protected, perhaps slightly over-indulged life, and is sensitive to all nuances of behaviour, fond of gaiety and laughter shared with devoted companions, it must be even harder to be grass-widowed by a cold and remote world which is, also, a constant threat to your husband's life. It is obvious from Vanda's diary that she missed the warmth and happiness of her family life at Babenwohl: she clung to it tenaciously all through her married life for comfort and reassurance. When she was left on her own, sadness would supervene: ". . . whether Sholto has any idea *how* I pass my life in grieving," she writes, while he is away hunting. She cannot be happy when he is not there: she spends a lovely summer evening with the boys in the Lutzwald, but in spite of their company feels so lonely that her heart aches. And then there is the danger, the ever-present knowledge that one day her husband may not return at all, the nightmare she had in 1872, when she dreamed she was staying with relations in London and discovered she was dressed in black crepe. Her father told her that all her weeping would not bring Sholto back; her mother offered her his last letters; Vanda fell on her knees and prayed for Sholto's restoration. Even her sister Adèle dreamed of the death of a man in a hunting jacket lying on the ground in front of a crucifix, with a broken back and a large wound in his head . . .

iii

This, more or less, was how Sholto Douglass was found one day in September 1874. Accounts of the accident vary in detail, but agree in principle that Sholto Douglass, ignoring all warnings, deliberately challenged fate. On 7th September he wrote to his wife, who was then away from home, that he intended to go chamois-hunting in the mountains between Lakes Formarin and Spüller: ". . . if I wait any longer, I may not be able to cross the high ground, because snow falls there so often and so early." Grete Gulbransson wrote that he was actually warned not to go, because there had been continuous heavy rain (which always makes for treacherous conditions on the heights). But he left on 14th September with several companions. They stayed the night in Dalaas, and early next day began the ascent to the high ground between the lakes, where one of the peaks, the Gamsboden Spitz (Gams-boden = chamois' land), seems to have been their main objective. At 2 p.m., presumably without having had any luck, Douglass blew his whistle to announce the end of the hunt. The intention was to make for Lake Formarin and to spend the night in the hut there before continuing the hunt next day towards the Spüllersee. The party was widely separated, Douglass at a much higher level than the others, set on a dangerous route. He could easily have rejoined them, and one of his huntsmen spent three-quarters of an hour signalling to him, trying to persuade him against continuing at the higher level which would take him near the edge of a thousand-foot cliff; but in vain. As two others of the party were making their way along the foot of this precipice, there was the sound of a shot and of falling rock. Believing that Douglass had killed a chamois, they hastened to look for it, but had not gone far before they saw Douglass himself lying face downwards, arms outstretched and legs doubled under. His face and hands were badly bruised and lacerated, but the worst wound was in his head. His own huntsman fainted at the sight. Douglass' jacket and waist-coat were missing, his rifle was broken, his alpenstock, cigar-case, and other possessions were scattered about. There was no doubt that he was dead.

The funeral procession wound through the villages of the Walgau from Falkenhorst to Feldkirch, where Sholto was buried in the Protestant cemetery, and "for the first time in history", as his son puts it, "the bells of all the countryside were tolled at the funeral of a 'Lutheran'". A wooden cross was erected – and renewed in after years – as near to the place from which he had fallen as anyone dared go; a plaque was put up at the foot of the Radonatobel; and to this day, in spite of the fact that Falkenhorst has not belonged to the family for sixty years, his mountaineering equip-ment hangs high up on a wall where it is shown respectfully to those who are interested.

At the time of the accident, Sholto Douglass was not quite thirty-six. In their ten years of marriage his wife had given birth to four children: John William Edward James (1865); Robert Ernest (1867), who died when he was six months old; George Norman (1868), and Mary (1871). When his father was killed Norman was five years and nine months old.

iv

He was known from the beginning as Norman, not George; and from the beginning was brought up in an atmosphere which, though kindly and liberal, recognised the particular significance of the first son, who would inherit the lairdship and estates. During the formative years of Norman's childhood this fact may never have been mentioned but its simple existence must have played some part, however small, in determin-ing parental and other attitudes. In the case of John and Norman there is no evidence for parental discrimination in affection, but the fact that John was nearly four years older than Norman in itself put a certain distance of another sort between them: Norman, in his childhood, tended to spend more time with his sister Mary, who was only two years his junior, than with John. The latter may soon have seemed to have a special relationship with his parents because he was frequently taken about with them on their incessant comings and goings, their almost weekly travels about the province and further afield. He was of an age to be taken without difficulty: the others were not.

To the mother, the first child cannot fail to have a special significance: every detail of the baby's behaviour and development is watched with intense interest, and often noted down. Vanda kept a little journal devoted solely to John. It consists largely of entries made annually on his birthday,

in the evening; these are mainly prayers of thanksgiving for his continued
existence and good health. The prayers are entirely extempore and sincere
in feeling, and are both touching and revealing of the time, in which so
many hazards threatened the early years. This journal covers the years
up to John's seventh birthday (1872) and contains some charming little
sketches, as do all Vanda's journals. Like them, too, it is shot through with
her love of the open air and all the sights and sounds and colours of
Nature.

Nature, and her children, are her chief sources of pleasure, to judge
by her diary for the years 1871–74, which begins with the birth of Mary.
She loves the Vorarlberg. She dislikes Scotland and old Mrs Douglass.
Her strong sentimental attachment to Babenwohl and Bregenz are evident, as is also her anxiety and loneliness at Falkenhorst. She feels sad
and listless as easily as she feels bored. One evening she looks out of the
train window into the houses it passes, by the light of their lamps: "How
many family groups, how many life stories, how much joy and sorrow
do those lamps illuminate?" The romantic-sentimental mood is always
latent, waiting to be evoked. Here also is recorded her prophetic nightmare about Sholto's death in all its stark reality.

v

In Vanda's diary there is a description of Norman singing "The Watch
on the Rhine", with her at the piano, at the age of two and (nearly) four
months. He knows the tune very well, and plays it – or helps to play it –
with closed fingers while rocking himself backwards and forwards and
singing most of the words with slight childish mispronunciations which
she carefully records: "The delightful smiling mouth and the little
teeth – too sweet!" She also writes down his remark – he was three by
then – about the dog Lasko barking: "Lasko should have his tail pulled
right off so that he can never bark again." (His sister had been told that if
she pulled her dog's tail *too* hard, it wouldn't be able to bark, which she
liked it to do.)

His own memories of childhood are described in some detail in *Together*.
Amongst much else, he remembered: being taken out of bed to the
window to see the *Nordlicht* (aurora borealis) in 1871; crawling, before
he could walk, under an immense walnut tree near the house; riding
down the steep slippery flank of a hill on the branch of a fir tree, seated
astride it between his brother and sister, all rushing home after roaming
about the hills above the church steeple whose bells obligingly rang out
at midday that luncheon was ready; smoking his first cigar, at the age
of six, on the Kloster Alp – "I puffed through an inch or so. Then without

any warning, death and darkness compassed me about. Death and darkness! The world was turned inside out; so was I. Not for several weeks did I try tobacco again; this time only a cigarette and in a more appropriate locality; even that made me rather unhappy." He remembered, lovingly, the Owl's Den, the Stag's Leap, the Bear's Cave, the Petrifying Brook and a dozen other secret or sacred places of childhood. And of course he remembered Alte Anna, the Douglass nurse . . .

Alte Anna was in fact not so old, probably about forty at that time. She had a pleasant face and an enormous stock of terrifying wolf stories which haunted Norman's dreams in his childhood and interested him in later years because they were evidence of the deep impression these beasts had left on the popular imagination. (The last wolf in the district had been killed in 1830.) Alte Anna specialised in other frightening phenomena, of which the *Dorftrottels* or village idiots were only one example. A couple of these whom Norman and his little sister Mary used often to see were two skinny madwomen sitting on a bench side by side:

There they sat, always in the same place. They were as mad as could be, and older than the hills. A terrifying spectacle – these two blank creatures, staring into vacuity out of pale blue eyes, with white hair tumbled all about their shoulders. One of them disappeared – died, no doubt; the survivor went on sitting and staring, in her old place. There was another idiot whom we liked far better; in fact we loved him. He was of the joyful and jabbering kind, and he lived near the factory. His facial contortions used to make us shriek with laughter. Sometimes he dribbled at the mouth. When he dribbled copiously, which was not every day, it was our crowning joy. The old Anna, of course, knew by heart every idiot within miles of our home . . . What she liked even better was anything in the nature of an accident, operation, horrible disease, or childbirth; she knew of it, by some dark instinct, the moment it occurred: she knew! and, being forbidden to leave the children alone, dragged us with her into the remotest peasant-houses and hamlets to enjoy the sight. Above all things, she had a mania for corpses, and the flair of a hyena for discovering their whereabouts. As often as there was a corpse within walking distance, she donned her seven-league boots and rushed towards it in a beeline, carrying my sister, to save time, while I toddled painfully after. Arrived at the spot where the dead body lay, she would first cross herself and then begin to gloat. We did the same. Who knows how many maladies, how many corpses, we inspected at that tender age.

He concluded that it was a sound education, as it made them familiar with death and suffering at an age when they couldn't grasp their full significance, and thus took away, for ever, much of their terror. He and his sister were never shocked by such experiences, "only interested – hugely interested".

All this took place within the vast amphitheatre of the mountains, in a secure and limited country – the Ländle – in which the Douglasses led privileged lives. Streams and woods, fields and peasants all were kind to these children, whatever the phantoms they might conjure up for themselves in the dark depths of the forest, or see sitting on benches in public places.

vi

With Mary, Norman could conspire. John may have been too solemn or conscientious, or too unenterprising to make a good conspirator; or too old for his age, or too much in charge of the situation; but Mary and Norman could lead each other on. They could thoroughly enjoy leading one another into temptation: baiting her governesses; wading fully clothed into the Montiola up to their necks; drinking themselves senseless on cider when they were respectively five and three years old; or straining at an enormous boulder up there in the hills until they dislodged it and watched it rushing down the hillside with "delirious leaps". It went clean through an empty but solid hay-hut, "tossing its wooden blocks into the air as if they were feathers". This destruction of some poor peasant's property, he wrote in later life in a characteristic mood of confession without contrition, was considered a great joke: "We laughed over it for weeks and weeks."

Yes, they could happily conspire – as in the doll's ritual. Misguided relatives used to send magnificent dolls to Mary by post. She would pretend delight, saying she must unpack the parcel, all alone, upstairs. She would then run eagerly out of the room, followed by Norman: "A glance, a single masonic glance, had been exchanged between us. It sufficed. I knew the part I was called upon to play." Upstairs, in some unused room, they locked the door. The doll was unpacked in ceremonial silence. When the last silk-paper wrapping had been removed, Mary would take the splendid creature in her arms and, with many false hugs and kisses, head for the garden. Norman followed. Not a word was spoken. On reaching a certain shrubbery, always the same one, she would pause and mutter ritual words into the victim's ear, then hand the thing to Norman. He took it by the legs, swung it through the air once or twice, and shattered its head to fragments against a tree-trunk. After that, they tore it limb from limb amid a shower of sawdust, and stamped on the remains, screaming with hysterical joy.

A few days later somebody might ask where the doll was. Mary would reply mournfully, in ritual words, always the same, that it was ill in bed. "Never a doll escaped assassination," wrote Douglas, "and nobody, I believe, found out what happened to them. My sister hated dolls with a vindictive, unreasoning hatred. And I, of course, was only too pleased to smash anything I was bidden to smash; and still am."

With Mary he could lie for hours under an enormous double bed in a remote bedroom contentedly munching cakes and crunching sweets which had been stuffed into the mattress to supply such needs, until the governess from whom they had fled, and who was unable to reach them in this refuge, implored them, "almost on her knees", to come out.

With Mary – one can be in no doubt about it – he was entirely happy; their childish exploits together are described by him in later years with an indulgent warmth of feeling. Later, she, like Norman and their father, also climbed mountains, an unusual accomplishment for a woman in those days. She was the first woman ever to reach the summit of the Zimba (2,643 metres) and probably the only one in those days ever to attempt the appalling "Hexenthurm". "These were the sports she loved; and I marvel to this hour what made her adopt the married state[7] – she who cared no more for the joys of domesticity than does a tomcat. Talked into it, I fancy, by some stupid relation who ought to have known better." No one who knows Douglas' work as a whole can doubt that these restrained phrases contain a profound regret – regret tinged with anger: Mary died of tuberculosis in 1903 at the age of thirty-two.

vii

John had started going to the local school, at Bludesch, before his father's death. Norman followed, and was there early in 1875. He has related how he trudged off every morning – "rather a long tramp for a child, across all those fields, especially through the fresh fallen snow of winter". The actual distance seems to have been less than a mile, and it is difficult to believe that Douglas would have complained about a walk of this length at any age if there had not been a school at the end of it. His only memories of the school were of endlessly writing out *schwimmmmen* with four "m"s, and of enjoying the view up the valley from the lavatory. He remembered Herr Som, the schoolmaster, who sometimes lunched at Falkenhorst, as "well groomed and gentlemanly", which probably means that he knew his place. Amongst a few documents that Douglas kept until his death was the school report written by Som, in immaculate copperplate, mentioned in *Together*.

It has been suggested that the boys might have picked up rumours at

school that Vanda Douglass had a lover. Gossip is said to have gone
further, and alleged that she had already had a lover – a local painter
called Jakob Jehly – during Sholto's lifetime; and that his death was due
to suicide on this account, and not to accident.[8]

I find this theory barely acceptable. It is unlikely that Sholto would
have continued to tolerate Jehly's visits to Falkenhorst, or that he would
have been seen with him in public, if he had even suspected his good
faith. It is also unlikely that Vanda, who was quite strongly religious,
could have been Jehly's lover in anything like the modern implications
of the term. She might have cast tender glances during Sholto's lifetime,
but is not likely to have done more. It seems to me that such rumours
probably occurred after Sholto's death, not before it, and that they were
due to the strong mythopoeic instincts of the local people. Douglass had
all his life been such a skilful (or lucky) mountaineer that, where no reason
could be discovered for a fatal mistake, it must have seemed necessary
to show that there was none, that his death was deliberate, the hero's
skill unblemished to the end.

His death, besides being a cataclysmic shock – such deaths always are
shocks when they occur, even when they have been anticipated in one
form or another for many years – had left much uncertainty about the
immediate future. His father had paid £24,000 towards buying back
Tilquhillie, but Jane Douglass, after Sholto's death, referred to the
remainder of the debt on Tilquhillie as "oppressive"; and advisers tried
to persuade Vanda to sell the business in Austria. There was bound to be
some doubt, too, at this time, about the future of the boys: John was in
his tenth year, and a school other than Herr Som's would be required.
Was it to be in England or in Germany?

viii

Intimations of these problems and of impending changes in the formerly
secure background of their lives must have percolated through to the
boys. Things were not what they had been, and might never be so again;
for which reason it may not be surprising that sometime in 1876 there
was an occasion which Norman regarded as a turning-point in his life.
He happened to be "all alone under the pines" at a certain place never to
be forgotten:

> [There], at the callow age of seven, I formulated, and was promptly
> appalled by its import, a far-reaching aphorism: There is no God.
> For some obscure reason (perhaps to test the consequences) those
> awful words were spoken aloud. Nothing happened. Who can tell

what previous internal broodings had led to this explosive utterance! None at all, very likely. The phenomenon may have been as natural and easy of birth as the flowering of a plant, the cutting of a wisdom tooth – which, as everyone knows, is nearly always a painless process. There it was: the thing had been said. Often later on, that little incident under the pines recurred to my memory. I used to ask myself: Why make such earth-convulsing speeches? And then again: Why not? Which means that periodical relapses into credulity, into a kind of funk, rather, occurred for the next few years. After that, my intellect ceased to be clouded by anthropomorphic interpretations of the universe.

"There is no God": there was certainly no Sholto any more, exerting his beneficent influence on the childish paradise of Falkenhorst. And that "kind of funk" of which Norman accused himself: could it simply have been a desire to return to former days of bliss, a desire to evade the inescapable fact of his father's death? His father's death, his absence, his desertion, must have seemed like a betrayal; the son may well have asked himself why God, if he existed, had not saved that apparently godlike and heroic man. How *could* there be a God?

CHAPTER THREE

―――――◆―――――

Vanda and Jakob:
The Secret Years 1876–1877

i

Writing of some of his more high-spirited escapades with his sister, Douglas comments: "Nobody need tell me what we required: a thorough good spanking. Who was going to administer it?" His father, who could spank "confoundedly hard", was dead; who else would have cared to lay a hand on these recently-bereaved children whose family was responsible for the employment and propserity of the entire neighbourhood? It is safe to assume that Norman and Mary were both to some extent spoiled in common with other children in similar situations: wilfulness, and expectations of indulgence were probably able to develop freely.

One person who might have spanked Norman was Jakob Jehly; but Jehly, although devoted to Vanda, is not likely to have had the natural authority of Sholto Douglass.

Jakob Jehly was the sixth of the seven children of a family of peasant craftsmen in Bludenz – a family which has an honourable place in the history of art and craftsmanship in the Vorarlberg. His grandfather and great-grandfather had both been local painters of renown, whose works decorated many churches and hung in private houses (examples of their work may now be seen in the Landes-museum at Bregenz). Jakob's father, in order to get a living in the wake of the Napoleonic wars, had perforce become a house-painter; but the family was devoted to a higher art, and when they realised that Jakob seemed to have inherited the gift of his ancestors, they did all they could to foster it. After the local art master had confessed that the boy had nothing more to learn from him, Jakob was sent to the Akademie at Munich. Some, at least, of the expenses seem to have been paid by his Heimatgemeinde or parish. That was in October 1870, when he was sixteen.

In the holidays, he returned to the Vorarlberg, where he made many sketches and paintings. One day Sholto Douglass brought back to Falkenhorst a portfolio of Jehly's work which he enthused about to Vanda, especially the mountain scenes. Vanda also thought them delightful, and he gave her an alpine scene in oils by Jehly for Christmas in 1872. Whenever she looked at it, says her daughter, her curiosity about the painter was aroused, and she hoped she would be able to meet him.

Sometime in 1874, Vanda's sister Amie came to stay at Falkenhorst, bringing with her a whiff of the Babenwohl atmosphere – in this case an infatuation with the idea of becoming a painter. Sholto thought immediately of Jehly. Amie, Vanda and Sholto drove to Jehly's studio to arrange lessons. Sholto brought the young man out to the blue and white Douglass coach, and Vanda looked upon him wonderingly for the first time. It was astonishing: he was a figure out of her own dream world. Long, golden ringlets of hair fell to his shoulders, and his limpid gaze was no less filled with wonder than that of the ladies in the big comfortable carriage. This meeting took place in the year of Sholto's death, by which time Jehly had started coming regularly to Falkenhorst to teach Amie.

ii

After the tragedy no guest was more welcome at Babenwohl, we are told, than Jehly, who was presumably continuing his lessons there. All the women were enchanted by him, and even the old Baron liked him because of his technical ability and his artistic judgment. They may also have found the situation pleasing, as most patrons do, who discover and foster young talent. Vanda was obviously fascinated by the young man, but no one thought she had feelings for him other than those excited by his gifts. In fact, she was falling in love with him.

Her love was deep and genuine, but it was strongly influenced by romantic notions, by the Babenwohl dream-world, a kind of neo-mediaevalism behind which lay the potent influence of Joseph Viktor Scheffel, the enormously popular re-creator of the Middle Ages, much of whose work – verse mostly, but a famous novel as well – was concerned with the country near Lake Constance. His novel, *Ekkehard*, centred on the old ruined fortress of Hohentwiel, has as one of its chief characters the Herzogin Hadwig, patroness of the monk Ekkehard whom she had chosen as her teacher and whom she tried to seduce. Scheffel also wrote a series of drinking songs about the legendary Herr von Rodenstein, one of which has as its refrain:

> Das ist der Herr von Rodenstein
> Auf Rheinwein will er pirschen
> [That is the Master of Rodenstein
> Who goes a-hunting for Rhenish wine.]

Consequently, in Vanda's own mythology (shared, or partly shared, with her family) Falkenhorst became Hohentwiel, Jehly (who liked his glass of wine) became Rodenstein, and she became his Herzogin. This intimacy, of course, did not happen all at once. Likely enough, it began as a game amongst the Poellnitz sisters at Babenwohl, with the household favourite.

After Vanda's return to Falkenhorst, the relationship with Jehly took a more serious turn. On a sunny day in April 1876, they walked up to the ponds which fed the waterfall, and there, says Grete Gulbransson, "without speaking, they knew that they belonged to each other". Years later Vanda wrote of the experience: "The stream ran gently by, birds were singing, now and then there was the long-drawn-out cry of a falcon poised high above us in the freedom of the sky. We two were so calmly happy, so happy that the memory of that time shines like a star through these many years."

Vanda was now set on a course from which she had no intention of being diverted, although she knew she would have to face tremendous opposition from Babenwohl, or at any rate from her father. To have Jehly about the place occasionally as a kind of court painter was pleasantly diverting; to have him as a son-in-law – a peasant who mostly spoke in the local dialect, a penniless artist, a Catholic, an artisan – was something that the Baron could hardly have been expected to dream of in his worst nightmares. Vanda knew she had a fight on her hands, and would certainly not have entered into it if she had had doubts. In fact, it seems likely that her love was a much deeper and more happily complete and complementary one than she experienced with Sholto. Her daughter, who lays the sentiment on rather thick, goes so far as to say that Vanda's life only began at this time. In June, on the eve of Vanda's thirty-sixth birthday, she became secretly engaged to Jehly. Jehly was twenty-two.

iii

Jehly's feelings can only be imagined. If he had been a woman one would say that he had been swept off his feet. He probably had little real idea – as Vanda had – of the difficulties which lay ahead; and he was hardly in a position to court Vanda openly.

Vanda realised this and saw that she would have to take the initiative. She began having art lessons with him so that they could have an excuse to be together; and whenever they were together in the company of others, she surrounded herself with friends or servants in order to camouflage her particular attachment. They made many expeditions into the countryside, accompanied by Vanda's maid and confidante, the raven-haired "Schwarze" Mariele. Mariele would take the children on a geological or zoological search so that Vanda and Jakob could be left to each other. Thus did Norman and John become acquainted (though not perhaps for the first time) with snakes and toads and salamanders, and with rocks and minerals. Miss Prime, the much-teased governess, would go on some of these outings, breathing heavily in pursuit of Mary, but apparently game and sporting enough to survive all ordeals. Vanda liked to play the accordion and dance in the mountain taverns. She was also religious: she and Jehly knew all the little churches and all the mountain pastors in the Ländle. She was also an untiring doer of good works. Her noblesse felt its obligations. She was known as "unserer heilige Elisabeth".[9] There was not a cripple or a pauper in the district whom she did not try to help.

When Vanda could not see Jakob, she wrote him endless letters from Falkenhorst. When she knew he was travelling past by train in the valley below, she put a lamp in a certain window. When she visited Babenwohl they were surprised that she got up so early: it was not like her. She got up to intercept the postman and hide her letter from Jehly.

So, in secrecy, it went on, sometimes in the Vorarlberg, sometimes in Munich; until, in 1876, just before Jehly began his fourteen months of military service, Isabella guessed her daughter's secret. She liked Jehly and wanted to help Vanda without betraying the Baron. She found ways of making Vanda's double life more endurable.

iv

The boys, meanwhile, or at any rate Norman, spent part of the year in London with old James Heywood,[10] Jane Douglass' first cousin by marriage. He lived at 26 Kensington Palace Gardens, now the commercial section of the Czech Embassy. Norman was probably there during the winter of 1876-7.

Heywood was one of several Kennedy connections with at least one foot in the Industrial Revolution, in his case in a gentlemanly and mildly intellectual fashion. He had written on the coal district of south Lancashire, addressed the British Association on economics, and served on at least one board or commission concerned with the extension of higher education. He was a comfortable, generous, kindly old fellow with a "noble paunch and a rosy clean-shaven countenance, softly beaming". Later, he always had a half-sovereign or a sovereign ready for Norman's return to school, after taking him to the theatre or a circus. Norman' earliest impressions of London were derived from these visits.

v

Through this winter and the spring of 1877 Vanda was living in Munich making preparations for the reception and advancement of Jehly when his military service should be completed. She renewed her friendship with Ludwig Steub, the Bavarian poet, who, when he had first seen her at Falkenhorst soon after her marriage, had romantically worshipped her and called her the "Rose of the Walgau". As he had influence in Munich she took him into her confidence and told him about Jehly, and her plans. He warned her to tread carefully, but enabled her to meet people who might be able to help the young painter. She inspected studios, met the bohemian world of the city, and, through her uncle Hermann von Poellnitz, made friends at the Wittelsbach court. In spring, after a visit to Babenwohl, she took her sisters Amie and Ella back with her to Munich.

vi

When the three sisters returned to Babenwohl, old Mrs Douglass had arrived for one of her long visits to Falkenhorst, and was staying with the Poellnitzes. According to Grete Gulbransson she sat staring negatively and without comprehension in her flinty grey eyes at the loving and lively reunion of the sisters with their family. She seemed "intent on extinguishing all joy".

Her grandson has written that nearly everyone who came from Scotland to the Vorarlberg – relatives and friends – was a source of terror, his grandmother most of all. She had a long upper lip and a high forehead, looked grave and serene and rather handsome. He remembered clearly that she had spanked him when he was an infant, before he could walk. Later, she punished "in the stern judicial manner . . . which is precisely the one way children should never be punished". He had no doubt she meant to do right; but that was an old pretext for doing wrong. She thought children should be "broken". She never broke him. Something else happened. But that was later . . .

The weeks at Falkenhorst with Mrs Douglass were extremely difficult and boring. To the grandmother, Vanda was an intruder who had imposed a way of life – the enjoyable, emotional, Babenwohl way – on the grandchildren whom she thought of largely in terms of the Tilquhillie inheritance. Vanda, as always, found her stiff and inhuman, formal and disapproving. As usual, the old lady did not leave before inviting Vanda and the boys back to Scotland. Vanda's heart sank at the thought of it, but she decided that they had better go, for diplomatic reasons.

They went, and the boredom of it has been described by Norman:

Dr Hutchinson's endless sermons and prayers for the "Highlands and Islands" and for fair weather, punctuated by the crunching of peppermint drops on the part of his congregation . . . the Paraphrases of the Psalms, ending in some line like "His holy Courts *unto*" . . . And then those drives! People with cars cannot realise what a torture it was for a child to sit for hours in a carriage, cooped up with a brace of grandaunts or suchlike, and be taken for interminable distances to see friends at Raemoir and Learney and Glassel and Crathes and Midmar and Ballogie and Deebank and even Aboyne and Glentanar, and Durris and even Stonehaven over that never-ending Slug road, and Park House, and Finzean etc, etc.

The great-aunts and other female relations were not merely boring, but were active nuisances to the children:

They never left us alone; they were always pulling us about, as if we had no nurses or governesses of our own to teach us how to behave. Always interfering! You mustn't eat this; you mustn't do that; little girls don't climb trees; little boys ought to know that cows are not made to be ridden about on; never jump down till the carriage stops; you know what happened to Don't Care? He was hanged; have you said your prayers? . . .

The grandmother wanted Vanda to become the next "dowager". She hoped she would wear the Douglass tartan and take her place as the dead laird's widow amongst his father's countrymen. Vanda would willingly have starved in the Vorarlberg, if it had been necessary to do so in order to escape such a frightful destiny. Her only worry was over the boys. Would they feel regret, even resentment, if she were to refuse this dowager-right? Quite by chance, her mind was set partly at rest by Norman. Wouldn't she rather, he asked at a formal meal complete with kilts and piper – wouldn't she rather be eating *käsknöpfle* with Rodenstein? *He* would. . . . She was so delighted that she gave him a great smacking kiss in front of everyone. Her doubts began to dissolve.

At the end of that summer, the boys stayed behind to go to school in England. Vanda returned to spend the autumn alone at Falkenhorst, secretly enjoying the thought of the winter in Munich, when Jehly would be released from his military duties.

vii

Yarlet Hall, the school to which the Douglass boys were sent was discovered for them by their grandmother, or by relations of hers in Lancashire. Certainly, by Norman's account, it could have been well calculated to "break" anyone. Its situation, four miles from Stafford, with a view to the Potteries, he found unattractive, although in fact this corner of the country – with little woods, thickets, streams and dells – is filled with as much quiet beauty as any Midland landscape. He hated the place and all it contained; therefore summer never came to the place, he wrote later, only winter and lowering autumn skies. "After a childhood in the Vorarlberg with its clear frosty winters and bright summer days . . . there I was – dumped down in this gloomy and menacing region, apparently for ever."

The school itself sounds fairly typical of its time and kind. The boys were herded together "like young savages" and kept in subjection by fear of punishment. This, of course, led to bullying; but there was also "a nagging and sneaking tone about the place": the staff were unwilling to do anything to help the pupils. Consequently, "we were a crowd of horrible little boys . . . made horrible by an environment over which we had no control". The Revd "William Bull", as Douglas calls him (his real name was the Revd Walter Earle), red-nosed and black-bearded, was a "pious hog . . . a worm in human form . . . a reptile", and manifestly unfit for his duties. So much did Douglas loathe him, then and even fifty years later, "that if somebody were to assure me officially that he had died of a lingering and painful disease I should rejoice from the bottom of my heart". People like Bull, he continued, had no right to inflict misery on children entrusted to them, and should be made to suffer for it. He admitted he was unforgiving. Why should he not be? Let others speak well of the man if they could. . . .

The diatribe against Bull is long, and seems excessive; there seems to be a touch of obsession, of mania, in the attack – especially when the only crime of which Bull is accused was that of making Douglas learn by heart, as a punishment, some of the twenty lines of Portia's "mercy" speech. But it is worth remembering that Douglas was extremely sensitive, in a quite objective and altruistic manner, concerning the unnecessary suffering endured by children. It looks as though he knew all about it from personal experience, and perhaps had his first taste of it at Yarlet.

CHAPTER FOUR

Vanda and Jakob:
Trouble 1877–1878

i

When he had completed his military service, Jehly took a flat in Munich with one of his brothers. He and Vanda were able to spend a good deal of time together, mainly on walks into the country, but also quite frequently in the city, although there, at parties and other functions, they often had to pretend to be mere acquaintances, and began to be exasperated by the need for deception.

Vanda pretended to Babenwohl and to some extent to her uncle Hermann and his family in Munich that the latter were a reason for her long stay in the city. To substantiate this invention she asked her uncle and his family to come and stay at Falkenhorst in the summer. This they did, and Vanda entertained them generously. They made many expeditions in the Walgau and saw a great deal of Jehly who, as usual, was at home in the summer. At the end of the visit Hermann stayed at Babenwohl, to see his brother Ernst. He had apparently kept his eyes open in Munich and in the Vorarlberg, and one day, as if the realisation of it had suddenly come to him, he banged his fist on the table and shouted: "Devil take me if Vanda doesn't marry that pink-faced painter!"

Blanche, Hermann's daughter, roared with laughter. The others were mostly alarmed or indignant. The Baron himself swore at Isabella and all her daughters for their accursed romantic notions that made such nonsense possible. When he realised that Hermann's ridiculous suggestion was being taken seriously, he went off to consult with old Baron Brockdorff, whom his second daughter, Mary, had married, and who lived in Bregenz. Vanda, of course, was at Falkenhorst.

The Barons arranged between them that Mary should be sent to that damned painter in Bludenz with the message that he was to give up Vanda at once. That would settle *him*. Then they would present Vanda with the *fait accompli*, and that would settle *her*. And that would be the end of the whole damned business.

Isabella managed to get a reassuring message to Vanda, with news of what was impending. Vanda blessed her mother, and waited to do battle with Mary. But when Mary arrived, Jehly was with her. She had given him her message, and he had agreed to give up Vanda, but only if Vanda wished him to. Mary suddenly realised what a truly good man he was, and decided to help him and Vanda. Between them, the three agreed that Jakob must go to Munich at once. Mary would stay two days at Falkenhorst, to give Jakob time to get there, and then return to the Barons and warn them to be reasonable with Vanda and try to meet her half-way: then she would add "as to Jakob, he is in Munich".

But poor Mary had no strength for such deceptions. She found herself trapped between two factions, bound by impossible conflicting loyalties. She lost her nerve, almost her reason. Perhaps, married to an old man, she was tortured by jealousy of Vanda's and Jakob's apparently idyllic love. "Haven't you given up that stupidity yet?" she asked Vanda bitterly one day – and Vanda's hopes of presenting her case to her family through the favourable recommendation of her sister were gone. All that secrecy, all those clandestine meetings, all that circumspect behaviour of the past, and every attempt on her part to present Jehly to her family as the worthy man he was, had been in vain! A showdown with the family was now inevitable. It was just a question of time.

ii

During this year – 1878 – the boys were in Britain, either at school, or, during the holidays, at the homes of relations in London, Scotland or Manchester. In February John was thirteen; in December Norman was ten. But sometime in 1878 or in the first half of 1879 there was a visit to Austria, at the end of which the boys were sent back to England with a somewhat irresponsible companion:

My Dear Mamma

I have arrived all safe at Yarlet. The gardener's brother got drunk at basle and paris, and when we arrived at London we asked him to take us up to Stafford, and he said he had *not* got *any more money* so I asked him where my 10 franks were and he said he has spent them. So we asked him about the luggage and he said he had left it at Paris. Johnnie will tell you the other part more plainer. Much love to all.

I am your loving
N Douglass

iii

In January 1879 Vanda could stand the strain no longer. She went to Babenwohl and announced to the whole family her intention of marrying Jehly. "Are you the Devil?" her father bellowed. "You must be mad to think of marrying that clodhopper! It could never work." When he had finished Vanda said: "And if you all tell me you'll die if I marry him, I shall say 'Die, then! I *will* marry him'." The women began to cry. The Baron, beside himself with rage, ordered Vanda out of the house, never to return. Isabella dared to embrace her and wish her well. She left, weeping copiously, amidst floods of family tears.

There was one consolation: the crisis, which had loomed for so long, was past; she had had the strength to meet it as she had hoped she would.

The Baron called up his heavy artillery. Jehly was bombarded with insults and accusations. He was told that he would make Vanda unhappy for the rest of her life; and the Baron went about telling everyone that a tragedy was impending. Vanda had warned Jakob what to expect, but under the assault he could be excused his doubts. Was Vanda sure, he asked her, that she would not rather change her mind? The responsibility for making so many people unhappy was a prospect that appalled him. She replied that her parents stood in the way of their happiness, and need not be considered. That was wrong, he argued; the children would never forgive him and Vanda if they made a tragedy unnecessarily. Vanda remained fearless and determined.

In the midst of the battle, Mary collapsed. Three doctors attended her; none knew what was wrong with her. At Babenwohl, also, casualties occurred: the Baron, Isabella, and two of their daughters were laid up. At Falkenhorst, Vanda, the enemy, received a telegram: "Come at once. Mary in great danger." She went, and was instrumental in saving – or prolonging – Mary's life; then she nursed all the Babenwohlers back to health.

Her mother, moved with gratitude, said how good Vanda was, and spoke also of Jakob's noble and loving nature; the Baron, overhearing her remarks, growled his agreement. Vanda returned to Falkenhorst, and with her, says her daughter, went everything mild, kind and agreeable. The Babenwohlers, rescued, returned to their mood of resistance and obstinacy. Mary relapsed – and died.

Vanda returned once more to Bregenz to comfort the bereaved, but stayed in an hotel. Then she and Jakob and Schwarze Mariele and Miss Prime and Mary Douglass all went on a walking tour in Bavaria. This was in the spring of 1879.

iv

The summer holidays lay ahead. She could spend them in England or
Scotland with the boys, or bring the boys back to Austria. That would
depend upon old Jane Douglass. Vanda, fortified and refreshed by the
Bavarian holiday, was optimistic: she decided to write to Jane Douglass
and tell her everything. Jehly was the only man for her, she wrote; she
loved him deeply, and was determined to marry him. She described his
worthiness, his sterling character, his art, his humble origin, and also
(which Isabella thought foolish) the opposition of her parents. She
could only come to Scotland, she wrote, if her plans had Mrs Douglass'
approval. Otherwise she would fetch the boys from school and bring
them back to the Vorarlberg.

That done, she tackled her father again, but he would neither consent
to the marriage nor forbid it; Mary's death seemed to have softened his
will.

Vanda waited four weeks for a reply from her mother-in-law. When
it came, it was even worse than she had thought it might be. Old Mrs
Douglass demanded that Vanda should give up, instantly and for ever, her
bizarre idea of marrying a working man. If she persisted with this intention, she would lose her children, her parents, her sisters, and all her old
loyal friends in Scotland. And since the young man was of the working
class, Mrs Douglass could not allow her grandchildren to visit Falkenhorst
in the holidays. Moreover, if Vanda was coming over to see them at
school, she would only be welcome at Feugh Cottage if she had by then
changed her mind about marrying.

On receipt of this ultimatum, Vanda ordered a carriage and drove
straight to the Guardianship Court in Bludenz. She reported the result of
this visit to her mother-in-law, probably with some satisfaction:

> I had better not say what I think of your letter. As soon as I received
> it I went to the Guardianship Court, where I was assured that as their
> mother I alone am responsible for the education and upbringing of
> my children, provided this is in accordance with their welfare and
> happiness. If there should be any doubt about my ability to look after
> them, then the Court, and the Court alone, has power to investigate
> the matter. Although you are their grandmother, I am their lawful
> mother, and as their mother, I wish my boys to come to me for their
> holidays.
>
> I was also told yesterday at the Court that I am free to marry again,
> and that if the man of my choice is an honourable one, and no objec-
> tions can be found to his character and way of life, I retain full rights

as mother and guardian of my children, let anyone dispute them who dares.

I would add this: it would be a shame, if my relations were not willing to comply with my wishes, if I were forced to seek justice in the courts, as I heard yesterday that law and equity are on my side.

If you remember the letter you wrote me, you will not be surprised at the manner in which my answer to it is expressed.

Vanda Douglass
geb. v. Pöllnitz[11]

But now, although she knew the law was on her side, she feared, in a sense, even more for her boys. The old lady might try in some way to get at them, or to set them against their mother. Scotland was out of the question; so she would go at once and fetch the boys from school, and bring them home.

v

She made the return journey in less than a week, and drove, dead tired but triumphant, from Nenzing station to Falkenhorst with her sons safely beside her in the blue and white Douglass coach. Their return was celebrated along the route by the firing of *böller* – little cannon that were used for salutes.

Vanda devoted herself to the boys, determined to give them a happy holiday. Their stone-hammers, butterfly-nets and specimen jars littered the hall table; and they spent happy hours scrambling over the hills. Sometimes, they could see their mother waiting for them at some lower level. They thought she was sketching, as she had taken her sketching-block; but usually she was writing to Jehly in Munich expressing all her hopes and fears for the future. Isabella was supporting her again, secretly, saying that as Vanda had gone so far, she must not give up.

Johnnie, as he was known in the family, was now fourteen. By the end of the holidays he would be fourteen and a half, and would be going to Uppingham. His mother decided to talk to him about her plans. When she said she was thinking of marrying again, he was delighted. He thought the marriage should take place as soon as possible; Vanda ought not to spend another winter alone at Falkenhorst. They should find a nice place in Munich. Meanwhile, Jehly should come on a visit, so that he, Johnnie, could get to know him well. "Trust me, dearest Mother; I shall never desert you!"

In due course the meeting took place. Jehly came from Munich, Vanda and Johnnie from Falkenhorst. They met at Rankweil where they would not be disturbed by neighbours or business. Johnnie swore faith and friendship to Jehly. He and Vanda, no doubt, discussed the date of their marriage.

The boys went back to England, Johnnie to his public school, and Norman, who would no longer have had even the solace of his brother's presence at the horrible Yarlet, was placed in the hands of Mr and Mrs Green, of Mowsley. Mowsley was less than fifteen miles from Uppingham, so the boys would be able to meet occasionally.

vi

At Mowsley Rectory, unlike Yarlet, it was always summer. That was because Norman's two years there were happy ones. He was among kind and friendly people, and he could be alone, "quite by myself, whenever so disposed". Such intervals of solitude were natural and health-giving to any boy, he wrote; and he remembered Mowsley in later years as an oasis in a desert of team-life.

The Revd Mr Green, who was supposed to be coaching Norman for Uppingham, did not overwork himself or his pupil, though he took him through a quantity of Cicero's letters – rather advanced Latin for a child of ten or eleven. He liked pottering about the garden or driving round the countryside behind a horse called Pilgrim. He was bearded, and a pipe-smoker; the smell of his tobacco filled his study, in which Norman had his lessons. His sermons were pleasantly short.

Mrs Green was a "frail woman with gentle ways" who had a lasting and beneficent influence on Norman. She played the piano and stimulated him to keep up his own playing. She encouraged his love of natural history. She allowed him to fill his room with chemicals, which occasionally produced the most vile smells throughout the house. But she must have done much more, for he wrote of her with exceptional tenderness: "the vision of her face was dear to me for many long years afterwards." In this phrase one can sense the devotional gratitude of a small boy, exiled from his mother, for a substantially satisfying emotional reassurance and a sensitive understanding of his needs.

Freed from the tortures of Yarlet, he had a placid and expansive existence at Mowsley. He made friends with children in the village, went bird's-nesting (rather too greedily, as was the custom then), found pleasant walks everywhere, and enlarged his collection of fossils. He made careful notes on all the birds and beasts he saw. He was a subscriber – his grandmother ordered it for him – to *The Zoologist*. And he had met Mr Matthews, Rector of Gumley, a neighbouring village, who was a keen ornithologist, and gave Norman a good deal of help and advice. In local farms he discovered the *raison d'être* of bulls and stallions.

Fifty years later, he remembered the exact appearance of house and garden, all the details of the countryside, and the names of farmers: ". . . I think of Mowsley and there steals upon me a sense of immemorial calm; all was verdant and reposeful . . . A retrospect of those two years is suffused with sunshine and kindliness."

A few letters have survived from the Mowsley period. The insistent reassurances in the following letter that his grandmother should trust him and do as he says are typical of the grown man:

May 14/80   Mowsley
Saturday   Rugby
My dear Grandmama,
   I got your letter quite safely, and I thank you very much for it. Those eggs will travel quite safely you may be sure without wrapping them in cotton wool even for the first reason because they are not as breakable as most eggs and for the second, yesterday I got from London two golden crested Wren's eggs, which are the *smallest* and *most breakable* eggs in England, and they were not wrapped up at all, they were simply laid side by side in a box which I got yesterday and they were not brocken nor cracked so you may be sure these will not even if you do not wrapp them up. There is no post going from here on Sundays so this must be your birthday letter, and I *wish you many happy returns of the day*. I got a letter from John this morning he is quite well and has got lots more stones. I am quite well also. Now I must stop. I remain your loving G.N.D.
P.S. I should like you to send the eggs very much, I will be blamed if they are broken.
P.S. The blots in the letter were made at the very last moment accidentally.

Remnants of the German language still cling to his English. He writes "brocken" for "broken", "wrapp" for "wrap", and says "I will be blamed if they are broken", meaning he will take the blame.

Another letter contains an example of a lifelong characteristic: imputing to the other person concerned the desire which he himself probably feels as strongly, perhaps more strongly, and (in certain instances) exclusively. This also is to his grandmother. "Johnnie will not be able to come here" he says in this letter

because the *Douglases* of Mk Harborough who are friends of Mr Green's have only got one horse, and that horse can only draw a certain carriage which only holds two people, and those two people will be Mr Douglass'es son, and a coachman and when they arrive at

Uppingham, the coachman drives the carriage back. He wants to come *so very much he has told me*, do not you think you could write to Mr Green to hire a carriage to take him from Market Harborough to Uppingham – for Mr Green drives him as far as Market Harborough?

No doubt Johnnie did want to come; but there can be no doubt either that Norman was at least as eager as John for the meeting.

A third letter, to his mother, illustrated with thumbnail sketches, gives a brief glimpse of his room at the Rectory:

My room here looks beautiful I have put up a lot of pictures, and natural curiosities, such as the weapon of a saw-fish &c and besides I have got large photographs of Beethoven, Mozart, Bach, Mendelssohn, Handel, and Hayden, and the two photographs of falkenhorst, some geological maps, pictures of antideluvian [sic] reptiles &c.

vii

While Johnnie was struggling with his first term at Uppingham, and Norman was gradually discovering that he was among friends at Mowsley, Vanda and her little entourage were preparing to leave Falkenhorst. The house belonged to Jane Douglass, and Vanda could not remain in it after her confrontation with the old lady, who, nevertheless, wrote calmly and mildly about the actual handing over. As Vanda would not be able to take the crested silver, the old lady offered her money instead, to buy silver with. Vanda looked askance at this apparent olive branch, and thought it false and out of character. In fact, it was probably quite genuine, and typical of the old lady, who seems to have had respect for anyone who stood up to her.

Ernst von Poellnitz was unrelenting. As soon as he heard about the preparations for closing Falkenhorst, he forced poor Isabella to write a warning, complaining, regretting letter to Vanda, full of apprehensions as to a possible future of poverty, hardship, and despair.

Vanda left on 5th November. It must have been a hard parting. Schwarze Mariele picked a last bouquet of flowers for her mistress from the Falkenhorst garden, and the little company set off for Munich: Vanda, Mariele, Miss Prime and Mary (who was now eight).

Vanda and Jakob were married at the (Protestant) Matthäus-Kirche on 4th December 1879. Jakob's brothers Hans and Michel were the only guests. An inscription on the wedding cake summarised the triumphant conclusion of the couple's long struggle to be man and wife, and provided an exhortation for such difficulties as they still had to face: NITT LUGG' LO, which, in Vorarlbergerisch, means NEVER GIVE UP.

CHAPTER FIVE

Vanda and Jakob:
Happily Married 1879–1883

i

During the whole of 1880 Vanda and Jakob seem to have lived pleasantly, in Munich, in a house or in part of it, built for himself by Georg Hauberrisser. Hauberrisser was an architect of distinction, responsible for the world-famous neo-gothic Munich Rathaus, which at that date was not completed. His house faced on to the Theresien Wiese, with the Bavarian Alps as a far-distant backcloth. He lent Jakob his own studio until a new one could be furnished for him. Considering their circumstances, the newly married couple could hardly have found more suitable or convenient accommodation anywhere. After about a year of it, though, the Jehly household, which included two Vorarlberger servants as well as Miss Prime and Mary, became homesick for the Ländle, and by the summer of 1881 they had returned to Bludenz.

It was not an easy homecoming for Vanda. Relations with Babenwohl were still greatly strained and, at a chance encounter with three of her sisters on the actual journey home, she was cut by them, which reduced her to tears. Also, she was forced, at the beginning, to live in cramped and uncomfortable quarters in a small hotel, besieged by the large Jehly family, who, though she liked them very well, could not really be expected to understand the predicament of a sensitive headstrong aristocratic woman who had never suffered material deprivation until she suddenly found herself homeless in her own homeland.

By luck or skill or both, Jakob found Die Halde, a pleasant house superficially not unlike a taller but smaller Falkenhorst. It stands just outside Bludenz to the east, not far from the village of Rungelin. He took a lease of it as soon as he discovered he could do so, and sprang it on Vanda as a surprise.

Vanda loved it. It was a house after her own heart. The furniture was brought from Munich and carried from Bludenz railway station by the Jehly brothers and their apprentices who, when the job was finished, immediately took part in a festive housewarming party. Vanda and Jakob

37

went to bed that night knowing they would wake with a view of the Mondspitz from their window; they were really home again, with their beloved mountains.

Vanda began to be happy in her new Vorarlberg life. She was reunited with Lasko, her faithful old black dog who had been looked after by the Jehlys while she was in Munich. She acquired a little squirrel called Hansele, who slept under her pillow or in her workbasket. She painted porcelain in order to bring in a little extra money. Miss Prime still had charge of Mary, who was now ten. Jehly was beginning to make a reputation as a painter. And it was now possible for the boys to come to their homeland for the summer holidays.

ii

After nearly two years of exile in England and Scotland, Johnnie and Norman arrived at Die Halde late at night on 27th July 1881, and found the rest of the family asleep. What their feelings were, on coming to a strange house five or six miles from their real home, and to a stepfather so different from Sholto Douglass – a stepfather for whom their mother had given up both her own home and the social position that went with it – it is impossible to say. At school, in the climate of acute snobbery then prevalent in such institutions, they may have suffered silently from feelings of social bewilderment. And Grete Gulbransson stated that they must have been horrified and ashamed to hear unpleasant and malicious remarks about their mother from old Jane Douglass while they were in Scotland. She added that John was unaffected by them, and determined to make the best of things. Certainly, the attitudes at Feugh Cottage, at Babenwohl, and at Die Halde were not disguised, and one can be sure that the boys took their mother's part.

Norman, who had formerly spent so much time with his sister, had by this time found a new intimacy with his brother. They had shared their exile in England, at least during the holidays, and were not far from each other in termtime. Their interests were similar: collecting stones; observing, shooting, and stuffing birds and collecting their eggs; hunting and collecting small animals; fishing. The day after their return to Austria, they went out together to a nearby quarry to see what they could find and were soon arranging specimens in their stone cupboards. In a notebook of zoological observations, Norman records that John shot nineteen creatures during these holidays; Norman himself "got" – whatever that may mean – five, one of which was certainly killed. Such were the modest beginnings of an adelphic campaign of slaughter in the years to come.

They must have enjoyed their holiday enormously: rushing up and down the Mondspitz (1,967 metres), going shooting and swimming, walking by moonlight up the Walserthal, visiting the Arlberg railway tunnel then being constructed and seeing the vast borer, the *Bohrmaschine*, sleeping in the Douglashütte on the Lünersee, or simply having a "grand battle with green apples in the Orchard, while Mama was working".

Norman must also have been delighted to be with Mary again, either just going for walks with her and the two dogs, Lasko and Sippins, or, during the Emperor's visit to Bludenz, having "great fun with Mary about some funny people". There may have been overtones of sadness which were not fully explicable to, or comprehended by the children. They went, for instance, to Falkenhorst: "Saw the garden, went about. House empty, sad and locked. All shutters shut." That was three days after their arrival; on another occasion they spent an hour and a half in Falkenhorst's garden; and they visited places that were to become, if they were not already, sanctified in Norman's memory – the Owl's Den, the Stag's Leap, the Lutzwald, and the church of St Anna: "Dear old St Anna with the Gate and two large trees and the Lutz Wald." A distance, both of time (during their absence in England) and of place had been set between the children and these familiar and beloved objects.

Jehly went about a great deal with his stepchildren, bathing, climbing, walking; but there was one expedition on which he did not go; that was when the three children and their mother visited Babenwohl. There is no mention by Norman of Grosspapa; only of Grossmama, who had always liked Jehly, and of Vanda's sister Ella. The "old cock on his dung-hill" was presumably absent or at all events unrelenting.

Whether or not the boys were in any way disturbed by the repercussions of their mother's romantic drama with Jehly, there is much to be said for Grete Gulbransson's view that they received positive benefit from it. According to her, they began, on this visit, to realise that all Vanda's struggles and sacrifices had been worthwhile to her, and that she was fundamentally one of the happiest people in the world, joyfully accepting her fate. The boys felt, according to Grete Gulbransson, that Vanda had fulfilled herself, and this realisation gave them an understanding of human values, and the ability to discriminate between what was and was not truly worthwhile and important. If this is correct, one can see that it could have had enormous influence on Norman's way of life: amongst other things it could have seemed to him entirely to justify the attitude: Do what you want to do, and be damned to everybody else.

In September, the boys returned to England, and at the beginning of this school year, Norman joined his brother at Uppingham.

Uppingham may not have been as bad as Yarlet, but Norman found it no more tolerable. It is likely that any formal scholastic institution in England would have seemed obnoxious to him after the homely atmosphere of Mowsley Rectory. He had just spent two happy months in his native country with his mother and sister, from whom he was now separated again by a sea passage and two days' journey; and, with the exception of Mowsley, his experiences in England and Scotland had been unrewarding; no one should have expected him to be riotously happy.

In fact, he could find no redeeming features in the place or, if he could, does not mention them. It was, he wrote, a matter of temperament: "Some few of us are born centrifugal. The herd-system and team-life, congenial to many, went against my grain. A mildewy scriptural odour pervaded the institution – it reeked of Jereboam and Jesus; the masters struck me as supercilious humbugs; the food was so vile that for the first day or two after returning from holidays I could not get it down."

He was also unlucky in his housemaster who, he alleged, was "a pompous sneak; he used to crawl about in noiseless felt slippers in order to catch us doing what we ought not to be doing." Years later he saw this man (the Revd J. H. Skrine) in the train between London and Carlisle on his way to Glenalmond, of which he had become headmaster: "I felt sorry for the boys . . . he was dressed in some absurd clerical costume, and looked more than ever like a skinned rabbit."

To say that there was no redeeming feature for Norman at Uppingham is not quite true: there was one, in the shape of a curiously wizened, prematurely old-looking boy called Collier – Harry Samuel Collier. He was a squat, undersized, unprepossessing child, whose appearance had not been improved by a cricket ball breaking one of his front teeth. His face was seamed with lines, and he was chronically constipated. Needless to say, he was known at school as the Bug.

This was the only boy with whom Norman became close friends. The Bug "played the violin and had a passion for music; he talked about other things besides games; he could laugh at that establishment which the other boys took so seriously". He and Norman sat together in the study of one or the other while the Bug would talk about such subjects as Schumann and his madness, or the organ in the Albert Hall in which a criminal had hidden himself (in one of the largest pipes) for nearly a week. They went for walks together, to the railway cutting at Manton where the vertebrae of Ichthyosaurus were to be found, or to Wardely Wood. The company of the Bug made his life endurable.

iv

The Christmas holidays of 1881 were probably spent either in Scotland or at the Kennedy stronghold of The Weaste, Eccles, Manchester. The Weaste, long since demolished, was situated just to the north of the Manchester Ship Canal on the opposite side from Trafford Park. Its chatelaine for many years was Margaret Tootal (née Kennedy), one of Norman's great-aunts, and the house was described by him as "a melting-pot of grand-aunts and grand-uncles, sisters and brothers of my grand-mother, who was also always there; wealthy and frowsy folk, every single one of them". This may have been the place, and these holidays the occasion of old Mrs Douglass' correction by her grandson, when the "something else" happened which saved him from being "broken" by her. The incident had better be told in his own words:

I was . . . all alone, perfectly comfortable and perfectly well, delighted to have escaped for a season out of some absurd school . . . when the old thing entered with an all too familiar silver tray, bearing the abominable mixture known as "Gregory's Powder". It was her universal remedy for every complaint of mine from a sprained ankle to a tooth-ache, the principle being that, whatever might be amiss, Gregory's Powder, by virtue of its villainous taste alone, must inevitably do good, if not as a medical preparation, then as an incitement to humility and obedience. This filthy poison I had hitherto swallowed like a lamb; and been made duly ill in consequence. On that particular occasion, however, the sight of the tray stirred me as never before; all the accumulated bile of similar torments in the past surged up; it was my first experience of "seeing red". Guided by a righteous demon of revolt, I seized a stick which stood in a corner at my elbow – an elaborate concern of hippopotamus-hide with carved ivory top, which some good-for-nothing uncle had brought from Natal – and therewith knocked the tray out of her hand and then went for her with such a dash that she fled out of the room. It happened in the twinkling of an eye. I knew not how the thing was done; it was plain, now, what people meant when they said So-and-so was "not responsible for his actions". On mature deliberation I decided, in the very words of the old lady, *that all was for the best*. There was an end of Gregory's Powder. That is the way to treat grandmothers of this variety. She dare not tackle me; she was too old, and I too tough, being then in the habit of winning most of the gymnastic prizes at school. As always before, she had tried to impose upon me by sheer strength of personality, and suddenly, for the first time, found herself confronted by a new and persuasive argument – brute force.

Well! To attack your grandmother with a walking-stick is not polite. On the other hand, there is no reason why boys should be needlessly tortured; they suffer quite enough, as it is. If I had not acted as I did, she would have continued to poison me with the stuff to the end of her long life. Why suffer, when you can avoid it? . . . For the rest, in her heart of hearts, she was perhaps not quite so "surprised and grieved" (a favourite phrase of hers, like "I sincerely hope and trust") as she professed to be; so strong was her family sense that she may well have been charmed with this premature exhibition of ancestral savagery; maybe she was anxiously waiting for it to appear, and chose Gregory's Powder as a kind of test or provocative. If so, it worked. One thing is certain: referring to the episode, she told another of those old women, who repeated it to me long afterwards, that I was plainly the son of my father – good news, so far as it went. . . .

v

The Easter holidays of 1882 were again spent at Die Halde. Vanda was expecting a baby, a prospect which had already given Isabella, her mother, the strength to ally herself secretly with Cis in a determination somehow to evade the Baron's interdiction so that she could be present at the birth.

Vanda's sister Adèle seems to have been sent as ambassadress. She visited Vanda in June or July, having also recently become pregnant, with her third child, and announced that she came with the consent of everyone at Babenwohl. "Papa as well?" asked Vanda unbelievingly.

Margarethe (Grete) Jehly[12] was born on 31st July. Both grandmothers were present, if not at the birth, immediately afterwards, and became firm friends. Relations with Babenwohl were greatly eased.

The boys spent their summer holidays at Feugh Cottage, presumably because Vanda's hands were full at Die Halde; and at Christmas Norman was at The Weaste once more, where he started an apprenticeship in taxidermy. The Revd Andrew Matthews of Gumley had told Norman that no collector was worth his salt until he had learned to skin his own birds. That was enough. He began lessons at the earliest opportunity afterwards, from a grimy old naturalist in one of the grimiest streets of Manchester, "a man who relieved birds of their jackets in dainty fashion with one hand, the other having been amputated and replaced by an iron hook". During this period the billiard-room at The Weaste became a dissecting-room every morning, "a chamber of horrors, a shambles, where headless trunks and brains and gouged-out eyes . . . lay about in sanguinary morsels, while the floor was ankle deep in feathers, and tables strewn with tweezers, lancets, arsenical paste, corrosive sublimate and other paraphernalia . . ."

Well, it was not actually Jane Douglass' house, but there is little doubt that she could have stopped such activities if she had wished to. She did not stop them. Nor do relations seem to have been affected by Vanda's defiant marriage, or by Norman's attack on the Gregory Powder. All in all, the old lady could hardly be called inhuman.

vi

The Bug was four years older than Norman, and both he and Norman's brother John were due to leave Uppingham at the end of the summer term of 1883. The thought of attempting to endure Uppingham without them must have been too much for Norman, and is almost certainly the reason why he delivered an ultimatum to his mother: either she must remove him from the school, or he would arrange to be expelled. How? That question was put to him more than sixty years later by Constantine Fitzgibbon, who was then intending to write a biography. "Was sodomy the threat?" "No," replied Douglas enigmatically, "sexual malpractice. Not sodomy."

The threat, if it existed, seems to have worked. It is not the sort of threat that most boys, even nowadays, and even in the freest families, would feel inclined to make to their mothers; and was it really necessary? Surely Vanda would only have had to be told that he was thoroughly unhappy, or was in danger sexually from other boys, to remove him? On the other hand, it is probable that she knew she would have to leave the Vorarlberg if Norman was to go to a day-school that would give him a really good education, and this both she and Jehly would have been reluctant to do, so some sort of threat is certainly a possibility, though it may well have been a good deal milder than Norman liked to make out.

If it was made, it worked. Norman and his brother left Uppingham together, before the end of the summer term in 1883. They went up to stay with their grandmother for a week before going out to Die Halde.

In October, the whole family packed up and migrated to Karlsruhe.

PART II

The Amateur of Natural Science
1883–1896

CHAPTER SIX

Karlsruhe Gymnasium
1883–1889

i

It is fruitless to speculate how different Douglas' life might have been if, like his father, he had been wholly educated abroad and had remained in his own home and native province, or if, like his brother, he had inherited the lairdship and the family business;[13] but it is a fact that the contrast between his schooldays in England and in Germany is distinct and sharp. At Uppingham he had been unwilling and resentful – "it reeked of Jereboam and Jesus"; and since it was a boarding-school in the mild countryside of Rutland, extra-curricular activities, though pleasant enough compared with Thucydides and mathematics, paled by comparison with the freedom and wildness of Austria. At home, also, time was of little consequence, whereas at Uppingham every vista was closed by a vision of assembly or the sound of the school bell. One receives an impression of loneliness from his accounts of his English schooling, and it is surely significant that a boy who, by his own account at least, was later to become so spirited and to choose friends who were also spirited, should have been obliged to seek the company of the despised Bug as his only companion. The fact is that he had been cut off by lack of common experience in home backgrounds, and to some extent at least, at Yarlet, by language itself, from his school-fellows.

At Karlsruhe, the change was immediate and fundamental. He was within a hundred and fifty miles of his home; he had a second home in the town, living in a rented house with his mother, stepfather, sister, and baby half-sister. The language of his childhood surrounded him; the food was at least familiar and palatable, if not always enjoyable; and above all, he was a day-boy, no longer subject to the petty disciplines, the idiotic horseplay, the bullying, and the fostering of the team-spirit which used to occupy so much of life at an English public school. At the Gymnasium he could drop purely defensive attitudes and relax; and in relaxing, expand.

The curriculum was a full one. He not only dealt with it satisfactorily,

47

but indulged in extras as well – Russian, Italian and French lessons, dancing classes, and the piano. His interests were as wide as his father's had been, and some of them – zoology, geology, and archaeology – were identical. During his years in Karlsruhe he laid the foundations of that versatility of knowledge on which, later in life, everyone who knew him made admiring comment. In his sixties, he was to wonder how he had found time for so many occupations, since boys in such schools were worked to their full capacity. Sometimes they were even driven to suicide by the strain of study, by fear of not passing an examination, or by a bad report. This could never have happened to him, he wrote: "a secret but healthy contempt for all education had been acquired long ago, in England; catch me killing myself for any school-nonsense!" Nor did he try to be near the top of the class: "without being set back, that is, losing a year, I was content to squeeze myself gingerly from one form into the next with a 'moderate – fairly good', and my final mark was the closest shave of all, namely, *Gesamtpraedicat: hinlänglich* [Final Report: adequate]. Those infernal mathematics! They gave me an infinity of trouble and often ruined my summer holidays. And the examinations in the heat of July were pitiless; they haunted my dreams for years afterwards."

He was at the Gymnasium for six years from the age of nearly fifteen until six months after his twentieth birthday. During these vital years of adolescence he achieved a great deal. Apart from becoming reasonably proficient in the subjects already mentioned, he reached what he called the height of his natural history mania – an enthusiasm which was to prove fruitful. It led him to learn Russian and, later, to go to Russia. It took him to the bay of Naples and Capri. It was responsible for his first appearances in print; and it brought him friendships which he remembered with affection many years later.

Intellectual interests apart, he also developed precociously in other ways.

ii

He started his first term at the Gymnasium in October 1883, and made the interesting discovery that he was in the same class as the only other foreigner in the school. This was Luigi Guerrieri-Gonzaga, a sprig of that ancient Italian family of which the Dukes of Mantua had been head. Norman and Luigi naturally gravitated to one another in the midst of so many German boys, and became great friends. "What fun it would be, he often said, if I knew Italian! We could then talk together without any of the other boys, or even the master, understanding a word of what we were driving at." Thus began Italian lessons with Frau Schenkh, who had travelled all over Italy, and in her gravely civil manner recommended

Norman not to miss seeing, among other things, the Neapolitan fish-market. She described its variety of grotesque sea beasts so vividly and with such enthusiasm that the eulogy remained fresh in his memory until he was in his sixties. It was she who introduced him to the writings of Gregorovius, which he became very fond of and thought he might have been influenced by; and when his sister also took up Italian and also read Gregorovius, she too became an admirer, to the extent of translating his *Insel Capri* into English.[14]

That was not all that was to follow from Norman's meeting with Luigi. Later, he often stayed with the Gonzagas, either in Rome or in their country house near Mantua. There were two young sisters "lovely girls whom Lenbach and others have painted" and whom their mother once took over to London for the season. Norman fell in love with one of them, and was engaged to her for six years.

Nor was that all. One day in 1892 the scene was to take place at Amalfi, while he was with these two sisters, that lost him an inheritance . . .

And still more was to follow. By the time of the Amalfi incident, Luigi had already become irritable and melancholy and suspicious of those around him. He gradually became more and more withdrawn and paranoid, drifting slowly into madness. He spent two years in an asylum, emerged briefly, subdued but sane, and then relapsed into violence and died in 1895. Four years later, Norman wrote *Nerinda*, a story based on the "disintegration of a personality". It embodied some of Luigi's actual words. "It was to be my first, and last, excursion into the domain of fiction" – or so he thought at the time.

iii

Diaries of the Karlsruhe period illustrate his growing preoccupation with natural history, and list a good many of the birds and other creatures observed, or shot, by Norman and his brother. The slaughter mounts steadily for several years, hampered at first by the "tragical end of Bijou", when his brother's air-gun was taken from him by a keeper. Of the summer sport in 1884 Douglas in old age wrote that it was a hecatomb, and quoted from his diary how he had occasionally blundered: "Shot, out of mistake, five goldfinches, young", or "Stoat, shot nearly in half". His mother, he added, did her best to stop him, but without success. Yet these beasts were not killed for the love of killing, he wrote. They were often preserved as skins or in alcohol; date and place of death were carefully recorded, as well as peculiarities or differences from the typical form: "I was a strange alloy of savage and scientist, with another ingredient as well which is not revealed in these diaries." Here also are listed the number of birds' eggs collected, 107 in one year, 179 in another, which he later thought "appalling". Statistics of other kinds also abound: there are 551 poplar trees in the *Allee* between Karlsruhe and Durlach; it takes 2 hours 5 minutes from Durlach church to Thomashof, easy walking; 4,874 paces will take you from near Strassenhaus railway station to the Hotel Kreuz, Bludenz. These larger and longer figures, which in some cases require for their procurement a considerable degree of concentration over relatively long periods of time can be seen as simple extensions of the careful records of zoological observations, or they can be read, as some psychiatrists would read them, as signs of anxiety, even if, as is possible, they were a kind of guessing game or the result of schoolboy bets with brother or sister.

The diaries also contain glimpses of himself in relation to brother John and sister Mary (in whose company, one guesses, he still found more happiness than with anyone else in the family), and a tolerantly critical remark about Vanda: "Mother is inclined now and then to fits of laziness and tells fibs by the dozen to make herself out a martyr." There are also some useful exercises in descriptive writing, such as: "Dodo River, Karlsruhe. Toad or frog caught making funny noise in bog, having very nice smell of varnished wood white black spotted stomach, brown slightly warted back, walking on tips of his feet very quickly."

iv

He kept up his piano-playing . . .

Wherever he might be – at Mowsley, or Uppingham, or staying at The Weaste, or abroad – he practised. It was an ordinary accomplishment, especially in those days, and in spite of some light-hearted pretensions which are ironic in tone, his seems to have been no more than a slightly higher than average ability, certainly not up to concert standard. No doubt he loved music and was moved by it; no doubt he was a competent performer; and perhaps he did actually compose a sonata as he said he did – it was a not unheard of accomplishment even amongst schoolboys – and perhaps it was numbered, as he said it was, 643, but it does not follow that it was preceded by 642 other compositions: it almost certainly was not. No doubt, also, he could have made more of his musical ability if he had devoted himself to the piano and dropped a few of his other activities. He did the reverse, and, as John Davenport wrote in a summary of Douglas' interest in music, it "simply got crowded out. There were other more important things to enjoy".

As a schoolboy he was a diligent pupil: of that one may be sure. Whether or not the "other things" were more important is a matter of opinion; it is fairly certain that Douglas must have found them either more useful or more satisfying, or he would not have dropped music in their favour. Speculations suggested by his life-long flirtation with music will be found on page 493.

v

At the beginning of the school year of 1886, in October, when he had moved up from the *Untersecunda* class at the Gymnasium and his family had left Karlsruhe to live in the house called Armatin at Bludenz, he was placed *en pension* with Professor Keim, one of the teachers in the school. Keim was a disciplinarian whose methods of supervision were too strict for Norman's liking; he had to be in at a certain hour, and do a fixed amount of homework – "all very tiresome for a boy of my age". However, he knew that it would be useless to complain about such matters in a letter home; it would never succeed in getting him moved elsewhere. He had better complain about the food and make sure he did it thoroughly. If anything would work, that should!

In *Looking Back*, he gives the impression that he wrote this letter without delay, but it is dated 25th June 1887, which he does not mention. This omission of the date is an example – there are others – of Douglas bluffing the reader into believing that he would put up with much less than he actually did put up with. He could be much more long-suffering and patient than even some of his close friends would have believed. The letter is of a kind not unknown to ingenious schoolboys or under-graduates, and a splendid example of its kind. After mentioning stinking sausage, scarcity of meat, and indifferent coffee, it continues:

> Also the bread seems to come from no very good backer [sic] the other day I luckily (just in time) unearthed a large brown backed [sic] beetle (Cockkäfer!) in a piece I was just going to eat. How many such I have already eaten I dare not conjecture. I will not speak of the butter, the little bit there is (or rather was) is mostly a pool of grease . . . The pat of butter (resp:grease) is always so hairy and dirty that it simply makes one sick to look at it, and I scarcely ever can touch it. The bread is always a hunck [sic] of black bauernbrod. But I am now quite resigned to my fate. I never buy "useless" things. Under such circumstances (i.e. the lack of *proper* food) it is not to be wondered at that I always if I am at the Stadtgarten or at Maxau for instance, eat something in the shape of a sandwich or sausages where other people, whose wants of this sort are all supplied at home, only take some beer . . .

The letter continues beyond this point (at which it breaks off in *Looking Back*, with a row of Douglasian dots), and this is another apparently trivial point worth recording: that Douglas' fundamental respect for textual accuracy was such that it nearly always compelled him to indicate omissions or incompleteness in this manner. It was a characteristic of which Mr Eames (in *South Wind*) would have warmly approved, and there are dozens of examples of it.

The letter continues:

> . . . take some beer. Hence one need not marvel at my spending *some* money on this sort of neben fütterung in the month.
>
> I wish you could tell me the number of your gloves. I wanted to get you some black ones but I had forgotten whether it was $6\frac{1}{4}$ or $6\frac{3}{4}$. I am glad you saw the Formarin see, it is very lovely but the road as you say is somewhat rough. Let me hear soon.
>
> Yr loving
G. N. Douglass

The gloves may have been a belated birthday present for 6th June, Vanda's birthday, but the apparent offer of them, which is not so much an offer as a history of intention, may look more purposeful than it really was.

This letter had the effect its writer desired. He found himself almost at once in the house of Dr Riffel, whose acquaintance he had already made, and whose place he had suggested as an alternative to Keim's. It was nearer to the Gymnasium, and Riffel was too busy to bother much about what Norman did or where he went. But even Dr Riffel's house did not come up to expectations, and Norman soon migrated across the street to an establishment kept by two old Prussians, Fraulein Nernst and Fraulein Beerbohm. There he stayed until he left Karlsruhe in July 1889. The house had peculiarities which suited him. Fraulein Beerbohm had taken to drink, was often speechless, and "sometimes not on view at all. One afternoon I found her tangled up on a sofa in a drunken coma." Consequently Fraulein Nernst had to do all the work, which, since she was the older of the two, tired her out completely. This suited Norman's habits:

> If I lunched or dined out, she was secretly delighted, as it saved her both money and work; if I brought some ambiguous friend into my room – the maid being well tipped – or stayed out all night, neither of the two ladies was aware of the fact; the Nernst was too tired to trouble about anything, the Beerbohm too drunk. Other clients dropped off, owing to Hetty Beerbohm's irregularities; I stayed on. Her alcoholism did much to sweeten that period of my life.

vi

That period of his life was also much sweetened by girls . . .

While he was en pension his sister Mary was attending the "high class Nickles pensionnat" as a day-girl. Mary had a great friend at the school called Mabel who came from London but lived with her mother in Karlsruhe. Norman, who in those days felt it was his duty to adore every girl he met, was a frequent visitor at the flat in which Mabel lived with her mother. The mother encouraged him to go to the flat whenever he liked; and she would play "Sweet Dreamland Faces" on the piano while Norman and Mabel waltzed round the room; she let Mabel go for walks with Norman. Mary Douglass had brought them together and egged Norman on "as only a sister can". Nobody, he wrote, had such golden chances of love-making as he had with Mabel, and nobody neglected them so scandalously. It was not that he didn't like her:

> I liked Mabel immensely and the notion of going a little further was always in my head; somehow or other, I never went any further. Was it the very ease of our relationship, the absence of risk or control? Nothing happened; not so much as a kiss. And Mabel was attractive beyond the common measure, with her dark eyes, slender girlish figure, and hair still worn down her back . . .

All the same, he was not going to be deprived of the pleasure of a glance from Mabel's dark eyes; whenever he caught sight of the Nickles school crocodile on its way to some exhibition or art-gallery, he whistled a certain four notes, which she alone knew. Madame Nickles had to send him a postcard telling him that in Germany one whistled at dogs, not at young ladies.

Norman introduced Mabel to Miss Long, who was a well-known figure among English-speaking people in Karlsruhe. "She was small and thin, about fifty years of age, and full of kindness." She kept a pension for a few English girls learning German or studying art. As she liked them to have a good time, she used to invite presentable boys to go there for tea, for informal little dances after dinner and inexpensive little picnics in the country, with herself and the girls. They were all fond of Miss Long; and in her pension were the two sisters Sisson, with whom everybody was in love "but, so far as I could find out, they were not in love with anybody in particular; no, not even with me. Such was my vanity in those days that I expected all girls to fall in love with me; one or two babyish successes, I suppose, had turned my head." The dissolution of this expectation was begun by Elsie McLeod, another of Miss Long's girls, and the only Scottish one:

Though I had no exceptional liking for her, I took it for granted that on grounds of nationality alone, apart from any consideration of my rare charms, she would conceive an instantaneous fancy for me. Nothing of the kind. During one of those excursions into the country I managed to segregate her from the troop and from Miss Long, and went into the matter. I ended by telling her that I felt very much like falling in love with her; what would she say if I did? She laughed and said I could do as I pleased. And what about herself? Oh, she didn't feel like that at all. Perhaps she would feel like that later on? Well, no; she didn't think she would. What, never? No, never; and she laughed again quite nicely. I thought it over afterwards and came to the conclusion that she was a unique girl, not worth falling in love with.

Elsie being unobtainable, and nothing happening with Mabel, the obvious answer was Violet Sherbrooke (or "Miriam" as she is called in *Looking Back*), a newcomer at Miss Long's who was less attractive than the other two, and yet . . . why should he long to write his name on that particular clean slate?:

The springs of love – who shall lay them bare? The inappreciable spell which determines an appeal to the senses – in what caverns of the soul does it lurk? Was I infatuated with the inflection of her voice, the charm of her rounded wrists? Possibly; such single traits have often turned the scale for me. A mutual enchantment there was, for Miriam responded . . . This was one of my most passionate love-affairs of the real kind; and one of the briefest . . . What risks we ran; what precautions had to be taken! It was too awful. The danger was so horrible that after a hectic month or two and some narrow escapes from detection I broke it off, determined that she should not get into trouble on my account, and thinking mighty well of myself for this chivalrous act of renunciation. The real reason, I have not the slightest doubt, was that I was in a terrible funk for my own skin. We remained firm friends, and years afterwards I went to see her at her home in Southport.

Miriam, if we are to take the Baumstark section of *Looking Back* literally, was one of three girls whose favours he was enjoying at more or less the same time, during his last two years at the Gymnasium. That was later . . .

vii

In his fifties, referring to the collecting passions of his boyhood and youth, Douglas wrote, "Butterflies were dropped when stones began . . . Stones were dropped when birds and beasts began." The statement need not be accepted as literal. There was, of course, an overlapping period as to the actual collecting; the knowledge and intellectual interest were lifelong. But he was still a keen collector of geological specimens right up to the end of his schooldays, and spasmodically for many years after that. A new stimulus was given to "stones" in 1886.

Every spring a local mineralogist, Professor Knop, used to take students from the Polytechnikum to the Kaiserstuhl near Freiburg. This "Emperor's Seat" is a volcanic region so filled with mineralogical curiosities that it is a "mineralogical museum, but only for the few, the very few, who know where to look for the exhibits. Knop knew where to look for them; I knew that he knew; I wanted to know too . . ." In 1886, therefore, at the age of seventeen, G. N. Douglass from the Gymnasium presented himself to the professor and asked whether he might join the expedition. "Why not?" said Knop; and Norman found that Knop was no less willing to talk to him, the baby of the party, than to the grown-up Polytechnikers, who at first looked upon him with misgivings.

The Kaiserstuhl consists of an isolated group of volcanic mountains with a number of villages on its vine-clad slopes. It rises out of the alluvial plain of what was once the Grand Duchy of Baden to a height of about 6,000 metres and has zoological as well as geological attractions. Norman was much taken with it, not only because it was a place of escape from Thucydides and mathematics "and all the other horrors of school life", but also because of the great variety, and in many cases the rarity, of its minerals. Their very names – two or three dozen of which he sets down with evident joy nearly fifty years after this first visit – rejuvenate him, and he sees himself "holding a rock fragment in one hand and peering through a strong pocket lens, made by Steinheil of Munich, into one of its tiny, labyrinthine cavities; exploring those recesses as one explores a darkened world, a world unknown . . . That speck down there, that barely discernible speck, big as the point of a needle – it looks reddish; is it, can it be, the almost fabulous perowskite?" He visited the place annually while at Karlsruhe, and even returned, during a short trip from London to the Continent, in 1890.

Geology had also taken Norman and his brother to Katzenbuckel in November 1884. Here the volcanic material had broken through red sandstone and produced, among other things, crystals of nepheline. But there were plenty of other minerals to be found: biotite, chabasite, leucite, augite and olivine. "Got up at 6" says the diary:

train 6.55, coffee at station, via Bruchsel and Heidelberg. Change at Heidelberg, get out at Eberbach, eat sausage and 2 wine, take guide (1.50 marks) and proceed for nearly 2 hours. Arrive at high plateau, change = dismiss guide, try to sketch but fingers *froze*. Near top some quarries. Get volcanic stones there and proceed to top. Big tower, 60 ft high, at top. Went up, and onto an erection in the middle, very breezy, lovely view over the Odenwald. Went down and along top to rustic bench and table of sandstone. Eat luncheon, very cold, ham eggs and spirits. Then light pipe which won't burn and proceed to examine crater (?) Go down, having finished examination, and carry bag which was very heavy in turns. Came down, refreshed ourselves, had three hours to wait, went into town along Neckar, threw in tub, which floated quickly past, came back, got into train at 6.12 p.m. arrived at Karlsruhe ... at 9 p.m. Came home and had some supper. Next day washed and sorted stones.

And there were a good many other such excursions during the Karlsruhe period: to Langenbrücken, Pforzheim, Ranmünzach, Annweiler, Eschbach, etc. A visit to Ubstadt in search of asphalt was unproductive; so also was a trip to Oeningen in August 1886, and all the more disappointing because of the great richness of its fossil beds. At the Lacher See he spent half a day breaking up lava blocks to obtain hauine of a particularly fine quality; and visited Hohentwiel for phonolite and natrolite. This last mineral he went in search of because he had read about it in Scheffel's *Ekkehard*. "I used to read his things," he writes typically and casually, and does not mention – which almost any other writer would have done – that Scheffel was a native of Karlsruhe and lived there for the last twenty years of his life, during Douglas' own years in the city. "Scheffel was a kindly and erudite old toper who toped himself into Elysium via countless quarts of Affenthaler." Scheffel, as Douglas might also have mentioned, was an important link, having been one of those Germans who in mid-century had completed an Italienische Reise and left a minor but indelible mark on Capri in the shape of the Café Hidegeigei, named after the cat which is one of the chief characters in Scheffel's *Trumpeter of Säckingen*, which he wrote on the island. He died in 1886, and could at least have been seen by, if he was not actually known to the young Gymnasiast. Vanda may have known him, since he was an old friend of Ludwig Steub.

viii

Hand in hand with stones went birds and beasts. With Wilhelm Händel, his classmate and most constant companion during his years at the Gymnasium, he began those studies of reptiles and amphibia in the neighbourhood of Karlsruhe which were to form the basis of his *Herpetology of the Grand Duchy of Baden*. As to birds, they were after them all the time, and became friends with Herr Fehsemaier, the Museum taxi-dermist. They not only collected birds and their eggs; they discussed biological problems of distribution, and why one of two closely allied species should become dominant over the other. They compared notes, and built up theories: "The relish one could derive from such things!" Why, for instance, should the blue tit have ousted the crested tit in Karlsruhe? What was the secret mainspring of the differentiation between closely allied species? Such problems seemed so important at the time, and for some years afterwards, that when he had left Karlsruhe, he entered into correspondence with Gädke of Heligoland about them. Gädke was then seventy-eight and had an international reputation as an authority on bird migration, but did not disdain replying at length to his young correspondent. From this Händel period also (1887) there survives in manuscript a treatise on the coloration of birds' eggs and the possible causes of their differentiation: eighteen foolscap pages which testify, as Douglas wrote many years later, "to a certain amount of thinking". Händel probably contributed to it; and may also have encouraged the production of an even longer treatise, *De Natura Hominis*. This is written in German, under Latin headings *de ingenio, de disciplina*, etc, in the manner of certain philosophers and is yet another example of the astonishing amount of extra-curricular activity that this knowledge-hungry young man crammed into his six years at Karlsruhe.

In 1886, James Harting, editor of *The Zoologist*, printed two very brief contributions from Douglas in the 'Notes & Queries' section of his journal. These, his first appearances in print, were seven-line and twelve-line notes on "Variation of Plumage in the Corvidae", and "Variation of Colour in the European Squirrel".

In September 1886, while visiting Honstetter, the taxidermist in Breg-enz, Norman saw there a beaver which had been shot on the Elbe and sent to a Dr Girtanner of St Gallen, who in turn had sent it to be stuffed. As Norman had lately read an article by Harting on "Beavers and their ways", he at once wrote off to Girtanner, referring him to Harting's paper, and then to Harting, enclosing an essay from Girtanner.

Correspondence with Harting continued. In November 1886 Norman sent him details of an Alpine marmot which had been shot in September. Its skull exhibited such "singular malformation of the teeth, that it may be worth while recording it in the Zoologist". What is interesting is the painstaking labour with which Norman described the specimen. The successive drafts of the letter to Harting in which he sets down his interpretation of the abnormality show that he had a good deal of diffi-culty in saying exactly what he wished to say, but through persistent application managed to do so. And the drawings he enclosed – "I am not much of a draughtsman" he commented in *Together* – are up to professional standard, "so very well executed", wrote Harting, "that one can see at a glance what has happened". They would have been too expensive, he added, to reproduce in *The Zoologist*, but Professor Flower, Director of the Natural History Museum (London), would like to acquire the skull if Mr Douglass would care to sell or present it. To which a draft answer exists: "I regret very much not being able to let you have the skull of the Alpine Marmot. I should have been most willing to do so had it not been a specimen from the Vorarlberg, but as such, I do not care to part with it."

His friendly relations with the Natural History Museum continued for many years. He presented it with various specimens, collected for it, and was a frequent visitor there. Eventually, it became the scene of an unfortunate occurrence – but that lay many years ahead.

ix

Douglas has given us the names of at least half a dozen of his school-friends, and told us something about them. Luigi Gonzaga was probably his closest friend to start with, although he spent much time with Wilhelm Händel owing to their common interest in natural history. A mutual interest of a different kind put him a good deal in the company of Arthur Baumstark. He was "an attractive boy", a keen student of Greek and a practical joker; but he and Norman seem to have been brought together by a precocious delight in the intimate companionship of girls. Some of their sexual experiences were acquired in the local brothel. Brothels were out of bounds; but as Norman slyly points out, "you could go there whenever you liked, because, if you did meet a professor on the premises – I never did – he was not likely to talk about it afterwards, was he?" However, he came to the conclusion that it "was really a horrible hole", and agreed with Arthur Baumstark when he said:

"A brothel is no place for a gentleman."
"Of course not," replied Norman, "I've given it up ages ago. I've got Ethel, you know." Ethel was a complaisant little English girl, a great favourite, who lived under hopelessly inadequate supervision with Frau M., where she was supposed to be studying German.
"Ethel?" said Arthur. "Ethel! Do you know whom I've got? I've got Louisa. Yes; Louisa."
"Impossible!"
How on earth, I wondered, had he managed to seduce Louisa? For she and her sister Auguste had the reputation of being, as we called it,

inaccessible as the "virgin moon". Their shop, a small grocer's, was opposite the gymnasium at the entrance of the Seminar Strasse and up two or three stairs ... Louisa was dark and decidedly pretty; Auguste fair and none too slender. Both the sisters were at least ten years older than ourselves: who cares about such trifles at our age? The shop was much frequented by gymnasiasts buying sandwiches in the morning interval; everybody was after Louisa, but she just laughed. How had Arthur done it?

"Yes," he went on, "Louisa has solved the problem of life for me. And if I were to tell you –! I will, one of these days. Now listen to me. Get rid of your Ethel, and take up with Auguste. I've talked to her sister about it. Everything will be quite all right, she says. So go ahead."

"I shan't get rid of Ethel. I can manage the pair of them, if it comes to that. Anyhow – thanks! I'll tackle Auguste on Saturday afternoon!"

"You can't. It's my day with Louisa."

"Sunday afternoon will do just as well, if she'll wait at the window for me, and then open the shop for half a moment!"

"You can't. It's my day with Louisa."

"I see. Sunday morning?"

"Very good. I'll tell her to look out of the window at ten sharp."

There was not much of the virgin moon about Auguste. But this double-barrelled arrangement had such grave inconveniences that relations between Arthur and myself were sometimes strained to breaking point. In the first place, there was only one door, the shop door; one had to sneak in when nobody was about, and they had only a single sleeping apartment at the back. Next, the door was not opened at night under any circumstances; they had to keep up their reputation for chastity. Lastly and chiefly, our half-holidays were limited to two, and Arthur was not long in discovering that it could not be "his day" on both of them; I wanted mine as well. On Sunday afternoons, however, when the shop was shut, there was perfect peace in the household. So friendly had we grown, and so unblushing, that we would retire together into that inner room, all four of us, a family party ...

A sound education for boys of eighteen to twenty. If some of my young English friends could enjoy its advantages, they would not grow up to be the flabby nincompoops they are, in the matter of sex.

Impossible, alas, to verify any of the foregoing now. In principle, there is no reason why it shouldn't all be true; but in practice, where there is dialogue in any of Douglas' non-fictional books, there is usually

elaboration or invention which is inclined to spill over into the intervening descriptive matter. But whatever that truth was during his last two
years at Karlsruhe, one need not doubt the zest and vivacity, the energy
and intensity of enjoyment he would have put into it and derived from it.
His zest for living, and his appetites, were vigorous enough in later life.
It can be assumed that they were certainly no less so between the ages
of eighteen and twenty.

x

Nineteen is a good age at which to see Italy for the first time – old enough
to appreciate all it offers, and young enough to return many times before
youth entirely vanishes. Norman's preparations for his first visit had
been made by March 1888, when he wrote to his grandmother:

> ... I had hoped to leave this town during the course of this week,
> but it appears that the inexorable set of professors will as little let me
> go earlier to Naples as they did in winter to England, at all events
> Mama wrote to the headmaster some time ago and I have not had any
> news yet from that quarter, which I look upon as a very bad sign. I
> shall just return all the later from Italy. I am looking forward to the
> short tour very much, as you may imagine, and making all sorts of
> plans and preparations. I have been studying my Baedeker very dili-
> gently, and already *seem* to know my way about Naples quite well. I
> was going today to pay a formal call on the Spanish Consul here, who
> had let me know that he would be very glad to help me in any way,
> but I could somehow not sum up the necessary courage, and have put
> it off till Wednesday. I am also looking up my Italian a little, as I daresay
> it will prove very useful. I have been offered 3 letters of introduction
> to families in Naples, but I only need one, to the director of the Aquar-
> ium there, *Dr Dohrn*, which a Russian friend of mine, his nephew, I
> fancy, is going to give me.

According to *Looking Back*, this trip was decided upon at a moment's
notice, but the letter shows that there was time for at least some preparation. "I shall just return all the later" strikes a typical note of defiant
independence which, in this case, may have been more literary than literal.
He probably behaved correctly in his dealings with "the inexorable set of
professors", but did not mind letting his grandmother know that he
thought them tiresome.

Norman and his brother left for Naples on 18th March 1888. The
vivid emotional impact of Naples itself as well as of the whole district of
the Bay upon this young man of nineteen may be surmised from his state-

ment that for eight years after this visit he had an "affectionate longing" for the place.

The two brothers explored the neighbourhood of Naples pretty thoroughly, beginning with the Phlegraean Fields. They went on foot, and slept in places such as Baiae, then a poor and fever-stricken place, and visited the Dog's Grotto, the Lucrine Lake, the Arco Felice, the Piscina Mirabilis, Lago Fusaro, and Cumae. They went up Camaldoli, Monte Gauro, Cigliano, and Monte Nuovo in the crater of which (only 20 feet above sea level, although the hill is 440 feet high) they found sea-shells which had been drawn upwards when the hill was formed in 1538. "How one enjoyed such discoveries!" They made three visits to the Solfatara; and went down to the Temple of Serapis, "where, unfortunately, there was a keeper. We should have liked to hack out of the columns one or two of those perforating bivalves, *lithodomus*, which proved that the building had once been submerged under the sea, but: 'man too sharp'."

On the south side of Naples they stayed in the Hotel del Sole at Pompeii, of which John Addington Symonds[15] has left an appetising description in his *Spring Wanderings*. It had not changed since his day; the place was still run by a retired brigand who, like others of his profession, had been pensioned by the Bourbon Government; a smiling old devil, who wore a red tam-o-shanter and died suddenly one morning, a few years later, while sweeping out his yard. Artists and archaeologists were the clients, and you paid four and a half francs (as the lira was commonly called in those days) for everything, including as much wine or beer as you cared to drink.

From Pompeii they went to Ottaiano and climbed to the top of Monte Somma. If there was a path they missed it, scrambling up through dank ravines looking for *Spelerpes fuscus* against a head wind amongst volcanic ashes. From the top they looked into the old crater, Atrio del Cavallo, a horrid prospect, and across it to the smoking and roaring cone of Vesuvius, erupting. They noticed how local lizards had adapted in colour to their surroundings; but the minerals were disappointing.

On 26th March, they first set foot on Capri "chiefly to procure the blue Faraglione lizard". They crossed from Sorrento, and were then rowed out in a tiny boat on a rough sea by Carlo Spadaro, who, while they were feeling seasick in the tossing boat, climbed slowly to the top of the Faraglione rock and brought down six blue lizards which were added to Norman's collection. (The Spadaro brothers were well-known Capri characters, one of whom figured in countless picture postcards as a typical old fisherman with large beard and clay pipe.) Next day Norman was on top of Monte Solaro, looking for Alpine swifts, but found none. It was too early in the season.

They seem to have spent only one night on the island; then back to Naples for a second visit to a Dr Johnston-Lavis,[16] who had already shown them his collection of minerals and reptiles, and back again to Pompeii and up to the summit of Vesuvius "in great heat", walking. Back to Naples, and a third visit to Johnston-Lavis and next, to Paestum to see the temples, and to be much beguiled by the local reptiles which in those days swarmed all over the area of the ruins: snakes of four different species, emerald lizards, wall lizards, frogs in a watery ditch, and the huge common toad *Bufo palmarum* "at least as large as a partridge". "Where are they now" asked Douglas rhetorically in *Looking Back*, "my pickled specimens from Paestum and all those other localities? Well, you cannot carry about from one domicile to the next a collection of seventy-five jars full of alcohol; all that now remains to me is a descriptive catalogue of their contents." The ruins of Paestum were soon dismissed, but two days were spent with the reptiles – a devotion partly due to the acquisition, a few weeks before the visit to Italy, of Eimer's book on the variation of the wall lizard.

Amalfi next, then up to Agerola, where the lizards had adapted themselves to the colour of the white rock; then through the newly-built tunnel down to Pimonte and Castellamare, and so back to Pompeii. Another dash into Naples and to Johnston-Lavis; then back to Pompeii again to inspect a new lava stream flowing above Boscotrecase, at night, by torchlight – "torchlight rather dearly bought".

Two days in Rome on the way home, where, to his later amused disgust, he found from his diary that he had "gloated" priggishly over the Laocoön in the Vatican Museum, and had been lost in "deep philosophic contemplation" on a bench overlooking the Forum.

Geology had the last word – at Sassuolo, Modena – on the subject of a mud-volcano and some petroleum springs, which occupied six pages of the diary.

He had packed a lot into three weeks.

xi

The usual crowded term intervened and then on 30th July he was off again on another trip abroad, this time with his friend Louis Wynne, who was British chaplain at Karlsruhe, and a dedicated cyclist. Wynne is described as tall, youngish (he was about seven years older than Norman), and rather bald, with a dark moustache. He was a little careless in the matter of clothes, a smoker of foul pipes who was apt to drop tobacco-crumbs all over the place. When he went with Norman to shoot grouse in Scotland, he was pronounced by old tobacco-hating Mrs Douglass as quite horrid. He was "no maniac for female society".

They set off from Karlsruhe, on high bicycles with solid tyres, for Stockach near Lake Constance. After passing through Rastatt and Freudenstadt, an accident occurred near Oberndorf. Norman lost control of his bicycle while going downhill: "You will say: why not apply the brake? Try it on, with one of those high bicycles! The brake grips the wheel and pitches you down head foremost on the road; it was a frequent cause of death at that period. The right side of the track being a steep downhill slope, which would have meant annihilation, I let the machine dash itself into a wall of rock on the left and landed against it like a bomb. The bicycle escaped with little damage (the rebound of the solid tyres, and also because the machines then were of stronger build than those of today), but my right wrist was gashed to the bone in saving my face from the impact; I bled like an ox." He had his wrist bandaged in the nearest village and they managed to get to the Vorarlberg, where Norman had to wait a fortnight for the wound to heal.

After this their journey took them over the Arlberg Pass to Landeck, then up the valley of the Inn to Finstermünz. They entered Italy through the Resia Pass, ran down the Adige to Spondigna, and continued via Trafoi to the Stelvio Pass (9,046 feet). Here, before descending to Bormio, they tied huge flat stones to their cycles, to act as brakes. In due course they reached Colico, on Lake Como – an outward journey of more than 300 miles, half of it in mountainous country. The return to the Vorarlberg was made via Chiavenna and the Splügen Pass to the Hinter Rhein, and then along its bank to Reichenau, and so via Ragatz to Feldkirch and back to Bludenz, another 110 miles or so. "Nothing of a tour, I dare say, with modern bikes," commented Douglas briskly in *Looking Back.*

xii

Norman actually left the Gymnasium in July 1889 after the final examination. This was in two parts, a written exam and an oral one, separated by an interval of about a week during which everyone was hard at work preparing for the oral – everyone, that is, except Norman.

Knowing that he was going to leave that part of the world for good, he had made up his mind to see Professor Leydig[17] before doing so. The oral must take care of itself: with luck he would probably scrape through somehow. "It was a risky thing to do, but I was always fond of doing risky things, and have sometimes paid dearly for it."

He had conceived, he wrote, "a kind of reverence" for Leydig, with whom he had already corresponded ("I possess a fair dose of reverence for the right kind of man"). Leydig, a well-known zoologist of the time, had worked on cell-structure, animal pigmentation, and "organs of a sixth sense".

What I liked about his books and pamphlets was not so much his minute histological researches, clear-cut description, and the admirable drawings done by himself; it was something else; his *asides*, his footnotes to the text, his generalisations. He would indulge in an excursus of "historical and critical remarks" on some species and even go into details about those artists who have successfully reproduced its shape; he would open up unexpected vistas, citing copiously from authorities old and new. This extensive documentation testified not only to wide reading, but to a wide outlook. His suggestiveness is what attracted me to Leydig. He was no ordinary Professor; he was something more comprehensive, more human.

Norman arrived in Wurzburg on 20th July and stayed until the 25th. As soon as he had booked in at a hotel he left a card on Leydig, and saw much of him during those five days. He came up to expectations. "He was wise and simple-hearted; nothing seemed to be beneath his notice." Several pages of Norman's diary were filled with what Leydig said, such as that his eyesight, once excellent, had by then accommodated to one distance only – the microscope's; and that of all his French colleagues only Lataste kept up his friendship after the war of 1870 – how absurd it was that this national nonsense should intrude itself into the scholar's study.
It was Leydig's strong emphasis on individuality which impressed Norman most. He was interested in differences of character between animals of the same species, and observed them among his dogs and among his pet birds and reptiles. He thought individuality should be fostered and not repressed, whereas scholastic institutions at that time tended to repress character.

He asked me: "Are you going to some University afterwards?" I said I had not made up my mind. "Let me beg you to avoid it if you can. It may ruin your individuality. Universities are downright monstrosities" ... *Universitäten sind wahre Monstrositäten*. This pronouncement coming from a University Professor, and one so venerable, gave me food for thought.

The five days at Wurzburg must have made a great impression on him. There can be little doubt that he remembered Leydig's "suggestiveness" when he himself began to write: this quality of continual reference to the greater world beyond the immediate subject, this "wide out-look opening up unexpected vistas" was to be one of the distinguishing marks of everything Douglas wrote from *Siren Land* onwards. "Nothing seemed to be beneath his notice": how like Mr Keith of *South Wind*, to whom everything was wonderful (and nothing miraculous). And the emphasis on individuality; Douglas must have been delighted to receive this approving comment on what was already more than a tendency in his own behaviour. "Some few of us are born centrifugal" was the starting point of his comments on Uppingham; he had never been one to follow the herd, and it must have made him happy to hear individuality extolled as a desirable end in itself by someone for whom he had so much respect. The visit to Leydig, in fact, was a kind of benediction and confirmation which came very aptly at the end of his schooldays and at the beginning of his adult life. "He marks an epoch," wrote Douglas; "my schooldays could not have been rounded off more appropriately." The emphasis on individuality supplied him with a formula "for avoiding those flat lands of life where men absorb each others' habits and opinions to such an extent that nothing is left save a herd of flurried automata. I think with gratitude of the old man . . ."

CHAPTER SEVEN

———————⇒⊂————————

Young Man About Town
1890–1894

i

After visiting Leydig he returned briefly to the Gymnasium, survived his oral examination, and left on 31st July. He probably went straight to Armatin, Vanda and Jakob's home in Bludenz, for a week later Vanda describes his departure from it:

> Yesterday I was so tired out by my son's departure and the preparations for it that as soon as he had left on the second fast train I went straight home – to bed! Towards evening I got up again, and was all right. But you cannot imagine the mess – two boxes and two trunks filled with lizards, snakes, toads and newts in alcohol; suits; a mountain of washing (which had to be washed, starched and ironed immediately, ready for the following morning!); minerals, pictures, socks, and three boxes full of books. I helped him unpack, re-arrange and fit in all these things – let no one say that I am idle! On the morning of his departure – he was to leave at 12.30 yesterday – none of the things that his lordship was supposed to take with him was packed . . . But we were ready in time, and I spent what strength I had left in seeing him off at the station.

What were his plans? He had told Leydig, a week or two earlier, that he had not made up his mind about going to a university, so it looks as though his decision to go to Scoones (the crammers in London) and work for entrance to the Foreign Office must have been taken after seeing Leydig. In September he received an invitation to stay in Paris, and arrived there early in October conscious of the fact that "a knowledge of French was going to be essential to me", so presumably by then arrangements had been made with Scoones, during August or September. It would seem that the pickled reptiles, the piles of books and the mountain of washing had travelled from Armatin either to London or to Scotland:

66

Feugh Cottage
Banchory   September 25.1889

Dear Mama,

I see that Mary writes so continually to you that I thought it would be unnecessary for me at present. I expect to leave for London in about 4–5 days, my address will be (till I get lodgings) Symond's Family Hotel, 34 Brooke Str, Grosvenor Square, London. I should be immensely glad if you would write to the old hags at Karlsruhe asking them to send off my box of books &c, which I left there to this address at once, per *Eilgut* as far as it will go. It ought then to arrive in London in about a week, but tell them to put on the address most carefully in 2 places, and to have a rope tied round the box. Perhaps they will object to doing this, but I do not know of anybody else who could besorg it, and I shall need the books as soon as I arrive almost. My ear is quite well again, only at present I have a little boil on my neck, which is rather a nuisance, but does not prevent me going out &c. Have no papers arrived for me from Karlsruhe? When you get bills for me be careful *not* to pay them, – but if you happen to have the blue envelope full of bills which I think I gave you, I should be very glad if you could send it here. I should be also awfully glad if Rodenstein could find time to paint the 2 reptiles in the *top* drawer of my stone cupboard. The one is a salamander and the other a frog. I should like them of course as near life size as possible, but I do not know whether oil or water-colour would be better. I almost think oil, as during *life* the animals are very sleek and juicy. The salamander is a very rare variety in which the yellow *spots* have been turned into lines down the back, as you will see. During life both the yellow and the black are more intense – they have faded a little in spirits, so it would not matter if R. made them slightly more brilliant. You will see that the salamander from being cramped into the bottle has got wrinkles and folds into its skin which in life are absent; it would be good to make these shew as little as possible and to give the whole animal a slightly plumper appearance as it will have shrivelled a little. I should like them to be painted as if they *were* in spirits, and Rodenstein could mark the outline of the bottle &c in his picture, even if the position of the animal did not prove that it was in an unusual position, but also, as if they had only just been put in, and had consequently still this rich colour and smooth appearance. It will be best to paint the salamander straight opposite, as the point about it is to shew that the *orange* lines *run parallel* to each other the whole way down the back, it is not necessary to paint the head &c carefully – only so far as the origin of the lines are concerned. The tail is also of little importance. The frogs are very rare, – I

discovered them near Karlsruhe and have since written a small notice
about them in the 'Zool. Garten' of July. The *smaller* and more brightly
coloured one is the one I should like painted. Its colours are much more
vivid in life than at present, the black and light colour are distinctly
separated. The spirits in which it is are rather dirty, so that perhaps
whilst being painted some new should be put in, in order that Rodenstein can see the colours more distinctly – but afterwards the old ones
put in again, as they are specially prepared. I should also like this to be
as if it were already in a bottle, but perhaps it will be good to take
a slight *side* view of the animal, as the black mottled markings on the
sides are very importance [sic]. *The stripes down the back and the colour
of the head is what is the chief point in this case.* The pointed shape of the
head is also characteristic. If he can manage better he might take the
animal out altogether out [sic] of the bottle and then just draw the outlines of a bottle round this painting to make it appear as if it were in a
bottle. I expect you will have had enough of frogs and salamanders by
this time, but I am just preparing my little work on those of Karlsruhe
and the paintings would be most acceptable. Your p. card came this
morning. Why not have Sippins made into Salami?

Much love to all

Yr afft

N Douglass

The careful instructions, about the box of books as well as about the
reptiles, are characteristic. Throughout his life, in letters of all kinds,
he was detailed and exact in his instructions, and prepared, if necessary,
to repeat them over and over again in a succession of letters. The "small
notice" in the *Zoologischer Garten* was a letter in the correspondence
section describing *Rana arvalis*. His little work on the frogs and salamanders of Karlsruhe would have been a section of what became the *Herpetology of the Grand Duchy of Baden*. This comprehensive article was serialised in nine separate issues of *The Zoologist*, beginning in January 1891.
Sippins, of course, was his sister Mary's dog, the beer-drinking and flea-
gathering Affenpincher, the "Chinese rat" described in *Together*; and the
casual proposal to convert him into salami was a typically terse Douglasian
tease.

ii

It was Gilbert Standen, a Karlsruhe friend, who invited him to Paris with
what Norman described as "an alluring letter". Standen was learning
French in a French family. There was a spare room and a charming

daughter called Lucille; wouldn't Norman join him? The idea was attractive, and Douglas arrived at 43 rue Vaneau on 7th October. "Lucille was
certainly an attractive girl and played the piano delightfully. . . . Four of
us youngsters were *en pension* there; the other two were an Englishman
and an American." They were always together – speaking English; yet
Douglas knew he had to learn at least some French as soon as possible,
also political economy and constitutional history, which he had already
begun to study. "I thought: a bicycle tour in the country should help;
nothing but French all the time . . ."

The tour was a U-shaped one through the central southern region and
was made partly by train. The route going south passed through Cler-
mont-Ferrand, ran up the valley of the Allier, and then on to Nîmes,
Montpellier, and Carcassonne. The journey north lay through Toulouse
and Limoges. The whole thing occupied the inside of a fortnight, the
second half of October.

He made, as usual, many observations of birds, and caught and ex-
amined many reptiles and amphibians on which he made copious notes
and even, in the case of the tree-frog, wrote a "long disquisition" on its
colour-adaptation. There were also notes on geology and on "micro-
cephalous individuals among the population" at Béziers. He had noted
the "desolate appearance" of Langeac in the mining country near Cler-
mont, and says it impressed him so strongly that he recalled it nineteen
years later when writing the nightmare at the end of Chapter 10 of *Siren
Land*:

> . . . coal-dust had crept over houses and roads and trees, and a murky
> cloud hung in the sky as though some demon, with outstretched wings,
> were brooding over the land. Troubled in mind, I wandered about the
> streets. Uncouth buildings, with a thousand chimneys and projections,
> towered into the sky; everywhere lay, in chaotic confusion, mountains
> of black mineral wealth, and carts, and iron contrivances of menacing
> aspect, whose purport I could not fathom. Pallid men and womens
> straggling home from the pits, scowled at me. It was all gloomy and
> evil . . .

Here one is made to feel some of the horror of industrial society as it
impinged upon the senses of this country-born and country-bred young
man: horror of the Blakean kind, or such as Shelley knew. The strength
of this impression must have confirmed, if it did not actually start, a
lifelong disgust with such places and with the society which permits and
actually creates them. The effects of such environments on those who had to
live in them must have been immediately obvious, and must have contributed to his distrust, which persisted through life, of town-bred people.

There had been a delay at Narbonne. A supposed German spy had been caught, and the police became convinced that Douglas was involved, perhaps because he talked French with a German accent. "They made themselves unpleasant, notwithstanding the fact that I was only twenty years old, and that I showed them several bags full of local reptiles . . . objects which do not form part of an ordinary spy's equipment." He was jeered at for collecting "des crapauds".

Back in Paris, in December, he celebrated his twenty-first birthday. A stock of food was laid in, cold meats and cakes and tinned provisions, as well as drinks of various kinds, champagne, Burgundy, Swedish punch, Benedictine. His friends squeezed into Douglas' tiny room where, because it was cold, an enormous fire was burning, and kept the feast going until all four of them were as drunk as human beings can be. "This orgy, one of the worst I can remember, ended in our boiling tinned lobsters in Benedictine; then eating the lobsters, and drinking the Benedictine. One must have been pretty far gone." He was sick on the slightest provocation for three days afterwards; nothing would stay down, and it looked as if the condition had become chronic. More than forty years later he was still unable to drink Benedictine, and even the flavour of angelica upset him. "Some slight alleviation was experienced at the time by tottering forth to the Morgue, which was then a public exhibition of dead bodies, most of them fished out of the Seine. The sight of those poor swollen corpses had a sobering effect."

iii

At the beginning of 1890 Douglas was living in Kensington. This London period, which was to last four years, was characterised by steady application to his work at Scoones, combined with as much social activity as a gay and energetic young man could encompass. The interstices, including holidays, were filled with the deployment and extension of his zoological knowledge. In these years he wrote and had published the *Herpetology* and the *Avifauna* of Baden, and wrote the substance of the *Darwinian Hypothesis*. He visited the Orkneys and the Lipari Islands. He first set foot in Greece and on the island of Santorini. These journeys were accomplished with a speed and energy that one does not normally associate with the period, but which are certainly characteristic of young men who are in a hurry to see and do as much as possible in order to satisfy an ardent curiosity and a desire for experience. This avidity for more and more experience and activity, which had so filled his schooldays that the remembrance of it later on amazed him, filled his young adulthood in the same way. Balls, dances, concerts, dining out, riding in the Park in the early morning, night clubs and music-halls, all contribute to a picture of unflagging zest and appetite for life, supported by a sizable income. His share of the family business brought him at this period about £2,000 a year,[18] and he lived without stint as a young man about town in a style which, together with his family connections and his eligibility as an amusing and handsome young man, opened, among other doors, those of Society. His diary for 1890 is filled with social engagements in and out of town. In these first months, he even visited family connections – such as Sir Edwin and Lady Chadwick[19] – because his Aunt Mary Kennedy had asked him to: "Edwin Chadwick was then over ninety years of age and a wonderful, though not attractive old man. If I am not mistaken, he laid out the drainage system of Paris for Napoleon III; that was his greatest achievement. The last time I went there was in the autumn of the following year. 'Never stop working,' he once told me. An awful doctrine!"

Old James Heywood, with whom he had stayed so happily as a child, still lived in Kensington Palace Gardens, and from time to time Norman would be invited or would drop in there. Heywood, though still as kind as ever, was becoming eccentric: "He wore wigs of different colours, white, brown, grey, and black, as the fancy moved him; he carried a supply of ginger-breads in his pocket because 'you never know when you may be hungry'; worse still, he took to mixing up one person with another, which was awkward, especially at dinner-parties; for he was obstinate about it, and stuck to his mistake." During Douglas' last visit, Heywood greeted him with urbanity but without affection. They discussed the prevailing epidemic of influenza; then after a pause Heywood observed:

"You're not asking me much about my symptoms, are you? Shall I keep up the treatment?"

"My God", I thought, "he is taking me for Sir Francis Laking.[20] And he'll be furious if I try to undeceive him. What's to be done? Clear out . . ."

"I must see you later, Mr Heywood, about that. I only thought I would drop in for a moment . . . it was on my way . . . to an important consultation (pulling out my watch) . . . good gracious! nearly four o'clock . . . Let me just feel your pulse . . . good; very good. Steadier than last time. Yes, do keep up the treatment. And now please forgive me for running away" . . . and with some such excuse, I made to depart. He caught me by the sleeve and said:

"Ah, but you're not going away without this", and took a weighty little envelope out of a drawer and gave it me.

When opened in the street it yielded five sovereigns and five shillings – my fee for professional attendance.

It occurred to me afterwads that an appointment may have been made for the real Laking to call on that same afternoon; if so, what about *his* fee?

Eccentricity of a different kind existed in a household at the other end of the Park. William Massie-Mainwaring, of 30 Grosvenor Place, was a cousin by marriage and a connoisseur who lived in a kind of animated museum: "... there was a streak of genius in Massie-Mainwaring, although, on occasion, he could be as normal or practical as you please ... yet you always felt yourself in the presence of an uncommon type of man. Antiques were his delight. The house was crammed with objects d'art collected by himself; new ones came pouring in every day; you seldom saw less than two dealers waiting in the hall." His speciality was Dresden China, but his tastes were catholic and drew him towards other branches as well – jewellery, prints, paintings, marbles, and even those watches with naughty mechanisms inside. He had in his household two *pièces de musée* in human form – his mother-in-law (through whom the relationship with Norman existed) and his wife.

Bella, the wife, "was the fattest woman in London, and Willie was going to be damned if he would let her slip into some rival's collection". She had the kindest heart in the world, made frequent jokes at her own expense, and played the piano with the touch of a fairy.

This was one of the most hospitable households I have ever known, and one of the maddest. Meals were going on all day long, and nobody seemed to care about moving into the drawing-room, a dreary sort of place full of monstrous Sèvres vases and Venetian mirrors. If, working your way through a cluster of dealers, you dropped in for lunch at four in the afternoon or for dinner at midnight, there was the table with an uncertain number of guests also arriving casually, and loth to leave each other. It stands to reason that they were curiosities one and all. ... Here I met Mascagni for the first time; here you might see the fierce Henri Rochefort, or Prince Polignac, or some famous American hairdresser, a Greek shipowner, Madame Novikoff, munching a vulgar apple tart and trying to look like a sphinx – or anybody, in fact ...

Now and then a newcomer would turn up and soup would be served to him; his neighbour could be seen dawdling over a French pear or a bottle of port; somebody over there had just reached the fish stage. And every five minutes a servant would come and whisper in the master's ear: "You're wanted, sir." Another dealer! A Greuze, a baroque pearl, a Capodimonte set, Frederick the Great's favourite snuff-box, the authentic *pot de chambre* of La Pompadour – a real bargain, which would be exultingly handed round the dining-room.

Meanwhile that all-too-amiable white collie would insist on jumping on your knee (rather a handful) and two or three Yorkshire terriers strolled up and down the table – on the table – poking their noses into any dish that took their fancy. The family was dog-mad.

Such households – all too rare – provided entertainment of a different order to that found in the company of old friends such as Harry Collier. Friendship with the Bug was resumed enthusiastically after the intervention of the entire Karlsruhe period. He and Norman went to concerts together, ate together, frequently at the Holborn Restaurant, and twice went on short holidays together. Norman also kept up with several of his Karlsruhe friends – Majendie and Ehlers and Binnie. With the last he went to Oxford, and stayed with him at Bradford, whence they made a walking tour over the moors. This was the year (1891) in which Binnie read a paper to the British Association on an Electric Self-Recording Rain Gauge. Norman himself had intended to read a paper to the same assembly, on Sexual Selection, but drew back at the last moment. His researches had led him to "conclusions of such novelty and, as it then seemed to me, of such earth-convulsing import – on the utility of useless characters – that I despaired of making my point clear before an assembly of this kind; I was shy of coming forward with my theory". (This theory was to be published five years later in a paper entitled *On the Darwinian Hypothesis of Sexual Selection* – see p. 93.)

In December he visited his Kennedy relations at The Weaste, and went on for Christmas to the Moore-Garretts at Wood Lawn in County Down. Mrs Moore-Garrett was his aunt Amie, Vanda's sister, who had once had painting lessons from Jehly.

iv

Douglas had completed the field work for his *Herpetology of the Grand Duchy of Baden* before leaving Karlsruhe, and since then had been putting into shape his sizable monograph on the subject. When this was ready for the printer, he wrote to James Harting and asked him if he would be interested in publishing any of it in *The Zoologist*. Harting replied that he was interested to hear of these papers on Reptilia and Batrachia; that they might possibly be suitable for the journal; and that the reason why so few articles on these creatures appeared in it was that few people seemed to be studying them – he seldom received such manuscripts.

After Douglas had sent the work, Harting replied:

I have read the papers and would suggest that as they stand they are a little unfinished for a Magazine article. They want an introduction of some kind, setting forth briefly the physical features of the Grand

Duchy of Baden, & especially of the Schwarz Wald, if any of your observations were made there. It is not enough to know that a particular species is to be found in a particular district or locality, unless we are also told under what conditions it exists there and the more you can tell the reader about the natural surroundings and the kind of places in which to look for a particular species with the best chance of finding it, the more interesting and useful will your paper be.

No sooner requested, than done. It is a mark of Douglas' lively intelligence (as distinct from his intellectual ability) that he seldom failed to learn the lessons which he felt were suited to his temperament; and thanks to Harting, the introduction to the *Herpetology* is the first instance of Douglas' ability to draw the reader into the subject-matter, however specialised it might be, with just those preliminary remarks which could best hope to claim his interest and attention. Harting had only to point out that such a preliminary sketch was desirable: Douglas was well able to do the rest. He was well able to do it because he had a natural eye for landscape and generalities as well as for indiviuals and particulars, and because he had been trained at the Gymnasium to collect and marshall his facts in a systematic and orderly fashion.

As to the *Herpetology* itself, it is, as Douglas later wrote, "not a bad performance for a boy fresh from school". Rather a good one, in fact, and according to a friend* to whom I am indebted for all the following critical and appreciative remarks (whether they appear in quotations or not), it "shows evidence of broad biological interests and an awareness of general problems which is remarkable in a man who was not a professional zoologist". Douglas' interest in colour variation and its biological significance (which had already been demonstrated by his notes in *The Zoologist* in 1886 and by his long manuscript essay on the coloration of birds' eggs) was a subject of great interest to naturalists at that period. The third footnote on page 156 (in Douglas' book *Three of Them*, which contains the *Herpetology*) makes a suggestion which "in a way anticipates modern ideas on the significance of colour and colour change in relation to temperature regulation in cold-blooded vertebrates". In other respects also, his work is forward-looking: "In the footnote on page 206, for instance, he points out that frogs and toads, unlike newts, do not regenerate extremities. This was probably generally recognised by continental workers at the time, but not very well known by English naturalists." In one instance, however, Douglas seems to give evidence of unwarranted

*Angus Bellairs, Professor of Vertebrate Morphology, University of London, Honorary Herpetologist to the Zoological Society of London, and author of *The Life of Reptiles* (2 vols. London, 1969).

credibility and of failure to discuss possible implications. This occurs in his remarks (p. 193) about maternal care. Dr Settari's alleged observations of smooth snakes swallowing and then regurgitating young lizards as food for their own young is uncritically accepted; and the old story that adders swallow their young in times of danger is "extremely difficult to believe; apparent evidence for it should not have been accepted as 'overwhelming'. This can be regarded as a definite lapse on Douglas' part, but the only one of any consequence that can be readily detected."

Although Douglas was perhaps past the peak of what he called his "natural history mania", he was still very actively interested, still a collector, and still an enthusiastic observer, describer and theoretician. By May 1891, when about half the *Herpetology* had appeared in *The Zoologist*, he moved into Walsingham House, which was only a few hundred yards from the headquarters of the Linnaean Society in Burlington House. Harting, who was also the Librarian of the Society, had apartments upstairs, where Douglas would be invited to tea with the family after lingering in the library below.

He had also made friends – as soon as he had come to London – with G. A. Boulenger, the Keeper of Reptiles and Fishes in the Natural History Museum. He liked him, and in later days had "lively recollections of his ruddy face and of those back premises which were his own domain – the rows of bottled specimens, the glass boxes containing live ones . . . He did an infinity of valuable work in the way of classification and description of species . . . He kept alive my interest in those animals and gave me a number of his scientific writings." During the first half of the Nineties Douglas seldom went on a journey abroad without offering to collect for Boulenger, and as a result a good many uncommon specimens found their way to the Museum through his hands.

v

Natural history was, in fact, still very much the deciding factor when it came to choosing a place for a holiday – given the fact that he had acquired, since 1888, a predilection for the South. Thus in April and May 1891 he first visited the Lipari Islands, attracted by Spallanzani's account of them, which he had read as a boy. No doubt the attraction was partly geological, but it was mainly zoological: he was looking for new varieties of lizards. What he found is described in a footnote in the *Herpetology*. Needless to say, he found much else. The guide Bartolomeo, who had shown Lipari to everybody for many years, was waiting for the steamer, and captured Douglas at once. Bartolo was small, badly-dressed, barefoot, and lame, but a great walker, who knew every inch of the island. While he and Douglas were still at the harbour, he pulled a grimy notebook out of his pocket containing testimonials from visitors who had employed him: "The first name that met my eye was that of Guy de Maupassant."

The flies, dirt and dust were disconcerting, and decent accommodation was almost impossible to find unless you were lucky enough, as Douglas was, to stay with such a hospitable family as the Narlians, who were Anglo-Armenians.

> Savagery and opulence touch hands on these waterless islands; I liked the quality of the landscape. I liked the harsh colours, the violent perfumes of earth, the monstrous cactus hedges, and all those scattered rocks that rise out of an incredibly blue sea and shift their profiles with every step you take. One thing alone is changeless and ever in its old place – the white dome of Etna. A panoramic region; it fills you with a sense of Homeric limpidity.

He speculated, as many others have, on the location of the kingdom of Aeolus, Lord of the Winds; if not merely imaginary, it should be, or should have been somewhere among these islands, possibly on land which once linked Panaria with its nearest islets, for here, and here only in the Lipari Islands, prehistoric implements have been found.

On Panaria he was faced with a dilemma. The natives saw him catching geckos, which are supposed to be medicinal, and thought he must be a doctor. They took him to a room full of people, in which a girl was bleeding to death. They explained that there was no doctor available, and would he kindly do something to stop the bleeding? "She seemed to be at the last gasp, and I thought that if she died while I was 'in charge of the case' there might be trouble: they were a rough lot. I did what I still consider to have been the right thing – jumped into my boat and cleared out."

vi

Not long after returning to London from the Lipari Islands he visited Uppingham – a strange thing to do considering his unhappiness there, but an early example of his lifelong habit of re-visiting places he had been to before. He was a compulsive "returner"; indulgence of this practice was as necessary to him as food and drink and fresh air. Sometimes he would go back in order to retrieve living scenes from still life, to meet himself at an earlier age and thus preserve as uninterrupted a vista as possible of himself backwards to childhood, presumably as a reassurance of his own identity in a changing world. In a largely extrovert character, this may have been his form of introversion. And sometimes he went back for purely intellectual reasons, out of sheer curiosity, to see what changes time had made to inanimate objects. And increasingly, as the years passed he would return to recapture memories of beloved companions or tender scenes. He went to Uppingham with Harry Collier. They stayed at the Falcon, and went for some of their old walks: "The wretched boys were still at it ..." Perhaps the two visitors wished to reinforce their pleasure at having escaped.

Later, in the autumn, Collier joined Douglas at Banchory, and they went together to the Orkneys and Shetlands, where Douglas wanted to see Foula. "We had a most stormy passage; the ship stank of vomit and fried mutton grease ... As to Foula, it was out of the question, since the weather grew worse with each day we spent on Shetland." He bought thirteen eggs of the Great Skua and collected four different species of slugs, which went promptly to the Natural History Museum; and noted that the climate had become so much damper that grain would no longer ripen, and former cornfields had become moors. The islands were "nightmarish regions, swathed in boreal mists ... On returning to Deeside, we felt as if we had entered the Tropics."

vii

His life was full, and his activities various. He was well off, and well endowed in every sense; he could order his life more or less as he pleased. For instance, he could at will, and immediately, "put a slice of sea" as he called it, between himself and a girl with whom he had become entangled. Such a girl was Cora, who worked in a milliner's shop in Richmond. His association with her began as a joke one Sunday afternoon and "rapidly developed into something different". Other entanglements, later in life, were to follow from similarly casual impulses, and sometimes led to far more troublesome consequences. He met Cora three times a week at the corner of Ellerker Gardens; they would stroll up Richmond Hill in the evening past the Star & Garter Hotel and into the Park, where they sat at the foot of an oak tree on a certain bench, on which they eventually carved their initials. This was in February and March 1892, when the weather was like June, and he "pushed the affair with youthful ardour, recklessly, till the seventh of March, when, just after breakfast, my Guardian Angel suddenly presented himself".

His guardian angel – the conversation may be read in the Introduction to *One Day* – told him that this affair with Cora must end: one more week and he would get himself into serious trouble. He had better clear out quickly. Why not go to Greece?

In spite of a grim struggle Douglas took this advice, and wished years later that he had done as much on certain subsequent occasions. Yes, thinking it over later, in Greece, he decided he had done right despite moments and "long hours" tinged with bitter-sweet regret: Cora had been so pretty, so different from the society girls he was used to pursuing, and had talked so endearingly. Cora, if she really existed, is an example of his lifelong interest in contrasts, in variety, in the individual, and not the class or the convention.

The mainland of Greece seems to have been of secondary importance to Santorini; and having planned thus far, he decided he might as well include Malta, in order to try and capture some Filfla lizards for his friend Boulenger. He was on Malta from 15th April until the 22nd, waiting for a favourable wind which would enable him to cross to the little islet of Filfla. Malta and its people he did not like – particularly "the bell-ringing Maltese bigots" – and would have been bored but for the fact that a fellow-passenger put his name down for the Club, where decent food, and dancing were to be found. Meanwhile he discovered a reptile and a batrachian he had not come across before; and on the 18th, he was able to get to Filfla. Fourteen of the famous blue-black lizards were bagged. He wrote a careful description of each for his own use before passing them on; and he concluded that Filfla was rarely visited by man, since he was able to catch three Great Shearwaters and two Manx Shearwaters by hand.

The *Oriental* took him to Brindisi, and on it he found a friend from London, a nightclub habitué called Cunningham. They had never seen each other in daylight, but were delighted to meet again. They drank steadily, with interruptions for eating and sleeping, until they docked. They were to separate at Brindisi, Douglas to cross to Greece, and Cunningham to go further east. They had a good dinner on board to celebrate their last evening together; then, after coffee, Cunningham announced that he must "see Italy". They discovered a young coachman who drove them about the streets and took them to two of his favourite wine-shops, where the three of them drank happily together. Soon the coachman grew mellow:

... he thought he remembered just one more place where the white wine was even better. It was; we took a bottle or two on board. Now Cunningham explained that, having visited the most noteworthy sights of the town, he felt it his duty to inspect the "countryside". It stands to reason that the countryside at this hour was in pitch darkness and everybody fast asleep; the coachman rose to the occasion. He had a married brother out there, a dear brother; one might wake him up and have another drink; it was a good way off, about six kilometres, but the horse was quite fresh ...

After an endless drive through the darkness, along lanes with deep ruts in them, we pulled up at a mysterious one-storied cottage. The coachman began hammering at the door and calling to his brother. At last a man appeared in his pants, armed with a gun. He took us within, lighted a small oil-lamp of antique shape, and produced some red wine and a loaf of bread; we sat on rickety chairs at a table glistening with a patina of age and dirt. Presently he opened a door into the adjoining room to show us "the family". Matrimonial beds are common enough: this was a patriarchal bed which nearly filled up the room; five grown-ups were sleeping in it – six, with the brother – and three or four children lay packed, cross-wise, along the bottom. Cunningham could not believe his eyes. He said: "God, I'll not forget that bed as long as I live. If this is Italy, I'm coming again."

Douglas' memory of the drive back was hazy, but he remembered helping Cunningham onto his boat and asking the steward to look after him. Douglas embarked on the *Venus* and sailed via Corfu and Patras to Athens. In Athens he expanded, "chattering in modern Greek" aided by memories of the classical language, and with the carefree impetuosity of youth plunging into conversation with success because he did not stop to consider whether or not he was capable of doing so in the way that he would have wished. He amused his café-acquaintances with his "European" pronunciation of Greek, and "they amused me with theirs". He met, among others Dr Botho Graeff, a connoisseur from Berlin of ancient marbles, who introduced him to the basement room at the Museum, in which statuary was kept which was considered to be too faithful to nature to be exhibited above. Graeff, like many Germans, was a great patron of the taverns, and cured Douglas once and for all, "so far as anyone can be cured", of his distaste for retsinato. He also met and found pleasure in the scholarly company of Ernest Gardner[21] of the British School. And day after day, in Athens, he sat in the golden evening light beneath the statue of Philopappos enjoying the marvellous view of the Acropolis and wondering whether he had done right to escape from Cora.

Five days out of his fortnight in Greece were occupied in visiting Santorini – three days on the island and a day's boat journey in each direction. Ever since reading a description of it he had made up his mind to visit this semi-circular island which was part of the cone of an ancient volcano,and had assiduously collected every scrap of information about it that he could get hold of. He found it as everyone else does, "a fantastic spot. Picturesque, or romantic, is too mild a term; the cliff scenery and the colours of sea and land made one catch one's breath. Under a bleak northern sky it would be a horrific kind of place; drenched in the glittering light of May it was fabulously beautiful." He spent three profitable days here, collecting and identifying the local fauna.

On his return to Athens from Santorini he visited Krüper, the German ornithologist, and went on a walking tour around Lakes Stymphalus and Pheneus with a guide provided by him. It was his first experience of the Peloponnese and was a revelation in more ways than one. He was surprised by the intellectual curiosity of these simple village people. They did not think it odd that he was collecting frogs and snakes; unlike the inhabitants of Narbonne they thought it praiseworthy. During this expedition he found *Rana graeca* and presented it to Boulenger, who refers to it on page 319 of his *Tailless Batrachians of Europe*.

Zur Fauna Santorins appeared in the *Zoologischer Anzeiger* of December 1892, and was at the same time issued as an offprinted pamphlet of three pages (the fourth is blank). Technically, or bibliographically, therefore, it is his first separately published work, as distinct from contributions solely confined to the pages of periodicals. It is a list of the local fauna observed during his three-day visit to the island. Its compilation and publication were occasioned by the fact that Santorini had been somewhat neglected in former descriptions of Cycladean fauna; but Douglas was the first to admit that the harvest was poor. He had a page of birds, four mammals, five reptiles, two or three snails and fourteen beetles – not much of a haul, especially as he was uncertain about one of the reptiles.

viii

He landed at Naples on 14th May, "feeling uncommonly fit". A week later he was with the family of his old schoolfriend Luigi Gonzaga. Luigi himself was not present, being at university in Pisa. Douglas and Luigi's parents and sisters drove from Sorrento to Positano, and thence by boat to the Cappucini Hotel, Amalfi, where they arrived late, after dinner, on 22nd May – a day that proved eventually to have been heavily loaded against Douglas by Fate.

When they had all finished supper, the parents went to bed after their tiring day, and Douglas took the girls into the garden for a breath of air. With one on each arm, he walked up and down, chatting and laughing, "and blissfully unaware of the fact that, from somewhere in the bosky recesses near by, two pairs of eyes were fixed on our innocent diversions".

One of these pairs of eyes belonged to Miss Annie Barff, "a white-haired she-dragon" who happened to be the dearest friend of Douglas' great-aunt, Mary Kennedy. Norman was Aunt Mary's pet. She was well off, had no dependants, and had never ceased to save money, all of which was to go to Norman. This was so well known in the family that Jane Douglass, his grandmother, had arranged to leave nearly everything of hers to his brother John. Unfortunately, Aunt Mary, the only spinster in the family, was terrified of any hint of impropriety; it was therefore a stroke of really bad luck that Annie Barff should have been sitting there in the garden in the dark on just that evening while Norman was strolling happily up and down the terrace of the hotel with a girl on each arm. If only she had made herself known she could have learned the truth and met the girls' parents next morning. If Norman and the Gonzagas had stayed another day, everything could have been explained. As it was, Annie Barff mistook the girls "for something utterly different, something worse than ambiguous, and wrote a long account of the incident to my dear Aunt Mary. . . . I can imagine Aunt Mary's face on reading this missive. She may well have fainted, for I had successfully trained her into the belief that I was the only chaste member of the family."

Douglas discovered all this when it was too late, after her death. He was then told that, on learning about the Amalfi episode, she had demurely remarked: "It seems that Norman has the tastes of his Uncle Archie." If she had only spoken or written to Norman about it, he could have explained; but she accepted her friend's diagnosis of the girls without question. She was "too pure, too horrified, too saddened, to approach me directly about such scandalous matters . . . The intensity of her grief became manifest when they opened her will, in which I, the pet, was not even mentioned. Thus I lost an income, thanks to that pestilential old frump at Amalfi."

ix

Fate had been both unkind and ironical in permitting Annie Barff to see Norman in such an innocent situation. He might have been seen at other times in other places in circumstances which could have justified all her doubts, confirmed her worst suspicions. The full life of a gay and enterprising young-man-about-town in the Nineties could hardly have been revealed in all its details to an elderly spinster. It is even doubtful if she would have approved of his staying out till four o'clock in the morning at nightclubs, which he frequently did. This was apparently the hour at which the Corinthian would close; and Douglas described himself and his friend Cunningham as assiduous clients of the place. He believed that the Corinthian was at one time the only institution of its kind in London, though there might have been "any number of low-class places". It had the monopoly of catering for the rich; consequently, the prices were extortionate, so much so that a small group of habitués, Cunningham and Douglas among them, eventually decided that they could stand it no longer. "Why not secede, and set up a rival establishment? Fortunately there were business heads in this informal committee, city men, bankers and stockbrokers, and it was through their efforts that the plan was carried out." They called it the "Gardenia", and as it was about half the price of the other place and just as lively, it immediately began to flourish, largely on former Corinthian clients. After his return from Greece, Douglas resumed his visits and kept them up until after he had entered the Foreign Office in March 1893. Then, one night when he was absent it was raided; everybody's name was taken down, and the premises were closed. "I fear the rules may have been relaxed too much, out of sheer hospitality towards the public. . . ."

He lived, as the young have always been able to, twenty-four hours a day. Whitmore, the surgeon, in the amusing interview recorded in *Looking Back*, lectured him on the speed at which he was living – as the middle-aged have always been able to: "going at that pace, he declared, I should be good for nothing at forty, and perhaps not even alive any more," and Norman in his sixties, safely past the dangers which this extremely amusing anecdote conceal, could afford to indulge a brilliantly ironic squib at Whitmore's expense. The truth behind it was pretty grim: Norman had, by one of those unhappy chances in a thousand, contracted syphilis, not from anyone who might have been suspect, but from a *lady*. Or so he said – and why should one doubt anyone capable of his frankness in such matters? This happened sometime in 1892, presumably after his return from Greece, "feeling uncommonly fit". The course of the disease, owing to the slow and uncertain treatment available in those days, unwound itself intermittently through the next six years of his life. Its effects, psychological rather than physical (for his constitution was otherwise superbly healthy and strong) are incalculable: to one who already liked "living dangerously" it could encourage an attitude of complete disregard for existing social conventions: "if *this* can happen to me in an approved milieu, with a partner of the approved sex, why bother any more about such nonsensical approval?" – something of that sort must occasionally have flitted through the mind of anyone in such circumstances, whose tastes were indulgent and uninhibited. Later, in Italy, when he began to use the services of a professional procurer, he insisted on virgins. The reason for this predilection could have been fear of infection as much as a particular preference, and there is some indication in *Looking Back* that it may have been the former.

x

At the end of January 1893 he sat his entrance exam "of candidates for one attachéship in Her Majesty's Diplomatic Service". There were seven candidates. G. N. Douglass, the successful candidate, scored a total of

3,158 marks out of a possible 4,150. The best of the unsuccessful candidates scored 3,076. Douglas was next to bottom in arithmetic ("those infernal mathematics") and in orthography, in spite of being only ten marks below the maximum. He was top (with a lead of 125) in German; top in Latin; and top by two marks in English composition. He was second in General Intelligence, with 125 out of 150; and third in French.

In March 1893, therefore, he entered the Foreign Office itself for his year of training before being posted overseas. When this year was almost over, and Barrington, the Private Secretary, suggested various places abroad in which attachés were required, Douglas unhesitatingly chose St Petersburg. Barrington was rather surprised. Did Douglas know that he would have to study Russian as soon as he arrived, as juniors had to pass a Civil Service examination in the language in order to be able to translate extracts from newspapers, etc? "I know Russian," replied Douglas; and Barrington was still more surprised.

For Douglas, Russia simply represented an opportunity of fulfilling an ambition that was by this time about ten years old: namely, that of discovering, like Pallas[22] before him, a sheltopusik. But for the sheltopusik, he afterwards said, his whole life would have been different. It decided the course of subsequent events.

The sheltopusik is a squamatous reptile about a yard long, commonly referred to as a "glass snake". It is no snake at all, but like its relative, our own slow-worm, a limbless lizard, and the biggest of them all. It has had at least fifteen names, as Douglas pointed out, but is now known as *Ophisaurus apodus*. His excitement about the creature when he first read of it may have been aroused by the uncertainty of some writers as to whether or not it had hind limbs, was a snake or not a snake. In the days when he had searched every manual of zoology he could lay hands on for descriptions of herpetological specimens, he read that the traveller Pallas had found this creature along the banks of the rivers Terek and Sarpa. "The rivers Terek and Sarpa: there was something glamorous about those names; they fired my imagination. 'Pallas', too, struck a note of distinction; not everybody can call himself Pallas."

Naturally, he had gone straight to the town library in Karlsruhe, and demanded Pallas. He had been given an enormous tome; but far from being put off by it, read and savoured every word. Before he was half-way through it he had decided that he must learn Russian at once, so that when he had finished his studies he could travel about that country and discover a new species of reptile.

He had been recommended to go to Alexander Ismailov, who was attached to the court of Baden, and thus met the first of a type he was to see more of in Russia – flat-faced, with long yellow hair, straggling beard, corpulent and greasy. "His clothing was always stained with droppings of food; they told me that he used to eat fish with his hands, and then wipe them on his hair. It may be true; hair like his must be an irresistible temptation." Nevertheless, Ismailov had been a painstaking teacher and had soon aroused his pupil's interest in Russian. But he had had one terrible failing – he had never even heard of the sheltopusik . . .

CHAPTER EIGHT

———————◦◦◦———————

St Petersburg
1894–1896

i

Douglas' hectic life in London, the effect of the spirochaetes in his blood and the treatment he was having for them, may have been responsible for changes in his appearance which can be seen in photographs of the period. The robust and aggressive-looking young man beneath the bowler hat of 1890 had been replaced by the delicate and pensive-looking embassy official of 1894. The Richmond photo of 1892 shows an intermediate stage. The two latter portraits are embellished with a thinnish rather straggly moustache of the overhanging variety, which may to some extent contribute to an impression of infirmity.

He arrived in St Petersburg in March 1894. How long he might have stayed there in the natural course of events one cannot tell; but he was to leave after two years and eight months, at his own request. He was not actually resident in St Petersburg for more than two years altogether. This seems to have been an average length of stay for anyone in the Diplomatic Corps in what was then the capital of Imperial Russia; for despite the fact that it was a superb example of eighteenth-century planning on the grand scale, it was in many ways an oppressive and unhealthy city.

The British Embassy, fronting the river Neva and looking across it to the gilded spire of the Fortress Church, was a noble building with an Adam-like interior including a beautiful white ballroom and Georgian plate valued even in those days at £30,000. It was also a busy place: St Petersburg was the chief port of Russia and supported a large colony of English and other Europeans engaged in all kinds of commerce and in the direction of public utility companies. The commercial section of the Embassy was always fully occupied with trading affairs; and the political section had its time filled largely with the work of ciphering and deciphering telegrams and despatches, translating relevant extracts from the Russian press and keeping in touch with Russian officials and departments. There were no typewriters, and all copies of documents, as well as originals and drafts, had to be made in longhand. Nor had this Embassy a telephone during almost the whole of Douglas' spell of duty.

ii

When Douglas had had time to become familiar with the routine of the Embassy he was given the leave that was due to him, and went off for the best part of a month, in June, with Major Arbin, an attaché from the Swedish Embassy. They made a journey through Finland, so that Arbin could show Douglas how Swedish occupation had improved life in Finland compared with conditions in Russia. "He convinced me; I was astonished at the relative comfort and the signs of civilisation we encountered everywhere." The route they followed is set down in *Looking Back*; roughly speaking, they crossed the country in a north-westerly direction from St Petersburg to Oulu (Uleaborg) near the head of the Gulf of Bothnia. "We happened to be here, almost on the Arctic Circle, on the 22 June; the sun behaved to our satisfaction." They returned down the coast. It was during this trip that Douglas heard of the freshwater seals of the Finnish lakes; and in the following spring he procured a specimen and sent its skull and skin to the Natural History Museum where they were received with effusive thanks by Dr Albert Günther, the Keeper.

iii

After returning from this leave Douglas seems to have settled down to a year's hard work at the Embassy, interspersed, as his work in London had been, with further zoological correspondence and an active social life. During the summer of 1894 and the following winter, he was preparing his paper "On the Darwinian Hypothesis of Sexual Selection", and there was correspondence with a Karlsruhe friend and with Boulenger on the subject of *Triton* (*Triturus*) *cristatus*; with Harting and Boulenger on the possible dominance of melanism (a hypothesis of his own); with the Scottish ornithologist J. Young on the mechanism of change in certain birds from summer to winter plumage and vice versa; with Harting about polygamy among pheasants; and with Alfred Russell Wallace about Recognition Marks.

Meanwhile, in his spare time, he was learning Russian. It had been obvious, on his arrival in Petersburg, that he had learned nothing positive from Ismailov except pronunciation, although Ismailov had also dispelled his initial fear of the language. Two students were now engaged as teachers; one for writing and grammar, the other for reading and conversation. He failed his first examination, the standard being still too high for him. At the second attempt he passed.

iv

The social life was full and satisfying, the hospitality sometimes over-whelming. Great families like the Dolgoroukis and the Demidoffs delighted to entertain the Corps Diplomatique and threw open their doors to them with lavish Russian generosity. Also "every lady", wrote George Fairholme, a first cousin of Norman's, from Bregenz, "has a *jour fixe*, and one meets a good many people in that way. One is always introduced to everyone in the room." Fairholme had been Acting Third Secretary seven or eight years earlier, and liked St Petersburg. Perhaps his pleasure in it had been communicated to Norman, and had reinforced his decision to go to Russia.

One of the hostesses whom Norman liked best was Countess Wolken-stein, wife of the Austrian Ambassador, whom he thought he must have met by presenting a private letter of introduction; or through Esterhazy, a particular friend of his who was Secretary of the Austrian Embassy. This building was in the street in which Norman lived, the Sergievskaia, and he dropped in there so often that the Countess told him he might just as well have been a member of her staff as of the British Embassy. "She was a friend of Cosima Wagner and, like all that set – Wagner himself is the typical instance – steeped in metaphysics; ready at the same time to discuss astronomy or agriculture, or sociology, or scandal. Solovieff [sometimes called the first Russian philosopher] was often to be met at her parties, as well as any literary celebrities who happened to be passing through the capital. She strove to be in touch with all European thought."

It was Countess Wolkenstein who arranged for Eduard Strauss (brother of Johann the Younger) to give a series of concerts with his own orchestra in St Petersburg, as she had heard that he was in straitened circumstances. "He came, a decrepit and painted mummy, beautifully dressed – he must have worn stays – with grey hair and moustache dyed coal-black. These concerts, which he conducted in jaunty style, were a tremendous success. The drum, with its nervous pulsations, is the life of such dance music, its very heart beat; Strauss' drummer, for accuracy of *tempo*, delicacy of touch, and rapidity of vibration was astounding, impeccable."

The English colony was also to be visited: there were tennis parties and visits to the ice-hills, and skating and sledging. The ice-hills – there was an English Ice-Hill Club to which all the Embassy belonged – were about forty feet high, built of solid blocks of ice watered every day. They were built in pairs, opposite one another, about 300 yards apart.

You climbed to the top of one of these hills with a small sledge about two feet long, lay face downwards upon it, legs trailing, and pushed off with feet and hands. The sledges were mounted on runners as sharp and polished as skates, and the slopes of the hills and the state of the ice were such that the speed of descent was extremely fast. One had only to climb straight up from the end of one's run, to be ready for the return journey down the opposite hill. Longer sledges were used when taking lady-passengers; the man sat cross-legged in front, and the lady, kneeling behind, hung on to him with her arms around him – so that the pleasure, for both parties, was not entirely confined to the actual sledging. But some ladies, even in those days, were dashing and tomboyish enough to challenge the men on their own ground, as solo sledgers. The acknow-ledged Queen of the Ice-Hills was Milly Carr, daughter of an English businessman. Norman teased her as a "stickler for propriety", called her "the backfisch", and spent a good deal of time with her, ice-hilling or skating.

Life, as usual, was full, and exhilarating. To his sister, now married and living in England, he wrote:

St Petersburg
Dear Meeri   23 Nov. 94
Have been fearfully busy lately else would have written sooner: but so much work and functions to get through almost driven to distraction.

I was muchly interested by reading Mama's letter – if you get another one you might forward it on here.

Glad you like Mildred Swettenham, though when you say she lives at Llandwrdcmch with her father that conveighs [sic] little to me except the semblance of high respectability. Glad you have been having rain and fog, – I mean sorry. So have we; and total darkness 3 p.m.

Glad cob clipped. Glad dogcart mended, – so am I after a bad attack of indigestion. Glad house dry – so am I – must go and get a drink soon. No time for music working at International law, exam next month. I don't know what I shd like for Xmas, etc. Cheque, after all, would not come amuck – I mean amiss – never does, curious to say.

Salutations
Tell Binnie I got his book (2 busy to write)

v

Life was full; yet more activity could somehow be squeezed in. In Decem-ber, for instance, he was asked by a Mr H. A. Macpherson for information about bird-snaring methods in Russia. Macpherson was trying to obtain fresh and unpublished information from all over the world as to the methods of catching birds. Many of these methods were of extreme antiquity, and were being forgotten. "If you share my interest in the matter," he wrote to Douglas, "I should consider it a pleasure as well as a privilege, to hear from you at your convenient leisure. I imagine the Russian peasants must do a good deal of snaring birds in the winter time." His intention, he added, "was to work out the evolution of the idea of fowling, as it occurred to prehistoric races; and to show how it had culminated in the Italian methods, which in Europe at any rate, were probably the most refined." No sooner asked, than complied with. Various friends and acquaintances were immediately asked for contributions, especially Michell, the Consul-General, and Mackie, his subordinate. A considerable amount of material was found within two weeks. Macpherson was interested to hear that there was an extensive literature on Russian Fowling. If it was only in Russian he would be glad of a translation, but he would like this to be typewritten. There, however, he was to be disappointed; typing was evidently impossible; Mackie, meanwhile, was to produce a manuscript translation. Other people were persuaded to help.

Macpherson's book, *A History of Fowling*, appeared in 1897, and in the following year he wrote to Douglas mentioning the fact but did not send him a copy. Douglas thought this rather mean of him, as he had taken a great deal of trouble (far more than has been mentioned here). There is a note from Michell which reinforces this opinion: "Mackie in my opinion has not been overpaid for his labour. Perhaps you might remind Mr M that translating from the Russian, and almost archaic Russian, is not the same as translating from Danish."

Boulenger wrote to say that he had sent copies of the *Herpetology* to a batch of internationally famous herpetologists – Eimer, Bedriaga, Peracca, etc; and Norman sent the manuscript of his *Darwinian Hypothesis* to Alfred Russell Wallace, who replied:

Dear Sir,

I have read your paper on Sexual Selection with much interest. The first more speculative part would I fear have no weight with those who follow Darwin in this matter; but the latter portion, dealing with the colours of the lizards of the Italian islands is very interesting and is a valuable contribution to the discussion. It would be worth printing in "Nature" or in some other Nat. Hist. periodical. I send you copies of two articles on another branch of Darwinism that you may not possibly [sic] have seen. I have returned the MSS as desired.

Yours very truly
Alfred R. Wallace

vi

Douglas had now completed his two years' probationary period as Attaché. Sir Frank Lascelles, the Ambassador, putting in to the Foreign Office for Douglas' commission as Third Secretary – a despatch written, or at any rate copied, like dozens of others, in Douglas' own hand – testified to the excellency of his services and stated that he had fulfilled all the conditions required. No doubt it was merely a matter of form, dated 3rd March 1895; for the letter commissioning "Our Trusty and Well beloved George Norman Douglass Esquire" as Third Secretary, when it arrived, was dated 1st March. So that was that. And now for the leave that was due – quite a lot of it. But while waiting for it to be granted there were the fruits of recent investigations to be forwarded: Despatch No. 57, Confidential, of 13th March encloses a Memorandum "by Mr Douglass on the proposed construction of a Russian Naval Port in the Northern Ocean which should be in railway communication with St Petersburg". This is a report of eighteen foolscap pages signed N.D., and it is followed on 28th March by Despatch No. 82, Confidential, consisting of "a further memorandum by Mr Douglass giving some particulars of Lieutenant Indrenin's recent expedition to the Murman Coast": five more foolscap pages. And of the same date, Despatch No. 83 contains a short memo of three pages on Prince Uchtomsky by N.D. Uchtomsky was spokesman for a group which advocated the immediate annexation of India, via Afghanistan, and is described in *Looking Back* as a firebrand. As to the information about the possible Murman port, it was supplied by Mr Kasi, a generous Russian friend.

Where he was to spend his leave had already been arranged. He was going to ride through Asia Minor with Law, the Commercial Attaché for Eastern Europe. Edward Fitzgerald Law was an Irishman, "yet more taciturn than the average Anglo-Saxon". He had a long pale solemn face, with a toothbrush moustache, "a noteworthy fund of naughty stories, and a noteworthy talent for telling them . . . it may have been this trait which drew me to him". They had got on well at St Petersburg ever since Douglas' arrival. Law wanted to write a report on English, German and French railways then being constructed in Asia Minor. They agreed to meet in Smyrna.

Douglas set out two or three weeks ahead of time, left some despatches in Warsaw, and found himself in Constantinople, where Sir Philip Currie was Ambassador. Currie had been Under-Secretary at the Foreign Office during Douglas' year there, and, after his appointment to Constantinople, had asked Douglas to look in there whenever he might be passing through.

This he now did, and was pleased that Currie seemed genuinely glad to see him. He exclaimed how good it was of Douglas to come: "I don't know how you found out, but we are dreadfully understaffed . . . I was wondering what to do. You don't mind putting in a day or two here, do you?"

"I should like nothing better, sir." And that, wrote Douglas, was how he came to be "nailed down in that infernal chancery". He might have spent the rest of his leave there, if someone else had not turned up later, allowing him to escape.

The fortnight at Smyrna before Law's arrival was one of the happiest of his life: "I was in a state of beatitude, and aware, not afterwards, but at the very moment, of that fact." Everything played its part, beginning with the robinia blossoms which drooped in creamy clusters against his window, and filled the room with their fragrance. To be drenched, after Russian gloom, in the brightness of an Oriental spring-time was exhilarating, and Smyrna seemed to be the most enjoyable place on earth. "That fascinating bazaar, the variegated crowds about the harbour, Eastern bustle and noise; or if you were in softer mood, there was the cemetery with its glorious cypresses, or the Greek quarter full of pretty girls, far prettier than those of Greece itself, because, I suppose, they are better nourished and less malarious. And what has happened to the British colony of those days, the Whittalls, Ogilvies, and others, who took me for such pleasant trips into the countryside?"

There was a flirtation, quite serious; and an expedition to Ephesus and Magnesia with the famous German archaeologist Humann. Also, near the harbour, there was that establishment which he so much liked and approved of:

> On the ground floor a cheap but attractive variety show was going on, with tables and chairs in front, on which coffee, Turkish Delight, and masticha, were served, and where, among the smiling clientèle, you could pick up a girl or anything else you fancied. Sooner or later you might be feeling ready for something to eat; if so just step upstairs to the next floor; it was a restaurant. After a hearty meal one is sometimes disposed, especially in the East, to have an hour's rest; if so, just step upstairs with your friend to the top floor; it was a suite of bedrooms. No questions were asked; you paid your money and got your key. Why are such delectable places not commoner?

On less frivolous evenings he went to see Truthful Freddy (Frederic Holmwood), the British Consul-General, a carefully got up old man who had marvellous tales to tell of Zanzibar and other places where he had been on service. They sat up half the night together, talking and drinking. It was here, at Truthful Freddy's, that he saw one evening a familiar figure he had almost forgotten: Major Law. He had arrived that very day, engaged a Turkish servant, bought provisions, and arranged for three horses to be brought round the following morning. He was sitting at the table, poring over some maps, and Douglas felt inclined to curse him for tearing him away from his life of bliss.

The requirements of Law's report sometimes took them off the main routes and led to zigzag movements; they went by train whenever possible, which was not often. They wound their way round about the centre of western Turkey and ventured as far east as Angora. "The going was pretty rough in places, and so was the accommodation; there was sometimes lack of food, but never lack of bugs. The natives were real Osmanlis, with red faces and prominent cheekbones, dirty and truthful, tough as the devil." The three travellers carried revolvers and Martini-Henry rifles, "more for the sake of appearance than for business", and used them only occasionally, to shoot at bustards, which they usually missed. They ended their journey at Constantinople, having got there via Broussa which left an enduring impression on Douglas, who found in its charm "an authentic smack of Paradise". At Constantinople he stayed this time at the Club, and "gave the Embassy a wide berth".

vii

This tour occupied "the better part of a month". A fortnight had already been spent in Smyrna, and the best part of a week (with the journey broken at Warsaw) had been spent in getting there. Six or seven weeks in all, which brings us to the last week in May. There is then a blank until 11th June, when he was in the Lipari Islands collecting, among other things, information which was embodied in a Foreign Office Report. Subsequently, it seems, he was ill with malaria at Genoa and in Venice, both in June; and went to the Vorarlberg in July, staying there most of the summer, apart from visits to England and Italy.[23]

He had handed in his Report on the Pumice-Stone Industry of the Lipari Islands to Sir Clare Ford, the British Ambassador in Rome, whom he had visited on previous occasions. He found him "pleasantly ga-ga, as every Ambassador should be", and "a *bon vivant* of the old school. . . . Sir Clare had a marvellous cook, and it was a standing grievance with him that not a single member of his staff cared for good food. 'I suppose they go to those restaurants,' he said sadly." If he and his visitor talked at all intimately, perhaps Sir Clare spoke of Effie Gray, Ruskin's wife, later Mrs Millais, with whom he had been in love as a young man. He had done his best, in those days, to seduce Effie from the path of virtue, "but after one rebuff he flung away and told her she would one day die of propriety". Young Ford had been a bit of a rake; Effie had reformed him, and encouraged him to work, with the interesting result that he had become Attaché at the Naples Legation within a year. Perhaps some reminiscence of Sir Clare's eventually gave rise to Mr Keith's remark in *South Wind*: "Ruskin. Good God! He's not a man; he's an emetic."

The Pumice-Stone Report was published in the Miscellaneous Series of the Foreign Office in August, and is worthy of a glance from anyone interested in Douglas' writing. It is an illustration (especially on pages 2 and 3) of how a technical subject may be made intelligible and interesting to the layman. The prime ingredient in the author is curiosity, a lively and enquiring mind; the second, an intellect trained to observe and describe essentials and characteristic particulars with precision and economy. Furthermore, the author should be furnished if possible with an extensive vocabulary designed to illuminate the subject without blinding or distracting the reader, and to provide a certain suppleness and variety of language which will ensure freedom from cliché and a turgid syntax. Douglas had these ingredients, and could apply this style to anything. It is essentially a *humane* skill, not normally found in those deficient in human sympathy or wide terms of reference. Douglas spent the first half of his life perfecting this skill, and it became the substructure, the skeleton, upon which the whole character of his writing was built.

As to the Report, Douglas wrote that the trade in London was annoyed with him for revealing the true prices of pumice-stone, "which I ascertained with a good deal of difficulty". As a consequence of what he wrote about the employment of children in the workings, an inspector was sent down to the islands, and child labour, which consisted of porterage, was replaced eventually by a mechanical conveyor.

With typical exaggeration and provocation, Douglas delighted in telling everyone that this was the *only* meritorious act of his whole life.

viii

In the autumn of 1896, the *Darwinian Hypothesis* was published, first of all in two instalments (November and December) of *Natural Science*, and subsequently as an offprint. Its argument is that decorative coloration, courtship, and sexual display, are products of excess vitality, and are not necessarily designed to please the female. Leisure is the prerequisite of all artistic activity and appreciation:

Without leisure no artistic product can be consciously evoked or appreciated as such; artistic worth does not exist, much less the taste whereby to criticise it. Whatever may be the potential capacity of mind of the "higher animals", I hold that their time is too preoccupied with the actual struggle for existence to permit the formation of the mental qualities ascribed to the argus pheasant. These are a luxury to which human savages, some of them, have not yet attained.

This, the most original and generally interesting of his scientific writings, was also the last. It fittingly marks a transition. Just as scientific speculation had already supplanted the merely observational records of his childhood, so now science itself had become an introduction to philosophy, aesthetics, literature; and this wider world was of such absorbing interest that science itself ceased to be the most important aspect of life. He never turned away from science or lost his interest in zoology, botany and geology; but he had begun to find a new, aesthetic, occupation. Having got two substantial monographs into print (the *Herpetology* and the *Darwinian Hypothesis*) which he had reason to be pleased with, he had perhaps begun to realise that he could actually write well. Even his diplomatic reports and despatches may have reinforced this impression; he may have begun to enjoy writing for its own sake. Although he has made no comment on the fact that he started writing in Russia, the fact that he did so seems to prove that he did not start writing merely to try to make money, as he says. The *Tale of Elba*, begun in 1897, of which he gives an extract in *Looking Back* would lead one to believe, from the extract given, that he made a gradual transition from fact to fiction; but this is incorrect, for in 1896 he was to begin writing fiction based on personal experience and not merely on research.

ix

In March 1896 his annual leave was due. He had nearly two months of it, and for at least part of this time was in London, where he entertained his mother who was on her way from Austria to Radnorshire to see Mary:

I left here on April 27th and on the evening of the 28th was in London where I was met by Norman at Charing Cross Station. He gave me an impression of "uprightness" [*gediegenen*] – he is tall and slim and of all three he is the most like his father. He was wearing a top hat and black frock coat and, as you can imagine, I was inordinately pleased to see my "diplomat", especially as he was very kind and considerate to me. In the evening we went to a splendid restaurant, The Holborn Restaurant, with bright lights and ornamental gilt reflected in enormous mirrors. The food was good, but fourteen

shillings for two was quite enough! The next morning Norman came
to breakfast, again in full dress, and got my ticket for me. I left Euston
at ten o'clock and was in Knighton by three, where Mary met me ...

x

Soon after his return to Russia, the Embassy packed up and went to
Moscow for nearly a month for the celebration of Nicholas II's coronation. "Crowded days and crowded nights; invitations four deep; functions
without end. The Coronation scene was admirably staged, especially that
culminating moment when, after placing the crown on his own head, the
Emperor turned slowly round and solemnly faced the assembly."

An atmosphere of fluster and flurry reigned at the Embassy. "Formal
dinners had sometimes to be given and knotty questions of precedence
cropped up, since Moscow was swarming with distinguished exotics
from every corner of the earth: how were they to be ranked? Li Hung
Chang, how – where should he be seated? Next to Madame Albani?
No; that would never do. And so on. ...." He met one or two people
whom he remembered, among many who left no impression: witty
Bishop Creighton, whose gorgeous vestments outshone all those of the
Russian prelates at the Coronation (where he represented the Church of
England); and an attaché from Paris called Blount, who commanded
Douglas never to order half a bottle of anything, "not even brandy. I
haven't drunk a half bottle in my life."

xi

His Russian had, of course, improved – in fact, he had passed an exam
in it. But he did not perfect himself in the language until towards the
end of his stay in Petersburg "according to that one and only correct
recipe for which the French have coined a vulgar but expressive phrase"
(*coucher avec son dictionnaire*). He was enabled to do this, he wrote, with
the help of "Colonel, or General, Obrucheff ... Governor of Transcaucasia or some other Central Asian region". Obrucheff was a "jovial,
herculean kind of man, tall and broad, brimming over with health; he
could drink anybody under the table, and his love-affairs were past
counting, despite the fact that he was more than sixty years of age".

Over their third bottle of sweet champagne one day, Obrucheff began
telling Douglas that if you wanted a girl in Transcaucasia and insisted,
as he always did, "on having a sound article", you must make a contribution to the family beforehand, or you will never get what you want.
You make a small annual payment to the parents, who reserve the girl

for you, and for you alone, till she has reached the proper age. You could pass her on afterwards to some husband, or send her back to the family. They were the most charming girls in the world, said Obrucheff; and his waiting-list was so long that there was always a fresh one ready for him. His staff did not follow this system; they picked up any girl they could find "and in so doing often picked up something else as well. . . . What they should have picked up, and what they failed to pick up by their haphazard methods, was a knowledge of the language. It was not his business to know this language but to administer the country and send reports to headquarters; it was theirs. Yet he could talk it familiarly, thanks to his system which entailed an intimate and lasting contact, and forced him to learn the speech of the natives."

Douglas said that this was just what he needed. He could only speak phrase-book Russian, and wanted to be able to use slang, to make jokes, to speak intimately and idiomatically. He was then in the midst of a most passionate love-affair with Helen Demidoff, but she never talked anything but French "even in the most expansive moments – if one could talk then at all". There were occasional liaisons with society ladies, but they always spoke French or German or English. He might have picked up a phrase or two of the vernacular by frequenting certain places, but he could not be seen doing that, even if he cared to go. He learned something, of course, from books and the theatre, and from Russian acquaintances; but what he really needed to complete his education was "one of those decent-minded, blue-eyed girls of the people whom you saw in thousands all over the place, who knew not a word of anything but Russian and were not procurable by any methods known to me". There was one in his own house, his maid Malasha, but he had learned to leave servants alone (his own servants at any rate) or the work was never done properly. Could Obrucheff help him to find such a girl? Obrucheff laughed and said a single word: "Postaraius" – I'll try.

About a week later, Douglas' man Ossip announced that a young girl was waiting to see him. Her name was Anyuta Ponomareva. She announced humbly that His Excellency had sent her, "and what could she do for me? I tried to discover how the trick was done," but Obrucheff had already left Petersburg, and it would have been "tactless to enquire of the girl by what arts he had contrived to do me this favour. Maybe he threatened to have her sent to Siberia if she refused to come to me; Russians will do a good deal to oblige their friends." If Obrucheff had passed the entire population of the country through a sieve, wrote Douglas, it would have been impossible to find anyone more to his liking: "There she was and there she stayed; not in my apartment, but at my beck and call. She lived with her mother and younger brother whose acquaintance, contrary to my present custom, I never even thought of making."

Although Douglas was seeing Anyuta and Helen concurrently, they never met. He found that they complemented each other perfectly. Each possessed "some little trait of temperament or physique which the other lacked; between them, they constituted one ideal whole. And I made both happy: what more could they want? I have often found it difficult to remain faithful to a single person, where women are concerned. Some lady-friends of mine seem to labour under the same difficulty, where men are concerned."

Helen and Anyuta were endearing companions. He could not separate them in his memory although they were as unlike each other as they could have been; they were "two emanations of the same spirit of joyous self-forgetfulness, of that wholehearted *abandon* which is commoner in Russia, among both men and women, than elsewhere".

In view of what happened later, it was fortunate that this dual affair remained secret. The only person of consequence who ever saw him with Anyuta was Count Campo Alegre, Secretary to the Spanish Embassy, his best friend in Russia; and completely trustworthy. Douglas and Anyuta sometimes used to go to his flat on the Fontanka Canal in the evenings to cheer him up, for he was then an invalid. "As to Helen – nobody knew of her relations with me save her bosom friend Princess Aurore Kara-georgievitch, who was not likely to talk about it, because . . ."

These remarks in *Looking Back*, ending with the enigmatic row of dots, are completed in the Berg copy with the annotation "she also had a boy-friend". Princess Aurore Demidoff married Prince Arseny Karageorgie-vitch in 1895, and was the mother of Prince Paul of Yugoslavia, Regent of that country from 1934–1941. As to the identity of "Helen", she is definitely named in the Berg *Looking Back* as a Demidoff. The most likely Helen Demidoff would have been Elena Alexandrovna Demidoff, not of the main Demidoff family of which Aurore was a member, but from a family of cousins, the Lopoukine-Demidoffs.

xii

"Your Anyuta-Helen love-affair is very interesting," wrote Milly Carr (Queen of the Ice-Hills) about forty years later, when she had become Mrs Feild and had read *Looking Back*, ". . . but how did you find time for so much activity? I took at least six hours per week of your valuable time. Did you ever eat and sleep?" Milly Carr never even kissed or was kissed by Douglas, though she would have liked it. She would not, because she had been warned by her father against him. "I was deeply in love with

Norman," she confessed, "but I think he regarded love as a sort of campaign and was not wholly spontaneous about it. Perhaps he was not very nice in that way." She led a very sheltered life, and at the impressionable age of seventeen found Douglas "so attentive and complimentary ... and altogether *such fun* that when you left St P. I felt very sad (not quite broken-hearted) and you vanished so suddenly out of my life – not even a 'goodbye' to soften the blow."

"A sort of campaign" – this was an astute perception of one of Douglas' attitudes to love; but it is only true of a part of his nature. Another part was only too spontaneous, and caused a great many complications in his life. The duality of his nature in this respect was matched in other ways: for example, no one could be franker than he, and no one more reticent. One has the impression that the hardened campaigner would sometimes be overtaken *in medias res*, and to his own surprise even, by the sentimentalist; the intellectual with love-on-the-brain (to use a Lawrentian expression) would find himself succumbing to a spontaneous physical impulse, set in train perhaps by some quite trivial circumstance – "the inflection of a voice" or "the charm of rounded wrists".

xiii

One would have liked to see Douglas and Anyuta cheering up Campo Alegre in his apartment on the Fontanka. The sitting-room:

> looked out upon the sluggish and discoloured water, and the furniture and other inanimate objects scattered about, their nature and disposition, gave you a hint of the uncommon personality of their owner. Campo Alegre, scholar and man of the world, impressed his character on all he possessed and all he said. Or so it seemed to me. I reckon him among the best friends I have had. He belonged to an almost forgotten race, the humanist; the man of boundless curiosity and boundless tolerance – of that tolerance which derives from satisfied curiosity, and can derive from nothing else. *Humani nihil alienum* ...
>
> Here were books, abundance of them, which he carried from one end of the world to another – the great writers of all ages, the real writers; for Campo Alegre had no sympathy for the commonplace, the mediocre, in literature or in anything else. Life was too short, he used to say, for anything but the best. On the other hand (he would add) he had enjoyed this life; he had taken it by the throat in many lands and made it yield every pleasure, legitimate or otherwise, which it had to offer. The civilised attitude! Your vulgarian cannot achieve this point of view. For all his effrontery he is a slave – a slave to his own poor soul, to a thousand prejudices and taboos.

Campo Alegre's previous post had been Tokio. He was inclined to blame Japan, and perhaps with reason, for his now indifferent health. He was threatened, he suspected, with some paralytic disorder which the best specialists in Europe had failed to cure. He could still move about and attend to his duties as *Conseiller* of the Spanish Embassy, but with a certain difficulty, and it was fortunate that he had a devoted Russian valet.

xiv

The last four or five months at Petersburg must have been extremely crowded, for it was in the midst of his Helen–Anyuta love-affair that he began to write his first imaginative and non-scientific work. It seems that he began to write it largely for therapeutic reasons. Sometime or other during his years at Karlsruhe, he had been nearly drowned. He does not mention the circumstances (perhaps this in itself is significant), but describes the experience as "one of the most objectionable . . . . of my life, and one – the only one – which has left a scar on my psychic constitution . . . the shock of that brief asphyxiation has endured, and no argument, no ridicule, no exertion of will-power, avails against it . . . Diluted, no doubt, by the passage of years, it persists to this day. Nothing would induce me to swim in deep water. . . . At that time, and for many years afterwards, the obsession of fighting for life and swallowing a lakeful of water never left me." It harassed his sleeping hours; it lasted through the Karlsruhe period, accompanied him to Paris, London and Russia; and at Petersburg, in 1896, he used the experience – with the help of Apuleius – in a short story called *The Familiar Spirit*.

In Petersburg he found an old French version of Apuleius' *De Deo Socratis*, and immediately became infatuated with the theory of an Attendant Demon. In the end, he had collected so much information about attendant demons, familiar spirits, genii, guardian angels, spiritual companions, etc, that he had become a specialist in the subject. (Much of it was used later, in the opening chapter of *Siren Land*.) The manuscripts of *The Familiar Spirit* were to grow to five in number between 1896 and 1900 from a first sketch, an outline of four pages, to a fifth version of over a hundred and seventy pages. "I was plainly fond of the theme to take so much trouble over it and carry it about so long."

The second version, dated Petersburg October 1896, extended to fifty-four pages. In the preface it was described as the tale of a man divided against himself, a man who succeeds in driving out his own Familiar Spirit or Guardian Angel. It consisted of three chapters, each divided into three parts – "a symmetrical arrangement".

It is the story of a man of rather dull intellect who, during a drowning accident, becomes aware of the existence of his own Familiar Spirit. In the course of time they hold converse together, and he gradually realises that his dullness is due to the presence within him of this Spirit, his *alter ego*, which is bent on crushing his ambitions. He takes a dislike to it. He gives hints of this state of affairs to his wife and to a man-friend, who endeavour to help him. He suspects that they are in league with this Familiar Spirit, and takes a dislike to them also. In a violent scene, he shakes off his Attendant Genius. "'Vampire' he stammered, '. . . you have lamed my energies. You have suppressed every aspiration that could raise me above the level of the animals. Go therefore, find some more subservient mortal. . . .' And he felt his Genius clinging, in fond despair, to his fibres, and sorrowfully quitting the mansion that was dearest to itself. With a groan it departed for ever. And an enormous chaos, black as night, suddenly yawned before his mind's eye. The lamp of reason was extinguished." His wife notices the great change in his nature, but is unaware of its cause. She tries to quiet him with gentle words. He accuses her of life-long perfidy, of having conspired with the Familiar to crush his spirit; the Familiar has been vanquished, and now it is her turn. He drowns her.

Some flavour of the style may be gathered from the above; extracts of greater length will be found in *Looking Back*, where Douglas' humorous self-disparaging remarks on the subject are agreeably well-balanced – not too harsh, not too indulgent. (After this second version the story was influenced by Le Fanu, and acquired an introduction and a new character, the friendly expert, in the Le Fanu manner. The fifth version was written in 1899 in Naples.)

It was no mean feat to have written fifty-four pages of this story in October, for his life was not only crowded, but had suddenly encountered an appalling complication: Helen was going to have a baby.

xv

In later years Douglas used occasionally to tell friends that if her family had discovered the true facts of the Helen affair, his life would not have been safe in Russia. There was only one thing to do and, by 17th October, he had made up his mind to do it. He had decided to "hop it", before it was too late; but as decently and as face-savingly as possible. In these circumstances, the subject of his story *The Familiar Spirit* – a man divided against himself – seems entirely fitting.

"My idea," he wrote later, "was to go on a long leave – *en disponibilité* –

for two years, till the storm which was brewing should blow over." The difficulty was to find some pretext acceptable to the Foreign Office. Joseph Chamberlain had proposed Imperial Tariffs, and Douglas suggested to the Foreign Office that his two-year leave might be devoted to the study of this question in the British Dependencies. He added that he was indifferent as to salary, and did not care whether juniors passed over his head or not. He was so determined to get out of Petersburg that he wrote: "If I am not allowed to go *en disponibilité* I should prefer to resign." At the suggestion of Foley, Assistant Private Secretary at the Foreign Office, Douglas sent in an official request; the reply (9th November 1896) was satisfactory: "Sir, I am directed by the Marquess of Salisbury to state to you that His Lordship agrees to your being placed *en disponibilité* for two years from the 15th instant."

In a letter drafted to Foley on 17th October, he had emphasised that he did not wish to resign if it could be avoided, but would like to get away as soon as possible. He had added: "I must go to England – if only for an afternoon – in the course of the next month or so to give evidence in the Queen's Bench (N.B. nothing discreditable!) and possibly it could be so managed that I need not return here."

It does seem to have been so managed, at the last possible moment. November 10th: Sir Nicholas O'Conor, British Ambassador at St Petersburg, to Her Majesty's Secretary for Foreign Affairs:

My Lord

I have the honour to enclose herewith to your Lordship an urgent application from Mr G. N. Douglass, third Secretary in Her Majesty's Embassy, to be allowed to proceed at once to England in connection with pressing legal proceedings.

Under the circumstances of the case I have ventured to give Mr Douglass permission to leave without waiting for your Lordship's official sanction.

I have the honour to be . . . etc . . .

He had done it – escaped in the nick of time, by the skin of his teeth! On the day before he left, he went round to say goodbye to Campo Alegre: "As I rose to depart, he said: 'Perhaps you'll accept this as a keepsake?' and he gave me a ring, a cabochon sapphire which he always wore. 'And – ah! I should like you to have one of my books as well. It may remind you of this room. Here is a small one. It will go into your pocket; it has often gone into mine: Petrarca's *De remediis utriusque Fortunae* – a worthless Rotterdam edition, you see, of 1649. . . . Those who judge Petrarca by his sonnets – how little they know about him! To explore, like he did, a trackless world and rediscover the old landmarks. . . . to make oneself lord of all the buried past. . . . I don't think we realise in what a state of rapture those men must have lived. . . . You'll glance into it sometimes?'" He reflected that Campo Alegre, conscious of his apparently progressive disease, never expected to see him again.

His retreat from Russia was the first important example of an emotional crisis changing the course of his life and forcing him to get across an international frontier as quickly as possible. There were to be at least two more of these, like huge re-direction signs planted squarely across his path, and oddly enough at intervals of almost exactly twenty years; and threats of others; and a scattering of minor crises of the same kind; for one of the extraordinary things about this apparently sagacious and self-possessed man was that he could have been said to veer wildly from one crisis to another in his private life. Not that this worried him, or ever made him think of changing his ways. On the contrary; and in this connection, with regard to the major crises, there is an interesting aspect of inevitability and of apparent pre-judgment about them. It looks as though he placed himself, unconsciously or subconsciously, in a position in which the only course open to him was the desirable one. It is difficult, for instance, to think of him remaining in Petersburg, or even in the Diplomatic Service, longer than he did. The time had come for a change, and it was as though he had forced the change on himself in a manner which left him no alternative: "Burn your boats! This has ever been my system in times of stress."

PART III

The *Amateur of Life and Letters*
1897–1908

CHAPTER NINE

———— ✦ ————

The Bay of Naples
1897

i

Ever since 1888 Norman had felt "an affectionate longing" for the Bay of Naples. This is hardly surprising. Who, having seen it, can ever forget it? Who, familiar with the classics as he was, could fail to be twice as deeply impressed by it as one who sees it simply as a magnificent visual effect? A tangible memory of Greek and Latin history, of myth and legend, and of the foundations of Western civilisation lies extended in a huge scenic amphitheatre of sea and land, in which various splendid natural features preside superbly over the human drama. Nowhere else even in the Mediterranean can the geological and historical past be seen together so vividly continuing their lethargic irruption into the present; nor can there be many places on earth more stimulating, more tempting to excess, or better calculated to induce in the indulgent an unrestrained dedication of the faculties to every kind of pleasure. Since the time of ancient Rome, and of Baiae, Pompeii and Herculaneum and Tiberius' palaces on Capri, men and women of all nationalities have practised here the arts of *dolce vita*, all that wealth, power, imagination and individual taste could encompass. Here, for a few, it has always been afternoon.

"Everybody," writes Douglas, "admires the Bay of Naples. Not everybody buys a house and grounds there without having looked at them." It was a measure of his desire for the South, and of his conviction that the Bay of Naples was the ideal place to live in, that he did so. The conviction could only have been strengthened by – indeed, it may have arisen from – spending two winters in St Petersburg. "In 1896, having some little money, I wrote from Petersburg to a German friend on the spot, Linden of the Zoological Station, and asked him to discover a villa on the Posilipo for me to buy." Linden found one – "I sent the money. The thing was done."

ii

At that time Naples was a city of about half a million inhabitants, the
most heavily populated in the Mediterranean, and one of about a dozen
of the largest cities in Europe; of these, it was in parts the most densely
packed with humanity. So much so that in summer at least life was lived
almost entirely in the streets – more than a hundred thousand people
were otherwise confined to *sottoterrani*: caves and cellars below ground.
To walk through the poorer quarters of the city, of which most of it was
composed, was like walking through a series of corridors in a single
colossal communal dwelling-house from which walls and doors had been
removed. These streets with their high terraces of tenement-like houses,
or overcrowded decaying palazzi, their black basalt paving without
sidewalks, their sky-high washing strung rank behind rank from one side
to the other, throbbed with vitality (as they still do) and with a rich
complexity of sights and sounds. Cooks with portable stoves dispensed
pieces of fish and meat; hawkers sold left-overs from restaurant tables or
a choice of cigar-ends carefully gathered from the main streets. Under the
arches of the Teatro San Carlo "public writers" waited behind desks for
commissions from analphabetic lovers; street vendors everywhere cried
their wares; medicasters with infallible cures for every known malady
delivered interminable lectures – and drew the teeth of passers-by; cows
and goats were driven through the streets to be milked at front doors;
singing, sometimes for money, more often for emotional release, here
and there rose and fell; funeral processions passed with baroquely-decorated
hearses and mourners belonging to secret fraternities disguised like
Klansmen; beggars, touts, prostitutes, pimps lay in wait for visitors;
anything could be bought; any pleasure, any curious taste could be
indulged; and everywhere all over the city children of all ages – many
of them almost or actually naked – wove their way in and out of all this
animated fabric like so many human bobbins. Above hung the same
sun and sea-breezes the Greek colonists had known seven or eight
centuries before the birth of Christ; Greek and Roman gods had been
accepted and Christianity adapted to pagan needs; Roman, Saracenic,
French, Spanish and Italian empires had come and gone, each in turn
confirming in a pleasure-loving but ironically-minded people a belief
in the vanity of vanities. The animation was half Hogarthian, half mediaeval; but the setting and the actors owed something to the kasbah and
the souks, something to the Levant, and to an incrustation of hopeful
excitement derived from a succession of baroque civilisations imposed
upon a people fundamentally rooted in a stolid and rather melancholy
form of pagan fatalism. The result was unique – a blend of independence

and originality described by Fucini as a spirit of primitive independence in which everyone does what he believes in and what he finds most convenient for himself, without caring whether he will appear ridiculous or whether it will bring further trouble in its train – a spirit that would certainly have appealed to Douglas.

In this enormous urban ant-hill, disease could spread unchecked. With its heaps of rotting garbage, its ancient sewage and water supply systems and its low altitude it was an ideal site for cholera. Between 1836 and 1884 there were seven outbreaks. Axel Munthe, later to become world-famous with his book *The Story of San Michele*, who had already worked on Capri and in the Ischian earthquake disaster in 1880 and 1881, worked also in cholera-ridden Naples in 1884, and his *Letters from a Mourning City*, published in 1887, helped to reveal the appalling conditions which then existed. Other writers, such as Mathilde Serao and Fucini, had already drawn attention to the plight of the Neapolitan poor; but it was not until after 1884 that any steps were taken by the authorities to improve conditions. The *sventramento*, or disembowelling, of Naples then began with some vigour, and has been continuing sluggishly and sometimes invisibly, ever since. At first whole areas were torn down and cleared so that new wide streets bringing light and air could be driven through the slums; a copious supply of fresh water was brought from Serino, near Lagonegro, more than a hundred miles away; the sewage system was improved. The poverty was still appalling, and there was still nothing that some of the poor would not do in order to earn money; but the cholera was held in check. The picturesque warren of Santa Lucia was demolished and replaced by a line of unbeautiful hotels. The prosperous, fashionable part of Naples, reaching out westwards towards the Posilipo and its delectable villas from the Castello dell'Ovo, and climbing the heights of the Vomero, was centred round the Villa Nazionale gardens. Here, in the evening, the *borghesi*, the well-to-do, and foreign visitors assembled on foot or in carriages to show themselves to each other, to enjoy the sea air beneath the palms, and to listen to the band. Here also was situated the Zoological Station founded by Dr Anton Dohrn in 1872. This institution, it may be remembered, was one of the attractions which had in the first place drawn Douglas to the South.

iii

The Dohrn[24] family came from Stettin. Anton's father, Karl August, was known throughout Europe as a great collector of Coleoptera; he had also become rich as the director of a sugar-refining business. There was there-fore a background of zoology on the one hand, and on the other, of that kind of amplitude of possibilities which money can bestow on talent and ambition. Anton Dohrn was born in 1840, and studied at Jena, where he was influenced by Ernst Haeckel, who became Professor of Zoology there, and later, a world-famous naturalist. After practical experience as a marine biologist in Scotland and, especially, in Sicily, Dohrn decided to devote his life to the creation of an international laboratory for marine research in the Mediterranean. He persuaded his father to give him the money he would have inherited, and with it built a deliberately imposing-looking building at Naples – a building that universities and governments could be impressed by. His idea was to lease research quarters, or "tables" as they were called, to an institution or a country, which would also provide for the expenses of the scientists it sent to occupy them. Thus the main burden of maintenance would be contributed by organisations which could afford the cost, and which, at the same time, would be able to give their scientists opportunities that existed nowhere else in the world. It was a simple but radical idea, attended by a large element of risk; but Dohrn made it succeed, and succeed brilliantly. He called the place a "station" (i.e. a place of temporary residence, a halting-place) because the international scientists who came to it would not be there permanently, and because he hoped that other establishments of the same kind would be set up all over the world, with researchers travelling from one to another.

The now world-famous Aquarium, and the Library, were the two chief features of the Station in its early days. They were backed by a large collection of pickled specimens, and by ever-expanding research at sea conducted by a steam yacht and launch, and a good many sailing and rowing boats. By 1888, when Douglas had first visited Naples, probably with an introduction to Dohrn, Herman Linden was Secretary of the Station. It would be interesting to know what kind of instructions Douglas sent him eight years later with regard to obtaining a house – whether they were detailed or general, grand, or merely practical. Whatever they were, Linden could not have made a happier choice: the Villa Maya is a delectable place, in a superb setting.

iv

Douglas' "affectionate longing" had taken him to the Bay of Naples at least once and probably several times between 1888 and 1896. He had been by boat, like Shelley before him, to visit the Scoglio di Virgilio, "a rocky point where the great Enchanter of mediaeval days loved to linger", and of which Shelley wrote: "Here are lofty rocks and craggy islets, with arches and portals of precipice standing in the sea, and enormous

caverns, which echoed faintly with the murmur of the languid tide".
The enormous caverns had given the locality its name of Gaiola, a corrupt-
tion of *caveola*. The Romans had excavated them when the sea level was
lower in order to obtain volcanic tufa for building the vast Villa Pausilypon which covered the whole seaward end of the promontory and gave
it its name. This place had been erected by Vedius Pollio, who is supposed
to have fed his lampreys on the flesh of slaves. He had left it in his will to
the Emperor Augustus.

Several of the rooms in Douglas' villa, and the large cellars, are of
Roman construction. It is described in Meade Falkner's *Lost Stradivarius*,
as the Villa de Angelis:

> The earlier foundations were, I believe, originally Roman, and upon
> them a modern villa had been constructed in the eighteenth century . . .
> Looking down upon the sea from the windows of the villa, one could
> on calm days easily discern the remains of Roman piers and moles
> lying below the surface of the transparent water; and the tufa-rock on
> which the house was built was burrowed with those unintelligible
> excavations of a classic date so common in the neighbourhood.

Norman changed its name to Villa Maya – Illusion. (As the letter Y
is uncommon in Italian, it became known as the Villa Maia.) "Illusion"
was a suitable choice of name. The name of Pollio's vast palace, Pausilypon,
had been derived from the Greek παυσων λυπην, avoidance of grief or
pain, the Epicurean recipe for happiness, reproduced in a later language
in the name of another villa near Douglas': Sans Souci. "Illusion" is less
confident, more ironical, a suggestion perhaps that his settling there was a
conscious experiment in hedonism which might or might not succeed.

The Villa Maya is bordered by sea on three sides and has a little beach
for bathing. Douglas later wrote that it would have been an idyllic
home "but for two drawbacks – some horrible low-class neighbours, and
the discomfort of the track . . . which leads up to the main Posilipo road".
He built a terrace all round the house: he could dine outside "facing the
Bay and enjoying the view towards Vesuvius, the Sorrentine Peninsula,
Capri, Ischia and Procida; lunch in more intimate environment on the
east side under a trellis of vines; and breakfast round the next corner,
looking into that small garden which I had contrived by means of a
sturdy sustaining wall on one side, and a second wall on the other as
protection from the gales. . . . Birds were encouraged here, and during
one spring I had no less than fourteen blackcaps' nests."

During the reconstruction of the garden, many ancient relics came to
light – "marbles of many kinds, including the rare breccia corallina;
amphoras buried deep under the soil which the neighbouring torrent had

brought down in the course of centuries (one of them with a thick paste at the bottom, a remnant of Roman olive oil); fragments of columns, capitals, and so forth. . . . What pleased me particularly was a piece of a glass vessel signed by the Greek artist Ennion, and two charming little pilasters in rosso antico." Roman pavements and four varieties of alabaster, part of a fluted column, and in all at least a ton of such stones were unearthed. Some were used for paving and for garden seats, and he took away sixteen sackfuls when he eventually left the villa.

The house had ten or twelve rooms, the most delightful of which was the library. It occupied the whole of the top floor of the house, Douglas having knocked three rooms into this one, whose "twin balconies afforded one of the finest views on earth . . . This was a welcome retreat from the world, with its leather armchairs and Persian rugs", its vaulted ceiling and rich moss-green flooring tiles. The entrance hall was also tiled by Douglas, with a superb design of scattered rose-leaves and rose-buds, hand-painted on a white ground. It was made to order at the Museo Artistico Industriale, and at the time was held to be the highest achievement of modern Neapolitan kilns and their artists. "While it was still on exhibition there, Queen Margherita happened to call, and Signore Tesorone, the Director and a friend of mine, ventured to observe that it would bring its owner good luck if Her Majesty would deign to be the first person to walk over it. She graciously condescended to do so," wrote Douglas some thirty years later, "and I am still waiting for the luck." Perhaps the luck has come to the present owner of the house, of which this very beautiful example of *trompe l'oeil* decoration of the Art Nouveau period is one of the most splendid features, still in excellent condition.

v

While the Villa Maya was being put in order, Douglas lived in the Villa Sarno, not far away. Here also lived another member of that team of scientists at the Zoological Station, Salvatore Lo Bianco. "He was a burly Sicilian with pronounced negro strains in his blood; I imagine his family name, 'the white one', is a playful allusion to this fact. It is no rare name in Sicily." Bearing in mind such origins, Douglas thought he perceived in Lo Bianco "the aboriginal African temperament, childlike and engaging, interested in everything, always ready for fun".

Lo Bianco was the son of the porter at the Palazzo Torlonia, in which Dohrn lived. Dohrn had room for an enthusiastic apprentice, so took him on largely to please the boy's father. That had been in 1874, when Salvatore had just left school. The boy was especially useful in dealing with the local fishermen, on whom the scientists were then dependent for obtaining specimens. He was soon made assistant to August Müller, the praeparator, who was in charge of the identification, preservation, bottling, and despatch of specimens to other scientific institutions. He learned all that Müller could teach him about the preservation and bottling of sea-creatures, and also experimented with new methods on his own account. He was apparently a gifted improviser. When Müller died at an early age, Lo Bianco, then twenty, was made praeparator, and found himself in charge of the department. "He knew all sea-beasts by name, down to the humblest and rarest, where they lived, when to catch them, and how to preserve the frailest of them in their original bright tints. He was a true student, never satisfied with his attainments. And there he used to sit, writing at an enormous table in a room which reeked of alcohol and contained hundreds of pickled specimens." His work was largely responsible for making the Zoological Station famous: scientific institutions all over the world wanted to know the secrets of his preserving techniques; but Dohrn would not allow publication of any of these secrets until 1890, when the world supremacy of his establishment was absolutely secure. Lo Bianco was made an honorary Doctor of Science by the University of Naples.

Douglas found him good company. They would often eat together at the Villa Maya, or at Lago Fusaro (oysters), or the Aquarium boat would pick Douglas up from his villa and take him off for the day, so that in the end he came to know every corner of the Bay of Naples, and a good many places beyond.

While he was at the Villa Sarno, Douglas also met Arturo Laconci. He was in the habit of lunching or dining at the Giardini di Torino where Arturo was one of the waiters, "but of another stamp; different manners, different accent, different appearance. His was so refined and intelligent a face that the idea occurred to me of taking him as my butler-valet later on. We made an appointment, talked it over, and came to terms. He produced his passport and drew my attention to the phrase 'father unknown', meaning to imply, I daresay, that he was the illegitimate son of a Prince or a Cardinal. That was quite possible. He was Tuscan by birth, about forty-five years old, clean-shaven save for whiskers, slightly bald, with large eyes, perfect teeth, and a paunch just sufficient to justify his rôle of *maître d'hotel*. He had a presence, and a grand manner. Arturo was in a class by himself. It was settled that he should come to me as soon as my place was inhabitable. Then he mentioned that he also had a wife, a passable cook . . . perhaps it would suit my convenience to take her too? It did suit my convenience, and she proved to be better than merely passable. But Arturo never gave his wife much credit for anything; he spoke of her in a feudal and half-commiserating way as 'my woman'."

The future of the Villa Maya was thus being studied with a certain amount of style. By December 1896 also, shrubs and trees had been ordered from Dammans, and Douglas had made the acquaintance of Carl Sprenger, the distinguished botanist who worked for that firm and had given his name to *Asparagus sprengeri*, and was later to give Douglas so many tropical orchids that they had to be removed in a taxi.

Preparations at the Villa Maya were going on so satisfactorily that he was able to join his friend Mrs Effie Wallace Carpenter in Paris for Christmas. Effie Carpenter had Cuban blood in her veins which showed in her sultry eyes and heightened complexion. She had been married at the age of sixteen to a rich English General, exactly four times as old, who had expired, not long after the marriage, in the arms of a Parisian *cocotte*. She lived in London in a luxurious house containing a Turkish bath and a notable cellar of wine, and there, after the General's death, Douglas had sometimes visited her in the early Nineties. To Paris she brought her maid and about four hundredweight of luggage. She and Douglas enjoyed each other's company so well that they arranged to meet again in the following year at Meran.

vi

The Parisian visit was presumably an occasion of spontaneous intimacy, uncomplicated by such arrangements and devices as had been necessary during his Helen–Anyuta love affair, which led Milly Carr to write of a campaign of love. But at about this time another campaign had been initiated. He became acquainted with a certain Maria Spasiano, who kept a dressmaking establishment in Naples. "I shall not," he writes with a niceness of distinction that is technically rather than essentially true, "call Maria Spasiano a procuress. She was a woman full of gaiety who took a fancy to me; like many others of her sex she did it for sport, for the fun of the thing. No doubt she earned a small commission; I have known English society ladies earn dreadfully big ones for performing the same service."

One day she told Douglas she had a niece of sixteen. Would he like to talk to the mother? If so, she was in the next room. He took an instant liking to the mother, a middle-aged woman of the old school, a widow, who told him that although poor she would never have let the daughter go but for her sister's recommendation of Douglas as a reliable person. "She wore no hat; this signified that she belonged to a certain social set which thought a good deal of itself and kept to its own traditions. A deep

and well-founded disrespect for all authority was one of them; the knife
played a leading part in their affairs."

Such contracts for girls were not at all unusual; they provided money
which went towards their marriage portion. "The rule used to be this:
whoever seduced a girl without the consent of her parents (a monetary
transaction) might look out for squalls; once that consent was obtained,
nobody, not even the nearest member of the family, had another word to
say in the matter. The age of the girl was not taken into account; she
might be a minor or even a child; she generally was."

Annetta was an exquisite girl, with pale complexion, full vermilion
lips, and darkly flashing eyes – all that his heart could desire. It was a
curious coincidence that her name was almost the same as Anyuta's and
that she also lived with a widowed mother and a younger brother, who
was fifteen. At the mother's suggestion he went to their home once or
twice. It was in one of those narrow streets that lead upwards in steps
from the Riviera di Chiaia. Mother and daughter were usually there;
Douglas never saw the young brother Michele, though he must have seen
Douglas. He was at work, learning to be a metal-engraver; Annetta
described him as hot-tempered and reckless. "Something awful will
happen," she used to say, "if he finds out about us."

Something fairly awful did happen. Douglas was hit on the head from
behind and dazed; his head ached as if it would split:

I sat down on a doorstep amid the usual crowd of sympathisers,
one of whom was kind enough to fetch a bucketful of water. It was
all over in a few minutes, save an enormous swelling, and then I did
what is unquestionably the right thing to do: beard the lion in his den.
For it was that young brother, of course, who had meanwhile evaporated. I found neither him at home nor his sister; the mother was
there, and she, on hearing what had happened, was disappointingly
calm about the accident to my head – a good stab in the liver might
have interested her – but trembling with rage at her boy, who had
broken all the traditional rules governing such cases.

"Only wait!" she said. "Wait till he comes home. And you must be
here too, sir. That boy needs a lesson, or he will never grow into a
man. You will do me a great favour if you come, because then he will
understand once and for all."

When I arrived in the evening, all three of them were there. The
boy hung his head; he had evidently been getting it hot. I looked at
him for the first time. He was like his sister, and even prettier; the same
red lips and pale cheeks, but the chiselling and pencilling were more
thoughtfully done and his eyes had a more troubling expression;

Annetta was a preliminary sketch for this picture. The mother scowled at the picture and said:

"Now, vagabond, have you had your lesson? What do you mean by bringing dishonour on our family and annoying (*inquietando*: a nice way of putting it, I thought) the gentleman who is a friend of mine, and a friend of your sister, and a friend of your aunt Donna Maria—"

"Just a boy's joke," I said.

"Are you going to behave reasonably in future? Are you going to understand that it is I, the mother, who commands in this house? If that good soul of your father were still alive, he would have broken every bone in your body. Now go down on your knees and kiss his hand and beg his pardon."

Which was gracefully done, while I laid my hand in playful benediction on his head. The incident was closed, and I stayed till quite late, talking about everything except the bump on my head. As I rose to depart, Michele was told by his mother to accompany me down the dark and slippery steps into the main street ... There he would have left me, but I dragged him further, observing that he was anxious to say something polite and did not know how to set about it. Crossing the street, we entered the well-lighted public garden and sat down on one of the benches near the Aquarium. He was abashed and monosyllabic, beginning a sentence and then stopping again, while I did my utmost to set his mind at ease and make him forget the nonsense of that afternoon, despite the fact that my head was now aching so much that I began to wonder whether he had not cracked my skull after all. It was an odd situation; there were moments when I felt like throttling him. Slowly he brightened up.

"That's a pretty stick of yours" he remarked, taking it in his hand. [This was a malacca cane with a silver top, engraved round the edge in Chinese style with a scene of mandarins. It had been a present from Anyuta. Michele liked the funny old men under the trees, but wanted to know why there was no picture on the top.] "Please, sir, let me engrave something there for you; it is the least I can do, after what happened this afternoon. You know that I am learning that trade. What would you like? A heart? Or I could also cut your initials, if you prefer ..."

The silver top was duly engraved ...

... not long afterwards the boy fell in love with me desperately, as only a southern boy of his age can do; so blindly that at a hint from myself he would have abandoned his work and family and everything else. It came in a flash, and he did not care who knew it. And the queer thing is (queer, at least, to our English way of thinking) that his mother and sister were not in the least surprised; they thought it the most natural thing in the world.

"L'avete svegliato," the mother said; you have woken him up.

vii

This preoccupation with Michele is the first instance recorded by Douglas of a homosexual interest; and in view of what was to follow later, one wonders if it was in fact his first experience of this kind, apart perhaps from transitory relationships at school which are common enough even among those who do not subsequently revert to them.

Unfortunately, the only evidence that can be consulted is circumstantial. Conjecture must take the place of fact; but in the first instance it is reasonable to ask: up to this point (in his twenty-ninth year) is there any evidence that Douglas was capable of a deep and lasting relationship with a woman? There is not: the relationships of this kind do not seem to have been begun until later; until about 1897 they all seem to have been transitory. As he told Bryher later in life, probably with a characteristically provocative relish, he had had "eleven hundred virgins". Even if one allows for exaggeration, the impression received is of a man more interested in satisfying a phsyical urge and sexual curiosity than in establishing a deep, lasting and complete relationship. These virgins, by the way, are indirectly referred to in his remarks about Raffaele Amoroso, who was apparently a famous Neapolitan provider of sexual entertainment:

"The tales this bespectacled and mild-looking old gentleman could tell – of the late Duke of Edinburgh, of the peculiarities of this or that Balkan sovereign, of what preparation had to be made when the British fleet called at Naples – they were a liberal education. His memory, like that of many uneducated people, was prodigious; it went far back, a store-house of real personages and real facts; facts almost unbelievable, many of them. Here was a man who should have written his memoirs! He had pet names for all his regular clients, mine being 'Lo Sposo', which requires no commentary." No comment was required, because Douglas, like the traditional fiancé, always insisted on his partner being a virgin. Whether this was due to fear or disease or to an insatiable appetite for variety it is impossible to say. In old age, he apparently told Constantine FitzGibbon that he had been "more or less satiated with worldly pleasures" by the time he went to the Posilipo. If this is true, it is difficult to believe that it referred to sexual pleasures; it is more likely that he had decided by that time to drop out of Society and its trivial but approved activities, and devote himself to study and to "indulging his genius", as he put it. If, at about the same time, virgins had begun to pall, then the meeting

with Michele may have seemed to be a reminder from his Guardian
Angel that a whole new world of endless possibilities was waiting ready
to hand if women should cease to please.

Possibly Douglas first came to know himself well in the company of
the Spanish diplomat Campo Alegre, whom he so much admired. Perhaps
he admired him so much that he came to emulate him, the "man of
boundless curiosity and boundless tolerance", the scholar and man of the
world who had "taken life by the throat in many lands and made it yield
every pleasure, legitimate or otherwise. The civilised attitude. . . ."

There was certainly no better place in which to indulge this "civilised
attitude" than in Naples; it had been catering, in the Amoroso tradition,
to the civilised caprices of the wealthy at least since the time of Propertius,
who begged his Cynthia to leave those shores:

> tu modo quam primum corruptas desere Baias:
>   multis ista dabunt litora discidium,
> litora quae fuerant castis inimica puellis:
>   a pereant Baiae, crimen amoris, aquae![25]

On these same shores, and in most of Italy, homosexuality amongst
boys was not associated with fear and horror, or looked upon as a sin;
and in men it was thought of as a harmless or unenviable eccentricity.
Douglas' "boundless curiosity" in other matters is well enough known;
that it should have extended to sex is only to be expected. The child of
seven who had denied God in the pinewood without being struck dead,
would never thenceforth have been deterred by fear of any of the consequences of this curiosity; and that the avid collector of objects should
have become the equally avid collector of experiences, of men and
women as objects of love would be in no way surprising. "Stones were
dropped when birds and beasts began"; "Birds and beasts were dropped
when girls began"; "Girls were dropped when boys began". None of
these statements is strictly true; none of them need to be a downright lie;
they may all be illustrations of a truth.

viii

In 1897 Vanda was widowed for the second time. On 27th March Jacob
Jehly succumbed to pneumonia and was buried in the new Evangelical
cemetery at Bludenz. Amongst those who mourned him was Vanda's
niece, Elsa FitzGibbon,[26] who paid her last tribute in verse. It is likely that
Douglas would have gone to see his mother, either for the funeral or
afterwards, and he would certainly have spent time with Elsa, by whom
he was greatly attracted.

In May he met Effie Carpenter again, as arranged, at Meran, and acquired the *brûle-parfum* in circumstances similar to if not exactly as described so amusingly in *Looking Back*. This was the decorated Japanese bowl – a reward for rescuing Effie Carpenter's dog – which he used later on as a receptacle for the visiting cards on which this autobiographical book was based.

ix

In July Douglas went for a cruise with Marion Crawford, the prolific American author of many popular novels, and some of his family in the *Alda*. This was a seventy-five-foot schooner built at Brooklyn in 1859 for the New Jersey Pilots Association, from whom Crawford bought it. He converted it into a comfortable yacht which he himself sailed across the Atlantic to Italy.

This cruise took them to Corsica, Elba, Porto San Stefano and Civita Vecchia, whence Douglas and Crawford travelled to Rome. They rejoined the *Alda* at Gaeta, and Douglas finally got ashore at Baiae. "Out of sheer joy at the thought of being definitely on land once more I walked the whole way home to the Posilipo over Pozzuoli" (a distance of about $7\frac{1}{2}$ miles).

They had stayed for a week in the harbour at Porto Longone (now Porto Azzurro), on Elba, whence Douglas explored the island in all directions. He made friends with the Porto Longone priest, who showed him the parochial archives, in which there was an astonishing entry for 16th March 1692, when a hermit was found dead and beheaded in his sanctuary at Monserrato. "Round this, the slaughter of a seventeenth-century anchorite in his solitary retreat among the rocks, could be woven a romance, an intrigue of love and revenge." Thus was conceived Douglas' second attempt at fiction, *A Tale of Elba*. At this time, he says, he had begun to see "a financial cataclysm looming ahead", and was looking for means of preventing it. Crawford managed to make an enviable income with one novel a year: why should he not do the same? After consulting many books on Elba and its history for background purposes he produced a hundred and three closely-written folio pages. He made the hermit hero a Spaniard, introduced a love-element, an Etruscan background, a voyage to Sicily, a dwarf, a Corsair raid, a French attack on Porto Longone, the iron mines of the neighbouring Rio, and a Peruvian emerald, "the shining green jewel that was set in a ring which Dona Maria brought with her from countries where her father had fought under Pizarro". There were ominous oft-repeated references to the Ides of March, the day on which the hero, who has sinned in his youth, awaits his destruction at the hands of the Avenger, Brother Martin.

I write in my cell at night. It is bitter cold among these moist rocks; although March has begun, the spring refuses to visit this dank and shady cleft. It is the fated year 1692. Why fated? I shall tell anon. And I am old – old and grey. The Destroyer has never left me for fifty odd years. Fifty years of terror, of broken slumbers, humiliation, dread. And my hands are stained with innocent blood. I am become a murderer, desperate of salvation. And he, the Avenger, knows all and waits, and waits . . . he waits for the Ides of March . . .

But have a care, my friend, how you cross a despairing man. This life of doubt must now end, and if you approach me with evil intentions . . . You are younger than myself and somewhat taller, but I will fight like the mountain cat, for seventy years have not dimmed my sight and my muscles are yet supple . . .

The style, he wrote later, was "a tiresome monologue"; and the story suffered from retrospective action in the form of voluminous reflections written by the Hermit.

Monks, monasteries, and priests were standard fitments of nineteenth-century fiction and the opera-houses of the period; but it may not be fanciful to detect Scheffel's influence here. The hero of *Ekkehard* was a monk; and in that book there was a strong love-interest, a famous description of a raid (by the Huns), several hermits, and descriptions of precious jewels and minerals.

As to Crawford's "enviable income" from one novel a year, it is strange to think that Douglas at this period so little knew himself as to imagine that with his temperament he could emulate Crawford, who was a mild but incurable embodiment of Juvenal's *insanabile scribendi cacoëthes*, and seems to have died, at the age of fifty-four, as the result of overwork.

x

Douglas had burned his boats in Russia, and perhaps the risk to Helen of a letter from himself that might be intercepted, prevented his writing to her; nor has he left record of receiving any communication from her. It seems, however, that he may once have spoken to Richard Aldington about doing so: "According to what he told me she was of so high a rank that any open scandal would have been death to them both. Norman got over the frontier just ahead of the Russian police, and when his train reached Berlin he was handed a long telegram from Petersburg in a language wholly unknown to him and the friends he consulted. It was, he assumed, a message from 'Helen', perhaps some message for them to meet somewhere, but as he could not read the message he was helpless.

Thirty years later he discovered (I forgot to ask how) that it was Siamese transliterated. The temptation to have it read was very strong, but he resisted, because to have found out what she had said might have brought one more endless regret." Aldington's book *Pinorman* (1954), in which this passage occurs, is unreliable; yet this would be a pointless invention on Aldington's part. On the other hand it is unlikely that Douglas would have confided in Aldington (of whom he was justifiably suspicious) rather than in an intimate friend; and the story has not come to light anywhere else. Perhaps he was amusing himself at Aldington's expense.

As far as the reader is concerned, Helen, abandoned in Russia, vanishes from Douglas' life. If she was the Elena Alexandrovna (Lopoukine) Demidoff (mentioned on p. 97), she married Pavel Mikhailovich Katkov, styled "Prince" Katkov-Kalikov, in 1901, lived in Paris after the Russian revolution, and died in 1949. Anyuta Ponomareva, her counterpart, did not vanish so suddenly from Douglas' life: two charming but rather sad letters survive. The first, from Russia, tells a little of her life with various men since Douglas had left Petersburg. "You ask if I am now happy . . . I have everything, I need nothing, but my heart is broken, and very often I am afraid of people, I would like to be without a heart, but I've still got one." The second letter, from Germany, refers to Campo Alegre, whom she has visited in Switzerland; his disease had become bad enough to make him resign from the Diplomatic Service and seek a cure there, at Divonne. Douglas went to see him in September.

The treatment had not done Campo Alegre any good; he had put on too much flesh in spite of it. After two or three days Douglas suggested that he should go back with him to the Villa Maya. "The notion appealed to him; he loved Italy, where he had not been since the days when his chief was Spanish Representative at the Vatican . . . It was September, that wonderful month when the melodies of summer linger on, as if for ever, in a tranquil *sostenuto*. My friend revelled in the calm and the sunshine, and spent long hours in my library at the top of the house . . . admiring its views over the whole bay." He stayed about a month, without improvement to his health.

At just this time, Oscar Wilde and Lord Alfred Douglas were living at the Villa Giudice, also on the Posilipo; and Mathilde Serao, writing in the *Mattino*, confused the two Douglases and their respective villas, and assumed that Campo Alegre – a big, heavy man in poor health – was Wilde. Rolfe, the British Consul-General, immediately corrected this false impression; but Mathilde Serao, not wholly convinced, wrote a second article speculating upon the identity of the supposed Lord Alfred's companion.

xi

The repercussions in England of Wilde's trial and imprisonment in 1895 were not long in making themselves evident among homosexuals: those who were free to do so escaped from the atmosphere of vicious intolerance at home, and stayed as long as possible, or settled, abroad. Italy received a good many, to join a fair number who already lived there, German as well as English and others. These Germans of an earlier generation, amongst whom a fervent Hellenism was often prevalent, had been drawn to Italy on this account, and found, no doubt, as many of their kind have found since, that it suited their tastes and temperaments more completely than other countries. Other Germans of similar interests followed later, notably Allers[27] and Olinda, who both settled on Capri where they were joined by what might be called the Wilde Goslings fleeing England. This was one of the ways in which Capri acquired a small homosexual colony – or colonies, since there were groups of both sexes, the female of which has been fictionalised by Compton Mackenzie in *Extraordinary Women*. It was in this year, 1897, that a wealthy young Frenchman, Count Jacques Adelsward Fersen, first visited the island, with his mentor of that time, Robert le Tournel, and decided to build himself a house there. His story also has been told by Compton Mackenzie, with great brio and little exaggeration or deviation from the facts, in *Vestal Fire* – a highly enjoyable novel which contains a splendid sketch of Douglas as "Duncan Maxwell". *Vestal Fire* was dedicated to John Ellingham Brooks, who symbolised expatriate life on Capri for many English and Americans. He too was among those for whom the island offered attractions other than climatic, as were "Dodo" (E.F.) Benson, who shared a villa with Brooks during annual visits, and Somerset Maugham, another regular visitor for a good many years.

Capri, which had already no lack of "characters", was now beginning to acquire them at an accelerated speed, though Douglas – an occasional visitor, no more – was not at this stage included among them. Later, there were to be rival claimants, at various times, for the title of the most forceful or high-coloured, sometimes with a resultant "disharmony" as Douglas might have called it, between possible claimants. And no wonder: it is a small island to contain at one time Gorky, Lenin, and ex-royalty; or Douglas, D. H. Lawrence, Compton Mackenzie, and Axel Munthe. As to the latter: some indication of Douglas's attitude to him may be gathered from the fact that he first wrote beneath the Axel Munthe visiting-card in *Looking Back*: "We have been friends since 1897," but corrected this to: "We have known each other since 1897." In both cases, that was all.[28]

xii

The year ended with Douglas embarking at Brindisi on the P & O liner *Ballarat*, "an incredible old tub, a kind of Noah's Ark", on 19th December, for his first visit to India. From Bombay by sea to Karachi; thence to Rawalpindi.

It looks as though this visit had been postponed for a year, for in the draft of his letter from St Petersburg to Foley, in which he had asked to be placed *en disponsibilité*, he wrote (and then crossed out): "I want to spend the winter in India."

CHAPTER TEN

Marriage and *Unprofessional Tales*
1898–1901

i

Of this first Indian visit, little seems to have survived. What his motive
was for going, what his impressions were, and how long he stayed, are
not recorded. He moved, he says, in military circles, having been asked
to stay with Captain H. P. Uniacke of the Gordon Highlanders, at Rawalpindi. Uniacke, a hero of the Afridi frontier war, was "a good-looking
little fellow with freckled face and reddish hair; well groomed, and very
proud, in a joking way, of his wonderfully straight nose". His wife, Flora,
was a daughter of Douglas' relation, Lady Isabella Keane, and was destined to play a not unimportant rôle in Douglas' life at a slightly later
period. Whether he had met her husband before going to India, or had
been given an introduction, is not known; but the visit to Rawalpindi
was important in several ways. Through it, Douglas first became acquainted
with the East and with a way of life totally different from the European.
It gave him a new vantage point from which to look at our own civilisation,
which, after many years, resulted in his most opinionated and controversial
book, *How about Europe?* In that book, he tells how he met the amiable
Mr Jacob, a connoisseur of precious stones (which he carried about
stuffed into his waistcoat pockets). Mr Jacob was instrumental in persuading Douglas to pay enough money to buy the dagger hilt of lapis-
lazuli which became one of his best known and most proudly displayed
possessions. Jacob was also the original of the "Mr Isaac" of Marion
Crawford's first novel, and a most obliging and well-informed companion.
Douglas learned from him more about India in a few days than most
people learn in as many months.

There was also Sita Ram, his servant, a grey-haired old man whose
"intelligence and devotion were not of this earth". He always anticipated
his master's needs and wishes, could cure his worst insomnia, and coax
a blazing fire out of iron-hard logs. On an upturned flower-pot in the
open air, he could produce a four-course meal out of nothing. As to his
curries, they were

of infinite variety. Thirty-one years and six months have passed since those days, and it makes me feel like crying to know that I shall never taste them again ... Curry is India's gift to mankind; her contribution to human happiness. Curry atones for all the fatuities of the 108 Upanishads. Go to India, young man, and may you find another Sita Ram! He was wonderful in his curries.

The most interesting comment on this India visit was made by Douglas in old age to Constantine FitzGibbon, who recounted it in his unfinished biography. It seems that Douglas spent most of his time at Rawalpindi in voracius reading, alone, in the regimental library: "He has said that it was during those quiet weeks that his true knowledge and understanding of literature was born and that the idea of himself becoming a writer first took shape in his mind."

ii

This "idea of himself" as a writer he attempted to realise immediately on his return to Europe. He began the fifth and final version of *The Familiar Spirit* in Naples. It resulted in "a huge folio manuscript running from page 154 to page 325 – quite a novelette. It begins in sprightly fashion at a London dinner party, goes on to Naples, and ends in England ... it slips along blithely, then tragically, with a sprinkling of platitudes and feeble witticisms. ... Poor stuff, though it shows some improvement on the earlier versions". He quotes the drowning incident, in the hero's own words to his wife:

"It was certainly no cramp this time. I only remember that I suddenly felt myself sinking, and that it was the most awful sensation – an agony, and of interminable length. I knew there was little hope. I was continually drawn down into bottomless depths, suffocating and struggling, and then slowly uplifted again. Whenever I rose I tried to regain the horizontal position, but it was useless endeavouring to strike out – I was numbed in all my limbs. And then I was sucked down again into the abyss, the green water gurgling in my throat and ears. I had cried out loudly each time I came to the surface, because I hoped that some men in a boat close by might hear me. And so they did, in the end; but I would have been already drowned, if—" and there he stopped.

"Well?"

"Do you really not believe in a Guardian Angel?" he asked, after a slight pause. "You may well smile," he added.

"It was a providential escape at all events," she replied, evading their last subject of discussion.

"I hardly think I have been saved through the customary providential methods," he retorted somewhat warmly. "Yesterday I was quite prepared not to believe in a Guardian Angel, but now his existence is as clear to me as it was doubtful before. I told you yesterday that I thought him remiss in his duty, and I have now found out that he is a coward as well. Yes, he dreads death! Laugh as much as you please, my dear. I feel inclined to laugh myself sometimes. But yesterday it was only a joke, and now—"

iii

Douglas was now twenty-nine, and perhaps, during those quiet weeks in the Indian regimental library, he had taken stock of his position in regard to life as a whole, and not merely with regard to literature. He had sown his wild oats, he had a capacious house in one of the most beautiful situations in Europe, and in spite of having foreseen the approach of a "financial cataclysm", he still had enough money to employ servants and lead the life of a gentleman. If he was now going to concentrate on writing as his main occupation in life, he might just as well settle in properly at the Villa Maya and get on with it. It may have seemed that a settled life would be altogether easier and more attractive with a partner. If, as he was to tell FitzGibbon, he was satiated with worldly pleasures by this time, he was without doubt neither cynical nor apathetic as a result, but, beneath whatever exterior manner might seem appropriate to the formal occasion, was warm-hearted, impulsive and passionate. Marriage and children, even if only for the sake of a new experience, may have been considered to be not incompatible with the kind of life he had perhaps begun to envisage. At the very least he may have decided that it was no longer necessary to flee precipitately from a possible future entanglement. Or, since the revelation which had apparently been made to him by his affair with Michele, he may have considered marriage desirable as a contrast, or for protection. He may have wanted children of his own. Who can tell?

What we do know is that George Norman Douglass married his first cousin Elizabeth Louisa Theobaldina FitzGibbon at Fulham Register Office on 25th June 1898. Elsa, who was twenty-two at this time, was a slim attractive girl with beautiful light auburn hair and large serious grey eyes, highly strung and imaginative, romantic and quick-tempered. She had written poems and stories; she had flirted, in what seems to have been a half-intellectual and half-mystical way, with Catholicism (in a Protestant family), and seems to have wanted to break out of the narrow confines of her family background, to a wider and more spacious world. She was ready, in fact, for someone to take her in hand and enable her to realise potentialities which seemed to have little chance of further development in Austria. Norman, if he was anything, was a born teacher, and just the man to do this for Elsa. They had known each other since childhood, and were on easy and familiar terms. Unfortunately, Elsa's mother Adèle (a younger sister of Norman's mother, Vanda) strongly disapproved of Norman, and called him "Anti-Christ". It may have seemed to him to be a compliment, or at least a confirmation that he had made his position abundantly clear; but it complicated his relationship with Elsa. So much so, that according to Constantine FitzGibbon (a distant cousin of Elsa), the couple were obliged to elope. Unknown to the family, Norman took rooms in a village on Lake Constance – Elsa presumably being along the lake at Bregenz, where her mother lived – until he carried his cousin off to London, returning on the day after the marriage to present the family with the *fait accompli*. Adèle was never invited to the Villa Maya.

So much for fact, and Douglas' verbal statements to FitzGibbon. But may not something – and possibly the real reason for the marriage – have been omitted? Regarding the preparations for the birth of their first child, Archie, we have the following uncompromising declaration on page 38 of *Looking Back*: "The event was expected and actually took place in February" 1899. Thus, the conception of this child must have taken place in May 1898, and since he was born on 2nd February, may well have taken place early in May. It begins to look as though the hasty marriage may have been necessary – whether it had been considered by the parties concerned or not – in order to avoid an appalling family row and possibly a complete estrangement. In this connection, there is a most interesting and intriguing remark in a letter from Douglas' cousin William Ernest Fairholme, written from London on 3rd May 1898. He had visited the Massie-Mainwaring household, and writes: "Elsa is with them and means never to go back to Bregenz no more." Something had obviously happened to her, either in Bregenz or in London, to make her so adamant – or apparently adamant; for she must have gone back if Douglas' account of the elopement to FitzGibbon is accurate. Elsa's temporary decision may or may not have been influenced by Norman's behaviour.

The marriage took place, and that was that; the honeymoon was said to have been spent on Ischia; after which, no doubt, Elsa was taken to the delectable Villa and installed as its mistress. There can be no doubt that husband and wife were very much in love, any more than there can be doubt that they were both temperamentally unsuited to withstand the strains and stresses and temptations of married life.

iv

Norman was taking no chances with his wife's first confinement; a nurse was engaged from a well known lying-in hospital in England; and was asked to arrive well in advance of the expected date of birth in case of any premature trouble. It must be remembered that the house was four miles from Naples, and that the only access was by sea (impossible if rough) or by a straggling path more than half a mile long that was dangerous in the dark. The trained nurse, therefore, was a sensible precaution – or would have been if she had not taken to the bottle as soon as she arrived. She was "a confirmed sot" wrote Douglas. What would happen if she were drunk when her services were needed? They decided to get rid of her and look for a local woman. Douglas put her into the train for England. She departed amicably enough, but soon he received a tremendous bill for wrongful dismissal, although she had been paid up to the day of her departure, also her travelling expenses. "To which I meekly replied that I would not pay another penny to a drunken slut who was a menace to her patients and a disgrace to her profession."

This statement was regarded as libellous by the hospital authorities, and affidavits began to fly between London and Naples. The situation looked black when Douglas suddenly remembered, through having studied International Law while in the Diplomatic Service, that his *animus revertendi* was not extinguished; he therefore had a Scottish domicile. "Let them tackle me in Edinburgh! Edinburgh, for some reason or other, was not to their taste. The matter was dropped." He heard no more about it: the *animus revertendi* had been a useful tool, and was to be even more useful on a future occasion.

He recovered his expenses in connection with the nurse by a lucky chance. He had written in good time to a firm in Dublin asking them to send an estimate for a layette:

> One day there arrived a wooden case, containing clothes sufficient not for one but for half a dozen new-born infants, and all of superfine quality; likewise a formidable bill for goods supplied as per order. As per order . . . a try-on! No order had been given, I wrote; they could have their layette back whenever they liked to come and fetch it; meanwhile I would charge them two shillings a day for warehousing expenses. They never fetched it. They never paid the warehousing expenses.

The layette was a great success.

It was used in due course by a son, born on 2nd February 1899 at the Villa Maya. He was named Louis Archibald, the second name being tradi-

tional in the Douglas family, and the first demonstrating Norman's belief
that one Christian name should be international.

v

He was in the Vorarlberg in August, probably with Elsa and the baby.
It was there that he received word from Campo Alegre that he was living
near Vevey, and would Norman call in and see him if he happened to be
passing that way? "He said nothing else, and I took it for granted that
there had been a change for the worse. Arrived at Vevey, I found Campo
Alegre with his bicycle. He always rode a bicycle, he explained; he was
completely cured. This was a surprise he had prepared for me. Not Divonne,
but some little up-country doctor, had wrought the mircale – for a miracle
it seemed to be. He had lost his superfluous flesh, regained his activity,
and looked twenty years younger."

Sometime in 1899 Douglas apparently made his first visit to Tunisia,
possibly accompanied by his wife. He was also writing the final version
of *The Familiar Spirit* and working on *Nerinda*.

He and Elsa were certainly together in India in February 1900, and
seem to have been in Ceylon in the same year. Douglas told FitzGibbon
that Elsa confessed to an affair with an Austrian officer in Ceylon while the
officer was on his way to help put down the Boxer rebellion in China.
The Boxer Rising took place in May, so if this story is true it points
to a fairly long stay in India and Ceylon. There appears to have been a
second visit to Tunisia this year, possibly with Elsa, and therefore perhaps
on the way back from India.

Of the Indian visit, nothing seems to have survived except, perhaps,
some of the comments in *How about Europe?* Memories of Ceylon, however, came back to him as he was writing *Looking Back*: the Galle Face
Hotel, rowdy, and with such vile food, that he migrated to the Bristol,
where the curries were famous, where his favourite waiter was called
Jesus, and where crows used to hop through the window, cock their
heads on one side, and watch him eating his breakfast.

He (they?) visited Galle, Veligama and Dondra Head, where the fish
climb out of the water to sun themselves on boulders. Frisky pied bullocks
drew the hackery, and the native children were "so mild-eyed and grace-
ful, so naked and frolicsome", that he longed to steal half a dozen and carry
them home as keepsakes. There was an excursion into one of the last areas
of primary jungle, from which he emerged streaming with blood, from
leeches. He remembered mimosa, vanilla, the scent of lemon-grass . . .
a cluster of rock-temples swarming with malodorous flying-foxes;
Anuradhapura and Mahintale, those colossal lost cities; "a brook in

some convent-retreat containing fish which came to be fed in such throngs that they thrust each other with noisy snortings into the air . . ." Adam's Peak confronted and challenged him so persistently that he could bear it no longer. With a young Tamil guide he began the ascent one evening after dinner:

All was dark on the topmost platform, and one felt a pleasant chill in the air, a sense of aloofness from earth. I stood among a group of shrouded figures, priests and pilgrims, with my back to the East; we were waiting, in the night, for a miracle. It came with the first streak of dawn, when that spectral pyramid, the shadow of the Peak, began to creep into the landscape, its flanks enclosing dusky leagues of hill and forest, its apex touching the rim of the visible world. There it outlined itself with geometrical precision, and lay distended.

So much for Ceylon. At least one other peak, in another land, was climbed during the same year, namely the Jebel Zaghouan, the highest in Tunisia. Douglas climbed this with his friend Rudolf Prietze, a traveller in Africa and a linguist like his more famous uncle, Gustav Nachtigal.[29]

vi

During the period between June 1898 and the spring of 1901, Norman and Elsa must have been working on what was to become a book called *Unprofessional Tales*, for the proofs of the book were ready by May 1901. It was published on commission in September of the same year.

Later in life, Douglas thanked God that the book had been published under a pseudonym. He was not proud of it, and in spite of various statements by him at various times, the details of its authorship are not entirely clear. In 1920 he wrote: "Not a single one of those things was written by myself; they are all by my wife who had an extraordinary (Irish) faculty – I wish I had it – for inventing plots and poems and things; but every one of them was re-touched by myself." This comment was in a letter to Ralph Straus; Douglas' first comment written for publication appears in McDonald's *Bibliography*:[30] "Only one of the stories, and the little anacreontic are entirely by myself." This story was *Nerinda*, which unlike most of the others in the book, bears the stamp of his clear and incisive style; it is indeed the first example of it. The "marked advance it displays" over *The Familiar Spirit*, or rather, over the fifth draft of that tale, may seem less difficult for us to account for than it apparently was for Douglas. Both were written in the same year, 1899; but whereas the one appears to have been verbose and turgid, finding difficulty in making its point, the other is clear and direct, and makes its point without fuss. It looks as though this is due to a greater fascination with the subject of the second story, so that the author lost self-conscious literary style in pursuit of his theme; and to the technique adopted, the story being cast in the form of a journal.

Nerinda, as Douglas himself explains in the Author's Note which he wrote for Orioli's separate-volume publication in 1929, is an imaginative attempt to describe the kind of progressive mania which engulfed his friend Luigi Guerrieri-Gonzaga, who died insane in 1895, in his late twenties. "The chief interest I now find, in glancing through these pages, is not because some of my friend's very words are enshrined in them; that ghost is laid. It is because they contain the seeds of much that I afterwards wrote about the country down there." This is our chief interest also, and not only for descriptions and comments on the country, but also on a number of other topics. It is interesting, for instance, to note that the protagonist of the story devotes three pages of his journal to Tiberius, regarding him, as did Tacitus and Suetonius, as a man-demon: "There is a stage when nothing short of the spectacle of tortures and rivers of red blood will prick the jaded appetite. I think I can understand a certain pleasurable emotion arising out of the sight . . ." This view of Tiberius may, or may not, have been designed to indicate a propensity for violence in the character of the protagonist. It is at least possible that Douglas, who had not yet begun his Capri studies, at this time accepted the traditional view of Tiberius. It is also possible that some of the opinions expressed through the mouthpiece of the narrator were Douglas' own: did he, for instance, regard Nietzsche's *Übermensch*, philosophically, as "a nugget of gold", and Maupassant's *Horla*, artistically, as a "priceless pearl"? Very likely. And it is of no little interest that these authors, like the writer of the journal, went mad, and one of them, Maupassant, had died (and may have become insane) as the result of syphilis, a disease of which Douglas, when he wrote *Nerinda*, had not long been cured. Did Douglas revel, as his creature did, in deceiving another person – possibly his wife? "Bertha remains unaware of this escapade, and it gives me pleasure to deceive her and to watch her face. Yes, it warms the cockles of my heart." Elsa must also have "remained unaware" of various escapades when, for instance, her husband spent the day in Naples, or was absent elsewhere.

There are certainly clues in this story which could illuminate the character of its author, if one knew for sure which they were. The section ending "Indifference, lack of faith, lack of enthusiasm – these be the real mortal sins, these be the outward signs of a moral fatigue of the race, these be the cankers that undermine the body social and politic" very likely represents Douglas's own beliefs, though why these should have been subjunctively expressed (even in the 1930 edition) is a mystery.

Nerinda is the best of *Unprofessional Tales*. The story has sufficient strength and realism to stand on its own feet, which is more than can be said for most of the other tales. It also contains little gems of descriptive writing, vignettes so fresh and clear-cut that he could never have improved them in later life:

> While we lingered, darkness came on with mysterious rapidity. The sun had set, but the sky, at first, still glowed with opalescent streaks of light that shone like flashing meteors strayed from their path. Suddenly they vanished and there was a great stillness. The landscape at our feet floated in an ocean of liquid pearl. Then a purple veil fell over all things. The evening star glittered overhead.

Other examples are not hard to find in the earlier part of the story.

Apart from *Nerinda*, the collection consists of the Anacreontic poem about a wagtail reprinted in *Experiments*; a fragment of blank verse drama in which the origin of socialism is ingeniously (and ingenuously) attributed to Satan; and thirteen more or less grotesque or gothic tales. Some of the latter are ghost stories, some are Grimm-like fairy-tales, some are psychological thrillers; and one is a dialogue between a disembodied spirit and the last human, in which the latter reveals how the rest of mankind was exterminated by gnats. Douglas claims authorship, though not necessarily invention, of this story in *Old Calabria*: "Thus I wrote, while yet unaware that such pests as anophelines existed upon earth . . ." Well, perhaps; but Ross had published his findings by 1898, and these tales were not printed until 1901. On the face of it, it looks as though this rather elaborate dialogue owed its origin to Ross' investigations, even if not to his actual findings.

The gothic tales are oddly assorted. Two of the ghost stories are feeble, but the third, *Elfwater*, carries some conviction. Then there is an atmospheric fragment (*Nocturne*) conveying a Promethean aura in the Shelleyan vein; a consideration by a house party of the most ignoble kinds of death, won by the tale of an old woman eaten alive by her cats (*The Ignoble*); a fairy tale of a woman consumed by a tree (*The Devil's Oak*); a fable accounting for the origin of the Faraglione lizard (*A Tyrrhenian Fable*); and, most interesting of all, *The Psychological Moment*. In this, an elderly husband enjoys watching his young wife fall in love with her music teacher. He obtains a vicarious sensual pleasure as he watches them rehearse "the drama that would be played immediately after his death". His wife, who knows he is watching, restrains herself, and although impassioned, behaves with decorum. The teacher cannot restrain himself and advances towards the wife with the intention of embracing her. Just before he moves, or as he moves – one does not know which – the husband "faints away", either from frustration at not having seen them embrace, or because the prospect of seeing them do so has excited him too much. Nor does one know – since he has been described at one point as having on his face what might be a kind of rictus – whether he is alive or dead. This story, leaving one with various interesting speculations, stands on its feet and makes an effect.

One other tale is worth mentioning: *To E.F.G.* (Elsa FitzGibbon?). It contains two epigraphs from Petrarch's *De remediis utriusque Fortunae* which, incidentally, was the book given to Douglas by Campo Alegre as a parting gift when Douglas left St Petersburg. *To E.F.G.* seems to be the beginning of a longer story (as do some of the other tales), possibly of a novel; and its title, together with much of the content, suggest that it may have been written by him, and that he might have drawn on members of his family, and himself, for certain passages describing character. There are whole sentences and paragraphs which fit himself and his father, and others in which he may have had his mother, father-in-law, or maternal grandmother in mind.

In spite of being glad that these stories were published under a pseudonym, Douglas was not averse from re-publishing five of them in book form, as well as re-publishing *Nerinda* twice, in a revised form. One feels that he had an attachment to these tales, or to some of them. And why not? They represent his first appearance in print as a non-scientific writer, they make his first actual book, and of some of them at least there was no need to feel ashamed.

CHAPTER ELEVEN

Norman and Elsa
1901–1902

i

When *Unprofessional Tales* was published, it was dedicated to Ouida. This name will convey little to most people under the age of fifty; and of those who are over that age, most will immediately think of one novel, *Under Two Flags*, and associate its author, by hearsay in their childhood, with the kind of great popular success which nowadays is so often thought by literary critics to preclude merit, especially if, as in her case, the subject matter is "romantic", the setting "exotic", and the characters are often "aristocratic". During the last four decades of the nineteenth century, Ouida made a great deal of money from her books. At the height of her career she was earning about £5,000 a year (a sum equivalent to at least £30,000 nowadays); but unlike so many other writers who have achieved this kind of success, she was a woman of great character who wrote with passionate conviction tempered by an incisive and well-informed intelligence. She possessed to a remarkable degree an intuitive recognition of what added to and what detracted from the essential dignity and nobility of man: there was no fumbling, no compromise in her morality, which embraced a strong code of honour, a glowing patriotism, and a conception of the relationship between men and women in terms of the highest chivalry. She was fearlessly independent in her views, and often shocked Victorian complacency and hypocrisy both by her novels and short stories and by the reputation she acquired for an extravagant and free way of living, made more scandalous to the orthodox by the fact that she was uncompromisingly opposed to institutional Christianity. She left England as soon as she could afford to, and from about 1872 lived in Italy in grand style for about twenty years; thereafter, extravagance and lack of forethought (combined with the failure of certain Florentine banks) gradually brought about financial difficulties, and her old age, particularly the last ten years of her life, was a miserable progression down the scale of living, via moneylenders and pawnbrokers, to a state bordering on destitution. She was forced to move from Florence to Lucca, from

Lucca to Sant' Alessio, from Sant' Alessio to Viareggio, to Mazzarosa and back to Viareggio, where in January 1908 she died.[31]

When Douglas first wrote to Ouida in the spring of 1901 she was living in the Villa Massoni at Sant' Alessio. Like its even bigger predecessors just outside, and in, Florence, this villa was large – it contained twenty-seven rooms – but by Ouida's standards was a cheap and fairly modest house. Norman sent her proofs of *Unprofessional Tales*, and asked if he might dedicate the book to her. He and Elsa may also have hoped that if Ouida were to enjoy the book, she might consent to write a foreword, or to recommend it in some other way. She replied (21st May) that she made it a rule

> not to read other people's Proofs; so pray pardon me if I return yours unread. But I can only feel it a compliment if you care to dedicate yr Book to me. But please to put no name except Ouida. Accept my compliments
>
> > Ouida[32]

Douglas wrote back – he had probably heard that she was living in reduced circumstances – offering the Villa Maya, presumably for a holiday, to which Ouida replied (30th June):

Dear Sir,
   The offer of yr villa sounds delightful & I thank you for the kind thought. But I should have to see it before entering on its habitation. When at leisure describe it a little. Only approach the sea must be a great charm & a guarantee against intruders.

> > Ever yrs
> > Ouida

In a postscript she asked him how long the sea trip to the Villa Maya took and how one got there. Thus began a correspondence which continued for two or three years, and resulted in 1902 in the exchange of about thirty letters and a number of telegrams. Immediately it had been begun, however, the correspondence was interrupted while the Douglasses were in Britain.

ii

It was probably in connection with *Unprofessional Tales* that Douglas went to England, some time in the early summer of 1901. He may have delivered the corrected proofs in person. He was joined by Elsa and Archie in July. After a short stay in London they left for Scotland.

One gets an impression from Elsa's diary of a pleasure-loving and
rather moody and volatile woman, highly susceptible to her environment.
Certainly the diary makes clear how much she disliked Scotland:

We arrived at Aberdeen, cat and all, this morning [July 23] at eight . . .
It was cold and there was a beastly drizzle that went on my nerves. When
I think of my Neapolitan blue sky and sunshine! We bought boots and
at ten went on to Banchory. We got a cab and drove up. The house is
very funny, all corners and gables and round windows with trees all
round that give it an anxious shivering appearance . . . A heavy grey
sky hung low down, all the trees look black and grey, not green, and
the air seems full of melancholy. Elsie seems a good old soul, but I
cannot understand one word she says . . . I think I shall go melancholy
mad in this awful atmosphere!

All next morning it "poured in sheets and was bitterly cold", and on
the following day it was "still raining as if all the water in heaven wanted
to come down". A few days and much more rain later: ". . . after the most
desperate struggle the sun came out today. We had the regulation Sunday
dinner at half past one, hot soup and cold mutton". They had food trouble
of this kind, or worse, throughout their stay; and the company in the
neighbouring houses was too often "dull and highly respectable", and
although the weather improved, Elsa suffered from backache nearly all
the time. The local doctor and a man in Edinburgh were both consulted
but "Nobody can or ever will make out my backache".

At the beginning of August they moved out of brother John's house,
Feugh Lodge, into a cottage. They ordered a piano (which arrived with
a packet "of the stupidest songs I ever saw, all more or less pious") and
hired bicycles. A regular bicycle round was instituted – down one bank
of the Dee to Crathes bridge, and back up the other side – and many other
excursions were made. And they walked, and pottered, and visited and
chattered; and quite often Norman was at his writing table; but one has
the impression that time hung pretty heavily. For instance, at a house
nearby: "about eight ladies there, all sitting round primly and fearfully
respectably in the garden drinking tea", or "dined at Feugh and it was
deadly dull", or "dined at Feugh. A hideously dull evening".

Archie was sent back to Italy in September, and early in October
Norman and Elsa went by train to Manchester, staying at the Victoria,
and the next morning they went, partly by tram and partly on foot, to
The Weaste. "It was very gloomy and drizzly, and the huge grey house
looked so forlorn in its neglected dripping garden. We went all through
all the rooms and grounds where I picked this little rose, then left." The
same night they were in London; the stop at Manchester must have been

solely in order to see The Weaste. Norman could endure, and even enjoy, any amount of bittersweetness derived from sentimental pilgrimages. One is reminded of that early visit to Falkenhorst: "Saw the garden, went about. House empty, sad and locked. All shutters shut", but Vanda, of course, had been responsible for that visit.

They stayed in London two weeks before leaving for Naples, which they reached on 24th October.

iii

There can be no doubt that Elsa, at least, was delighted, and relieved, to be back again. A sirocco was blowing next day, but she called it in her diary "the dear homely wind". While Norman was in Naples she had a day of "general rummaging and unpacking" enjoying Archie's jolliness and talkativeness. There were masses of cyclamens in the garden and a few narcissi, and the air was as soft as could be.

Life resumed its Villa Maya pattern. Norman and Elsa would often dine at the Giardini di Torino, sometimes with Lo Bianco, and they might all go on to listen to the band in the Galleria. Once, soon after their return, Lo Bianco bought Elsa a little white dog in the Galleria; and he frequently sent her, or bought, masses of flowers ("I wish he'd stop that, though it's polite of him") and once made the musicians at the restaurant sing "Terezza d'oro" thirteen times ("He was quite screwed").

Early in November they went by the Aquarium boat to Capri: "We got to Capri at 10.30 and walked up intending to go to an hotel, when we met a Herr and Frau Andree. They are German millionaires and have a house in Capri. They asked us all to lunch, so we went with them . . . We looked at the garden which has a pretty view to the rocks of Solaro and over olives to the piccola marina, but is awfully stylisiert, full of little grottos and silly surprises. We had an excellent lunch, soup, then a delicious fish, very tender beefsteaks, snipe, and chocolate cream, then coffee, liquur [sic] and cigarettes." They then went to see the new road built by Krupp, and drove to Bitter for tea: "The sunset was divine and one could see the Siren Islands, like crimson rose leaves." Next day Elsa and Norman "walked up to Anacapri by the steps. It was very steep and hot. Lots of narcissi were flowering among the roks [sic] but we only managed to get two. We passed Munthe's house and went past Mon Plaisir, then down an awful little road into Anacapri, and back again by the steps."

On Elsa's birthday (13th November): "Twenty six today, oh my Gawd! All the same I felt intensely festive, and it was a lovely birthday all round. It was a fine day, soft and warm and full of good smells. In the morning there were tremulous congratulations from Kathi and the Nurse, also

Archie murmured his little 'gratulations mother'. At ten N. went off to Naples. I employed my time usefully cleaning the buffet silver. He returned at two and first we had an excellent lunch, Schweins cotelleten mit Bohnen und Kartoffeln and a most lovely birthday cake also a bottle of our best Nocenso. Then when we were going to have our black coffee, I found the very sweetest Geburtstagstisch in N's room. Two lovely little vases, books, scent and oh joy, an amber necklace, everything surrounded by tufts of tuberoses. We had coffee and smoked and I generally enjoyed myself. Then we started planting twenty tiny cypress trees and two tujas. Fifteen were put in the Sternleweg[33] with my best birthday blessings."

The Marchese Valiante (called by Douglas "that perfect botanist") came quite frequently – more frequently, in fact, than he was welcome – and sometimes stayed the night. He and Lo Bianco were their most frequent guests – indeed, they hardly seem to have had others at this time – and Valiante was obviously less entertaining than Lo Bianco. And from time to time, like anyone else, Norman and Elsa could have too much of the same company. There was the day when they drove all the way from the Grotto to Fusaro, "the sea below Baiae like a sapphire, and on the vines still the few leaves that shone in the sun like red and yellow jewels. We got there at half past one and found Valiante and Lo Bianco already there. We had a beastly lunch, bad tiny oysters, rotten pheasants and putrid fish. The wine was vile. Then we got rowed across the lake to Torre Gaveta and went up to the old farm where N. got a well carved white marble capital. We went to the beach too and found a few nice pieces of marble. Then back to Fusaro. We couldn't face sitting with those two for another hour and a half, so we N. and I said goodbye to them and walked to Baiae an old man carrying our marble. It was a lovely walk, very warm, with lovely moonlight glittering on the sea. At Baiae we found a cab that took us in an hour to the Grotto. The guardian carried the marble home."

Norman's birthday: "I arranged a garland of laurel leaves and narcissus round his plate with my presents. Then we wandered about the garden. After lunch I sat on the terrace and already at three Valiante came. They always come *hours* too soon. We arranged a very nice supper. Archie was worse than ever today, crying, naughty, fretful and miserable. At halfpast four Lo Bianco came with three of his children and four musicians. I was nearly driven mad at first, Kathi with no help in the kitchen, Archie yelling upstairs, and these many people about. At six we dined, and then they played, the violinist really beautifully. Afterwards we went into the drawing room and danced and got quite festive. They left at eleven, Valiante stopped overnight. Archie yelled till about one, then went to sleep."

Archie was upset because, together with his mother and Kathi, he had been vaccinated. Scotti, their doctor, said there was a lot of smallpox about, especially in the neighbourhood of the Gaiola. They all suffered from swollen arms and felt quite ill. Norman, who for some reason was not vaccinated until a fortnight later, seems to have been the worst affected: either the vaccination "took" with great severity, or it triggered off some other illness, or the latter came on coincidentally. He spent the last ten days of the year, including Christmas, in bed. On Christmas Eve the tree was placed beside his bed: "After five I lit the candles, and arranged Archie's presents on a small table in front of the tree, the little piano, gardening tools, a sailing ship, reins and whip, and trifles, also the things for the servants, each a warm jersey, a flannel morning jacket, writing paper soap, the nurse cigarettes Kathi chocolate, and each a lot of Lebkuchen. Then I rang the bell and Archie trotted in. He was delighted. I gave the females their things and they went away. I was dead tired." Christmas Day was awful, bad weather and all three Douglasses feeling ill.

The New Year began badly with Norman, who had been in bed for ten days, being taken to hospital. January 2nd: "At about 10.30 the Aquarium launch came with Scotti Lo Bianco and Linden. Scotti said N. must go to the Hospital at once to have an operation. I nearly fainted. Poor poor Goldie. When they had gone I packed his bag and dressed him. He nearly fainted several times, but was awfully brave. He was as white as a sheet, and so thin. At two the launch came and he managed to crawl down. They arranged a couch for him and off we went. At the Rotonda was a carriage and we drove slowly to the Hospital. I put him to bed, and then he sent me home to be in before the sun set. I felt miserable at leaving him all alone." He remained there for a week, suffering bad rheumatic pains in all his joints. Elsa, who was ill herself with a bad cough, visited him daily; he had lost his appetite, and the hospital food didn't help to bring it back; he also felt "dull and lonely". By the 7th he was a "trifle better, he can move his hands now", and two days later he had so far improved that Scotti said he could go on an expedition to the Siren Islands which Lo Bianco was arranging for the following day: "At twelve we arrived at the Siren islands, covered with Narcissus and blue and lovely as ever. We all sat down and lunched. At two we left again, and I had to lie down again. It was a fearful bore, but I felt too bad. Arrived here at six with a most tremendous bag of Narcissus bubls [sic] and a huge bunch of the flowers which Lo Bianco and a nice young man Herr Wendt (whose father[34] had been N.'s professor in Karlsruhe) had gathered for me. N. went back to the Hospital, but he is coming home tomorrow thank heaven."

During the following week, Herr Wendt took over Valiante's rôle by

turning up a little too often. There was an abortive expedition to Vesuvius
which only got half way off the ground – a gale force wind was blowing
the ashes so strongly that no one could go to the top. Torre Gaveta was
revisited and "N. got a whole sackful of marble"; another day at about
three "suddenly Wendt arrived. We couldn't face keeping him all the
afternoon, so we started for Naples" – a ploy familiar to all who have
tried to lose a guest – but it was late before they "got rid of W. at last and
then we drove home and lost the key." There was an evening with
Linden "and the everlasting Wendt" at a crowded Salone Margherita
(in the Galleria) to watch La Belle Otero[35] dance. Wendt's time was
eventually up, and they saw him on to his boat with his friends the
Meisners: "I went to Frau Meisner's Cabin and saw her baby, a hideous
little boy. Then we went up to dinner which was very good with a jolly
band playing. Afterwards walking through a passage I suddenly met
Jim Fairholme![36] I was surprised. He was going with friends of his to
Cairo. We talked a long time together, but at last had to go . . . Then
straight to the Hotel de Londres where we routed Adelkind [Fairholme's
sister, Adèle] out of bed and sat talking to her a long while. It was funny
to get all old home news so direct. Then we said goodbye to her . . . and
went to the Pshorrbräu where we had sausages and beer. Then home at
last." On the following day they "mooned about and were dull and
melancholy" – homesick, perhaps, for the Vorarlberg? or had some
fundamental emotional disturbance occurred and begun to work its way
to the surface of their lives? and could this have been connected with the
fact that Elsa was now pregnant for the second time? A day or two later,
at any rate, Elsa, without making mention in her diary of any symptoms,
went to Scotti and was told that she had a gastric ulcer. She was laid up
for three weeks. Norman had raging toothache for about a week, but
brought lilies of the valley and violets from Naples for her; and also, on
8th February came back "with the *dreadful* news that poor Campo Alegre
is dead. It is too sad". When Elsa was up and about again, they began
looking at various properties in the neighbourhood – which seems to
suggest that they had thoughts either of leaving the Villa Maya or of
investing money in another place, either to let or sell it; but at the same
time, Norman was buying a good many shrubs and flowers for the
garden. Had he hopes, perhaps, of selling or letting the place to Ouida?
He evidently still hoped that she would come on a visit:

Feb 22

My dear Sir,
    I am most deeply touched by yr kind letter. I shall hope ere very
long to see yr classic home. The rains & cold here (Tuscany) for the

last 5 months have been almost insupportable. I am going to ask you if you could help me in a moment of extreme distress as you are so kind as to say you wd be glad to do me any service. Wd it be posible to lend me fifty pounds at once? I am in great difficulty from money

£50

failures and if you could do this for me I would return it you in a few weeks. Meantime I could give you as security the copyright of the Massarenes. Pray do not deem this strange or wrong. I am in great distress momentarily & yr kind letter makes me venture to ask you this. Pray regard it as confidential.

Ever yrs
Ouida

I wrote to you in the Highlands last Aug.

iv

The letter that Ouida wrote him when he was in Scotland was probably the following short undated acknowledgment of *Unprofessional Tales*: "Dear Sir, I find yr volume of stories on my return here. Thanks for it, also for the offer of yr villa at Posilippo [sic] Yr much obliged Ouida." Douglas' statement that she wrote him much about herself and about *Helianthus* is as nearly true as makes no odds; but when he adds that "in return" he dedicated to her a book of short stories, he is reversing the sequence of events and must surely have known that he was doing so. His usual regard for the truth in such matters may have wavered under an obligation which he felt he owed Ouida not to reveal the large part which money played in their correspondence: unable to be wholly and freely truthful, he may have been careless about the partial truth. Or, presuming that Ouida's letters and their contents would never be published he may have decided to let readers assume that she, of her need, had freely confided in him and that he, in acknowledgment of her trust, had courteously dedicated his book to her. It should be pointed out, though it need not be emphasised, that there was occasionally a willingness in Douglas to let the reader assume that his knowledge of certain subjects and his intimacy with certain people was more profound than was actually the case. But the mention of this fact makes it all the more necessary to point out that the exact opposite – a very rare quality – was equally true and much more generally characteristic: namely, that he could be extremely modest about his accomplishments and knowledge, and extraordinarily reticent where personal relationships were concerned. This was one of the stronger features of his character, and an example of it can be given by almost everyone who knew him well.

His reminiscences of Ouida are a splendid example of Douglasian defence by attack and invective; and anyone who doubts that Douglas himself shared the warmth of feeling, the geniality, the wide outlook, the freedom from cant, and the generous humanity of Ouida, should read them. They should also read Ouida's *Views & Opinions* and *Critical Essays*, which deserve the praise he gives them. As to her influence on him, it would be easy to overestimate it.[37] There can be little doubt that Douglas' attitude to life was either influenced by Ouida's to a noticeable degree, or, alternatively, that she expressd his own attitude on many subjects so felicitously that he was on one or two occasions irresistibly drawn into adopting her manner of expression. It would be foolish to say more, and no more needs to be said.

Ouida's repeated appeals to Douglas for financial help stemmed, of course, from her outrageous extravagance. (During a visit to London in 1886, for instance, she spent two hundred pounds a week on flowers.) It was as much a part of her nature as her generosity and her brimming talent: without it she would not have been that "unique, flamboyant lady". Nor would she have appealed so readily, as she seemed to do, to her friends. Lady St Helier, whose reminiscences were published only two years after Ouida's death, mentions these petitions, which had given rise – as such measures always do if they are frequently repeated – to charges of lack of conscience. Lady St Helier denies this charge, giving as proof an example of an apparently substantial short-term loan repaid promptly on the appointed day.[38] But as far as Ouida's appeals to Douglas are concerned, this was not typical.

To the first request, in February 1902, Douglas replied instantly with a cheque for 500 lire, written on notepaper; but a day or two later Ouida wired him that she could not cash the cheque, and he sent a printed replacement. She wrote that she was most grateful for it and "intensely touched" by his sympathy; she did not need legal advice, which he had apparently offered to procure for her, but only "that precious and necessary good – ready money". A week later, returning the duplicate cheque she replied: ". . . Only pray believe that you have done me an immense service. Wd it be possible should there be great occasion for you to send me 200 francs more during next week? I should only ask it if I have not had other funds and do not know where to get any for the moment."

Douglas immediately made another 500 lire available to her, and was rewarded thus:

23.iii.02

My dear Sir,

The B[anco] d'I [talia] paid me the second 500 lire making a 1000 lire for which I am your debtor. When I shall have repaid it, I shall remain nevertheless yr debtor for one of the kindest & noblest actions which ever illumined a cold & dark world. To me at this moment it is very cold & very dark. It is sad how one becomes indifferent to people as soon as one no longer lives amongst them and entertains them.

I came to this Eremo Verde as I call it some years since when I lost nearly everything I possessed & my beloved home near Florence, but it was a mistake perhaps, as it is altogether out of my Monde. I should be so glad to talk to you for one can say so little by letter. Yr kindness and confidence have been very consoling. Please now tell me a little about yrself & the villa.

Ever yrs sincerely

All this was very well, and for the moment satisfactory; but it had given Ouida the idea that Douglas, who had recently had his own vision of an approaching financial cataclysm confirmed – it had given her the idea that he was rich.

v

Spring was well established, and Norman and Elsa were delighted to discover two birds' nests in the garden – one of them a blackbird's. They had a few good days, but on the whole do not seem to have been happy. Elsa, four months pregnant, was not particularly well, suffering from headaches, giddiness and lassitude; and both she and Norman not uncommonly felt "frightfully low and dull . . . almost too bored to live".

Norman's brother John and his wife Olga came on a visit for three weeks in April, and the two couples made a short visit to Capri, though they stayed in different hotels. Norman left a card on the British Liberal leader, Lord Rosebery, at his villa, and Rosebery called at the Villa Maya when Norman was out: "He was very nice," Elsa records, "sat and talked and wandered round the garden with me. Then he left, and went straight to his yawht [sic] and off to Sardinia." He brought Conan Doyle with him, and Elsa thought Doyle looked like a bounder, but didn't say why. Norman, who seems to have visited Rosebery at his villa, and to have entertained him at his own on a good many occasions, has left a delightful informal sketch of him in *Looking Back*.

On the day before Rosebery wandered round the garden with Elsa, the "great Mr Maund"[39] had arrived from Egypt, pitifully ill. The Douglasses went to dinner with him in Naples, and were shocked by his appearance:

His skin was drawn tight as parchment over a face the colour of earth, there was no flesh on his hands, the voice was gone, though fire still gleamed viciously in the hollows of his eyes. That raven-black hair was streaked with grey and longer than ever, which gave him an incongruously devout appearance. He had taken pitiful pains to look fresh and appetising.

Maund then came to stay at the Villa Maya, and was there on and off for a month, attended daily by his doctor. He left on 2nd June, and died less than a fortnight later on his way to England.

The interesting thing about this visit is that Elsa's account of it day by day in her diary does not tally very exactly with Norman's trenchant and amusing description in *Alone*. There is no mention of Maund's irascibility and offensiveness, nor of his devastating effect on the household staff, nor of the boy-messenger with a face "like a boiled cod-fish", in Elsa's diary; furthermore, she confirms Maund's charge that the servants drank his wine, which Norman does not actually deny, but calls an "outrageous" accusation. This would seem to be a case in which, to use Douglas' own phrase, "truth was mixed with untruth". The stories of the sow methodically engulfing the rat, and of the codfish-faced messenger boy, may be invented;[40] the story of "the benefactor of the human race" may be exaggerated; but how right they are in spirit, how fittingly the untruth (if untruth it be) is inlaid into the truth!

vi

It had been Elsa who had complied with Ouida's request for a description of the Villa Maya and its owner; but when about a month had passed, and the Douglasses had heard no more, one of them must have written or telegraphed. Ouida replied by telegram: "Infiniment touché par toute. Ecrirai. Mille choses affectueuses à madame. Ouida", and three days later wrote to Norman, and then to Elsa, showing typical warmth and interest:

Dear Lady,

I was infinitely touched by yr most kind invitation & all the trouble you took to explain to me your position. I shall hope ere the year is out to see you. But I never inflict myself on people as a guest of long duration for I knew I must be a *seccatura*; having many fancies and habits engrained in me, having been mistress of my own home since I was very young. I think you must get tired of not having the beach, & not having walks and drives. I suppose you have your own boats?

Do you see anything of Axel Munthe when he is at his house on Capri? Or of Marion Crawford? He has made the fiasco he merited with his Francesca.

I think your husband said you were going to spend all this year at Posilipo without going to England or Scotland? It must be rather a tiring journey for your little son. Let me assure you once more how deeply I feel yr infinite kindness and with warm regard, believe me ever yrs

Ouida

May 1 Have you nightingales? There are many here. I hope your Husband had my letter three days ago.

There is more about birds in a later letter: "Don't go away till your birds have done nesting which will not be till July, & swallows go on longer. There are many nightingales in these grounds; to be so shy they (yours) are worried probably by cats, snakes, or men. They are *not* shy birds; tutt' altro."

About a week before this was written, Elsa had noted in her diary that there were "*nine* nests in the garden one in the process of being built, and one quite absurdly near the road so that one can see it sitting with its tail and head nearly on a level". The loss of the beach, referred to in the earlier letter, was due to reconstruction being carried out by workmen under Douglas' direction. Considerable quantities of marble were being unearthed, or raised from below water, and steps and walls were being built between upper and lower levels on the property. It was at this time that Douglas was served with "a kind of writ" by his Italian neighbour, Signor Acampora, over a right of way, which also involved Douglas' other neighbour, Nelson Foley.[41] The details and repercussions of this case are described in *Looking Back* (pages 101-3 and 375-6) with a certain amount of satisfaction and amusement, for Douglas, lucky or well-prepared in law, won this case as he won others. The marbles were jealously guarded, and carefully washed and handled by their owner who, with typical appetite, sought for even more elsewhere, going to Torre Gaveta as he had on many another occasion, to see what was to be had there. There was an Antiquaries' business somewhere in that district at which he occasionally bought pieces, and sometimes he and Elsa simply took a sack and picked up what they could find lying about. These marbles, together with the flowers and birds, were the objects chiefly loved and cherished at this time. But on 1st June disaster struck: "This has been a quite unhappy morning. When we walked through the garden after breakfast we found the birdsnest in the Sternleweg that we had been watching with such interest and affection, *destroyed*, and all the little newly hatched birds gone. I couldn't help howling it made me so miserable and spoilt all my interest in the other nests. It had been so lovely watching the little mother bird who had always looked at one so full of trust and confidence. It must have been that cat last night, or else a rat." In the evening Norman shot a rat, and he and Elsa laid down poison "for those infernal cats" – only to find, on the following day, that four dogs had died of it. What are we to make of Norman's brisk and businesslike account in *Looking Back*:

> . . . during one spring I had no less than fourteen blackcaps' nests. To achieve this end, the cats had to be destroyed. I shot them remorselessly, much as I like the species. Stray dogs were also a nuisance; they left their visiting-cards on the terrace. This terrace drained in a pipe down to the sea-level thirty metres below, where I had excavated a cistern from which water could be pumped up for bathroom purposes; the other water, as is customary in those parts, being supplied from the clean roof. If I was to enjoy my bath, those dogs had to go. They went, with the help of strychnine which was laid down in appetizing ham *patés*. This happened about once every month and I often killed six or eight in a night; an occasional cat was also bagged. Before beginning operations I sent word to the neighbours to keep their own dogs at home that evening, if they had any. The strange thing was that these roaming beasts were quite unknown; the oldest inhabitants had never seen them; they came from God knows where, scouring the country by night, like wolves in search of what they might devour.

Is this an example of the masterful, no-nonsense, ruthlessly capable image which he liked to display from time to time, or literal truth? Elsa's diary shows that four dogs – whether from far or near – died by accident rather than by design. Norman, of course, could be referring to other occasions.

On 3rd July Ouida wrote saying she was still unable to pay back the 1000 lire, referred to the pirating in America of *Under Two Flags*, and ended with an enquiry: "I suppose there wd be no chance that yr Bankers, if you spoke to them, would lend me a little money? I want it, still, *very much*." On the following day, she added, on one of her green gilt-edged cards (enclosed in an envelope): "P.S. Of course it was foolish to think that yr bank wd lend anything to a stranger but wd it be possible to get 2 or 3 hundred francs for the immediate moment? Wd Axel Munthe do you think?" A few days later another green card arrived in another envelope. It offered some sort of proof that she was expecting money for an article from the *Sphere*, and asked: "Cd you lend me a hundred francs by return, & I will send it back when I receive this little cheque which will be on Monday or Tuesday. Pray forgive this. Ever yr O." The Douglasses do not seem to have replied.

vii

In June they decided to go to Bludenz, presumably so that they would be there in ample time for the birth of the second child, due in August.

Elsa's pleasure at escaping from the Neapolitan heat was equalled by her delight at once more plunging into the old haunts of childhood with Norman, who at intervals through the years had shared so many walks and expeditions with her in this corner of the world. "Deliciously cool and grey" was her comment on the weather when they arrived, and she exulted in the smell of mown hay from the fields round about Armatin, the house of Vanda, her aunt and mother-in-law. Elsa and Norman walked together every day, revisiting some favourite place such as the Halde Wässerle or a special little ravine in which nightshade grew ("The same sweet woody poisonous smell"); but after a few days it became almost as hot as Naples, though stuffy and oppressive; the air was filled with horse-flies which drove her almost to tears, and their bites kept her awake at night. She longed then for the sea-breezes of the Gaiola. On the last day of June, when Vanda had gone down by train to see Elsa's mother at Babenwohl, Norman and Elsa wandered up the Obdorf road and into the woods and "sat where the big Föhren are a long while, it was quite indescribably lovely, the sunlight glittering in the Föhrenzweige, the air so soft and sweet-smelling". Another nightshade was found, and they continued their walk, coming back, as usual, by a different route. Vanda had not returned when they got back to Armatin, but they apparently thought nothing of it, had supper, and went to bed.

Next morning, when Elsa came down from her bath, "N. told me that Viva [Elsa's sister, Violet] had arrived early in the morning to say that aunt V. was dead. She had left Babenwohl to come home by the last train and had fallen down on the road where a man found her. She was taken first to the Spital, then to Babenwohl. They say she did not suffer at all."

Two days later, the Rose of the Walgau was laid to rest beside her second husband in the new Evangelical Cemetery – a beautifully-sited plot of ground tucked under the foothills of the Furkla and looking across the valley of the Ill to the great wall of mountains opposite. Norman and Elsa visited the grave the following day, and then again a week later. Norman's feelings have to be imagined; he suffered for two days from "a most terrible headache"; and he or Elsa had evidently written to Ouida, who replied:

My dear Sir,

Accept my most intense sympathy. It is an immense an undying sorrow. It is the loss of one's truest friend. I had that sorrow ten years ago . . .

This was deeply felt, as anyone will agree who cares to read about the circumstances of Madame de la Ramée's death; but with a certain firm but gentle pursuit of continuity, Ouida's letter goes on:

I have not heard from you since I sent you "The Sphere" letter. Perhaps you never received it? I thought you were offended & so [you] did not reply.

I know the Brenner route well and love the Tirol but I cannot leave here yet, – for reasons you know.

Ever yr most indebted

9th July Ouida

and a week later, referring to the fact that she had not answered a question of his about her likes and dislikes, she sets them down:

Well, the chief is that I must have a big hot bath to begin the day; then I must have cream with my tea, & be allowed to make & use my own tea; then I like to go to bed early or late, according to my feelings; and I fear I cannot be called sociable! This is to reply to yr kind enquiries. But there is no chance of my putting you to the ordeal of myself because I cannot leave here *yet*; & should I be able to do so, I want very greatly to go to England. I feel it is so wonderfully kind of you & yr wife to invite me as you do. I shall certainly try to see you in the winter. Ever yrs gratefully

In Norman's reply to this letter, he must have asked Ouida if she knew of a suitable house to be had in her district, with running water. She was at that moment ill with dysentery and vomiting "due to wrong use of copper saucepans, always forbidden by me", but she would make enquiries. What schemes were afoot in Norman's head at this time? As to the Vorarlberg, it was becoming intolerable; one feels that it had little to offer him after his mother's death. Elsa was becoming ever more restless and irritable in the appallingly muggy weather as her time approached. She and Norman had one or two good days together, as for instance on an expedition by train and landau to Falkenhorst which was itself "awfully hot and glary and unpleasant", but after coffee at about five o'clock, she and Norman set out on foot "for the beloved Mufflwald. The first part through the fields was rather hot, but the view onto the hills quite exquisite. In the Mufflsumpf N. found some delicious orchids that smell like Brunellen. We picked a huge bunch. In the wood of course it was lovely, golden sunlight glinting through the trees, and a delicious deep woody silence. We sat down twice and the second time made a little goodsmelling fire. The carriage with Archie arrived the same time as we came out of the woods, and we drove back to Nenzing having a glass of milk on the way . . . N. picked me this leaf." Ten days later, he was on his way to Naples – whether by previous arrangement, or from some immediate need? – but returned before 17th August. His second son, Robert Sholto, known to the family in the Vorarlberg as Tussi, and later by his own wish as Robin, was born on the 20th.

On 21st July Elsa had noted: "N. very busy packing as he goes to Naples tomorrow. It's awful, I shall be so lonely," and on the following day, after he had gone: "Felt awfully blue and miserable . . . I had my supper feeling miserably lonely." Her mother and young Grete Jehly came to see her, so did her sister Viva; but in the light of future events one feels that something irrevocable had happened in her relationship with Norman without the real volition of either party.

viii

During the last five months of 1902 there are some fifteen extant letters from Ouida, slightly less than half of which are to Elsa. Ouida is interested in the new baby and twice prescribes for it the names Ronald Alan Kenneth ("Pray don't give the little new-born an Italian name. I sent you three beautiful Scottish names"). She begs Norman to send her 200 francs (or even 100) by return: "I shall lose some beautiful enamels at the Monte di Pieta here if I do not redeem them on the 6th. Pray, pray do." It looks as though Norman answered this prayer; also, apparently contemplating research involving both corsairs and the Pisan archives, he enquired about Pisan libraries. Ouida regrets, with obvious sincerity, that she cannot help him. A journey to Pisa and a possible meeting there with Ouida, was discussed over a fairly long period, and it seems that Norman and Elsa may have vistied Pisa on their way from the Vorarlberg to Naples at about the end of September. Ouida sent messages at the last minute, excusing herself, and Florence was tentatively proposed as a rendezvous some time in the future. She asked if there was anybody who could send her oranges in the winter from Naples: "They are so good for the throat."

A week later came an urgent request to Norman for 100 francs in order to avoid "extreme unpleasantness"; and the next day, explaining that her taxes have been increased by one third, and that she is afraid of sequestration, she asks instead for 200 francs, if possible, "by return".

She will pay him back "early next month". This two-day letter was not answered, and three days later she sent two telegrams: "Prière aider moi si non chiens vendus", and "Prière aidees [sic] selon lettre si non toute chose vendu [sic]". No response; therefore, four days later, another letter:

31 Oct

My dear freinds [sic]

Last Saturday I wrote to you. On Monday I sent you two telegrams. I have had no reply. Of course you may have been totally unable to do anything but surely you wd have answered? The horrible sale is remitted to the 3d Nov. I will explain when I hear you have had letter & telegrams.

Ever yrs

I hope the babies are not ill?

Presumably, on this occasion, Norman regretfully declined – producing figures, perhaps, to show that he was no longer in a position to help:

12 Nov

My dear Freind [sic]

Burn my letters & telegrams of the last few weeks; I have burnt yours received yesterday. I am infinitely more touched by yr kindness in the spring now that I know you are not rich as I thought. It is a pity to sell the Posilippo villa. What price? What architecture? What kind of grounds? – I fear you will suffer in Austria; the endless rains & the long winters are insupportable; the Country is beautiful but one can so seldom see it. I have suffered horribly in the last affair, & I only received the money at noon yesterday! ...

She sends her love to Elsa, and asks, on the back of the envelope: "Combien à louer la villa à vous?" It is sad to think of this splendid woman being reduced in her old age to subscribe to those Edwardian standards which made of poverty and necessity a disgrace rather than a misfortune. "Burn my letters ..." – the very inscription of the phrase on paper is enough to ensure their preservation – even amongst the most loyal of friends. Ouida, with her knowledge of the world, should have known that. And yet – there was a vein of innocence in this otherwise sophisticated woman. It was one of her most endearing characteristics.

CHAPTER TWELVE

Capri
1903–1908

i

For the years 1903 to 1906 facts are in short supply. Two things are certain: they were unhappy years for Elsa; for Norman they constituted a period in which he laid the foundations of his career as a writer, and began to become one of the best known inhabitants of Capri. To that extent they were constructive years, and not unhappy for him. Writing about his series of Capri pamphlets, which was published between 1904 and 1915, he mentions that prolonged stays on the island did not begin until 1902, and adds: "It was a serene period on the whole, with blissful streaks in between."

For the earlier part of the ten years during which he was based on Capri, he was a tenant of the Villa San Michele (which was situated near the town of Capri, and was not Munthe's villa in Anacapri). This villa belonged to Prince Caracciolo, "a delightful old man, bearded and ever youthful", who lived on the ground floor and "in the pauses between superintending his vines and procreating fresh children" – of which he had about a dozen – "would amuse himself with painting images of Madonnas and Saints for churches, and not at all bad ones". Here Douglas began his intensive study of all aspects of the island, starting presumably with the Blue Grotto and the forestal conditions, since these were the subjects dealt with in his first two monographs. He would have been working on these in 1903, though he probably began his investigations at an earlier date, while living on the Posilipo. On those many visits to Naples recorded in Elsa's diary, he must have spent a considerable amount of time in the Biblioteca Nazionale.

This Eames-like scholarly occupation, combined with physical exploration and a social life when he desired it, suited him admirably; but he had to feel free from conventional obligations in order to be happy. There are countless instances in his life of a refusal to commit himself to projects or appointments. When meeting people for the first time, he liked to inspect them first at some café or restaurant so that he could, if he felt

149

like it, "evaporate" without further involvement. He changed his mind about travelling arrangements, about projects of all kinds, and particularly about meeting people – even old friends. Yet constancy to certain friends, certain themes and opinions, certain loved places, was stronger in him than in most of us: once again in his character opposites are united, and live happily together. The mercurial part of his temperament, though of Sterne-like proportions, has been understated in favour of the dominating masculine decisiveness. The light-hearted, volatile, irresponsible, snuff-taking part of his character was also the creative part. It might never have produced anything but extremely entertaining conversation without the drive and determination, the diligence and sense of purpose supplied by the scholarly pipe-smoking steady-paced mountaineer. He was equal parts of both, and this may account for his unsuccessful marriage, for marriage demands steadiness and requires some demonstration of it almost daily, as well as week by week, month by month, year in and year out. It is unlikely that Douglas could ever have succeeded in such an enterprise without denying half his nature. The constraints of marriage and the financial responsibilities connected with the Villa Maya and with children were too restricting. These facts in themselves would have been sufficient – perhaps they were sufficient – to break the marriage.

When the marriage had in fact broken, though the rupture had not then been formally recognised in law, he only stood to gain by separation. He began a new life, the serenity of which seems to have started immediately, for at the Villa San Michele he had "a little maid from the neighbouring farm" who was "the most faithful and attentive creature in the world":

> Whenever I was obliged to go on one of my visits to Naples, she would insist, even on pitchblack wintry mornings and in pouring rain, on accompanying me at 4.30 a.m. to the piazza where a cab might be waiting – the funicular was not yet built – to catch the early boat, and if there was no cab she walked the whole way down to the harbour: all on the pretext of carrying my diminutive bag which weighed perhaps five pounds. Catch an English maid doing that! Hers was a happy disposition and she deserved to enjoy a long life and give pleasure to others instead of dying, as she did in 1913 and while I was in London on the *English Review*, during a local epidemic of typhoid. *Requiescat*.

For his own contentment of mind, he perpetuated her name – Enrichetta – in *South Wind*. This was a sentimental and agreeable habit which was also applied to Anyuta.

ii

The first of his "prolonged stays" on the island in 1902 may have been the three weeks during which he was away from Armatin just before the birth of Robert. Or afterwards, at almost any time, although it seems that Norman and Elsa were both in the Vorarlberg for Christmas 1902 and that Norman did not leave there until the following February.

On 2nd February 1903 he went to Capri and stayed there ("detained" according to his divorce statement) until 2nd May. During this absence of three months his wife is said to have become the lover of Baron von Stengel. After Norman had returned to Bludenz in May, Elsa, pleading ill-health, went to stay with an old school-friend at Strasbourg, and did not return until July. According to the divorce papers, which cannot be relied on, a few days after her return she apparently confessed to Norman that she had committed adultery with von Stengel and had miscarried a child of his while at Strasbourg.

Douglas told Elsa he would have to divorce her (after apparently trying unsuccessfully to arrange a separation), and that she would have to leave his house (presumably Armatin). At her request he allowed her to stay until 7th August, when she went to her mother at Bregenz. This period of about ten days must have been the one referred to in stories of the break-up, apparently emanating from Douglas himself, during which he is supposed to have replied to all Elsa's remarks with either "Miaou" or an imitation of a clucking hen.

On 16th October Ouida, writing to Norman on Capri, says that she has heard with "inexpressible regret" of his approaching separation from his wife. From this date onwards he seems to have been established on Capri.

Whatever the effect on him of his marriage breaking up, the years 1902 and 1903 had brought three deaths which must certainly have affected him deeply. Campo Alegre and Vanda died in 1902; and in June 1903 his sister Mary died of tuberculosis. She, who had been so close to him in childhood, died at the age of thirty-two, and was buried near her mother in the same churchyard.

With regard to the death of his mother, an interesting line of enquiry suggests itself: had Norman during her lifetime attempted to conform to a modicum of the conventions for her sake? Did he in fact marry Elsa because there was a baby on the way, and he did not wish his mother to be involved – as *his* mother and *her* aunt – in a family scandal? Did he "keep up appearances" at the Villa Maya for the same sort of reason? And did he feel, when his mother had died, that since there was now no one whom he minded hurting, he could do as he pleased?

iii

In 1904 the first two monographs on Capri were published: *The Blue Grotto and Its Literature* in February; and *The Forestal Conditions of Capri* in April. One hundred copies of each were printed in London.

It seems most likely that Douglas was in England for the printing of both these pamphlets, which he would have seen through the press with his usual care, and picked up in bulk to take back with him to Italy, for his divorce case was heard on 18th March, and he had then to be in Edinburgh. Elsa, the defendant, was found guilty of adultery with the co-defendant, von Stengel; she was therefore divorced and separated from Norman, the Pursuer:

> his society fellowship and company in all time coming ... and Find and Declare the Defender to have forfeited all the rights and privileges of a lawful wife, and that the Pursuer is entitled to live single or to marry any free woman as if he had never been married to the Defender or as if she were naturally dead ... and hereby Find the Pursuer entitled to the custody and keeping of Louis Archibald Douglass and Robert Sholto Douglass the children of the marriage. . . .

For the second time, the law of his ancestral land had done for him exactly what he had hoped it would do; but it is doubtful if his pleasure on this occasion could have excelled that which was to come from another court on a day almost exactly four years later. For the moment, however, considering that he and Elsa had agreed to divorce – and would have been technically guilty of collusion if their concurrence had been discovered – for the moment he must have been gratified.

iv

At the end of 1904 Joseph Conrad (who had completed *Nostromo* in the autumn) was looking for a place in the sun to which he and his wife, who was recovering from an operation, could go for a few months. They were recommended to go to Capri, and decided to do so. This decision, which neither of the Conrads could have thought would affect anyone but themselves, was to have an important influence on the life and future career of Norman Douglas.

The Conrads arrived on Capri in January 1905 and had certainly become acquainted with Douglas by the end of March, and probably much earlier than that. Douglas would soon enough have mentioned his literary ambitions, though he would hardly have introduced them into the conversation in anything but a genuinely or apparently casual manner. The two men had taken a sufficient liking to one another by the time the Conrads left, for Douglas to feel confident of Conrad's help if he should need it.

It looks as though Douglas went to England not long after the Conrads returned there. By the end of May Douglas had either delivered or sent to Conrad a manuscript referred to by Conrad as *Nelson* which was almost certainly a preliminary draft for *Blind Guides*, published in the *English Review*, May 1913, and reprinted in *Experiments*. He wrote that he had just read it and thought it very good though perhaps Douglas assumed too much knowledge on the part of his readers. This was the first gentle revelation to Douglas of what he, Conrad, thought of the reading public (more trenchant opinions would follow). As usual, Conrad was not well; he had gout and other troubles; but he would try to place *Nelson*. On 21st June he wrote again, about a manuscript referred to as *Sent: Love* – presumably meaning Sentimental Love, which may have been the basis for *Men and Morals* (*English Review*, August 1913). He liked it, but (as usual) everything was "going askew just now". Edward Garnett and H. G. Wells, whose interest and help he had hoped to enlist on behalf of Douglas and his work, had failed to turn up to lunch; and Pinker, the agent, who had been asked to place Douglas' work, had gone to the USA: "Believe in my fidelity, quand même. Jessie's kindest remembrances." A month later *Nelson* and *Sent: Love* were with Garnett: "Patience and Perseverance must be our motto. Life is hard my dear fellow and not only hard. But," he declared, as if he deserved a medal for his resolution, "I am not going to groan." A week later he encloses Garnett's remarks on the two articles or essays. (Unfortunately these seem to have vanished.) Conrad will try *Nelson* on Lippincott: "I run the risk of being kicked downstairs by the average British editor. You don't allow enough for the imbecility of human nature." By the way, could Douglas find out if Conrad's walking-stick was at the Hotel de Genève in Naples?

The first campaign (as above) has failed, writes Conrad in October, but he will open the second in November when in London. He hasn't had more than three weeks of decent health since leaving Capri, etc., and let Douglas not forget that "People don't want intelligence. It worries them – and they demand from their writers as much subservience as from their footmen, if not rather more."

In the absence of surviving documents one must assume that the faithful Conrad continued through 1906 and 1907 to try to effect some kind of meeting in print between the despicable British public and its literary-minded citizen on the Italian island, but no real progress in this enterprise seems to have occurred until 1908.

v

In 1906, meanwhile, several interesting things had happened to, or been arranged by Douglas. In the first place, he had relieved himself of the responsibility of his children. In May he arrived at the house of his old friend William Nelson[42] in London, with Archie and Robert. "I left my father's home and guardianship *forever* in 1906," wrote Archie Douglas. The boys were then seven and a quarter and three and three-quarters years old respectively. Archie remained with the Nelsons. William Nelson "undertook all my maintenance and English education at 3 or 4 schools, and was a most wise, kindly and generous man." Little Robert was soon afterwards taken into the household of Mrs Flora Uniacke.

Douglas seems to have been devoted to his children and to have wanted to do the best he could for them. He had looked after them on Capri for as long as he could – in her very old age, Mrs Romaine Brooks[43] still remembered him going about the island at that time with "two sons in a baby carriage" – but he may have felt that he could do this no longer. Difficulties would anyway have arisen about Archie's schooling, and the boys must have represented a constant threat or actual impediment to their father's freedom, at a time when he had set himself to work regularly, not only at the completion of the Capri researches, but also at the more ambitious project of breaking into the literary world. He must have realised that he could never hope for a more influential sponsor in that world than Conrad, and that he must make the most of the opportunity which chance had given him.

There may also have been another quite different reason for Douglas taking his children to England. Their mother had apparently tried to remove them from Capri. Douglas had managed to defeat or evade these attempts; but constant vigilance against the possibility of further attempts could only have been another irksome task which would necessarily have hampered his freedom.

vi

1906 was also the year in which Douglas' researches on Capri, "such as they are, may be said to have terminated". He explained that it was not his "original intention to bring this series of disconnected papers to such an abrupt close . . . I saw no reason why I should not continue to browse a lifetime among such literature as might be expected to deal with the island, producing every now and then some fresh monograph . . . With this end in view I had already accumulated details for further contributions dealing with Saint Costanzo, with the Faraglione lizard, with the descrip-

tions of Capri left us by the numerous writers of the Romantic period –
the Anglo-French occupation – the Arcucci family and their Certosa
the change of place-names – the Sirens." He was also particularly interested
in the iconography of the island. Why, then, the "abrupt close"?

He implies that he had to stop when his library of Capri books and prints
was sold; but elsewhere we are told that this did not happen until after
March 1910. So what happened in 1906 to put an end to his researches?
There are several possible answers to this question, any one or all of which
may be correct.

Firstly, he was certainly short, or running short, of money. This may
even have been the main reason, or a contributory one, for his taking the
children to London. In 1907 he was giving lessons at the rate of about
ten a month, and he never gave lessons unless really in need. Secondly,
he may have thought at one time that his researches would enable him to
write a more popular book on Capri as well as the monographs, and thus
enable him to draw a small but useful income from sales to visitors.
If this possibility had occurred to him before 1906 it must have seemed
much less feasible after that date, when Harold Trower's *Book of Capri*
appeared. This was a sufficiently comprehensive guide book to most of
the ground covered by Douglas in his monographs, but without his
characteristic literary quality, or his meticulousness and judicious opinions.
Thirdly, he may have realised at about this time – he had certainly begun
to do so by the beginning of 1908 – that if he was ever to make a living
from writing (which he states in several places was what made him take
it up) he must either present his specialised knowledge in a manner that
would appeal to a wider public, or write fiction, or combine fiction and
fact. The monograph as such would have to be abandoned; but the
essence of it, written as an essay, might surely find a place in an intelligent
weekly or monthly journal. It was not until 1908, at the earliest, that he
first considered the possibility of combining these facts with fiction in an
entertaining whole. Fourthly, lack of any significant new contributions of
fact, of the sort of original discovery which every writer on a special
subject hopes to make, may have discouraged him: "On the whole, I
confess that going through the eight monographs I have already written,
and remembering the fateful industry employed upon them, I am surprised how few additions I have been able to make to the literature of this
Island", and a few lines further on he adds: "Fabio Giordano cost me a
good deal of trouble."

It was this latter pamphlet and the *Three Monographs* (*The Lost Literature
of Capri*, *Tiberius*, and *Saracens and Corsairs in Capri*) which appeared in
July 1906. All these pamphlets, unlike their predecessors, were printed in
Naples, and 250 copies of each were issued instead of 100.

vii

What else happened in 1906? "I was at that time in the throes of an all-consuming love affair, and suffering the torments of the damned at every hour's separation from the idol of my heart." The object of his love was "a Capri girl, about 1906" according to an annotation in *Looking Back*. Also in 1906, if she remembered correctly, he first met Muriel Draper, then Muriel Sanders.[44]

Muriel Draper wrote with a vivid impressionism, and an energy and colour, which combine to give a lifelike portrait of Douglas at this period. She is worth quoting extensively:

I saw him for the first time one late afternoon . . . as he was walking down the Anacapri road. I was between [Mrs Webb and Elizabeth Cummings], and they seemed anxious to keep me there as this rugged sensitive figure greeted them in one of the most iridescent male voices I have ever heard. He spoke rapidly but very distinctly, with a slight shaping of his words on his underlip, that just escaped a lisp. The infinitely varied inflections of his voice rose and fell on a constantly sliding scale so that even his pauses were a vibrating sound-bridge between words. It was magic, and I was enchanted. He looked old enough to my youthful mind to make it seem a little unkind to those two dear ladies to keep me so buttressed. There was, for instance, a young Count with whom they often left me alone . . . And here was this one, with a terrifying intelligent humorous gleam in his eye, a nice Merrimac Valley kind of walking-stick in his hand such as my father used to walk to early Communion with on Sunday morning, an indescribably rich "know" flowing from him, and that voice! Something had to be done about it. So I did something. I said, from between those two virtuously flanking ladies, in a rather gasping voice, "Won't you come to tea?"

He looked at me for a searching moment.

"Tea? No," he said; "but I will take you to see some trees, the only real trees there are on this hellish little island. Come along."

And regardless of the restraining arms and reproving voices of those two good ladies, I just slipped out from between them and . . . went, never daring to look back.

"That's a good girl. You shouldn't sit up in that cold hole drinking tea. *Tea*, my God! Who let you come over here with those two old women? American parents don't know the first thing about bringing up children. Have you read *Plutarch's Lives*? Do you learn a column of the dictionary every day by heart? Well, you should. Tea indeed –

come along . . . I suppose you've met the Count? I might have known! My God!"

So we went, stumbling and scolding, along the road. When we reached the little grand opera piazza of Capri we struck off through some arcades and on to a stony path that went straggling up a hill. Everybody walks in Capri, and we passed several members of that motley crew of English, Danish, Polish, German, American estrays who people the island and chatter from tea-party to tea-party. Most of them I had met and, therefore, greeted them in passing. Each salutation brought forth some lively comments from Douglas, and ribald criticism of the social standards of Mrs W. and E.C.

"So you know that old thieving harlot, do you? I don't care if she *is* very well known in America. Look out for your purse and your lovers when she's about. Haven't got any? Well, you *should* have. Oh! These American parents!" And another passed . . . "Beware of that young Danish doctor now. He is here because he just murdered his old uncle for a paltry thousand pounds . . . Yes, he did too."

And still another.

"Frantic for three days she's been, that one, because she's expecting a new supply of drugs on the Naples boat and it hasn't come. The captain is probably holding it up for blackmail. Nice place you've picked in which to finish your education. Where *are* your parents, if you have any, which I'm beginning to doubt . . . Where are they? I'll write them a letter and give them what-for. No, I won't. Serve them right if you come back a murderer, a drug fiend and a thief, to say nothing of . . . Ah, well never mind. Come along."

And I came along.

Finally, the stony little path stopped before a gate in a high wooden fence. Douglas took a key out of his pocket, put it in a lock of the gate in front of us, turned it, opened the gate and pushed me in.

"There", he said. "There are some trees – the only ones on the island. You call all these orange stands trees? Go in there and look at these – I own them. They, and the land they grow on, are the only things I own in the world. I'll come back and get you when I think you've been there long enough," and he shut the gate in my face, turned the key in the lock and started down the path muttering, "Tea, my God, tea!" as he walked away.

I went into the trees.

After a while, he returned, rapped on the iron gate with his walking-stick, let her out, and saw her to the foot of the hundred and forty-four steps which led up to the Villa Torre Quattro Venti, where she was staying. She suggested that it might be just as well if he didn't take her to the door.

"No fear," he answered. "I wouldn't face those two witches tonight for anything you could offer me! Mind you learn a column of the dictionary tonight by heart, and tomorrow I'll come [and] take you for another walk," and he waved his cane in the air and walked quickly away.

But the next day a note came:

Dear Mew (that is all I understand of your name), I can't come [to] take you for a walk to-day. I must go [and] see Conrad who is here and ill. He has learned his dictionary and has excellent whisky. I enclose the key to the trees, if you want to go by yourself. – Yours, and Aunt Eliza's (which is all I understand of your duenna's name), in Jesus, N.D.

The Mrs Webb was, of course, the rich *poulet effrayé* who is described at some length in *Looking Back*. Her daughter had married one of Muriel Sanders' brothers. Mrs Webb and Elizabeth Cummings had brought Muriel on her first visit to Europe.

The property to which Muriel Sanders was admitted by key was the Petrara, Douglas' last attempt to establish himself permanently in the Bay of Naples.

viii

From 1907 onwards Douglas' pocket diaries have been preserved. In these he noted briefly where he was, who he wrote to, certain appointments, and occasionally other items that he wished to record so that he might refer to them later if he wished – items such as "butter ordered", "whiskey begun", "X owes me 30 frs", or "Y" – (who may have been paid in advance, or would have to be paid later by the hour) – "came/did not come", or "Z left". These little diaries form an invaluable skeletal record of his life.

The diary for 1907 shows his main preoccupation to have been with his Petrara property. This apart, the names which recur with most frequency (at least once or twice a week) are "Nelson" and "Tunnicliffe", and they are associated with affidavits, registered letters and packets, and telegrams, throughout the year. Douglas seems to have been collecting information, some of it legally attested, which he had been sending to these two men, one of whom was his solicitor. A third person involved, possibly locally, in Naples, is "Costa".

After three weeks in May spent in England, he begins "watering plants at Petrara". He notes how long the site is exposed to the sun ("sets 5.8 from terrace behind Citrella. Over *inner* Farag [lione] last at 6.15") and there are records of basket-loads of *pozzolana* being carried thither, presumably for building purposes, as described in *Looking Back*. He cherished the place, which he has called "the fairest spot on Capri", with loving care, had it always in his mind even when abroad, and, if fearful that the burning sun was threatening it, would send a card or telegram to a friend with whom he had left the keys of the place, to have a look at it, and please to water it if necessary:

It was an aboriginal corner of the island, untouched by man; a specimen of the landscape as it used to be, like those oaks of Serpentaro near Olevano which William of Germany rescued from the axe. Arrived on the spot, you found yourself in a cup-shaped hollow embowered in self-sown pines and surrounded by rocks, through whose gaps you looked southward over the Tyrrhenian, and westward upon the formidable cliffs of Monte Solaro ... One of many attractions was its inaccessibility. And yet, I thought, once a path has been constructed ... you are within a few minutes' walk of the piazza, the centre of such life as there is. Go to that centre, if you wish to see fellow-creatures; lock your gate, and wall up that fissure in the rock higher up, and only a bird can reach you. An aerial situation; you are poised between earth and sky. Here, if anywhere, one might still find peace from the world; here one might gather together the wrecks of one's belongings and dream away the hours, drinking the heady perfume of the pines and listening to that Theocritean melody of theirs, which is not truly a whisper, but an almost inaudible breathing: summer music. Here, if anywhere, one might –
The temptation could be resisted no longer. The site was bought and a path of access built; I struck out a noble terrace southward from which you could let your thoughts wander across leagues of sea to Africa and the torrid regions of the Garamantes and where godlike Aethiopians dwell; a smaller terrace looked westwards, down a sheer precipice; there were paths, and a cistern for catching the rains of winter. Thereafter we began, in the kindly shade of those trees, to dig the foundations of a villa adapted to my simple needs ...

Alas! the villa was never built. Money ran out, work was suspended for three years, and eventually his beloved Petrara had to be sold: "Calamities of this kind had occurred before; they have occurred since, and I am fairly seasoned: Kismet!"

ix

In August he made his first visit, lasting a week, to Calabria. What it was that persuaded him to make this journey into a region that he was to revisit so many times, he does not say. It seems likely, in view of his later practice when living in Florence, that it was a desire to escape from the burning summer sun into lofty valleys and pine-clad hills, for his visit was confined almost exclusively to the Sila. In these geologically ancient hills he was reminded of Scotland:

> There is the same smiling alternation of woodland and meadow, the same huge boulders of gneiss and granite which give a distinctive tone to the landscape, the same exuberance of living waters. Water, indeed, is one of the glories of the Sila – everywhere it bubbles forth in chill rivulets among the stones and trickles down the hill-sides to join the larger streams that wend their way to the forlorn and fever-stricken coastlands of Magna Graecia. Often, as I refreshed myself at these icy fountains, did I thank Providence for making the Sila of primitive rock, and not of the thirsty Apennine limestone.

The country was as refreshing in summer as the Vorarlberg, which he was to revisit annually at a later period – but nearer at hand from Naples. The Sila, also, was a remote hinterland little visited by travellers. If he had it in mind as the subject of an article or essay, he would have few, if any, rival writers to contend with.

His original paper on the Sila was written between 7th and 12th September, while his impressions were still fresh in his mind. Within a fortnight it was on its way to New York, together with an article on Ischia. At this time also he had begun his investigations into the *Adamo Caduto* of Salandra,[45] of which more – some would say too much – was to be heard during the course of a life which embraced so many other interests.

x

In October the affairs that were being handled by Nelson, Tunnicliffe, and Costa reached a stage of maximum activity. It is evident at this period that an alignment of forces had taken place. On the one hand were two individuals, Goldsmith and Saunders, allied with the enemy – presumably the unfortunate Elsa attempting either to procure evidence against Norman or to obtain re-possession of her children – and on the other were Nelson, Tunnicliffe and Costa, acting for Norman, and presumably steadily filing away evidence against Elsa. In October Goldsmith and Saunders were closely observed by Norman consorting with Harold

Trower, the British Consular Agent on Capri. The luckless Trower, who would almost certainly have observed what Romaine Brooks called Douglas' "rather faunesque liking and pursuit of young boys about that island", had now committed an offence far greater than that of publishing his guidebook to Capri: outraged moral sensibility, or officious rectitude, or both, probably led him to seek some kind of official restraint of Douglas, or perhaps his removal from the island, or imprisonment. At all events he was on Elsa's side, and that in itself was probably enough to secure for him an immortality he could not have desired: a few years later he was to be gloriously transformed into that superb caricature of British expatriate seediness, Mr Freddy Parker of *South Wind*.[46]

In January 1908, Douglas went to London. The main reason was probably so that he could be present at the actual moment of what he must have hoped would be his triumph: Lord Chief Justice Warrington's decision in the High Court of Chancery in the case referred to as "Douglas (infants)". Alas, it has proved impossible to obtain records of this hearing, which was held in camera in His Lordship's private room on three successive days – 4th, 5th and 6th March. After the decision had been given, Douglas sent a telegram to Costa. He had won

Douglas was in Capri by 14th April, and by the 25th was spending that "lovely week" on Ischia with Olaf Gulbransson which is described in *Looking Back*:

> I was still simmering with joy at the recent turn of events; bubbling in tranquil fashion, all to myself, day and night. All to myself; for Olaf knew nothing about that affair, and catch me telling him! . . . Certain folk had been damned; it was enough to make anybody bubble with contentment.
>
> One night after we had gone to bed I was bubbling myself, as usual, into a beatific sleep over their discomfiture when, for the first time, the full comicality of the situation dawned upon me. It had never struck me in that light before . . . Straightway I over-bubbled; I caught myself laughing. I thought: I'm in for a good laugh this time. Who can laugh in a sordid bedroom? Open spaces are required for such a purpose; the hills, the stars, must be witnesses of my mirth and have their share of the fun. So thinking, I dressed again and went out noiselessly in the direction of Ponte d'Ischia, Ischia proper. It was half-past one or two in the morning and a dark but cloudless night; not a soul in the streets. That main road, so noisy by day with passing carriages and screaming children and the cries of fish and fruit vendors, was mysteriously calm. Soon the ground began to rise – I was on the slope of the old lava stream of 1301; then level again, with ailantus

trees dimly discernible on either side of the paved road. I wondered: shall I laugh here? No; who can laugh on a paved road with human habitations every few yards? I must be away from the works of man and in touch with elemental things; I must have nature to myself, if I am to laugh as befits the occasion. . . .

Houses were soon left behind; there was a pleasant chill in the air and an aromatic perfume of wild herbs and volcanic earth; silence all around. Here was the place for me. I sat down on a heap of stones by the roadside, and began to laugh. The hours passed. I laughed through the whole of that moonless night; the more I reviewed the situation, the more laughable it proved to be, the comicality consisting in a fact which had never struck me till then, namely, that it was they, the others, who should have laughed. In the bubbling exuberance of my glee at the turn of events, I had forgotten what this signified to them. They had expected to laugh, and rightly. Instead of that, they had been damned, damned for good and all – yes, and wrongly damned! This was the divine joke. How I laughed . . . That April night was surely one of the most blissful of my life.

A sense of humour is a weird and personal idiosyncrasy; but just how weird and personal in the case of Douglas one might never have known if one had not read these paragraphs, knowing what they refer to. There can be no doubt what they refer to: it is explicitly stated in a note on page 294 of the Berg annotated copy of *Looking Back*, written by Willie King: "The author had won a lawsuit against his wife." Who would have thought that a man in his fortieth year, with many friends, and many interests in life, would have found a whole night's-worth of laughter of a purely vindictive kind, as the result of a lawsuit which had been decided five weeks earlier? "He was to speak of his wife with great bitterness" wrote Constantine FitzGibbon in his *Pictorial Record*: and great bitterness must have produced that Ischian laughter; it cannot have warmed the night air with merriment. It cannot have been far removed from hysteria.

xi

Some light may be thrown on the mysterious activities connected with affidavits, which are such a prominent feature of Douglas' 1907 and 1908 diaries, by a German novel published in 1910. This novel by Kurt Aram, *Violet: the Story of a Mother*[47] is a fictional portrait of Norman and Elsa at the time of their divorce. There can be no doubt about the real identity of these two characters in the story. Elsa is called Violet (her sister's name); she is described as tall and slim with large silver grey eyes and thick red hair; she is her husband's first cousin; they have a little son called "Archi"; they live by the sea, on the Mediterranean; and Violet's grandfather is a Baron who lives in the Vorarlberg. Her husband, Baron Herbert von Strehlen, is a tall heavy man, also with red hair; in the past he has been in the Diplomatic Service in St Petersburg; he is devoted to the birds which have nested in his garden by the sea, he hates and destroys his neighbours' dogs, and loves flowers. He divorces his wife for adultery with an army officer: the case is heard in an English, not a German court because the Baron has taken English nationality in order to be ready for just such an eventuality as this. After the divorce, Violet goes to Munich; and her mother (in real life Mrs FitzGibbon) is called Mrs Fitzalan. If any further doubt could possibly exist as to the identity of the chief characters in the book, it is dispelled by the fact that two letters exist proving that Elsa knew and worked for the author of it. One may fairly conclude that *Violet* is the last shot fired by Elsa or on her behalf in a prolonged matrimonial battle which must have lasted several years.

The novel shows how Strehlen (who represents Douglas) had great influence over his cousin. Before their marriage, he had become her teacher and adviser, whom she trusted. But his love for her became more and more passionate, and eventually he made the mistake of declaring it. She was shocked and upset that he, whom she had regarded as superior to other young men who had tried to become her suitors, should not have differed in this respect. His intellect and liveliness, however, enable him to regain this lost ground, and he becomes more important to her than anyone else, and more important than he had been previously, because she now knows of his love, however she may have reacted to his declaration of it.

Strehlen is shown throughout the novel to be cunning and crafty. His wooing is calculated: he shows himself off as gay, brilliant and sophisticated, takes Violet to dances and parties, talks intoxicatingly, and sweeps her off her feet. Before she knows what is happening, she has become his wife. He has brought his campaign of love to a successful conclusion, but does not know whether he has really conquered Violet or only won her by a trick, whether she has really given herself to him, or has only pretended to do so.

After the marriage Strehlen begins what he calls the "refining" work on his wife's mind, intending by this means to subject her to himself completely.

He reads the Greek classics with her to see if she will be enthusiastic about them. When he sees that she is, he reads her Lucian and other satirists in order to destroy her enthusiasm. He repeats this process with many other writers until he has suppressed her natural impulsiveness and spontaneity, and implanted in her a tired sceptical vanity-of-vanities outlook on life in which she is entirely under his influence. He has just completed this process to his satisfaction when their son, Archi, is born; and at one stroke everything she has learned, everything he has so pains-takingly taught her, drops from her with the accession of motherhood.

She begins to devote herself more and more to the child, and Strehlen has to take second place. His influence over her has vanished; she has become a typical ordinary woman, contented with being a mother.

Soon the couple discover that they are no longer in love. He suspects her of infidelity, and apart from feeling jealousy, feels neglected and scorned. Violet accuses him of mishandling and frightening Archi during her absence. He has no heart, even for Archi, she tells him; as far as she is concerned their life together is finished; she cannot stand it any longer, and will certainly not let Archi be subjected to Strehlen's cruelty. She goes to bed and locks the door of her room.

The novel goes on to show how Strehlen disregards the child's natural impulses and tries to impose his own will and a system of reasoned behaviour, as he had done with Violet. He also tries to make his son do unpleasant things in order not to be a slave to fears and dislikes.

Violet has been visiting a man whom she believes herself to be in love with. She and Strehlen discuss their matrimonial impasse. Supposing he were to agree to a divorce, asks Strehlen, then what about Archi? She begs him passionately to let her have Archi. "That too!" He rounds on her and asks if she thinks him a complete fool – to give her up to the man she loves, and give her Archi as well: "What do you take me for? D'you think I've got red blood in my veins, or not?" He loses his temper, but regains it. "And if it were a question of either the lover *or* Archi, what then?" She would never give up Archi. "So it seems your love is not so great after all!" He tries to convince her that this love is only a passing fancy. She denies it, and asks again if he will not release her. He says he will not. If he tries to keep her against her will, she says, she will escape. He will prevent that, he replies. She will find ways and means, she answers, and anyway, children belong to their mothers. "Not in English law," retorts Strehlen.

Violet packs, ready to leave, but is advised not to flee with Archi, as this could be an unlawful act, and the consequences of it might ruin all her chances of happiness. She unpacks. The attitudes of both parties harden. Strehlen refuses to let her go with Archi even if she promises not to marry again – this is due to his pride – and if she should go nevertheless, he will have Archi brought back wherever she takes him. "For spite?", she asks. "Yes, indeed."

Strehlen now agrees to divorce Violet if she will agree to declare herself the guilty party. It will be less awful than it may seem, he tells her; mainly, it will mean that she will not have to appear in court or take any part in the case except a passive one. She objects that it would be a lie. "I will not quibble about that. The court will not consider it to be a lie, and that is all that matters." He will let her take Archi if she agrees, and only if she agrees: "If you do not agree you will never see Archi again even if you succeed in getting a divorce." She retorts passionately that she will let anything happen to Archi rather than agree to such a condition. He gives her twenty-four hours to think it over; and on the following morning she agrees: she will go to her mother, and take Archi with her.

Violet is divorced; and shortly afterwards Archi is kidnapped by Strehlen, who has had his wife watched from the day she left him. When he receives reports of various other men visiting her flat in Munich, he sees a way of hurting her with the greatest possible effect. Hence the kidnapping. Violet asks Strehlen under what conditions he will allow Archi to return to her. There is only one condition, he answers: that she should return to him. This, of course, Violet will not do.

Strehlen next cuts off her income; he is not compelled by law to keep her. It now becomes impossible for her to pay solicitors and court fees. She writes for help to her father in London – described in this novel as living with a mistress – but receives no answer. She has to exist as best she can on an annuity. She writes stories and sketches and attempts to give English lessons, but earns very little.

The novel ends with Strehlen's death. In a moment of quixotic idealism he has intervened between a Neapolitan and his donkey, which the man is beating violently. Strehlen loses his temper, and hits the man; the man buries a knife in Strehlen's chest.

He dies, unrepentant, bitter, sardonically amazed that he, who thought he had everything under the control of his will, should have been laid low by passionate feelings occasioned by a donkey.

That, briefly, omitting complications and other characters, is an outline of *Violet* in so far as it seems to be immediately relevant to Douglas and Elsa. The chief interest of the novel as a clue to what actually happened lies in the fact that Strehlen makes the bargain with Violet which resulted in her declaring herself the guilty party, and that he cheats her over it with regard to Archi. Something similar may have happened between Douglas and Elsa. Why else should he have written, with reference to that Ischian laughter:

   . . . the more I reviewed the situation, the more laughable it proved to be, the comicality consisting in a fact which had never struck me till then, namely, that it was they, the others, who should have laughed.

In the bubbling exuberance of my glee at the turn of events, I had forgotten what this signified to them. They had expected to laugh, and rightly. Instead of that, they had been damned, damned for good and all – yes, and wrongly damned! This was the divine joke.

"They had expected to laugh, and rightly ..." This suggests that Douglas had either double-crossed Elsa over Archie, as in the novel, or that he had been guilty of whatever charges she may have brought against him, after the divorce, in an attempt to show that he was unsuitable to have custody of the children.

PART IV

Professional Writer
1908–1916

CHAPTER THIRTEEN

Siren Land
1908–1911

i

By the end of May the elation of his victory in the English courts had at last been assimilated: the Gelächterfest with Olaf Gulbransson had been his greatest celebration of it. By sheer vindictive diligence, by unremitting energy devoted to countering the counter-attack, he had won! He was free as he had not been free for years; Archie and Robert had gone, and he no longer had to watch his behaviour in order to present a reasonable case in the courts; he could do as he liked and be damned to the lot of them!

On 21st May, with this new freedom singing in his blood, he began to write *Siren Land*, while living in the Yellow House ("The House of the Spirits") at Nerano, attended by a peasant-boy, "a laughter-loving child" (laughter of a happier kind) whose surname was Amitrano. He had reached a turning-point: he had never thought much of conventions for their own sake, and had always tended to ignore those that might spoil his pleasure. One of his pleasures had now changed radically: henceforth he was to find fulfilment in love more and more with members of his own sex, not merely with males, but with youths and quite young boys. He was not merely a homosexual, as well as a heterosexual, but also a paederast, in the original sense of the word. His attitude to life had for a long time been that if a certain course of action seemed likely to result in pleasure, and was unlikely to do harm, then why not give it a trial? "Why not? Warum nicht?" This practical attitude to conduct was basically a sceptical and scientific one, the attitude of a man who is not prepared to accept received ideas of behaviour any more happily than he will accept fundamentalism or the notion that the moon is made of green cheese. He is prepared to put everything to the test. If the experiment is successful and adds to the richness of life, then society can be left to approve or disapprove as it wishes: it can be ignored. This was the mental climate in which Douglas' robust appetites flourished. Try it! See what happens! Why not? It should be emphasised, though, that the mainspring was

169

emotional, spirited, not calculating, not the result of attempting to stimulate a jaded sexual appetite with dishes of increasing spiciness and complexity. All his appetites were in excellent condition, and needed no prompting. His pleasures were simple and straightforward, but for the age in which he lived, one of them was unusual. In the Graeco-Roman world, it would have passed without comment. In Italy itself, in Douglas' lifetime, it was not generally regarded with the fierce moral reprobation with which it was greeted in the Anglo-Saxon world where, although it was quite prevalent among certain classes of men – such as schoolmasters, choirmasters, and scoutmasters, who suffered an occupational temptation – it was tacitly assumed not to exist, except amongst a handful of men whom the public was encouraged to regard as monsters. In South Italy, on the other hand, where the concept of sin is scarcely more than skin-deep, a more humane attitude prevailed.[48] Everyone knew that boys went through a phase of homosexuality, and no one ever considered anyone else to have been the worse for it. It was thought unfortunate that an individual should grow up fixed in that mould – unfortunate, that a grown man should have to seek his pleasure from mere *bambini*: a case for commiseration, not condemnation, unless cruelty or callousness could be proved. They cannot be proved. One may deprecate Douglas' habits as strongly as one likes; one can wish, as the present writer would have wished, to keep his young sons from too great an intimacy with Douglas; and yet, in the particular cases of close and lasting attachment between himself and young men or boys of which a good deal is known, his influence seems to have been beneficial. In the first place, he loved them truly, for their own sakes. To be loved thus, strongly and truly, for oneself, cannot be anything but an enhancing experience for anyone, at any age. As well as loving them, he educated them, as he educated everyone who spent any length of time with him. He broadened their outlook on life, made the whole of his experience and knowledge available to them, taught them out of books, saw that they got (if possible) satisfactory jobs, remained friends with them when they married, and may even have encouraged them to marry if doing so seemed likely to promote their happiness. He stood in relation to them like a combination of the type of inspiring schoolmaster one never forgets and the most companionable father that can be imagined: and if the sexual passion which may originally have been responsible for the relationship subsided, friendship remained.

This sort of pattern is true of the half dozen or so of his friends of whom quite a lot is known. There were undoubtedly dozens of others, acquaintances of an hour, a few days or a week: at worst, they may have been forgotten; if so, one can be sure that they were not ill-treated, or

approached in a furtive or sneaking manner; on the contrary, a Rabelaisian atmosphere would have prevailed, a climate of enjoyment. It is
probable that these boys and young men were treated with a good deal
more love, consideration, and respect than were commonly shown at
that time by the average heterosexual man to the girls he casually picked
up.

The Yellow House at Nerano was known as the House of the Spirits
because it was supposed to be in the possession of a malignant spirit, and
for this reason had not been inhabited for years before Douglas went to
live in it. It stood alone, in the midst of olive groves, and "the small but
efficient peasant-boy" who feared no ghosts

revealed himself as an inexhaustible mine of that lore with which
every nook of the district is saturated. *Siren Land* owes much to him,
and so does the eighth chapter of *Old Calabria*.

For setting on foot a modest work of this variety what more pro-
pitious spot could have been chosen than my retreat among those
exquisite surroundings? No friends, no neighbours; olives on every
side and the sea far below, with views upon the Siren Islets, the distant
mountains of Lucania and the Amalfitan coastline; the smile of that
devoted little fellow who would wake me in the mornings with a fresh
bouquet of vanilla-scented orchids gathered along the pathway over-
head? I must have found myself in responsive mood to the promptings
of the *genius loci* when I wrote in *Siren Land*:

"Here, on these odorous Siren heights, far removed from duty's
sacred call – for duty has become the Moloch of modern life – it may
not be amiss to build a summer hut wherein to undergo a brief period
of *katharsis*, of purgation and readjustment. For we do get sadly out of
perspective with our environment in the fevered North, out of touch
with elemental and permanent things; we are forever looking upstream
... To dream in Siren Land, pursuing the moods and memories as
they shift in labyrinthine mazes, like shadows on a woodland path in
June; to stroll among the hills and fill the mind with new images upon
which to browse at leisure, casting off outworn weeds of thought with
the painless ease of a serpent, and unperplexing, incidentally, some of
those 'questions of the day' of which the daily papers nevertheless know
nothing – this is an antidote for many ills. There is repose in Siren
Land; there is none of that delirious massing-together in which certain
mortals, unable to stand alone, can lean up against one another and
so gain, for a moment, a precarious condition of equipoise."

These lines, extracted from *Late Harvest*, are of much interest. The self-
indulgence implied by that delicious little tableau of Douglas being gently

woken by his acolyte bearing sweet-scented flowers is sufficiently characteristic: "one owes oneself something, n'est-ce pas?" It is almost
narcissistic. And the actual words from *Siren Land* are a revelation once
one knows the circumstances in which they were written. "A brief period
of . . . purgation and re-adjustment": a period, one might say, of sexual
re-orientation. Then comes the false contrast between South and North,
as though country people in the North were unable to stay in touch with
"elemental and permanent things", and as though Southerners were
never "fevered". Finally, there is matter apparently for self-congratula-
tion, surely hardly necessary in 1908 in a member of the leisured classes,
that he can stand alone and does not need the delirium of massing-
together. It is almost as if he wished to give himself Nietzschean stature,
up there among the olives, looking down on the idiot activities of man.
It was a fairly harmless attitude to which he occasionally reverted later
in life.

"For months," he continues in *Late Harvest*, "I was alone with this
friendly child learning what is not to be learned out of books and 'casting
off outworn weeds of thought with the painless ease of a serpent'. It was
a cleansing interlude, one of those moments in life which must have left
their mark, for even nowadays, after all these years and all their changes
and chances, I never pass along the familiar tracks without a certain little
heartache."

"Casting off outworn weeds of thought . . ." The implication would
seem to be that he was learning to see with the eyes of a child who was a
product of the soil, of the traditional local culture. No doubt this was
chiefly in his mind when he wrote these words; but "outworn weeds of
thought" – how well the phrase applies also to habits of life he wished to
abandon; and "learning what was not to be learned out of books" – how
well that applied to habits he very rapidly acquired, and never relinquished.

The Amitrano boy is a good illustration of Douglas' love for the young
of his own sex, and of his continuing interest in their lives. He often
came to see Douglas on Capri, and one can be sure that Douglas visited
him on many of his short trips to the Sorrentine peninsula. In 1916 he
joined Douglas on Capri for a good many weeks, and cooked for him while
he was writing *South Wind*. "Then he was drafted into the army and died
later at home after long suffering, the result of the War. A month before
leaving Italy, in April 1937, I looked up his widow and the child. They
were pretty comfortable. . . . They would be faring better, if he were still
alive."

This crucial year of 1908 was full of happiness for Douglas. The last
unhappy vestiges of his marriage, which had taken place ten years before,
had been successfully obliterated in March, and he had made a fresh start.

It was a year of release, the year when his way of life for the future was first entered upon in freedom, the year when the pattern of companionship and independence that he was to follow for the rest of his life first began to emerge. It was, significantly, the year also in which he first embarked wholeheartedly upon a writing career. By the end of the year he had published no book that was entirely his own, nor any articles other than his monographs and the Salandra article; but he had written a sizable part of what was to become *Siren Land* and had already, in June, projected another book on Calabria. Furthermore, he knew that his work was good: Joseph Conrad had left him in no doubt about it.[49] He was forty years old; he had no money to speak of and not much prospect of earning any; but the days were slipping along very pleasantly.

ii

All through 1908 Conrad had enlisted the interest of other literary men in Douglas' work. By the end of the year Edward Garnett, Pinker the agent, E. V. Lucas, Reg Smith of Smith Elder, and Ford Madox Hueffer, had all been sent or lent the articles on Ischia (*The Island of Typhoëus*, reprinted in *Summer Islands*) or Ponza, and Douglas himself had sent these, and other articles, to the USA. At the end of September Conrad wrote:

> Just a word to say that your *Isle of T* is accepted by the Editor of the *English Review*. The life of that publication will begin on the 25 Nov with its December No. Your paper will appear in the third issue – that is in Febry 1909. It was impossible to arrange it better as in the first issue *W. H. Hudson* writes on *Stonehenge* – in the 2d issue Cunninghame Graham on *Andorra* and you in the 3d on *The Isle of Typhoeus*. Hueffer the Editor (and my "intime") asks you most heartily to call on him in a friendly way at *84 Holland Park Avenue* as soon as ever you arrive in London.

Hudson, Cunninghame Graham – and Douglas: Conrad had succeeded in bringing him into port alongside two impressive names, and as Douglas' name began to appear in the literary journals in 1909 it became obvious that there was every justification for printing these excellent pieces. The essay on Poe; the *Island of Typhoëus*; the *Brigand's Forest* (which became part of Chapters XXVII and XXVIII of *Old Calabria*); *Sirens*; and *Tiberius*; were all printed for the first time in this year. The last three appeared in the *English Review* which was glowing with well-assembled talent under the editorship of Hueffer, who deserves to share with Conrad the credit for launching Douglas. "Douglas," wrote Douglas Goldring, "had been one of Ford's discoveries, and I shall never forget the unfeigned

pleasure and excitement with which Ford hailed his first contribution.
This absolutely pure love of good writing for its own sake is a quality in
Ford which ought to outweigh any of his shortcomings." And more than
twenty years later Ford himself described *Sirens* as "the most beautiful
thing we printed".[50]

All through these early years of Douglas' writing career, in 1909 and
1910 particularly, but also right up to 1916, Conrad was steadfastly there,
rock-like, crotchety, hypochondriac, generous, affectionate, and abundantly helpful with advice, encouragement, and influence. The copious
and detailed criticism, and the warm appreciation and encouragement of
this already eminent writer were poured out unstintingly in letter after
letter to the amateur, twelve years his junior, who was trying, at the age
of forty, to earn a living by writing. What Douglas gained from this
friendship is obvious: what Conrad gained is not so clear; but during the
years from 1905 to 1916 Douglas spent many weekends with the Conrads
and visited them frequently for the day from London, and was always
genuinely welcome. Certainly he was good company, especially as a
guest, never stayed too long, and always made himself exceedingly
agreeable to Mrs Conrad, who described him as "a unique personality, a
man of great charm of manner and conversation. His chief attraction for
Joseph Conrad lay in his wonderful erudition. His presence was . . . a
distinct flavour to any company. His success with my sex was certain and
assured."[51] In addition to his fascinating and amusing conversation he
had travelled widely and known all kinds and classes of people, as Conrad
had. He was full of zest and spirit; yet could always be trusted never to
betray a confidence, and always to fulfil any commission he might undertake. To a hard-working author buried in a remote village in Kent, continually half ill, and often helpless with gout, all this was probably more
than enough. The fact that Douglas from time to time was able to assist
Conrad with short-term loans of money – always scrupulously repaid –
would have been consequent upon the depth of friendship, and would
certainly not have played any part in attracting Conrad's interest. In one
way it was a strange association: the older man having an extreme regard
for right conduct – including duty, that "Moloch of modern life" – and
the younger continually questioning the validity of any kind of moral
restraint imposed from without, and eventually writing a book to show
that murder could be justified. As Conrad was no fool or innocent, one
may assume that he peeled off and discarded the outer layers of Douglas –
the Ninetyish, dandyish amoraliser, the romantic trifler – until he came
to that core of absolute sincerity of regard for love and independence, for
place and person and landscape, for fact and truth. This quality in Douglas
could be called reverence: it was serious and devoted, though never

ponderous, and it called forth, incidentally, a private morality, a sense of obligation, and a code of behaviour that were as undeviating as any of those prescribed by conventional ethics. The difference was that in Douglas' case, he accepted only what he felt to be true, and only what he thought he could fulfil. To approve rules of conduct which one had no intention of following, he rightly regarded as hypocrisy, and "humbug" was one of the most condemnatory terms that he ever used about another person, though even then it was uttered dismissively, not righteously.

Conrad would very soon have recognised this quality in Douglas, and would have realised that, in essentials, their moral attitudes had something in common.

iii

Having established a firm foothold in the literary world of London with three sizable pieces published in the *Cornhill* and the *English Review* in January and February, Douglas left for Capri in the middle of May 1909. On arrival there he heard such appalling tales of the suffering that was still being endured nearly six months after the colossal earthquake in the region of Messina, that he determined to make whatever contribution he could to relieving it. This earthquake – one of the worst ever recorded in Europe – had occurred in December 1908, devastating the towns of Reggio and Messina and all the country round about, and killing 96,000 people. As soon as reports of this colossal disaster had been received, help had started to flow in from all parts of the world

> yet the misery was still such that one could hardly believe one's eyes. One reason for this was that the money filtered through committees, and many families might be starving before they received their share. I . . . therefore determined to do a little distribution of charity on my own account. No committees for me; the money was to be personally handed over to the victims. Furthermore, I decided that only foreigners should contribute to this fund, since the Italians had their own channels for rendering aid, if they cared to do so. With this end in view, and knowing nearly all the foreigners on the island [Capri] at that time, I managed to cajole or blackmail most of them into giving something, however little. During this operation I had occasion to observe, not for the first time, that when it is a question of relieving distress the poorer folk are more generous, relatively speaking, than the wealthy ones. Even so, the total sum raised was so insignificant that it was hardly worth carrying to Messina: a drop in the ocean.

His trump card was held in reserve. Mrs Webb happened to be on the island. He went to her with his list of subscribers and asked her to glance through it, after he had talked to her about Messina as he had known it, and as it was now. Could she think of any worthier object of charity? She gave him twice as much as all the others put together: "No doubt she could afford to give it. But . . . the point to note is that she did afford to give it."

Having collected the money it only remained to deliver it. Douglas left for Calabria on 3rd June. He was joined at the last minute by a young American from Capri called Vernon Andrews (portrayed in Compton Mackenzie's *Vestal Fire* as "Nigel Dawson"). Andrews was

> so ladylike, not to say effeminate, that I never understood why he should insist upon coming with me at half an hour's notice – "just let me rush home and get a bag" – on a wild tramp of this kind. He did insist, and I had no objection whatever. He proved a good companion; he could walk; he could tell improper stories about his life as a boy in Honolulu; he could waste a morning in trying to teach me the correct American pronunciation of "hot-water bottle" – an impossible feat; he could eat things swimming in grease, which is another achievement beyond my powers.
>
> He gave our muleteer a bad shock in the Pollino district. We had just finished luncheon in a picturesque part of the forest of Janace near a patch of snow, when [Vernon] drew forth from his bag a mysterious box and began, mirror in hand, to powder his cheeks and touch up his lips with rouge. The man was speechless; I daresay he crossed himself on the sly.

The whole trip was packed into ten days, two and a half of which were spent in Reggio and Messina, the rest in Calabria.

It was the middle of June when Douglas returned to Capri and wrote the eye-witness account of those two devastated towns which appeared in the *Cornhill* in September 1910 and was subsequently incorporated, as Chapter XXIX, in *Old Calabria*. While writing this account, he received from Conrad a letter entreating him to try and throw his impressions of Messina into the form of a story. There was no need to make it a conventional novel or story: "Just try to invent some action and hang a picturesque rendering of your impressions upon it." Such advice was to be repeated on at least one other occasion: Conrad, from kindness of heart, wished Douglas to write fiction because he thought it would bring Douglas more money. This exhortation to introduce elements of fiction into factual observation was not ignored. If it did not initiate, it certainly encouraged a tendency which became more obvious as Douglas' work progressed. By mid-September, for instance, he had written a piece called *The Locri Faun*, which was sent to *Harper's*, to the *Century*, *The Smart Set*, and to *Sievier's Monthly*, but which did not get published in a periodical. It appeared eventually in 1917 incorporated into some of the later chapters of *South Wind* where it became the raison d'être of one of the most delightful episodes in the book: the battle of wits and double bluff between Count Caloveglia and the millionaire, van Koppen.

iv

During the last week of August and the first week of September Douglas was in Scanno, retreating, as he often did, from the burning south, and on this occasion to the cool uplands of the Abruzzi.

At about noon of the day on which he left Capri for Scanno, a slender and immaculately dressed young man came up to him and introduced himself. He then began, very politely, to ask for a small loan of money:

> There was something childlike and forlorn about him. His manner was ingratiating but not cringing; an unaffected, offhand manner, as if he spoke about the weather or the latest scandal.
>
> "My dear sir," I said, "you have just come to the right person for a loan. And who is the damned idiot that recommended you to apply to me?"
>
> Nobody, he vowed. He did not know any one in the island. That was just it! If he only had some friend in the place, he would probably not have ventured . . . But he had noticed me once or twice in the street, and I looked so "kind" that . . . oh, quite a small matter, only a few francs, sufficient to enable him to run over to the mainland where he was expecting remittances which must have arrived from New York by this time . . . Couldn't I manage it?
>
> I said: "I wish the devil I didn't look so kind. Anyhow, you won't get me to lend you money; I never do. It makes enemies."
>
> "Dear, dear—"
>
> "But I have been known to give, on occasion. Let me see—" pulling out my pocket-book grumblingly and counting up all I could spare – "would thirty-seven francs meet the case?"
>
> It was enough, he declared. Nearly one pound ten; it was more than enough! Then, after some further protestations: "Can you really spare it?"
>
> "Of course I can't. But I suppose I shall have to."
>
> "I'll never forget your kindness," he said.

This was Maurice Magnus, who was to become a bone of contention between Douglas and D. H. Lawrence; who had already been business manager to Isadora Duncan and Edward Gordon Craig; and who was to die tragically some eleven years later. Douglas did not see him again for eight of those years; but when they re-met, Magnus was to prove that he had not forgotten the kindness mentioned here.

v

Through that summer and autumn Douglas worked on *Siren Land*, showing his work, as it progressed, to his friend John Ellingham Brooks, and posting off completed chapters to Reg Smith of Smith Elder, who was also editor of the *Cornhill*. As usual, he made frequent trips to the mainland. He had a deep attachment to the countryside at the western end of the Sorrentine peninsula, returning countless times during his long life to Sant' Agata, the central point of this district. He never seemed to tire of it. From time to time he became weary of or impatient with Capri and Florence, and there were times of the year when he did not wish to go to Calabria or, later, to the Vorarlberg; but there is no record of any impatience with Sant' Agata or its neighbourhood. If he was doubtful where to go next, or had gone to some other place not too far distant, only to be disappointed when he got there, he would make with confidence for Sant' Agata, as though returning home.

It was at this particular time that he first showed a practical concern, as well as affection, for a small individual item in that countryside. This was the abandoned eighteenth-century chapel at Scola, which contained, beneath a broken roof, a floor of hand-painted majolica tiles. The scene represented was the expulsion of Adam and Eve from Paradise, and the place had tender memories for him: "I hated to think of the rains of winter pouring in upon a sanctuary where so many happy but unhallowed moments had been spent." So the motive for his vain attempts to save the place from ruin, as described in *Looking Back*, was characteristically a personal one. Had that picture on the floor some indefinable symbolic significance in his own life?

Just at this time, also, he had met a Miss Iseman, ". . . young and fair, with a naughty little face. Altogether a provoking person. Fortunately, I was not in the marrying mood just then, though she was . . . as usual on such occasions, I put a slice of sea between her and myself."[52]

"I was not in the marrying mood . . ." Perhaps the picture on the floor at Scola helped him not to be. The "slice of sea" was that between Naples and Tunis, where he arrived on 22nd December. He had £50 with him and meant to stay until he had collected sufficient material for, or had actually written a book on Tunisia.

vi

His itinerary in Tunisia was roughly the same as that described in *Fountains in the Sand:* Tunis—Sousse—Gafsa—Metlaoui—Tozeur—Sfax—Sousse—Tunis. At Gafsa he met a Herr Daniel, a schoolmaster from Düsseldorf, "tall, young and attractive". They got on well together, and presumably found lodgings (off the market-place) which they shared, since for two months "we lived together, agreeing splendidly, and making tours of the Seldja gorge and elsewhere". Some of the best photos in *Fountains in the Sand* were taken by Daniel with a cheap German camera. He followed Douglas' example in making a collection of prehistoric flints, Douglas, with typical energy, soon accumulating four hundred of them – a heavy burden to carry home; but one that turned out to be not entirely impractical. Whether Daniel also followed Douglas' habit of smoking a pipe or two of hashish is another matter, not disclosed. As Douglas himself wrote, the effects vary with the individual, "so far as I am concerned the inhalation of hashish has beneficent results; beneficent and clarifying; intellectually provocative."

Without it, he declared, *Fountains in the Sand* would not have seen the light of day:

Ideas stole forward like phantoms . . . visions put on flesh and blood, they crystallised into enduring shapes . . . Count Ponomareff, for instance . . . is a *kif*-product; this and other figures owe their lives to the gentle ministrations of *cannabis indica.*

So he asserts; and there is no reason to doubt his sincerity; but the Tunisian setting seems to have been as much of a stimulant as the drug itself. He used to smoke it mostly in an Arab café, the later disappearance of which he felt to be a personal loss:

Never a European darkens its door . . . Within that windowless chamber eternal twilight reigns, and your eyes must become accustomed to the gloom ere you can perceive the cobwebby ceiling of palm-rafters, smoke-begrimed and upheld by two stone columns that glisten with the dirt of ages. . . . A spirit of immemorial eld pervades this tavern. Silently the shrouded figures come and go. They have lighted the lamp yonder, and it glimmers through the haze like some distant star.

Here you could stretch your limbs on the floor and saturate yourself with the *genius loci* . . .

But he never had any difficulty in saturating himself with the *genius loci* anywhere, hashish or no hashish.

On returning to Capri Douglas found that he had spent all the fifty pounds he had set out with, "and, as usual, there was nothing coming in from anywhere. Now Mrs Webb stepped into the breach. She bought for fifty pounds the collection of prehistoric flints I had brought together." However, he kept back the best stones and sent them in a parcel to his brother John.

The rest of the summer was spent on Capri, working at *Siren Land* and the Tunisian book, and living as economically as possible.

vii

At the end of the year, he was in London again where he stayed nearly two months in lodgings near the British Museum; he also spent four weekends with the Conrads and visited his son Robert in Yorkshire. Douglas sent out a few articles, such as *Intellectual Nomadism* and *Tyrrhenian Shores* and some chapters from the Tunisian book. Smith Elder had not committed themselves to publishing *Siren Land*, and Conrad advised Douglas to take up an offer from Dent; it would make him feel better to have the thing settled.

The Dent offer came about through a young man who was a reader of manuscripts for them, and was also an assistant editor at the *English Review* offices. He had read Douglas' contributions to that periodical with as much excitement as Ford himself had done, and perhaps with even greater appreciation, since he had deep roots in the ancient world which Douglas so skilfully evoked. His name was John Mavrogordato, and he was to become a lifelong friend.[53]

During this London visit, Douglas made another lifelong friend: the Eric to whom *Looking Back* is dedicated.[54] The prefatory letter to that book implies that he and Eric met for the first time on 5th November 1910 at the Crystal Palace Fireworks Display; and this seems to be confirmed by the annotation (Berg) "A pick-up", and by a special marking in Douglas' pocket diary. Eric was then nearly twelve and a half years old, and it has been suggested that Douglas' relationship with him, which became closely intimate, was so unusual that Eric must have been a natural son. This possibility looked for support to a certain facial resemblance later in life, and to a remark made by Douglas to Constantine FitzGibbon when the latter was proposing to write his biography. Douglas offered no objections, provided FitzGibbon told the truth, but added: "I don't know how you're going to get round Eric." What was there to "get round" in Eric's case that did not need "getting round" in the case of others? In all probability, nothing. Douglas may simply have been thinking of Eric, who was then still alive, and consequently of possible difficulties about telling the truth; or he may have been thinking of that relationship in those early years and realising that it was indeed extraordinary, something he could hardly "get round" or account for completely in his own mind. For Eric became virtually his third son. Douglas even tried to adopt him, but his mother would not let him go completely. It was not extraordinary to adopt a child although unusual to adopt one from a humble background such as Eric's. What was extraordinary in Douglas' case was that he should have taken up with a "third son" for whom he became largely responsible in every way when, although devoted to them, he could not afford to look after his own sons. The conclusion, that this was a devotion of a different order from the usual father-son relationship, is unavoidable. It proved to be a wonderfully happy and successful one for both parties.

Eric was an attractive boy, whom everybody liked. His parents, who lived in the back streets of Camden Town, came to like Douglas very much, and saw that he offered the means by which Eric might enter a world of greater possibilities than they could provide.

As soon as Douglas had left England for Capri, late in November, the postcards started to flow into Camden Town, at least once a week. This stream of letters and postcards continued with great frequency for many years, just as it did to Archie, and to a lesser extent, to Robert. Even when pressure of work was great and there might be fifteen other letters to write on the same day, they were never forgotten. There was a fund of deep devotion and allegiance in Douglas, never overtly expressed (catch him!) but absolutely unquestioning and faithful. It makes nonsense of accusations of "irresponsibility", "selfishness" and "wickedness" – words that are anyway meaningless without further definition.

viii

From January until 4th March 1911 he was in Capri, still working on the Tunisian book and on parts of what was to become *Old Calabria*. He arrived in London on 7th March, the day before publication of *Siren Land*, having spent a day with Conrad after crossing the Channel. This was to be a short visit of less than five weeks, which must have been made partly so that he could be present at the time of publication and partly because he had in mind a rather bold and unusual plan. As to the first matter, he subscribed to a press-cutting agency and sat back in his lodgings to wait for notices. They were not long in arriving and they were good. The general view was that *Siren Land* possessed unique qualities. It was "a happy combination of literary grace and philosophical clarity", and like a good sparkling wine had "style and breeding, wit and a malicious sanity".[55] This is true; it also has the maturity and mellowness of a good wine, for it is based on years of research and personal knowledge and experience of the Sorrentine peninsula and Capri.

When submitted to Dent's for publication, the book consisted of twenty chapters, seven of which were omitted by the publisher as being "too remote from human interests". Of the thirteen chapters published, two had already appeared as monographs in the Capri series. These are *Sister Serafina di Dio* and *Tiberius*; and although they were substantially revised for inclusion in *Siren Land* they are not quite in key with the rest of the book. They are written with greater concentration on the subject than the other chapters, which are all discursive. The one is an exercise in sustained ironic exegesis, and the other a well-reasoned and lucid brief for Tiberius contra Tacitus and Suetonius, for Tiberius as a sage and not a monster.

The general tone of *Siren Land* is in the manner but not quite in the language of conversation. It is discursive, moving from one topic to another, a series of brief disquisitions ranging lightly and speculatively over the whole extent of a capacious, enquiring and well-stocked mind. The movement within the book is circular or haphazard, and this is true of all Douglas' books except the three novels where the movement has to be progressive and linear in order to develop the story; but even in these cases it is worth noting that *They Went* was written in the most out-of-sequence order of chapters imaginable, and *South Wind* was written in two halves, the second first. Only *In the Beginning*, a tightly-knit and invisibly-jointed story, contains "no loose ends", either because it was written carefully in sequence from beginning to end, or because such joins as it may have contained were carefully polished out afterwards.

This disquisitional method is, in *Siren Land*, more that of a raconteur than of a conversationalist; it represents musings rather than opinions or speculations so phrased as to provoke reactions from the reader or from some companion (who exists here only in embryo form compared with others in later books). The author is addressing mainly himself: "I am only dreaming through the summer months to the music of the cicadas . . ." The mood is serene, more so than in any other of his books: "An azure calm, a calm of life, streams down from on high, permeating every sense with tremulous scintillations of vitality." The mind, although stimulated to attention by the sun, is yet at rest.

In this, the first of his own books, all his chief literary characteristics are at once displayed. The preoccupation with an intellectual problem – who were the Sirens? The pursuit of this quest through such literature and legend as has even the remotest bearing on the subject while dropping references and allusions, information and speculations into the reader's ear with casual prodigality and unusual skill at stimulating interest; the building up of a three-dimensional picture in the reader's mind of the countryside concerned, so that it is almost made evident to the senses, from broadest outline to minutest particular; the revelation, feature by feature, usually obliquely, but sometimes in a forthright statement of opinion, of the author's personality while always withholding something, always hinting at unlimited reserves of ability, knowledge, and experience; the high spirits (the chase of the hen at the end of Chapter VIII); the touch of pedantry; the inclusion if possible, of a fairy tale or tales, or the use of repetitive passages or phrases as in many fairy tales, to unify what would otherwise be disjointed material ("And still it rains" in Chapter VIII); the craftsmanlike openings and endings of chapters, the one provocative, the other satisfying; the use of a row of dots to indicate a suggestive thought which the reader is tactfully left to complete for himself; and several other typical Douglasian characteristics.

In *Siren Land* there is evident the author's own enjoyment of using words not merely as serviceable instruments of exposition, as in his previous writings, but as sources of delight in themselves. In this book one feels that he has begun to revel in the use of words for their own sake for the first time: there is a certain amount of flourishing, a certain amount of self-consciousness in their use to build up effects, something slightly hothouse and overripe or artfully designed. This is only to say that the book contains brushmarks of the period in which it was written. What it contains that is untypical of the period is far more important, and preponderates. With an almost classical mastery of economy, restraint and sense of proportion and with an unique ability to entertain, inform and fascinate all at once, he makes the reader so aware of the essentially poetic qualities of that sunsoaked and legend-haunted promontory, that one can feel nostalgia for it without ever having been there.

There is a blitheness, to use a favourite Douglasian word, an engaging freshness, a quality of loving identification of the author with his subject matter, his environment, that never recurs in his work in quite the same way, because never with quite the same feeling of serenity; and this adds a second, personal, element of nostalgia. It is impossible not to have a special affection for it, not necessarily greater than for his other books, but of a different kind.

ix

The rather bold and unusual plan which Douglas had had in mind was that of taking Eric with him back to Italy. There were numerous places in Calabria that he wanted to see or to revisit for the purposes of the book he was writing, and there was something about Eric's companionship that was irresistible. Why not take him out there, if his parents did not object? Why not?

They left London on 12th April, and did not return until August. Eric kept a diary of the trip. (Douglas always made, or tried to make, his friends keep diaries of his and their journeys together.) The twelve-year-old Eric, though constantly interested and impressed by his first visit abroad, preserves a note of what might be detachment or urbanity in an adult, but which in his case is almost certainly an indication of that unquestioning trust in an older person which is one of the most endearing traits of childhood. "I said Good bye to England because it might be the last time I shall see her," he writes, without really believing what he is writing. "I was very glad I had a seat at the window so that I could have a glance at the country as I past, because it was my first time I had been in France. As soon as we were out of Boulogne the country began to begin." After dinner in Paris, "Slowly pasted the hours severn to eight" before driving across the city to take the train to Modane. And going along at night "it seemed if you were travelling under the earth and soon I fell into a deep sleep". The self-possession of this young Cockney who was travelling rapidly further and further away from the streets and parks that were familiar to him, in the company of someone he had known only a few weeks, is delightful. It is also a compliment to his travelling companion. "I woke up next morning amazed to see the train among mountains" . . . Some phrases, but not many, may have been suggested by or unconsciously copied from Douglas.

They went to Sant' Agata, to the Pensione Petagna, for three weeks, after which the itinerary was roughly that of *Old Calabria*, with omissions. Douglas only made concessions that were absolutely necessary to the size and age of his companion: very long walks were avoided; but there were no substitutes for wine and the ordinary food of the country ("Salami" wrote Eric, "is a kind of sousage it is very beastly"); nor could fairly rough conditions be avoided; but Douglas, who knew what he was doing, was well aware of the huge delight and pride that young boys derive from being treated in some respects as adults:

At this place [Spinazzola] we slept the Town was to far away from the station so we had to sleep at the station. It was a tiny house and contain 4 beds to of them we [re] occupied and so we took the others and slept as best as we could. Not troubling to undress we layed on these beds and as soon as I got on mine I began to scratch any way at last I fell into a slumber. My friend woke me at 4 o'clock because we had to catch a train going to Taranto.

At Taranto Eric was invited by local boys on the beach to join them in a raw-crab feast. They were walking along the strand dismembering these creatures, breaking open their shells and stuffing the contents into their mouths. Eric had no hesitation in declining the invitation. At Morano "as soon as I got in bed I had to get [up again] because it was smothered with bugs. I did not sleep any more that night so I went and dressed myself and waited". They went up Monte Pollino (7,450 ft), and descending to Terranova, spent nine hours on muleback. Echoes of Douglas' conversation with Eric can be heard faintly at intervals: at the end of July, for instance, "we were getting sick of Cotrone and sick of Italy and sick of everything in it"; the river Neto "had once been a very important river and now it was a poor old miserable puddle"; "Going along you smell cheese that has been locked up to stop it running away."

In due course they reached the centre of an extensive coastal belt in which Anopheline mosquitoes found huge breeding places in the swampy estuaries (malaria was endemic all over Calabria). Here, or hereabouts, they were infected, and thereafter soon began to live in what Douglas called a dazed condition, though not, apparently, knowing what they were suffering from. Somehow, they managed to get back to London:

> I deposited Eric with his parents, who were none too pleased with his looks and sent for a doctor ... while I tottered to Museum Street and took a room.
>
> Next day I happened to glance at myself in a glass; I was yellow, like a canary. Jaundice, I thought; it will pass. It passed. But the heat ... Not thirst; sheer heat. My body was like a furnace; my mind had ceased to function. By day and night I dreamed of icicles; of the joy of embracing a glittering column such as might be seen to hang down the whole length of Niagara Falls in midwinter. What would I not give for a good shiver! Full of this fevered notion I staggered forth and bought at a pub an enormous block of ice to take to bed with me. On the stairs I met the maid, who asked me what I was doing with it.
>
> "Taking it to bed."
>
> "Lord! You must be a hot gentleman."
>
> There came a lucid moment when I thought: this must end. All my friends being out of town, I went to Joseph Conrad near Ashford – or rather found myself, somehow or other, at his home.

x

Conrad had referred to Douglas as "one of my two most intimate friends",[56] which is no doubt why Douglas "found himself" at Capel House; but even the most intimate of friendships is likely to feel the strain when one of the parties concerned totters into the house of the other in a semi-delirious condition and keeps everyone in it awake for four or five nights, and alarmed during the day. Conrad wrote to Galsworthy about it:

                                                        Capel House . . .
                                                        Friday 11 am
                                                        [18.viii.1911]

Dearest Jack,

Providence is looking after me with a vengeance. Last Saturday Norman Douglas (who had returned to London from Italy 4 days before) came for a week-end. But he arrived in a state of high fever and hardly able to stand. We put him to bed and sent for a doctor. On Monday we sent for a nurse (after Jessie and I had been up with him for two nights and a day). To-day he does not recognise anybody, his temp after most appalling ups and downs has reached 105°, – and here we are.

His "oldest friend" (a solicitor in London) and his brother in Scotland return evasive answers to my letters and telegrams. They say they are "shocked". And the "friend" has bolted off somewhere north for his holiday without sending me his address. He is "very sorry".

All we know *for certain* of D's illness is that it is not typhoid. At first we thought it was a heat-stroke. Now we doubt it. The doctor says – how can I tell? There are no other symptoms but fever. And suppose it is brain fever? He can't be moved and indeed where could one move him? One can can [sic] hear him moaning and muttering all over the house. We keep Jack ouside all day – or as much as we can. Borys begins to look hollow-eyed – his room is just across the passage – six feet from the sick man's door which is kept open for air. I've never seen Jessie look so strained. She knows what it means for all of us. Last week I haven't written a line. My head swims – and in truth I am as near distraction as is consistent with sanity.

Should he die I shall have to bury him I suppose. But even if he recovers (which we still hope for) it will be a matter of weeks. All my work, all our plans and our little pitiful hopes seem knocked on the head. I have seen and tended white men dying in the Congo but I have never felt so abominably helpless as in this case . . .

Douglas was moved to Ashford Hospital the day after this letter was written, and was well enough, two days later, to sit up and write letters. He returned to the Conrads (24th) for four days before going up to London on the 28th. Eric, also, was recovering, but the *plasmodium malariae* reasserted itself, as it will. Douglas was ill again in London. He took Eric away for a week to Yarmouth, hoping that the sea air would do good. It didn't. Then Douglas had to return to Capri for a fortnight, leaving Eric in London. On his return they took rooms at Leigh-on-Sea and stayed there until mid-December.

The landlady was a good cook, but swindled us frightfully in her coal-bills, which was a serious matter, as we required huge fires on account of our shivering fits. Presently Eric began to have a bad time of it. His curly hair dropped out till he was nearly bald, and a sight for the gods; his spleen swelled to such an extent that the doctor vowed he ought to be exhibited at every hospital in England; worst of all – so far as the general public was concerned – he developed a disconcerting trick of being sea-sick, without a moment's notice, in the middle of a street or wherever else he might happen to be.

Before leaving Leigh Douglas spent a weekend with the Conrads. He had apparently been feeling depressed, perhaps as a result of malaria, but perhaps also because he realised that he might have to get work in England in order to survive financially; or perhaps merely as the result of post-publication blues, when even the most sanguine authors sometimes feel a sense of loss: the book which should have set the Thames on fire seems only to have glimmered briefly like a match:

I am sorry you feel so discouraged. Don't give way to the feeling of having written yourself out. That will pass off, and my dear it's really unreasonable to give the game up before it's fairly begun. You have only published one book after all. We can't possibly tell how far you may be successful. At any rate you may just as well keep on with that as fold your hands. Colvin is always enquiring most tenderly about you. But as you did not seem to care to let him do anything I did not keep him up to the mark. What is it precisely you would like? Anything is difficult to get but one could try.[57]

Conrad's question "What is it precisely you would like?" may have received as answer: "a steady job, or reviewing", for it was at about this time that Douglas began regular reviews of books for the *English Review*. His second review (of volumes of poetry) which appeared in print in February 1912, was sent in by mid-December, before he and Eric left Leigh. He was at Banchory for Christmas, and went to see Robert in Yorkshire on his way back home.

CHAPTER FOURTEEN

London: The *English Review*
1912-1913

i

A new period in his life had now begun. He had settled down to regular work for the *English Review*, and later in the year became a member of its staff. In January he migrated from 9 Coptic Street in the neighbourhood of the British Museum, in which he had always lived in recent years when in London, to 248 Kew Road; then to 27 Selwyn Avenue, Richmond, and later to 15 Chiswick Road and 150 Sutton Court, Chiswick. Eric was more often than not with him; and during the years from 1912 until March 1916, when his job on the *English Review* came to an end, he was never out of England for more than a month in the year.

From the literary point of view, this period of five years is an important one. During it, he had three books published, one of which was *Old Calabria*, and almost completed a fourth, which was *South Wind*. He wrote innumerable reviews and a score or so of articles for literary periodicals. He exceeded his promise and achieved a success which few, perhaps, had expected, or expected so soon.

Regular work for the *English Review*, with constant visits to the offices to pick up books, resulted in his getting to know members of the staff and an ever-increasing number of contributors. As he was already a personal friend of Conrad, and through him knew Edward Garnett (and had indeed known Ford, who had made the reputation of the journal), and was generally considered to be one of the *English Review*'s discoveries, he was respected as much for his associations as for his abilities. But, as always, he was eclectic in his choice of friends, not necessarily choosing those whom one might have expected him to like. Amongst those whom he met through the *English Review*, one of the first was Edward Thomas; James Elroy Flecker, another poet, also; and later, Edmund John; and Rupert Brooke, whom he knew only slightly. They were all poets.

It has frequently been said that he disliked poetry, had no feeling for it, and never had a volume of it in his possession. It is difficult to know how such an opinion can be reconciled with what he has written, or with other evidence. He has written of having passed through "a Shelley period"; he wrote at length on the Greek Anthology; he seemed to like Horace, and greatly admired Lucretius. He himself wrote a sprightly "Anacreontic" which shows an understanding of the metre and rhythm of his choice, and as late as 1943 wrote a poem in a mixture of Italian and Portuguese (which was inscribed in a copy of *South Wind* given to a friend, Mrs Claire Bergqvist, who lived in Portugal). A large proportion of the reviews he did for the *English Review* were of volumes of verse, not necessarily because no one else would do them (which was sometimes the case) and he felt sorry for the poets; nor because they were an easy means of writing an amusing anti-review; but often because he was genuinely interested. He was one of the first in England to praise Robert Frost, for instance; and if there was even a hint in the work before him that a true if minor poet existed, he was generous. Thus he wrote of Wilfred Gibson: "If any of our moderns have the Theocritean touch, it is he"; and he seems to have preferred Edward Thomas' work to that of Rupert Brooke, which shows good judgment at that time.

He certainly liked Edward Thomas the man at least as much as he liked or respected his poetry (". . . if only he could have published one slender volume every two years, and nothing else whatever!"). He found Thomas "so austere in the matter of food and drink, so conscientious, so incurably monogamous, that, differing fundamentally from each other, we agreed perfectly". They were both badly off, and talked of escaping from the literary rat-race into a village shop, an "everything shop". Thomas said he would find the shop if Douglas would find the capital. "This is precisely what I failed to find and the project was abandoned." Thomas had been caught in the economic trap, had to produce three books a year, all hack work, in order to keep afloat, and did not write the poetry he is remembered by until the last two or three years of his life.

What Thomas lacked was a little touch of bestiality, a little *je-m'en-fous-t-ism*. He was too scrupulous. Often, sitting at the Horse Shoe or some such place – often I told him that it was no use trying to be a gentleman if you are a professional writer. You are not dealing with gentlemen; why place yourself at a disadvantage? They'll flay you alive, if they can. Whereupon he would smile wistfully, and say that another pint of Burton would be my ruin.

Douglas liked people of character, people whose idiosyncrasies had not been worn away to polished surfaces. He never knew Rupert Brooke

well enough to fall under his personal spell, as did so many others. Indeed, I had a feeling that, if we two were left stranded on some desert island, we should sooner or later have come to the end of our conversational tether – we should not have struck sparks indefinitely. The fact of the matter is this: I like somebody whom I can dislike, or, at least, with whom I can quarrel. There was no disliking Brooke. There was no quarrelling with a supremely contented man.

He was a dear, transparent, social creature whose attitude towards everyday things reminded me of a Newfoundland puppy entering a strange room, and sniffing at all those unfamiliar objects with delighted tail-waggings. Another Brooke might have emerged in course of time, had the chance been given. . . . It was with Brooke not a question of intellectual clarification, but of readjustment and appraisement of experience. Likely enough he would have realised the dream of his friends and admirers, for he possessed what is lacking in many, in too many, in far too many, of his craft: a spinal column. Brooke was vertebrate. His was a positive gift, a yea-saying to life – the poet's first requisite. The animal in him was not atrophied, as in so many of us.[58]

No; it cannot truthfully be said that Douglas disliked or had no use for poetry. No one who had could have written with such underlying respect, perception and tenderness of poets. It is far more likely that he did not trust himself emotionally in that sphere, that he was afraid of having too much sympathy with a bad poet rather than none at all with any of them. Also, of course, Elsa had been a poet . . .

ii

In his capacity of Assistant Editor Douglas was evidently sympathetic enough to be appealed to fairly frequently, as there were a good many people who could not get on with Austin Harrison, the Editor. The difficulty with Harrison, from Douglas' point of view, lay not so much in trying to persuade him to print something one thought good – sometimes one could; more often one couldn't – as in trying to get him to come to a decision at all. James Elroy Flecker,[59] in particular, was badly treated: "He was consumptive and by no means well off; a small cheque or the prompt return of his offered contribution, would have meant a great deal to him. Yet Harrison never could decide what to do with his things . . ."

Whatever his sympathies, however, Douglas had a job to do, and had to find his own ways of dissuading would-be contributors for whom there was no space. Cecil Roberts[60] gives a glimpse of Douglas at work:

After the departure of Austin Harrison I found myself in conversation with the assistant editor, who shared his room. Tea, that admirable institution which permeates British business, was served. I found myself listening to an astonishing monologue from the assistant editor, who was speedily transferring manuscripts into a tin tray labelled "Rejected", where so often mine must have been committed. He was a heavily-built, florid-faced man of about forty-five years of age, with sandy hair and a most affable manner. He gave me a grave warning on the folly of writing verse, which few read and no one bought. His talk had a learned, whimsical twist, which later, transferred to a book, was to bring him fame as the author of "South Wind" . . . He was so fascinating that I forgot my real mission, to dispose of some poems that were curled up in my pocket. After a few minutes nothing would have dragged out of me the confession that I had brought him verses to read, so sweeping had been his denunciation of people who wrote them.

Well, that was one way of doing it; no doubt more direct methods had to be applied to less impressionable poets, or to those who thought themselves geniuses.

Douglas had already begun to drop in to the informal literary luncheons at the Mont Blanc or Villa-Villa restaurants in Soho before he became Assistant Editor. At these luncheons, which took place about once a week, five or six would be gathered together – people such as W. H. Hudson, Garnett, Edward Thomas, Stephen Reynolds, Thomas Seccombe, Perceval Gibbon, Richard Curle[61] – they would all attend fairly frequently, and be joined on rare occasions by Conrad, when he was in London.

Hudson, whom Douglas may have met and had certainly corresponded with before 1912, was the eldest (seventy-one in 1912) of those who were usually present: "It was then a source of surprise to me that the author of books like *La Plata* and *Green Mansions* and those others, so delicately phrased and so full of original observations, should still be badly off." Hudson said little at these luncheons; he seemed to be remote, rather than reserved: "Maybe his thoughts were on the Pampas. He sat there like an old hawk on its perch, observant and silent. His resemblance to a bird of this kind was marked, and sometimes he struck me as not altogether human." He was also thought birdlike by Douglas Goldring, who had been Ford's editorial assistant when the *English Review* was started. Ford had called his attention to the fact that Hudson, who was tall, thin, care-worn and bearded, "moved like an Indian. Going up and down stairs, he was almost as swift and noiseless as a bird." "Not altogether human" is an impression one could easily gain from *A Crystal Age* and certain others of his books, although his style at its best is one of the quiet glories of English literature.

Of the others, Edward Garnett was the talent and genius spotter, the

most exceptional publisher's reader of his time, so zealous for good work
and good writers that he broke the traditionally anonymous rôle of the
reader, and when he found a good thing, went out and found the author
of it, and did everything he could to protect, encourage and foster him
until he could stand on his own feet. Countless authors of the day –
Conrad and Lawrence among them – owed a great deal to his paternalistic
interest. He seems to have done his best to interest editors and publishers
in Douglas' work.

iii

Fountains in the Sand was completed by the end of 1911 at the latest, and
possibly before the end of 1910. Douglas says that he wrote most of it in
Tunisia; but he returned from Tunis to Capri in March 1910, and in July
(6th) wrote to his friend Mather: "I am getting on with the Tunis book,
but slowly." He was in Capri until October, then came to London. He
could not have shown the manuscript to Conrad (as he says he did) until
this time; so until about the end of 1910 *Fountains* must have remained in
its original form – that is to say, in sixteen chapters instead of twenty-four,
and having, as Douglas wrote, "a story running through it: a kind of
romance. I showed the thing in this form to Joseph Conrad, who read it
carefully and then said: 'What is that woman doing in here? Take her
out!' Out she went with all that belonged to her, and the book became
what it now is."

"Take her out!" must have been a disheartening command for Douglas
to hear. It had been Conrad's more than any other influence which had
induced Douglas to make his descriptive writing carry a little fiction when
it could. Now here he was ordering it to be removed! It says a great deal
for the respect which Douglas must have had for Conrad's critical judgment that he unhesitatingly (as it would seem) obeyed him. It is just as
well that he did – and for two reasons. In the first place, the plot is the
plot of *South Wind*. Douglas, having removed most, but not, as he claims,
quite all of it, kept it by and used it again in an improved version. Secondly,
Fountains was too short a book to carry this melodrama satisfactorily; the
book's value is in its comprehensive descriptive faithfulness to the actuality of Tunisia; fiction would almost certainly have dulled the impact of
this reality and detracted from the freshness and truth of its images.

Having known *Fountains* in its final form it is not easy to judge what
impression the original might have made, especially as the manuscripts
are patched and mended to an extent which makes it impossible in places
to know exactly what sequence the text would have followed; but so far
as it is possible to judge, it may be doubted whether Conrad ever issued

a more salutary command in all his days afloat or ashore. *Fountains* in its original form could easily have got itself into the same sort of category as *The Garden of Allah* or any other stagey romance of the desert.

The revised manuscript was sent to John Murray early in January 1912 – Garnett had promised to put in a word for it – but a young man of twenty-nine who had just started publishing was already interested in getting the book for his own list. This was Martin Secker, who was to become one of the outstanding publishers of the century.[62] After a year's experience with Eveleigh Nash he had set up on his own, starting in January 1911 with the simultaneous publication of Compton Mackenzie's *Passionate Elopement* and Richard Llewellyn's *The Imperfect Branch*. Secker possessed a rare combination of talents. He was enterprising and courageous and discriminating, and a level-headed businessman as well; also, and this was perhaps his greatest advantage over his rivals, his books were simply but beautifully produced.

In 1911 or early in 1912 John Mavrogordato introduced Douglas to Secker, and in February 1912 Douglas signed a contract for *Fountains in the Sand*, which Secker published on 16th September.

Generally speaking *Fountains in the Sand* is a less meaty and concentrated book than *Siren Land*. The author, though interested in it, did not love the country as he loved Siren land; and the culture associated with it is alien to the European tradition. In Italy the ancient world merges perceptibly into the present one through a continuous series of gradual changes. In North Africa the old Roman civilisation has left nothing but its impressive ruins, of which there are few in Tunisia. A once fertile country had been all but buried in the sand: "its physical abandonment, its social and economic decay, are the work of that ideal Arab, the man of Mecca. Mahomet is the desert-maker." Upon this desolation and Arab fatalism the French attempted to impose their own cultural ideas including a modern and successful business enterprise, the phosphate industry, all drive and purpose. The contrasts of these two cultures and of the ancient and modern environments are sufficient to defy the efforts of the most skilful synthesiser: the book lacks the intrinsic harmoniousness of *Siren Land,* both country and book. It also lacks something else: there is little scholarship in *Fountains*; it is not backed by those years of research and thoughtful deliberation which give to *Siren Land* its constant and lively preoccupation with the associative value of every stone and symbol, every flower and legend and earth or sea creature. Such personal and historical familiarity with a country makes for a closeness and richness of texture which is not to be found in grains of sand, and which Douglas has no inclination to look for in oasis or kasbah. No Muslim he! Where *Siren Land* is the work of an exceptionally knowledgeable and affectionate insider, *Fountains* is a visitor's account, much of it apparently written on the spot, and some of it, particularly the sections dealing with the phosphate industry and French official and unofficial attitudes to the natives, is in the nature of the best kinds of reportage. He described what he saw and heard clearly and trenchantly, without suffering from the political ophthalmia that was endemic at the time. Seldom has the ethos of a colonial capitalist enterprise been so firmly and uncompromisingly or so objectively described. As to Douglas' observations on the terrain and on the customs of the natives, they were evidently of a faithfulness and accuracy that still proved useful thirty years later.[63]

The most successful part of the book from the literary point of view is the latter part of it, from Chapter XIII onwards. All traces of the original fictional content which, in its residual form, merely irritates the reader by suggesting an indecisiveness of purpose, vanishes; the purely descriptive and speculative rôles of the author are foremost, and, becoming strengthened as the book proceeds, end with the unobtrusive but unequivocal conclusion that the desert and its attendant miseries are due to the religious and philosophical climate of Mohammedanism. It is the summing up of the whole book, delivered with the quiet finality of a door gently but firmly closed.

There are one or two points of interest here with regard to Douglas himself. He writes: ". . . no doubt there is such a thing as a noble resignation; to defy fate even if one cannot rule it. Many of us northerners would be the better for a little *mektoub*." No need to refer everything to the will of Allah – that would be ridiculous; but, as "Monsieur Dufresnoy" suggests, were the Arabs not right to bow the head before the inevitable rather than commit suicide? Was not suicide simply the result of a neurotic condition? "How easily things could be bridged over, or repaired, or even endured! The most hopeless invalid could testify to the fact that some pleasure can still be extracted out of a maimed or crippled existence; a man, however impoverished, might still live in dignified and fairly cheerful fashion." He thought that in Europe we were deluded by conceptions of honour and duty and that the Arab philosophy of *mektoub* "pointed to an underlying primitive sanity which we would do well to foster within us".

Remembering Douglas' love of life and his assertion even in his eighties, when he was suffering physical deprivations, that he would still like to live as long as possible "even if both my arms and legs were cut off", the above remarks are interesting as an indirect admission of the stoical side of his character. It was quite pronounced, but he did not often comment on it.

In most – perhaps in all – of Douglas' books there is at least one moment

that seems to stand outside time, a moment of absolute contentedness
when the author seems to be completely at peace with himself and the
world. These are the times, one feels, when he was truly happy, with a
happiness half-brooding, half-wistful and made all the more palatable by
the merest minim of melancholy – the happiness of a true solitary even if
the mood should occur, as it sometimes did, in the company of another
person. In *Fountains* such a mood occurs when he is at Old Tozeur, and it
is worth noting that it is induced by two ingredients – the "soporific,
world-forgotten fragrance" of the place itself where there is no market,
"no commercial or social life, save a few greybeards discussing memories
on some doorstep", and a swarm of lively young boys playing hockey. The
old, and the young: it was a combination he liked; and if there hung about
the locality, as here, some connection, however faint, with Greek or
Roman antiquity, so much the better. He is invited to join in the hockey
game, and accepts. "I made one or two strokes, not amiss, that called
forth huge applause; and then returned, rather regretfully, to my sand-
heap [on which he had been sitting] to meditate on my own misspent
youth, a subject that very rarely troubles me." Alas, but not unexpectedly,
we are told nothing more about these meditations. Instead, we are treated
to several paragraphs explaining with sympathetic understanding the
decline of ancient Tozeur and its people – "There is nothing like systematic
misgovernment for degrading mankind" – to their present state in a "land
of violence, remorseless and relentless" where even the beetles scurrying
about in the sand at his feet, he thought, did so with "an air of rage and
determination". And yet, surprisingly, the mood of happiness supervenes:

So I mused, while the game went on boisterously in the mellow light
of sunset till, from some decaying minaret near by, there poured down
a familiar long-drawn wail – the call to prayer. It was a golden hour
among those mounds of sand, and I grew rather sad to think that I
should never see the place again. How one longs to engrave certain
memories upon the brain, to keep them untarnished and carry them
about on one's journeyings, in all their freshness! The happiest life,
seen in perspective, can hardly be better than a stringing together of
such odd little moments.

This definition of the happiest life comes, one may be sure, from a man
well practised in *mektoub*.

iv

In February Douglas had moved from Kew to Richmond, where he remained until August, except when he was in Italy (Capri and Calabria) in
May. Eric was at the Richmond flat with him much of the time, and Eric's

mother and his sister Violet often used to go out there to lunch. And so occasionally did his brother Percy, who remembers going to an Italian restaurant in which Douglas, of course, spoke fluent Italian.

Among expeditions which Douglas and Eric made together were the visit to Stoke Newington in search of Poe's schoolhouse – described in *Looking Back* – and one to Mowsley, described by Eric:

> Mowsley is a very small village and has only got about 400 people in it. We caught the train to Rugby and it got there in 1¾ hr. At Rugby we ate something and then caught the train up to Theddingworth a place 3 miles away from Mowsley. When we arrived at Theddingworth we walked up to Mowsley and we never got any rooms until 6 o'clock before six we went for a walk and gathered a lot of fossils. We came home and then we had supper and got to bed. In the morning we went to the Mowsley fishing ponds and there we saw a water rat. We then laid down until dinner time in a field and we went home and in the afternoon we slept and a little thunderstorm came over and went away again. After this we got up and went to a little brook and got some fossils we then went along until we came to a big reservoir and from there we went home . . .

Two more days of similar activities are described, until one morning – replete with fossils, including "some jolly fine ones" – they "got in the trap and went to the station".

At about this time Robert, who was now ten, was sent to a boarding school, and began to spend most of his holidays with the Conrads at Capel House, referring to Jessie Conrad as "Mum", and having as his companion, John, her younger son.

v

Sometime in 1912, probably in July, Douglas and Muriel Sanders met again in London. In 1909, in America, Muriel had married Paul Draper, the wealthy brother of Ruth Draper, the diseuse. Later, they went to Italy, settling in Florence where Draper was studying opera-singing, and where Muriel gave birth to Paul junior. Paul Draper discovered that he was not an opera singer, but a singer of *Lieder*, and in 1911 the Drapers had come to England so that he could study with Raimund von Zur Mühlen, reputedly one of the great teachers of *Lieder*. By the summer of 1912 the Drapers had established themselves at 19 and 19A Edith Grove, where, in two houses knocked into one, they provided for the next two or three years some of the finest musical entertainment to be found in London. Casals, Ysaye, Arthur Rubinstein, Chaliapin and countless other musicians and singers played and sang for pleasure, sometimes after giving a public concert. Beginning late in the evening, the music often lasted till morning, when everyone would adjourn to the dining room for breakfast. Sargent, Gertrude Stein, Henry James, Henry Ainley and his friend the Baroness von Hutten; Cortot and Gertrude Bauer; Eugene Goossens and Thibaud; Monteux and Moiseiwitsch, even Nijinsky – they all came, either to perform or to listen. Edith Grove was one of the oases of culture in Edwardian England, of which Arthur Rubinstein has recently written, ". . . it remains in my memory as the supreme musical euphoria of my life".

At about the time that No. 19 was being converted, Muriel learned that Douglas was working on the *English Review*. Remembering his instructions to her when she had last seen him, to learn a page of the dictionary every day, she wrote him a note:

> Dearest Doug: I have married, marrow, Mars, marsala, Marseillaise, marsh, marshal, marshalsea, marsupial, mart, martello, marital, Martin Paul Draper and live at 19 Edith Grove, grovel, grow, growl, growth, groyne, grub, grudge, gruel, gruesome, gruff, grumble, grume, grummet, grumpy, Grundyism, grunt, gruyère, grysbok. Will you come to tea, teach, teague, teak, teal, teamster, teapoy, tear, tearing, tease, teasel, technic at once (I have got some excellent whisky), and stay to dine, ding, dong, dinghey, dingle, dingo, dinosaur, dinothere, dint, diocese, dioptric, dioxide, dip – Yours, Mew!

Such an invitation was irresistible. "He came that afternoon," wrote Muriel, "The same rugged sensitive figure, his voice of an even greater flexibility, eyes more deeply humorous, and hair just beginning to silver at the temples":

> "Well, Mew, so you're married and have a son! Where is he? Let me see him. If he has been bad today I'll give him a penny, but if he has been good I'll give him a sound smacking. . . . So this is he," and he looked down at Paul Jr standing by me on tiptoe with excitement at this incredibly wicked and anarchistic grown-up. "Well" – looking him over with an appraising eye – "here's a penny for you. Any day you've been really bad come to me and I'll give you another. Never mind your mother. She's like all American parents, doesn't know a thing about bringing up children. Only now beginning to learn the dictionary. For God's sake, don't let her fill you up on tea. Run along now and play with some matches, and if you can't find any, pick all the nice flowers in the window-boxes. There's a good boy."
>
> When we were alone, we sat down and began to talk. We talked through tea, through whisky, through dinner. Through the night.

Italian newspapers, American glaciers, English letters, sexual relations in Sicily, blood relations all over the world, music, Russian ballet (then in Paris), Russian emperors, more music, Nietzsche and back to English letters again. . . .

Douglas, she says, scolded her for her fanatical admiration of Henry James, although, according to her, he was in no doubt of James' "considerable gifts". She adds that when Douglas and James met at Edith Grove "the conversation between them was of the most desultory character. They were too fundamentally divergent in their approach to life, and diametrically opposed in matters of style and technique even to bring about conflict between them, to say nothing of agreement."

With the coming of dawn, Douglas left, telling her to "start that boy of yours off in the morning with a really sound thrashing. He has been damned quiet tonight." It was the first of many visits which she hugely enjoyed. She wrote later of his

> exceptional powers of destructive criticism, Spartan standards of intellectual discipline and Babylonian standards of moral tolerance . . . Humour ran the whole gamut from the subtlest shades possible to be conveyed by a pause, to the most solid salacious outbursts that can be expressed in the splendid coarseness of the English language. Particularly adroit was he in the use of good old Anglo-Saxon words of one syllable. Servants were in a state of shocked adoration, even the miracle maids, imperturbable as they were, finding it at moments difficult to serve him in perfect solemnity. As for the Irish angel, she would snatch Paul Jr into the safety to be found behind a locked nursery door, crossing herself as she flew upstairs with him the minute Douglas entered the house. But she would come down in an amazingly short time again on some perfectly needless errand or other, and hover about the premises, her face scarlet with embarrassed delight and murmuring, "Glory to be God, madame, he's *terrible*."
>
> This would bring a chuckle from Douglas that was the most satisfactory sound one could hear . . . I crossed the ocean three years ago [1926] to hear it and came back refreshed.

vi

From 1913 Douglas lived for nearly four years in Flat 63, Albany Mansions, Albert Bridge Road. This was for him a record stay in one house in London, and in fact he only twice stayed longer anywhere else in his life on both occasions in Italy. The Albany Mansions flat has been described by his son:

The triple-windowed living room of my father's flat faced the greenery of Battersea Park and this landscape was one of the chief reasons for his renting a flat in a somewhat down-at-heel neighbourhood. Another reason was its cheapness. The rent was so low that he could afford to lock the door with a clear conscience of not being extravagant when he went abroad on one of his long trips . . . There was no central heating nor was there a constant hot water supply; nor were there doormen and liftmen – there was no lift. The flat was well built and comfortable and the living room particularly inviting with its foreign appearance. The furnishings were a précis of his wanderings. The room gave an immediate impression of faraway places, being cluttered up with little statues and bronzes he had excavated: fragments of marble and Roman tiles; amphorae and other vases somewhat smaller; daggers and curios of all kinds; and rows upon rows of bookshelves, reaching from floor to ceiling and occupying at least two-thirds of the available wall space; and there were hangings of Indian silk and brocade wherever it was possible to place such splashes of colour. An outsize specimen in desks, a comfortable writing chair, two or three easy chairs, a table or two, and the anthracite stove that heated the room with amazing efficiency . . .

Once he had settled in, the outsize desk was used amongst other things for carrying on a new correspondence, with Hugh Walpole.[64] He had met Walpole at lunch not long after Secker had published *Fortitude*, towards the end of January. Walpole, who had just moved into a cottage in Polperro, had just finished reading *Fountains in the Sand*:

Dear Mr Douglas,
 . . . No travel book has interested me so much for a long time and I know no book that I have read for ages that has shewn both the writer and the place so sharply. Most travel books are concerned with travel. Yours is also concerned with Norman Douglas and so one gets a double thrill.
 At any rate I must thank you for furnishing my mind with a new picture.
 This place, as I told you, is adorable. I've just furnished a cottage and intend happily to work here until June. If, in about a month's time, you were to come this way I could give you a bed and eggs and bacon and show you some beautiful places. I would like to do something in return for your beautiful book. I remember what you said about writing letters but you must make an exception this once.

Yrs sincerely,
Hugh Walpole.

In his next letter Walpole wrote:

I'm immensely glad to hear about your forthcoming book. I can't
get the other one out of my head and I think it was the things you *didn't*
say even more than the things that you *did* that remain with me.

Don't bother to answer this (You see I still remember your words
about letters) but I should be glad to hear.

Yours sincerely
Hugh Walpole

"I think it was the things you *didn't* say. . . .". Here, as Lytton Strachey
was to do ten years later, Walpole put his finger on one of the secrets of
Douglas' charm as a writer. This power of suggestion on the printed page
was the equivalent of "the subtlest shades . . . conveyed by a pause" in
his conversation, mentioned by Muriel Draper.

Douglas went up to Cambridge for a night at the end of March
and wrote to Walpole from that town, in which he had apparently
drunk enough to be admonished in a wonderfully typical letter from
Walpole:

The Cobbles
Polperro
Cornwall

Monday [31 March 1913]
Dear Douglas,

I'd quite thought that I should not hear again – but the fact of the
matter is that however much one may loathe writing letters (and I
loathe it) there is nothing in the world so fascinating as writing to someone you've only seen once (your smile is the only thing I can remember
about you) whose tastes are congenial (loathesome word) and who is
the right age. I can't bear my own immediate generation as a rule except
for playing with, but you're just that little bit older – six years I should
guess – that enables you to tell me all sorts of glorious things and to
give me lots of respect for your opinion. As for the vice versa, of
course it's fun to find someone who is eager for your opinions and
experience.

So it's all very pleasant and from Saturday next until the end of the
month I shall be waiting to be told of your arrival here. You can edit
your old "Review" down here with the aid of the sea-gulls and you
can write a glorious book about Cornwall. I'm very happy having
finished the first part of my next novel on Saturday. (Don't by the way
if you come across them read anything of mine yet written 'cept
"Perrin and Traill". They're all very 2d coloured. The last one has a
lot of "2d coloured" me in it (me very young).) I've finished arranging

the cottage and Henry James sent me last week the loveliest old Bureau on which I now write. The water is light green under my window and two blue boats are washing up against an old sea-wall. I've never known such happiness as I've now got. I make enough now to live without loathesome journalism. I've got the most fascinating art in the world to learn. I've got the most splendid friends – and I've got a person I don't know to write to.

Do come down and see someone in this blissful condition. Come before the end of the month.

Now I've written enough nonsense, and please, be more unlike yourself than ever and answer it.

Also send me as soon as possible "Siren Land". I wanted to ask you but hadn't courage. Send it *soon* as I want to read it before I get at my book again.

Why do you get drunk at Cambridge? – such a conventional thing to do. Come down not by aeroplane but in your squashy hat.

Yours whensoever

Hugh Walpole

The reply has survived:

63 Albany Mansions
Albert Bridge Road
S.W.
14th Apr. 1913

Dear Walpole,

Thanks for your card and the magnificent letter.

I will send you tomorrow a copy of Siren Land, warning you beforehand that there are one or two misprints and that I was not allowed to have a hand in the compilation of the Index which was evidently perpetrated by some enemy of mine, and also that the book is, in a way, merely a *torso* – incomplete, that is, because it really contains not 13 but 20 chapters, seven of which were cut out because it would have made the thing too long for the ass of a publisher who plainly did not know a good thing when he got one. I am working the remains into a book on Calabria – some of it, that is – which is now nearly finished. If you can think of any periodical that might serialise some of them, perhaps you would drop me a line. The Cornhill which takes my stuff, is now out of the running, as there is a dark feud on between the English Review and Smith Elder, and Harrison does not like me to have dealings with them. As for the English Review, I am booked for literary & sociological stuff there. He (Harrison) does not care about the other kind of stuff, tho' I did cram a short Italian paper into the April number.

And how are you? I am beastly cold and altogether rather grumpy. Spent the day yesterday with Joseph Conrad – you know him? How is your novel progressing? Are you still as happy as ever? Beware! the gods are envious. Remember Polycrates. You had better offer some sacrifice before it is too late.

Yours ever
N. Douglas

Douglas never did get down to Polperro to stay with Walpole.

vii

Friends that Douglas had made almost as soon as installed at the offices of the *English Review* were Compton Mackenzie and his wife Faith. In 1912 Mackenzie was in America with the play adapted from his novel *Carnival*, for nearly six months, but early in 1913 had been struck down for the first time with the sciatic pain that was to plague him at intervals for the rest of his life. A picture in their hotel room in New York of the Faraglioni rocks, and vivid memories of Douglas' *Siren Land*, persuaded the Mackenzies to return to Europe via Southern Italy: perhaps the Mediterranean sun would prevent a recurrence of the sciatica.

They reached Naples about the end of March, and while there or at Sorrento received letters of introduction for use on Capri from Douglas. They decided to go over to the island, for a weekend at least, if only to make use of their introductory letters. "The moment we emerged from the funicular in the Piazza we felt that nothing must prevent our living in Capri," wrote Mackenzie. "We were so perfectly happy immediately that we sent across for our trunks before we had explored Capri . . . It was, for me at least, falling in love, irrevocably." Within a few weeks they had taken a year's lease on a house called Caterola.

One of the letters of introduction was to the Misses Wolcott-Perry[65] – an introduction that did not produce its richest reward until 1927, when Mackenzie's *Vestal Fire* was published by Secker. This was the (barely) fictionalised story of these passionate old ladies and their relationship with Count Fersen,[66] set against the background of Capri society.

viii

During part of the time when the Mackenzies were beginning to enjoy the rich, sensuous, and intriguing tapestry of life on Capri which Douglas knew so well and had introduced them to, he himself was not far from them. He took Eric to Sant' Agata for three weeks and then for a week to Ischia.

Since Eric was now two years older, almost fifteen, longer walks were possible on this visit abroad than on the previous one. They made a little three-day tour, for instance, walking from Sant' Agata to Positano, where they spent the night, and then walking on the following day to Agerola. On the third day they got up at 4 a.m. and walked with a guide to the top of Mte Sant' Angelo (4735 ft). The guide pointed out their path down the mountain, which took them to Moiano and Vico Equense, and then returned to Agerola. At Vico they caught the tram to Sorrento, and a carriage took them back to Sant' Agata.

They visited Crapolla, where Eric met a character from *Siren Land* for whom Douglas had much affection:

> Crapolla is only a little place with a few huts of Fisherboats. There is also a very old man whose name is Garibaldi he has lived in this place for years and he is very bad he will not be alive next year. When we got there no fishermen were there only old Garibaldi . . .

They returned to Crapolla a week later, but did not see Garibaldi. He died in the following year, in September. Douglas kept the notice of his death – written by hand on a piece of cheap writing paper, but in the usual formal style – until the end of his own life. No one could have wished for a better epitaph than the few lines Douglas had already written about Garibaldi (whose real name was Giuseppe Persico) in *Siren Land:*

> . . . no one knows better how to catch the wary *cernia* as it lies hidden among the rocks; if he wished, he could be as rich as a king. But money slips like sea-water through his fingers, and when he makes a good catch, he prefers to treat his friends. For forty years he has known no other life than this . . . carving out a quiet existence for himself in this secluded nook, where he now potters about, blithe and loquacious, in his leaky black tub. So he lives, this *cigale* of seventy summers, reckless of tomorrow and often gaily fasting for days together when his purse is empty. All too soon, I fear, he will be found lying lifeless upon the stone floor of his hut (his bed was pawned thirty years ago and never redeemed) and there will be one gentleman less on earth.

Brooks came over from Capri for the night and either brought with him or collected on the mainland a certain Pasqualino whom Eric refers to as "my Italian friend". They all four went short walks together, idled in cafés, talked and smoked . . .

Douglas and Eric were back in London by June 9th.

CHAPTER FIFTEEN

London: Albany Mansions
1914

i

Douglas had completed *Old Calabria* by the end of 1913, possibly earlier, though the manuscript may not have been ready to send out. He was working, of course, at the same time, at intervals, on *South Wind*. But in spite of all this and his work for the *English Review*, he had begun, in his evenings and weekends, to collect London street lore, a quest which he pursued with all the ardour he had once put into the collection of stones and birds and reptiles. The first fruits of this pursuit were printed in the *English Review* in November 1913 under the title *In Our Alley*.

His own children, as opposed to those in the streets, were flourishing, but he did not have a great deal of time to devote to them. He visited them when he could; and from time to time they visited him; but when they did, they were liable to have to fend for themselves. Robert, his younger son, remembered arriving in London from school to spend a few days with his father before travelling north to Yorkshire for Christmas. At St Pancras there was no sign of his father; but a large policeman asked if his name was Douglas: "Your Dad asked me to give you this; he got tired of waiting." On a slip of paper was the address of the *English Review*. The office was closed when Robert got there, but pinned to the door was a note which read: "Gone to Gennaro's for dinner. Follow." When at last he found the restaurant, three hours after his arrival, it was nine o'clock. Gennaro himself welcomed him: "Ah, your pappa is gone 'ome ten minutes ago. 'E leave this note for you." It read: "Gone home, what's the matter with you?" And when Robert finally reached the flat in Albany Mansions: "Ah! There are you . . . Are you hungry?"

Douglas' position as a father was difficult. He had to spend many hours a week at the *Review* offices, and when he was not there, he usually had at least two books on hand that he not only wanted to write, but also needed to write in order to earn what little extra money they might bring him. Thus he was either out at work, or working in the flat. In either case, it was his habit to give Robert half a crown and tell him to go out and not return until six or seven o'clock. The son has described how his father would then struggle into a clean starched collar and dress to a running commentary on "the idiocy of all men for allowing themselves to be imposed upon to the extent of wearing the clothes they do". Then out would come his antique Russian snuff box of silver in which he kept his sovereigns and half sovereigns, and they would set off out for dinner. As like as not they would go to Gennaro's and meet friends such as John Mavrogordato, Conrad, or George Thomas:[67]

> I would eat a vast quantity of spaghetti followed by an indigestibly large portion of Neapolitan ice cream, and then, without further ceremony, I would be dumped into a nearby motion picture house until such time as my father and his friends had finished their conversations. A tap on my shoulder in the dark of the movie palace would startle me as I sat enthralled at the sight of Red Indians surrounding the covered wagons. Thus was I collected, and home we went, about midnight. If either of us were hungry then, and usually enough we both were, he would fix up a snack of some kind. For bedtime reading I was handed "Tales of Mystery and Imagination" by Edgar Allan Poe. Thus did my father complete his contribution to my education for life.

Whether or not the last sentence is intended to be sarcastic, it is certainly ambiguous; but from one point of view, not necessarily the worst, all these experiences undoubtedly were educational.

ii

If they were not going to Gennaro's, they might be setting off for Edith Grove via Battersea Bridge and the World's End Passage. The latter was a long narrow ill-lit alley running through the slums of Chelsea, shabby, stinking, and occasionally dangerous. Sounds of brawling from outside the pub at one end, and the deep shadows cast at night by three street lamps, were in particular frightening to a boy who spent nearly all his time either at boarding school or in the countryside; but the place "never failed to inspire my father to unprecedented heights of reminiscence":

> "Just here" he said musingly, while he tapped with his walking stick against a doorway surmounted by barbed wire and broken bottle glass, "Just here, a woman had her head bashed in by some chap who must have thought she had a shilling in her purse. He cut her throat too; with a piece of that glass!" We walked on a bit farther. "You see all those cats? Well, every now and then, those restaurant fellows come down

here and catch all they can and kill them. They use cats' brains to make that whipped cream you're so fond of!"

The cats' brains story (sometimes varied to horses' brains) was a favourite tease; and such "recollections" as he here made of death and villainy in the World's End Passage were apt to punctuate the memories of his walking companions like milestones. All through life he was accompanied by this desire to shock and possibly frighten; it went with him wherever he went, like a small shadow or an outer skin; sometimes it seemed to be a means of warning off bores – an *épater-les-bourgeois* attitude; more often it was a deliberate provocation of friends and companions – to mention in their presence some subject which he knew or guessed they disliked; sometimes it may have been his personal equivalent of the practical joke that was endemic in the Edwardian era amongst the middle and upper classes; and sometimes it was just one more means of expressing "knowingness", of demonstrating that he was no fool, that he knew his way about, and that no one could pull the wool over *his* eyes.

Robert's account of an evening at Edith Grove, though it may be slightly self-pitying, and may consciously or unconsciously wish to demonstrate that his father was not a model one, is worth quoting at length:

I was a silent, utterly silent, spectator at these gatherings . . . I usually sat in somewhat miserable loneliness on a hassock, which always, by some mischance of the devil, managed to move itself, with me on it, into the centre of the big studio. My father, observing my unhappy face, would call out from the piano:

"Do you want a chocolate? Give him a cigarette, Mu! One of your good ones. Nothing cheap and nasty!"

"But it'll make him sick, Norman!" Muriel Draper would protest.

"What of that? He looks sick now! Give him two – he might as well learn to smoke now as later on!"

I was given the cigarette – and was not sick. After all, at the age of eleven, in a roomful of strange people, buzzing with talk of incomprehensible things . . . jokes that I could not understand then but would appreciate now, music that was far more incomprehensible than Greek to me, filled with the scent of fat wax candles that threw their flickering light into the shadowy corners of that warm, human arena of artistic lions, the aromatic perfume of burning birch and cedar logs on the enormous hearth . . . decidedly I could not refuse a cigarette, and I owed it to my eleven-year-old dignity not to be sick, not in front of all those people. . . .

The studio was built out into the garden and there was a steep flight of stairs connecting it with the dining room which was part of the original house. At the appropriate time I would go to the dining room, hovering as close to my father as I dared without annoying him and saying nothing until he was aware of my existence – which he acknowledged by passing me a plate heaped with selections from the entire buffet table. Everything from lobster mayonnaise and gelatine of chicken to ice cream and Gorgonzola cheese was piled on one plate and I was bidden to go and eat in the now deserted studio: "And don't you dare to be sick! It isn't at all the thing to be sick in front of other guests! There's a big fireplace in the studio; remember that: if you haven't time to get to the you-know-where!"

iii

While Robert was being stuffed with food, his mother, who at the beginning of 1914 was living in Munich, had barely enough to eat. This, by her own account, was the seventh consecutive year in which she had had no news of any sort of her children. She had very little money, perhaps only what she earned from writing stories and sketches, and from translating. In this respect her case seems to have been at least as bad as "Violet's" – in the novel of that name – if not worse. In January she wrote to her sister that she was dreadfully depressed, and had no one to talk to: "I often feel it would be best if I took an overdose of Veronal, and so found peace at last." She was plagued by a multitude of little problems that drove her half mad; but the immediate cause of her troubles was Aram, author of the novel *Violet*; he was also a journalist for whom she worked. He had given her ten political articles to translate and had made her believe that they were written to order for a newspaper: she had therefore expected to be paid as soon as the translations were done:

I worked like a maniac the whole day to get them done, as I required the money more necessarily than ever before. Today he writes that the articles are not yet accepted, and also require "filing" . . . It now seems to me, as if these articles were not written to order at all, in which case God knows when I shall be paid, or else that he is trying to cut down the payment by saying *now* that they are not sufficiently well translated. I had firmly counted upon getting that money. A few days ago Dora got my last 20M for the household, and since about a fortnight I have given up having any lunch at all, so as to save. When those 20M are done, I have'nt *as yet* the faintest idea what we are going to live on, or how we shall buy coals.

As it is, I only have a fire in my sitting room. My bedroom is like an ice cellar, which is very bad for my lung, and my cough is *much* worse. Besides all this, I ought to pay 50M for my typewriter this month, else I risk that it gets fetched by the shop, and then I am absolutely done for . . .

Forgive me for writing all this, but you know that it does one good to speak openly to someone who loves and understands one.

No doubt better times will come, and if only my health holds out, I daresay I shall fight it through, as I have fought through worse things. But if my body is underfed, and my lungs ill treated by ice cold air – well if I do pull through, I am tougher than I thought.

It is terribly cold, and today snowing again.

Write me a few consoling words, for love is the only thing that can give one courage. And dont tell the mother of my condition, she has botherations enough of her own.

With endless hugs and kisses I am ever your own darling

Elschen

"More necessarily than ever before" is an eccentric usage; so also is "filing" when most English people would have written "polishing"; and so is the definite article in front of "mother". If Elsa translated Aram's articles into this kind of English, he would have had cause for complaint. It is therefore possible that Elsa was not entirely blameless in this distressing business, although she evidently felt herself to be a victim of deliberate deception or scheming. One suspects that reduced health and circumstances may have prepared the ground for a slightly paranoid outlook. She returns to the theme of Aram's apparent unscrupulousness in her next letter, written on the following day – the response to the first one had obviously been instantaneous and generous:

My own most adored one

If I had known you were going to do a thing like that, I would never have breathed a word of my present difficulties. Darling, it is *wicked* and angelic of you, and I assure you, if it were'nt for Dora and the dogs, I would have sent it you back, because I know you have'nt got it to spare either. At least I can send it you back the instant I get this infernal Honorar. Meanwhile, let me bless and hug you a hundred thousand times . . .

It is all Aram's fault; he pretended I should receive the money the instant that the articles are translated – I nearly hetzed myself to death to get them done, and now he calmly writes some alterations must be made, and heaven knows when I shall get paid.

Meanwhile I have got quite used to having no lunch, in fact only one meal a day, and it is extraordinary the amount one saves by that.

And I don't think this starvation cure will do me any harm, and will certainly teach me to be more careful than ever, when these "seven lean years" are over. But thanks to you my own beloved, we can at least eat, and need'nt freeze . . .

"Well, if I do pull through, I am tougher than I thought": that phrase, in the first letter, is pure Norman; as also, in the second, is "this infernal Honorar". As to pulling through, no one can say for certain, in the light of what was to happen, whether she succeeded or not.

iv

If Douglas could be held to be largely responsible for Elsa's plight, he could, on the other hand, be credited with having enriched the lives of many other people – such as the Mackenzies. They were now established on Capri not only in Caterola, but also in a tiny but delectable house called Rosaio in Anacapri which Compton Mackenzie used as a writing place; Caterola was given up to the entertainment of visitors. One of these was Martin Secker, who came out soon after Christmas 1913. Arthur Eckersley of *Punch*, and a friend from Mackenzie's Oxford days, also came.[68] Likewise Bertram Binyon, the singer, whose mother had been a Capri girl; and later John Mavrogordato.

Mackenzie was received into the Catholic Church. Edwin Cerio[69] finished building Casa Solitaria, perched high on and over the edge of a precipitous cliff, which the Mackenzies would also occupy. Munthe told Faith bluntly that her husband would never get rid of his sciatica as long as he lived in Caterola; and

> Norman Douglas was there too that spring. He had injured an ankle and rode about like Silenus on his ass, with Rosina the donkey-woman, the prettiest wife on the Piazza, magnificently and it seemed perpetually pregnant, digging lustily at the haunches of the lagging beast . . .
>
> Spring, 1914, was a variation on spring, 1913. There were no gay parties at the Villa Torricella, for the old ladies [the Wolcott-Perrys] were touring the world with Count Jack. 1914 was rustic and more amusing. Norman Douglas knew all the best places to eat in Capri and Anacapri, and a few bottley lunches and dinners on vine-shaded terraces convinced me that in the right company here was the most enjoyable form of entertainment.

E. F. Benson[70] was also in Capri that spring in the house which he shared partly with Brooks and partly with Somerset Maugham, though all three were hardly ever there together. The news of the assassination at Sarajevo, he wrote, caused only a ripple in their serenity; but Compton

Mackenzie wrote later: "I declared that this murder would mean a European war." He had signed a contract with Edwin Cerio for Casa Solitaria, and when the Mackenzies left the island in July Cerio was having special dinner services made for the new house:

> He was as excited about the house as we were, and would have it all furnished and ready with linen when we returned from England in the autumn. Caterola was evacuated without regret, Nannina . . . was left in charge of Rosaio, and we went back to stay in Martin Secker's home at Iver, a perfect Queen Anne house called Bridgefoot.

At Bridgefoot Mackenzie sat up all night and every night for two months, writing the last three hundred pages of *Sinister Street,* but towards the end of August he took a day off to visit friends in the country near Tring, and they all went over to see D. H. Lawrence, who was living in a cottage not far away. He and Frieda had been married for only five or six weeks, and war had descended on them; as Lawrence wrote later, his soul "lay in the tomb, not dead, but with a flat stone over it". Mackenzie suggested that he should return to Italy (where he and Frieda had lived for seven or eight months before the war), and offered him Rosaio, adding that everyone thought the war would be over by the spring. Lawrence said he would remember the offer; and five years later, when he went to Capri, he did.

At the beginning of November the Mackenzies returned to Capri, to live in Casa Solitaria, Mackenzie having failed so far to get himself into the war. They found the house

> quaintly furnished by Edwin Cerio with a set of ceremonial Venetian arm-chairs of surprising discomfort, Maxim Gorky's writing-table, which was about seven feet long and covered with green baize, a divan the size of a small room, from Gorky's Capri house . . . From [the] terrace we could see the moon rise over the Sorrentine peninsula and watch the dolphins playing round the Monacone rock below us . . .

v

Three months later, in February 1915, *Old Calabria* was published. It was at once recognised as "one of the few genuine solid books of travel of this century", and as perhaps more enjoyable than any of the others. Reviewers and critics welcomed it, with lavish praise. R. A. Scott-James[71] who reviewed it in the *English Review*, also wrote a note to Douglas: "It is a *great book*, my dear Sir, exquisite and inimitable", and Eden Phillpotts[72] interrupted his reading of it:

It is a comely, beautiful book, & reading it I feel this must be the absolute & only way to write travel. A cunning, crafty book, for never was matter arranged with such tact to carry its full weight & balance the natural humour & subtle levity of the scribe. How the devil do you do it? You'll get some good healthy rapture from the critics, who, though purblind beasts speaking generally, do manage to spot a superlative thing when they've broken their shins over it. The learning alone must challenge. I do congratulate you on this most distinguished & beautiful book, Norman Douglas. . . . And I do gratefully thank you for the gift of it. And I honour the labour & the rare art. Do come west & favour us with a visit if only from Saturday till Monday. Now to return to "Old Calabria".

Another congratulatory letter which has survived came from Compton Mackenzie:

Dear Duggie

Your book is great, and I havent so well enjoyed the quality of your reading for a long time. You won't sell a copy, and you're very lucky because you may hope to escape being drowned in a vomit of undigested criticism. I've concluded that popularity is a curse. I'm worrying [illegible] about our joint travel book and I hope its going to come off.

Now what about coming out here? Are you coming this May. I shall be finished with my work and we can have a really amusing time. Love to all

Yours ever
MCM

The joint travel book was never written . . .

Richard Curle let Douglas know that he was going to review *Old Calabria* for the Times Literary Supplement. "That sounds very nice," Douglas replied, ". . . and I am sure you will do something noble. But as that paper is run (insidiously) on ultra-Catholic lines, I would suggest your saying nothing about my Voltairean principles, else it might make them look up the book and cut out the whole review (nothing about my treatment of saints etc)." After this warning, Curle evidently wrote asking Douglas to say what he would select as the chief virtues of the book, or what he would like mentioned or emphasised in a review. He was not left in doubt:

63 etc
3 Mar [1915]

Dear Curle,

That's rather a puzzler, you know! What the Hell am *I* to suggest? You might advert to a certain golden humanity and equipoise running through the whole – breadth of outlook; to the suggestive and original scholarship displayed in chapters like IV, XIV, XXXVIII; to the intimate knowledge of Italian conditions revealed in chapters VIII, XVI (postscript), XXXIII; sympathetic treatment of landscape and personalities – vignette-fashion – thumb-nail sketches; intellectual rather than emotional tone running through the whole; that the book gives a stimulating account of Calabria, its history and scenery, and yet is, essentially, rather a human document than anything else – the revelation of a complex but charming personality etc. There you are! Put it on as thick as you like; only don't touch those real masterpieces chapters X,XXXI. You might say that it is astonishing what a literature has gathered round south Italy, of which the ordinary Englishman knows nothing, p. 181 & 186, and of which *I* give glimpses. The Milton discovery ought to be mentioned; also what the Ital. Gov't are doing about malaria. You might say that it is creditable to Secker to bring out a book of this kind just now. That the final chapter gives the keynote of *pagan serenity* which runs through the whole. What I say about Horace p. 42; about English and Italian mentality p. 91 – in fact, damned if I can tell you any more. Index will help you to get one or two things. Zestfulness of the whole – natural history, legends and lore, colour-sense of peasantry, brigands, deforestation, eucalyptus-trees, suicides – see index! Love of elemental things: sun, forests, mountains, women (p. 205), torrent-beds 292, wine 307. Glowing and gentlemanly patina of erudition. Chapter on "Musolino and the Law". I am sending you a letter from Eden Phillpotts which may stimulate you: please return it. That the book contains an entire philosophy of life – a guide to conduct. There! I can't think of anything more *nice* to say, and I will leave you to discover – as you doubtless have done – its many deficiencies.

Conrads were here to tea yesterday. I wrote you to No 95 – nothing important; merely to say that I expected you on Monday.

Yours

N D

P.S. Why are you A. B. Curle?
And why no Esquire?
A.B. – what's that?
Able-bodied Seaman?

Yes; Curle had recently become an Able-bodied Seaman in the RNAAS, and a description, in his next letter, of his duties, aroused in Douglas a certain schoolboyish humour which lay very near the surface of his personality ever ready to be tapped by any sympathetic stimulus:

63 etc
5 Mar

Dear Curle

Thanks for yours, with the atrocious handwriting which the devil only can decypher and which – as much of it as I could read, at least – caused me to chuckle inwardly. But after all, you *are* doing something; and seeing life from another aspect, even if you do nothing but clean out shit-houses all day (By the way, you might come and have a look down *my* drains, when you get a day off: there is the hell of a stink coming up from those regions and I rather fancy that the lady in [sic] the floor above mine has got rid of an illegitimate infant and rammed its remains down the WC, where they have got stuck for the last 3–4 days, sending up these pestilential odours; a brief examination by a specialist like yourself will soon clear up the matter)

How much longer are you staying there? You had better apply for a DSO on the ground that altho' you may not have seen active service in the trenches, you are nevertheless one of those humble heroes who, by clearing out shit-houses, are plainly in the same category with the great Hercules and his performance at the Augean stables.

What comforts are you going to get? Bronco-paper? Or do you still have to use your hands, and if so, which hand? I enclose you one sheet of bronco-paper, just for auld lang syne – you can dangle it in front of your adjutant-general or whoever your boss may be, and tell him that altho' he may be a bloody patriot and use only his hands, you are going to set an example in the matter of cleanliness and hygiene to the rank and file (more *rank* than file, eh?) and you will halve the sheet with him if he undertakes to get you a VC by the end of next week.

No wonder you don't feel inclined for Calabria under such excremen-tatious and stercophile conditions. But you should see the shit-houses in Calabria and, above all, you should smell them! And the long white worms – intestinal – wriggling about among the decomposing ordure and complaining bitterly of their cold environment after the warm nests they have left behind. There is a good notice of the book, by the way, in this week's Punch (talking of shit).

The Conrads leave tomorrow. I hope to see them for a moment this afternoon, but I may not get off. You had better write that review in sections, and begin with a prelude to the effect that the war has its inevitable effects upon the literary profession and that doubtless many other critics have found themselves in the same patriotic fix as yourself – to wit, with a pen in one hand and a gallon of liquid regimental shit in the other, both clamouring loudly for your attention etc. etc. You might write something quite "tasty" on those lines.

Yours ever
N D

Most critics pronounce *Old Calabria* Douglas' masterpiece, differing, as such people often do, from the popular preference, which is for *South Wind*. *Old Calabria* therefore has acquired through the last five or six decades a reputation disproportionate to the number of people who have read it. For my own part, I think his non-fiction is in a sense indivisible as to the quality of the writing. Yet certain works have in addition an excellence of shape and form which makes them almost perfect: *London Street Games, Summer Islands, Some Limericks, Paneros* – it is difficult to believe that the subjects with which they deal could have been treated more successfully by their author in any other way. It may be said that perfection is not difficult to achieve in such a small scale: what of the longer works? Of these, I would say that *Siren Land* comes almost into the category of perfection; but that the remaining travel books fall a little behind this level, though they may make up in substance, depth, or charm for what they may lack in architectural unity. It is the latter quality which I find deficient in *Old Calabria*.

It is a weightier and more encyclopaedic exploration of its area than his two previous books of travel were of theirs. It is also a good illustration of Douglas' well-known definition of what a travel book should be:

> It seems to me that the reader of a good travel-book is entitled not only to an exterior voyage, to descriptions of scenery and so forth, but to an interior, a sentimental or temperamental voyage, which takes place side by side with that outer one; and that the ideal book of this kind offers us, indeed, a triple opportunity of exploration – abroad, into the author's brain, and into our own. The writer should therefore possess a brain worth exploring; some philosophy of life – not necessarily, though by preference, of his own forging – and the courage to proclaim it and put it to the test; he must be naif and profound, both child and sage.

The progression towards this ideal can be traced from *Siren Land* to *Together*. The first book starts from the traditional point of view with more landscape and more history than self-revelation. Apart from the two biographical chapters, it has a close unity of time and place – the time, whatever episode of the past may be under consideration, always being firmly united to the present, to the actual physical aspect of the Sorrentine peninsula and Capri. *Fountains in the Sand*, again, is wonderfully strong in impressing the senses: the figure of the author, collecting prehistoric flints, suffering from the cold, smoking *kif*, meditating, looms a little larger than in the first book. When one has finished reading *Fountains*, one has become acquainted with a distinct individual who begins to take shape in the mind.

Material rejected by the publisher from *Siren Land* finds its way into *Old Calabria* which also deals with the southern half of Italy and here, while there may not be proportionately much more autobiographical material in the sense of factual information about the author, we are treated to a good many fully expressed opinions on a large number of subjects and are given a fairly extensive notion of his philosophy. By the time of *Alone*, written in a much more relaxed and mellow style, conversational rather than literary, a beguiling informality enables the author to slip in and out of the autobiographical mood with perfect ease, and also to refrain from giving us those extensive dissertations on certain specialised subjects which have sometimes proved a shade tedious. In *Together*, the opposite extreme from *Siren Land* is reached: autobiography replaces landscape and history as the principal feature of the book, although all these elements are successfully integrated with each other, and the book gains much from concentrating on a small area.

Old Calabria, then, stands midway in the series of travel books, and is one of four books deriving from his experiences and researches in southern Italy, the others being *Siren Land, South Wind*, and the Capri monographs. It is a portmanteau into which he crammed almost all the material on South Italy, available at the time of writing, which might conceivably be thought of as likely to appeal to an intelligent reader. The material, as usual, is of two kinds: that which derives from research, and that which derives from observation. Sometimes the former is presented in large un-adulterated chunks, such as whole chapters which alternate with chapters of personal observation – for example, x and xi, or xxxi and xxxii – but more often in smaller sections or even in successful mixtures. The general effect is of the table-talk of a polymath richly endowed with all the know-ledge necessary to recreate an impression of life as it was in those parts at any time in the past, from the palaeolithic to the parliamentary age, and with a perceptive eye for the present and the future. The wide learning displayed, the entertaining speculations and comments, the prodigious capability of the author both as traveller and unraveller – these are the virtues of Douglas which have been so often and so justly described and praised. That characteristically Douglasian appreciation of the things of the soil, a sensuous, intellectual, and intuitive enjoyment of simple tradi-tional tasks, of time-honoured ritual, and of the weather-beaten people who through unnumbered generations have doggedly transmitted this basic culture to us through countless natural and man-made disasters, is evident here as in *Siren Land*, but is less generally pervasive. This particular flavour, of humanity as a continuation of antique man, close to earth, in a large landscape seen steadily and un-idealised, may be found in such chapters as viii, xix and xx which, to my mind, are those which best convey to the reader the sensation of being in Calabria. The question is whether, from an artistic point of view, so much, of so diverse a nature, should have been put into a single book. There is not much continuity of mood, nor even a mild concentration of purpose overall, to unify the material here brought together. There is not even any logical sense of progression in the author's actual travels from place to place; his movements about the country are haphazard and zigzag. The book is more like an anthology of all the author's notes and writings which can be justified by the title. Here and there he has written in linking passages in an attempt to disguise this fact; but otherwise we are asked to take it or leave it.

One cannot have everything, but where so much is given, one would have liked more, just that little more that might have been given by a great artist, but which Douglas only seems to have been able or willing to give in his novels. He seems to have been content to leave his travel books without much form. Why, for instance, is the Milton article dropped into the book unmodified, so that it sticks out of its context like a priest in a playhouse; and why are we told so much – too much – about St Joseph of Copertino, and about Southern Saintliness – all these three subjects being treated in a style of writing different from that of his observational chapters? The answer probably is that he either could not be bothered to try and reshape this material (in which he may have been right; perhaps it would not have been possible, or successful) or that he was reluctant to jettison the details of his findings after so much research. Again, why is there no introductory chapter which might help to unify the book? The book has an end, and a good one, but no beginning and no middle.

The end of the book, the last twenty-five pages or so, give it what unity it possesses simply by setting a mood, a valedictory one, and although not sticking to it, by returning to it. It is a mood of treble valediction through which we discover that we are not only saying good-bye to a unique guide who is saying good-bye to this actual Italian countryside, but he and we are both also saying good-bye to the whole of antiquity:

> From these brown stones that seam the tranquil Ionian, from this gracious solitude, the reader can carve out, and bear away into the cheerful din of cities, the rudiments of something clean and veracious

and wholly terrestrial – some tonic philosophy that shall foster sunny mischiefs and farewell regret.

Thus only towards the very end of the book do we discover the reality of the pilgrimage we have made through time and space. In retrospect the apparently disjointed information and impressions we have received appear to coalesce. They appear to; but it cannot truthfully be said that they do, for while we are reading the book we are only conscious of a great number of disparate pieces of information, relating both to the present and the past. It is hardly – as one reviewer claimed – an apprehension of what Goethe called "that living life which shifts and fluctuates about us"; that description better fits D. H. Lawrence's *Sea and Sardinia*. Nor does *Old Calabria* supplant Gissing's limpid and immaculate though lighter-weighted account of the same country; by a multiplicity of images and information it confuses as much as it clarifies. It would never do as a work of reference, and will not quite do as a work of art. It is an omnium-gatherum of everything more or less relevant to the subject, displayed with characteristic pride and prodigality by the collector. The guiding principle, or lack of it, reminds one of the contents of the trunks and boxes described by Vanda (p. 66) or of the lists of assorted objects he made when preparing for a journey.[73] He carried just such an odd assortment, of information, in his head. It is the book fundamentally of an eccentric, but it provides intriguing glimpses of actual places and engaging details about living or historical people, and scans dark corners of the past with an intelligent and illuminating eye. It stimulates, but does not quite satisfy; visiting Calabria, one would rather take Baedeker and a set of the ancient classics and work out one's own salvation. The treasures which intrinsically belong to this book, as part of the actual travels and observations, and not part of a theoretical book on Calabria, are autobiographical: the walk over the Sila and across Aspromonte, the eyewitness account of the mountain festival, and the philosophical reflections at the end, remain vividly in the memory. Much of the rest smells too much of ancient folios.

This, I am aware, is a heretical opinion, not generally shared by Douglas enthusiasts, and the reader had better look elsewhere for contrary views.

CHAPTER SIXTEEN

London: Tribulations
1915–1916

i

The obscenities of excessive patriotism, which were a distinguishing feature of that war, penetrated even the peacefulness of Capri. Faith Mackenzie, whose husband had gone to war in the Middle East in May, got into trouble for continuing a nodding acquaintanceship with a Prussian lady who was married to an Italian, and an Englishwoman on the island "boasted that she had put out her tongue to the Prussian woman". A friend had gone out from England to keep Mrs Mackenzie company after the departure of her husband, and the faithful Brooks was frequently in attendance, but by mid-July she had gone to London where she engaged in war work, packing books or making slippers for wounded soldiers. She saw a good deal of Douglas at this time, dining with him at Gennaro's or exploring London in his company. It was

> some compensation for the loss of Monty's perpetually diverting society. Norman was looking for war work of some kind, which meant that he had plenty of time on his hands, and so had I, between shifts at the canteen.
>
> Ribaldry was the basis of our friendship, and I don't know a better one. It is a solid foundation. Whether we were sitting under a tree in the strange little back garden of a pub somewhere near Strand-on-the-Green, or plunging through a swamp in the middle of Richmond Park on a pitch dark night after a bottle of Tokay, or sitting late over dinner at Gennaro's, the tang of his salty conversation delighted me.
>
> "Are you Satan, perhaps?"
>
> "Perhaps."

In November Mackenzie was given leave, and wired for his wife to join him on Capri, which she was only too glad to get back to. Douglas, who did not leave England at all in 1915 – the only year of his life until then lived wholly in England – must have wished to go with her.

"Norman was looking for war work of some kind", wrote Faith

Mackenzie. Exactly when he began looking for such work, how hard he tried to get it, and how long he persevered, we do not know. The introduction to *Alone*, which, when published separately, was called *The Tribulations of a Patriot*, need not be regarded as true word for word, though in spirit it almost certainly is. It recounts an experience, or a series of experiences, that were only too typical both of that war and the later one. It is probable that Douglas offered his services in some capacity he thought suitable – for a position in which his knowledge of languages or his experience in the Foreign Service would have been useful – and that when he encountered the wastage of talent, the confusion of purpose, and the crass pigheaded obstructionism of bureaucracy, he didn't press his claims. He was, after all, one quarter German, both his parents had lived all their lives in Austria, and Austria more than anywhere else was his homeland. He was therefore in a better position than most people in England to know what utter nonsense and infamy was being perpetrated in the name of Allied propaganda. In 1923, referring to his book *Alone*, he wrote that during the war he had "really felt *alone*, surrounded by a legion of imbeciles hacking each other in pieces." This sounds, and is meant to sound, devoid of sympathy and compassion; it is Douglas justifying his reasonable (and incidentally, kind and considerate) self by a harsh and emotional criticism of others. It is Douglas converting a defensive position into an attacking one which becomes so exaggeratedly offensive (the desire to shock seizing the opportunity) that he exposes himself to greater criticism than he would have if he had been content with the initial statement, for he continues: "An exhilarating sensation: and one that has not quite faded away. May it never do so". His real feelings are revealed in his restrained lamentations for departed friends such as Rupert Brooke, Philip Baynes, Edward Thomas, the Amitrano boy, and a good many others.

The Tribulations of a Patriot is Douglasian irony *con brio*, and stamped with the hall mark of his individuality, particularly the refrain "Tried the War Office? I had", and in the ending, which sets the tone for the book which follows:

So luck pursued me to the end, though it never quite caught me up. For bags were packed, and tickets taken. And therefore:
"What did you do in the Great War, grandpapa?"
"I loafed, my boy."
"That was naughty, grandpapa."
"Naughty, but nice . . ."

This delighted and unashamed acceptance of escape to pleasure, coming as it does after numerous pages describing the dreariness of officialdom at work, and of a country groaning under the burden of an appalling national effort, has a wide significance beyond its immediate context, as Douglas' whole attitude to life exemplifies. All that is relevant at the moment is the experience described – or caricatured – in this effective piece of irony. Whether he endured everything described may be doubted; but two of the people designated by capital letters existed – one was a Rothenstein,[74] and the other, who revealed in print that he had recognised his portrait, was Humbert Wolfe. Bearing these two gentlemen and their names and race in mind, a regret must be expressed that Douglas should have found it necessary to insist that there was a high proportion of young Jews in those safe bureaucratic jobs: "Was there some secret society which protected them? Or were they all so preposterously clever that the Old Country would straightway evaporate into thin air unless they sat in some comfortable office, *while our own youngsters were being blown to pieces out yonder*?" (My italics). Making all due allowances for the climate of opinion at the time, when "Jew" was still a term of abuse applied to anyone who drove a hard bargain, or swindled or cheated, it is sad to see Douglas, who was the least prejudiced of men, inviting comparison with common opinion about the Jews.

The subject of Douglas is introduced with typical suavity into Humbert Wolfe's artificial reminiscences of Arnold Bennett.[75] Scott-Moncrieff[76] is present as well as Wolfe and it is the former who speaks first, referring to Douglas, whose name Wolfe has mentioned:

"And if I admire, like any man of taste and intelligence, that great author, do I, may I inquire, incur your censure? Possibly you know a better contemporary writer. Perhaps indeed you write better yourself." "Young men, young men, young men" Arnold intervened. "Young," fumed Scott-Moncrieff, "the man's fifty if he's a day. Or do you think," he turned to me, "that you would be admitted to the Ballila?" "You are perfectly right about my age," I replied, "but you know the saying, those whom the gods love die young, those whom Norman Douglas dislikes are born old." "And why did he dislike you?" inquired Scott-Moncrieff; "though, mind you," he added generously, "I do not in the least blame him." "I don't blame him myself. Have you read 'Together'?" "It is not a favourite of mine," said Scott-Moncrieff, "but I have glanced through it." "There is a passage," I said, "in which Norman Douglas records how in search of a job during war-time he was introduced to the room of a certain *embusqué*. 'A plump, though not ill-looking, young Hebrew was Mr W.' But it seemed that in spite of his plumpness, his comparative absence of ugliness and above all his Hebraic ancestry he could not 'place' Mr Douglas. The writer permitted himself to wonder why this Jewkin was not dispatched to the front."

"And why weren't you?" asked Scott-Moncrieff. "You were indispensable, I suppose." "No," I said, "merely indistinguishable." "And because of this incident wholly discreditable to yourself you venture to deprecate the author of 'South Wind'." "On the contrary, I adore him. I would almost as soon have written 'South Wind' as Shelley's 'Ode to the West Wind'. I ventured indeed to dedicate a poem 'The Locri Faun' to Mr Norman Douglas without his permission 'from his unknown admirer Mr W'. He never acknowledged it." "It was probably a very bad poem," suggested Scott-Moncrieff. "Certainly, I should think." "But it does not explain why you did not get him a job." "Well, no – as to that – there was this reason and that reason. It had been indicated to me that at that particular moment in England he would not be a success." "Success," shouted Scott-Moncrieff; "do you think a man like Norman Douglas needs success? Why success has been chasing him all his life and, thank God! never overtaken him."

"It had been indicated to me . . .", etc. This remark suggests that Douglas had become sufficiently careless in his conduct to allow of little doubt, at least in informed circles, about the more obvious objects of his personal interest. If no more was known, it was surely understood by this time that he was very much addicted to the company of young boys. An annotation in *Looking Back* makes it clear that by December 1915 at latest, even the office boy at the *English Review* was "one of his boys". As Douglas himself would have known, it is always dangerous to mix work and pleasure in this way. People notice, even when you don't think they do; and they talk; and word gets round and spreads to the most unlikely places.

ii

Archie, now seventeen and in his last year at Uppingham, wanted to study medicine. Whether he could or not was a question for Nelson to answer, since he would have to pay for the training. Nelson, alas, could not go quite this far in generosity; in fact, he was leaving London to live in the country in order to economise. He told Douglas that the best thing for Archie would be to sit for a Civil Service exam, a second division clerkship. Robert, who had failed an exam for direct entrance to the Navy, was destined for the *Worcester*, the training-ship which provided another means of access to both Royal and Merchant Navy service.

Douglas wrote at the beginning of the year (1916) that he was "fussed to within an inch of my life" – a phrase that he was to use many times in that life. Sometimes it meant that he had more to do than he thought he could cope with, sometimes that he was worried, and sometimes that he was suffering from the consequences of his pleasures: being harassed by police or busybodies or other actors in the drama of "living dangerously". Or . it meant that he was ill: rheumatism had a habit of occurring at such times; also at other times. And, as usual, there was no money. He asks Archie to join him at dinner with Mrs Le Butt at Gennaro's "but have a good tea beforehand as I *can't* afford a decent dinner" ("can't" is underlined eight times for emphasis); and "I have just remembered, by a miracle, that tomorrow is your birthday. I will try to find something for you, but probably, as you know, won't succeed. Money is not only tight, but extinct as the Dodo." Worse was to come: "I am leaving the E.R. at the end of this month," he writes in the middle of March. "Don't know in the least what will happen to me. It's rather awful." And on the 22nd: "I have left the E.R. and am looking out for some other job ... Don't write me any more to the E.R.; or call there, or ring me up there. I have done with it, and will not be there again. So don't go near the place." Reason for leaving – not known. What is known is that the *English Review* owed him money.

Money was tight, certainly; so much so, that he had sent out stories (under pseudonyms) from *Unprofessional Tales*, and during the course of the year four of them, by "Wilfrid Hale", "Edward Morris", "E. F. Lyubin" and "Albany Clifford", appeared in a journal called *Ideas*, which, incidentally, changed their titles. He had even asked Pinker to try to place *London Street Games* in America, surely a desperate undertaking. And Archie was put off in the Easter holidays: "I have nothing to eat in this place and nothing to drink; no cooking done beyond maccheroni [sic] & eggs. There is no bedding or pillows to spare. I must work all the morning." And, "If I don't hear, I will be at *Gennaro's* on Thursday at one o'clock. Put me off in time, if you can, as I have an awful lot of things to do. I won't wait after 1.30, and there will be only 2/- worth of food, so you had better have a good breakfast." But that was only one aspect of the letters. They arrived, wherever Archie might be, at the rate of four or five a month, advising and encouraging, admonishing and trying at least to be understanding. They testify to parental responsibility of the right kind – Douglas showed that he was interested and concerned, and not merely conscious of his duties (which he may or may not have been). They also offer glimpses of Douglas in a characteristic moment of exasperation, as for instance with a doctor who had taken pains with an injury of Archie's at Uppingham: "What fools these English doctors are! X rays! What next. Everybody knows what that is: 2/6 would cure it. We deserve to be beaten by the German for being such damned idiots ... Did you, or did you not, show those blasted fools of doctors the prescription of the London man? I can, of course, believe anything of an English doctor. When I had malaria, which is the most *prevalent* disease on earth, they diagnosed it, in the *hospital*, as typhoid. Shits!" ("Hospital" is underlined four times for emphasis; and "shits!" it should be said, meant, in those days, or at any rate in Douglas' usage, "fools.")

"Have not found a job yet," he wrote to Archie at the Nelsons' on 16th April. "Things are heading for a crisis. Hope you are all doing well? Give my love to Auntie"; but less than a month later, he was in Capri: "I have a huge house to live in, all to myself, for which I pay nothing. Meals, gratis, for the most part . . . I am trying to finish writing that thing, and I make Mrs Mackenzie type it for me as I go along." "That thing" was *South Wind*, and he was living in two rooms of the empty Villa Behring. He had written four chapters of the book in January, and had hoped he would get through six more in February; so he would have gone out to Capri with a substantial portion of the book begun. At first he did not think he would be away for more than two or three weeks, he told Archie; but later he found that his writing became rather spasmodic "owing to the heat and owing to the laziness of Mrs Mackenzie who won't type as fast as she might. I have got through a lot here 35 chapters out of 50. Two more months ought to finish it." Faith Mackenzie, who typed what he had ready, recorded she "had hired a large and noisy Erard Grand from Naples, and this he used to play delightfully. Once he had studied music seriously in Germany, and his technique had rusted very little. Chopin, Bach (a lovely Chorale that no one ever plays was my favourite), and actually a number of hymn tunes which he played with enormous feeling, while I sang in my choirboy's voice, just faintly sharp all the time, 'Lead Kindly Light' and the rest."

Eventually, he arrived back in London on 15th August.

iii

London Street Games had been published in July, a handsome and sturdy little volume in thick boards covered with buckram, and printed on a good substantial paper which gave it an attractive bulk. He had finished the book during the previous summer, and sent it to Andrew Melrose, making the point he makes in the Preface, namely that he merely wishes to demonstrate the inventiveness of the children, not to write a professional treatise. "I think it stands on four legs, as a social document, without any further elaboration or expenditure of erudition. Five legs would be neither necessary, nor beautiful." "Dear Douglas," replied Melrose some three weeks later, "It is simple fact that your *Street Games* fills me with admiration for it as a literary achievement of the most difficult kind triumphantly done. It would be sheer humbug though to say that it is a publishing 'proposition' which any publisher wd venture on with the view of making money. In short I can't see a public for it & therefore I cannot submit it for my partner's approval. You know how gladly I shd publish something of yours?"

Several other publishers had been tried, with much the same result. For a while he had put the book aside, and concentrated in his spare time from the office on what was to become *South Wind*. Eventually, "with the help of a friend", he had had it published on commission by The St Catherine Press. The friend was Sir Lees Knowles, to whom the book is dedicated, and who also put up the money for the two final monographs on Capri: *Disjecta Membra*, and the *Index*, both of which had been printed in London in editions of 100 in January and May 1915.

Much is made of Douglas' scientific interests and writings, of his ability as a pianist, and his command of languages and dialects; it is usually forgotten that he could claim to be something of a sociologist as well.

His investigation of what might be called amateur poetry is not, as might at first appear, an excuse for having a bit of fun at the expense of sincere but unskilful writers of verse; it is a serious glance at that kind of buried literature which no one had bothered to look at before. It is the sort of study – or sketch for a study – that George Orwell might have undertaken, or that Mrs Queenie Leavis might have attempted as a successor to her admirable *Fiction and the Reading Public*.

Modern Minstrelsy was published in the *English Review* in January 1913. Ten months later, in November, it was followed by an article entitled *In our Alley*, about street games. Much of the material – and probably the idea – for this article came as a result of Douglas' friendship with Eric. This is virtually proved by Douglas' statement that he had been occupied with the subject since 4th November 1910, the day on which, or the day before, he met Eric. Eric's sister remembers Douglas giving her ten shillings when she was about twelve years old because she had helped him gather information about street games, and telling her that he would "buy her a beautiful pair of butterfly corsets when she was a lovely young lady", which latter remark made her mother dissolve into laughter. No sooner had a beginning been made, than collector's mania took over. His appetite for new specimens of games became insatiable; he pursued them all through the southern and eastern boroughs of London:

The collecting of these games gave me unbelievable trouble as well as pleasure; I found stalking these shy East-End (and S.E. and N.E.) children, and winning their confidence, the most arduous and exciting sport I had yet undertaken, especially in the case of the boys, who are far more distrustful than the girls. Those of them who could write described the games in their own fashion on scraps of paper . . . I made them control each other's descriptions, and these holographs, which I still possess, form a bundle weighing nine hundred grammes.

His son Robert has described how his father would leave the flat in Albany Mansions in the morning "with his pockets stuffed with rewards in the way of sweets, toy pistols, small dolls, cheap watches, and pennies with which to bribe the suspicious urchins to divulge their invented games". Notes in his pocket diary suggest that he may have got in touch with schoolteachers, presumably to ask them to collect descriptions of these games from their pupils, in the latters' own words. He certainly did this himself, and the result must be one of the earliest examples of field research, verbatim, in a large city. It anticipated the type of record that was made about twenty years later by Tom Harrisson's Mass Observation in numerous other subjects. If he had produced a treatise, he wrote, he would probably have found a publisher without much difficulty: "There is always a public for stodgy professorial dissertations on out-of-the-way subjects . . . That was not my aim. I wished to produce a social document, however unpretending. My point, my only point, was the inventiveness of the children. That is why I piled up the games into a breathless catalogue which, to obtain its full momentum and psychological effect, should be read through, *accelerando*, from beginning to end without a break."

The moral of the book is this: "if you want to see what children can do, you must stop giving them things. Because of course they only invent games when they have none ready-made for them, like richer folks have . . ." This moral is one that is much better known today than it was in 1916.

This is the least known of Douglas' books, and although not of such general interest as most of them, one of the best. In fact, it is difficult to see how it could be better, and I would have much less hesitation in calling it a masterpiece (as one perceptive reviewer did) than in applying the same term to *Old Calabria*. It achieves perfectly what it set out to do; it is most skilfully presented, so that the author's comments match the style of the "breathless catalogue" in tone and local colour; and it is just the right length. The concentration and intensity achieve a result which could fairly be called brilliant; and the recognised authorities on children's games* have called it a "pioneer work and social document of first importance":

It is a skilful prose-poem fashioned out of the sayings and terminology of Douglas's urchin friends; and we must admit that it was only after several years, when we ourselves had become familiar with the

*Opie, Peter & Iona, *The Lore and Language of Schoolchildren*, OUP 1959.

argot which the kids still speak in London's alleyways and tenement courts, that we appreciated the book's finer points.

The Opies reported that seventy-eight percent of the chants Douglas recorded were still being chanted in 1959.

Amongst those who liked the book was Edward Garnett: "I hugely enjoyed it. Warm congratulations! It is a fine piece of literature – the work of a scholar & it has all the delightful spontaneity of Rabelais in his list of Mediaeval Games. I shall want you to annotate my copy with one or two of the improper versions!"

After Douglas' return from Capri to London in August he simply had to "stick it out" and finish *South Wind*; but he was bored and missed his friends. Faith was in Capri; the Drapers had gone to America. Eric also had gone, swept away by the war, joining the army under age, and actually landing in France in June 1916, just before his eighteenth birthday. And how vile was London in the infernal gloom of war, compared with Capri! He got out of it when he could, especially to Wimbledon Common and Richmond and the Surrey hills; but in wartime London itself there was not much to be done, except "live dangerously". One could always go out and see what one could pick up. . . .

iv

On Tuesday 12th September in a column of brief news items in the *General Anzeiger* of the *Münchener Neuesten Nachrichten* the following item occurred:

> A woman living in Horscheltstrasse who was smoking a cigarette while lying in bed suffered extensive burns when her bedding accidentally caught fire. She was taken by ambulance to Schwabing Hospital.

On the following day, in the same column of the same journal, there was a further report:

> The death is announced in Schwabing Hospital of Elsa Douglas, who, as we reported yesterday, was severely burned on Monday in her apartment in Horscheltstrasse. Whether in fact there is a question of carelessness while smoking a cigarette, cannot be established. At all events, the unlucky woman had the misfortune to be burned while asleep, otherwise she could easily have called for help, since an electric bell was within reach of the bed. At eleven o'clock in the morning, according to the maid who looked after her, Mrs Douglas was still asleep. At a quarter to twelve the bell rang, and the maid, who had hurried to the room, found her mistress already severely burned. It is thought that the unlucky woman may have struck a match in order to see what the time

was – the window shutters were closed – and then have thrown the match away carelessly. In this way the bedding may have caught fire.

It would be difficult to think of a worse death; one must hope that what may have been the basic cause of the accident may at the same time have mitigated the suffering: for how could one be burned in one's sleep without leaving one's bed unless one were drugged, whether with alcohol or a sleeping draught or some other inhibitor of the senses?

Elsa had described herself as tortured by money worries and wondered if her poor health could stand the strains imposed upon it. "You my dear Mother know that I was always full of energy and steadfastness . . . I have lived for nine years without knowing if my children are still alive or have been ruined; I do not even know where they are, and now all my energy has gone and I am completely exhausted. I am no longer young and much too much alone."

Her elder son says her last words were: "Mein – Kind – in – England"; but there seems to be doubt as to how these words were conveyed to him. According to him they came from Elsa's sister, (Mrs) Violet Fairholme; but whether she was present at the hospital seems doubtful, for Violet's son says she never left Switzerland (to which she had moved on account of the war). Elsa's mother, Mrs Adèle FitzGibbon, was in England. No notice of her death appeared in England until 13th October, a month after her death, when it was announced in two places in *The Times*. And we do not know when Douglas himself first heard. He told Archie in October, and, Archie felt, "with a certain hint of spite. I expect you've heard he professed, half jokingly, to have the power of the evil eye. He showed me the Times announcement." It seems unlikely that he would have withheld the news from Archie, and therefore likely that he himself only heard the news in October.

It is true that he believed in the power of the evil eye;[77] there is written evidence that he went out of his way to avoid a certain witch because he believed she had the power to do him harm by means of the *jettatura*. As to his own power in this respect, it is impossible to tell whether he believed in it or not. Certainly, many times later in his life, as will be seen, he offered to "put the evil eye" on the enemies of his friends: "Sometimes it takes a long time", he would say, "but it works in the end." There is no evidence of any kind for any of this before the death of Elsa; it could well be that this half-serious belief, in so far as it existed, stemmed from this intimate and devastating example. If he had wished her dead, and even performed some simple home-made ritual in order to emphasise the deliberate "wickedness" of his desire, he would afterwards, undoubtedly, whatever his statements on the subject may have been, have felt desolated

by the manner of her death. To have felt guilt would have been insupportable, to have felt successful, after so long a time, might have seemed
ridiculous: yet the notion was not without its attractions, and it would be
interesting to see if it would work in the future. If he could make it work
once or twice, in such a manner that its power could hardly be doubted as
a reality? Meanwhile, better to treat the matter lightly – let those who will
believe him, and those who will not, believe that he is joking. He was to
tell certain friends, including Mrs Edward Hutton, "I burnt my wife . . .";
and would add, sweetly, as if conferring a blessing, ". . . but she *deserved*
it, my dear."

The notice of Elsa's death appeared in *The Times* on 13th October. On
17th October Douglas went down to the Linden Hall Hydro, at Bournemouth, and stayed there for the best part of a week. Was there any connection between the two events, and if so, did he go there to celebrate, or
to recuperate from the ghastly end to a long-drawn-out personal tragedy?

There was an odd epilogue to the story of Elsa's death. It was the
occasion of a strange comment allegedly made shortly afterwards by a
relation. According to Compton Mackenzie (*Octave V*, pp. 51–52), writing
of the year 1916, he asked Colonel W. E. Fairholme (cousin of both
Douglas and Elsa, and at that time Military Attaché at Athens) for help in
trying to get Douglas out to Greece for intelligence work:

"'That blackguard' he exclaimed. 'Never! Do you know I've just heard
that his unhappy wife whom he treated so abominably was burned to
death recently in a Munich brothel?'

"'There are two sides to the story of Douglas' marriage,' I objected."

Apparently the word "brothel" did not surprise Mackenzie. Either he
interpreted the word as meaning a cheap hotel; or he was so well prepared by Douglas' version of the marriage and its aftermath that he was
ready to believe that Elsa was willing to be taken to, or worked in, a
brothel. Mackenzie, at any rate, leaves the reader to assume what he or
she pleases. Considering that Elsa lived and died in her own apartment,
and that Fairholme, according to Mackenzie, was a stupid man, this un-
willingness to protect Elsa from an extremely damaging suggestion is less
chivalrous conduct than might have been expected from Mackenzie. In
spite of claiming that there were two sides to the story of Douglas'
marriage, he seems only to have listened to one side.

That there were faults in both partners of the marriage can hardly be
doubted: Violet Fairholme indicated as much to Angus Wilson, who visited her a few years before her death; and there is a letter from Elsa's
father, Augustus FitzGibbon, to the same effect. Nevertheless, in anyone
less generous than Mackenzie one would suppose the "brothel" aspersion
to have been introduced solely for the purpose of discrediting Elsa.

V

Douglas returned to London from Bournemouth on 23rd October, and a month later, almost to the day, was arrested at South Kensington Underground Station. That was a Saturday, and he first appeared in court on Monday the 27th. It was reported in *The Times*:

REMANDED IN CUSTODY

At Westminster Police Court yesterday, before Mr Francis, NORMAN DOUGLAS, a well-dressed, middle-aged man, described as an author, of Albany Mansions, Albert Bridge-road, Battersea, was charged by the police as a suspected person. There was a further charge against the prisoner of assault on a boy of 16, whose schoolmaster signed the charge-sheet.

Detective-sergeant Cogging said he kept special observation on the prisoner on Saturday afternoon at the Natural History Museum, South Kensington, where he met a boy, for whom he purchased a shillings-worth of cakes. The pair were followed for some time and the prisoner was arrested. He then said: "I've just been with him to a lecture." The boy made a statement as to visiting the prisoner's house on the previous Saturday.

MR FRANCIS remanded the prisoner, who asked for bail.

Detective-Inspector Bedford said he was directed to oppose bail, as there might be serious developments in the case.

Bail was accordingly refused.

There was a more detailed report a few days later in another paper. The detective-sergeant (Goggin, not Cogging) and the boy had been waiting in their separate places in the Museum at two o'clock. Douglas arrived, walked down the central hall, and after waiting a few minutes crossed over to the boy, who was sitting on one of the seats. They went round various rooms of the Museum together, presumably shadowed by the detective, and shortly before three o'clock left the building together. At South Kensington station they went into the ABC shop, where Douglas bought the shillingsworth of cakes and gave them to the boy. Goggin stopped them outside and said to Douglas: "I am a police officer. What are you doing with that boy?" Reply: "I have just been with him to a lecture." Goggin: "You have been with him in the Natural History Museum some considerable time, and there has been no lecture on. This boy says you took him home last Saturday and assaulted him." Douglas: "No. I only took him there to find an address. I suppose it is no good my saying anything?" He was told that he was being taken into custody for being a suspected person frequenting for an unlawful purpose. At the police station he was told of the additional charge and said: "This is a serious charge. I have two boys of my own at home."

Douglas' solicitor asked for a remand, and one of eight days was ordered. Until 5th December, therefore, Douglas was locked in a cell.

Faith Mackenzie was one of those who read the report in *The Times*. In her memoirs she says she "wrote to him in prison assuring him of my belief in his innocence"; but when she tried to turn the experience into fiction, her belief in his innocence was less evident:

> "Described as an author." That was pretty good. Conway himself would have laughed at that. But was Conway laughing now? What was happening to him. She couldn't imagine Conway in a prison cell with a warder outside. She tried to conjure him up, sitting there with that hunted look that came into his eyes sometimes and his hands with their fleshy palms and tapering fingers turning over the little pocket book he always carried to note down ideas. Perhaps he wouldn't even be allowed to keep that – in prison. What was the technique when a friend went to prison? What did one do about it? Did one write "So sorry to see about you [sic] bad luck in the Times", or "Distressed to hear the bad news." And anyway, where did one write? Bron knew of no precedent.
>
> She had dined with him only a few nights ago, and such was their intimacy that she had said: "You are an ass. You'll be run in one day", and he had poured himself out another tumbler of Chianti with his devil's laugh. "Take away this porcheria Luigi and now bring me something to *eat*. No my dear, I'm not such an ass as you think. Rather not!"
>
> "But you are if all the fairy tales you tell me are true. Perhaps they're not."
>
> "Good gracious, but I don't tell you everything! No fear!"
>
> "Very well, then," she had said rather annoyed. "Then you certainly will be run in."

At the second hearing the boy said that on the Saturday afternoon before Douglas' arrest – namely 18th November – he had attended a lecture at the Natural History Museum. The lecture finished at four o'clock, and as he was walking towards the door to leave the building, Douglas, whom he had seen at the lecture, spoke to him: "It's very early to close the museum. It's a pity. I was just getting interested." He went on to ask the boy if he had any ambitions in connection with natural history – "There are lots of good posts for boys of your tastes. . . . I know plenty of good jobs you can get. Suppose you come round to my place and talk things over?" They went first of all to the ABC shop, where Douglas bought him some cakes, as on the second occasion. "Come round to my place and eat them," he said; "It's not far." They took a cab, nevertheless, and Douglas told the boy he was lonely as his wife was out. He also asked him if his parents were hard to manage, and whether they would let him go in for natural history.

On getting into the flat the prisoner lit a gas fire, sat on a chair, and then committed the offence complained of. Witness did not say anything, but tried several times to get away, but prisoner pulled him back. Prisoner kissed him and gave him a shilling, also a screwdriver, telling him the latter was a keepsake from him. After that he took witness to a bus, and he proceeded to the school in this.

Douglas had asked the boy to meet him at the museum on the following Saturday, and he had promised that he would; but at the first opportunity the boy had reported the incident to one of his masters at school. There had been an interview with Goggin on the following Friday, and the set-up in the museum on the next day. Douglas asked him to go to his flat. On the way, he said, "We'll go and get some cakes, shall we? You didn't tell anybody about last Saturday, did you?" The boy said he hadn't.

It was said that the boy had struggled, but did not call out; that he agreed to a further meeting because he did not think Douglas would have let him leave the flat if he did not agree. Outside, he was said to have looked for a policeman, but could not see one. His schoolmaster said he had an excellent character. The prosecution asked for remand for a week, and if no further evidence was produced, that the case be sent for trial. Douglas' counsel submitted that there was no case for committal, as the boy's story of the alleged assault was entirely uncorroborated. Mr Francis: "In my opinion it is obviously a case that should go for trial." On this occasion, bail was allowed – a surety of £100, or two of £50.

Compton Mackenzie: "At this moment practically all Douglas' friends avoided him, but two of them did stand bail for him; Joseph Conrad refused to do this." (Mackenzie himself was in Athens at this time, and unable to help.) Borys Conrad knows nothing about the bail refusal, but claims to remember that his father's instant reaction on seeing *The Times* report was "We must have the boy to stay, at once" – meaning Robert Douglas. Faith Mackenzie wrote: ". . . he turned up at my flat on bail, and asked me to help him with an important work he had to finish." He wrote to Secker asking him to come and see him at Albany Mansions: "Faith will cook us something." He wanted to see Secker about two things. Secker was unable to go at the time Douglas suggested; but one of the two things was *South Wind*, so very nearly, but not quite, finished.

Remands continued now for a month, so that the third hearing did not take place until 2nd January 1917. The prosecution was looking for further evidence. Meanwhile, Secker asked him to spend Christmas with him at Bridgefoot.

> It was a green Christmas, and rather muggy. We went for walks a lot of the time, and all the talk was of what to do. It looked as though the case was certain to go for trial, and he would probably have got nine months at the Old Bailey. He thought he would be bored by nine months in the Scrubs, but to go abroad would be like "cutting off his head" as he called it. In the end he decided to clear out.

At the third hearing he was charged with further offences in July against brothers aged ten and twelve, also at the Natural History Museum. His counsel asked for a week's remand so that a witness could be called who would effectively refute these charges. This witness was Faith Mackenzie, who duly appeared at the fourth hearing on 9th January to testify that Douglas had been on Capri at the time of the alleged offence, and had actually lunched with her there two days later. His passport also showed that he had left England in May and had not returned until August. Verdict: Alibi proved, and case of mistaken identity on the part of the brothers. Prisoner discharged. "He awaits trial therefore, on one charge only."

He decided to leave, as soon as possible.

On 10th January he moved into the Ivanhoe Hotel; on the 11th he obtained a visa for France; on the 12th, a visa for Italy. Archie helped him pack, and on the 13th he was seen off at Waterloo by Faith Mackenzie and Archie, went down to Southampton and crossed to Le Havre. This effectively put an end to his patriotic tribulations – such as they may have been – for as he wrote later,

> I . . . might for the next three years have been kicking my heels, like any other patriot, in the corridor of some dingy Government office at the mercy of a pack of tuppenny counter-jumpers, but for a God-sent little accident, the result of sheer boredom, which counselled a trip to the sunny Mediterranean.

He was forty-eight years old; he had no money worth speaking of; he was known as a writer only in limited circles; and this was the second country he had had to leave in a hurry. It was not to be the last.

PART V

Italy, France, Italy 1917-1920

CHAPTER SEVENTEEN

Italy and *South Wind*
1917

i

He arrived at Le Havre the next morning – 14th January – travelled straight through Paris and stopped at Levanto from the 16th until the 26th. On the 18th he was granted permission to stay for seven days, "for reasons of health", in this part of the world, which was a defence zone. On the 26th he moved to Siena, and was beginning to get anxious about the proofs of *South Wind*:

> Dear Secker
> Thanks for your card which I found on my arrival here this morning. No proofs have yet arrived – I will let you have them back by return of post. I think, on the whole, they had better be sent registered, as printed matter. Anyhow, I will return them registered. If you have any letters waiting for me, you might send them on now – after the 1st Feb. Also tell Archie to write to me – if you see him; likewise Faith to whom I will write in a day or two. This place is shrouded in a boreal mist, icicles are hanging from the windows and the snow lies about 3 ft deep in the streets: temperature at least 10 below zero. The few people who dare move out of doors are wrapped in sheepskins. It is like Tobolsk – in other words, the usual "sunny south". They have given me a bedroom as large as the Albert Hall and no heating whatever except a small charcoal pan the size of a tea cup at the bottom of which can be discerned three little red specks, like cigarette-stumps. My beard is frozen to my jacket. Haven't been so cold since – since when? Since I was last in Italy. Impossible to do anything except mumble disconnected prayers for sunshine which God probably can't understand. It is 3 p.m. and I am going to bed – the only chance of getting warm, especially if the chambermaid - - - -

Siena being too arctic, he moved on 1st February to Pisa, whence he returned one set of proofs to Secker, wondering whether perhaps the book should be published anonymously. "I see they have put my name on the title page. Personally, I don't care one way or the other, but there is the question of press-notices to be considered. Punch, for instance, might hesitate if the name were there; whereas appearing anonymously, I think Eckersley would feel he could say what he liked about it." He only stayed two days in Pisa, then went on to Viareggio: "Please send everything in future to the above address, where I hope to stay for a good while" (but in fact stayed less than three weeks). The third lot of proofs had arrived, he told Secker, but the second had not: "They must have got lost in the post. You had better send me three fresh pulls, and *drop me a card, at the same time, when you send them off* . . . It is damnable, this postal dislocation, and who knows what will happen with the 'blockade' . . . If Faith comes out, she had better bring them (proofs). I have not heard from her for ages. What is she doing? And how's your influenza? . . . *Don't forget the proofs p. 49–80 inclusive* AS SOON AS POSSIBLE." Two days later, another letter to the same effect, with the additional information: "Damn the post. Beastly cold here. I am still wearing, indoors, two pairs of socks, 2 pants, 2 vests and 2 waistcoats. DONT FORGET to cause chapter 24 to terminate near the TOP of the page. How do you find this stuff reads?"

On 19th February he moved to Florence. His energy was undiminished: postcards, as well as letters, had been, and continued, whizzing across France to Secker like bullets, asking for duplicate proofs for America, announcing the despatch of corrected proofs, damning the post, demanding news of the next lot of proofs, listing further misprints discovered later and commanding Secker "Drop me a line if you hear of anything that may interest me." "Don't forget" he ordered, as though any printer could arrange the matter without difficulty, "that Chapter 24 should end in the top half of the page; and chapter 38 not lower than 8–10 lines above the bottom of the page. DONT FORGET THIS." "I shall stay on here, now" he wrote from Florence on the 24th. "I don't much care about the place; never did; I don't like the Tuscan character. But I shall sit tight for a month, during which I hope those proofs may at last dribble in . . . Viareggio was absolutely *impossible*. Bloody hole." Would Secker send 5/- to Robert on the Worcester and 10/- to someone else, name enclosed, but lost to us: "Don't omit to do this, whatever you do. Faith may not be in town any more, else I would have asked her; and other people I cannot feel certain about. Don't forget! At once. Thanks awfully."

It was at this time, in Florence, that he met Edward Hutton:

Norman was sitting at the next table in a restaurant or café, trying to balance an egg on one of its ends. He was tight, of course – tight, not drunk; I've often seen him tight, but never drunk. "Can you do it?"

he asked me. I said I was sure I could not. Then he showed me how to do it. You shake it hard and break the yolk, and this runs down inside to make weight at the bottom and keeps the egg upright.[78]

Once they had got to know each other, they talked and talked endlessly. One would see the other home, to flat or hotel; and then they would walk back again to the other's place, and so on, backwards and forwards perhaps four or five times in the early hours of the morning. And – as others have testified – no matter what had happened the night before, Douglas would be up and out, pink-faced and fresh, at nine o'clock the next morning, having done all his correspondence for the day.

Through Hutton he met Reggie Turner, and through Turner a whole section of the more Bohemian expatriate society of Florence. "R. Turner has not read Harris' book" Douglas wrote to Secker at the beginning of March, "and would be greatly obliged if you could get him a copy and let him know what he owes you. . . . Brook Kerith? Thanks; no. I've no use for gentle Jesus, and, as seen through the eyes of George Moore, he becomes more of an emetic than ever. Besides, I waded through the damned thing – and liked it, *in parts*. But if you can send me any other kinds of books – except poetry; any other kinds!. . . . Here are one or two corrections which please get into the revise: it is worth doing the thing as well as possible isn't it?. . . . I made a small enlargement to Chapter 24: I hope the printers won't make a mess of it? That chapter is so good that it *deserves improving*. . . . It is still cold here, but I have got some wood at last and am now thawing for the first time since 6 weeks. So sorry to hear you can't get rid of your cold. Why not drink half a gallon of hot whisky every night? Works like magic."

By 8th March all the proofs had been corrected: "Let me know how the thing progresses and when you expect to get it out. . . . Send the first copy you can get hold of to the 'Punch' man [Arthur Eckersley] to his *country* address. . . . I think this may be of use as other people take their cue from him, and if it is sent to the Punch office, it may get into the hands of another man." Later, he added that the second copy should go to Garnett; between the two of them they should give the book a good start. Meanwhile he had noticed in *The Times Literary Supplement* that *Fountains in the Sand* had been remaindered: "Do I get anything out of that transaction? I have only had £15 out of that damned book so far, you know."

ii

All the proofs had been corrected: now the question was, what next? A curious idea had taken hold in his mind – curious because in those days it could hardly have hoped to reach print in England in any effective form:

"I am wondering whether my recent London experiences could be fashioned into a sort of novel. One might say one or two interesting things (about police methods etc) and bring in one or two interesting characters. Think it over and *let me know*. Certain things, of course, would have to be turned [toned?] down. There would also have to be a love-element, which I could easily invent. So meditate upon this and tell me how you think it might be done. Not more than 60,000 words, I mean." Did Secker know E. S. P. Haynes?[79] – "Let me hear about this". The idea was still in evidence a month later. He was thinking, he wrote, as far as he could think at all with violent toothache and insomnia, "of that novel of situation, which I wanted to contain more elements of my own recent experiences. A propos of Haynes, I wish you could drop him a line to say you read with much interest his letter in the 'New Witness' of March 22 about perjury by the police and that you would be very glad if he, who seems to know all about their system, could put you on the track of some of the more flagrant recent cases; (I imagine the cattle-maiming case, as well as the recent Lloyd-George poisoning affair, are to the point); or could tell you where you could find out about them. Don't mention me, of course."

It is evident that he felt he had a score to settle with the police and with public morality in England. "How would you like," asks Mr Keith in *South Wind*, "to be haled before a Court of Law for some ridiculous trifle, which became a crime only because it used to be a sin, and became a sin only because some dyspeptic or impotent old antediluvian was envious of his neighbour's pleasure?" Douglas obviously did not like it, any more than anybody else would, and was prepared to fight back to the best of his ability; but there was to be no cant or hypocrisy about it – he was not fighting back on behalf of other people, or conducting a campaign: he was fighting back because the activities of the police impinged on his own activities and threatened a pleasure which he considered harmless. He was no zealot for reform; but if he was pinched, he was prepared to cry out. Furthermore, he was prepared to cry out at that particular moment even more loudly than usual because there had been reverberations of that affair in London which might affect him here in Italy. Faith Mackenzie wrote about it to her mother:

> Casa Solitaria
> 10 April 1917
> ... After dinner tonight a most beautiful capitano of the Caribinieri [sic] came to visit me sword & all. I had written to the Consul General at Naples who is a great friend, that I had been asked impertinent questions by the Head of the police here about N. Douglas. The result being that this exquisite person was sent over from Naples to enquire

into the matter. My wrath having by now died down I begged him to be lenient with the poor old Head, who is really a dunderheaded contadino. But I was very angry with him at the time.

Three weeks later Douglas said there was no further news "as regards what Faith wrote about. I have not moved. I imagine things are quieting down." It looks as though someone on Capri – presumably a reader of *The Times* – had been nagging at the "dunderheaded contadino" (who was, of course, Capolozzi, the Capri magistrate who appears in *South Wind* as Malipizzo) to ban Douglas from the island, or even perhaps to try to get him kept out of Italy.

Through March and April he remained in Florence. In May he began those wanderings in the Latium which are delightfully but rather obscurely described in *Alone* in the chapters "Olevano", "Valmontone", and "Alatri".

iii

Early in June, *South Wind* was published. It was an immediate success. It would have been a success at any time, but coming as it did in the midst of an appalling cataclysm, a long hard dreary desperate war, it was received with all the more joy for being entirely unconcerned with "the wearisome actualities of life". Some readers disapproved of it for this reason; it seemed to contain profanities of customs and beliefs commonly held sacred; and these objectors, by their very stuffiness, helped to recommend the book to the young, and to those who were or wished to be emancipated. As it was Douglas' first book to earn him a reputation outside the purely literary world, so it was the first to associate him with "naughtiness", the first to give rise to a Douglas-cult.

The success of the book was due, of course, to its greatest virtue: its tremendous zest and high spirits, its excessiveness, its completely amoral devotion to fun, to the indulgence of moods and appetites for their own sakes, its explosive satyr's laughter and malicious wit – all embodied in the most urbane and civilised forms of communication: conversation, and polished ironical treatises and disquisitions. Perceptive critics noticed the plot, and dutifully described it; none thought it of great importance; one went so far as to declare that there wasn't one. This annoyed Douglas, who wrote a three-page defence of it in *Alone*, and, excessive as ever, retorted that the book was nearly "nothing but plot":

How to make murder palatable to a bishop: that is the plot. How? You must unconventionalise him, and instil into his mind the seeds of doubt and revolt. You must shatter his old notions of what is right. It is the only way to achieve this result, and I would defy the critic to point to a single incident or character or conversation in the book which does not further the object in view. The good bishop soon finds himself among new influences; his sensations, his intellect, are assailed from within and without. Figures such as those in chapters 11, 19 and 35; the endless dialogue in the boat; the even more tedious happenings in the local law-court; the very externals – relaxing wind and fantastic landscape and volcanic phenomena – the jovial immoderation of everything and everybody: they foster a sense of violence and insecurity; they all tend to make the soil receptive to new ideas.

If that was your plot, the reviewer might say, you have hidden it rather successfully. I have certainly done my best to hide it. For although the personalities of the villain and his legal spouse crop up periodically, with ominous insistence, from the first chapter onwards, they are always swallowed up again. The reason is given in the penultimate chapter, where the critic might have found a résumé of my intentions and the key to this plot – to wit, that a murder under those particular circumstances is not only justifiable and commendable but – insignificant. Quite insignificant! Not worth troubling about. Hundreds of decent and honest folk are being destroyed every day; nobody cares tuppence; "one dirty blackmailer more or less – what does it matter to anybody?" There are so many more interesting things on earth. That is why the bishop – i.e. the reader – here discovers the crime to be a "contemptible little episode", and decides to "relegate it into the category of unimportant events". *He was glad that the whole affair had remained in the background, so to speak, of his local experiences. It seemed appropriate.* In the background: it seemed appropriate. That is the heart, the core, of the plot. And that is why all those other happenings find themselves pushed into the foreground.

As a rational defence this is plausible enough, but it sounds more like a retrospective explanation developed (with typical vigour) in order to appease critics, than an outline structure on which the novel was carefully built, and the plot, when carefully considered, is seen to be more or less irrelevant. It is true that in so far as every novel – at any rate in those days – was expected to have some line of development, the bishop provided one; but it is also true that the reader cannot be bothered with Mr Heard, the bishop, let alone identify himself with him. Mr Keith, Count Caloveglia, van Koppen, the Duchess, Mr Freddy Parker, the Russians, even Mr Eames and such minor characters as Marten, Angelina, Miss Wilberforce, and the old boatman are all so vastly more interesting and entertaining than Mr Heard that one does not care very much what Mr Heard thinks. And when it comes to the point, he is hardly credible as a character. The progressive inroads made upon his moral stamina by the Nepenthean climate, both geographical and social, are mere marks upon paper. They constitute an event so improbable as to be even more un-important than the murder itself, for the fact is that men like Heard, who have reached episcopal status and have lived for years amongst primitive people in tropical conditions without abandoning their principles, do not suddenly drop them within the space of a fortnight owing to the influence of an exotic atmosphere.

The reader who can accept the "conversion" of the bishop to a view of murder as being irrelevant in this case, where it seems to be justified by self-defence, will also be likely to accept the bishop's change of attitude as irrelevant, because either illusory or incredible. In any case, the motives of Mrs Meadows and the bishop are profoundly unimportant compared with the remaining ninety-five percent of the book. Douglas probably fought to protect the validity of his plot because it had given him a great deal of trouble to weave the thin thread of it into the large and complex tapestry of the book as a whole. He was probably disappointed that the craftsmanship involved in doing this – which was considerable – had not been acknowledged, or in some cases, even noticed, by critics.

South Wind, like the travel books, but unlike the other two novels, is composed of numerous short essays and disquisitions on a great variety of topics, some little more than paragraphs, others much longer, even whole essay-chapters or themes recurring at intervals through the book. These are all skilfully knitted together and interlaced with a great deal of other, purely fictional material, and the whole is scattered as it were in the Piazza of Nepenthe amongst a crowd of fascinating individuals who take up the various subjects discussed, play with them in their several characteristic ways, and then relinquish them, having perhaps helped to carry the plot an inch further towards its alleged goal of "making murder palatable to a bishop" – but the fact is that one does not care, and it is not in the least important, whether they have advanced the plot or not. What they do, and particularly what they say, is sufficiently fascinating in itself.

South Wind is another portmanteau book, like *Old Calabria* and *Alone*: into it are crammed the author's knowledge and opinions on politics, edu-cation, religion, literature, and the general business of living. These views are stated uncompromisingly through Mr Keith's forthright, teasing, energetic utterance, or more gracefully and subtly through the urbane serenity of Count Caloveglia's benign and avuncular detachment. Other facets of Douglas also appear – Marten, the geologist, healthily ruthless and realistic, who believes that chastity is an unclean state of affairs, and who pursues and obtains the delicious Angelina whom Denis, the undecided public-schoolboy would have liked, but is too shy and diffident to approach. Mr Eames, whose life-work is to annotate Perelli's *Antiquities of Nepenthe*, represents perhaps the scholarly side of his creator, combined possibly with a pinch of Douglas' friend Brooks, whose life-work it was to translate the poems of Herédia, and who had once formed an association (resulting in marriage) with an unsuitable companion (although Romaine Brooks could not be called a *ballon captif*). Eames has a certain poignancy, due to his vulnerability combined with his singleminded devotion to his task. In his character one may catch a glimpse of Douglas' attitude to scholarship.

If, as Douglas maintains, everything in the overcharged canvas of Nepenthe could be said to play its part in making the bishop qualify the sixth commandment, *South Wind* could in a sense be regarded as a defence of an anarchistic or nihilistic philosophy in which the struggle for existence which Darwin had demonstrated in the animal world is recommended as a substitute for the social contract observed by most societies. As Professor Dawkins wrote later, Douglas believed in "the inevitability . . . of the struggle for life in its fiercest forms; he is what the French . . . have sometimes called a *strugforlifeur*, and one of the most uncompromising kind. Too much energy, he has said in more than one place, is now spent in keeping alive people who had much better be dead."[80] And in educating people who are incapable of benefiting from it. And in trying to promote the happiness of the greatest number, instead of the happiness of those who are best fitted to be happy. This totally unacceptable social philosophy, based upon or perhaps derived from Nietzsche, he pertinaciously continued to believe in, even after the Second World War. Though he hated the Fascist régime and was appalled by the Nazis and lived in the democracies by choice, he would stand no argument about cause and effect in democracies: they were wrong, and that was that. It is a large question, only mentioned here in order to show that the radical element of subversion, which is so often forgotten or ignored, certainly existed in Douglas' mind. His three novels are in varying degrees pleas for it – utopias of a kind; and there are other indications of this attitude too numerous to leave one in doubt about it. He saw clearly that three-quarters of the beliefs and laws of society are superfluous or irrelevant or absurd, and with his usual excessiveness was willing to do away with the lot. At times. At other times, he was only too ready to make use of them, for he was never a consistently rational man, though he sometimes liked to give the impression of being so, and was successful to the extent that countless readers have thought of him as the embodiment of rational sagacity. Sometimes, but not very often, he was.

The subversiveness of the plot in *South Wind*, both as regards the act, and the subsequent attitude to it, would convert nobody. The truly dis-integrating force in Douglas which blasts away at the foundations of society, and at the whole history of man from the birth of Christ onwards, is Douglas' sardonic zest. His irony, his wit, his satire, his brief caustic comments, are frequently referred to; he is also occasionally a brilliant comic writer and always an impressive one, as for instance in his treat-ment of Miss Wilberforce or Mr Freddy Parker, or in describing a depu-tation solemnly waiting upon Mr Keith at breakfast while he detains them with a long exposition of the benefits of costiveness. Some of the actual phraseology is in itself humorous, embracing both the polysyllabic variety ("stolid pachydermatous obliquity") and the ridiculous ("a dusky dame of barn-like proportions"). H. M. Tomlinson said that Douglas had told him, while he was writing *South Wind*, that he intended to put into it all the sins which have ever been committed and some that never have been. He must have changed his mind; but what he could have said with truth was that he had put into the book every kind of writing calculated to amuse the reader, from the most polished Wilde-like epigrammatic wit to the broadest knockabout farce, ranging through every form and variety. There cannot have been many books, if any others, in this century that are so entertaining, and give such repetitive pleasure at the fifteenth as at the first reading.

Entertaining, yes. Yet as much pleasure comes from the strong, earthy percipience and discernment, the canny (perhaps Scottish) level-headedness and seriousness, which makes nonsense of assertions that Douglas was *merely* frivolous or scampish. Keith is something of a Johnsonian figure, and the Count is something of a Chesterfield. Between them, they have as much to offer the young – or the young in heart – as any practical philo-sopher who has ever lived. Eleanor Roosevelt, one of the last great liberal Americans in the grand tradition, knew this, and when she had written a whole book at the end of her life which was designed to answer the ques-tion "What have you learned by living?", and had read it through again with some despondency, fearing that she had discovered nothing new to pass on to her readers, she remembered her favourite passage in *South Wind*, and ended her book with it. The Count is talking to Denis about his "old teacher", whom one presumes he has invented as a means of advising Denis unobtrusively:

"What did he say?" asked Denis.
"The old teacher? Let me see . . . He said: Do not be discomposed by the opinions of inept persons. Do not swim with the crowd. They who are all things to their neighbours cease to be anything to them-selves. Even a diamond can have too many facets. Avoid the attrition of

vulgar minds; keep your edges intact. He also said: A man can protect himself with fists or sword but his best weapon is his intellect. A weapon must be forged in the fire. The fire, in our case, is tribulation. It must also be kept untarnished. If the mind is clean, the body can take care of itself. He said: Delve deeply; not too deeply into the past, for it may make you derivative; nor yet into yourself – it will make you introspective. Delve into the living world and strive to bind yourself to its movement by a chain of your own welding. Once that contact is established, you are unassailable. Externalise yourself! He told me many things of this kind. You think I was consoled by his words? Not in the slightest degree. I was annoyed. It struck me, at the moment, as quite ordinary advice. In fact, I thought him rather a hypocrite; anybody could have spoken as he did! I was so disappointed that I went to him next day and told him frankly what I thought of his counsel. He said – do you know what he said?"

"I cannot even guess."

"He said: 'What is all wisdom save a collection of platitudes? Take fifty of our current proverbial sayings – they are so trite, so threadbare, that we can hardly bring our lips to utter them. None the less they embody the concentrated experience of the race, and the man who orders his life according to their teaching cannot go far wrong. How easy that seems! Has anyone ever done so? Never. Has any man ever attained to inner harmony by pondering the experience of others? Not since the world began! He must pass through the fire.'"

"I had no teacher like that," observed Denis. "He must have been a man of the right kind."

"Oh, he meant well, the old rascal," replied the Count with a curious little smile.

There is more, much more, of the same kind to be found in *South Wind* as well as in other books by the same author. In *South Wind* it often comes direct from the mouths of certain characters, as here, and gains dramatic force by doing so; but it was always there, in Douglas himself as well as in his books, for his friends and his readers to draw upon.

This depth, no doubt, was another reason for the book's success, a reason which contradicts the reviewer who thought it merely superficial. On the whole reviewers shared this opinion, being blinded by surface brilliance to those deeper truths which the book contains. Even his friend Eckersley, in a review of only twenty-five lines in the *English Review*, thought the book deserved to live "on account of its ironical and deep-biting wit"; but Virginia Woolf in *The Times Literary Supplement*, in a half-page review, saw that the book was rich in humane values; and

George Saintsbury, Professor of English Literature at Edinburgh University, who was as widely read in English and French as any man of his time, and had no reason to flatter, wrote to Douglas the famous letter that was printed (with his permission) in later editions:

February 23, 1921

Dear Sir,

Permit me to be tedious, as well as illegible. I am seventy-five. I have read more novels than a man of seven hundred and fifty ought to have done. For some twenty years I used to review hundreds or thereabouts of English and scores of French as they came out. For another twenty, the first of this so-called age, I have come across just two new novelists who have given me something that I can recommend to a friend. The author of "South Wind" is the second in order of time, not rank.

As to sales, they were very satisfying. Up to August 1915, when the first American-printed edition was published, 15,500 copies had been sold. Thereafter, of course, the sales rocketed away until they reached six figures; but Douglas, alas, did not reap much financial reward from them. The bulk of them were American, and he was not protected by copyright in the USA.

A word must be said about this vexed question since it deeply affected Douglas' pocket, and undoubtedly exaggerated his already strong suspicions of publishers, literary agents, and the normal method of publishing on a royalty basis.

Until the 1950s, permanent copyright protection of books and periodicals in the USA could only be obtained by having an edition printed in that country from type set up there. Temporary copyright protection (similar to "patents pending") could be obtained under certain circumstances, which included registration almost as soon as the book was published in England, evidence that an American edition was being negotiated, and the inclusion of a "copyright reserved" notice in all copies of the book sold in the USA.

Responsibility for obtaining copyright in the USA would normally rest with the English publisher, or, if the author employed one, with his literary agent. Douglas' agents were Hughes, Massie & Co; and their acting in this capacity absolves Secker of all blame in regard to negotiations – or lack of them – with the USA. Not that "blame" is quite the right word; it was more a matter of luck, or sometimes of good or bad judgment. Right up until 1943 Douglas believed that Massie's failure to have the book copyrighted in the USA could be explained only "on the charitable and perhaps correct assumption that – so I was told – he was too ill at the time to attend to business, dying in fact, shortly afterwards". This belief was apparently erroneous. Massie, it seems, had "done his

utmost to induce American publishers to take up the book, but failed",
and Douglas apologised in print for his former imputation (also in print)
that Massie had not tried.

The dilemma was an acute one for an English publisher or agent. If
they could not make arrangements for more or less simultaneous publication (including typesetting and printing) in the USA, they had to risk
losing copyright by selling sheets of the English edition to an American
publisher. Once these were bound up and distributed in the USA, all right
to legal protection was lost. And after the importing publisher had paid
for his sheets and published them, *any* American publisher was free to
issue an American-printed edition without legal financial obligation to the
author. Reputable firms usually paid a courtesy royalty, but it was often
merely nominal, and seldom amounted to what the author could have obtained from a copyrighted American edition. Some firms were notorious
for paying a royalty for a short time, and then ceasing to pay it, or for not
paying one at all.

South Wind sold in great numbers in the USA in at least seven editions
and a considerable number of impressions. The Modern Library edition
alone had amounted to 120,895 copies by the time of Douglas' death.
From 1932 onwards, although they had formerly agreed to pay a courtesy
royalty of 5 cents per copy, they cancelled this agreement and paid nothing,
which left Douglas the poorer by nearly $4,000.

iv

Apart from going to and from Rome in his walks amongst the hills to
the east of it, Douglas also spent a fortnight in the city itself, in August.
One day a fastidiously dressed little man stopped him in the Corso, and
reminded him that he, Maurice Magnus, had borrowed money from
Douglas at the time of their previous meeting, eight years earlier. "And
now," he added, "you must let me do something for you in return, if I
can; you really must."

> He was pretty flush just then, and I on my beam ends and altogether
> run down. He installed me in his apartment, cleared out of his own
> bedroom and gave it to me, bought me a new outfit and fed me like a
> prince. There I stayed, putting on flesh again; and . . . from that day
> onwards till his death there was nothing he would not do for me; he
> seemed to delight in anticipating my smallest wishes.

There is not much doubt that Magnus had soon, or at once, after this
second meeting, fallen for Douglas, who amongst other things probably
represented the strong paternal masculine element that was lacking in
Magnus's life. For he was the only son of an adoring mother from whom

he had seldom been parted until her death. She claimed that she was the illegitimate daughter of William I of Prussia, and this claim was left visible in the words on her tombstone: *Filia regis*. Douglas says he gathered that her death, which occurred when Magnus was thirty-six, was the tragedy of his life. "He told me she had never been able to deny him anything", and thought that this could well have accounted for the recklessly extravagant habits which led to his undoing. His mother's death had left him with a sadness of expression in unguarded moments such as Douglas had never seen on the face of anyone else: and probably accounted for his absolute need of the consolations offered by the Catholic Church, to which he had been converted. Nothing seems to be known of his father; he was presumably an American, since the son was a citizen of that country.

In appearance Magnus looked rather less than forty years old, "spruce and youngish in his deportment, very pink-faced, and very clean, very natty, very alert, like a sparrow painted to resemble a tom-tit . . . he stuck out his front tubbily, like a bird, and his legs seemed to perch behind him, as a bird's do". He was "a little smart man of the shabby world" who knew "all the short cuts in all the big towns of Europe", and his voice was "precise and a little mincing and it had an odd high squeak". "He was finicky and fussy and fastidious to a degree, especially about his wearing apparel; he never used any save the finest cambric handkerchiefs, and . . . made a fine art, almost a religion, of the folding-up . . . of clothes." This little man, with his pince-nez, his jewel case, his religious medals and his pyjama bag trimmed with lace had felt a desire to play a part in the war. Soon after Italy had entered the war in 1915 he had tried to join the Red Cross in four different countries, without success. He then, in Douglas' words, "committed the nightmarish blunder of enlisting in the Foreign Legion where a natural refinement in habits and manners and language intensified his sufferings a thousandfold". He had arrived in North Africa in March 1916, where he very quickly discovered what a mistake he had made. After a few months, during which he was lucky enough to be transferred to Lyon, he had deserted and escaped into Italy. In the summer of the following year, when he and Douglas met for the second time, he was starting to write the story of his experiences, which he called *Dregs*.

The text was different from what it now is; it contained many allusions, expunged later on, to certain ultra-masculine peculiarities of legionary life upon which I shall not expatiate here. Me they amused, these little incidents; they struck me as a natural result of local conditions; but their bestial promiscuity and utter lack of idealism horrified the fastidious Magnus more than any of his other unpleasant experiences out there; they made him sick ... ready to vomit. Yet he put it all down with names and dates and places.

Douglas helped him write *Dregs*, and gave him advice about "toning it down" so that some publisher might at least consider publishing it, which they certainly wouldn't, said Douglas, in its original outspoken form. (When eventually it was published, it had been expurgated too much, Douglas complained. Some indication "for the initiated" as to what had been omitted, should have been provided.) Douglas would have helped him further "but for the fact that in October ... I had to hop over the frontier".

Whether he had to "hop over the frontier" for the usual sort of reason, or whether it was to do with the unfriendly efforts of someone on Capri, or was for a purely technical reason connected with the expiration of a *soggiorno* in wartime is not known. But that he may have been rattled while crossing the border – rattled or annoyed, so that he temporarily lost his usual sense of proportion, seems likely:

... on the 13 October 1917, I was stopped on my way from Italy to Paris by a horrible Commissaire at Modane – one of those Frenchmen with whom one is instinctively driven to quarrel, because they wear a sententious parting down the middle of their beards – who vowed that my authentic explanation of having gone to Italy "to amuse myself" was inadequate, and who summoned some British officer, likewise a spy hunter employed by both Governments, to find out what it was about. When I told this person the correct method to end the War, namely that, before beginning to shoot spies, they should shoot every newspaper editor in Europe, he grew seriously alarmed for the welfare of the British Empire, and it was only after poking his nose into all my papers (a damned piece of impertinence; and besides, who can imagine any spy in his senses carrying documents ...)

etc, etc, etc. The expostulation, especially in wartime, seems a little disproportionate to the occasion, although, as Douglas had been taken off the train, he was delayed twenty-four hours, and says he missed "a delicious appointment" in Paris. All the same there seems to have been a certain amount of provocation, seeing that officials of this kind are notoriously short of humour.

On his last day in Rome Douglas was still trying to persuade Magnus to "tone down" *Dregs*. It seems from the following letter that Magnus had been working on the book at a monastery, probably Monte Cassino. In view of future events, this letter is of interest. It reveals the state of

Magnus' mind, and gives a brief glimpse of his needs, his fears, and his affection:

Dear N.   Oct. 5, 1917

Thanks for yours just received. I am in Paradise – what more can I say. It is the only place – the only life! I only pray I may be able to settle all my affairs soon & be permitted to stay always. The peace – the quiet – the services – the monks and work – it is that "which passeth understanding". It is a real thing in the soul – no explanation possible. There is no other life more real – for me. I have a beautiful room – large – overlooking the valley & mountains. I rise at 6 I work at 7, after breakfast: coffee milk bread, at 8 mass – at 9.15 work again until 12 (I work at the chapters all morning). At 12 lunch (soup, good soup, meat vegetable fruit and wine), nap until 2 – at 2.30 vespers – after vespers library – talk with monk – at 3.30 work (translating chapters from German, historical work on Monte Cassino, for monk) until 5.30 or 6 – then walk with monk garden or mountain until dark. Then read what I feel inclined until 7.15: benediction & 7.45 supper: wine, soup, meat, vegetable, fruit. 8.45 compline – then 9.15 my room, read until bed at 10 or 10.30. Sleep peaceful – heavenly – never slept 8 hours before anywhere. That is my day. Today S. Placido – most momentous ceremony: solemn profession of a monk. Quite wonderful and mediaeval and gorgeous. The only place where one lives in unchanging time – the only life where one lives according to all things such as we are born with.

Sorry – so sorry you are lonely – you know I am sorry. Come here for a few days but announce yourself first to the Revnd Padre Prière. You say nothing what Cobb said. [sic] *Am afraid to write* – don't want anyone to know where I am.

Remember our last conversation in cab? Well it was early and I wasn't good at answers – here is the answer – society such as it is organized today is not compatible with religion. And it is the world that forces itself upon us first.

What about your affairs. What results Monday? Consul? Carbone? news from Assoli?

Look for slippers *under* bed wardrobe, *under* tables in studio where you put your shoes on, in corner next to sofa – under bookcases. Certainly I did not hide them – poor dear!

                                                               Ever & ever thine
                                                               The worried one

A week later, with Douglas on his way to Paris, Magnus must have felt even less secure than he had done when this letter was written.

CHAPTER EIGHTEEN

Paris and St Malo
1917–1918

i

Life in Paris during the war was not unlike life in any other large city behind the lines, although there were two notable differences: enough money could still buy almost anything; and the polish and glitter, the assembled talent at the service of the man with money, were still superior to those of any other French city. For the majority of people, though, blackout and restrictions of all kinds enveloped the city in gloom and in small daily sufferings on which were superimposed the appalling losses and injuries at the front, so that there was probably not a family in France without its dead or maimed.

Instead of taxis, elegant broughams, carriages and cars going up and down the Rue de la Paix and the Rue de Rivoli, there was a steady stream of Red Cross motors with wounded, with officers, with nurses. The shops looked sad and forlorn, the streets empty, the people looked serious, every second person was in mourning, and mourning was written on the faces of those who did not wear it. At night all was dark, the restaurants were difficult to find, not a ray of light emanated from window or doorway . . . The few taxis which were about were driven by crippled young men. Parts of the big hotels were turned into hospitals. There was a feeling of depression everywhere . . . One had the impression that everyone expected the worst to happen, as if one were in a doomed city.

During the year that Douglas lived in Paris there were occasional air raids at night and Big Bertha shells exploded in the streets in daylight. His friend Wade-Browne,[81] who was tired of living through these war years, actually went out on these occasions hoping to meet death half way. Wouldn't Douglas like to join him? "Not likely!" Douglas would dive into the Métro for shelter, fascinated by the crowd he found down there "representing every section of society, huddled together for a few mo-

Sholto Douglass, Norman's father

Vanda Douglass, Norman's mother

Falkenhorst

John, Sholto, Vanda and Norman Douglass

Norman

In 1878, aged nine

In 1882, aged thirteen

In 1890, aged twenty-one

In 1892, aged twenty-three

Norman

In 1894, aged twenty-five

At Armatin: (*left to right, above*) unknown, Jakob Jehly, Grete, Mary, Norman;
(*left to right, below*) John, Vanda, unknown

Elsa Douglass, painted by
Olaf Gulbransson (*photo
Bayer. Staatsgemäldesammlungen,
Munich*

Elsa Douglass

Ouida in 1878, aged 39, a crayon drawing

Douglas on Capri, 1912

Capri photographed from Siren Land by Douglas

Jessie and Joseph Conrad with their sons, 1908

Robin Douglas and John Conrad

Eric Wolton

Martin Secker, photographed by Hoppé
in 1912 (*photo Martin Secker*)

John Nicholas Mavrogordato, *c.* 1920
(*photo Martin Secker*)

Faith Mackenzie and Douglas, in 1925

Maurice Magnus

Edward Hutton (*photo Peter Hutton*)

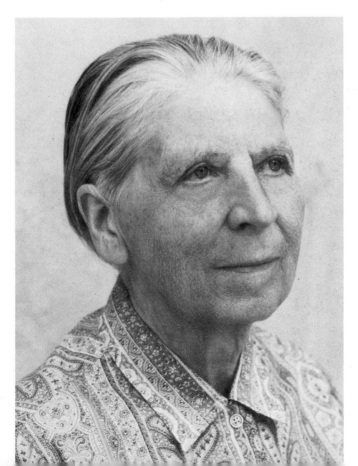

Bryher (*photo Islay Lyons*)

Douglas and Pino Orioli on a
walking tour in the Vorarlberg

Pino Orioli capering with a Calabrian idiot

Douglas making a face to amuse a friend

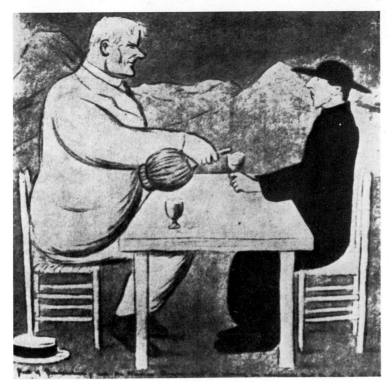

Cartoon by Max Beerbohm: "A flask of Bombarolina, and Mr
Norman Douglas bent on winning an admission that the rites
of the Church are all a survival of Paganism, pure and simple."

Reggie Turner, Douglas and Orioli listening to D. H. Lawrence read from the manuscript
of *Lady Chatterley's Lover*. Drawn from memory by Collingwood Gee, 1933

Douglas painted by Desmond Harmsworth (*photo Iconography Collection, Humanities Research Center, The University of Texas at Austin*)

Douglas on Capri, *c.* 1948

Archie Douglas and his first
wife

Robin Douglas

Auntie, her niece, Oscar Levy

Nancy Cunard

Douglas with Kenneth Macpherson,
c. 1948

Douglas at eighty looking back
at himself at the age of ten

Norman Douglas (*photo Islay Lyons*)

ments and then never to meet again; what hearty but ephemeral friendships were made!"

Wade-Browne was one of those curious characters who flit in and out of
the half light at the back of the stage acting as linkmen to those whose
names are better known. "He possessed a rich store of memories and a
crapulous turn of mind; he was obscene to the marrow. He was obscene
from a kind of ancestral necessity – obscene in a heart-sick and unmirthful
fashion." He was lean and cadaverous, had been a schoolmaster and a tea-
planter (and it was he also who had discovered Corvo dead on his bed in
Corvo's Venetian apartment, in which Browne had a room).[82]

Browne and Douglas were equally broke in Paris and used to meet at a
cheap restaurant to eat what they could afford. Sometimes Douglas could
not afford a proper meal at all, but had to make his lunch off a few roasted
chestnuts, and very often had to sit as long as he could in some cheap café
in order to try to get warm, since there was no heating in his room. It
was not pleasant, either, to be dependent for tobacco on gifts from Allied
troops. But, as he always knew, all these deprivations were flea-bites compared to the sufferings of others. Eric, to whom he still wrote at least
once a week, must frequently have sprung to mind when Douglas felt that
life was particularly hard – Eric "somewhere in France" within sixty miles
or so of Paris, and "in the thick of it" . . .

Fortunately, life was not unremittingly hard, at any rate during the first
few months, while Mrs Webb was in Paris. True, she was not in her most
generous mood, and he had actually had to *sell* her the large emerald he
had been given in Russia by the obliging Mr Kasi, and for far too little;
and her cheques, which were not nearly large enough, were to be regarded
as *loans*, she said, and what was the use of borrowing from people who
expected to be paid back? Nevertheless, without Mrs Webb, he would
literally have starved; as it was, his stomach had contracted and he was
by no means always capable of doing justice to a good meal if it was
offered. Edward Hutton, who went up to Montmartre to find him at the
end of 1917, took him to Durand's and gave him a porterhouse steak,
which made him ill: "I realised then that he was starving."

"I cook my own breakfast and luncheon over a spirit-lamp; my room
is full of Bugs" he wrote to Muriel Draper; and to others he wrote that
he was starved and frozen to death and that he couldn't get tobacco or
even get drunk because wine was too expensive. ". . . if you have any
money to spare, send it me as I am almost at the last gasp – which may
sound very amusing on the other side of the Atlantic, but does not amuse
me at all. No money coming in from anywhere; not even a cent from
publishers. I live in conditions more like a pig than a human being; as to
food. . . . Therefore, if you have a couple of dollars to throw away, chuck

them over here." Mrs Webb, he added, had often asked him for news of Muriel "as if I were your wet nurse. Wish I were. Makes me wet – the very thought of it. You will be glad to hear I have reformed at last; *nearly*." Perhaps she could find a publisher in the USA for his new book, nearly finished, and like *Old Calabria* "but in lighter vein and more aphoristic. ... Think about this, as I am ¾ in the grave."

Though poor, he was not without resources, but then he never had been and never would be. He always had friends who were eager to help him, and some of them were in a good position – not necessarily financially – to do so. Hutton, for instance, who had official connections in Italy, had been planning an Anglo-Italian Review, and as soon as he was certain it would appear, he wrote to Douglas asking for contributions for it: "When your book is finished, if you will send it to me I shall no doubt be able to use some of it in the Review, and unless you intend giving it to Secker, I might try and arrange its publication here and in America for you, but I do not in any way want to deprive Secker of it." Hutton also offered to do, or get done, any research that Douglas might like to have made in London libraries. He also had access to an Italian courier, and at Douglas' request sent over his typewriter after extracting it from a box (of which more will be heard) which Douglas had left in Secker's care. The type-writer was deposited at Cook's, where Douglas picked it up towards the middle of May. The writing of his new book was pretty well completed by this time, and at the end of the month he went to St Malo, where he began typing it out.

ii

His choice of St Malo may have been influenced by his old friend Dr Mann[83], whom he had met again in Paris and who was himself going to Dinard, just across the river from St Malo. Douglas had known Mann since the beginning of the century, a Scotch Canadian who had made enough money in America as a surgeon to retire at a reasonably early age and lead a mellow contemplative life. He was a translator of poems – Petrarch and other sonneteers – and a keen student of prehistory.

St Malo was not a great success, but at least there was fresh air, the effects of war were less evident, and the food was better. "Not bad" was his first verdict, a week after arriving; but of course such a judgment could not stand: a month later the place was "a rotten hole, and I would clear out if I knew where to go. No walks whatever; nothing but a beastly sea-beach, which stinks like Hell, as they all do. No country; and what there is – most unappetizing; flat as a billiard-table. I had looked forward, in Paris, to woods and streams and cows." Also, he confided to Ralph

Straus, no "inspiration" was discoverable "which is something of a record, for a town. . . . The Paris inspiration was immovable, I am sorry to say. Even had it been otherwise I should never have had the money to pay for the necessary transportation; as I used to do in olden days."

There were compensations. One of these, as was almost habitual with Douglas, derived from a study of the locality in which he was living. Brittany was thick with legends, and after a brief glance at some of them, he decided to dissect a few to try to show that they were accretions gradually accumulated through the ages, in which the various experiences of different epochs might be identified. He decided to start with the legend of the Roi d'Ys, the local version of the drowned-city story which is found in other parts of Europe. The ingredients of the tale fell into place: an aboriginal story of a lustful and domineering woman; an equally primitive conception of a personified sea seeking revenge; a bronze-age concern with metals, architecture and crafts; then a Roman period, and lastly, the intervention of a Christian saint – all the elements were clearly traceable, as expected. The trouble was that the pristine vigour and originality of such legends were often disguised by the material added in Christian times, by monks and other chroniclers. Concentrating on this analytical aspect, he forgot about other legends and asked himself at what point in its progress through the ages the Roi d'Ys legend, and it alone, "could most profitably have been arrested; at what step an artist might wish to see it crystallized for ever, stereotyped, in order to be seen in its most attractive light. Was there still room for improvement? What characters or incidents could be added? Were any of the existing ones superfluous?"

Such meditations led to the gradual evolution in his mind of a story set in Brittany about 400 AD – and tentatively thought of as *Theophilus* – into which he could inject, without too much improbability, the moral theme of amorality which had become the main thesis of all his imaginative writing. It was, he wrote later, a pleasant mental exercise for a summer holiday.

He used to discuss the matter with Dr Mann. They would take long walks together, during which Douglas would talk of the fifth century, and Dr Mann of the Magdalenians "as though they were of yesterday, Stuarts or Hanoverians". The subject also occupied his mind occasionally when he was with another friend – that Mme Rollet whose character he admired so much and has sketched in *Looking Back*. They used to walk round the ramparts in the summer evenings, and then "retire to her small apartment for a dinner of eggs and bacon, or fish, or cold meat; then she played . . . a sonata or two of Beethoven, while I sat at the open window, gazing across the water towards Dinard, thinking of *Theophilus*, and smoking. . . ."

That was another compensation that St Malo offered – in addition to legend, Dr Mann and Mme Rollet – English tobacco, and as much of it as he could smoke. He had met the amiable Captain Dowie, whose boat *The City of London* made regular trips between Southampton and St Malo, and who brought him not only tobacco, but also – after the usual detailed instructions had been sent to Secker, who had them – Douglas' brown bag, containing his clothes, and his overcoat. By the time he returned to Paris, early in September, he was better dressed than he had been for nearly a year, and took with him several pounds of tobacco.

iii

As to why he returned, perhaps he found lack of any "inspiration" too frustrating. Or perhaps, as the war looked like ending, he wished to be ready to leave – in whatever directions he might decide upon – from a Paris terminus. It is even possible that St Malo, like how many other places, had – at any rate for the moment – outlived his patience with it. When he arrived in Paris he went back to his old lodgings at 45 rue Pigalle, but after a few days moved to the rue Buffault in the same arrondissement. This was quite near the rue de l'Agent Bailly, at the corner of which the "passionate farewellings" took place that are mentioned in *Looking Back*. As to when these occurred or who the other party was; when he threw his watch defiantly into the Seine much as Rousseau had once disposed of his; when he began giving lessons in French to American Ordnance officers at Vincennes, or was cajoled into entertaining the girls in a brothel and emerged – this was during one of his two Parisian winters – to find a cab horse standing with each of its four feet firmly planted on newspaper to stop it slipping on the icy road – *when* these incidents occurred hardly matters: they are essential threads in the tapestry of his Parisian life as described in *Looking Back*.

Essential threads: these, incidentally, were what were missing from parts of his frayed overcoat. He should, he wrote, have thrown it away, but in the circumstances took it instead to a tailor whose place was not far from the rue Buffault:

We had a short preliminary conversation on the horrors of the War, in the course of which it was discovered that both of us had sons at the front. This sentimental reason prompted him to make me an unusually moderate offer for doing the job; something like thirty francs. It was kind of him. What was still kinder was that when I came to pay for the coat and laid down a fifty-franc note on his counter, the dear old man mistook it for one of a hundred francs and gave me change accordingly. At any other time of life I should instinctively have pointed out this error on his part; at that moment, however, I succeeded in dominating the impulse to be honest, pocketed the change, and wished him good morning. The tailor might be poor, but he was richer than I was, and here, in any case, was one square meal, dropped from the sky. Disgraceful conduct, which I should not hesitate to repeat if my stomach were as empty as it then was.

This is one of several passages – a mild one – in *Looking Back* which may have prompted the critic Raymond Mortimer to point out, pertinently, that in this book Douglas "coolly admits to odious conduct that anyone else would try to forget". Mortimer, who of course is also well aware of the book's merits – frankness of the above kind being one of them – here draws attention to Douglas' shamelessness, and thinks he may never have met anyone so unregenerate. The passage about the tailor has been quoted with this in mind as an example of Douglas' curious and apparently uncharacteristic taste for "naming himself in public". He is not merely shameless: he deliberately displays his shamelessness. In the same way, he is not merely atheist, but anti-theist; not merely homosexual (as well as heterosexual) but a paederast; and he did not merely come to dislike his wife, but took every opportunity of vilifying her to others even twenty or thirty years after her death. If there is one adjective which fits him like a glove, it is "perverse"; he was not only contràry, in the old homely sense of the word, but went out of his way to suggest that the unusual tastes which he made so much healthier than so many other people by his robust and zestful attitude were sinister or wicked. And he delighted to hint at or describe various amusements that might shock his listeners or readers.

Douglas' son at the front was, of course, Archie. He had arrived in France early in 1918. In October he was "blown up and slightly gassed" near Cambrai, and his father obtained a three-day casualty permit to visit him in hospital in Amiens. It was here that the "brief but convulsive love-episode" occurred which is alluded to in *Looking Back*, and amplified in a Berg annotation by William King: on the way to the hospital Douglas "encountered a Madagascan soldier who was lying dead-drunk in the gutter and who if he is still alive is unlikely to realise that he was once buggered by the writer of *South Wind*".

About two months earlier, during a big advance from the Allied lines Eric had found himself in charge of two messengers who had to be sent to the front line. They were killed. Two more were sent and were also killed. Eric then refused to send any more, and took the message himself. He was lucky enough to get through, and for his bravery was mentioned in despatches and awarded the Military Medal.

iv

At the beginning of September, perhaps just before he left St Malo, a complete typescript of the book that was to be published as *Alone* was sent to John Mavrogordato, for criticism and general comments. With his usual uncertainty about titles, Douglas had provisionally called it, or accepted Mavrogordato's suggestion of calling it, *Sunshine*.

The typescript was composed from a rearrangement of the manuscript version, most of which had probably been written before he left Italy. It differs from the published book in two main respects. Firstly, it contains about forty (manuscript) pages – which were actually half-foolscap pages, in accordance with his custom of leaving room for corrections and additions – on the subject of Tuscan blasphemies, alluded to in the footnote on page 176 of *Alone*. Secondly, it also contained about eighteen manuscript pages devoted to the Greek Anthology. These two subjects were distributed in sections through the book in Douglas' manner; he was supposed to be reading and commenting on the Greek during the course of his travels, and to be gathering information about Tuscan swear-words from a certain Aldo, whom he supposedly met in Florence from time to time during the three months he spent there from February to May 1917.

Mavrogordato liked it better than *South Wind*, but thought that perhaps the "swear-words subject" was overdone: ". . . there is too much of it in quantity: and in making too much of it you are in danger of the schoolgirlish air of thinking the subject of swearing an inexhaustible joke." This home truth probably made Douglas remove the whole subject, although, as three years were to pass before the book was published, it is possible that he suppressed it after deciding to live in Florence.

Meanwhile, instalments of the book had begun to appear in Hutton's *Anglo-Italian Review* in August (1918), and the faithful and admiring editor made certain that each number of his journal – for a year – contained a chapter or section of Douglas' book. "Nothing will induce me, my dear Douglas," he wrote, before receiving the first contribution, "not to print it." When it arrived, it turned out to be *A Traveller of the Twenties*, a description of Crauford Tait Ramage, the English eccentric who explored the "Nooks and By-ways of Italy" dressed in a white merino frock coat, and carrying an umbrella. "Anything," wrote Hutton, "from your dear old hand would have been welcome, but this gorgeously humorous account of a book and person, who I suppose never existed, is as fine a creation in its own way as anything in your novel."[84] He was apologetic about payment, but could not get Constable to agree to more than three guineas. On the other hand, he himself was determined to do more, and arranged with Secker to insert a free advertisement for *South Wind* in the

Review; and wanted to commission someone to write an article for it on Douglas' work. Was there anyone whom Douglas would like to do this? Douglas sent him the names of three people; Eckersley was one, and the other two were probably Garnett and Straus.

v

Ralph Straus[85] had written one of the earliest reviews of *South Wind*, anonymously, for the *Bystander*; and two months after its appearance had written to Douglas revealing that he was the author and apparently sending either a description or a photograph of himself or a friend, asking if Douglas had a copy of *Old Calabria* to spare for this person. Douglas said he only wished he had, but he hadn't:

> I think if you sent the card to Mr Rafael Sabatini (Secker's partner) one might get a copy at trade price – possibly cheaper: who knows? Possibly for nothing. But I won't hold out hopes. Money is tight. I wish I were.
>
> Yes; Secker is slinking about Hounslow and Rotherhythe in a false beard, pretending to be a Dutch pimp. On fine nights he sleeps in the Green Park, and he always walks into houses backwards, so as to make people think he is coming out. Artful, eh?

This bit of tomfoolery was obviously an over-enthusiastic response to a suggestion by Straus that Secker was "crafty" or something similar. Straus had apparently nailed his colours to the mast and could be trusted with certain intimacies. Possibly he had even been vouched for by Faith Mackenzie who knew his mother. At any rate, the friendship by letter developed rapidly and led to the exchange of about 300 letters of considerable frankness during the next four or five years.

Apart from a certain subject, which was discussed with all the more relish because its details were thinly disguised, there may be traced in this correspondence Douglas's suspicion, then his distrust, and finally his desertion of Secker. The animus against Secker begins – the first indication of it is in the letter which has been partly quoted – before sheets of *South Wind* had been sold to America at the end of 1917, and therefore does not originate with any copyright problem connected with the USA.

Straus had been working in a hospital in Kent: "So you are examining conscripts for hernia! Well, you might do worse. Clever of you, to have got that job . . . I too have walked the Hospitals. I killed my first patient, a girl, in the Lipari Islands. R.I.P. . . . Lots of good hernias here, if you are homesick for them." Straus was also a Petronius enthusiast, and was urged to write the missing portions, and "When you set up your printing press, I will persuade you to print for me a selection of 500 limericks with notes explanatory and otherwise. The notes will be of the ripest scholarship, and the book will prove a sociological document of great value for future generations."

Straus had suggested that Douglas might like to write something for the *Bystander*, and Douglas had said that he would like to: "A few guineas is *just* what I want at this moment." So would Straus send him a few extracts from the *Bystander* that would give him some idea of the general tone of the paper? And did Straus know anything about getting into the Indian or Shanghai police forces, as Douglas had a young friend in the trenches who had decided to join one or the other of them after the war and would like some information?

It was at about this time, in September, when Douglas was back in Paris, that the campaign against Secker warmed up:

Secker's account of the sales of South Wind has reached me, from which it appears that my total profit out of that book is £71. I have sent it on to my agent Hughes Massie (to whom Secker, of course, ought to have sent it) who may be able to pick a hole in it – as the profits strike me as ridiculously small for a book which is now in its fourth edition. [i.e., impression]

In short, I anticipate a row with Secker which will not be the first, though it will certainly be the last. I must get another publisher, if I am ever going to write again.

Now Secker has, in his office, a tin trunk of mine containing manuscripts, family letters, some old curios and so forth which I put there, considering them too valuable to be sent to a depository. This box must be got out of that office before the row begins: the decks must be cleared for action. Can you fetch it, and take it to your abode and keep it for me in safety? In that case, I would send you a letter authorizing you to take it away and write simultaneously to Secker to that effect. You would have to take it to your place in a taxi; there would also be the expense of porterage, all of which I would be only to [sic] happy to re-fund you, if you can get hold of the damned thing and *sit on it* – i.e. put it in some safe place in your house – until I can see to it myself . . .

That seemed all right; but then it occurred to him in a postscript on the following day that "hostilities *may* begin at any moment", because he had already written to Hughes Massie, and if Massie found that "things were not as they should be", he might tackle Secker at once:

That is why I am enclosing you this paper authorizing you to carry off the box, which, if you can manage it, please do as soon as you can, even if you can't continue keeping it at your house. (We can easily think of some other place in a week or two) I have written Secker to say that a friend of mine may be coming to Paris soon and will bring the box over here to me, as I need it badly. So don't forget: *you're going to Paris!* I hope that's clear? I should be eternally grateful if you could arrange this. I don't like the idea of that box being stored with Secker if I am to have a row with him – it would put me under an awkward kind of obligation . . .

By 19th September Douglas has heard from Straus that the latter has successfully "raided" Secker's office and removed the tin box:

> You ask whether it be worth burgling? Yes, it is worth burgling, and that is precisely why I wanted to get it out of that neighbourhood before the row begins, if there is to be a row. It *is* worth burgling, and *don't you* touch it, because there is a spring gun inside, which goes off the minute you open the lid, unless one knows the trick, which I am not going to tell you. SO BE WARNED.

He reports in the same letter that he has only received £15 for *Fountains in the Sand*: "What do you think of that? I can't go on being an author at this rate . . . The new book is done. But I'll be buttered before I send it to Secker." Mavrogordato, in a letter of about the same date, referring to Douglas' complaints about *South Wind*, says "Secker is so timid that he probably printed very small editions [i.e. impressions], thereby losing custom (because of the interval between each edition [i.e. impression] during which the book is unobtainable) and increasing his own expenses. This is just what he has just done with Monty's book, in spite of advice threats beseechings from M. . . . I think M. will kill Secker if he comes home."

This is all very well, from the writers' point of view; but let the writers see how courageous they would be if the positions were reversed. Secker was by no means timid; no one who was timid would have started his list with *The Passionate Elopement* or have published *Old Calabria* in the middle of a war, or, later, would have re-issued Lawrence's *The Rainbow*.[86] He was prudent, as all who care about quality must be, since the books with large sales come to them only by chance. In fact, Secker started *South Wind* off with an impression of 997 in June, followed it cautiously as most publishers would have, with a further 516 in August, and when all doubt about its immediate success was removed by that second impression selling out, printed another 980 in November. Considering that 1500 was considered a good sale for a well-received novel in those days and that Douglas had published no other novels, this record of nearly 2500 copies issued in six months is one that any publisher would have been justified in thinking creditable.

Hughes Massie, naturally enough, found nothing wrong with Secker's figures. Douglas left Secker nevertheless: he had simply made up his mind to do so, with or without proof of his suspicions. That is why *Alone* was not published by Secker.

vi

As to *Theophilus*, he had begun it, and had asked both Straus and Eden Phillpotts if they could suggest dailies, weeklies, or monthlies in which it might be serialised. As it happened, the book was held up almost as soon as he had made the enquiry:

> I found it impossible to warm my imagination to the required pitch on an insufficient dietary. Some of us are supposed to produce our best efforts under the stimulus of privations; such a state of affairs paralyses my initiative. I must be well fed, like those mousing cats who capture mice not to still the pangs of hunger but for sport. No starving cat will throw its soul into the task of sitting in front of a mouse-hole motionless, hour after hour, for the fun of possibly seeing a mouse emerge. Hunger has made it listless and apathetic; it drifts away. Even so, here in Paris, I drifted away from *Theophilus*.

Apart from *Theophilus*, there had been Straus' invitation to write for the *Bystander*. This had not turned out well. He had asked Douglas to write, simply; but Douglas had asked, in turn, for "a few subjects", and something on "the German professor" had been suggested by Straus. This, or what seems by inference to have been this, was written and sent off, with strict injunctions that it was not to be signed with his name. "Lasko" was suggested as a pseudonym. The piece was never printed, probably because – if it is that *Plea for the German Professor* of which a copy has survived – its irony verged rather on the side of savagery than of light-hearted fun, and was therefore perhaps thought to be too unpatriotic for the time.

The last few weeks in Paris were unpleasant. The "relative opulence" to which he refers as being the consequence of teaching French, came to an end with the Armistice, in November. Thereafter his circumstances seem to have dwindled until they were worse than they had been at any previous time in Paris. On 7th December he moved from the rue Buffault to a back room across the river in the rue Servandoni, near the Luxembourg Gardens, and it seems to have been depressing or squalid or both, at any rate cold and gloomy. "Marcel still came to see me when he was in the mood, to cheer me up. I had given up bothering about other people."

vii

Marcel was a plump but ragged *voyou*, a tough little product of the under-world, angel-faced, with a profile of "gem-like purity and thick-clustering curls". He was amusing, unstable emotionally, and liable to fits of genero-sity, when he would take Douglas out to the circus or stand him drinks. Douglas never asked where his money came from nor what he and his family did; he never even asked Marcel what his surname was, being fairly certain that answers to such questions would have been lies. For Marcel was probably an "implement, a decoy, who for some reason or other took a momentary fancy to me". There was something feline and sinister about him, which moralists would have disapproved of. Douglas found him instructive, and his society "a liberal education".

Part of this education occurred soon after Douglas had moved to the rue Servandóni. He needed medicine from the chemist, but felt too ill to fetch it, so asked Marcel if he would get it. Douglas only had a 100 franc note. Marcel said he would be back in a moment with medicine and change; but he did not return – the temptation had been too much for him. Douglas, who says he was more attached to the money than the boy, determined to try and find him just for the satisfaction of telling him what he thought of him. The money, he knew, would be gone. He began look-ing in Marcel's usual haunts . . .

Meanwhile Douglas had decided – a sudden resolution, he calls it – that if he were going to become a derelict, he would become one in the sun. He sold every superfluous asset, crammed what was left into a single suitcase, and decided to leave on the 12th.

On that very day, he discovered Marcel in a café, dressed in a handsome new overcoat, and gave him a mild, though sarcastic rebuke, referring to the overcoat and the money with which it had been bought; but Marcel was frightened by Douglas' threat to tell his confederates about him, and implored him to leave. Douglas said he was leaving – for Marseille.

In the evening when he arrived at the Gare de Lyon, Marcel was waiting for him – to say goodbye. He was dressed in his overcoat and had a skin disease on his hand, which Douglas guessed would soon appear on his own. When Marcel realised that Douglas was actually going, a sudden change came over him. "He set up a terrific howl. Nothing I could say in the way of consolation had the slightest effect, and his chubby little face, all streaming with tears, attracted more attention than I cared about. He wanted to come too; he implored to be taken into the carriage. Everybody sympathised with him as he leaned against the outside of the compart-ment, sobbing as if his heart would break; there were some ugly looks in my direction, for it was a clear case of an Englishman giving pain to a poor French child. A burly fellow, standing next to me, asked quite indignantly: 'What! Aren't you taking the little one with you?' How I longed for the train to start! In its small way, this was one of the most disconcerting scenes I can remember."

At last the train pulled out; Marcel disappeared from view; and an appalling journey began.

It took him three nights and two and a half days to reach Menton. He had to stand the whole way, packed so tight in the corridor that everyone supported his neighbour: "the hopelessness of obtaining any kind of repose or of abandoning your upright posture – it became an agony; one was ready to scream . . . our only relief being when we could move about for a short while on the platform of some station." The agony was worse for Douglas than for his fellow-travellers because he had slipped in the roadway near the Gare de Lyon, and a taxi, "swerving in the nick of time to avoid my stomach," had run over his leg.

CHAPTER NINETEEN

———————◆◇———————

Menton
1919

i

He arrived at Menton on Sunday 15th December with 61 francs in his pocket. A little money might soon begin to trickle in, but very little; and he did not despair of finding work of some sort in Menton; but he was unwilling to spend any of the money in his pocket on a porter or cab, although carrying his heavy suitcase in his weakened condition was now impossible. He looked around him at the station for help, and noticed a group of schoolboys who were saying goodbye to a friend. Perhaps one of them . . .?

"It took a little courage to ask an unknown schoolboy of good family to carry my bag and, what made it far worse, in front of his companions; I was desperate. I went into the matter. I spoke of the horrible journey from Paris, of the preceding night spent on the floor of the Nice refreshment room, and how that I was too weak to carry the bag myself and too poor to pay for a porter: *voilà*! Would he be so kind as to help me, after he had seen his companion off? This was a pretty severe test also for 'Mr R.'. Something inspired him to say 'Je veux bien'."

The boy's name was René – René Mari – and he was so obliging and helpful, finding for Douglas a cheap hotel of just the kind he needed, that he went home – he lived with his parents in Ventimiglia – with a note from Douglas to his father saying how grateful he was and regretting that he could not come over to meet the father himself. The result of this was that both parents came to see him on the following day, and his acquaintance with René developed easily and naturally from this good start.

The miserable Parisian period of deprivation had ended and an exceedingly happy relationship began that was to last a good many years. René was fourteen at this time, and was very quickly taken under Douglas' wing. Soon, instead of commuting every day from Ventimiglia to Menton to his school, he was staying in Menton with Douglas. He:

... is with me all the time. He goes to school here and his parents live across the Italian frontier. He goes to see them every 2–3 weeks (it is only a few minutes in the train) and they come here now and then and bring me Italian cigars and other delicacies. The boy never did a stroke of work formerly; now, the headmaster says, it has been a *regeneration*. What it is, to have a kind heart! This is not the first miracle of its kind I have performed ... I have a perfect genius for teaching and inspiring the young ...

In some respects, possibly in more respects than is the case with most people, Douglas knew himself exactly; certainly, he never wrote more truly of himself than in this last sentence.

The effect of the relationship upon René's school work had made itself manifest within three months; and its effect upon Douglas is also obvious within the same period. His letters to Straus, which are so frank and unreserved, take on a note of revived high spirits and facetiousness, of fresh attack and purpose. He was once again "indulging his genius", and the other activities of his daily life were beginning to fall into place. His life was easier, happier, and once again held promise.

ii

One of the good prospects was of a visit to Greece in order to write a book about the country on the lines of *Old Calabria*. The suggestion that such a book should be written by Douglas had been made to Venizelos, the Prime Minister:[87] "The result of this suggestion? Venizelos was delighted. And what would I be pleased to accept by way of remuneration? Three hundred pounds. Done! Government money, of course." At this point Douglas seems to have been undecided about accepting the offer: for one thing, he had not finished *Theophilus*, and for another, nothing, he wrote to Straus, would move him out of Menton: "I would sooner be cut into a million pieces." Nevertheless, as was often the case when he was at his most hyperbolical, he almost immediately began to envisage the opposite extreme – in this case the journey to Greece – and informed Secker a fortnight later that he would probably stop at Sant' Agata on the way. Perhaps it was Hutton who convinced him – Hutton who had for months been trying to get him to accept an offer of £100 in advance from Constable (Hutton was one of their readers) on his new novel – and would go on trying to the end of Douglas' days to help him in any way he could:

If I were you I should accept the offer of £300 and go to Greece. You can easily spend the whole of the summer in Greece on £300 and have a delightful time I should imagine. Surely one could live there for £2 sterling a day at the present rate of exchange but I strongly urge you to get the money into your hands, the whole of it mind you, before you start. I have very little faith left in Italians and still less in Greeks.

By 18th April he had the cheque: "I ought to go to Greece and write a book about it – my expenses being defrayed by the Greek Government, who have already (foolish ones) sent me a cheque of £300 in anticipation." However, he could not move until his novel was off his hands, because once out there, he would probably stay a long time; and it would be a terrible wrench to leave Menton, "not, I may mention, on account of the scenery or climate". In the end, he did not leave Menton until the end of August; and did not get to Greece for nearly a year. Meanwhile, the prospect was pleasant to contemplate.

Immediately, though, when he had sent the cheque off to his bank in London, he did two things: sent cheques to Hutton and Straus asking them to send him English notes – a request that was made to various people all his life when the exchange was good – and went with René for a short walking tour in Provence during the Easter holiday.

Certainly, prospects were improving. René was a great solace; and soon after he had met him, he had found money too. A letter suddenly arrived out of the blue from William Arkwright, whom Douglas had never met, but had corresponded with. Arkwright said he had heard that Douglas had financial troubles: would he accept a cheque (enclosed) for £20? Douglas replied that he would be delighted to accept it, and while thanking Arkwright, said that he hoped he was not inconveniencing him. Not at all, replied Arkwright; he had plenty of money. In that case, Douglas replied, would Arkwright be so kind as to send him £20 a month till further notice? Arkwright did this, and it enabled Douglas to give up looking for work, and also to leave the Hôtel d'Italie. Now he felt ready to tackle his novel again.

The trouble with that was that *Theophilus* was hung up. It simply would not go:

I have now been exactly a year, writing 50,000 words, and I can't get the damned job finished. It WONT come right: simply won't. It is a task beyond my powers; *outside* them, I should say, for it would be child's play to any one else. God knows what will happen.

What happened was that *Theophilus* got itself finished somehow within about three months.

After various Italian wanderings in August and September, he arrived in Florence on 20th September. The date is worth mentioning because his wanderings were over – in the sense of having a permanent place of

his own to which he could return – although he would not know this for
several months. Florence was to be his headquarters for more than eighteen
years, until the summer of 1937. There were many journeys away from
Florence in all those years – he may not have spent more than fifteen of
them in the city itself – but it was his centre, his workshop, his domicile,
the nearest substitute for a home that he had ever had since the days of the
Villa Maya and the insecure years on Capri which had succeeded them.

iii

During the preceding months at Menton, the anti-Secker feeling had persisted. Early in February Secker had written enquiring what Douglas' plans
were:

> You ask after my plans. I have no definite ones; Greece may materi-
> alise; whatever happens, I shall not stay here more than another month.
> As to work, I have all but finished a short novel about which I have
> not made up my mind save that it is no [sic] worth publishing under
> conditions like those of *South Wind* which has now, in two years, pro-
> duced me £16 or £8 a year. Not good enough. I mean, not worth the
> bother of correspondence and proof-correcting and waiting at conti-
> nental post offices – not worth the postage. I shall sit on it, if I can't
> get better conditions, and my children in due course may utilise the
> MS to wipe their behinds with.
> The same with travel-books. Some day you must explain how I
> managed to get on [sic] £15 out of *Fountains in the Sand*. As to *Old
> Calabria*, which you say is out of print, I don't know how we stand at
> all; I am so discouraged about publishing such things that no reader
> would ever have known of the existence of my last book if Edward
> Hutton had not begged for some extracts out of it for his Anglo-
> Italian Review where it has been appearing every month since August.
> He has got enough material now to outlast his paper, and the MS will
> go in about a fortnight's time together with my other heavy and more
> valuable stuff to a friend in Paris, while I depart to Greece or Sardinia
> or Tunis, or possibly Hell.
> If you like this stuff – Mavro, who alone has seen the MS, says he
> prefers it to *South Wind* – if you like to publish this whole book you
> must make up your mind quickly and send me £100 advance on royal-
> ties together with the two contracts in which you can follow that of
> *South Wind* save that the royalties must be 20% on the first 2000 copies,
> that the editions must be stated to consist of 1000 copies and that you
> undertake to copyright the book in America. I will let you have your

contract and the MS back by return of post. But don't do yourself any violence about this; the thing will be perfectly happy in Paris where it can stay, for all I care, till the moon is made of ripe green cheese! I don't leave Mentone till I hear of the arrival of these things in Paris. And I shall leave Mentone as soon as ever I can.

As to writing novels for £10 a year: *I* can't do it! I wish I could, for in that case perhaps I would.

Too damned knocked up to write any more just now. Filthy weather here and I am as sick as a cat.

This is a not unreasonable letter from a disappointed man. It contains a few threats of the kind that are sometimes used in business; it replaces what might have been self-pity with bravado; it makes an offer. But behind it lay the same suspicions – namely, that he was on the one hand being swindled, and on the other, whether being swindled or not, was not having his interests looked after: the eternal and neurotic complaint of the author to his publisher, sometimes, but rarely, justified. The feeling against Secker could always be warmed up in correspondence with Straus:

Much obliged for what you say about "Old Calabria". Secker has just written to me that 1000 copies were printed, of which 500 (!) went to America. Do you believe this? I don't! Why should he send 500 copies to America – and if he did, why the bloody fucking hell don't I get any money for them? He is a slippery beggar.

This is followed by a repetition of the complaint that he only got £15 out of *Fountains in the Sand* which Secker "naïvely confesses, is now out of print. I wish somebody would buggar [sic] him with a *pineapple*. Will you do this for me? I should be ever so much obliged." No sooner had this extravagant request gone off to Straus, than a further enquiry came from Secker. He received a curt reply to the effect that he could judge the quality of the book that was to be called *Alone* from the sections printed in the *Anglo-Italian Review* and that Douglas was "not keen to print this book just now, as a new novel would do me more good at this moment, and also because I can go on serializing it with Hutton or elsewhere for another year or more. It is simply a question of getting some money in hand ere I leave Mentone. That thou doest, do quickly." Straus was asked, in a later letter, why that pineapple should "be considered to be *wasted* after the operation on Secker. Nobody, surely, need *know*? As to its not fitting him: that is exactly what I want. Anyhow, I am not taking any further notice of him, and have left his last ridiculous proposal unanswered." In spite of this bawdy fun with Straus, Douglas does not seem to have had any personal animosity towards Secker, simply a dislike of him as a man of business, and this dislike largely engendered by disappointment with the financial rewards of being an author: "Damn contracts: I am sick of all such things. As I said, the correspondence, proof correcting and posting etc etc involved in publishing a book is such an infernal nuisance that almost nothing, nowadays, will make it worth my while, even if I have to starve"; but in the same letter, having heard that Secker may be coming to Italy, he adds: "If so, we may be able to meet. You could come by this Riviera route. Above address always finds me, meanwhile." And there is another friendly note in September. In November, from Florence, he writes that he will be glad to see Secker, who is in Italy, "on your homeward way, if you can manage it":

That novel has to be serialized first. No use talking about it for another year. Besides, you know, publishing novels with you is a luxury for millionaires. I haven't yet received the miserable few pounds due to me since June of *last* year. And why the blazes don't you ever advertize?

If you like meanwhile to print my Italian travel-book, you can have it. £100 in advance on royalties, and contract on the lines of that for *South Wind* with a few alterations and improvements (for myself, of course). It has about seventy or eighty thousand words, and no illustrations. About half the book has appeared in scattered form in the Anglo-Italian Review, and I could let you see these printed extracts, nicely bound together, if you swear before God Almighty to let me have them back within a month. They would give you an idea of the tone of the whole. The best portions were reserved for later issues of that Review and cannot now be serialized, as that infernal concern has just changed hands and is now devoted entirely to trade matters. But don't do yourself any violence about this. I have had offers for it from two other London publishers, but as they don't even hint at an advance on royalties, I'll see them damned first.

And that reminds me. You must, you really must, reprint *Old Calabria*. I alone, within the last ten days, have received letters from three people complaining that they cannot obtain it anywhere – or ask at Hatchard's whether they don't get frequent demands for it. So hurry up. Why on earth did you print only 500 copies? If you won't reprint I must jolly well find somebody who will, in accordance with that rotten contract of ours. As Hughes Massie is responsible for that part of the business, I shall get him to write you in the same sense. Losing money all the time! And I can't afford to lose it. You seem to forget, my dear fellow, that I am not Monty, or Alexander von Humboldt, or Mr Gladstone, or Conan Doyle, or Victoria Cross, or even the Archangel Gabriel, but only

Yours sincerely

Norman Douglas

A fortnight later, after hearing from Secker that a new edition of *Old Calabria* was being prepared, he is still fairly severe with him:

> Glad to hear about *Old Calabria*. I wonder, by the way, whether that reprint of *Fountains in the Sand* is ever coming off. It was Massie who told me that only five hundred copies of O.C. had been printed. He wrote "it would appear that the first edition was of 500 copies". He probably forgot his 500 American ones.
>
> So you see that not only authors, but also literary agents, may be sometimes mistaken.
>
> And possibly even publishers. You, for instance, when you say that "South Wind royalties are paid up to the end of last year". I have certainly not received anything due since June 1918, and Massie's account to me, dated Feb. 4, 1919, encloses a cheque for royalties on S.W. "up to June 1918" Furthermore, he wrote me on the 10 Feb. 1919 "Mr Secker writes that he is unable to make the return up to December 31 at present as his book-keeping department is in arrears". How am I to reconcile your statement and his? It can't be done! Do look up the matter when you get home.
>
> The fact is I have so much trouble, and give so much trouble, trying to rake in the few shillings which I imagine to be due to me that, if I ever perpetrate another book – damned if I don't sell the copyright and have done with it.
>
> I'll send you those Anglo-Italian Review things as soon as I get them back – in a day or so. I hear you have just published "the hottest book on record". For shame, for shame! *Do* send me a copy.
>
> Much love to Monty
Yours always
Norman Douglas.

Nevertheless, the game with Straus had to be kept up because only in these letters could Douglas make Secker the scapegoat for his outraged feelings:

> Secker is in Capri with Compton Mackenzie and threatens to return to London via here. If he does, I am going to poison him and throw his corpse into the Arno . . . But please keep this between ourselves. These things oughtn't to be too much talked about.

The scapegoat, true to custom, was innocent – or almost innocent; a little dilatory about payment, perhaps, and possibly not as aware as he might have been of the continuing – and growing – demand for Douglas' work; but on the whole, doing his best for an author who was becoming more and more difficult and demanding. It is probably true to say that

Douglas could not make up his mind whether he wanted to be published by Secker or not; and Secker could not make up his mind whether publishing Douglas would be worthwhile in terms of the haggling and argument and fault-finding that would almost certainly follow. The closer Douglas clung to Straus, the less chance there was for Secker anyway; and in April 1920 Douglas signed a contract for *Theophilus* with Chapman and Hall, through Straus. Secker, who had put Douglas on the map as a writer, published no more of his books.

iv

Throughout the Menton period there had been invitations to Straus and Hutton to visit him there. Straus had also been introduced, at long distance, to Eric, who had left the army. It appears that Straus got Eric his job in the Ministry of Pensions, in which both Eric and his sister Violet began to work; but Eric did not like it, although perhaps he did not discover this at once, or if he did, disguised the fact from Douglas, who wrote to Straus that Eric seemed to "relish his work, and it is awfully good of you getting that job for him". But a month or so later Straus seemed to think that Eric was so fed up with his job that he might leave it. Douglas reassured him: "Eric will not leave his job. I will talk to him, and he always listens to what I say. The fact is, life in the army ruins a man for every other occupation." Nevertheless, Eric had "behaved like a brick all through life, and does me the greatest credit. If I left behind me nothing but him, as a memorial, it would suffice to prove to posterity that I had not lived in vain."

Archie, also, had been sent along to see Straus while on leave from army duties in Germany, and Straus had fed him and looked after him. When he had returned to duty, his father wrote to Straus:

> As to Archie – I have had no news from him whatever. He seems to have forgotten my existence. I *presume* he is in Germany, but – who knows? You might, however, note this: that the next time he sends you any money to buy tobacco with, buy it by all means, but send it to me, not to him. On second thoughts, you might as well send me the money too . . . Wish you could have come here! There is something you would be interested to see.

René, of course, was the something that Straus would have been interested to see; and just as Straus had helped Douglas with Eric and Archie, so he had also obligingly contributed to the happiness of Douglas and René. He had been asked – it was a request that was made to various friends at intervals throughout Douglas' life abroad – to obtain "an ordinary cricket belt of the best quality: blue by preference, though any other colour would do". These peculiarly English articles of dress played an almost ritualistic part as tokens of Douglas' esteem for his young friends. C. K. Scott-Moncrieff was one of those to whom Douglas applied for help in obtaining such belts. He informed his friend Vyvyan Holland that Douglas

> wrote the other day asking me to get him three cricket belts, uso inglese, with snake clasps; I did so, but asked him whether it was a secret society (the shop seemed quite used to supplying my friend in Florence): I quoted the lines which you may remember:
>
> > a cricket belt was round his waist
> > and light and brisk his tread
> > but I never saw a boy who looked
> > so wistfully at the bed.

CHAPTER TWENTY

Lawrence, Magnus, and Greece
1919–1920

i

In Florence, Douglas lodged in the Pensione Balestri, and began to show signs of settling down: "I am going to take lessons in modern Greek; meanwhile, I peruse endless books on that country which one can get out of a vast circulating library here. There is also the British Institute where you can read papers and go to sleep in armchairs"; and in a burst of personal revelation, he tells Straus that he must go and get something to eat, as it is 12.15 but must first of all shave:

> Once I am shaved and washed, I can't do any more writing or even thinking; *I must be dirty*. It's awkward, but there it is. Are you like that? I fear not. You probably have a lovely wash the minute you get out of bed. So do I, when I can afford it. But when I have to work, I must be dirty till 12.15 p.m.: see?

For "I must be dirty" one should read "I must not be distracted from my writing by premature activity"; there was probably never anyone with less *nostalgie de la boue,* in any sense of the expression, than Douglas, as the unfailing correctness of his appearance in public always showed.

Although now virtually settled in Florence, he went to Rome for four or five days to see Faith Mackenzie, who was on her way from Capri to England, and helped her with passport trouble. He and Hutton saw her off on her train to Paris, then Norman returned to Florence and the Vieusseux Library: "I read one book on Greece every day, and will soon know the country and the language so intimately that it will be sheer waste of time and money going there."

ii

On 15th November, 1919, D. H. Lawrence left England for Italy, having asked Douglas to find him a room in Florence:

I knew him before his marriage, in *White Peacock* days, and still hope that a certain photograph of him taken at that time may be reproduced somewhere. It was a charming likeness, with an ethereal expression in those youthful features. Then he came to see me with his newly-married wife; I cooked, in her honour, a German luncheon.

Since the Lawrences were married in July 1914, Douglas must have entertained them at Albany Mansions. Thereafter they would have met occasionally, perhaps, when Lawrence came to the *English Review* offices, just as they may have met originally in the earliest days of that journal's life under Ford Madox Hueffer:

He sometimes turned up at the *English Review* office with stories like the *Prussian Officer* written in that impeccable handwriting of his. They had to be cut down for magazine purposes; they were too redundant; and I was charged with the odious task of performing the operation.

Douglas was excited at the thought of seeing Lawrence again, and even more excited when Lawrence actually arrived. His friends were informed that Lawrence was with him and, judging by letters he wrote at the time to Straus, Reggie Turner, and Hutton, they appear to have enjoyed each other's company, though both were on their guard against traits in the other's character that they did not approve of. Lawrence wrote that Douglas never let him down, and the quality that Douglas admired in Lawrence is best described in his own words:

He was a man of naturally blithe disposition, full of childlike curiosity. The core of his mind was unsophisticated. He touched upon the common things of earth with tenderness and grace, like some butterfly poised over a flower – poised lightly, I mean, with fickle *insouciance* (for his books contain strange errors of observation). This, once more, was the direct reaction, the poet's reaction; the instantaneous record. No intervening medium, no mirage, hovered between Lawrence and what his eyes beheld. These things lay before him clear-cut, in their primordial candour, devoid of any suggestion or association. It was his charm. There was something elemental in him, something of the *Erdgeist*.

And there was something in Douglas that responded gladly to the call of the *Erdgeist*, the spirit of the earth.

Frieda Lawrence had returned to Germany for a visit to her parents – the first since 1914 – in October; but Lawrence had refused to go with her and had decided to go to Italy, where she could join him later.

He arrived at Florence with £9 in his pocket, and only a slightly larger sum left in the bank in London. He hoped that when Frieda joined him, she would bring another £2 or £3, but they would have to go carefully if they were to stay in Italy through the winter. He had written to Douglas asking him to find a cheap room, and leave a note about it at Cook's. Florence "seemed grim and dark and rather awful on the cold November evening", and he must have been reassured by the note at Cook's. He set off towards the address Douglas had provided, and had just passed the end of the Ponte Vecchio when he heard Douglas' voice:

"Isn't that Lawrence? Why of course it is, of course it is, beard and all! Well, how are you, eh? You got my note? Well, now, my dear boy, you just go on to the [Balestri] – straight ahead, straight ahead – you've got the number. There's a room for you there. We shall be there in half an hour. Oh, let me introduce you to M——"

I had unconsciously seen the two men approaching, D—— tall and portly, the other man rather short and strutting. They were both buttoned up in their overcoats, and both had rather curly little hats. But D—— was decidedly shabby and a gentleman, with his wicked red face and tufted eyebrows. The other man was almost smart, all in grey, and he looked at first sight like an actor-manager, common. There was a touch of down-on-his-luck about him too. He looked at me, buttoned up in my old thick overcoat, and with my beard bushy and raggy because of my horror of entering a strange barber's shop, and he greeted me in a rather fastidious voice, and a little patronisingly. I forgot to say I was carrying a small hand-bag. But I realised at once that I ought, in this little grey-sparrow man's eyes ... to be in a cab. But I wasn't. He eyed me in that shrewd and rather impertinent way of the world of actor-managers: cosmopolitan, knocking shabbily round the world.

He looked a man of about forty ... just the kind of man I had never met: little smart man of the shabby world, very much on the spot, don't you know.

"How much does it cost?" I asked D——, meaning the room.

"Oh, my dear fellow, a trifle. Ten francs a day. Third rate, tenth rate, but not bad at the price. Pension terms of course – everything included – except wine."

"Oh no, not at all bad for the money," said M——. "Well now, shall we be moving? You want the post-office, D——?" His voice was precise and a little mincing, and it had an odd high squeak.

"I do," said D——

"Well then come down here——." M—— turned to a dark little alley.

"Not at all," said D——. "We turn down by the bridge."

"This is quicker," said M——. He had a twang rather than an accent in his speech – not definitely American.

He knew all the short cuts of Florence. Afterwards I found that he knew all the short cuts in all the big towns of Europe.

I went on to the [Balestri] and . . . was taken to my room.

. . . After an hour or so someone tapped. It was D—— coming in with his grandiose air – now a bit shabby, but still very courtly.

"Why are you here – miles and miles from human habitation! I *told* her to put you on the second floor, where we are. What does she mean by it? Ring that bell. Ring it."

"No," said I, "I'm all right here."

"What!" cried D—— "In this Spitzbergen! Where's that bell?"

"Don't ring it," said I, who have a horror of chambermaids and explanations.

"Not ring it! Well, you're a man, you are! Come on. Have you had some tea – filthy muck they call tea here. I never drink it."

I went down to D——'s room on the lower floor. It was a littered mass of books and type-writer and papers: D—— was just finishing his novel. M—— was resting on the bed, in his shirt sleeves: a tubby, fresh-faced little man in a suit of grey, faced cloth bound at the edges with grey silk braid. He had light blue eyes, tired underneath, and crisp, curly, dark brown hair just grey at the temples. But everything was neat and even finicking about his person.

"Sit down! Sit down!" said D——, wheeling up a chair. "Have a whisky?" . . .

The room was dreadful. D—— never opened the windows: didn't believe in opening windows. He believed that a certain amount of nitrogen – I should say a great amount – is beneficial. The queer smell of a bedroom which is slept in, worked in, lived in, smoked in, and in which men drink their whiskies, was something new to me. But I didn't care. One had got away from the war.

We drank our whiskies before dinner. M—— was rather yellow under the eyes, and irritable; even his pink fattish face went yellowish.

"Look here," said D——. "Didn't you say there was a turkey for dinner? What? Have you been to the kitchen to see what they're doing to it?"

"Yes," said M—— testily. "I forced them to prepare it to roast."

"With chestnuts – stuffed with chestnuts?" said D——.

"They *said* so," said M——.

"Oh but go down and see that they're doing it. Yes, you've got to keep your eye on them, got to. The most awful howlers if you don't. You go now and see what they're up to." D—— used his most irresistible grand manner.

"It's too late," persisted M——, testy.

"It's *never* too late. You just run down and absolutely prevent tnem from boiling that bird in the old soup-water," said D——. "If you need force, fetch me."

Magnus went. He was a great epicure, and knew how things should be cooked. But of course his irruptions into the kitchen roused considerable resentment, and he was getting quaky. However, he went. He came back to say the turkey was being roasted, but without chestnuts.

"What did I tell you! What did I tell you!" cried D——. "They are absolute ——! If you don't hold them by the neck while they peel the chestnuts, they'll stuff the bird with old boots, to save themselves trouble. Of course, you should have gone down sooner, M——."

Dinner was always late, so the whisky was usually two whiskies. Then we went down, and were merry in spite of all things. That is, D—— always grumbled about the food. There was one unfortunate youth who was boots and porter and waiter and all. He brought the big dish to D——, and D—— always poked and pushed among the portions, and grumbled frantically, sotto voce, in Italian to the youth Beppo, getting into a nervous frenzy. Then M—— called the waiter to himself, picked the nicest bits off the dish and gave them to D——, then helped himself.

The food was not good, but with D—— it was an obsession. With the waiter he was terrible – "Cos'è? Zuppa? Grazie. No, niente per me. *No – No!* – Quest'acqua sporca non bevo io. I don't drink this dirty water. What – What's that in it – a piece of dish clout? Oh holy Dio, I can't eat another thing this evening ——"

And he yelled for more bread – bread being war-rations and very limited in supply – so M—— in nervous distress gave him his piece, and D—— threw the crumb part on the floor, anywhere, and called for another litre. . . .

Next morning Lawrence saw Magnus in his room, "a little Pontiff" in a blue silk dressing-gown "mincing about" with many cut-glass and silver-topped bottles on his dressing table, pomades, powders, an elegant little prayer book and life of St Benedict. "All he had was expensive and finicking." Douglas told Lawrence a little about Magnus – how he had been a manager for Isadora Duncan, and had edited the *Roman Review* just before the war. He admitted that Magnus seemed to be smitten by him: "All the better for me, ha-ha! – if he *likes* to run round for me. My dear fellow, I wouldn't prevent him, if it amuses him. Not for worlds."

A few days after Lawrence's arrival, Magnus' birthday was celebrated with a feast, at Douglas' insistence. Lawrence helped Douglas choose a small present for Magnus, who left on the day after his birthday, for Rome. He travelled, as always, first class: "Why should I go second? It's beastly enough to travel at all?"

It was a fortnight before Frieda arrived, and a further week before the Lawrences left the city. Lawrence had had ample time in which to become acquainted with all the local expatriates whom he sketches so vividly in *Aaron's Rod*.

iii

René came to Florence on a visit, arriving on Christmas Day, and it was at once obvious that he was ill. Douglas got him to his pensione as quickly as possible, put him to bed, and sent for a doctor. Pleurisy was diagnosed, and "things were quite critical at one moment: there was talk of an operation". He had to remain in bed for a month. "Now," wrote Douglas to Straus on 24th January, "he has turned the corner but can't, of course, move for a long while to come. The pension-bill is already over 600 frcs, quite apart from medicines and extra food: what the doctor's bill is going to be I tremble to think! Nor have I the faintest idea where the money is coming from. Let me have your prayers. I ought to be on my way to Greece by this time. A fix: if ever there was one. His school began on the 3rd January: the doctor won't hear of his going back to school for a long while, or even travelling . . . My only way out of it is to sell the copyright of *Theophilus*. Which is the most honest: Heinemann, Macmillan, or Constable? Which would be most likely to accept a book from me? Which would pay most? To which of them in other words would you advise me to apply?" Meanwhile, he had sent a typescript (of *Theophilus*?) to Curtis Brown in America for possible serialisation; and on the same day he wrote to Hutton to ask if he could sell Constable the copyright of *Theophilus*, warning Hutton that he would make the same offer to another firm and also to "Martin Secker who, *blackguard as he is*, may be prepared to pay fairly well with a view to not interrupting his Douglas series. Even then, he will probably succeed in letting me down somehow." Hutton was not informed of the nature of Douglas' predicament: Douglas could be tender and discriminating in respecting the susceptibilities of his friends, and Hutton, as an ardent Catholic, need not be thoughtlessly presented with the facts about René which would probably embarrass him and severely test his admirably liberal outlook and warm affection.

He was certainly a good deal frustrated and distracted. For a month at least, he had hardly ever got out of his room because of René's illness, and

for a further month his movements were restricted while René recupera-
ted. And anxiety about money, and parting from René to go to Greece.
and dentist's bills, all played their part in feelings of desperation: "Poverty
is terribly demoralising. I feel as if I could murder any old woman just
now, if she had money in her pocket and there was no fear of being
found out."

Constable, through Hutton, offered for the outright sale of *Theophilus*
(excluding US and Canadian rights) the sum that Secker had offered in
advance royalties; so that was no good (but it did not make him think
any more generously of Secker!). At the end of February, however,
Chapman and Hall, through Straus, offered an advance of £200; this, as
Douglas said, sounded as though it was as good an offer

> as I might dare to expect. All the same, didn't they see their way to
> buying the English copyright? I wish they did; firstly because just now
> I need as much money as I can ever get hold of, and secondly – well, it
> is a temperamental matter. I am constitutionally unfitted for correspon-
> dence with publishers or agents, for grappling with royalties and
> percentages. These things send a chill through my bones, each time I
> have to think of them, and *incapacitate me from work* ... They have
> taken years off my life and wasted hours and days and weeks of my time.
> When I have finished writing a book, I want to forget all about it as
> fast and as soon as I forget about my after-breakfast shit: I want some
> benevolent old gentleman to present me with a cheque, and then tell me
> to get on with something else. The mere thought that I might have to
> write to Chapman and Hall, on any subject whatever, once I have
> seriously settled down to my work in Greece, is enough to take off the
> edge of my appetite for that next job. Therefore: can't they be tempted
> into that other proposal?

As bait, a new edition of *Street Games* is offered and an option on the
new Italian book, which Douglas thinks is better than *Old Calabria*. "I
can hear your blasphemies," he ended (to Straus), "across half Europe, and
in spite of the closed windows and the din of the tramcars. A nice job
you've let yourself in for! Well, well – may the Lord requite you, for *I*
shall never live long enough. Let this be a lesson to you, in future, to be
very careful what kind of people you correspond with. Think how comfortable you might feel, at this very moment, if I had never been born."

By 10th March Douglas was in Rome, had accepted the Chapman and
Hall offer by telegram, and was waiting for two things: to have his fare
to Athens paid by the Greek Minister in Rome, and, with luck, to receive
and sign the contract with Chapman and Hall before leaving for Greece.
The publishers had objected to *Theophilus* as a title, and they or Straus

had suggested *The Lonely Unicorns* or *Get Thee Behind Me*. Douglas didn't think much of the first suggestion; as to the second, he did not dislike it as such, but thought the words "might be suggestive of a movement which would provoke a smile on the part of the prurient-minded"; furthermore, there was a Biblical flavour about them, and *Theophilus* was not at all a Biblical sort of devil, but the devil as he ought to be. The word summed up the "gentle non-morality of the whole book. It is easily pronounced, looks well in print, and has a certain air of distinction . . ." Later, Straus suggested *They Went*, and Douglas thought it "quite an inspiration", but still wanted *Theophilus* if they would have it. They would not, so *They Went* it became.

iv

He arrived in Athens on 25th March, and stayed at the British School of Archaeology. With its assistant director, Stanley Casson,[88] he went to the unveiling of Rupert Brooke's tomb on Skyros on Easter Monday, 5th April. He did not care for Skyros: deforestation, he wrote, had years ago dried up the water-springs and eroded the topsoil. Sterility was followed by poverty, and poverty by depopulation; but Rupert Brooke's grave, in a dell of olives sloping gently towards the sea, "was such as a poet might well long for . . . There is solitude in this favoured hollow, a solitude so intense and so kindly that one might imagine the Genii of Earth and Air still deigning to hold communion here with lovers of mortal clay . . . Hoopoes flitted about, and the grove was loud with nightingales and the twittering of goldfinches." Also, the tomb itself was all that it should have been.

The tomb was all it should have been – but the British School was not. It was comfortable, but suffered from an "Oxford atmosphere; not very Rabelaisian . . . I have done nothing improper since my arrival in this country – nothing to speak of." For this sort of reason, life in the British School, he decided, would injure his health in the long run. Also, he found he could not get on with the language which he had chattered in so happily in 1892, and engaged a teacher, but after six or seven lessons "it was apparent that I was too old to learn, too old or too stupid, or both." And then there was the formidable library: "Greece from too many angles. I was appalled at the task before me. Would I ever be able to assimilate all this material and fashion it into a readable book, seeing that *Old Calabria* had taken several years to write and many months of weary research?" And finally, there was the food, of which the less said the better: "The Greeks eat nothing, and drink less – and *they look like it*." By the middle of May, he could stand Greece no longer, and decided to go to

Sant' Agata as soon as possible to write up what he had so far seen and read. As to longer-term plans, he had finally decided to make Florence his permanent home: "It has grave drawbacks, but all the other places on earth that I can think of – and I have thought of all possible ones – are still less attractive to me, for one reason or another. I shall try to get a couple of unfurnished rooms, send to England for my few remaining books, and then instal myself there . . ."

He reached Sant' Agata on the 27th, and would not, he wrote to Hutton,

> go back to Greece if they paid me my weight in gold – which wouldn't be very much just now, owing to the systematic starvation one undergoes in that country . . . Keep my whereabouts *entre nous*. I shall stay here till I have recovered my spirits and rotundity, which may take several months . . . So glad to be back in this place after the desolation of Greece, with its sulky malarious inhabitants and filthy food. What a relief to come to a place, a green oasis, with views over the sea on both sides, where everybody smiles at you and where you can eat and drink till you burst, and where all the boys look like angels, and mostly are! Yes; I shall be needing cricket-belts very soon . . .

Greece was finally dismissed when he shaved off the "huge moustache" he had grown specially for his visit: "It is the only thing to be done in this country, unless you want to be raped by Albanian Shepherds *and* their dogs. I wouldn't mind the dogs so much, but one must draw the line somewhere." Removal of the moustache, he told Hutton, was a great pity from the artistic point of view, but he really could not stand it any longer.

CHAPTER TWENTY-ONE

Magnus
1920

i

Sant' Agata was deliciously cool, after Greece, and there were endless walks in pleasant company. "There is a great festival tonight at a neighbouring village which of course I have to attend; I shall probably spend the night in some cave, God knows with whom. This, let me tell you, is perfectly permissible on such occasions – unadulterated paganism, which it is one's bounden duty to keep." But the little place had grown popular, and prosperous, alas, which sent up the prices. The projected three months turned out to be three weeks, and he arrived in Florence in the middle of June instead of in October.

Florence was very pleasant and relatively cheap, but surprisingly crowded, and it seemed impossible to find a couple of unfurnished rooms to settle down in.

As to business, John Lane had proposed a book on Venice, a text of 50,000 words to accompany illustrations by Frank Brangwyn – for which he was prepared to pay 100 guineas for all rights; Massie seems to have been in trouble of some kind and Douglas was delighted: "Send me a wire if he dies, and I shall get drunk for a week. But if Secker expires you had *better not let me know*, as my access of joy might bring on an apoplexy. Break it to me gently", but a month later a paragraph from the contract for *South Wind* was being quoted to Straus seemingly as a model of clear and satisfactory author–publisher relations.

The proofs of *They Went* had not yet arrived. By 12th July Straus thought Douglas would have had them, but "I haven't, by God! . . . I will wait for tonight's post. God help you! And me. Because I can't live in the smouldering heat of Florence much longer." The night's post came, but no proofs. On the 14th, 15th, 16th, 17th and 19th Straus was bombarded with postcards informing him that the proofs had not arrived, had probably got lost, ought to be replaced by ordering a new set, and that Douglas was fast melting into a grease spot in the heat. On the 22nd a letter to the same effect. On the 26th two postcards, one before 11 a.m., cursing, and one at 11 a.m.: "Proofs arrived. Returning them today", followed by a letter:

I thought to have corrected the proofs during this afternoon. So I would have, if they had been normal proofs. But what am I to do, when those people only give me an eighth of an inch of *blotting-paper* to write my corrections in? Damn and blast all publishers, to Hell and back again! I did not ask for galley proofs, knowing that it would involve them in the horrible expenditure of about fourpence halfpenny, but they might at least have given me a margin on which a fellow can write a one-syllable word. Well, this job is going to take me a week or so, and you had better let them know right away that I shall charge them a guinea a minute. I am not only losing my time and temper over this fucking freak of theirs, but seriously ruining my eyesight. Such things have to be paid for. You might let them know, once for all, that I am *not a miniaturist*. If you could hear me cur[s]ing at their blasted paper and non-existent margin! What do they think I am going to do about it? Am I going to get blind . . ."

etc, etc, and ending: "I have lost half a stone of good fat since eleven this morning, from sheer blaspheming. No more just now. Yours ever." The proofs were returned (on the 30th), not, needless to say, without a certain amount of criticism. Some "comma-maniac" had been at work: "It is quite disheartening, when one has taken such endless trouble with punctuation, to have it fooled about and spoilt by some blasted illiterate . . . He also 'thinks' too much. He *won't* write strumpet (p. 230): he calls it trumpet . . . He also dislikes putting in any dots . . . He *won't* reproduce my dashes."

ii

By this time, however, René had arrived, and there was an end to cursing for a couple of months while they went on an extended walking tour ending with nearly three weeks in Scanno before returning to Florence. There, rooms in which Douglas could settle and work through the winter were no easier to find, and he decided he might just as well live at Menton and be near René. He hoped he might write another novel while there, and that perhaps Straus might be persuaded to come that far, as it did not seem possible to get him to Florence, and they could work together at Straus' novel, *Volcano*. He stayed there until 22nd December.

He had refused Lane's offer for the book on Venice politely, but to Lane's friend, who had suggested Douglas for the book, he said he considered Lane's offer a "pigeon-plucking proposition". Lane raised the offer to £150, and Douglas thought he and Straus might do it together, if only Straus would come out; but they did not. No, he did not mind Straus coming out with a maiden aunt – quite the reverse: "I should probably make myself so infernally agreeable to her that she would not only pay all my expenses and cut you out of her will, but, ten to one, end in adopting me"; and Straus was thanked for interesting an African vice-consul in Eric. Eric had for a long time been fed up with his job, and Douglas hoped that this kindness of Straus' might lead to something.

iii

They Went was published in September, and was received with respectful acclaim, but not with the enthusiasm accorded to *South Wind*.

They Went is less than half the length of *South Wind*, and lacks the variety of mood and subject, the extended leisurely conversations, and the learned disquisitional air of the earlier book. It lacks also the hilarity, the excessiveness, the sharp clash of personalities, the delight in knowledge for its own sake, the "jovial immoderation", and the "overcharged canvas" of *South Wind*. *South Wind* seems to be written from the inside, by one of the inhabitants, and in this way gains an apparent authenticity and seems to be more immediate and actual than *They Went* which seems to be written from the outside, as if by a stranger. We do not know enough about the city of Ys and its inhabitants, and that critic may have been right who suggested that the story would have been improved by expansion. *South Wind* is a whole history, *They Went* is a sketch, an essay, a traveller's tale.

South Wind is concerned, amongst much else, with morality in action. In *They Went* moral judgments of actions are neither given nor called for. No one, for instance, is interested either way in the use made by the Princess of the Great Drain. This withdrawal of interest in the moral behaviour of individuals is inimical to the very stuff of which novels are made, and results in a dangerous depletion of general interest and verisimilitude to life. This is in no way compensated for by the realisation that the novel is an attempt to consider the rival claims of art and morality, that the subject of the book is "the conflict between beauty and betterment". Neither really wins, although goodness survives, and beauty is drowned. Beauty is not condemned, as goodness might have liked it to be, to bring about its own downfall by wickedness and luxury: the disaster is the result of the malevolent ambition of a single human being. Beauty's peril is thus shown to lie not in the temptations which assail the devotees of beauty, but in the envy of those who are not devotees, and to some extent in the very freedom from mundane affairs and practical concerns which are so often the concomitants of an artistic temperament. Whether Douglas intended it or not, the allegory is here at its best: beauty is by nature to some extent imprudent and always vulnerable. Perhaps if it were not, it would be unbearable; in its vulnerability lies that poignancy, that seasoning of sadness that beauty so often contains.

South Wind leaves one warmed and reassured, delighted with the place and with many of the people. There is hardly a page of the book that one would not wish to see come to life, largely because the whole thing makes a great appeal to the senses. In spite of the fact that the physical beauty of the city of Ys is of such importance in *They Went*, there is little appeal to the senses in the book, nor are the characters, with one exception, in any way endearing. Most of them, incidentally, are tinged to some degree with sadness or uncertainty; they lack the definition and incisiveness of those others, of Nepenthe, and they are the duller for it. The Princess, who ought to have been the irresistible, totally desirable, completely fulfilled mistress of all she surveyed, comes out in the end as a kind of reluctant undergraduate, half wilful and half submissive to her tutor Theophilus, the Devil. Even Theophilus is wrong, an anaemic devil, with the suggestion of a conscience and a deprecating, almost a self-doubting manner. Aithryn contains more explosive and powerful forces than all the rest of the characters put together, but is somewhat inhuman or non-human, perhaps deliberately, since Douglas insisted that there "is an infusion of the extra-human" in the book, which is true, but is also surely one of his red herrings. Kenwyn, the Christian missionary, is, curiously enough from Douglas' point of view, made into one of the least uninteresting characters; he is seduced by the Princess and duly thrown down the Great Drain when she has finished with him, as are all her lovers. This exalts him, and gives to the otherwise earnest Christian what character and interest he possesses. It also suggests, as the whole book does, that Douglas was in a less cynical and decisive mood when writing it than he had been when writing *South Wind*. If he had wished to defeat Christianity, he should have made Kenwyn a figure of ridicule, enslaved and mocked at by the Princess until he became a laughing stock in the city. Similarly, if he wished to defeat goodness and betterment, he should never have created the arch-druidess, the "quite-too-chaste-and-venerable" Mother Manthis, who makes all the other characters seem like cardboard figures. She, one can believe, had a mind, depth, humanity, wisdom; she also had drive and decisiveness, a lively concern for education, an understanding of others, and a desire to find and hold on not merely to the unimaginative traditional stereotyped good, to the good for its own sake, but to the good because the simple wisdom of the ages seems to have proved it to be a practical means to a happy life.

The quite-too-chaste-and-venerable Mother walks away with the book in her pocket; or rather, when the somewhat pathetic devil escapes from the flooded city with his equally pathetic princess – they are like confidence tricksters who have to move on to the next pitch – the Mother remains, undisturbed, not particularly jubilant at the fall of the sinful city, and yet augmented in strength of character by the disaster. To this extent it can be said, surprisingly, that goodness wins hands down and – even more surprisingly – with Douglas' tacit or unconscious approval. Yet even Mother Manthis is somewhat tinged with disillusionment.

iv

No one would have supposed that the encounter between Lawrence and Magnus at the Florentine *pensione* at the end of the previous year held any promise of development, but it did. Magnus had gone back to Rome, and later moved to an expensive hotel at Anzio, as a result of which he appealed to Lawrence for money. Lawrence sent him £5 and they met at Monte Cassino where Magnus was staying, and which Lawrence wanted to see. Magnus showed Lawrence the manuscript of his memoirs of the Foreign Legion, then called *Dregs*, and confessed that he had paid his hotel bill at Anzio with a dud cheque. Lawrence thought *Dregs* had merit, and persuaded Magnus to improve it. The Lawrences then went to live in Sicily, at Taormina.

Suddenly the blow fell on Magnus. The guest master at the monastery told him that the police might come for him at any moment, gave him money, and advised him to flee. Magnus fled to Taormina, where he began begging and imploring Lawrence's help. Lawrence gave him enough money to enable him to get to Malta, where he had friends, and from which he hoped to get a boat, later, to Smyrna, where there were other friends: "If anything happens in the meantime," Magnus wrote to Douglas, ". . . look for my grave there in the foreigners' cemetery – and *I leave all my manuscripts & papers to you – and their proceeds.*" All these events had taken place while Douglas was in Greece. He reached Sant' Agata a few days after Magnus arrived on Malta.

Magnus felt safe on the island. He had a little house at a rent of £5 a year, and friends, and still a tenuous connection with Monte Cassino. Having finished *Dregs*, he started writing further memoirs, beginning with Russia, and had the first section, on St Petersburg, finished by July. Would Douglas like to see it when it had been typed?

Douglas was touring with René, so the first part of the Russian memoirs did not reach him until September, when it was also sent to Alec Waugh at Chapman and Hall. *Dregs* had gone to a literary agent, who replied that he did not want a "war book" which showed, said Magnus, that he could not have read it. The second instalment of the Russian memoirs followed the first, to Douglas, with a letter asking for various pieces of information and ending on a rather forlorn note: "I haven't any energy left to get up and go chasing madly through the world . . . I am tired. I want to be quiet & sit still and just go on writing in my own little way. But I don't see how I am going to live on that unless some one subsidises me!" He had written, he said, to the Queen of Spain, to give him a room in one of her empty houses or a cell in one of her monasteries: "No answer – not that I expected it – but I thought it wouldn't do any harm trying. There are so few queens left now!" But Douglas' letters had a tonic effect: "Some how your letters are like an elixir to me. I am glad you like the memoirs. Your judgment is the only one I care about . . . I wish you were here – it gives me courage to see you and I look at things differently." Certainly he seems to have been as much unfortunate as foolish: "I wish I could get hold of some publisher to pay me *something*. How can one continue to live like this. I have *60* manuscripts out (including translations) at least ten of them accepted and not one paid. This is irrespective of the stuff I am doing now, or 'Dregs'."

v

While Magnus could not sell what he had written, Douglas was complaining that he could not write: "A complete blank – a sterility approaching cretinism – has fallen upon me. What's to be done? Money is fast running out . . . and none coming in at all . . . I have tried to write an article on Greece. Two pages in the better part of a week. They read like a Board-School exercise. Don't know what is happening to me."

He was expecting Straus, together with Straus' sister and maiden aunt, on a definite day now – 25th November – and sent his usual detailed instructions about the journey, offered to book rooms in hotels in Menton or a room with his own landlady for Straus himself; anyway, Straus must have breakfast with him and René; and as Straus' aunt is bringing luggage will Straus please try to bring Douglas' tin trunk. Straus also received instructions on how to treat his family:

Why on earth do you take any trouble about aunts and things? Haven't you yet realized that they are mere encumbrances? It always makes me sad to hear a grown up man talking about his "relations". I had dozens of uncles and aunts, but I saw through the whole fraud of "family life" between the ages of 11–15 and dropped them all, dead! like hot potatoes; likewise my grandmothers, my mother, sister, and brother – *the whole boiling lot*; and I have *never* regretted it. What on earth is the use of relations? You never get a kind word – much less a kind action – out of any of them; they only use you. In this case, your aunt simply discovers that you are useful for tickets, cabs, porters etc etc – that's all! And when she dies she will bitterly regret that she is forced, for the sake of what people might otherwise say, to mention you in her will. And now she refuses to pay for your life in the hotel!

Well, if you were ½ a man, you would tell her that you do not propose to act as her courier and travelling servant for nothing, and unless she undertakes to pay *every item* of your expenses, you will leave her to manage her journey alone, and will come by yourself to Mentone, what time suits you best [sic], and stay where you please and do what you like and return to London when the fancy takes you. That will bring her to her senses. And if it doesn't, why, you will be rid of a damned nuisance, that's all! Send her to Hell. That's where she belongs – with all other "relations".

And could Straus get him a copy of Doughty's *Arabia Deserta* – the full text just about to be published – at a reduced price. He needs it "more than any other book on earth", and is ready to go to any lengths to oblige anyone who can get it for him: "I will for example, present them with an inscribed copy of any of my works, or anybody else's works . . . I can't think of anything I wouldn't do to oblige such a person, even to the extent of —————————————— [sic]". The same request was made to Hutton, in more restrained terms.

Chapman and Hall had offered £50 in advance on the Italian book, but Secker, in spite of Douglas having published *They Went* elsewhere, had offered £100 advance "on any damned thing I care to write". This was obviously more advantageous, but Straus need not mention it to Chapman and Hall: "I'm in no hurry whatever! To get that Italian book into shape, what *I* call shape, would mean 3–4 months' hard work. We can talk about it when you come." However, before he came, Straus wrote to say that he had heard unofficially that Chapman and Hall would offer £100: "They don't want Secker to have any more of yours." At about the same time, Straus accepted, on Douglas' behalf, an offer of £100 advance on an American edition of *They Went*.

These items of good news, the company of René, and the anticipation of Straus' visit engendered in Douglas what was on the whole a sunny mood, but there was a rumble of thunder occasionally:

I am meditating a trip to Monte Carlo this afternoon. What for? *To buy matches*. There are none in Mentone, and there haven't been any for a week – and a smoker like me, you know, can't put up with that sort of thing indefinitely. But Mentone is full of such drawbacks, and if you ever want an article cursing the Riviera up and down, from every point of view, just let me know. I'm your man. Loaded up with venom just now.

And relief from the rituals of Riviera life was occasionally very thoroughly indulged:

Just now, as a matter of fact, I am in the Hell of a rage, having burnt a huge hole into my last remaining decent jacket. Why must *I* be singled out for these calamities? Why couldn't you burn your jacket, instead?

I have also a slight headache. Fact is, yesterday having been Armistice day, there was a general holiday which *we* utilised to climb into a mountain village and there get drunk – really drunk, I mean, so that we fell down every few yards on the homeward way. We *forgot* to have any dinner and slept for 12 hours on end. After luncheon we shall both be quite fit again; if it weren't for my blasted jacket.

vi

Douglas returned the first part of Magnus' Russian memoirs – the Petersburg section – early in October, but no acknowledgment of it had reached him a month later: "Where are you?" he wrote on a postcard on 6th November, "Wrote you last on the 29 Oct and before that on the 22nd October"; and two days later (8th November) another card said: "Crimea just come. Will return it together with 2nd article tomorrow", but he didn't, because on the 14th Douglas wrote a letter saying he had been "fussed to death with all sorts of bloody botherations which are not over yet. But I will despatch your two Russian things tomorrow with as many suggestions as I can think of. I think they will do very well, tho' you might put in a few more conversations . . ." There had been a possibility of Magnus going to Morocco: Douglas said he might be going to Africa also, but to Tanganyika, where, it seemed, Eric had probably got a job. "Sorry to hear," he added, "that *Eugene Onegin* is by Tschaikowsky. I thought the music rotten, and I am very fond of his things as a rule. I hoped it was by that ass Rimsky Khorsakoff, or whatever his name is." He expected Magnus was leading a very low life on Malta . . .

A few days later came letters from Nathaniel Cobb in Rome and D. H. Lawrence in Sicily to say that Magnus had committed suicide.

Magnus died on 4th November. As Douglas wrote later: ". . . they pounced on him at Malta, and, in a moment of supreme weakness, he killed himself rather than fall into their hands."

Magnus had had as much as he could take, and his letter of 23rd September in which he says "I am tired. I want to be quiet & sit still & just go on writing in my own little way" illuminates a true personal tragedy, for just at the time when he seemed to be at his most productive and might well have gone on to establish himself as a writer, the consequences of his past caught up with him. He had so many times managed to evade the effects of living beyond his means, that he had continued as though he could either run for ever or always find someone to help him out. He knew all the short cuts in all the principal cities of Europe, and in the end took the shortest cut of all, the one that would end the necessity of taking any more.

The circumstances which led to his suicide originated partly in Italy and partly in Malta. He was wanted in Italy for defrauding an hotel in Rome (or Anzio? or both?) and according to Douglas he had been betrayed to the police for this offence by a malicious acquaintance. On Malta, in order to comply with the law, he had to find a guarantor, or deposit a sum of money with the police in order to avoid deportation at the end of his first three months. As he had no money Walter Salomone became his guarantor. When a friend, Michael Borg, informed Salomone confidentially that Magnus owed money to him, Borg, in the local shops, Salomone withdrew his guarantee. Magnus asked the Commissioner for three weeks' grace in which to prepare to leave Malta, but received no acknowledgment. "Then," says Salomone, "he decided to prepare for the last act of his drama."[89]

On the morning of 4th November, two detectives in plain clothes met him in the street. "One of them quite casually went up to him and said very civilly that the inspector of police wished to see him *re* a guarantee or something, and that he was to go with him to the police station." (In fact, the detective had a warrant for his arrest and extradition to Italy.) Magnus replied that as he was in his sandals he would dress and go with them immediately. They accompanied him to his house and allowed him to enter. He locked the door behind him, leaving them outside.

"A few minutes later he opened his bedroom window and dropped a letter addressed to Don [Mauro] which he asked a boy in the street to post for him, and immediately closed the window again . . . Some time elapsed and he did not come out. The detectives were by this time very uneasy and . . . decided to burst open the door. As the door did not give way they got a ladder and climbed over the roof;" they found Magnus in his bedroom dying from poisoning outstretched on his bed and a glass of water close by.

Death was certified to be due to hydrocyanic (i.e. prussic) acid poisoning. He was buried on his birthday, 7th November, when he would have been forty-four.

Nothing was known at this time about a legal will. Papers were left expressing his wishes:

> In case of my unexpected death inform American consul.
> I want to be buried first class, my wife will pay.
> My little personal belongings to be delivered to my wife.
> My best friend here, Michael Borg, inform him.
> My literary executor Norman Douglas.
> All manuscripts and books for Norman Douglas. I leave my literary property to Norman Douglas to whom half of the results are to accrue. The other half my debts are to be paid with.

Mrs Magnus was unable to pay for her husband's funeral at the time, but subsequently reimbursed those who had paid for it. Nor was there any immediate means of paying Magnus' debts, and until they were paid the American consul was obliged to hold Magnus' possessions as security. If a legal representative of Magnus' estate could be found, and was willing to settle the debts, then these possessions could be handed over; if not, they would have to be sold. Douglas, therefore, was unable to obtain Magnus' manuscripts; but he wrote to Grant Richards who had a manuscript of *Dregs* under consideration, and possibly part of the Russian memoirs, to keep them and get in touch with him about them.

In his letter to Douglas informing him of Magnus' death, Lawrence wrote:

> I heard from Don Mauro the other day that Magnus had committed suicide. Today I receive the Malta newspaper with a paragraph – he was found in a white suit dead on his bed in his room at Notabile, having taken poison. En voilà fini.
> Here it rains heavens hard and I get rather sick of it . . .

Later, he wrote that when he received the full account of Magnus' death from Walter Salomone "the world seemed to stand still for me. I knew that in my own soul I had said, 'Yes, he must die if he cannot find his own way.' But for all that, now I *realized* what it must have meant to be the hunted, desperate man: everything seemed to stand still. I could, by giving half my money, have saved his life. I had chosen not to save his life." He added that after the passing of a year he still thought he had done right; he still would not save his life.

Douglas wrote to Straus – the correspondent with whom he was most intimate at this time – that he was "terribly upset" about Magnus' death; and later he wrote "If only he had told me the complete truth!"

As to that "En voilà fini", nothing could have been more mistaken.

PART VI

Florence: Settling Down
1921-1927

CHAPTER TWENTY-TWO

Nardini
1921

i

On the last day of 1920 Douglas and René left Florence, where they had spent Christmas, to return to Menton. On the way they spent two days at Marseille with Eric, who was on his way to Tanganyika where he had obtained a job as Assistant Inspector of Police at a salary of £325 a year. "Not bad," was Douglas' comment, "and, when you consider it carefully, all my work. He will get six months' leave in two years, and hopes to have saved about £250 by that time."

Three days after returning to Menton from Marseille he developed what he thought was gout in his ear. It hurt "like Hell", and turned out to be the first manifestation of erysipelas. "My face is swollen to twice its natural size and covered with thick black ointment and wrapped up in cotton-wool, allowing just one eye to peep through. And the thing gets worse every day. If it gets much worse, I shall have to call in some other doctor or go to a hospital. I spend the time in bed, and have *nothing what-ever* to read! It's absolutely damnable." However, the disease did nothing to diminish the flow of his correspondence. He still wrote with the same vigour and crustiness, especially of Secker: "He has sent me on his account up to last June (all faked, of course; but all his accounts are faked) . . . Everything is faked! But he knows, all right, what's coming in! . . . Don't imagine Secker is an *ordinary* villain like John Lane, or Dent, or Fisher Unwin."

By the third week in January, the erysipelas had gone, and on the 29th, Douglas was in Florence, where someone – he had asked everyone he knew there – had found him a place to live in, "two microscopic rooms . . . so small that I can't even get all my *clothes* in, though the walls can be lined with shelves for books and there is just room for a table & chair in one, and for a bed in the other. Damned sight better than nothing, and only £18 a year, including service and electricity." He intended to start living there at Easter, he told Archie in a letter which also contained advice on how to get a book back that you have lent to a friend.

Archie, against Douglas' wishes, had lent Straus a copy of *Unprofessional Tales*:

> As to *Unprof. Tales* – I hope you'll get it back! But he is a book-collector, you know! The best way is not to ask for it but, when he is out of the room, calmly put it in your pocket (my system): the real collector has always some reason for not giving it back. (Perhaps that is why he is now abrupt – *get rid* of you, in order to *keep the book*). I am glad you have vowed never to lend books again, (though you will find the vow difficult to keep) but sorry you should have learnt that lesson with *Unprof. Tales*, of which there are only 2, or possibly 3, copies in the whole world, and which, if I make any kind of reputation, may be worth, as curiosities, their weight in ten pound notes. But don't ask for the book except as a last resource. *Try to find where it is, and then steal it.* And then write a sweet letter saying that you forgot to mention that, while he was out of the room, you took back your property, "as he has doubtless read it by this time".

The plot of this one-act melodrama was kept alive by Douglas in subsequent letters (e.g., ". . . it's the only way, according to my long experience; also, it avoids friction and rows. After that, never lend a book again. You only make enemies"), but when Archie very sensibly refrained from such action and apparently got the book back simply by asking for it, Douglas, unable to name Straus guilty, charged him with incompetence: "I fear Straus is not as much of a bibliophile as he professes to be, else he would not have disgorged so easily."

Archie was also given a brief glimpse of Robert, who had failed an exam in the army, and was in hospital at Aldershot with blood-poisoning: "He is yearning to get out of the army. Flora don't seem to approve of the idea." (Mrs Uniacke, it will be remembered, was the widow of an army hero.) A little later, Douglas had a letter from Robert to say "he simply couldn't stand the military life any longer – no wonder, if it be true, as he says, that he gets only 7/- a week!" And it was Archie who was given a neat and probably truthful summary of his father's relations with his ex-publisher: "As to Secker, we write each other, but I fear there is not much love lost. He is furious that I dropped him, and I am furious that he ropped [robbed] me: that's all there is to it!"

ii

There followed another instalment of the Tin Box serial which had begun in Secker's office. The box had been removed from there by Straus to "clear the decks" for aggressive action by Douglas; but Straus' family was now obliged to move into a flat in which, it seems, there would be no room for it. What was to be done with it? Elaborate instructions were issued, and Hutton was asked if he could very kindly find room for it. He could, and did, and within a week had it in his house. The final episode occurred in April, when John Mavrogordato brought it out with him to Florence on his way to Greece. So that was that; but as is the way with serials, the end of this one was succeeded by the beginning of another and similar one; for in the same letter announcing the arrival of Mavro and box, Douglas asks Archie to

think hard, and to dive into memories of January 1917. This box, namely, contained all my precious old silver things and such-like, and still contains them. Therefore it has not been rifled. But there lacks what I require just as much, namely, a bundle of printed monographs on Capri and one book – The Life of Sister Serafina – an old decrepit-looking Italian book, very rare. You remember we re-packed this box together in my hotel at the last moment, the earlier box having shown signs of giving way. I can't think where those books etc can be – indeed, they can't be anywhere – unless I gave them you at the last minute to take care of for me, they being more precious to me than all the silver in the world. I would have given them to nobody but you. Did I? And have you got them? Please think carefully before saying *no*, and try to remember the circumstances of our packing in that hotel in Blooms-bury. Think hard and then let me know. If you haven't got them, they are simply evaporated. But I hope you have!

These instructions, with variations on the same theme, were repeated to Archie *ad nauseam* in letter after letter over a period of seven months.[90] The only things Douglas required were the Life of Sister Serafina and a bundle of pamphlets, tied with string, by Bedriaga, Maugham, Eimer, Bergamo etc, just one book and a bundle the size of another book: that was all! Couldn't Archie at least find out definitely whether these things existed? Couldn't Archie make a list of what a trunk, which he had mentioned as being in a repository, contained? The matter was *urgent*. The book and pamphlets were of priceless value, and Douglas needed to refer to them before he could finish the book he was working on . . .

There seems to have been an extraordinary obtuseness and procrastination on Archie's part. By 6th September and the eighth letter referring to the subject, in which the whole situation is explained in more detail than ever, it seems that Archie has not even looked in his trunk in the repository. On 7th October (tenth letter) Douglas writes: "Do let me know as soon as you can whether you have those books etc of mine. If not, I shall probably hang myself"; and on 4th November (fourteenth letter): "As

to those books – I am in sheer despair. *Twice already have I written you a list
of them* ... worth more than their weight in gold to me, and also to the
British Museum, as they are all unique copies. If you haven't got them,
God knows where they are." But that seems to have been the end of it.
Archie came out to Florence a few days later, and may have brought them
with him.

The interesting point about the foregoing is the patience – the almost
complacent equanimity – with which father treats son most of the time,
whereas with almost anyone else Douglas would have been erupting with
incandescent curses; and the extraordinary ineptitude of the son towards a
father whom he undoubtedly loved and respected. And to whose other
requests – for snuff, tobacco, collar studs that did not "waggle in all
directions and make me perfectly mad", and joss-sticks to drive out the
smell of paint in his newly decorated rooms, making them smell "like a
third-rate whore-house (far preferable!)" – he had been quite promptly
responsive.

iii

Douglas' quest for *Arabia Deserta* had been successful. He could not
afford the copy that Edward Hutton had offered to obtain at a slightly
reduced price, but had arranged to write a review-article of the book for
the *London Mercury*. He had begun this work with a 1,000-word article in
mind, but Squire, the editor, suddenly wrote asking for 5,000 words, much
to Douglas' expressed annoyance ("They take me for a sausage machine,
evidently"); but judging by the finished work it looks as though he must
have enjoyed the stimulus. He complained that it took him nearly a month
to write it – he was a slow writer, and nothing could be done about it –
whereas "anyone else could have done it in three days, easy!" He received
£14 for the article, enough to pay the rent of his new flat for nearly ten
months, and it is one of the most pleasing and characteristic that he wrote.
It contains his credo on the writing of travel books – as exemplified in
Doughty – which has already been quoted on page 214.

At the same time that he was working on Doughty, he was going
through the typescript of Straus' novel *Volcano*, which they seem to have
discussed so thoroughly while Straus was in Menton (during the last week
of November and the first half of December) that Straus referred to their
"collaboration"; but Douglas refused to let his name appear on the title-
page. For a time, indeed, Straus was reluctant to let his own name appear
there. He seems to have been genuinely afraid that the book was outrageous or even indecent or obscene. Douglas saw it for what it was – a
mere joke, or frolic that was hardly likely to offend the authorities; but he
told Straus that if he felt worried about it he had better tone down what

he thought outrageous. Straus, by all accounts, was a snob, and was probably afraid for his reputation in the stuffier circles which he may have carefully cultivated.

Douglas' "microscopic rooms" were on the top floor of the Nardini Hotel, where he had stayed for many weeks intermittently during the previous year, and it was to the Nardini that he went on 16th March to supervise the decorating of his rooms. There were the usual delays, and he did not actually get into the rooms until early in April. Meanwhile René was with him for about a week, and Douglas was "delighted to be out of that blasted French hole and away from its filthy inhabitants"; Florence was very gay and full of people, and the food was much better, and cheaper, than it had been at Menton. He had unpacked all his London belongings, surprised at what he found in the trunks that had not been opened for so long; and his books "look quite nice in their new shelves, but the place is too small – so small, that I haven't even room for a wardrobe, and can't think where to hang up greatcoats etc". The prospect of at last – after four years – having a place of his own with all his books and other possessions about him, filled him with excited anticipation, and made even the prospect of work almost enjoyable: "I am going to devote the whole of tomorrow to a careful consideration of Chaphall's Contract for *Alone*," he wrote to Straus, and sure enough the latter soon received a 1,200-word typed commentary on, and criticism of, the document in question. It is one of Douglas' most reasonable and truly businesslike documents which shows that in moments of calm and goodwill, he could serve his own interests at least as well as any agent. The changes he asked for or suggested were nearly all agreed to by the publisher, and he signed the contract before the end of April. He had estimated with typical exaggeration that it would take him nine months to put *Alone* in good shape for publication; then he reduced the estimate to seven months; and actually had a typescript ready in less than four months.

iv

Some of the people who helped to make Florence gay and full were H. G. Wells, Rebecca West, Aldous Huxley, and D. H. Lawrence. Lawrence was on his way to join Frieda, who had been called to Germany on account of family illness. He arrived in Florence late on a day when Douglas, Reggie Turner, and Rebecca West had all lunched together: "To each of us," wrote Rebecca West years later, "different though we were in type, it appeared of paramount importance that we should go and pay him our respects at the first possible moment",[91] and she describes how they found him in a small room at the Balestri "tapping away at a typewriter. Norman Douglas burst out in a great laugh as we went in, and asked him if he were already writing an article about the present state of Florence; and Lawrence answered seriously that he was. This was faintly embarrassing, because on the doorstep Douglas had described how, on arriving in a town, Lawrence used to go straight from the railway station to his hotel and immediately sit down and hammer out articles about the place, vehemently and exhaustively describing the temperament of the people. This seemed obviously a silly thing to do, and here he was doing it. Douglas' laughter rang out louder than ever, and malicious as a satyr's."

The comedy of the situation dissolved when Lawrence set himself to entertain them, and in particular to be a good host to Rebecca West, whom he had not met before. His audience sat on the bed, entranced.

On the following day, Lawrence, Douglas and Rebecca West went for a walk into the country, past the Certosa, and the two men talked of Magnus "with that grave and brotherly pitifulness that men who have found it difficult to accommodate themselves to their fellow-men feel for those who have found it impossible". They moved easily together along the road, she noted, and were on good terms.

v

Douglas finished *Alone* on 23rd August, and sent it off to Straus with instructions about proofs with wide margins on hard paper, and many another detail about which he felt strongly. That "damnable Italian book . . . has taken *years* off my life" he wrote to Hutton: a perfectly normal comment for him to make after finishing almost any book. As soon as *Alone* was in the post, he and René set off for the Vorarlberg.

He had been planning this visit for several months. It was a double escape – from the oppressive heat of Florence in the summer to the cool uplands of the countryside farther north, and from the "wearisome actualities" of trying to make a living to the enchanted land of childhood in which every stone and tree was an extension of his own past life. Added to which, Austria was incredibly cheap: "We have an enormous room for -/10d a day; each meal costs about 2/- (for both of us) – and so on; in fact, one can live on the fat of the land, and drink till one bursts, for about 5/- a day, if one is alone." An additional attraction, undoubtedly was the thought (and later, the act) of showing to someone he loved all the intimate scenes and objects of his homeland. Straus and Archie were bidden to come out. Archie was told that a week there would pay for his ticket, but "you are probably playing tennis with some long-toothed and addle-pated English girls and imagining you are enjoying yourself". Archie had lost his job, and become engaged.

"As to your engagement," his father wrote, after he had returned from Austria, "– *of course* it is always the women who propose to us. Don't take it too seriously, and don't write passionate letters, or any that might be construed into a definite promise of marriage on your part (not that it greatly matters, but *still one has to be careful*); a public row might lose you your job. Why the devil do you still have dealings with females, at your age? Disgusting, demoralising. Use them: don't let them use you. Do you find them intelligent, or devoted? If so, you must be very young still. They are out to catch us; that's all. *Don't be caught.*"

A week later, back in Florence, he wrote to Archie saying he feared he had written rather snappily. He had been "fussed to death over . . . a letter from Robert asking me to give my sanction to his marriage. I enclose you my answer to him. It applies equally to you, tho' I think yours is a more hopeful case. (You are far too good to be thrown away on any damned woman just yet). Keep it in your family archives."

Florence
14 Oct. 1921

Archie ⎫
My dear Robert ⎭

Many thanks for your surprising letter of the 3rd and the charming photo.

Since you are your mother's son (I happen to know this, as I assisted at your birth) there is not the slightest chance of your ever listening to advice; I won't therefore waste time in trying to give it you. I will only ask you to use, for a moment, your powers of observation. Look around you and count up how many young fellows of your age are married, and how many aren't. Then ask yourself: why aren't those others married? The answer is, of course, that they're not such – well, damned fools. Quite useless, I suppose, telling you that you – both of you, I mean – will bitterly repent this imbecility after a short period of married life? Enough! You are looking for trouble, my son. You'll get it.

You don't inform me, by the way, what Bettie's people say to this. If they give their blessing, you can certainly have mine.

Much love to Grannie.

Your considerably alarmed but ever faithful
Dad

Robert ⎫
Here comes a letter from Archie ⎭ to say that he, too, is engaged to be married. God Almighty! What a brace of luscious idiots I've generated . . .

Perhaps Archie decided to follow his father's example in "putting a slice of sea" between himself and his fiancée: having considered a job in the Indian Forest Service, he eventually decided on an Assistant Inspector-ship in the Customs Administration at Port Sudan, and in the middle of November he came out to see his father on the way to taking up the appointment. They spent a few days together in Florence and also in travelling down to Naples, where Archie got on a boat for Egypt.

As to Robert, who was not yet of age, he was forbidden to marry and told to break off his affair, and "the sooner the better". His father even threatened to have the law on him if necessary, and asked Robert to let him know when he had done as instructed.

vi

Now that he was known to be resident in Florence, there were few writers who came to that city who did not wish to try and see him. The number, of course, was to increase through the years; and out of sheer self-protec-tion he had already begun to adopt a practice of never divulging his address except to intimates, of using Cook's as his postal address, and of agreeing to meet people only in cafés or restaurants from which he could retreat quickly if he did not wish to prolong the acquaintance. On the whole, it is remarkable how many new friends, as well as the old who returned again and again, he managed to fit into a busy life in which he always had work in hand, and what a large correspondence he managed to keep in circulation with the apparently effortless dexterity of a juggler – always with an elasticity that could fit in a new weekly letter of a page or two to an appreciative or interested correspondent without forgetting the long-established friend. A new correspondent at this time, who was an especial admirer of *They Went*, and who became a lifelong friend, offered a problem in identification, and had to be answered ambiguously:

c/o T. Cook & Son
Via Tornabuoni
Florence
20 Oct 1921

Dear Sir (or Madam)

Many thanks for your charming but rather Delphic epistle of the 5th. You don't even give me a chance of guessing whether you are male or female. Not that these things matter greatly, nowadays! You also give me an address in a region of London so *recherchée* that it occurs to me that you may be a Peer of the Realm. Unfortunately the British Institute here possesses no London Directory or even telephone-book. If you are a Duke, please forgive my informal mode of address. Your handwriting, what there is of it – far too little – is so extraordinarily like that of a dear child I used to know ages ago, that I should take you to be him. But your learning seems to be so prodigious, and your *reverence for me* so exiguous, that you can't be *him* [or *he*]* (much as I might wish you were).

Now do tell me this. It appears you are a civilised person. How on earth, in that case, can you live in a loathsome hole like Montreux? I wouldn't allow my worst enemy's cat to be buried there.

Yours sincerely
Norman Douglas

The writer of this letter had presumably, as was her custom, simply signed with the one word "Bryher". Hence Douglas' doubts, or assumed doubts, about gender and ducality. In fact, Bryher is the legal name (assumed by Deed Poll) of the lady who was formerly Miss Annie Winifred Ellerman, daughter of the first Sir John Ellerman, the shipping magnate.[92] During the Twenties Bryher became known to the few, particularly in avant-garde literary and film circles, as a patroness whose publishing house "Pool", at Territet in Switzerland, was responsible for producing some of the brighter experimental literary talent of the decade and for providing what still, even today, could be regarded as perhaps the most exciting of all serious journals devoted to the cinema – *Close Up*. Both before that time and since, Bryher has written poetry, novels, and criticism. In 1921 she had written a novel, *Development*, and a critical appreciation of Amy Lowell, the poet. She had become a close friend of another American poet, Hilda Doolittle, or H.D.; and she was about to settle in the neighbourhood of Montreux, where she has remained ever since. She is now known as an historical novelist; and in 1921 it was this fascination with the living actuality of history and the attempt to present it in terms of art, which made her feel that *They Went* might have been written for her. "I loved it, laughed at it, and immediately wrote to Norman Douglas." They soon became, and remained, friends for life.

vii

Alone finally made its appearance in November 1921.

It is the mellowest, the most relaxed, of all his travel books, and the author's favourite:

> Were I forced to spend the remaining years of life on some desert island with no companion save one of my own books – unenviable

*The square brackets are Douglas'.

fate! – I should choose *Alone*. A nostalgic and multiherbal fragrance hangs about those pages. They conjure up a legion of friendly phantoms – memories that are fading away, towns and villages never to be re-visited, voices that I cannot well hope to hear again. The book is too short for my taste; I would have it longer. One craves to savour more keenly the delights of those hours and to discover yet more details, however insignificant, of what befell during the months when, at the age of fifty, I exhaled the last breaths of an inconstant youth by the wayside of a beaten track in Italy. There are moments when the yearn-ing for that past life grows insistent and hard to bear . . .

Those words were written in wartime England when he thought he might never see Italy again. As for *Alone*, although it was the last sub-stantial work that he wrote about Italy, it had all been written by the end of, or very soon after the end of, the First World War. No wonder it enshrined memories. These memories, moreover, were not solely of the countryside, nor even only of his companions, but also of himself. He liked to look back; he liked to commemorate friendships and love-affairs; he also liked to see himself in these sentimental vignettes. Thus he writes here with tenderness of Malwida von Meysenbug,[93] because he is entranced by the picture of himself, at the age of twenty-one or twenty-two, wander-ing arm in arm with her about the ruins of Rome. He writes of her with affectionate charm, with a kind of compassionate indulgence, that strikes a new note in his work. And of her he writes the astonishing sentence: "It is good to pause awhile and etherealise oneself in the neighbourhood of her dust" – a reminder of his belief in the magic of place and asso-ciation.

In similar mood, it is here that he confesses to having had a "Shelley period", and writes the remarkable passage about the "wistful inter-mezzo" of Brahms (see Appendix, p. 493). All these are instances of a softer attitude than his readers had been accustomed to, an attitude which is also reflected, but only in part, in his spirited and magnanimous defence of Ouida, in which he quixotically accuses Henry James of being "feline and gelatinous".

The book is full of portraits of all kinds: the "gorgeously humorous account" of Crauford Tait Ramage (mentioned on p. 256), which was Douglas' first contribution to Hutton's *Anglo-Italian Review*; a brilliantly polished profile, glittering and hard, of John Oakley Maund; a contemp-tuous dismissal of an English acquaintance, Mr. P. G.,[94] whose behaviour, though not markedly different from the behaviour of others away from home whom Douglas might not have castigated, is given such short shrift that one must conclude that he had offended in some other way as well.

And intriguing little sketches of landladies and a shopgirl, of those typically atrophied Englishmen Brown and Potter of Olevano (who are inventions), of Atillio and Giulio, two agreeable youngsters; a snapshot of Magnus; a carefully arranged portrait, indoors, of Mrs Nichol, an impressive feminist seated at the card table – who, alas, did not exist in the flesh. And the memorable, but also fictional red-bearded fellow who had such a profound distaste for work and managed successfully, with the aid of women, to avoid it.

Informal, beguiling, and controversial, *Alone* is the most confiding and bedside of his books before *Looking Back*, written almost as if it were a journal. And perhaps, with *Looking Back*, it is the most representative of his character, containing as it does an almost complete range of his interests and moods and manners, and blending together, fact, fiction, and semi-fiction in a completely satisfying whole. "The variety of moods in it," wrote Lytton Strachey, "is indeed extraordinary; and yet the totality of the impression is completely preserved ... How did you manage to fill it with that romantic beauty?"

The romantic beauty of Rome, which seems, in retrospect, to occupy the centre of the book, is conveyed with an effortless ease and indirectness by mere suggestion, by concentrating on the details in the foreground – the starving cats in the Forum of Trajan, the flora and fauna of the Coliseum, the superb description of the fountain in the Borghese gardens – these things are involved in a mellow enchantment, a blissful summer afternoonish glow of contentment. They are counterbalanced by the dewy refreshment and invigoration of walks in the Italian countryside with young companions:

They are not standardised. They are more generous in their appreciations, more sensitive to pure ideas, more impersonal. Their curiosity is disinterested. The stock may be rudimentary, but the outlook is spacious; it is the passionless outlook of the sage. A child is ready to embrace the universe. And, unlike adults, he is never afraid to face his own limitations. How refreshing to converse with folks who have no bile to vent, no axe to grind ... who are pagans to the core; ... who are not oozing politics and sexuality, nor afflicted with some stupid ailment or other ...

Perhaps, in that interlude between leaving London in January and going to Paris in October 1917, when most of *Alone* was written, his happiness had been intensified by the fact that he had escaped not only the unpleasant consequences of a trial, but the whole atmosphere of English puritanism and hypocrisy, which he hated, the English climate, English wartime food and patriotism, and the whole shrivelling process of trying to fit himself into a way of life that went against his grain. He had burned his boats, and for the following eight or nine months at least, could revel in the freedoms, mental and physical, which his flight to Italy had given him. He could find himself again, and "indulge his genius". *Alone* is, above all, the book of a man who knows exactly how to do this, and does it with style, sharing his pleasure with the reader.

viii

It may be remembered that the position at Magnus' death was this: he died owing money – £55 – to Michael Borg (and a small sum to his typist). His funeral expenses had been paid by friends. None of his possessions could be released until the debts had been settled. When Douglas wrote to the American consul in Malta to enquire what progress had been made in settling the estate, he was informed that Magnus' effects had been sold – to pay his debts – to his principal creditor. Borg, whose attention had been called to "Mr Magnus' last wishes respecting the disposition of his writings" had been given Douglas' address, "and will doubtless communicate with you at once". Mrs Magnus had reimbursed those who had paid her husband's funeral expenses.

Borg did not communicate with Douglas either then or later, though Douglas certainly wrote to Borg about three weeks after hearing from the American consul; but Borg got in touch with D. H. Lawrence about publication of Magnus' manuscripts. Lawrence very properly replied that as Douglas was executor, he would no doubt get the manuscript of *Dregs* published. "The reply came from Malta, Borg would never put anything into the hands of Douglas," but would like Lawrence to try to get *Dregs* published. Long and tedious negotiations followed, involving Douglas, Lawrence and Grant Richards, the publisher, about what to do with the manuscript – how and by whom it should be edited and expurgated, what price it would fetch in America and England, how the proceeds should be split. Nothing had been decided when, in March 1922, Lawrence sailed for Ceylon without having received the manuscript from Borg. However, in 1924 *Memoirs of the Foreign Legion* by M.M., with an Introduction by Lawrence, was published by Martin Secker.

CHAPTER TWENTY-THREE

Orioli
1922–1923

i

In February 1922 Douglas had started writing *In the Beginning* "... a fantastic novel, which will take me 18 months at least. How to live up to the time when it shall be finished – that is the problem which confronts me at this moment. I have enough for 3–4 months, and not another penny coming in from any source that I can think of." His references to the book make it out to be far naughtier than it is; but this was only to be expected; if the occasion offered, he liked to hint at scandalous behaviour either in himself, in others, or in his work.

He really did not know how he was going to manage financially until he had finished another book. *Vanity Fair* wanted him to write "little dialogues, or comments on foreigners in Italy, or indeed almost anything at all that is not erudite or technical", and would have paid extremely well; but as usual Douglas, who had nothing suitable, would not sit down and write to order. Apart from preferring to be independent, and to choose his own subjects and write about them when he felt like it, he also wanted, at this moment, to get on with what he had begun, without interruption. He wanted to "sit tight" as he called it, "... and swot all the time, and not get drunk more than once a month".

Archie, still in the Sudan, was somewhat perturbed at the thought of possible pressure – perhaps even a breach of promise case – being brought against him by the girl in England to whom he had become engaged. His father advised him to

write letters, ever fewer and further between, sufficiently amiable not to create a deliberate row, but not committing yourself either for yes or no; let the thing die out naturally, if it possibly can die out. In other words, *insert a wedge of time*. Time is the great healer, and often the only one. Note this: no modern girl can possibly get "compromised" by going to dances with you or with anybody else; and also this, that you are at perfect liberty to ignore, and even send to Hell, her "father's female friends". Unless they are very vulgar people, there is no possible danger of an action for breach of promise. Never be *downe'd* [sic] by any woman; down *them*, by wriggling, or lying, or anything else. Be as astute as you can; a marriage after such a misunderstanding (or semi-row) would be a ghastly failure. Of course I know NOTHING WHATEVER about her – not even her name; but, *a priori*, I always take the man's part in these things, because it is he, and not the girl, who has been led into it, and is now asked to pay for his stupidity.

No; I didn't see Princess Mary here. As I have shaken hands both with her father and grandfather, I consider I have done enough for that bloody family . . .

Robert, to whom Douglas had given an introduction to Chapman and Hall via Ralph Straus, was advised, via Archie, that he was "an ass to trouble his head about that Worcester affair.[95] If you get a chance, tell him not to cultivate a conscience – it is the most pestilential attribute of man; and never to regret *anything*. Tell him to send the Worcester and everybody else to Hell." Robert's literary project at this time seems never to have been made clear to his father even by Robert. Within a few weeks he announced by post that he was going to become an actor; and later, that he had joined a dance band at Folkestone.

Douglas was getting up at 7.30 to work and "keeping to himself" till the evening: "I never go to the British Institute," he wrote to Hutton, presumably in answer to a query, "it is crowded day and night, with frowsy old English pension-cats, who occupy all the chairs and read, each of them, five newspapers at the same time. The King of Italy has just arrived. Looks more of a shit than ever. I am getting *terribly* old, and grumpy . . ." Grumpiness erupted suddenly onto "those *Who's Who* inquisitors" who had apparently asked Straus (or Chapman and Hall) to ask Douglas for the relevant information for an entry: "I loathe them and their bloody yellow-journalistic prying methods. Why can't one live in peace?"

ii

He arrived in Menton on 24th May to coach René for his English exam, and stayed about a month, loathing it. For one thing, he was lonely, only being able to see René on two days of each week; he asked both Straus and Hutton to come out and join him. "I live in a cockroach-haunted attic at a price which would enable me to rent a palace in any other country; the heat is stifling; clouds of mosquitoes; food and drink not fit for human consumption; loathsome inhabitants (real French *worms*) and prices 3 times as high as Florence. So be it! One does one's duty – or tries to." (But, presumably, not because one has a *conscience* . . .) He hadn't done a stroke of work all the time he was there, he told Archie just before leaving – conditions were too miserable. He was looking forward to being roasted to death in Florence.

He had had a mild attack of erysipelas at Menton, and one of the worst attacks of stomach trouble he had ever had, shortly before. These may, or may not, have contributed to "one of the beastliest months of my life"; and he feared – rightly as it turned out – that his sacrifice had been in vain, and that René would not pass his exam as Douglas had not been able to teach him what he ought to have been taught: "Not my fault! I have done my best; and paid for it, in discomfort and loss of time and of *money* (everything here is 4 times as expensive as in Florence; and 10 times as bad)." He returned to Florence towards the end of June, went down to Rome for a few days, and then, in the middle of July, was joined by René in Florence. They went off to the Vorarlberg together, as in the previous year, but this time stayed for the whole visit in Thüringen.

Douglas delighted in the rain after the heat of Florence, and he took René up for "a several days' excursion into the mountains . . . above the region of vegetation, among the snow, and I think it did my pupil good. He is not quite right just now, won't sleep properly, or even work, or even eat; I fear that failure in his exam has done a good deal of harm. We shall see. Meanwhile, we take it easy." They took it easy, and Douglas wrote to everyone in England he could think of – such as Straus, Hutton and Secker – to send him tobacco, as there was none in the Vorarlberg. Everything else was splendid, and wonderfully cheap. He even began a new book: "The novel has been laid aside for the moment; it is too difficult; but I shall take it up later again and am beginning something else, short but sweet, in the meantime." Thus began *Together,* in which his two visits to the Vorarlberg with René are telescoped into one.

The visit certainly did René good. He put on weight. Alas! Douglas had to cut his visit short in order to get his pupil back to school again in time for another exam: "I shall be roasted in that bloody fucking room of mine at Florence – what the mosquitoes leave of me, I mean: Simply Hell. I was just settling down comfortably and hoping to stay till October at least."

iii

At the end of May Secker had written suggesting a limited edition of *South Wind* – 50 copies signed by the author. Douglas told him to go ahead, he would autograph them "and you shall sell at £2-2- and give me 20% royalty. Why not print on turquoise paper? However, please yourself. It only upsets [underlined six times] me to think that these few mistakes in the book are never to be corrected." Couldn't Secker let him correct them? Yes, it seemed that Secker could, and in the letter which contained this pleasing news, he suggested printing 100 copies instead of 50. Douglas added: "I suppose you are dead against a blue coloured paper for this edition of *South Wind*? Yet it is the ideal book for reviving this custom." He also had a copy of the letter from Professor Saintsbury which he had received in 1921 that he thought would do very nicely for printing opposite the title page of this new edition of *South Wind*. And while Secker was about it, why not ask three guineas for the book instead of two? "People who are so wasteful as to spend two could easily screw themselves up to three." And perhaps, he conceded in his next letter, Secker was right to propose printing the Saintsbury letter in the new ordinary impression – the eighth – that he was about to bring out, rather than in the limited edition; and he agreed that Secker could "easily risk printing 150 copies at three guineas; you might consider, even, whether 200 would not meet the case. There are so many Americans and lunatics about just now." By the middle of September, he had sent back all the signatures to Secker. Relations between publisher and author had never been better: each made suggestions and accommodated to the other's point of view when necessary. The blue paper edition appeared in November, and was praised by Douglas ("Very choicely got up! Distinguished"). At the same time the eighth impression of the ordinary edition was printed, bringing the total number of copies thus published to 7,500. It is no coincidence that these agreeable dealings between Secker and Douglas should have taken place in the year when the latter's friendship and correspondence with Straus had dwindled rapidly.

iv

The book on which D. H. Lawrence had been engaged when Douglas, Rebecca West, and Reggie Turner had burst into his room at the Balestri in the previous spring, had duly appeared in June. It was *Aaron's Rod,* which, in its sixteenth and seventeenth chapters, contains vividly recognisable portraits of Norman Douglas, Reggie Turner and several other Florentine expatriates. Douglas' reactions to this are of interest in relation to subsequent events. He wrote to Straus (5th July) that it was "a silly – really silly – account . . . Such tosh I never read". This was the first reaction of which we have any record. The second, in a letter to Archie, seems to show a decision to treat the thing as a joke: "There is a funny description of me . . . I haven't got the book, and shall probably not get it. Turner and other Florentines also figure therein." Hutton was informed of a "droll description in Lawrence's last book . . . which I don't possess but have heard about. He has also got Reggie into it, and others. Reggie is slightly annoyed, I fancy." Three weeks later, Bryher received a longer account: "Have you, by the way, read *Aaron's Rod* by D. H. Lawrence? There is a caricature of me in it, they say, under the name of Argyle. It is sure to be pretty rotten stuff, saturated with the wrong kind of sexuality (the negative kind) and without any humour or even humanity. But he gets off a good sentence now and then, when he least intends to do it. In fact, people in Florence are very furious with him for this book; he has put a lot of them into it, in a rather cat-like fashion."

Archie, fed up with his job and the climate and society of Port Sudan and Sinkat, sent in his resignation. "Couldn't you have exchanged with somebody in another part of the world? Or got a job first, and then resigned?" his father asked, forgetting perhaps his own impetuous decisions in similar circumstances; and regretted that he couldn't help Archie – who thought he might like to be in the Consular service – with the Foreign Office, with whom he had no influence whatever. It appeared that Archie would be coming back to Europe via Constantinople, Brindisi, and Venice, and tentative arrangements were made between father and son for a reunion in Italy, which took place after Christmas.

v

The most significant event in Douglas' life in 1922 was the establishment of his friendship with Pino Orioli, the bookseller. In his autobiography Orioli says that he first met Douglas in the spring of this year "at a small party given by Miss Wilkins, one of the innumerable rich old maids" living in Florence; and according to the book the occasion was commemorated by Douglas deliberately shocking Miss Wilkins in typical style, and incidentally demonstrating that the "well-bred cad" of the Nineties had not entirely vanished.

Orioli at this time was thirty-eight, some fifteen years younger than Douglas, but with an equally adventurous, if different life behind him. He was the seventh child of a pork butcher and sausage-maker (salami, mortadelle, coteghini, etc) in a little town called Alfonsine, south of Bologna. Here, at the age of twelve, young Giuseppino was put to work as a barber's assistant – an excellent position in which to hear the whole gossip of the town and acquire a thorough education, at second hand, in the ways of the world. Here also he began to read anything worth reading that he could get hold of. Two years later an older brother who was already working in Florence, found him a job in a barber's shop in that city, where he remained for the five years until he was called up for his military service.

When his period in the army came to an end, in September 1907, he was twenty-three, and for the first time in his life had a sum of money in hand. It was not enough to start a business with, but sufficient to keep him for two or three months. He decided to visit Paris and London and try to get work there. Paris did not come up to his romantic expectations of it, and apparently could not provide him with work, so he fairly soon went on to London. Here, seeing that his money was about to run out, he began giving lessons at a language school, but was forced at first to augment this income by singing in the street and forming part of a *claque* at the Alhambra. Further teaching of Italian, especially to private pupils, and an introduction to the antiquarian book trade, which he took to with enthusiasm, enabled him to pay his way; and through these two kinds of activity he met Philip Woolf (younger brother of Leonard Woolf), Irving Davis, and a Miss Minasi. Woolf and Davis, who were undergraduates at Cambridge, invited him to stay there, where, he says, he met Lytton Strachey. Miss Minasi, a middle-aged spinster, housed and looked after him in London, while he worked in the Polyglot bookshop in Charing Cross Road.

When Irving Davis had taken his degree, he and Orioli persuaded Davis' father to set them up in a bookshop in Florence. They stayed there three years, most of the time sharing a large flat with the obliging Miss Minasi, who had emigrated to Italy. In 1913 they returned to London and opened a shop at 24 Museum Street, and by the time the war started were well known in the antiquarian book trade both in London and abroad as specialists in incunabula and early Italian books.

Davis had friends in Cornwall where Orioli, on a visit during the early part of the war, met D. H. Lawrence. In the summer of 1915, Orioli was called up, and joined the Italian army at Bologna. A year or so later, through the intervention of a friend, he was appointed to the Italian Military Mission in London, later becoming King's Messenger between England and Italy. At this time he lived in London in the household of Irving Davis, who had a job in the War Office.

Through his Cornish friends he met Harold and Laura Knight, the artists, and Alfred Munnings; and through Laura Knight's interest in ballet, Lopokova; and Ronald Firbank. In the spring of 1920 Orioli went over to Florence and opened his own shop without abandoning his connection with the London shop, run by Davis. He found a good site on the Arno, in the centre of the city, and he, and Davis having built up a large connection both in the trade and amongst collectors, did well.

It was not only knowledge of his subject and genuine enthusiasm for it which accounted for Orioli's success, though this was astonishing enough considering his origins: his personality – so warm and alive, so vividly amusing, spirited, generous and refreshing, as well as having in it a strong

vein of harmless scurrility – appealed to everyone. He was much loved, as
may be gathered from the reminiscences, spoken or written, of all who
knew him; the mere biographical facts here given cannot hope to convey
anything but a faint background impression of the man with whom Douglas
was to become so closely associated during his Florentine period – the
man without whom he most probably would not have even remained in
Florence.

Douglas was trying to settle down; he had, amongst other things, a
horror of being alone in the evenings, and wanted a close and permanent
adult friend in Florence with whom he could be completely at ease without being passionately involved, "and there," as Richard Aldington says,
"was Pino with his boundless vitality and gift of entertainment, his stories
and his memories of peasant life, always at hand". Orioli, for his part, was
glad to become the intimate friend of Douglas, and was apparently "very
proud of it, nearly as proud as he was (in 1930) of his friendship with
Lawrence . . ." Aldington, not unexpectedly, cannot resist adding that
Orioli was a much more lovable person than Douglas, and more amusing
and attractive; his faults were those of a naughty child, easily forgivable.

Douglas and Orioli had enough in common to ensure a strong foundation for friendship. They both liked and had a wide knowledge of good
food and drink, of literature, anecdote and gossip; they both had a Rabelaisian turn of mind; they both, in their different ways, were without
pretensions; both, in their different ways, had boundless curiosity; both
liked travelling; and both were interested in the younger members of their
own sex, though in Orioli's case, less young than in Douglas'.

vi

Archie was with Douglas all through January of 1923, and it was probably
largely owing to him that his father decided that he must get out of his
summer-roasted and winter-frozen flat in the Nardini and try to find something less extreme in temperature. He found such a place in the Via
de' Benci. It would not be free until 1st May, but he didn't know how he
was going to raise the money for furniture and electricity which it lacked,
or how he could possibly pay for redecorations and the move, unless
Bryher should come to the rescue. Meanwhile, now that *Together* was
finished and had been vetted and approved by the faithful Mavrogordato –
who said that he liked it better than *Alone* – Douglas was ready to forsake
his hermit life, and indulge himself once more.

"Tonight is Blaker's dinner" he wrote to Archie; "I have eaten hardly
any lunch in anticipation of it"; and later in February there was a "frightful binge . . . Everybody drunk. R. Turner was sick all over the dinner

table! Nearly put me off my food, but not quite. I had to take him home afterwards, where he was sick again."

It was at this time, when he was once again open to social engagements, that Osbert and Sacheverell Sitwell introduced Nancy Cunard[96] to him. She was twenty-seven, already a legendary figure and of striking appearance, with enormous sapphire blue eyes set in a face as taut and trancelike as a ballet dancer's. Her long slender body and small-boned arms concealed up to the elbows by enormous African bangles of wood; her simple but richly decorative clothes; her passionate steel-like will and devotion to causes; her inflammable poetic heart – they all contributed to a personality that was as formidable as it was feminine, attractive, dangerous, disarming; a human dragon-fly with a tender, but unsentimental heart. While waiting for Douglas, however, she seems to have been mildly apprehensive, and could get no satisfaction from the Sitwell brothers who teased her with hints and implications: "I should be *careful* if I were you", or "Well . . . er . . . there's that little box of his . . ."

Suddenly you were there beside us, having entered unseen, and you had a perfectly normal, if dignified and courteous presence: tallish, broad-shouldered, well-set, a man of fifty or so, I thought – with a fine head, very clear-cut features, sharp tip to long nose, piercing blue-grey eyes of aquatic flint under thick, curving eyebrows, a rather florid or high complexion, an admirably neat outline of head and perfectly-trimmed, close-cut partly grey hair – dressed in a macintosh over a thick, well-tailored tweed suit – very forthright and straightforward in manner, as was at once apparent. Not in the least formidable! Beautiful bearing and beautiful breeding – *beaucoup de branche*, in fact.

You came and sat down beside me and after a moment pulled out an exquisite little *tabatière* and offered me some snuff. At this, Osbert's and Sachie's eyes gave a leap – "There now, see?" – as I took some for the first time in my life, you telling me how it should be done, the right spot on the hand. I had a good sniff; it was strange and delicious. As I continued not to sneeze, I wondered if this would seem a sign of anything in particular to you. Apparently not!

We had a good, long look at one another. I remember *that* moment extraordinarily well.

"What do you find to do here?" you presently asked me.

"I've been in Florence two weeks now, and oh the rain! This year however, it seems to come regularly every alternate day and I've been going by that. So, the fine days I do excursions, and picture galleries and churches in Florence the wet ones. It has worked out beautifully, so far."

"Pictures . . .," you repeated, "excursions – where?"

"San Gimignano, for one. What a wonderful place in itself! and of course, the Benozzo Gozzolis there, those frescoes . . ."

"Benozzo Gozzolis!" The name of this painter set you off. "*What on earth for?*"

"Because I love his painting – that's all."

(I asked myself if you were playing at being a bit of a Philistine. Did I seem somewhat puzzling to you?)

". . . And Piero della Francesca, and Signorelli. These are my three favourite painters."

This was too much!

"What next?" you exclaimed, and offered me some more snuff.

(*Were* you playing at being a bit of a Philistine? A tweeded Scot, pooh-poohing at art? I was nonplussed now).

"Isn't all that rather *Cinquecento*, my dear?" you asked suddenly.

It must have been an expression well known to Osbert and Sachie, judging from the laugh that went up, which added to my bewilderment, although it made me laugh as much as them. What could it mean, used thus?

She defined "Cinquecento" later on, when she had known Douglas for some time, as an expression "of sublimated scorn applied to all those who, without being duly qualified, commonly express themselves in Art-jargon, emitting flatulent opinions and catchwords current in the Art circles of Florence and elsewhere. Pretentious, snobbish, gassy amateurs, phoney collectors, or ponderous critics who are bores. All that is *précieux*", but she found the application of the word by Douglas – as others did also – elastic enough to be used as gentle ridicule of all sorts of situations. Douglas maintained that a good luncheon is worth all the Benozzo Gozzolis in the world; but he soon ceased to tease her in this fashion – a sure sign that he had accepted her as a friend.

vii

Bryher, that other daughter of a shipowning family, had been in Egypt and had invited Douglas to meet her at Naples on her return to Europe, but he demurred to this suggestion: "I hate that town and all its neighbourhood which is saturated with memories that I don't want to revive, and it would be torture to me to go about there. I would like, if I could, to hop on board a boat and go to Sicily, which is relatively unsaturated, spending only 25 minutes at Naples!"; but in the end Capri was chosen. In spite of his remarks about Naples, Douglas went down from Florence a day early and tortured himself satisfactorily (one presumes) by going

out to the Gaiola. On the following day he joined Bryher on Capri. He had
not set foot on the island since August 1916, before the publication of
South Wind, but he seems to have returned in style. Bryher was at the
harbour to meet him:

> The news of his arrival spread from mouth to mouth. I have never
> seen a political leader enjoy so great a triumph. Men offered him wine,
> women with babies in their arms rushed up so that he might touch them,
> the children brought him flowers. I slipped away as he walked slowly
> through a crowd of several hundred people, shouting jokes in ribald
> Italian, kissing equally the small boys and girls and patting the babies
> as if they were kittens. The *signore* had deigned to return to his kingdom
> and I am sure that they believed that the crops would be abundant and
> the cisterns full of water as a result.

On the following day she received an invitation to dine with him, but
when seven o'clock had passed and there was still no sign of him in his
hotel lounge, she began to wonder what could have happened – he was
always punctual to the minute. Finally she sent a message up to his room
asking if there had been a mistake. "He tottered down, looked at me with
considerable vagueness and asked, 'What time is it?' I should have been
warned." When she produced his invitation-note, and reminded him of the
time, he instantly came to, slapped her on the shoulder with a hearty
intimacy she was entirely unused to, and growled "Kept you waiting, did
I? Never mind. I'll take you now to a brigand's den where there's been a
dozen murders", and, he added, to the best cook on the island. On the
way he sometimes leaned heavily on her shoulder, and in his best Newgate-
Calendar manner told her that every inch of the island had been steeped in
blood several times over. "They're a crowd of cut-throats", he flung back
his head and pointed at his throat alarmingly, "Proud, you know. We're
near Africa." She was puzzled why they never seemed to walk in a straight
line . . .

Eventually they were seated, and an enormous lobster was set before
him. He talked entrancingly of Capri long ago, a place "of straw hats, long
skirts and uninhibited passions that had ended even for him soon after
1900". So enraptured was his listener that she did not notice until too
late that he was beginning to chew the lobster, shell and all. "Tough, my
dear; how wise you were to stick to the omelette." He was rescued by the
patronne of the establishment, and Bryher at last realised that he was
"wildly, gloriously drunk".

She was afraid she would never get home; but of course Douglas knew
the way by instinct. He proposed that they should go up Monte Solaro
and make a night of it. Bryher, unused to such proposals, thought not:

"'Another day,' I murmured, five steps more and I should be safe. 'Another day! What is the matter with you this evening? How do you know you will live to see it? You may be stabbed or fall off a cliff.' I did not answer. I guided Douglas as gently as I could towards the safety of his room." But at that very moment he noticed three Englishwomen who seemed to be schoolteachers: "He broke away from my grasp, pranced towards them, taking off his hat, and said courteously but in a voice that could have been heard on the other side of the Piazza, 'Well, my dears, and whom are you tucking in with tonight?'"

Nancy Cunard arrived on the island, and Douglas and Bryher went to meet her at one of the cafés. Douglas entertained them with descriptions of how to deal with bores, and Nancy Cunard particularly enjoyed his method of dealing with a woman who had pertinaceously pestered Douglas for advice on what to drink. He had recommended an aperient mineral water: "... she had tried this mineral water – with most satisfactory results. She had not been seen for two days." This is one of many anecdotes – most are not in print – that illustrate (if true) the casual nastiness of which Douglas was occasionally capable; and the imbecile admiration which such acts could arouse amongst his more fatuous and sycophantic admirers.

His fame as the author of *South Wind*, and the imprecise but awe-inspiring reputation that was generally attributed to him as a person, were responsible for attracting a good many of the bores from whom he had learned to escape either with precipitate rudeness or by more subtle means. It occurred to him that there might be a sale for *South Wind* and *Old Calabria* on the island – tourists were beginning to come in their thousands – and he sent to Secker for five copies of each, to be addressed to Edwin Cerio. Either Cerio himself or someone else would act as agent in this matter, and Douglas might make a small income from it, as he obtained the copies from Secker at full author's discount. "Sooner or later," he advised Secker optimistically, "I daresay there will be some more required." But it did not work, and he had to confess to Bryher some months later that only four copies of *South Wind* were sold in spite of advertisements: "I don't think it worth while continuing that speculation, especially as the man charges 15 % on commission." The experiment is of interest as an example of his enterprise in trying to break the chain which binds author, publisher and bookseller in a bondage which he, in common with other authors, but to an almost obsessional degree, found so irksome. Within a year or two he was to find a typically unusual answer to this problem.

viii

After three weeks on Capri, Douglas migrated to Sant' Agata. "I am not alone," he informed Archie, "have an infant with me who is learning to cook and will, if he behaves, be my servant in the new Florentine apartment." Archie was asked to find Robert and send his father a full report on him, for Robert had suddenly written that he was in urgent need of money. Douglas had sent him £3, but feared "he was a bad egg". To Robert, now first addressed by his own request as Robin, Douglas wrote:

> I don't think my publisher will care about the title of your novel. Too lurid. He will probably ask you to change it. You want to make money? All you must do is to send me every one of your short stories (good *and* bad: what you consider mediocre may just suit my purposes, so don't leave it out) and I will arrange in my manner those I can arrange and put my name to them and try to dispose of them in America or elsewhere. We go halves. I shall not get *less* than £20 for any story of mine over there. That means £10 for you, without any trouble whatever. I am always being asked for short stories by those fools over there; and I can get rid of your stuff, or any one else's, if I put my name to it; and if I can maul it about to resemble my own writing. So don't be an arse, but send the whole damned lot along; AND DONT OMIT THE BAD ONES. Later on, you can reprint them under your own name, and I will write a jocular preface explaining the situation.
>
> Have you seen Archie?
> Where is Flora?
>
> > Your afft
> > Dad

> I have just finished a book called *Together* on the lines of my *Alone*. It is dedicated to you and Archie.

Robin had made friends with Mrs Tippett, who had dramatised *South Wind* in a play of the same name which had its debut early in April. He was also about to get himself – perhaps with the recommendation of Mrs Tippett – a job in the film department of Curtis Brown the literary agent, and was proposing to try and sell *South Wind* to a film producer. If he succeeded in that plan, his father wrote, he ought to get a third of the share of Mrs Tippett and himself combined, but the exclusive rights of filming would be Robin's.

He arrived in Florence on 7th May, "bloody tired, . . . I am going straight to bed. Tomorrow begins the removal into the new flat, which will take years off my life and waste at least 8 of my precious days – to say nothing of the precious money required to buy the endless things necessary to house-keeping." However, he was amply compensated by the great joy he got from informing Nardini that "I was leaving this place at the end of *this* month. He waxed green with rage, but couldn't say anything. Thought he had nailed me down here to the end of my life. He and his bitch simply *glowered* at me later in the evening. Ha, ha!"

ix

He had hardly got settled in his flat before he was off again – heading for the Vorarlberg with his cook. They were held up at Milan by passport difficulties, but the boy was "$\frac{1}{2}$ delirious with joy at the prospect of getting out of his country", and Douglas seems to have taken a companion for him – presumably so that he could work more easily while the boys entertained each other, or possibly he had the idea that two might seem less compromising than one.

In the zoological terminology that he used with Bryher, the boys he had with him – and any others in whom he might be interested – were Crocodiles, or Crocs. "The crocodiles like the place" he wrote, "and smash something new every day", or "The Crocodiles are out of doors all day, helping with the haymaking; I shall hang on here as long as I can." He was working, yes; but at a snail's pace; "I am dribbling along, about 35 words a day, with a religious novel" – this unlikely but marginally justifiable classification of *In the Beginning* was perhaps designed to please Edward Hutton, to whom he was writing.

Correspondence with Robin continued: he had become officially engaged to Miss Winifred Nelson Gott (known as Pip); it had been announced in an Eastbourne newspaper. And Robin, who seems to have been the kind of young man who is desperate to succeed quickly, had taken what he presumably hoped would be a short cut to success. He had chucked his job at Curtis Brown and started an agency of his own. "I heard the news from elsewhere," wrote his father, who got a good deal of pleasure from letting his correspondents know that he had information about them that they were unaware of.

How goes it? You will have to be pretty nippy; there are a lot of *other blackguards* in that field already, as you doubtless know. What staff have you got? What capital? Anyhow, I shall drink to its success at luncheon today, which happens to be the festival of our village saint.

As to writing memoirs – no! I can't write anything to order, otherwise I should be rolling in cash by this time. The offers one gets from

America! To Hell with them. I must plough my lonely furrow. For the rest, my next book, *Together,* is all memoirs.

I don't at all mind writing a foreword to your novel if you can get a publisher to accept it . . . If you really want to sell your book with the help of a foreword from me, the best foreword I could contrive for that purpose would be a humorously-*murderous* review of it. Sentimental puffing would be fatal. You may tell the publisher that I am ready to do a preface of 1000 words or so, if he lets me have advance sheets. If you are not too proud, I will also go through your proofs (in pencil). There!

There was a certain gruffness, a certain suggestion of amused contempt, definitely a lack of tenderness, in his attitude to Robin as compared with Archie, for whom he quite as obviously felt great solicitude and concern. Robin, of course, had not kept in touch as Archie had; he had not helped his father pack when he left England, as Archie had, having been still at school; and he had not fought in the War, which seems to have made Douglas feel particularly compassionate towards Archie. Archie was a slower, more solid, more careful person; Robin was more volatile, impatient, restless, and ambitious; but in each these characteristics may have been reinforced by Douglas' own attitude. He had not seen Robin, who was now twenty-one, since he had been a boy of fourteen. One has the feeling that Robin, who was born to parents who agreed to divorce before he was weaned, was a constant reminder to his father of those unhappy days, or that Douglas identified in him, or thought he identified, or sought to identify, some of the characteristics which he disliked in his wife. On the whole, his attitude to Robin was one of duty; to Archie, one of easy intimacy and some pleasure.

x

Early in August he heard from his new landlord that the flat in which he had barely settled, was required for the landlord's son, who was getting married. "This is a real disaster for me, as I had spent all my savings (such as they were) on getting into it, and expected to live and die there. I have no idea what to do now, or where to go."

Back in Florence in September, having delivered the Crocodiles to their homes, he began flat-hunting. "Crocodiles are flourishing," he informed Bryher. "No 1 has learned a little Austrian cookery; No 2 is at home again (round the corner here) and his people are delighted with his improved appearance." "No flat discoverable," he wrote to Archie on 12th November, "save at fantastic prices. I try to get other people to take a share in one or the other, but nobody cares to. Unless a miracle occurs, I start packing about the 20th; shall store my things here, and go away – don't know where to. This is dislocating my life . . .''; but the writing of this very letter was interrupted "by Orioli coming in to announce his discovery of a flat for me. We went there and *I have taken it* at once. Will need tons of repairs etc, etc but that can't be helped." The flat was a rather "tumble-down sort of place; no kitchen," sanitary arrangements "on the prehistoric system, and other drawbacks," including very low ceilings, but the price was reasonable. It was just on the other side of the Arno, in the Via San Niccolò, and looked south into a garden. He moved into it, after having had it painted, on 19th December.

xi

Together had been published at the end of September.

There is a legend, fostered by certain Douglas admirers, that each of his books was written while he was inspired by a particular love-affair. Like many anecdotal stories, it has an element of truth, as may be seen from his admission to Brigit Patmore when she told him she wished he was writing something: "'I can only write if I have *this*'" he answered. My forearm was resting on the table and he gripped it hard. I knew he didn't mean *my* arm or me, but the confiding closeness, that ardent heightening of mind and senses through love or passion."

This confession illustrates his attitude. He needed to be in love, but not necessarily in the romantic way implied by the anecdote, devoting himself to a particular individual who would elicit from him by some obscure chemistry of the personality a distinct creative response. He simply needed to be in love, in the same sort of way that he needed reasonably good food, and drink; but even as one knows that he could do perfectly well on very simple or poor food when necessary, one suspects that the books continued to be written through gaps between love-affairs – supposing that such gaps existed. Some books, certainly, owed allegiance to several successive companions: *South Wind* is one of them. The Amitrano boy helped greatly with *Siren Land*; *Old Calabria* must be forever associated with Eric, but no doubt with others, unknown, as well. Some of the mellowness of *Alone* is due to René; and to René also, and above all, is due the leisurely and attractive ease, the wistfulness and joy, the concentrated homogeneous atmosphere of reminiscence in *Together*.

Together was the result of two successive visits to the Vorarlberg with René, in 1921 and 1922. It was written easily and quickly, between the end of July and the end of December of the latter year, and with three kinds of love – in the present, for his companion; for present sights and

sounds and experiences; and for the past, for his childhood and its associations. The dialogue between himself and René, their happy leisured
progress through the province, with good-natured mutual teasing, is just
the right foil for the more serious business of examining and mentally
caressing the past, or for setting down longish footnotes filled with historical or philological or zoological information. Although these two
elements, the autobiographical and the observational, remain more or less
separate, they combine to make a delightful whole. Here the mixture is, as
it were, folded in, and not completely blended, as in *Alone*.

These visits to the Vorarlberg, after so many years' absence, produced
a flood of autobiographical reminiscence that must have astonished readers
accustomed only to brief and reticent asides concerning himself and his
family. Here, suddenly, we are told a great deal about himself as a child,
about his father, his grandfathers, his paternal grandmother, his sister
and her governess, and various local people who played some part in his
early days – the Brunnenmacher, Mattli and Alte Anna. But the information is carefully selected; we are told nothing about his mother,
nothing about her second husband, nothing about their child Grete,
nothing about his brother John. One has been told a little about why his
brother does not make an appearance, but nothing – alas! – that accounts
for Vanda's absence.

Together is in a category of its own amongst his travel books. It is an
exploration of a limited geographical area and of its history, geology,
botany, zoology and sociology in his usual manner, that is to say in a
table-talking or random or conversational mode with dips here and there
into wells of erudition that give one an impression of massive underground resources of knowledge. It is also an exploration of his childhood; and finally, of himself exploring his childhood. It has much depth,
and gives an impression of calm and secure happiness. It was to be his
last real travel-book, and his last non-fictional work of any weight until
Looking Back (1933).

Together pleased both friends and critics and brought Douglas some
delighted tributes in the press and some appreciative letters. Amongst the
latter was one from a fellow-writer, who thus began a correspondence
which was to continue intermittently for five or six years:

Oct. 29th, 1923

Dear Mr Norman Douglas,
   I have for long wanted to write to you to express my admiration of
your books. I'm afraid you will be bored by the remarks of a stranger,
but my enthusiasm has now overpowered my discretion, and I can no
longer forbear to march in where angels, certainly, if they had any

sense – but have they? – would fear to tread. This boiling over is the result of my having just finished "Together" . . . which seems to me to be perhaps the most subtly composed of all your books. I believe I have now read everything that you have published – except "Siren Land", which I am told is out of print. I think it's difficult to appreciate one of your books properly without reading several of them . . . now the slightest of your phrases gets me into the right key at once, and the thrill that only you can give goes down my back.

I think "South Wind" is the most brilliant of your books, and "Old Calabria" the most imposing but I have a special love of "Alone". How did you manage to fill it with that romantic beauty? The variety of moods in it is indeed extraordinary; and yet the totality of the impression is completely preserved. In these decidedly lean years it is the fatness of your kine that is so particularly striking. Your books are so full; there is . . . so much learning, so much art, so much humour, so much philosophy, and so much proof that there is so much, so very much, more underneath, that is unexpressed.

Will you forgive these expatiations? They are at any rate sincere . . .

This letter from Lytton Strachey was no doubt as sincere as it announced itself to be; but it is also evident from later letters that Strachey had recognised that he and Douglas had interests in common other than literature, and this knowledge undoubtedly added something to their rather excited, almost gushing correspondence.

Douglas was delighted by Strachey's unexpected letter: "I value your opinion more highly than that of any English writer" he replied, and sent him a copy of *Siren Land*. "I cannot tell you what joy it has given me," Strachey answered, ". . . I shall return to it again and again . . . Your story of Dent's pulping that book is appalling. The idiotic fiend! He ought to have been pulped himself." He was rather sorry about Tiberius, he wrote – "sorry to exchange that dramatic monster for such a respectable old person"; but Douglas' learning was positively terrifying. Incidentally, if Strachey could do any odd jobs – "references taken or copying out, etc" – for Douglas he would be "extremely glad to be able to do you the smallest service. I am often at the British Museum, and can be a diligent transcriber." Nothing could testify more strongly to Strachey's genuine admiration for Douglas than this offer, which no writer will idly make to another. Douglas' return civilities extended to the hope that Strachey would write a biography of Heliogabalus: "Come here, and we'll do it together. Or the private journal of the Emperor Claudius."

Another writer who felt moved to send his congratulations on this book was E. M. Forster. "I like 'Together'" he wrote. "Very beautiful, and unlike anything that you or any one else has done, I thought. That capacious envelope, the past, needs very careful filling. Keep the pathos down, yes, keep it down . . . 'Together' impressed on me more than ever the vastness of your resources."[97]

There was also a charming letter from his old friend W. H. D. Rouse,[98] and Robin, who had apparently enquired about the Douglas family as a result of reading the book, was not entirely discouraged: "The worst of it is, there is nothing of the slightest interest to know, so far as the priceless *family* is concerned." Nevertheless, Robin could ask any questions he liked, and his father would answer them, if he could.

The short stories which his father had asked Robin to send him for rewriting had been left in France while Douglas was in the Vorarlberg. He now went through them, but concluded rather petulantly "*I* can't do anything with them. They won't let themselves be bent with my manner. Am therefore returning them, registered." He did not think Robin's story in the *English Review* was "'tripe' at all, not at all, at all. Write some more. But that is just the kind of thing that I can't twist into my style (as aforesaid) . . . How's the Daily Mail? Great people for sucking your brains and then giving you the chuck." The letter was quite affectionate in tone; and for Christmas he wrote him another, which was slightly tetchy, and contained one of those rare hints of something close to self pity: ". . . I hope you are feeling more comfortable than I, with the damp plaster on the walls which (aided by the petroleum stove) may mean pneumonia for me at any time." In this letter he quoted his favourite obscene limerick, about the Virgin, the Ghost and the Lamb, evidently hoping that it might shock the "Victorian" notions of morality which Robin claimed he had developed.

CHAPTER TWENTY-FOUR

Printing His Own
1924

i

The finding, by Orioli, of the flat in the Via San Niccolò, and the reasonably quick entry into it must have been a great relief, after Douglas had been faced with the possibility of having to lead a "portmanteau life" again. He was just fifty-five at this time, and did not relish the idea of having to move. "You see," he wrote, "what I want (at my age) is to settle down definitely. I have a hankering to be at rest." Of course! He had always had a hankering to be at rest – spasmodically. His books are interspersed with descriptions of stillness and peace in remote places, and in some of the descriptions of landscape there are suggestions of emotions which in other people might have led to transcendental or mystical speculations, but which in Douglas' writing owe their peculiar charm to a momentary suspension of intellectual preoccupations, which are resumed after an interval in which the senses alone are feasted – resumed in an entirely matter-of-fact and undramatic manner. Douglas, with all his zest and impulsiveness, his appetites and impatience and determined self-indulgence, was at the same time also a fatalist. He was partly hedonist, partly Epicurean, partly Stoic; one of the maddening things about him is the inability to pin him down – maddening and admirable, since it constitutes his peculiar individuality. The business of life was to enjoy oneself, and there was to be no truck with utilitarianism – one could enjoy oneself sufficiently without the majority doing likewise; in fact, the consciousness that the herd was a fool, and not enjoying itself might make one's own enjoyment all the greater. That was hedonism. But how did one enjoy oneself? In one particular, at least, the sexual, a good deal of danger and trouble and vexation – what would definitely have been classed as pain by Epicurus – were involved; and Epicurean enjoyment consisted in the avoidance of pain, so sometimes love involved a kind of stoicism. He was Epicurean when he went without lunch in order to enjoy a special dinner all the more; or when he led "a hermit's life" in his room in order to finish some work and thus avoid the pain of not having it done at the

323

right time. But by and large he accepted life on its own terms which he knew backwards having wrestled with them since childhood, and took what came and made the best of it in whatever way seemed to offer the most promise of happiness. He had led a pretty rackety life, sustained by a splendid constitution and regular habits. He had been tough and energetic and had lived mentally and psychologically, if not always physically, among the hills and in the ancient world; but now, at the weakest point in life – in middle age – he had come down into the valleys and settled in Florence, and had begun to lead more and more the self-indulgent hedonistic life. Food, drink and sex became more and more the chief preoccupations of his existence; intellectual activities occupied less and less of his time; life in general, as it will in middle age, became more mechanical and less spontaneous. In the fourteen years between 1923 and 1937 (when he left Florence), he published a number of books. After *Together* (1923) eleven publications appeared before *Looking Back* (1933). The only substantial one of these was *In the Beginning*, which had been written by 1925. The rest of his creative work during these years could have been put quite easily into one modest-sized volume. It was book-making, either editorial and commentatory, like *Birds and Beasts of the Greek Anthology, Some Limericks*, or *How about Europe?*; or reprinted material, as in *Experiments, Nerinda,* the *Capri Materials,* and *Summer Islands*. The original pieces which appeared in these years – the Lawrence–Magnus pamphlet, *One Day*, and *Paneros* – were all brief, about 12,000 words each. It is hardly an exaggeration to say that the main stream of his work ended virtually with *In the Beginning*; *Looking Back*, six years later, was an afterthought, and a very splendid one. But the Florentine period, during which he became famous and much visited, and notorious and much flattered, against his will, had an effect upon him which was not entirely to be welcomed; for even in resisting sycophants – not all of whom were foolish nonentities – he reacted to them, and to that extent became the victim, in some small degree, of his own legend. In this Florentine period Uncle Norman – rather portly, rather inflamed of countenance – was characteristically encountered in a restaurant autocratically overseeing the production of the food he was about to eat, treating the waiter as his personal servant, exacting lieutenantship from Orioli, his personal Fool, weighing the wine, and letting nothing pass that did not meet with his absolute approval. It became a sight that all who were interested were determined to see; and those who succeeded in seeing it were often rewarded, alas, by Uncle Norman performing as required. Not that he did so in order to entertain, or please – he'd have been damned rather than do that – but because his natural inclinations lay in that direction, and because no one whom he respected disapproved. On the contrary, most of them one way or another, actively or passively, encouraged him. His talk, on the whole, appears to have been largely of food and sex, and as time went on, became more and more spattered with predictable ejaculations, such as "What next!" His arteries did not actually reveal that they were hardening until the very end of this period; but his thoughts were becoming less elastic; his reactions were becoming more and more mechanical and predictable. He was settling down into a "character". He was content, on occasion, to be co-buffoon with Orioli. These two men, with such utterly different backgrounds and characters, had become very close friends by 1924 and were destined for another fifteen years and more to bring out the best and the worst in each other, to become indispensable to each other, and indissolubly linked.

ii

This crystallisation of the Florentine period was just around the corner in 1924; but one of the prime ingredients in it – the establishment of Douglas as a "collected" writer – had already begun with the publication of the *South Wind* on blue paper. In the summer of 1923, an enterprising London bookseller, W. Townley Searle, had written to ask Douglas if he had any copies of his Capri monographs for sale. He had; and thus began one of those small business transactions in which he took a disproportionate amount of interest. Searle was supplied with a good many more pamphlets which Douglas obtained for him when he visited Capri. But Searle, as it turned out, performed two other functions: he obtained a contribution from Douglas to a journal called the *First Edition* which he edited, and he proposed reprinting the Capri monograph on *Forestal Conditions*, if it could be brought up to date. Douglas, referring to it deprecatingly as a "stodgy little performance", replied that he could not revise it himself, but Searle might apply to Edwin Cerio: "He writes English as easily as he does Italian, and with great charm, and no living man knows more about this subject or takes a livelier interest in it." He was both surprised and gratified by Searle's interest in the monographs.

More was to come from Searle, including some revelations of an unpleasing kind. In August Douglas replied to a letter from Searle which must have contained the news that Searle had been offered some of Douglas's Capri monographs for sale by Louis Golding. There was no chance, Douglas wrote, that Golding could have got a single one of the monographs except by misappropriation, the circumstances of which he explains. "The inference is perfectly plain and not altogether lovely."

Golding's misbehaviour was not the first chance disclosure made by

Searle. In July, Douglas had written to him, concerning another: "It is very kind of you to forward me that pearl of a letter. But I want the young fellow to understand that documents of that kind are not to be hawked about. Does he know that it has been through *your* hands? If not, what would it matter if he knew that it were now in mine? I shall do nothing till I hear from you." This refers to Robin, who had sold Searle one or more letters from his father. Quite apart from the fact that Douglas did not like having his letters "hawked about the streets" at all it is said that this letter was a particularly private one, giving Robin intimate advice, at his own request, about one of his women. A few months later Searle was offered more of Douglas' letters, almost certainly by Robin; he bought them, and informed Douglas – may even have sent them to him. Douglas wrote: "So kind of you buying those letters of mine, but you really must not put yourself out like this. If he offers you any more, just tell him, *from me*, to stuff them up his (exhaust)-pipe . . ." Shortly after this, Douglas wrote to Archie: "'No news from Robert. I never write him."

This episode marked a turning-point in Douglas' attitude to Robin. He simply "dropped" him, wrote only if it was absolutely necessary, and did not really forgive Robin for sixteen or seventeen years. It is possible that Robin's lapse even made his father doubt – though not perhaps for the first time – his son's paternity, if his words in old age are to be taken literally and not merely as an idiomatic expression of outrage: "No son of mine could have done a thing like that!" Certainly, Robin had acted foolishly, no doubt through need of ready money, which may have been particularly necessary to him at that time, since, as he had informed his father early in the year, he had married. "Bloody fools, both of them" was his father's comment to Archie; and although he had scraped up a reply to Robin containing the word "congratulations" he enclosed no cheque or hint of a present. His next letter, in April, had told Robin not to be "in such a damned hurry" about a wedding present, and after a long complaint about lack of money from his books, ended bad-temperedly: ". . . print all my letters and put in as many *fucks* and *damns* as you please", which suggests that Robin had thought of publishing his father's letters before he thought of selling them. This kind of negative permission from his father, which could fairly be called petulant, occasionally erupted from him in circumstances over which he felt, perhaps, that he had no control. He cared greatly about the publication or offering for sale of private letters, but he seems to have been damned if he was going to say so, or, if having said so, and been disregarded, he was going to remonstrate or show anger. He would pretend not to care, let the other fellow get himself more deeply in the wrong, and then simply drop him.

At this date Douglas approved of Townley Searle, probably not so much on account of the actual services rendered as because Douglas had been enabled by them to indulge his pastime of surprising – in this case – Robin with knowledge of his activities. The greater the distance intervening, the greater the triumph in finding out. Not that he exploited such discoveries in an unpleasant manner: they simply gave him satisfaction.

iii

One of his boys, Mario, possibly one of the two whom he had taken to Austria, who was now his cook, had elected, or was persuaded, by Douglas, to go into the merchant navy. This required "endless formalities and documents"; but Douglas persevered. Evidently Mario had become a nuisance. When he had gone, Douglas packed up and went down to Rome and district for a week, then to Calabria for a week, and came to rest as he had so often done, at Sant' Agata. But here, no sooner had he settled down and begun to get into

> my old frame of mind, when I got a letter ... from Mario, who says he missed his steamer at Constantinople (he probably got the sack) and was repatriated by the Italian consul and *is now at Florence*. Cook's girl, needless to say, gave him my address and he talks of coming out here at once and joining me. If so, I shall never shake him off again! So I have written saying that I am going elsewhere, and only hope he won't turn up before I go. This is all *perfectly damnable*, and of course I can't go back to Florence, else he will catch me there. What's to be done? I may spend a week or so in Capri or on Ischia, deciding what to do; but catch me telling Cook's girl where I am. I shall have my letters forwarded by her to some other place, where I can just call for them: it will mean delay, but it can't be helped ... What a life, my dear! Why can't people *leave me alone*?

Three weeks later, having met the Mackenzies while crossing over to Capri for the day, he was staying with them in Casa Solitaria:

> I can't go back to Florence at present, for fear of being caught by the Crocodile, and never let go again. The girl at Cook's – damn her – told him I was at S. Agata; he promptly came there and *is there still*. I had left 2 days before his arrival. I wrote to him to say I could not have him or see him, and told him to get work in Rome or anywhere else and sent him money for his ticket there and said I was going back to Florence and that he could write to me there. By this means I hope to

lure him out of these regions. But the whole thing is too damnable, and also too complicated to explain in a letter.

iv

From Capri he rushed off to Scanno and then Sulmona; but there was struck down with "a kind of bloody rheumatism". He could not move out of bed, but did not think the attack would last long, and was not unduly perturbed: "The hotel is good and I have a nice English youth, as well as a little Capri boy, to look after me." Five days later, when he had returned to Capri to collect his luggage ("wish I had let it go to Hell") he was "suffering torments", and had decided to go to Rome, where he had a good friend in Victor Cunard, and get himself into a hospital. He arrived in Rome on 3 June, was overhauled by a good doctor, and ordered to take the baths at Fiuggi. The rheumatism was as bad as ever, he wrote a few days later, but Cunard, with whom he was staying, took good care of him. He was in pain all the time.

Meanwhile, a few days before the onset of this attack, he had learnt that René had

> bolted from home and his school and, according to a telegram just received, should be at the Hotel Nardini in Florence. He did all this *without ever consulting me*. Now if his father discovers him in Florence I may be involved in very serious complications, police or otherwise. Would you [he wrote to Orioli] please find out if he is there . . . and point this out to him and get him out of Florence as soon as ever possible. Nardini, who is now a great enemy of mine, will do his best to stir up trouble. Tell him that if he had only consulted me before taking this step, I could have arranged everything. It is a veritable *coup de folie*. I cannot come back to Florence now: tell him this. Tell him also that on receipt of his previous wire and letters I wrote him at once to the *Sud-bar* address he gave me. Get him out of Florence or it may mean mischief for both of us . . . Tell him that I would have written him myself, but am afraid my letters might fall into the hands of Nardini.

This scare was dissipated a few days later when Douglas heard, presumably from René, that his father knew all about his leaving home. Douglas hoped that René might be able to wait in Florence until he could join him there, if René had money: "I have *none* left. Never been so hard up since the war." What actually happened was that René joined him at Fiuggi. The only surviving letter from René reveals some of the charm which everyone who knew him remarked on:

Fiuggi le 10 juin 1924

Mon cher vieux Orioli

Je suis en ce moment-ci avec Douglas à Fiuggi (mais "acqua in bocca" n'est-ce pas?)

Norman doit suivre un régime ici. Ni vin, ni viande et ne boire que de l'eau de Fiuggi. Ça ne l'amuse pas beaucoup.

A Rome c'est très difficile de trouver du travail. *Peut-être* j'aurais une place de journaliste ou de secrétaire, mais il y a avant un tas de complications. Il faut par example attendre une réponse de Paris etc etc . . . Ça sera d'ailleurs très long et d'ici là . . . Vous qui avez des amis influents et qui connaissez tant de monde à Florence ne pourriez-vous pas me trouvez quelque chose. Je ferais *n'importe quoi* sauf "tapette" bien entendu . . . Voyez . . . je connais trois langues (à peu près . . . Il est vrai) Mais je crois tout de même qu'avec cela ce ne sera pas trop difficile. Voulez-vous essayer, je me contenterai de tout, même si c'est en dehors de Florence (ça ne fait rien du tout . . .) Je serai toujours content. Ecrivez-moi à propos de cela et je vous remercie infiniment.

La santé de Douglas n'est pas très bonne. Il a des rheumatismes un peu de partout mais j'espère que Fiuggi lui fera du bien . . .

Encore une fois pensez à moi, et écrivez-moi tout de suite à propos de mon travail. Je vous serais tres reconnaissant.

Toujours à vous
René Mari

By the middle of June the rheumatism was better. Douglas and René travelled up to Rome together, and the next day René left, presumably for Menton or Ventimiglia. Douglas hoped he might get a job near an old friend, Basil Leng, the botanist and landscape gardener, who lived on the Riviera, but happened to be working in Guernsey. Orioli was thanked for looking after René, and warned, repeatedly, not to let Mario know where Douglas was.

v

In late summer Douglas was once again in the Vorarlberg, where, despite still persistent rheumatism in hand and foot, he was able to get on rapidly with his work. This consisted of "scraping together old articles etc which I mean to get published here at Bregenz, in 250 copies at £2-2-0 each. Who knows? There may be a hundred fools to buy a copy each." He went to a printer, had a specimen page set up which was satisfactory except for margins that were too narrow, but could not find a decent paper. The type was too large for the size of page. Printing in the Vorarlberg was abandoned as a possibility. Archie, who was in Italy swotting up his Italian in order to sit for a Consular exam, could not get money to come to Austria, so his father decided to join him on Capri.

Archie, meanwhile, had been offered and had accepted a job in the Passport Office in Prague. It was a safer bet, as his father pointed out, than risking all on the Consular Service exam, which he might not pass, and could not take twice. After a short time together, they went their separate ways, Archie to London and Douglas to Florence, where the latter at once began to hunt for a printer for his volume of miscellanies. Hutton was asked for a title – there was always trouble about that – and suggested "Shepherd's Pie", which, Douglas replied, "sounds charming. But what is Shepherd's Pie? Is it the abomination we used to get at school, with a forbidding crust of mashed potatoes on the top, and inside, a collection of heterogeneous fragments of meat which ought to have been thrown away weeks ago? If so, the title will exactly fit the book: the suggestion, I mean, of dishing up antiquities."

He had been intending to visit Eric in Africa ever since Eric had taken the job with the Tanganyikan police. Eric now wrote that he wanted to get out of Africa and asked for letters of introduction to Australia or New Zealand or South Africa. Douglas did not know whether he would be able to go to East Africa to see him or not; but in case Eric would still be there, he decided to try to raise the fare by selling his autographed Joseph Conrad first editions, and the manuscript of *South Wind*. The sale of these items, to the famous American bibliophile Abraham Rosenbach, was negotiated by Walter Lowenfels, a young poet, son of a butter millionaire, and friend of Muriel Draper. In 1922 or 1923 he had made the American grand tour pilgrimage to Europe and he and Douglas had met, introduced no doubt by Muriel Draper.

My dear W. L.,

... I will go through my Conrad correspondence, to see if I have any letters of his relative to his books. But I greatly fear I haven't. He always (as we were so often together) just handed them to me. If I find any, I will send them along tomorrow.

... The MS will have reached you by this time – in two parts, alas, as it otherwise would not have conformed to the postal regulations. I don't think there will be much trouble about re-binding it. ... Anyhow, it is genuine, which is more than can be said of certain other MSS, about which I can only speak to you by word of mouth (whereupon you will chuckle softly).

By the end of October he had received subscriptions for about 75 copies of *Shepherd's Pie* from America alone; others were reserved in England, for instance by Townley Searle. Early in November its title was changed to *Resurrection Pie*, then to *Partialities*. He was busy correcting proofs and preparing for his visit to Africa.

Towards the end of October he had asked Secker to send him a copy of Magnus' *Memoirs*, with Lawrence's introduction: "If you expect a 2nd edition, I might also write an introduction (little memoir): say 4000 words." Secker replied that he had just reprinted the book, "but I should be so delighted if you could write a supplementary memoir of 4000 words or so as you suggest. I will include it in the next printing, at the same time making any reasonable payment you suggest for the use of this." Having suggested the idea, however, Douglas did nothing to implement it; he tried half-heartedly to get a journal interested in publishing it first; but when there was no response to this idea, or possibly even before that, he must have decided to write the thing and publish it himself as a pamphlet. He had evidently consulted Leo Stein (brother of Gertrude) about this project, and had asked Secker to send Stein a copy of the Magnus book, as Stein seemed inclined to write on the subject: he was one of the Florentines who had figured in *Aaron's Road*, as Walter Rosen.

Towards the end of November his rheumatism returned, and with it an abscess on the jaw "as large as a cocoa-nut". He sent two despairing notes to Orioli, asking him to send someone to cheer him up. "I sent a bottle of whisky to cheer him up," wrote Orioli. It was the same thing as last time, Douglas informed Archie after consulting his doctor, not rheumatism but neuritis. On the night before his birthday he was up all night poulticing his jaw; he was feeling no worse than on the previous day, he told Orioli, and hoped to be at Betti's in the evening.

He enjoyed his birthday dinner enormously; his neuritis was better, but not gone; and he was only waiting to finish an article (probably for the new book) before dashing off to Syracuse.

He also wrote to Stein saying he hoped he had received Magnus' book: "If you write anything about him, don't confine yourself to this book but let it be, if possible, a dissection of his nature and literary activities in general. Tell me, also, whether you want it printed under your full name, your initials, or merely with an explanation from myself hinting at its authorship."

To Bryher he wrote explaining that the title of his new book had been changed again, to *Experiments*, and that work on it was proceeding: "But I am interrupting it. . . . in order to print off swiftly a pamphlet which I am now writing and which I shall distribute myself at 5/- a copy; promises to be *pretty juicy*. I shall put an advert in the 'Times Literary Supp^t' about it, and hope to get rid of a good number of copies, once it gets known . . ." That was why he had gone to Syracuse, he added – to work absolutely undisturbed.

He stayed ten days, in the ideal conditions described in *Late Harvest*, working with satisfying speed and concentration, and then went straight to Capri to see Faith Mackenzie: "Here you are, my dear: read this. Is it strong enough? I don't want to mince words." Mrs Mackenzie was able to assure him "that no words were minced. It was a cut off the joint steaming and pungent. A brochure worth having . . .". She added that she was fairly sure that what had "got him on the raw" about the Lawrence introduction to the Magnus *Memoirs* was the anecdote about Douglas having the wine weighed.

CHAPTER TWENTY-FIVE

Africa
1925

i

D. H. Lawrence & Maurice Magnus: A Plea for Better Manners was advertised in the *Times Literary Supplement* on 21st January, by which time it was ready for distribution.

The subtitle reveals the angle from which this forceful but by no means virulent or devastating polemic is written. Douglas is offended rather than angry, vigilant rather than swashbuckling. He brushes off Lawrence's caricatures of himself in the introduction to Magnus' *Memoirs* and in *Aaron's Rod*, but objects strongly to, and refutes, the statement that Douglas despised Magnus. Also untrue is Lawrence's accusation that Magnus had spent "over a hundred pounds of borrowed money" and had "guzzled" with it. He defends Magnus with examples of his compassion, his generosity, his capacity for hard work, his faithfulness and courage, while also admitting that the fussy, finicking, pompous side of his character shown by Lawrence, is true. The trouble with "friend Lawrence" is that he has "the novelist's touch", picking out this or that aspect of a person to suit his purpose, and blinding himself to the rest. There is wrong feeling nearly all through Lawrence's introduction – an inappropriate bitterness, which may have been caused, Douglas suggests, by the fact that Magnus had borrowed money from Lawrence. Lawrence's presentation of Magnus lacks humanity.

Douglas then broadens his attack to condemn Lawrence as a symptom of the times: novelists and journalists writing familiarly of their friends, "personality mongering" – a disease to which *Who's Who*, among other influences, contributes – encouraging the "squeaky suburban chuckle" and spawning a school of "cerebral hermaphrodites". There ought to be a limit to this sort of thing: it is "not only bad literature but bad breeding".

The pamphlet, written with considerable brio, makes entertaining reading, although it must be admitted that one smiles nowadays occasionally at Douglas' expense while reading it: his "gentlemanly" attitude, never very convincing even in his lifetime, has long been obliterated by writers

with much less scrupulousness than Lawrence. In regard to the contro-
versy the pamphlet aroused, it should be remembered that the advantage
was with Douglas throughout. Lawrence's views were so unorthodox, his
behaviour was so eccentric and cantankerous, his morals were so suspect
to the ignorant – above all, he was so open, so honest, so vulnerable – that
everything he did and said was liable to be turned to sensational account
by the press. He lived under the arc lights, on the stage, in full view of all
the prurient scribblers and scandalmongers of the time; whereas Douglas,
the nature of whose morals was known to few, was known, if he was
known at all, only as the author of an acceptably naughty novel about
la dolce vita in the Mediterranean. Douglas, whose bearing and manner
were courteous and gentlemanly, and who never openly threatened the
status quo, must also have seemed to be the embodiment of the voice of
reason and moderation, the decent, restrained citizen with whom the
average reader of the weekly review could identify safely and comfortably
in opposition to the disturbing and anarchist-minded Lawrence. Such
views of the two men were not confined to the reading public: they were
shared by a number of writers. H. M. Tomlinson,[99] for instance, wrote to
Douglas:

> Lawrence is a writer who has never got beyond the age of puberty,
> & the queer thing is his transition state is that of a girl. Some of the
> silliest trash that has been printed of late is his. *Moreover he is a mean &*
> *treacherous man, I should guess,* [my italics] who would do anything that
> suited him with a confidence.
>   . . . I don't like the idea of Lawrence being chucked at me as a pleb.
> I'm a pleb. And Lawrence – worse than having no manners – has the
> mind of a hen.

Alas, it is no credit to Douglas' mind that he marked the first paragraph just quoted, and kept the letter until his death. Why should he have
felt the need of shoring himself up with such fragile material? It seems
that it can only be because he too, like so many others, was genuinely
puzzled and uncertain when confronted by the phenomenon of Lawrence,
and occasionally took nourishment from people like Tomlinson for no
good reason other than that he seems to have needed the reassurance they
may have provided. Occasionally, a shaft of malice would be allowed to
fly, as in the following comment in a letter to someone he only knew by
post: "Lawrence is all wrong about my room; *table* obviously untidy: as
to my keeping windows shut, I can afford to do so; I haven't got a
syphilitico-tuberculous throat like he has."

This waspish invention, not at all typical of his attitude to Lawrence,
was added as a postscript to a harmless and genial letter on a day when he

wrote twelve or more letters and excused himself in this one for a "scrawl". It is as though the bile had suddenly risen in him, and demanded immediate discharge. The resentment here can only have been due to Lawrence having made available to the public a glimpse of Douglas in what the latter considered ought to have been the sacred privacy of his room. There is never any suggestion that Lawrence is lying, and the evidence that he is misrepresenting by only showing a part of the whole, is thin. All writers are bound to select; the trouble with Lawrence was that what he selected, he described with such vividness and accuracy that it was inclined to remain for ever photographically embedded in the memory of the reader. That obviously – and especially to a man of Douglas' tastes – could be dangerous.

It must have been obvious to Douglas that Lawrence's photographic eye and apparently limitless recall of conversation was the one kind of writing which could do him great damage without setting a foot anywhere near the laws of libel.[100] Lawrence had only to take it into his head to describe Douglas in the company of Mario, or Silvio, or Alvaro, or Emilio, for the entire relationship to open itself out before the reader's eyes. What Douglas did not realise was that Lawrence, as much as or perhaps even more than, anyone else writing at the time, had also a sense of the fitness of things. It is unlikely that he would ever have published anything that could have got Douglas into trouble.

It cannot truthfully be said that Lawrence in his *Introduction* was unfair to Douglas, except in the one matter of charging him with despising Magnus. The kindest interpretation to put upon this would be to say that Lawrence mistook a gruff and derisive jocularity on Douglas' part towards Magnus' fussiness and attentions to him, for a kind of contempt; whereas there can be little doubt that Douglas was fond of Magnus – but catch him letting Lawrence see it! The other main personal grievance that Douglas had against Lawrence, as mentioned in the pamphlet, namely that he showed Douglas in *Aaron's Rod* as talking unpleasantly about his friends, is made too much of by Douglas, and dragged in as extra ammunition against Lawrence.

As to Lawrence being unfair to Magnus – it may be true; but if so, it is true only of about four pages out of more than eighty. On the whole, the portrait is convincing if one makes some slight allowance for Lawrence having been driven to a state of exacerbation by Magnus' insistent appeals to his charity. He got the amount of Magnus' debts wrong, but may have been wrongly informed.

Magnus and Lawrence were bound to misunderstand one another. To one luxury and paternalism in some form were almost a necessity; to the other luxury was odious, and any kind of exterior authority oppressive.

One was too urbane, too mediterraneanised (as Douglas might have said) to be easily shocked; the other was as puritanical in some respects as an old spinster. In these matters, you could call Magnus a typical Latin, Lawrence a typical Anglo-Saxon. Douglas was an amalgam of the two: Compton Mackenzie could think of him as a Catholic manqué, and he can also be thought of as an inverted Calvinist. Strangely enough, both descriptions could be applied, for different reasons, to Lawrence. The differences between Douglas and Lawrence were prodigious, and have frequently been pointed out; the similarities do not seem to have been mentioned, yet they exist.

Both men were devoted nature-worshippers, with a great love and an extensive experience of the observation of plants and animals. Their works are full of descriptions of them – the one tending to rhapsody and imaginative perception, or writing as a poet; the other observing with the steady scrutiny of a scientist, and describing with the inclusive knowledge of a polymath; the one arriving at his truth by a series of repeated (and often repetitive) sallies and withdrawals, the other by methodical progress from one point to the next. The one spreads his emotions with gothic prodigality all over the page; the other contains them with classic restraint within the boundaries of a phrase. They might be Shelley and Landor, so alike, so dissimilar.

Both men travelled widely, perhaps, as Rebecca West suggested of Lawrence, "to obtain a certain apocalyptic vision of mankind"; both were highly individualistic and ex-centric; both were revolted, in their different ways, by the prurience of the morality of their time, to which both reacted in print by treating of sex, in their different ways, in a radical and unorthodox manner; both were capricious, changing their superficial emotional reactions to people and places frequently with the accession of a mood; both exaggerated wildly, one with a kind of hysteria, the other with a kind of wry fatalism or outrageous humour; both were absolutely loyal, in their totally different ways, to the tender core, the essence, of life; both saw, in their different ways, how it was so often smothered by civilisation; both liked simplicity – the one to do daily household chores, the other to talk with unsophisticated people. Lawrence had an unconquerable spirit, Douglas an unquenchable thirst for living . . .

Douglas, like anyone else who knew Lawrence, often found him difficult and unsatisfactory; but however much he may have disliked certain aspects of Lawrence, Douglas did not doubt his gifts or attempt to denigrate them, as many did; he saw through the prickliness, the over-sensitive reactions, the hysteria, the occasional absurdity, to the spirit behind it, which he honoured and admired. He was glad to help in such small ways as he could ("Douglas has never left me in the lurch"), which he would certainly not have done if he had wholeheartedly disliked or disapproved of Lawrence in the same sort of way that he disliked and disapproved of Henry James. And yet he was wary of Lawrence in a way that differed from the wariness, or the exasperation, of other people. It has always seemed to me possible, even likely, that Douglas recognised in Lawrence a quality of lyricism and spontaneity – the Shelleyean, the Blakean streak – of which he himself, at one point in his life, might have been capable, might have developed, if he had not progressed in another direction, and that perhaps it filled him with a kind of nostalgia for what might have been, a kind of envy. Perhaps this hypothesis would also illuminate Douglas' lifelong interest in and association with poets, although he professed to dislike poetry.

Lawrence, for his part, must have recognised in Douglas what he may have regarded as a fallen angel or spoiled priest of nature; must have recognised his knowledge of animals and plants, and the tenderness of his regard for them; must have admired not all the hardness in Douglas, but certain independent, self-reliant aspects of it; and may possibly have known an occasional momentary flash of envy of the mild and easily accommodated kind, of Douglas' masculine side, his ability to cope with situations of almost any sort.

If these suppositions are correct, or more or less correct, the two men would have had enough regard for each other – as they seem to have had – to wish to get on with each other better than they did; but were fated by their experience of each other, both through the influence of others, and when they met, to find that the obstructions to friendship were greater than the access to it.

ii

The Lawrence pamphlet had been gratifyingly successful. In the first fortnight he sold 500 copies, and there were two further printings. The whole thing had gone well: from starting to write it until having its 13,000 words in print had occupied less than a month. It was also easy to distribute: merely a matter of slipping it in an envelope.

Experiments, unfortunately, did not go so smoothly. It gave endless trouble, both in the preparation and in the result: "Out of 312 copies, *fifty-six* are unfit to be sent away (a loss of about £100 to me: just when the thing was beginning to be profitable: so that I am only the merest shade better off than if I had not printed at all . . .)"

Experiments was itself experimental, as Douglas wrote. And not only in production. The privately printed version contains, in addition to the stories and essays, a number of book reviews that were not reprinted in

the English commercial edition of the book, but does not contain the reprint of the Magnus pamphlet which is included in the English edition.
The American edition is the most complete, containing both book reviews
and the Magnus pamphlet. A good many of these book reviews subsequently appeared in *Late Harvest*.

Some readers will think he scraped the bowl rather too thoroughly in
the making of this anthology. The stories from *Unprofessional Tales* are
mere stuffing. The review article on *Arabia Deserta*, and the appreciations
of Poe, Waterton, and Isabelle Eberhardt are well worth having in permanent form, however, and few authors collect only the cream of their
scattered writings. The stories were probably inserted – he was ever
considerate of the reader – as light relief, or at any rate change of tone,
from the essays and book reviews. Some of the former and a good many
of the latter remain uncollected, and one would like to see a comprehensive volume devoted to them.

Experiments justified itself as a publishing experiment, in spite of all the
difficulties and the spoiled copies. He seems to have cleared the whole
edition before going to Africa; and he learned useful lessons. The English
edition also did well; but the American version failed – about half the
copies of an edition of more than 2,000 were remaindered thirteen years
after publication. Not that Douglas cared: under his new system, he had
sold the thing outright.

The first copies of *Experiments* had come to him on 29th March; by
2nd April, he had received his ticket for his passage to Mombasa. Presumably it was paid for out of money received for the pamphlet and
advanced on *Experiments*. More money was due to arrive any day. As a
matter of fact, he had actually had some of it, and could have had all of
it, in January or February, if he had not sent back what he had because he
was particular about the manner of payment.

iii

On 5th January he had received a cable from Muriel Draper telling him
that she had sold his Conrad books and letters to Rosenbach for $600
and was forwarding a draft. This was followed by a letter:

My dear Doug:

   As I cabled you on January 6th, Dr Rosenbach has bought the six
Conrad books and seven Conrad letters which you sent over to W L to
dispose of for $600. I have repaid W L $100 which he tells me he advanced you on this sale as you will see by the enclosed copy of my letter
to him, and am forwarding you $250, per enclosed draft, and will

forward you the balance due you of $250 as soon as received. So much for business.

This took me three weeks, Doug darling, 7-gold tipped [sic] cigarettes (which I hate), 2-hours [sic] with Dr Rosenbach (whom I do not love) in his vault, the reading of the entire correspondence between Oscar Wilde and Lord Alfred Douglas, to say nothing of some mouldy Elizabethan Anthologies, the original manuscript of the Meister Singer, with the sickening sight of $72,000 worth of unsold Conrad manuscripts always before me. However, I would have undergone much worse with joy and only wish I could have obtained a larger sum for you ... I am attacking the sale of the manuscript of South Wind next week ...

Douglas had sent interim thanks for the news contained in the cable, and promised to drop her a line as soon as the draft arrived. The line he dropped her was not a short one, nor particularly gratifying to an old friend who had reason to suppose she had done rather well by him:

> FLORENCE
> 24 Jan. 1925

My dearest Mew

Thanks awfully for your letter and all the trouble you have taken. But this check is no good to me at all. I am going to Central Africa, and what is the use of all those bloody Italian lire's to me? Besides, the *Banca di Credito* is the rottenest bank in Italy; they give the worst exchange, and keep you waiting *ONE WHOLE DAY* in ice-cold corridors and places before they will cash one cent. If Rosenbach pays in dollars, why the Hell should I have these filthy Italian notes which are not even good enough to wipe one's behind on? And why the devil should I be told where to cash my checks? If I had received an ordinary check in dollars I should have sent it to my bank in London, (and left them to do the rest) Therefore, my dear, please send me the whole five hundred dollars in one check and let me cash it where I please. This is how it should be made out: only in dollars,

---

	32 Feb 1993
	Barclays Bank Ltd
	93 Lombard St. E.C.
Mrs Muriel Draper	
Five Thousand Pounds	
£5000—0—0	A de Polski

And no damned Banca di Credito Balls. Don't have it made out in pounds, or lires, or francs, or kronen, or marks; but in dollars. Trust me to change them.

And now, my dear, just listen to this. I sent the *South Wind* MS to W.L. on the 24th *September,* at the same time telling him that I must get to Central Africa in spring and needed the money, and that if Rosenbach did not want the thing he need only say so. I thought that he (R) would either take it or leave it. Well, since then I have had two other offers for this MS., and, *entre nous,* am damned sorry to have sent it to R., because, as I told you in my last, Eric is leaving his present post in Africa in spring, and wants me to come to him at once – and I can't buy the ticket because I haven't got the money for that infernal MS. Don't you think this is very vexatious? Rosenbach has had the thing since early October, and kept me dangling all this time. That is un-businesslike – because it is not a question of thousands of pounds where, by delay, he might have got the interest on his money. What is the interest on £200? Not worth talking about – not for him, at least. And tickets to Zanzibar have to be bought a good two or three weeks beforehand. *You can't think how annoyed I am about this.* Now if you know Rosenbach at all well, I wish you would give him to understand the following: if he wants the MS, he should pay for it at once for the reasons above stated; if he does not, he need only advise me to that effect, and I will send him a check of £20, to recoup him for the trouble he has taken in the matter, and for the warehousing of the MS during these months. I SHOULD BE DELIGHTED TO SEND HIM THAT CHECK, because then I might still be able to carry out my intention of going to Africa. I can sell the MS, and get the money for it, within one week of its arrival here from America.

　　　　　Read this page over again

Thanks so much for the *South Wind* cuttings. Boni and Liveright are going to push it properly in their Modern Library Series, to which I have written a special Introduction.

By the way, there was a woman who felt rather ill and went to consult a doctor. She entered what she thought his house, met him on the stairs, and explained her symptoms. He said: "Just step into that room, Madam, and take off your clothing. I'll be with you presently." When she was quite undressed, he came in and said: "Now, Madam, bend forwards all you can." He had a careful look at her behind and then said: "Well, Madam, there are just two things I ought to tell you. Firstly, you have the dirtiest backside I have ever seen; and secondly, the doctor lives next door."

No more for today. I am too bloody angry about R – these business-like Americans . . .(?)

Delays occurred, as they will in matters of this kind, and in the end he went off to Africa without the money and also, surprisingly, without having written more than two additional letters of complaint to the unfortunate Muriel.

iv

At Marseille he picked up a "wonderful medicine-box" which Bryher had had sent to him from London: "I daresay I shall require one or two of its appetizing ingredients before I am done with Africa: in fact, I shall begin with quinine five days before landing." He had worked in Florence over the pamphlet and *Experiments*, and entertaining and looking after various visitors such as Archie, Booth Tarkington, and Mr Gelber, an American bookseller, and now he meant to cut himself off from all but his intimates, and perhaps not even write to them, and relax. Archie, who had chucked the job in Prague and had decided to try the Consular Service, and had asked for advice on how to study and prepare for the exam he would have to take, had been briefed as follows, in a specially typewritten and registered letter:

I will now jot down all that strikes me as regards examinations.

Perfect health is an essential; everything should be sacrificed to getting *and keeping* it. One can't do anything if one is ailing, or liable to be ailing.

Next, maintain an absolute routine of life: one day exactly like another, and make no exceptions for Sundays (you haven't got the time). Avoid all social functions for those few months, all gaieties and all excesses. Not worth while. (Time for that later on.) A regular-routine-life is tiresome only for the first few days; after that, it becomes positively pleasant.

Passing exams is largely a psychological affair and that is why one goes to a high-priced crammer. He must know the psychology of the examiners, their bent of mind. He must know the sort of thing they are likely to ask you; and not only that. He must know the *sort of thing they are not likely to ask you*, the sort of thing, therefore, over which you might lose a lot of time otherwise.

Light luncheon; as heavy a dinner as you like. Never work more than one hour at each subject. Then switch off on to another one. Learn vocabularies (not grammar, but only vocabularies; and not more than 12–15 fresh words a day) last thing at night. Go through them again first thing in the morning. If you can get in an hour's work before breakfast – on a self-made cup of tea – you will have an enormous pull over others. That one hour is worth 2½ hours of afternoon work, and once you have started on this system you will find it perfectly easy.

You can work very hard so long as you work regularly. That is *a great secret.* It is the interruptions that make the subsequent work so difficult and trying. You had better make up your mind to live a few months of monkish self-retirement; arrange a regular schedule of work and free time, which accounts for every hour in the whole week – including Sundays. As little tobacco as possible: makes one nervy. No wine (hardly) except half a bottle of the finest hock just before going in to exam.

Handwriting very important. Illegible words make examiners MAD.

Translations should be done with a certain elegance. "Enfin, je *m'efforçai* à sortir du lit." At last, *with an effort,* I got out of bed.

And that is all I can think of just now.

Will write again before leaving (about box at Consulate etc).

Your loving

Fa

You might do worse than get a volume of Marcel Proust (ridiculous writer) – say "Du côté de chez Swann" – and Scott-Moncrieff's translation . . . You will learn a lot if you compare the two, going through French and English *one paragraph at a time.*

The proper time for bed was between ten and eleven p.m. Douglas told Archie a few days later, writing about sleeplessness; and on 10th May, from Djibouti, added a detailed recipe for writing essays:

As to essays in exam: they are sure to give you 2–3 subjects to choose from. Choose by preference the most difficult: there will be less competition for that subject. Take at least 5 minutes to read over titles and find out what examiners really want: very important, else you may write an excellent essay all beside the mark. Then 10 minutes writing down your ideas on the subject. Then 5 putting them into skeleton shape. Then rough draft. Then re-reading (with corrections). Then fair copy. Then 10 minutes at end, final corrections: proper stops etc. Do all your subjects – papers – *by the watch*; exactly timed, as in exam. Don't write a word more than you are required to: it only annoys examiners to get longer essays than necessary.

Pino also received a note from Djibouti – the third of its kind since Douglas had left Florence, where he had failed to see Orioli immediately before going. He hoped he had the leather box he had left for Orioli to look after, asked him also to keep an eye on René and cheer him up and lend him 200 francs (of Douglas') if necessary. He said he would be sending Orioli his Loeb Greek Anthology and his lexicon for safe keeping. It was infernally hot at Djibouti, "impossible to go on deck on account of the sun, in spite of double awnings ... Love to Reggie and the other brethren in Jesus. Yours perspiringly, N.D."

v

He arrived at Mombasa on 18th May. It had no surprises for him, except the baobab trees. Later, when he saw the size of the jungle specimens, which dwarfed all their neighbours, he learned to regard them with awe – "aged monsters whose seed might have dropped from another planet while man was yet unborn". From Mombasa to Voi by train, and thence up to Moshi by car. There he was met by Eric, who took him to his place at Arusha, passing immense herds of game on the way, and "some picturesque Masai shepherd boys leaning on their lances". At Arusha, living in the Boma with Eric, a regular routine began. They met for lunch and dinner, also at teatime for whisky and soda and the discarding of sun helmets. In the morning and afternoon, while Eric was at work, Douglas explored alone and on foot. There was a wooded hill not too far away, from the top of which one could look "across leagues of country to the majestic dome of Kilimanjaro glittering with snow. At the foot of this hill, to the west, lay a patch of forest full of birds and butterflies, all of them new to me; there I often went, when too lazy to climb."

Arusha is situated amongst the foothills of Mount Meru, an extinct or at any rate dormant volcano 4450 metres high, with a lunar landscape to the south of it, "a nightmarish mountain". One could walk pleasantly in these hills, even in an equatorial region, watching carefully for the approach of sunset, so as not to be stranded in darkness at the mercy of a chance leopard or lion. On one occasion he and Eric went over to a neighbour's place to help scare away a lurking leopard. The man was an official, and when the leopard seemed to have gone, they sat up half the night telling stories and drinking. "At such moments these people unbend and grow human; then, next morning, they are officials once more." That was the trouble, he told Nancy Cunard – he was confined to the white colony by barriers of language and convention: conversing with natives, even if he had known Swahili, would have been considered eccentric, "and it is easier to be eccentric in Bournemouth than in Arusha". He should have left his countrymen alone, and picked up a native guide at Mombasa who knew the country and could have acted as interpreter; they should have camped out and he would have got his guide to initiate him into the life of the natives. Then he might have learned something. As it was he had to content himself with strolling down to the market-place, "a perennial source of joy", and simply watching the teeming life.

He saw antelopes, zebras, wildebeests, ostriches, giraffes and baboons; no lions, or elephants, or rhinos. There were several trips across country – to and from Dodoma, where he and Eric stayed for about ten days; and to and from a coffee-plantation. Douglas stayed at an hotel kept by a Greek at Dodoma; "our chief afternoon amusement was being driven along the railway line on a trolley and shooting game for [Eric's] table, the small dik-dik antelope for the most part, which is good eating; a silver jackal was also bagged." He noted that in the lower regions lack of timber from deforestation was already a problem; and that the civil servants did not educate their cooks and house boys to be economical or even to be interested in producing appetising food. The planters made themselves more comfortable. He also saw the potential threat of the Indians, a divisive and disturbing element.

He left Mombasa on 6th July in a German boat. One imagines that he was not sorry to leave Africa – loyalty to Eric would have obliged him to exert more self-control than was enjoyable for an extended period – but glad to have been there. "Africa did me a lot of good," he wrote to Booth Tarkington, "Just what I wanted; a spring-cleaning."

vi

He arrived at Genoa on 22nd July and went straight to Florence, where amongst an enormous pile of letters he found a cheque for $500 from Muriel Draper, representing the proceeds from his sale to Rosenbach of the Conrad books and letters. It was just as well, as he had spent more than twice as much money as he had expected to spend in Africa, and was "completely high and dry again for a change". The heat in Florence was "far worse than Africa", and he longed to get away to the Vorarlberg, but could not, or would not, because he had set his mind on going there with Mario's brother, and Mario's brother was not available, "not even in Florence . . . So Austria is off, ten to one". After visits to Sant' Agata and Capri, he returned to the job of flat-hunting, and found a flat – a flat to buy, from which he could not be ejected – at 14 Lungarno delle Grazie. He at once put down a *caparra*, a deposit, on it. As usual, this one also needed renovation, and what with the usual delays, he did not finally get into it until after Christmas. Towards the end of November he moved into temporary rooms in Borgo dei Greci which he described as a street of brothels. Meanwhile he had been afflicted once again with "an enormous abscess in my jaw"; Symmonds, his dentist, said he must have it X-rayed, as he was not "satisfied as to its origin (? cancer)". A week or so later he wrote to Archie: "Didn't go to the x-ray man. Funked it" – and no more was heard of the business. His capacity for surviving "enormous abscesses", "frightful neuralgia", erysipelas, and being run over by a car, was quite remarkable.

CHAPTER TWENTY-SIX

Lungarno Delle Grazie
1926–1927

i

Douglas was pleased with his flat, which, after partial redecoration, was ready for occupation early in January 1926. For several months he had been making notes, which often required a great deal of troublesome research, on the fauna of the Greek Anthology. In the security of his own place, invulnerable to the whims of landlords, he pushed this work forward, intending to publish a book on the subject as successor to *Experiments*, but making a more professional job of the production. He hoped to have a manuscript ready by the end of February. Meanwhile, he was having trouble, he told Bryher, in finding a decent hand-made paper. But most of his correspondence at this time was concerned with actual researches into the birds and beasts he was trying to write about. Edward Hutton, in particular, was recruited for this work and Douglas' friends Atchley and Petrocochino in Athens. Perhaps the connection of all these people with Greece was what prompted Hutton to ask Douglas if he would accompany him on a tour of the country. "I can't possibly manage Greece" Douglas replied, "my finances being as low at this moment as during the war, and not likely to look up, till I have done that damned Anthology book", but two days later he is writing that it is so nice of Hutton "carting a useless old crock about Greece", as though all was arranged. Brisk practicalities followed:

> You will want a strong stick in Greece, with a sharp steel point for the dogs: this is essential. Old boots. I can't think of anything else. If you don't get the stick, you may share the fate of Euripides and dozens of others. They are a real terror, those dogs . . . You will also require a knapsack which should be *got in England*. And flea powder.

In less than a fortnight Hutton arrived in Florence; and before they set off together, his wife, who had written to Douglas evidently fearing that her husband might be exposed to danger in Greece, was given a dose of Douglas' shock-treatment:

Edward arrived here in perfect condition and we leave on Thursday morning. You may be sure that nothing can happen to him in Greece. The weather is still too cold to encourage even the fleas or bugs and the food is quite all right. The dogs are rather a nuisance in certain places, but if you can spike them in the eye or in the open mouth they generally leave you alone, and I am rather good at that game (though I don't want to boast).

Their visit lasted about three weeks and was succeeded by correspondence referring to the writing of a book about the country in collaboration: ". . . the terms you mention sound admirable," wrote Douglas, "but it stands to reason that I don't take more than a percentage of the profit, since you are doing *all the work*. It wouldn't be fair otherwise; not at all, at all. My attempts at writing about Greece are all failures anyhow." By this time he had written an Introduction – "dreadful tosh" – for the book, which Hutton seems to have criticised, since Douglas says that "Cora must of course come out". It looks therefore, as though his introduction may have been a first draft of what subsequently became the opening pages of *One Day* (which was dedicated to Hutton). In July he signed a contract:

I sign the contract but, my dear, I cannot write a book about Greece; if I could, I should have written it long ago. But I think I can collaborate with you in an ineffectual, not to say futile, fashion. If you will do what they call the *rédaction*, and send me the chapters one after the other, I will *write* all I can into them. That is the only way, I fancy, since the rédaction must be done by one person, and you can do it, and I can't. I haven't the data, to begin with; and I haven't the energy. I am an old man, and don't you forget it! But I will write all I can (probably tosh) and you will have to discard what won't fit. The contract strikes me as very good.

The collaboration continued busily all through the year and into 1927. Douglas received his cheque for the work – £50 – in September.

By this time, Hutton had apparently made arrangements already for a book to follow on Italy. "After that" wrote Douglas, "we'll do the Riviera, Sweden, Poland, Crimea, Yucatan and Iceland . . ." But even in his letters, Douglas' enthusiasm sounds too pumped-up and feverish to be durable; and in fact, it did not last.

ii

The English commercial edition of *Experiments* had been published by Chapman and Hall at the end of October 1925, and was reviewed, rather belatedly, in the *New Statesman* of 13th February 1926. This review was seen by, or brought to the notice of D. H. Lawrence and led to the writing and publication of the well-known letter in which he said he was "weary of being slandered". He had been in New Mexico, he wrote, when the Magnus pamphlet first appeared, and "it seemed too far to trouble". But since it had appeared in permanent form in *Experiments*, it was time he said a word about it.

Lawrence's main concern in this letter is to deny the implication in Douglas' pamphlet that he, Lawrence, had greedily obtained the manuscript of the *Memoirs* for publication in order to make money from it, thereby doing Douglas, the executor, out of his rightful share. Douglas had misrepresented the true financial situation with regard to Magnus' manuscript and book. He had presumably forgotten that he had told Lawrence (26th December 1921) to "pocket all the cash" himself if he succeeded in getting Magnus' book published, for in his pamphlet (January 1925) he had written: ". . . I hope that I, who am entitled to half the proceeds, will in due course receive something on account." This sentence, implying rapaciousness if not worse on Lawrence's part, was easily refuted by Lawrence quoting parts of Douglas' letter, including the relevant phrase about pocketing the cash, underlined by Douglas himself. Lawrence also emphasises that he wrote his Introduction solely "to discharge an obligation I do not admit", and that he could probably have made more money, if that had been his object, out of the Introduction published separately as a study of Magnus, than as preface to his book. When publishers to whom the manuscript had been submitted had suggested this, Lawrence had refused to let the introduction be published without the Memoirs. "As for Mr Douglas," Lawrence's letter ended, "he must gather himself haloes where he can."

It was a strong and extremely effective letter. What Douglas thought of it he did not write down – or if he did, it has not come to light. Scott-Moncrieff, writing to Vyvyan Holland, said he had seen Douglas, who was "rather piqued at Lawrence's onslaught on him in the *New Statesman*". Perhaps his pique, if it existed, wore off in Tunisia, to which he went with Basil Leng, the landscape gardener, at the beginning of March. By the time Douglas returned to Florence from Greece in May, the Lawrences were just about to move into the Villa Mirenda, a few miles south of the city. Here, in the autumn (1926), Lawrence was to start writing *Lady Chatterley's Lover*. The first version did not satisfy him; he produced three drafts altogether, working at the story intermittently until January 1928. It was the third version which contained the four-letter words, and which he was determined to publish whether an expurgated edition was done or not; and it was Orioli who was to publish this, the most provocative and scandalising of Lawrence's books. In one form or another the novel, or parts of it, was read to an audience consisting of Orioli, Reggie Turner, Norman Douglas, and Collingwood Gee; but that must have been after Douglas and Lawrence had patched up the cracks in their relationship which had been caused by the Magnus affair.

They were reconciled, according to Aldington, in Orioli's shop, probably in this winter of 1926–27. Orioli had apparently mentioned the subject to both men previously; then one day while Lawrence and Frieda were in the shop, Douglas entered. After a small tight silence, Douglas held out his snuff box with the usual invitation: "Have a pinch of snuff, dearie." Lawrence took one, saying "Isn't it curious" – sniff – "only Norman and my father" – sniff – "ever give me snuff." Then, according to Aldington, the friendship was on again; but it may be doubted whether it was on on quite the same footing as before.

iii

Family matters continued, if not to preoccupy, at least to interest Douglas. He had heard early in 1927 that Robin had separated from his wife and appeared to be flourishing. "Somebody keeping him, I suppose. What ho!" was his comment. Unlike the good-natured Archie, his father had stopped even acknowledging Robin's occasional letter. The following, to Archie, probably refers to Robin:

> Very interesting – his going to stay with that old mischief-maker abroad. She'll fill him with nonsense to bursting-point. If I were you, I would not bother about replying to him (that is my – time-saving – system). A tarnished person who cannot do you good in any way and is liable to turn round on you at any moment. What do you gain by writing? A reconciliation, I take it, will inevitably be followed by a second rupture. Why waste time on such people? Anyhow, don't send me his letter. I have other fish to fry!

The "old mischief-maker abroad" would have been Archie's and Robin's maternal grandmother, Adèle FitzGibbon, who is referred to in another letter to Archie: "Had a letter from Robert from Vorarlberg where he is probably staying with that venerable tart of a grandmother. Am *not* answering it." Archie himself had visited her in the previous year, and been gently reprimanded for doing so:

> I think you make a mistake in going to see "old Adèle" after the filthy way in which she behaved not only to me but to her husband, my father-in-law; I should have been miserably dead long ago, if she had

succeeded in doing what she wanted to do. However, I am not going to warm up old broths, tho' it would have been more in accordance with Douglassian consistency not only to have dropped that whole brood, but to have *told* them to go to Hell, where they belong. Please yourself! And don't talk to me about them any more. Sentimental and mendacious carrion.

In March Archie had started work in a bank in Paris, and was given warnings by his father about the various unpleasant consequences which might befall those who were heedlessly promiscuous in that city, which, he said, was the worst in the world for "claps". Archie mentioned a divorcée in whom he was apparently interested. He was immediately told that "All divorced women are disappointing and dangerous, without exception" – rather a sweeping statement, even in those days, when divorces were fewer. "By all means get married" wrote his father, "but not an American, because you won't get any settlement out of them: and not a divorcée, because they generally can't fuck. To get proper fucking, one must *bring them up oneself*. And the same applies to the other thing. Nothing like a virgin, when all is said and done, male or female."

In the intervals between jobs, Archie had been obliged to apply to Nelson for money, when he needed it; and as might be expected with even the most dutiful, generous, and patient of men, Nelson, after twenty years of responsibility for him, must occasionally have wished that Archie could stand entirely on his own feet. His father wrote Archie a long letter about it:

I will tell you what I think – in quite a disconnected way – about this whole Uncle W business; from being a vague suspicion already some years ago, it has now grown into a conviction. But this is not advice; it is just my opinion. I don't think you will be morally (perhaps not even physically) well, until you have got rid of this nightmare. He may say that you are a kind of vampire on him, because you drain away his money. But he is worse than a vampire on you; he drains away your self-respect. It would be a great thing, for *both* of you, if you could say to him *Go to Hell* (financially); it would clear the air. The present position of affairs strikes me as anomalous (unnatural) and humiliating. By all means get money out of men or women – to any extent! But I should have done, once and for all, with Uncle Willie's money, even at the cost of some pinching. You [sic] present relations with him strike me as *harmful* to you; and you were doubtless right in what you said in your first draft to him, about the "weakness" you felt when dealing with him. *He* is the vampire.

Note that he is not a man of the world in any sense of the word; for all his merits, he is a worm-like creature, hide-bound, and *frowsily parochial*: in fact, he does not belong to the present generation at all. Then think how little he gives, and how grudgingly it is given – and accompanied, too – by an overdose of gratuitous and quite unreasonable advice and reproaches. I know that *I* wouldn't put up with such letters as his last to you – not for anything! I would do what I actually once did with such a letter (not his) – wipe my arse with it, and send it him back, *registered*.

If you break off with him financially, once and for all, you will feel completely rejuvenated. He is sucking out your *amour propre* with those few miserable pounds: it is ridiculous to be dependent on any one for so little, and to have to swallow so much dirt by reason of it. Only think of the time you have wasted in writing your last letter to him. Your time, if you have any to spare, can be wasted far more pleasantly. In fact, I don't think you will get your worldly values right, until you have done with this undignified and discreditable relationship. It exposes you to perpetual advice, as if you were a child. I wouldn't take advice from anyone, unless I asked for it. Anyway, that is what *I* think. Have done with that nightmare. It is wearing out your *morale* to be financially indebted to persons not of your standing – and Uncle W is an upper-better middle class Englishman, who has not a grain of imagination and understands absolutely nothing except his own little miserable business. Outside! And get well again.

Your loving
Fa

TEETH
DO YOUR WORK

It is difficult to defend the Douglas who wrote thus of his oldest friend, who had done him countless good turns of one sort and another quite apart from raising Archie from the age of seven as though he had been his own son. At best, his father may have been trying by deviousness to make Archie, who could be very obtuse, determine resolutely to become independent, for the sake of all concerned; this would not be untypical of the means Douglas sometimes employed in an attempt to manipulate others, and is a likely possibility. At worst, Douglas may have felt the resentment and splenetic bloody-mindedness he expresses. In either case, the remarks about Nelson are inexcusable.

iv

The collaboration with Hutton was in full swing during January and February. Hutton was sending out his manuscript chapter by chapter, and Douglas was making his comments and returning it chapter by chapter. He thought the conversations in the book might be more frequent, and "on any subject whatever, provided it *begins* with Greece. If you will start them, *I will end them*. . . . I have to be *fecundated*, you know." He would make them as long as Hutton liked, and he thought they ought to be a commentary on life in general; some of them should be absurdly short. They had cost him more trouble than Hutton might believe; they were the best he could do: ". . . they can be sharpened up, but a little interval of time is necessary."

Hutton, whom Douglas described as having the energy "of 50,000 devils", and was the sort of professional writer who could get a full-length book done in a fortnight if necessary, was evidently working rather too fast for Douglas' liking; by the beginning of February the first hints of exasperation begin to appear in his letters: "When you have got this material, I have still 2 dialogues to do . . . When I have done those two, I hope to get a day's breathing space, in order to have a wash and a shave, which I badly need. Also a little sleep . . . The Delphi dialogue which you will get tomorrow has given me grey hairs and nearly landed me in a sanatorium . . . By all means come out here when you can. I hope you will find me still alive . . . Very tired just now (58 years of age, don't forget; and a tempestuous life behind me, which is now finding me out) . . ." And to Archie he complained that Hutton "with his bloody Greek book is assassinating me by inches". Nevertheless, he had finished *Birds and Beasts of the Greek Anthology*, and gave it to the printer in the third week of February.

There was discussion with Hutton, by post, as to where they should meet to go through their work. And for how long? Hutton thought three weeks, Douglas three days. That was on 25th February; he was overworked and dead tired, frustrated by having to do this work instead of his own, and perhaps bored. These were the sort of conditions which predisposed him to indiscretions, and sure enough, on 5th March, Archie, who was now living and working in Rome, received a telegram: COME HERE TONIGHT IF POSSIBLE. He replied IMPOSSIBLE COME UNLESS YOU ARE ILL REPLY URGENT and was finally informed NOT ILL BUT LEAVING TOMORROW NIGHT. Not for the first time, he had judged it wisest to hop it, quickly. Not for the last time, he fled to Menton.

He pretended to Hutton that he had had to go to Menton to meet a friend who would be arriving by boat at Marseille; but told Bryher

a little later, that he had fled for "crocodilean reasons", which was
true. However the break gave him the resolution, or impelled him for
purely physical and practical reasons, to cease the collaboration with
Hutton:

> I don't think – after mature consideration and taking into account
> what you say of my humble (and small) contributions – we had better
> do this book together at all. You cut out – or leave in – what I have
> done and let it be your book; I have slaved myself to death over the
> damned thing – never worked harder in all my life, and am now going
> to have a rest and not write another line.

He enclosed a letter that Hutton could show the publishers; and he
would let Hutton have the money back as soon as he approved the letter.
"It will cost me a refund of £100" he wrote to Archie. "Can't be helped!
At least I am free again. No more collaboration!" He stayed in Menton
nearly three weeks, keeping in touch with events in Florence through
Walter Lowenfels, who was living there with his wife, and Orioli. He
returned to Florence on 29th March, and on the previous day wrote from
Milan: "Things all right *so far*, but I am terribly knocked up." He had
certainly had a bad fright, was doing no work and had bad nights and
harassed days. However, he hoped the affair would end satisfactorily:
"*I have deserved it.*"

v

The boy involved was called Luciano, and the trouble arose from his
mother, who lived in Florence – where, of course, she may well have
heard stories about Douglas. The father lived in Monza and worked in
Milan. Douglas seems to have hoped to persuade the father to let Luciano
be his pupil; meanwhile Hutton came to Florence, which must have been
awkward and annoying in its way, though their friendship was strong
enough to survive even subjects that Hutton did not want to discuss but
must have known about; and shortly the air was menacing again in the
Luciano business. "I am not out of the wood by any means! Things are
clouding over again"; but he and Hutton were "trying to patch up that
collaboration," on Douglas' terms: "I need the money!"

Douglas was in touch with Luciano's father, who came to Florence
towards the end of April. Douglas talked to him about Luciano, and the
father "decided not to put off again the taking-away-from-Florence of his
son". He did it at once. Douglas went out to Pistoia separately, so that
he need not be present at Florence Station while Luciano's mother was
saying goodbye to the boy: "I join their train . . . and we three go together

to Milan (father, son & self) ... From which I hope you will gather that the battle is won (*the toughest of all my life*, and I have had a good few) ... a fight which lasted from 19 Feb to 27 April and which has left me financially impoverished and physically shattered." He would stay one day in Milan, then return to Florence to get on with his work. "I shall get drunk – the occasion is worthy of it – but must keep my wits about me ... Have you understood this letter? *It marks an epoch*." And in his pocket diary he wrote "Treaty of Monza" so that the epoch would be truly marked; but, alas, like so many treaties, it was to prove disappointing.

He and Hutton finally came to grief over the book. At Hutton's request, Douglas wrote an introduction for it. ("I would sooner eat shit than write another one" he told Walter Lowenfels). Was this the original, with Cora removed, or something new? When it was done, Hutton said it didn't "fit in". (Of course it didn't, wrote Douglas suggestively to Orioli; what did he expect?) "So the collaboration is off for good, and *thank God*! I can do my own work at last."

vi

By the first week in May he was getting ready to leave Florence again. He would be going to Monza to stay. "Florence is over, I imagine, for a year or two." The strain of the situation had told on him: "My hand has got so shaky that I daren't shave myself – not from drink, but worry." He sent Archie full instructions about the Florence flat, where the keys were, and where his valuables could be found. And soon, after he had arrived in Monza and Luciano's passport had been applied for – he meant to take him to the Vorarlberg – he sent, or began sending (for they continued for the rest of the year) instructions to Orioli, about looking after his interests at the Giuntina, where *Birds and Beasts* was being printed, and about numerous other matters, including Emilio, for whom he felt very tenderly and wanted to provide as well as possible.

After a long delay, he discovered that a passport could now only be obtained for Luciano if there were proof that he was going to study at a school abroad. Such proof could not be provided in a manner that would satisfy the Italian consul at Innsbruck. "A lunatic asylum, the whole business," was Douglas' comment. So he and Luciano went off to Sant' Agata and then to Capri, ending up in mid-July at Pistoia, and then San Marcello near by. This was the best Douglas could do without actually returning to Florence which he dared not do on account of Luciano's mother. He could at least go into Florence without much difficulty from these places, to attend to his business – which he did. Money was running

out, and he had to pay a pound a day for himself and Luciano at San
Marcello Pistoiese: "I am prepared for a catastrophe. Shall mortgage or
sell the Florence flat: can't be helped!" But somehow, as so often before,
it could be helped, and he did not have to take such drastic action.

By the middle of August he had finished the novel *In the Beginning* and
sent it to Mavrogordato to be vetted. "I have begun something else," he
wrote to Archie, and from Tomlinson received advice about his "Reminiscences", so it looks as though he had already begun to write parts of
what eventually became *Looking Back*.

The first copies of *Birds and Beasts of the Greek Anthology* were sent off on
12th September. By this time he and Luciano had already moved to Prato,
even nearer to Florence, so that he could commute to Florence daily to
attend to all the business connected with sending out copies of the book.
"Florence is taboo for me . . . at present," wrote Douglas to Lytton
Strachey. "I am living at Prato and only go in for an afternoon now and
then, thickly veiled and wearing blue glasses and a carroty beard. This
will last, I daresay, till after Christmas." (This is just the type of con-
fessional double-bluff from which Douglas gained much quiet pleasure –
the thought that Strachey would think *all* that he had written was invention, whereas it was only a caricature of the truth.) Emilio had joined
them for the last ten days or so at San Marcello, and occasionally came for
the day to Prato, and got on well with Luciano. Orioli and his young
friend Carletto, who became his servant and assistant and general factotum, as Emilio was Douglas', also came sometimes, and there was a
"family party" atmosphere which may have drawn Douglas to the other
three and away from Luciano to some extent, or Luciano may have felt a
little superfluous or have become sulky. It was perhaps a change in the
emotional air which led Douglas to declare to Archie that he was "fairly
sick of life". He made arrangements with Archie, who was to write him
an urgent letter, when necessary, telling him that his (Norman's) brother
was dying and wished to see him. "Look here," he wrote Archie at the
end of November, "L is getting quite impossible – going mad, in fact,"
and instructed Archie to write the urgent letter, which his father wrote
out for him. It may never have been used, for on 14th December, Douglas
wrote to Archie: "Took L to Monza, having a good excuse. I leave Prato,
then go to Florence for a week – unavoidable on account of book; then
Menton probably, so as to be *out of the country*." He was not pleased to get
rid of Luciano; on the contrary – it was a wrench– but he knew he had to
make that decision: "Have written to Luciano, hinting that I may not
be able to keep him any longer. Very difficult and disheartening. It has
quite upset me . . . He got unmanageable, in spite of all my prayers and
efforts."

vii

Birds and Beasts had flopped, in spite of his having sent out nearly a hundred circulars about it. It was an unpleasant surprise: and he doubted if it would even pay its expenses. Advertising it in the *T.L.S.* did not help either.

The lack of orders for *Birds and Beasts* may have been a surprise to Douglas, but cannot have been much of a surprise to the general reader. Not everyone, even amongst his most ardent and faithful admirers, could have been expected to share his own enthusiasm for such specialist monographs. He, as he has shown in *Late Harvest*, could devour them wholesale, but he was probably forced to realise that he could not expect to carry his readers nor even all his collectors with him. He himself called either the book, or the additional notes he provided for it, "dull reading, except for a naturalist". He could more truthfully have written "except for a small number of naturalists". However, as it is his, one looks through the book carefully. It has a certain charm, and as one perseveres much of that ancient tapestry in which gods and men and other living or fabulous creatures meet upon a common ground of legend and mythological wonder is painstakingly illuminated and occasionally brought vividly to the notice of our unaccustomed modern eyes – as, for instance, in the cases of the Dolphin, the Cicada, and the Cricket. Sometimes, also, Douglas steps forward and lets fly with a particularly characteristic prejudice, as in the case of the Bee: ". . . from time immemorial men have held in veneration this cantankerous and fussy insect which, by dint of specializing in communistic habits, has lost every shred of individuality." It was not, of course, so much a matter of regretting that bees (and ants, which he disliked even more) had lost their individuality as that they provided examples in Nature from which men could draw moral conclusions that were extremely obnoxious to him, about the benefits of industry and socialism.

viii

After the disappointment with *Birds and Beasts* it was fortunate that *In the Beginning* was ready within three months, for it went off well. Orders rolled in, and all expenses were paid by the time the book was ready to send out, early in December or late in November.

In *They Went* goodness survived the battle with art: the praying Manthis was left with her chaste seminary perched upon an infertile rock while the splendidly adorned city with its artists and craftsmen was buried by the waves. In the next, and last novel, *In the Beginning*, nothing survives:

". . . everything, artistic and ethical, goes to ruin", all charmed into the
desert, "the dear desert, of long ago". The charmer, of course, was Aroudi
the demon Haunter of Outskirts, the spirit of the wild and untamed
corners of earth, of the jungle and sand which wait at the borders of civilisation ready to encroach at the least relaxation of vigilance.

Douglas had sympathy with this spirit, as may be gathered from various
passages in his books. He was distressed by the persistent foolishness and
shoddiness of man's behaviour both to his fellows and to his environment. Aroudi prophesies that even the Earth-god will tire of mankind
"when every fair spot has been scarred by their hands and deformed to
their mean purposes, the rivers made turbid and hills and forests levelled
away and all the wild green places smothered under cities full of smoke
and clanking metal; when the Sun himself . . . will refuse to peer down
through their foul vapours". The romantic streak in Douglas was never
far beneath the surface, but superimposed upon this sense of wonder and
devotion there was a sense of defeat, of disillusionment. He was held in
perpetual tension between the two states, though the tension was not
noticeably inconvenient in strength. He never became a true cynic, nor an
earnest satirist. Too blithe for the one, he was insufficiently disgusted
with humanity for the other. Nor did he often lapse into sentimentality. A
more typical and recurrent mood was that of Ecclesiastes, of the vanity
of human wishes and deeds. Or a pungently sardonic attitude, sometimes
tempered by compassion:

> Observe, Azdhubal, what is happening. They are neglecting their
> tasks, and letting city and country go to ruin, and hacking each other
> in pieces, because they cannot come to an understanding about good
> and evil. The simpletons, to draw lines where no lines can be drawn,
> to go delving into themselves, instead of into the world around them . . .
> If they had the wit to see through their witless gods, they would know
> better than to tear the spirit away from that body which should be its
> guide and friend; they would soon realise that nothing is good for the
> one save what also benefits the other, and that nothing can be a bane
> to one unless it harms the other at the same time.

"Because they cannot come to an understanding about good and evil . . ."
But did Douglas ever seriously try to "come to an understanding about
good and evil" with any adult whose moral views were opposed to his?
Of course he didn't, for he must have known how utopian the idea of
doing so is. How easy, therefore, and how innocent (to put the kindest
interpretation upon it) is the comment made by Nea-huni. How innocent;
but how convenient for Douglas, who can thereby opt out, and refuse the
responsibility of an adult member of his race while assuming the bland

features of compassionate sagacity. The truth is that goodness, from which
he had suffered so largely in childhood, had to be a villain. If it were not,
he might have to admit that his family – those tiresome aunts and great
aunts and cousins who "never left us alone and were always pulling us
about and generally interfering", and all those righteous schoolmasters –
he might have to admit that they were right, in principle. Their application of the principle had made him cut loose from all temptations to
impose morality on others, and refuse all attempts of others to impose
morality on him.

In the Beginning is Douglas' final verdict on mankind; and in a sense a
valediction. It marks the end of his fantasies or fairy stories about human
behaviour, and it is a great shame that it does, for the tale is beautifully
told, without a loose end or an untidy comma, and contains some lovely
passages, such as that in which Nea-huni so tenderly remembers Azdhubal;
some deliciously fresh, sun-warmed, sparkling descriptions of Theocritean clarity and innocence; and – among many other delights – a stupen-
dously over-ripe scene of debauchery described, to Douglas' great pleasure,
as "pure Gorgonzola" by Edward Garnett. It is a book that one can read
over and over again with pleasure, yet which never quite reaches the level
of satisfaction which one continually hopes, from page to page, that it will
achieve in the end. Why not? Possibly because the death of Linus removes
half the interest of the book, and the arrival of the goodness germ makes
the rest too much a matter of determinism. Yet it can be read as an allegory
of the ages of man or of the rise and fall of a civilisation. Strangely, goodness once again, in what seems like an anti-goodness morality, very nearly
wins – perhaps does win in a sense, though too late, by undermining.
Goodness defeats Symira and leaves her ancient court of harlots exhausted. We could have been shown younger people recovering from the
goodness germ and enjoying the fruits of a sinful life, but we are not; we
are presented with a picture of total fatigation and moral bankruptcy. It
looks as though sin is not preferable to goodness, as though all striving is
in vain, and as though at the end a great emptiness awaits us, a nihilism as
extensive and capacious as the desert. Or perhaps the book suggests that
both gods and humans suffer from an ineradicable capriciousness and inability to moderate their conduct; that only Satyrs, those perfect Epi-
cureans or Stoics, know how to lead reasonable and contented lives. Only
they are to be taken seriously. Only they are fit to be consulted, or to
give counsel.

Five years later Douglas wrote: ". . . This is not the moment to write
things like *In the Beginning* . . . It lacks the admixture of saccharine which
is prescribed by the taste of today. Its anti-democratic and uncompromising outlook is disquieting: 'too awful to contemplate' writes [a critic],

'especially the last chapter' . . . He would have liked me to insert a touch of that 'hopefulness' with which the present generation loves to delude itself, in defiance of the teaching of all history."

It took him five and a half years, off and on, to write it, and he had good reason to be pleased with the result. The earlier part of the novel, in particular, describes, with great beauty and economy, a more or less idyllic Theocritean scene of the kind we associate with the spirit of the pastoral Greece of mythology, a scene of the kind which moved Douglas deeply – a paradisal simplicity with "infusions of the extra human". It is difficult to think of any book written in English in this century which seems to embody that spirit so well. It has the lightness and clarity, and the sensuous outlines of an Attic-vase design, the scent of fresh river water seems to rise from it, and its air is laden with the warm breath of Derco, goddess of love.

ix

During Douglas' absence in Prato and Menton, the redecoration of the flat on the Lungarno had been completed, and stood awaiting his return, invitingly. But little else, apart from the novel, had been satisfactory in this abortive and uncomfortable year. Walter Lowenfels, for instance, had compiled a substantial book of extracts from Douglas' work – four hundred selected passages varying in length from a sentence to a page or more, arranged for days of the year. Douglas had written a preface for it, but it too was a victim of this bad year, and in fact was never published at all;[101] but it was the forerunner of both the *Almanac* and of *Late Harvest*. Nevertheless, *In the Beginning* was really very pleasing and had only, as far as its author could see, one misprint. Time was getting on: on 8th December, 1927, he entered his sixtieth year.

PART VII

Florence: Uncle Norman
1928–1937

CHAPTER TWENTY-SEVEN

Orioli, Publisher
1928–1930

i

Douglas had been in Menton – it was to become an annual event – for Christmas; and seems to have thought it safer to continue to stay out of Florence as much as possible. His programme, outlined to Archie, was to go to Florence for a few necessary days in the middle of January, then return to Menton to work, "then (?) to Jerusalem ... about end of February, or a little earlier". His address out there, he happily told several correspondents, would be c/o Judas Iscariot Esq, The Poplars, Golgotha.

Meanwhile his teeth were so bad that he dared not travel far afield without having them seen to. Early in February he decided to go to Paris and consult a really good dentist. The dentist's verdict was *"terrible – formidable"*, and on the 10th he began having his teeth removed, and replaced with an artificial set. Altogether he was in Paris for about three weeks, and it was during this period, right at the beginning, when the dentist had only just begun his work, that Lytton Strachey came over for a night to meet him.

Correspondence and mutual admiration of work had been exchanged intermittently, and with enthusiasm, by Douglas and Strachey since October 1923.[102] Douglas had sent him various of his books, and Strachey's enthusiasm was such that he even claimed he had read every word of *Birds and Beasts* with the greatest interest. It was Douglas who suggested a meeting, first of all in Italy, later in Paris. After explaining about the dentist, he added that he was "sure you are the very person to hold my hand. Besides, we can go to Prunier's in the intervals." In spite of hating Paris, Strachey couldn't resist the invitation, he wrote, and would come over for one night; but having committed himself, was thrown into confusion: "I am excited and terrified. Good God! The crossing! The cold! The streets of Paris! and – most serious of all – Norman Douglas! Will he be charming, vulgar, too talkative, too vague, or what? – Perhaps a womaniser after all! Who knows? And what, oh what, shall I say? How am *I* to carry it off?'

He took his young friend Roger Senhouse with him to help in the carrying off and also to play the part of expert in the filthy and obscene limericks which Douglas had asked Strachey to bring with him or collect for his forthcoming anthology. They had a rough crossing, and Strachey arrived feeling like "a mere piece of wet brown paper", dreading the coming meeting. As soon as they met, though, his fears dissolved in the warmth of Douglas's sympathetic understanding and amiability. They had dinner at Prunier's, and all seem to have enjoyed themselves. Strachey noticed, as others did, the dominie in Douglas; he reminded him of

> one of those odd benevolent unexpectedly broad-minded school-masters one sometimes comes across. Superb in restaurants, ordering food, and so on. A curious, very marked accent – partly Scotch, perhaps, partly – I don't know what – distinctly fascinating. The talk was mainly on a certain subject. Roger played up admirably, quite admirably, and made everything go much more easily than would otherwise have been the case. He seemed to be not particularly literary – which was slightly disturbing; and I think just a trifle too old – I mean belonging to a generation almost too distant for really intimate approach – a touch of Sickert . . . A slight effect you know of not having been very well treated by life . . . One would like to surround him with every kind of comfort and admiration and innumerable boys of $14\frac{1}{2}$.

Douglas insisted on going to the station to see his visitors off, paid for all meals, and even tried to tip the porter. "Apart from the first moments of exhaustion, I enjoyed it all more than I can say – and how am I to thank you for all your extreme kindness? We were both overwhelmed – longed to stay on – and could not bear leaving you on that wretched platform."

Within three days of this visit, Strachey demonstrated his gratitude and his regard for Douglas in an extremely practical manner. "It infuriates me to think of Alone and Together having such miserable sales," he wrote to their author, "they ought by now to be coming out in cheap popular editions"; and he wrote on the same day to Charles Prentice, of Chatto and Windus, his own publisher, suggesting that Douglas was "exactly the sort of writer your firm would like to be connected with, and that he on his side would benefit greatly if this could happen". As a result of this generous thought and action, Chatto and Windus soon became Douglas' publishers. "Lytton Strachey came, and went," wrote Douglas to Orioli, "We got on very well . . ."

While Douglas was in Paris, Archie got married, in England. Douglas wished, he wrote, that he "could come over", as though it would be easy enough, "but *time* is against me. Every week counts" (he wanted to be in Jerusalem when the weather was suitable) "and once at Dover I should have to go and see a few people in London etc." They would be sure to meet, he suggested, somewhere on Archie's travels: "Where do you go to?" But this apparent insouciance concealed a nagging doubt about his official reception in England, as one who had fled from the law in 1917. He would almost certainly have liked to make a quick dash to England, to see Archie and his wife, and perhaps even to stay with Lytton Strachey at Ham Spray House, but he had either to put the idea out of his mind or institute enquiries that might prove embarrassing. He put it out of his mind, and thought about Jerusalem.

ii

Thinking about Jerusalem, he came to the conclusion that he had better not go there. He couldn't trust himself, he told Hutton, perhaps ironically, to "write a decent book about it; and if I don't, I shan't get back my expenses". So once his teeth were fixed he decided on Damascus. He would go overland by train, via Stamboul and not go to Damascus at all, but to Baalbek. He found the train journey through the salt desert and the magnificent scenery of the Cilician Gates, in the comfort of a wagon-lit, fascinating and impressive.

Of Baalbek's famous ruins he has left no written impression. This is typical: he left the famous sights well alone on the whole; if they were mentioned at all it was usually in some unfamiliar context. The Colosseum, for instance, is introduced as a subject only so that its flora and "fauna" may be mentioned; Paestum for the same reason.

He was three weeks at Baalbek. He visited the grove of Cedars of Lebanon – the last remnants of a vast forest of them – on the Mediterranean side of the Jebel Libanon mountains. It was a long climb up through the snow-line to Cedar Col, more than 2,500 metres high, from which the Cedars may be seen, "a strange-looking black patch", rocky desolation all around. Within the grove, where the largest tree had a girth of seventeen metres, he noticed that no saplings grew. Seedlings sprouted, and were killed by the frost, indicating a drastic change of climate.

In the mornings he worked in his room on a new novel called *Love among Ruins*; and in the afternoons walked, sat down somewhere, and thought out the next chapter or two. *Love among Ruins* "pictured in brief flashes the development of every variety of human love I could recall; love of the young and of the old, love connubial and promiscuous, conventional and unconventional, heterosexual and homosexual, idealistic and carnal; love of God, of fellow-creatures, of self; and all these love affairs ended blissfully for the persons concerned. In the background hovered the shades of Lucian and Meleager – Syrians both."

Only the first two chapters out of a projected fifty seem to have survived. He does not say how many were actually written. From what survives, it is difficult to see how he would ever have come to grips with his subject except in a tedious and inferential manner. Perhaps it is just as well that he "sent it to perdition".

iii

One might gather from his remarks that he had enjoyed himself sufficiently on his holiday. He was proud of his pilgrimage to the Cedars of Lebanon and had sent "boast-cards" of them to his friends; but the novel had turned out to be abortive, and one has an impression at this time of a more general sense of loss or emptiness, a disorientation. He was evidently conscious of this, and wrote some weeks later that his life had "grown very *scattered* lately, and I don't seem to be able to pull the ends together". Lawrence, with his unfailing and relentless perception, had noticed this before Douglas left for Baalbek: ". . . was in Florence yesterday – saw Douglas – looking very old – off in a week's time to Aleppo – or so he says – by Orient Express. . . . From Aleppo he wants to go to Baalbek – and then, presumably, to rise into Heaven. He's terribly at an end of everything."

Douglas' work seems to have been as scattered as he thought his life was. Limericks were piling up; there was the "pamphlet"; there was reference in March to a possible contract for *In the Beginning*; Nancy Cunard was printing a facsimile of the Foreign Office *Report on the Pumice Stone Industry* (this was distributed in June) and before the Limericks were sent to the printer in mid-October, he was working on aphrodisiacs for *Paneros* or *Venus in the Kitchen*. Book-making and catering for the collector's market had begun to take precedence over original work. One gets the impression of the rather frantic and fragmented activity of a man who may have felt that much of his zest and drive and intensity, perhaps even some of his interest in and curiosity about life, had begun to evaporate. He seems to have been drifting ever so slightly into a kind of acquiescent silliness, playing up to the frivolities and puerilities of some of the more imbecilic of his admirers, to follow rather than lead, and to be directionless.

It took a shock to make the sincerity and feeling in him instantly recognisable.

This occurred when he was in Paris early in July. He was handed a telegram from Emilio telling him that the boy's mother had had a serious accident. She had in fact been knocked down in the street by a truck, and the accident proved fatal. Douglas wrote at once to Orioli:

Dear Pino

Just got a wire from Emilio, and have wired you asking for details. If she's dead, *the boys can stay with me*: Please tell him that (if she's dead). No time for more. I am expecting your reply wire. Will be in Florence Tuesday or Wednesday. Please give E this 100 frcs as soon as you can – waiting for your wire before I write to him. Got the mail from Cook this morning. Make it clear to E that I shall do all I can. Can't write more – room full of people. Both the boys can come to me: *make that clear*.

Far from waiting for Tuesday or Wednesday (he had written on the Saturday), he set off for Florence the same night, and was there the following day. Anyone to whom he had given his love and affection, and who had responded in the same way, could rely on him utterly in a crisis. He saw Emilio and his younger brother Alvaro through the next difficult fortnight in Florence, and then, partly because he himself could not stand the city in the heat of July and August, but mostly no doubt to alleviate their sorrow, he took them down to Scanno for three weeks. It was typical of him that he should give the impression in a letter to a friend in America – whom he knew well enough to have been truthful with – that he was behaving naughtily: "I have fled with *two* kids into the Abruzzi . . ."

iv

Some Limericks was ready for distribution about 1st December in a limited edition of 110 copies, 100 at five guineas and ten at ten guineas on special paper. It could not be advertised, but by writing letters to selected friends, and friends of friends, he was able to ensure that word of it got round in the right or in likely circles. A typical letter described it as

> extremely obscene and blasphemous – one of the filthiest in the English language, I should think, and written only for the *Dirty-minded Elect* . . . I should like to have an assurance from you that you have realised this fact . . . Please don't mention its existence to people like booksellers because, through them, the police and the customs might be put on the track, and then I should . . . certainly have trouble . . . It goes off slowly as I have no means of making it known. If you like it, perhaps you would mention its existence to other scholars who might like a copy.

Purchasers were urged to the greatest discretion in showing the book to others, asked to open the parcel themselves, and send a card acknowledging its safe arrival.

Whether Douglas really believed that a hundred and ten people, many of them living in England (which at that time was the laughing stock of Europe for its Grundyism), could keep the book secret from the authorities is doubtful, especially as a good many of the purchasers would, by their nature, be lovers of scandal and have tongues that wagged only too easily. It must be assumed that as far as Douglas was concerned, this was another act in the drama of "living dangerously". If this is correct, he had trailed his coat very successfully, for before the end of the month, Kyrle Leng was visited by the police in London, who were making enquiries as to how he came to possess an immoral book. Others, also, were said to have been questioned. Leng wrote to his brother Basil, in France, to pass on a warning to Douglas.

The curious jealousy and rivalry – probably completely unconscious – which seems to have existed in Douglas with regard to D. H. Lawrence, may have hastened the production of *Some Limericks*. The idea had been in his mind since 1917, but for years he did nothing about it, though he may have put aside a few limericks ready for the day, should it ever dawn, when he could find someone to print them. His eagerness to get on with the book only became evident at about the time when he attended readings of *Lady Chatterley's Lover*; or at the time when he wrote, as near to being scandalised as he could get, that Lawrence was "finishing one of the filthiest books I ever read. The word 'fuck' occurs eight times on the last page, which I happened to see in print." He seems to have been of the opinion that Lawrence, not being a gentleman, would be bound to abuse the freedom of four-letter words. Hence his insistence that *Limericks* was for the Dirty-Minded *Elect*, meaning no doubt, gentlemen – gentlemen of discretion who could be relied upon to keep their filth in its proper place, i.e. in the smoking room, club, or other exclusive ambience; that is to say, keeping it *at a premium*, in such a way that its force and effect would not be reduced by dissemination amongst a broad public. "Our own half-starved classes. ... know not these poems," wrote Douglas. "The well-fed youngsters of the universities and the stock exchange, commercial travellers for good houses, together with a wise old scholar or two – these are the fountain-heads." And not only the fountain-heads, but the sort of men to whom this book is addressed, curiously enough public-school men for the most part, men of the middle and upper-middle classes and upwards, for whom "friend Lawrence" was definitely *not* writing: "'Scholars and men of the world will not find much inspiration in [his] novels. Lawrence opened a little window for the bourgeoisie. That is his life-work." Therefore Lawrence could not be trusted; he would very likely devalue the privileged world of the smoking-room by removing the door and windows altogether so that anybody could stroll in or out as they pleased and become a party to what was recounted there, or worse still, discover that with the access of fresh air all such hothouse growths had begun to wilt and shrivel. Therefore the sooner he, Douglas, could get out his collection of Limericks, the better – before the democratisation of such a sub-culture should deprive it of all its force and vigour.

Lady Chatterley's Lover was published by Orioli in June; *Some Limericks*, by Douglas, in November. It is a curious picture – Lawrence and Douglas, living within a few miles of each other, the one sick beyond recovery and the other bursting with Rabelaisian health, both battering side by side at the doors of respectability; and it is strange to see that it is the sick man who is really concerned, who has the courage of his convictions, whose every blow is sincere and desperate; the other stands there making his clownish faces, and making a fuss over lighting a little squib.

It went off all right, was a great success with many. Scott-Moncrieff called it "one of the most laughter-provoking things ever produced"; but Scott-Moncrieff was probably biased by sharing almost exactly the same taste as Douglas' for the scholarly bawdy. The book was pirated very soon after publication, and has gone into innumerable editions, and will doubtless go into more.

The limericks are filthy enough and blasphemous enough for most tastes, and the scholar-like notes, drily ironical, concernedly helpful, or esoterically informative, could not have been better done, both as to length and general tone. The index, likewise, is a good example of the mock-serious. As to the introduction, it has its serious points to make, and makes them with typical economy and lightness. Limericks, in effect, are part of our sub-culture, and worthy not only of investigation, but of preservation: "He must be a quintessential fool who does not realise that the following fifty limericks are a document of enduring value." They are irreplaceable – and like London street games, modern minstrelsy, and the oaths of Florentine cabmen, ephemeral. So may they be justified in the eyes of sociologists as worthy records; meanwhile let us also enjoy them.

For all their evidence of zest and vitality it is difficult nowadays to dissociate these "lyrics" as Douglas rather wryly called them, from an unpleasant illiberal background in which the male population of the middle and upper strata of society shut itself away secretly to seek reassurance about the anxieties of love-making or of certain other bodily functions. In other words, as Douglas points out in his introduction, these things are evidence of the psychological desire to be free of puritanism. It is somehow typical of him that he should have liked these "lyrics" for themselves, and have preferred, apparently, having them to having an unpuritanical state of society in which safety valves were superfluous, as he hints may be the case in Catholic countries. Most people today would be more inclined to agree with Aldous Huxley than with Scott-Moncrieff: "Did you ever see that collection of pornographic limericks that he had privately printed? It was the only way, poor fellow, that he could make some money. It was a terribly unfunny book."[103]

v

At what precise time *How about Europe?* was conceived, it is difficult to say, but it was certainly under way by December 1928, and began to move rapidly forward during the first few months of 1929. By the middle of August it was finished. It cannot have been a difficult book to write, being a kind of scrap-book of newspaper cuttings, statistics, and extracts from books all threaded on a string of prejudice and opinion. It is only about 45,000 words in length.

This little book was ready for distribution before the end of November, but Douglas complained that he was "getting slower and slower. Old age, I suppose." He had begun to use the phrase "putrefying as gracefully as I can"; he had become "Uncle Norman"; but he was keeping his end up by getting out a book of some kind every year. Nevertheless, he was still a vigorous walker who could leave many younger men exhausted on a tramp through Calabria or elsewhere; and it was to Calabria that he and Orioli went for a holiday in April. It had been planned for some time, and was the first of many such holidays that the two men were to share. No doubt it celebrated Orioli's first venture as an independent publisher, as opposed to his more truly managerial rôle in the case of *Lady Chatterley*. This first volume of Orioli's was *Nerinda*, slightly revised by Douglas, and published in April; it was well received by the bibliophiles.

In the summer, Lawrence came to stay with Orioli; he fell ill on arrival at Orioli's flat in Florence and within a few days he was so ill that Orioli thought he would die, and telegraphed to Frieda in England. She came out, and Lawrence recovered. When he was well enough to leave for Germany with Frieda he invited Douglas and Orioli to a farewell luncheon. Unfortunately, they had inadequate time in which to enjoy it, for suddenly, after the first course – which had been long in coming – Lawrence cried out that he and Frieda must rush off or they'd never catch their train. Douglas found himself paying for meal and taxi, and it dawned on him that this might not have been entirely accidental: he had recently induced Lawrence to pay for some drinks for himself and Orioli ... As the train drew out of the station he thought he might have detected on Lawrence's wan face "the phantom of a smile".

As soon as he had finished *How about Europe?*, Douglas started working on an introduction that Orioli had asked him to write to *The Last of the*

Medici, the biography of Gian Gastone, translated by Harold Acton.[104] Orioli, meanwhile, had decided, says Douglas – though he was quite likely persuaded – to reprint Douglas' Capri monographs, and at the end of the year Douglas was revising them for this purpose, correcting proofs. At this time also, he was apparently intending to write an introduction to a cookery book.

This latter arose out of a little paper-covered volume which Orioli flung on to the table one evening in Florence when he and Douglas and Faith Mackenzie were sitting down to dine. It was called *La Cucina dell' Amore*: "'If you'll translate that, I will publish it' he said. He had picked it up on a bookstall. Its subtitle was *Manuale culinario afrodisiaco per gli adulti dei due Sessi*. It should be called *Venus in the Kitchen* or *Love's Cookery Book*. I spent a winter at Jethou translating it. When the cackle, of which there was a good deal, was cut, it was a good collection of rich recipes. To these Mrs Boyte added some of her choicest works of art, Orioli dug out some old ones in Florentine notebooks, and the result was a diverting gourmet's manual."

The book was never published, added Mrs Mackenzie (writing in 1940), because of copyright complications; but she had been well paid for her work. In fact, the book was never published in just the form she would have had it published in; but *Venus in the Kitchen*, sub-titled "Love's Cookery Book" eventually appeared in 1952, edited by "Pilaff Bey" (i.e. Norman Douglas), with acknowledgments to Faith Mackenzie and another friend. It was the last book Douglas worked on, and came out posthumously.

In 1929 also, in July, *One Day* was published by Nancy Cunard in a total limitation of 500 copies, some signed, and some not, costing three guineas and thirty shillings respectively. Douglas had been paid £300 for it by the Greek government in 1919, and subsequently calculated that it had cost Greek taxpayers only a fraction of a farthing each. The book, he wrote:

> was not imposing perhaps as to bulk, but crammed with shrewd and suggestive observations, exhaling a candid love of their race and fatherland and a reverence for its traditions; a book written by a countryman of their national hero, Byron, and in a style, moreover, which no critic will call displeasing: all this for the fraction of a farthing! Not a bad bargain from the Greek point of view.

The book was, in fact, less than 12,000 words long; and of these more than 3,000 were devoted to the Greek Anthology, which may have surprised the Greek government if – ten years later – it was still interested. Economical as ever, Douglas carried most of this particular material over from the first version of *Alone*; and the Cora episode from his abortive introduction to Hutton's *A Glimpse of Greece*. Nancy Cunard would certainly have paid him something; the thing was sold to the magazine *Travel* in the USA; and appeared yet again in 1930 in the book *Three of Them*. He did not do badly out of it.

Nor did his readers, for as Douglas himself says "the writing slips along easily". One gets a benign impression of Greece, ancient and modern; an evocation of the heat, the stones, the barrenness, the clarity of air and outline strikes up at one out of these few pages with a strength and faithfulness to landscape all the more powerful for concentration in a short space, although in a reminiscent and relaxed tone. One also has the pleasure of spending another half hour in the company of a fascinating and intriguing writer who can slip so easily into and out of the autobiographical mood, who can impart information and opinion with such civility and geniality and who can make the essence of a well-spent life – as in the Greek Anthology section – seem so simple, so natural, so plainly dignified, so intensely enjoyable. They are heart-warming pages, all too few.

He was in Paris for ten days in November, having his teeth finally attended to. Archie came over for a weekend; Robert, who had married the daughter of a rich American, had been visiting the Vorarlberg with her. Grete Gulbransson thought Uretta "very nice", and any recommendation of hers was enough for Douglas, who received the three of them when they passed through Florence on their way to the Bay of Naples. They intended to settle there for two or three months and get some work done; but Robert was struck down with appendicitis at Capri, and he and Uretta rushed back to Paris. Robert was operated on.

At this time Douglas had thought – or was it Nancy Cunard who had the expectations? – that they might make a visit together, with Henry Crowder, her American Negro friend, to West Africa. Her account of the talks she had with Douglas about going there, of his willingness, but insistence that she should make all the arrangements, of his objections (on reasonable grounds) to her successive suggestions, of his raising the subject again when she thought it had been dropped for good, and of still more objections – these pages in *Grand Man*, her book of reminiscences of Douglas, show a side of his character that is not often recorded. From them one can only conclude either that he was too sentimentally considerate to risk offending Nancy Cunard (and perhaps Henry Crowder) by saying that he did not want to go; or he thought two would be company and not three; or he did not like Crowder enough; or he was in such a state of indecision that he was only willing to go if it was made so easy for him that he need do nothing but get on a boat when the time came. Evasive and provoking he certainly must have been; and behind Nancy Cunard's account one can detect an impatience and bewilderment on her part that are not surprising in the circumstances. "I think the African trip will fizzle out" wrote Douglas to Orioli on November 10th; and a few days later, "Africa is *off*". Perhaps he had doggedly manipulated the situation so that she would make the decision, out of sheer exasperation, that he wanted, but did not wish to take responsibility for. His behaviour represents a departure (by no means unique) from that dominating masculinity which many people regard, erroneously, as one of his immutable characteristics.

vi

In December, *How about Europe?* was ready to be despatched to subscribers, not many of whom could have known what they were going to get.

Of the earliest version of *Alone*, Douglas had written to Straus: "It pretends to be an impromptu, but is really an artful Gospel of Revolt." Some things in it, he thought, might be "too naughty for our public". Unless he was referring to the Florentine blasphemies, which were not noticeably offensive except to Christian believers, and then only in the space of a few lines, one would have to look very hard nowadays to justify this comment on the book. That was in 1920 or thereabouts: nine years later he made no such apologies for *How about Europe?*, in which he drops artfulness and says exactly what he thinks about a whole range of our customs and beliefs. If the other book was a Gospel of Revolt, this is a verbal guerrilla war against occidental civilisation. It has been criticised as "the least satisfactory of his books, for the violence of the tone, and particularly the sneers at Christianity. . . . Perhaps only a man who had no home land . . . could have attacked his civilisation so bitterly, and perhaps that is why this book is in many ways so unsatisfactory."[105] The book is not entirely satisfactory, but for reasons other than "bitterness"; and if a man may not attack his own civilisation, what right has he to attack anyone else's? I do not see the attacks on Christianity as sneers, but as valid criticism. "Two thousand years of believing the impossible" and "a devastating epidemic of unreason" seem to me to be mild descriptions of the darker side of any systematic and illogical belief to which masses of people subscribe although some, as Douglas suggests of Buddhism, are probably less harmful in their effects than others. The book seeks only to point out deficiencies in our civilisation; it is not an attempt to balance the good in it against the bad.

The pretext for the book was another book, *Mother India*, by an American journalist called Katherine Mayo, famous in its time, less known now. Douglas thought that what Katherine Mayo had to say of India was sad and unpleasant – but how about Europe? Could not just as many abuses, even if of a different kind, be found there? One thing was certain: Europe was growing steadily smaller, had lost its smile, and was becoming balkanised – i.e. explosive and hectic. It was a "frowsy and fidgety little hole", and a young man would do better to go East, where the way of life "engenders self-respect and ease of soul", especially in a "gentleman's country" like India. Easy enough, of course, to make fun of the slightly petulant phraseology and the "gentleman" fallacy, but not so easy to invalidate the basic argument of the book, namely, that life in Europe had become progressively more harassed and exacerbating, particularly since the First World War. It would not be easy to refute this charge at any level of society: other arguments or implications might be called, finally, class judgments, and these, of course, would include many of Douglas' comparisons of life in Europe with life in India as seen from the sahib's point of view. Nor would Douglas have had changes made: he approved of the caste system, and also said he had no patience with ameliorative policies designed to keep thousands of people alive who had much better be dead. As to his injunction "Stop this breeding!" (the urgency of which is now trebled), he is wise enough not to try to offer any advice as to how it might be put into effect. "The reader will find no suggestion of remedies in these pages," he blandly announces, "I observe and pass on." All right! Destructive critics do occasionally justify their critical freedom by recognising and naming weaknesses which others overlook.

The chief targets in *How about Europe?* are Christianity, education, antiquated or absurd legislation, war and its effects, and petty restrictions of all kinds. These are no unusual objects of criticism, but in the course of a random attack on them, Douglas makes some refreshing comments. The superiority of polytheism over monotheism is illustrated not only by reference to the Greek pantheon but also to Roman Catholicism, with its division of God into three parts, its host of local Madonnas of this and that aspect of life, and its vast gallery of saints. The degradation of women by official Christianity, which hardly exists in the Latin Catholic countries where the Madonna is worshipped, has been perpetuated by Protestants, and is one of the greatest indictments of the faith. As to other matters, "imperialism is an undiluted mischief"; the Press, in moulding public opinion, inevitably appeals to the least desirable emotions; mass education tends to produce a type instead of a character; standardisation and state-worship, both of which Douglas thought (correctly) were gaining in momentum, derived from "those self-inflated *parvenus*, the Romans", on whom, in consequence, he launches a refreshing attack. It was their "ingrained vulgarity" which was responsible, he thought, for accepting "imported pinchbeck like Christianity".

A good many of these thoughts and opinions derive from Nietzsche, who "made a clearing in our jungle of unreason; one of those bare, sporadic patches where the sun can penetrate to earth, and where a gentleman can take his pleasure"; but Nietzsche is firmly taken to task for anthropocentrism – always a cardinal sin in the Douglas ethic – and for scorning evolutionists like Spencer and Darwin.

The book did not pretend to fullness; it was to be read as a collection of footnotes or marginal comments suggested by a reading of *Mother India* – nothing more. The footnotes could be enlarged into volumes, but it is just as well that they were not, by Douglas. Emotional and prejudiced, he was never a systematic thinker where such semi-philosophical and political matters were concerned, and could easily have been demolished by logic. Nevertheless, these footnotes, being highly provocative and stimulating, will at least make many readers consider problems they might otherwise have ignored. Crotchety, bad-tempered sometimes, and occasionally absurd, the book is also generous-hearted, tolerant, and in places more genuinely objective than would be expected. It is the product, as he himself would have said, of someone with red blood in his veins, and not one of those anaemic dissections of fact and opinion that are so often served up to the apprehensive enquirer into such matters. A splendid Landorian scorn is apparent here and there, most effectively displayed perhaps in the withering exclamation: "Can cretinism go further? Of course it can!"

In its general backward-looking, or sideways-looking nostalgia for a simpler and more dignified way of life, the book is a characteristic product of its author. In attacking the creeping blight of a highly successful technological society hurrying towards Hell over the corpses of human dignity, peace of mind, gentlemanly leisure, and freedom from petty restraints, it ignores such benefits as may have accrued to the masses during the development of this process. It implies that a return to a simpler and more dignified way of life, even if it were basically a feudal system or a society incorporating slavery, would be preferable – at any rate for a gentleman. The starting point for such attacks on European society must be a deep regret for lost innocence – the expulsion-from-paradise syndrome to which we are all subject from time to time. It does not seem to me to be stretching the evidence too far to assume that in Douglas' life this syndrome was central and important.

How doubly sad it must have made him feel to see India become more and more industrialised, more and more devoted to demagogues and ideologies, to nationalism and socialism, and perhaps worst of all, to the gradual adoption of a Western way of life. Before the pace of this change was accelerated, however, he was to visit India once more, in 1934–5, with Orioli as companion.

vii

There were advantages for both Orioli and Douglas in their close association, although Orioli's health may have suffered to some extent as a consequence:

Douglas said you were ill, but he didn't say how or what. I do hope it isn't bad. I expect you got yourself thoroughly upset Christmassing at Nice and Menton. When you were here I knew from your voice that you were knocking yourself up. Why are you so silly? Why do you think you want to razzle and drink like Douglas? It doesn't agree with you – and you are only miserable. Remember that by family you are born moral, and so you'll always be miserable when you go off the hooks. You'll merely kill yourself if you try to live up to Douglas' festive standards. You're not made that way. There's a preach! – and all the time, here I'm in bed too.

These are the words of a man who cared greatly for the inner psychological health of his friends, and himself. But was Lawrence aware of the state of his own health? ". . . and all the time, here I'm in bed too" was written at the end of January. Almost exactly a month later, Lawrence was dead.

Douglas and Orioli sent telegrams immediately to Frieda, and both of them went to see her though it would seem likely from subsequent remarks of hers that she only wanted to see Orioli, whom both she and Lawrence, like so many other people, had found so warming and sympathetic. However, as money was an urgent necessity, Douglas' hardheadedness may have been of some use to Frieda, though his advice was typically wayward and opinionated, to judge by a letter he wrote her after he and Orioli had returned to Florence:

Florence
29 March 1930

Dear Frieda,

Pino has just shown me some of your correspondence. Don't make any mistake: now is the moment to print everything that D H L ever wrote. In a few years' time there will be very little demand, except on the part of 5–6 collectors. *Ich versteh' mich drauf.* The psychological moment for printing Lawrence is *now*, or never. And Pino's system is by far the best. It is the same as mine, and I have tried all systems. But I am afraid you are infected with *Tazzelwurmimania* if you think you can ever get £25000 for his manuscripts. You won't get £2000, and if you delay, you won't get £250. Get them *printed* by Pino; then sell them to a publisher like I do. It is the only way to get money. Do you want money? Then follow my advice. Otherwise, if you get mixed up with those thieves of publishers and agents, you will repent it (*bitter bereuen!*) when it is too late to repent. Get your money now; you will get nothing in 5 years; you will also get nothing if you serialise (I've tried it!) you will also get nothing if you go on the royalty system with those cut-throats . . .

Yours ever
Uncle Norman

Conrad, a very important writer, is completely forgotten now. A manuscript of his, *which I have*, is not worth £5 (five pounds): nobody will buy it! Try, my dear, to get over your illusions, else it will cost you dear. You have seen D H L's accounts from publishers: £40 for 12 books! Don't have that system again . . .

Orioli went again to visit Frieda several weeks later.

Lawrence was forty-four when he died. Some four years younger, Charles Scott-Moncrieff, prince of translators, scatological wit and child-like purveyor of scandalous anecdotes, died at about the same time, miserably, in Rome. In the middle of February, when he was very weak, Douglas went down to Rome especially to see him and found him "at the last gasp. . . . He is shrivelled into a monkey, and not recognisable. They *say* he can last another 2 weeks. I don't see how he is going to do it."

viii

Robin and his wife Uretta were in Florence in February with her sister and mother; and some steps seem to have been taken towards a reconciliation between father and son. Douglas liked Uretta's mother, old Mrs Campbell; and relations between her and Robin seem to have been satisfactory enough not to require the invocation of the evil eye, which he had tried to bring to the aid of Walter Lowenfels whose wealthy parents were, in Douglas' view, particularly ungenerous to their son. He had invoked it also on behalf of Archie – but in neither case did it seem to be working. "I'll see what I can do about that mal'occhio," he wrote to the latter, "I think the ma-chinery is getting rather rusty", and a month later reported: "Mal'occhio is now *turned on*." So that was that; but the people against whom it was directed continued obstinately to flourish, or at any rate, not to decline . . .

Archie, miraculously, was still in the same job at the Royal Horticultural Society, facing the responsibilities of a married man but not necessarily enjoying them. He was given some fatherly – and presumably unsolicited – advice about women:

I should make it my business not to be broken, but to break other people. That can be done, if one sets about it scientifically. Be hard; and take your time over it. Once you have made up your mind, I should never be soft again. It is the continual half-nagging and then making it up again which wears one out. I should have none of that, once you have decided on your line. All women are vampires – all, *without exception* – if you give them a chance. I should vampire them; slowly and systematically. It takes time and study, but the results are worth it . . . No good allowing oneself to be eaten raw. To Hell!

The same man, meanwhile, was asserting that he was 'loaded up with love-affairs, as never before! All that will be over soon, so I make hay while the sun shines. Very good hay, too." The succession of his more enduring and nobler loves had been continued beyond Eric and René, by Emilio; but there were many others, who fulfilled humbler and less durable rôles, as Orioli's diaries of his holidays with Douglas were to make clear.

There can be no doubt about Douglas' gratitude to Orioli for publishing his *Capri Materials*; he called it "a *heroic* undertaking; no ordinary publisher would have touched it". It was ready for distribution in July 1930, solidly and handsomely produced, and was thought to be the largest volume in English ever published in Italy. After all expenses had been paid, Douglas reckoned that he and Orioli were left with £30 profit between them. As soon as all the ordered copies of the book were despatched, he and Orioli fled the heat of Florence and went to the Vorarlberg.

ix

Here Orioli kept what seems to be the first of that series of diaries which he made of their holidays together. It is written in Italian with a few phrases in English; and it sets the uninhibited tone for all the other diaries. These impressions of their life together from the inside are highly illuminating and contain intimate details which could never have been discovered elsewhere.

A small percentage of what Orioli wrote in his diaries would certainly have been unprintable until quite recently, and sooner or later the reader of them is bound to ask why Douglas not only encouraged Orioli to keep these diaries, but also why, having read them himself, and in some cases having typed them out or corrected them, he should have allowed them to survive, especially as Orioli died before he did. In themselves and taken as a whole they do not damage Douglas' character, and could be said to enlarge it; but in the hands of an Aldington or some other insidious vilifier they could be made harmful. Perhaps his allowing them to survive is another instance of his respect for the truth; perhaps it is another example of his sometimes "naming himself in public" (to posterity); or perhaps he simply did not care, knowing that these things were not malicious or untrue, and that anyway they could not be published during his lifetime.

This first diary shows that a good deal of time was spent with, or looking for, young companions who might or might not be admitted as regular intimates during the course of the holiday, and perhaps also of subsequent holidays in the same district. Douglas, master of the necessary languages and dialects, and born teacher and inspirer of the young, found boys with consummate ease, seemed in fact to conjure them out of the air or ground. Orioli, who was less masterful and knew no German, did not so readily find companions in Austria.

On this particular holiday Douglas' friend was a boy called Fifo – a fairly constant companion who came regularly to the Hirschen at Thürin-gen, where Douglas and Orioli were staying, for what Orioli euphem-istically calls his "lesson". The nature of the lesson can hardly be doubted since when it took place in Douglas' room it required that the windows be screened; but it often took place *al fresco*.

This was Orioli's first visit to the Vorarlberg, and he was introduced to its secret and special places. Douglas's obsession – it seems fair to call it that – with the ritualism of place and happening is illustrated by his never failing to mention, at a certain spot, how, as a child, he had fallen out of a coach or carriage there. He seems to have felt compelled to refer to this incident every time he and Orioli came to the place, which was almost every other day, until Orioli became at first exasperated, and then fatal-istically resigned to it: yet Douglas persisted, though in the end simply by gesturing at the spot and pronouncing the one word "Here!".

Another ritual referred to in this and in the next Vorarlberg diary is that of the "Woolley-Woolley" (or Voolley-Voolley, as Orioli called it in conversation). This was a monster which peragrated, or a spirit which haunted, and perhaps ravaged, the neighbourhood. It could be placated with gifts of flowers and sealing-wax, and it seems that it could be sum-moned or charmed by music. It was at all events "a potent but capricious deity". Its name could not be uttered, nor even be written down, it seems, without risk of retribution. This mythology, which must have derived from Douglas' childhood, was still very much alive in his mind, and there can be little doubt that he either believed in it, or was so determined to be reunited with his childhood that he acted the part of superstition with complete conviction. Aldington thought it mere fun on Douglas's part, but Orioli disagreed: "My dear boy, you do not know how superstitious is Norman."[106] Orioli had direct experience of it, during both this visit and a subsequent one. On this present occasion Douglas asked him not to arouse the nameless one (represented in Orioli's diary by a blank) by playing a certain tune on his mouth-organ when they were in a vulnerable position under the Hanging Stone, lest the —— should tumble the stone down upon their heads, which, said Douglas, it was sufficiently powerful and malignant to do.

The boy who had denied God (aloud) at the age of seven was evidently unable to deny this other deity. All through life he carried on a protracted skirmish or running battle with the Almighty and his "priceless Son", as he called Him, often with great vehemence, but sometimes with a contemptuous buffoonery and a trivial offensiveness which most adults would have been ashamed to indulge. He and Orioli, like two naughty schoolboys, would egg each other on in these, as in other matters. One evening, for instance, after they had come in soaked to the skin, they sat in Douglas' room smoking before going to bed. Orioli, who found himself sitting in front of a crucifixion scene carved in wood, could not resist sticking his smoking cigarette in the open mouth of Christ's slightly hanging head. He and Douglas exploded with laughter, and went on laughing and laughing and laughing: the Christ, thought Orioli, looked almost human, and exactly like a gigolo.

There was plenty of rain, as there so often is in the "Ländle", and it was sometimes impossible for them to go out. Douglas would urge Orioli to work at his diary: it would be difficult, wrote Orioli, to find anyone who was more ready to encourage him to work than Douglas, although it was he, Orioli, who had already done a morning's work in replying to letters of all kinds and attending to orders for the *Capri Materials*.

It continued to rain. "What's to be done?" demanded Douglas.

"You can copy out twenty German recipes for your book," answered Orioli with evident alacrity. "Don't forget that *Venus in the Kitchen* has got to be published."

So they worked. The room filled with smoke from Orioli's cigarettes and Douglas' pipe. Orioli went to open a window.

"Whatever you do, don't open the window. No fresh air for me, otherwise I stop working immediately."

"Alright, alright, go on."

And the window, says Orioli, stayed shut; "and we suffocated with smoke."

Douglas is also shown, in this diary, at a rare social disadvantage. He and Orioli were cornered, after eating at the Traube, by two English-women who were staying there:

You must forgive me, but knowing you are N.D. I cannot resist not to tell you how I admire your works. I am here in Vorarlberg after having been enchanted by your book about these places. I am one of your greatest admirer, etc. etc.?

N. is quite red in his face and shy. I nearly giggle, knowing how he dislike these kind of complements [sic] and how he detest these kind of women running after writers.

The holiday ended, with a crisis, earlier than planned: Douglas had gone for a night to Lech with Fifo while Orioli went to Feldkirch with some-one else. At Lech there was what Orioli calls "un terrible patatrac": the local policeman wished to see Douglas' passport, and unfortunately chose to make this inspection while Douglas was giving Fifo a lesson.

Douglas, understandably, was nervous, but more concerned for Fifo than for himself. What was to be done? Orioli advised flight.

The next day they bolted.

x

The writing of the preface to *Venus in the Kitchen*, which had been under way for some months when the Capri book was published, had required a good deal of research. As time passed, Douglas seems to have forgotten the original purpose and to have become engrossed in the subject for its own sake. More and more material accumulated, and after six months of work – not exclusively on this subject – something quite different resulted: a treatise on aphrodisiacs in a pastiche of seventeenth-century prose style.

This essay (entitled *Paneros*) was completed by the beginning of Octo-ber, and Douglas had already decided with Orioli that the latter would publish it as No. 5 in his Lungarno series, as a separate volume, although it was less than 12,000 words long; he would charge – on the strength of the subject matter and the reputation of author and publisher – the somewhat extortionate price of 3 guineas, in an edition of 250 copies. This was the same price as the de luxe edition of the Capri book, which contains 366 pages and numerous illustrations. On the other hand there is a less urgent demand for information about Sister Serafina and the Forestal Conditions of Capri than there is for means of stimulating sexual potency. So perhaps the price was fair enough – except that, as Douglas knew, and explained to friends, all oral aphrodisiacs are useless: "The best aphrod. *I* know," he wrote to Hutton, "is fresh blood; variety. It works!"

Printing and distributing his own books had proved, on the whole, both profitable and expeditious. Referring to an offer via Richard Curle (who was in the USA) from an American publisher, Douglas replied in the negative:

If I had offered him this last book, "How about Europe?" for a private edition, I should have got 250 dollars down, and then had to wait for further royalties till Doomsday . . . Now the book (350 copies) priced £1. 6. 0, only came out in the last week of November and, although Christmas got in the way, it is already sold out; not a single copy is left, and I have netted £450, *which are in my pocket*. Why, under these conditions, should I be such a damned fool as to publish with —, or with those others who are always applying to me and never mentioning terms? Not likely! They may be Americans, but I am not a Scotsman for nothing.

Financially, his own venture had been successful, particularly as the rights of his books were afterwards sold to English and American publishers for another lump sum. But there were disadvantages as well. A great deal of work was involved in choosing type and layout, supervising printing, doing the same for the binding, circulating all likely buyers through the post; and finally, packing and despatching, often by registered mail. This labour was at least halved, and with the help of Emilio and Carlo, probably quartered, when he began to publish under the Orioli imprint. It also helped to consolidate Orioli's steadily growing reputation as a publisher of limited editions, which, in its turn, was beneficial to both men. *How about Europe?*, therefore, was the last of the six Florentine publications that he brought out himself.

This satisfactory arrangement with Orioli was accompanied by an equally agreeable business situation in England, where Douglas now had a devoted publisher in the person of Charles Prentice of Chatto and Windus, to whom Lytton Strachey had written after his meeting with Douglas in Paris. As a result of this letter Chatto's had produced the English edition of *In the Beginning* in June 1928, and had followed it up with *Three of Them* in February 1930, and with *How about Europe?* four months later. In 1932 they would buy the four Douglas titles published by Chapman and Hall (*They Went, Alone, Together, Experiments*). Charles Prentice and Pino Orioli guaranteed Douglas a kind of security.

The consolidation with Orioli was taken a stage further when Orioli bought the flat below Douglas', which he moved into at the end of the year.

xi

As to health, with Orioli it was his liver that made itself felt; with Douglas, his teeth and his neuritis. In spite of all that had been done in Paris quite recently, he still had tooth trouble, and decided to go to the Parisian dentist again. But when he arrived in Paris he discovered that the dentist was temporarily inaccessible. So he plunged into a round of social activity. Nancy Cunard, with Henry Crowder, and Harold Acton, were there:

Norman was fond of Nancy in his bluff way. . . . [but] he wished to sample as many gastronomical specialities as Paris could provide in a limited time, and he refused to be kept waiting. Himself punctual to the dot, he looked forward to his next meal with a ravenous appetite: "I'm in the mood for *kebab* today: I've heard of a first-class Turkish place, the most de-leeshus coffee you ever tasted. Come on!"

"But what about Nancy?"

"We'll knock at her door on the way."

We would knock in due course, to find Nancy's room as crowded as if a party were going on, dense with cigarette smoke, books scattered over the bed. "Nothing doing. This is no place for us. Let's hop it," Norman would say. He disapproved of Nancy's hangers-on and grew more and more avuncular in their company. He enjoyed, however, making them sneeze: "A soupcon of snuff, my dear? Try it. It ought to clear your head." If this failed, he would offer a *Toscano* cigar, a real stinker, hoping it might act as an emetic. "In Burma the cheroots are rolled by young women between the breasts and thighs – deleeshus! That accounts, of course, for their fragrance."

Nancy was making arrangements to show a Surrealist film in London, which involved more confabulations in cafés than Norman was prepared to put up with. Rather grumpy, he was dragged along to visit André Breton. After one horrified look at the Dali dominating Breton's room – an intricately demoniac picture of William Tell in his underwear with a bright phallus protruding, and such details as the carcass of a donkey on a piano with a horse galloping over it – Uncle Norman said sharply: "I can't stay here. That picture will spoil my dinner. See you later, I must get some fresh air at once." Nobody could detain him. He had come to Paris to enjoy Nancy's company, but there were limits.[107]

His days were crowded. Mavrogordato was there; also Oscar Levy, and Victor Cunard; also Walter Lowenfels; and he met Desmond Harmsworth, and liked him. With so many people anxious to entertain him, he lived excessively, if not well: "We dine and lunch at the most expensive restaurants, and I shit 3 times a day and spew half the night" he wrote to Orioli.

As to the dentist, he never saw him at all before going off to spend Christmas with René at Marseille.

xii

Orioli's 250 copies of *Paneros*, at 3 guineas, were to be succeeded in the following year by a commercial edition of only 650; consequently, the book has been a scarce – and costly – item ever since. This is a pity, since it contains Douglas' philosophy of love and to some extent his philosophy of life, in its most positive and benign form. There may be an occasional sly irony, but there are few concessions in it to cynicism or misanthropy. Paradoxically, and typically, this short treatise written in seventeenth-century prose style, though whimsical in conception, contains little whimsy. It is a serious examination of the subject, and an unequivocal confession of belief. It contains some of the true passion of Douglas conveyed in urgent yet decorative brevity:

> Collectors of dusty things spend their wealth in the garnering of pictures or statuary; they will have you admire this antique trash, and crave to possess it. Why amass with dear money the masterpieces of art, when a friendly word will purchase those of nature? Why set your heart upon dead copies, when you may have originals throbbing with life?. . . . Seek masterpieces not in merchants' houses, but on the road-ways.

> Would you be young? Then live with the young, and flee the old with their aches and pains, fretfulness and valetudinarian makeshifts.

> Learn to foster an ardent imagination; so shall you descry beauty which others pass unheeded. The spark of desire is born in the head . . .

> At home dwells monotony; you take today what was given yesterday and shall be given tomorrow; the performance has grown to be weariness of the flesh. Why stay at home when you may walk abroad? There you encounter variety, to gladden your soul and fill your veins with fresh youth . . .

> Give love to the young, who requite you with kisses; take no thought of HIC JACET, which takes no thought of you.

> Cherish the living, whose hearts may yet be gladdened. There is no gladdening a corpse, try as we may.

An elixir of love may be a chimaera; but many passages in this book are an elixir of Douglas' wisdom – the wisdom of the heart, and of a munificent common sense that has been acquired by going deep into realms to which no one governed solely by common sense would dream of going – a golden mean, a balance acquired by going to extremes, an excellent example of "that tolerance which derives from satisfied curiosity" and of that sanity of practice which comes from knowing one's own capacities, desires, and limitations. It is Douglas in an incisively positive mood, half patriarchal, half avuncular. It is also the message of a happy man, who has got his values right for himself and knows it. It is his advice – though he would never have called it that – to the young; his legacy in word, as his life was in deed.

It would be foolish to suggest that "intimations of immortality" never

for a second entered Douglas' head. At the heart of all life is a mystery
which every lover recognises and salutes in his own way, even if it be by
silence, just as the mystic salutes it in his. Between Douglas and Sir
Thomas Browne – who in this book must surely have been his model –
there was much in common in intellectual curiosity and respect for life
in all its manifestations. Perhaps there was less philosophical difference
than might at first appear to be the case. One thing is certain: he and
Douglas shared a like attitude (though for entirely opposite reasons) to the
pomposity of mausoleums:

> "That cenotaph! Let me devour mine, while daylight
> lingers, with some tender darling; then pitch me,
> after death, into what Acherusian swamp you please."

> "... 'tis all one to lie in St. Innocent's churchyard,
> as in the sands of Egypt. Ready to be anything, in the
> ecstasy of being ever, and as content with six foot as
> with the *moles* of Adrianus."

CHAPTER TWENTY-EIGHT

Aldington, Prentice, Orioli
1931–1932

i

While Douglas was in Paris, Richard Aldington had arrived in Florence with Brigit Patmore, hoping to find Douglas. As he was not there, they were delighted to have the company of Orioli, whom Aldington had met two years previously in Florence and had known slightly since 1913. Orioli was doing his best to help and advise Frieda Lawrence, who had come to Florence to spend Christmas in his company. She wanted him to publish small limited editions of Lawrence's hitherto unpublished manuscripts, including *Apocalypse*, and also wanted to discuss the question of a library edition and publication of his letters. Aldington, who joined in these discussions, soon realised that they could do with some professional advice, and asked A. S. Frere, who was then managing director of Heinemann, if he would come over from the South of France. He did so, and after a long discussion

> agreed that he would issue the Letters and other posthumous works (allowing Pino his priorities and paying Frieda well for them), and also if possible take over all the other books and keep them in print – all of which he carried out loyally.

Reference to these negotiations, and other remarks about Lawrence, in Orioli's *Adventures of a Bookseller* were to be described by Aldington as a travesty, and he was convinced that Douglas, not Orioli, had written them. He was almost certainly right.

Douglas arrived back in Florence on 27th December, and sometime not long after this met Aldington and Brigit Patmore:

> Pino had given us some warning that Douglas would join us for lunch next day at Bianca. We had just sat down and were looking over the menu when a tall, powerfully-built, white-haired man came into the restaurant, glanced quickly round, and then made for our table. He introduced himself as Norman Douglas, apologised lightly for "in-

386

truding", and asked if he might sit at our table. As if he needed to ask! I was attracted by the neatness and exquisite cleanliness of his person – an aristocratic refinement of toilet – and by his manners. No plebeian ever achieves that seemingly effortless courtesy which puts one instantly at ease without the slightest trace of condescension. And yet the meeting was unconventional and bohemian, and the place a restaurant for commercial travellers, *contadini* and tradesmen of the quarter . . .

At that date Norman Douglas had just passed his sixty-second birthday. He was tall, heavily built without being fat, moving with the stiffness of age, but always straight-backed and dignified, walking always with a stick and the unhurried tireless stride of a mountaineer. From a distance and especially from the rear view, he looked very Scottish . . . His features were no longer handsome, though you saw he must have been very handsome in youth, but they were clearly marked. His nose was large and prominent but well-shaped, his lips well-formed and firm, the line of his jaw and chin full of power, his ears set close to his head, and his comely white hair still parted in the middle as it had been since he was a schoolboy at the Karlsruhe Gymnasium. His eyes, though lacking the strange beauty of our friend Lawrence's, were very expressive, especially in so old a man, and enlivened his whole face to animation when he was amused or interested or indignant. The coloured drawing of Norman Douglas by his friend Otto Sohn-Rethel gives a startlingly true likeness of his appearance in the 1930s. It gives his features exactly; and also his red complexion and the dissipated look which made the puritan Lawrence describe his face as that of "a fallen angel" . . . But that Sohn-Rethel sketch also preserves a curiously unhappy expression which was habitual to Douglas' face in repose, above all when he thought he was not observed. It was a look of suffering as well as of discontent.

Douglas seems to have liked Aldington and Mrs Patmore, and they stayed talking long after they had finished eating. Aldington had just written an appreciation of *Paneros* in the *Sunday Referee*, and there was a good deal of discussion about this and other books published by Orioli, and a good many meetings at Bianca or Betti's or Piccioli's followed. They observed at first hand his passion for grey truffles and cheese, the effluvium of which reminded Aldington and Mrs Patmore of acetylene gas. They were not allowed to try the jugged hare (which Douglas had given Charles Prentice not long before and which Prentice had praised so highly) because Douglas had become "convinced that Florentine hares were all cats, a prejudice which no argument could remove. We offered to buy him a hare with its pads on and take it to the restaurant. 'Pah! they'll steal it for themselves, and serve up the kitchen cat as usual'." Frere agreed that "he always said rabbit and hare was cat. It amused him to see the English reactions."

Equally characteristic were the notes . . . sent over by the hand of one of his friends among the street urchins, or left by himself, with some such warning as this: "Don't forget. Fusi at 8 sharp. Pino insists they have *abbacchio*, which he has ordered." *Abbacchio*, of course, is spring lamb; and what Norman liked – indeed insisted on – is that we should club together to order a whole fore-quarter or hind-quarter to be roasted at Fusi's . . . When the moment came he loved to take charge of the carving, for then he could cut himself the morsels he liked best, and not be at the mercy of the restaurant. The assertion in his note that Pino had "insisted" on lamb and had "ordered" it was one of his fictions. Most likely Pino would have preferred to invite us all to dine quietly with him in his flat, where he was well looked after by an old peasant woman, the mother of his assistant, Carletto. Pino's hankering after spring lamb was a convenient myth.

"He could cut himself the morsels he liked best . . .". This was the final action in a series in which his chief interest was undoubtedly "looking after Number One". If you ate with him, you had to eat the food he ordered for you, you had to put up with his management of the staff (or run his messages, not always by any means pleasant ones, as Magnus had discovered) and you had to be content with the portion he served you with. Aldington describes an occasion when Pino rebelled at this treatment. Douglas had "handsomely given everyone else what he didn't want himself, and having carved out the morsels he did want had slyly helped himself to both the kidneys":

Pino at that moment was drinking wine, but on perceiving this. . . . was overcome with indignation. Putting down his glass, and hastily and rather noisily wiping a wet mouth on the back of his hand to save time, he sprang to his feet, pointed a denunciatory finger . . . and declaimed: "Look at him! Because he have written *Sous Wind* he is a great man and steal our kidney!"

Frere says the story is apocryphal, and that Douglas enjoyed the story and used to encourage Pino to tell it.

ii

Early in the year, Pino went to London with Frieda and was away about three weeks. *Apocalypse* was prepared for the press, and published by Orioli on June 3rd. *Paneros* was going off moderately well; about half the edition had been sold in the first month. Chattos were contemplating a cheap edition of *How about Europe?*, were going to do an English edition of *Paneros*, a new edition of *London Street Games* as part of a series of short books called Dolphins, and in the same series had been promised an appreciative essay on Douglas by H. M. Tomlinson. Meanwhile Professor Richard MacGillivray Dawkins was preparing a paper on Douglas which would be published by Orioli and become the most interesting study of Douglas' work made in his lifetime. *Summer Islands* was to come out, published by Desmond Harmsworth in October. And Douglas was visited early in the year by Miss Carlotta Petrina, who was making drawings for an illustrated edition of *South Wind* in America.

Meanwhile, he was working hard, whatever remarks he may have made suggesting the contrary (as, for instance, telling Edward Hutton that he was apathetic, and doing nothing; or Bryher, that he found it hard to be interested in his work; or confessing to Aldington – so Aldington says – "that at times he spent much of his morning sitting down with his eyes closed and his head leaning against the wall because there was nothing he wanted to do"). He was not only working hard, but also working – no one can doubt it who reads *Looking Back* – with enjoyment; and writing better than at any time in the previous ten years. By the middle of September he had written two-thirds of this long book; and he certainly stuck to it with admirable persistence, spending less time this year out of Florence than ever before.

He was conscious of being in his sixty-third year – the year of the grand climacteric. It appears that he was somewhat superstitious about the seven-year periods into which life had been arbitrarily divided by ancient astrologers and soothsayers. He felt that on reaching the age of sixty-three he would reach a critical stage in his life; and as the grand climacteric was formerly associated in men's lives with a change in sexual activity and capacity comparable to the menopause in women, it was commonly believed that potency seldom survived the crisis. Douglas may well have shared this belief; as the sixty-third year approaches, and proceeds, he writes more of his age than previously, asking his correspondents what can be expected, in effect, of old age, and he tells Archie that he is "getting impotent, slowly and gracefully, but *surely*. It is a bloody nuisance, but it can't be helped". If it is true, he may simply have found what he was expecting; but a year later Orioli complains that Douglas, though always saying that he is impotent, "goes on like a bull".

Archie spent almost half the year in Freudenstadt, in Württemburg, having lost or given up his job with the Royal Horticultural Society. His marriage had also reached a crisis and he was full of domestic troubles. Robin, after making a good deal of money running booze across the

border from Canada into the United States, was caught and subjected to
the third degree; his car was confiscated, and he was deported. He arrived
in London a month or two later; and he, too, seemed to have come to the
end of his (second) marriage. It was not a good year for the Douglas
"children", actual or adopted; Eric had got involved with a married
woman; René was seriously ill with consumption; and Emilio had been
suffering from severe eye-trouble for several months.

iii

Douglas "stuck to it" (to use his own expression) admirably through the
cold Florentine winter, and finished writing *Chips of a Life* or *Yesterday* or
Looking Back, as it was finally called, in February 1932. It had been an
effort, this book of 170,000 words: "I have been working hard . . . ever
since we came back from Calabria," he wrote to Kenneth Macpherson,[108]
Bryher's husband, in January, "and am getting about sick of it. I am too
old to work, and I never liked it at any time of life. To Hell with work!"
It was typical of him, all the same, that he did not allow himself to get sick
of it until he was within a month of the end.

  Looking Back is a worthy book for anyone to have written at any age and
forms a fitting climax to Douglas' writing career. It is an impressive book
almost on the scale of *Old Calabria* and *South Wind*, yet his touch is so light
and elegant and his method so informal, that it easily escapes recognition
as one of the most memorable books of reminiscence written in the first
half of the century. Memorable – but incomplete, deliberately and most
ingeniously so. The notion of picking visiting-cards at random out of a
bowlful which had accumulated during his lifetime, and writing about the
people who had left them – and therefore about himself – was perfectly
suited to his purpose. Of certain periods in his life, or certain events, he
need say nothing. He could write with spontaneity and freedom, neither
more nor less than the mood of the moment dictated. So some names
from these cards are quoted – some, perhaps are invented – with only one
line of comment, and a few are followed by nothing but a question-mark;
still others produce several pages of reminiscence. The range and variety
of response called up by the cards is wide and typical, embracing every
mood and interest and activity of the author, and many of his travels. The
same characteristic combination of frankness and reticence is here displayed as in *Together*, but in sharper and more forceful contrast.

  Parts of the book had probably accumulated over the years, as the cards
had. The beguiling introductory pages are an elaboration and improvement of anecdotes rejected from the early version of *Alone*, most of which
was written in 1917; and parts of the longish article on Lawrence may have

been drafted at the time of the Magnus pamphlet. There are also extracts from abandoned manuscripts such as *A Tale of Elba* and *Love Among Ruins*, and from diaries and letters.

Consistently interested, he is consistently interesting: the broadness of his outlook, his sense of proportion and of humour, his zest and vitality without heartiness or conceit, his urbanity without smugness, his Rabel-aisian-Falstaffian-Boythornian excessiveness, are all combined, triumphantly and entertainingly in the "outrageous sanity" of his work, of which *Looking Back* is a splendid example.

For a book that was intended to be available to all, unlike *Some Limericks*, it is also the boldest of his books, for in it, here and there, he does not spare himself but "coolly admits to odious conduct that anyone else would try to forget". Boldness of a different sort, which would pass without question of its propriety nowadays, is also to be found in this book. He himself had such doubts about one passage that he wrote to Edward Hutton saying that it could not be printed in English:

> Do you know any really good latinist, who can translate this English sentence for me? I should have tackled it 50 years ago, but my Latin is gone to the dogs, like so much else. Quite an innocent sentence as it stands, but the context is such that it *can't* be printed in English: "So friendly had we grown, and so unblushing, that we would retire together into that inner room, all four of us, a family party . . ."

This is just one example – there are half a dozen others – which shows how he could over-estimate the immodesty or scandalousness of certain of his writings, or exaggerate the prurience or shockability of the public. The sentence duly appeared, in English. No one complained.

As to the truth of this episode, who knows? Douglas often told friends in later years that much of *Looking Back* – sometimes exaggerated to all of it – was fiction: "Made it all up, my dear – not a word of truth in it!" But that, of course, is nonsense. Douglas' saying, often repeated to Kenneth Macpherson, "Truth blends very well with untruth, my dear", may be borne in mind.

iv

The success of this book was in part due to the fact that Douglas had, in effect, a patron whom he was fairly sure would publish it. There can be little doubt that this knowledge gave him the confidence to undertake a book that was much longer than it would have been if he or Orioli had been publishing it; and gave him also the feeling that he could relax and stretch himself, and take what time he needed in order to obtain the finest distillation of experience that could be combined with holding the readers' interest. This "patron" was, of course, Charles Prentice of Chatto and Windus, who in the three and a half years since the publication of *In the Beginning* had become an assiduous and discerning friend as well as the publisher of nearly all Douglas' later books. Whenever business permitted, he liked nothing better than to snatch the opportunity of a few days, or a week or two in the company of Douglas and Orioli. On such occasions, they formed an indivisible trio, the existence of which was recognised by Richard Aldington who chose it as a convenient basis for his malicious and spiteful attack on Douglas in *Pinorman*.

"I am greatly excited to hear that Norman has really finished his book," wrote Prentice to Aldington in February. "I was chary of worrying him with questions myself, but now I'll send him a line." Douglas was probably quite aware of Prentice's excitement; and was determined to make the most of it, for he was also aware that this was probably the last substantial book that he would write. He was determined to sell it outright, and sell it dear. The proceeds, if sufficiently large, might be invested in some security that would at least bring him in enough income to cover his day-to-day expenses. He hated the royalty system, largely one suspects owing to his bitter experience with *South Wind* in America (though the proper object of hatred in that respect would have been the non-validity of the copyright laws in the USA); and he constantly advised his son Robin and various friends, to do as he did, and sell outright. All the same, his last two ventures, he wrote to Lowenfels, "were a *dismal* failure; none of them bought, and I am not going to bring out any more private editions".[109] The only course remaining that had any attraction for him was to sell outright for as much as he could get. He could not only expect to get a sizeable lump sum, but would also avoid the income tax which had lately been extended to authors living abroad; and as the gold standard had been abandoned and the pound had depreciated, he would ask for gold pounds. This is what he did. He asked for a thousand gold pounds, but as these could not be paid in actual gold, the sum would amount to more than a thousand depreciated pounds.

Chattos thought about it for quite a long time. Charles Prentice was keen to get the book, but he had to persuade his co-directors that Douglas' was a special case; and had to think of ways and means of trying to ensure that Chattos would get their money back. In the end they decided to do it – Douglas received his cheque for the first half of the sum in July – and to emulate Douglas' practice by bringing out a limited edition. This was to be in two volumes (£2-10-0) printed from the same setting as the ordinary commercial edition at 16/-. The whole of the limited edition (535 copies) was sold prior to publication, and in this way Chatto's knew that they were home and dry before the book appeared in the shops. The whole affair was a triumphant vindication of the Scotch canniness of the two principal protagonists – Douglas and Prentice – and a fairly spectacular success, since the whole business was carried through in the teeth of the worst economic crisis of the century.

As soon as he had a presentable manuscript, he went for a short holiday to Tunisia with Kenneth Macpherson. On his return he set about trying to reorganise his financial affairs. Most of his money – what there was of it – was in War Loan, which didn't seem to be very productive. He wrote for advice to Archie and to Hutton; and in the end decided to sell it and invest the money in an annuity which Hutton arranged for him. During the course of the next twenty years this annuity stood by him through all kinds of crises, and undoubtedly saved him from real need and embarrassment. He was always most grateful to Hutton for putting him on to it.

V

There was a time after he had finished *Looking Back* when he thought he was going to embark on another book; but this seems to have been only a flash in the pan, and he was soon alternately complaining that he could think of nothing to write about and that he would probably never write again. It would not be long before he claimed that he had written himself out, which was virtually true. He may have believed that the grand climacteric would affect his ability to write even as he believed it might affect his sexual potency; but a more likely reason for the feeling that he had written himself out is that necessity had imposed upon him in the years between 1924 and 1932 a surfeit of book-making. He had contrived books, had published and distributed them at considerable cost in physical and nervous energy, and had deliberately set out to tap the first-edition and collector's-items market, both of which he despised. He had succeeded better than anyone could have predicted; but at the cost of making himself thoroughly sick of the whole business of writing, presenting and selling books. He'd had enough! If he could manage to live without writing, he would; and he could, and did.

Douglas had never suffered from an irresistible urge to write – far from it – and just now he seems to have done as little writing of any kind as possible, correspondence included. He refused to write an introduction to Robin's book *Well, Let's Eat*; and used this first refusal as a useful excuse for not writing an introduction for Hutton ("*In any other circumstances I should have been delighted . . .*", etc); and to Bryher, who wanted him to review a book, he offered 100–150 words.

There was as yet no real reconciliation with Robin. When he arrived back from America and wrote, apparently rather morosely, of his experiences which had left him short of money, his father scraped up a fiver, but treated Robin to some gratuitous and rather sour home truths:

You seem to have mucked yourself up properly. Is it lack of realism? I suppose so; lack of the capacity to appreciate a good thing when it comes your way, and to turn it to profit. Any Italian boy with half your chances and half your talents would have feathered his nest long ago. Well, I hope you may still live to feather your own – and mine too, if possible.

He seems genuinely to have admired Robin's ability as a writer. He thought the section of his book *Booze-Runner* that had been previously published as an article on the inquisitional technique of the American police, excellent: "I don't think you can improve on it; I wouldn't alter it for anything ... admirable in style *and in tone*. A person who can write like that is very lucky." Nor is there any doubt about his genuine concern when Robin appeared to be seriously ill towards the end of the year.

vi

After the signing of the contract with Chattos, Douglas and Orioli went off to the Vorarlberg for nearly three weeks. Once again, Orioli kept a diary, in English this time, and vivid enough to convey a strong impression of Grete Gulbransson, his "fat step-sister" as Douglas was beginning affectionately to call her. The occasion (also mentioned in Orioli's autobiography *The Adventures of a Bookseller*) was a performance of Grete's play, *Battlog*:

We arrived at Schruns at about 3.30 a real parade of men and women in their local costumes are at the station with N's sister. The man have a rough top hat with large breams the woman have a curious hat which gives me the idea of Russian hat. Grete is just the same bitch as N says. Ach! Mine Bruter – Ach Pino – well come to Schruns and there is a mixture of German English and Italian and also French. We are introduced to the man who has written the music for Grete's play. The first actor and a good many of the actor and actresses are introduced to N and I.

A great success my dear Pino such a success is my play – you must crie – oh yes my dear, you must crie, and N must crie – oh, I count on all the tears – oh. Such a success. Here I am, Norman – Great – Great – You must crie.

Grete explain me the play is a local folkloristic play – a man from

Schruns who was a judge under the Napoleonic invasion and use to judge from his heart and not from the law. What happen to Herr Battlog of Schruns I don't know, as N and I we had enough of 5 minutes of the play. I did not understand a word and N the same as a large part of it was in Vorarlberg dialect.

There is a moment's steady contemplation here, too, of Douglas in a mood mentioned by Aldington as being typical of him at this period which might be considered by those who are unable or unwilling to discern the passages of unadulterated truth in *Pinorman*:

> In the all it was a dreary tyring day – a real fiasco I considered. N was very sade. He has been very sade all the time. I have not found out what troubles him. He say he is not happy not havin anything to do. He get much more tyred than usual, and is much more keen for a sleep than he used to be. A little fidgeting, not wanting to meet or see any one. I don't think he is enjoying as much as two year ago.

In the middle of their holiday they were joined by Charles Prentice for a week. In excited anticipation of meeting him within a few hours, Orioli wrote to Aldington and Brigit Patmore that he was putting on his best clothes, "a cordaroy complete which I had made in Florence on purpose for Charles, a bright yellow shirt with a blue tie . . . Charles' room is full of shealling-waxe, flowers and kind of charms against the W.W." This W.W., of course, was the Woolley-Woolley.

Douglas' "sade and tyred" mood is not heard of again; but there is a splendid picture of him in his better known rôle of energetic and vigorous walker, capacious eater and drinker, and in the seldom mentioned but quite frequent rôle of good-humoured and entertaining clown:

> Dinner ready at about 8. They are always very long here at Schlin, the charming proprietress is in very good mood today and this please N who is very fond of her. She never gives much to eat, but to day I had to much – I am very fond of her preserved home made prunes. I begin to feel frightfully tyred and stiff and sleepy, and I think then that we have to walk to Thuringen, Tsuring as the Alemanics say, and through the w.w. walley which is one of the worst for swamp. N has on the rook sack and he is going to put on galoches at the beginning of the valley. Charles and I we have our boots greased as if we were wading across the channel. The matter of fact N is very disappointed when we go through to find that no svamp is there at all and the going through is comparingly easy. Only a little accident, N would mention w.w. in the middle of the valley and pum down he went, stumbled and fell down, the lanterne went out. For a moment I tought that w.w. was in a real rage with us and

something terrible would happen. But I through my piece of sealing wax in the wood and we are left in peace. We light the lanterne and we go on. We come out of the valley thank God for that.

In my room there is nearly a litre and a half of good whyte wine so we sit there drinking with N making faces. We painted with black a pair of moustace on N's face and put my hat on one side, my God what a face. How we laugh. I laugh so much that I could not control a huge fart coming out and N with that face saying Farting! This went on for nearly two hour, till Charles and I were bursting with laugh and N went on saying: Go on go on I don't care what you do. Go on.

The "grand man" could relax in a most informal and appealing way. Perhaps he had to be appealing, in however grotesque a manner: as one grows older one becomes more dependent on others, both emotionally and in other ways.

vii

Among other ways in which he was dependent, the financial took first place. It cannot have been pleasant for so impetuous and freedom-loving a man to have been obliged by necessity in this way, but there is little doubt that he was. Nor is there much doubt that he made the most of such opportunities as were open to him, among his richer friends, of obtaining financial assistance. It can be taken for granted that he disliked the position he sometimes found himself in, when he was not only dependent on freely offered largesse, but was obliged to indicate a particular need to those who did not necessarily know that it existed. It was difficult to do this in an inoffensive and undemanding way while also sounding a note of urgency. In such a situation it was always the urgency of the need that was omitted from the appeal; the appeal itself was often no more than an indirect hint – he never asked outright for financial help. A typical example of this "hint-dropping" technique occurred during the autumn of 1932, when he kept on telling Kenneth Macpherson, in letter after letter, that he had tooth-trouble and was thinking of trying the dentist at Vevey. The inference is obvious: he hoped he would be invited to stay with the Macphersons or in a hotel at their expense, as had happened before, and that possibly even his fare and treatment might be paid. When these hints were apparently ignored, he had to refer to his financial situation: "This blasted pound sterling is sending me to *Hell*. I have to live *like a pig* nowadays – losing 25–30 lire every day, as compared to the old rate." In the end, he had to go to Paris: ". . . I have written to Kenneth 2–3 times without getting an answer, and simply *daren't* write any more. It's a nuisance, as Paris will cost me twice as much; but I've done my best."

Age was making itself felt: "I can't even *read* any more" he complained exaggeratedly to Archie: "Breaking up! Also, *all but* impotent: I give myself another 4–5 weeks. Bloody!" He also wrote at length about his "so-called neuritis", naming his remedies, but adding: ". . . the numbness in my hand has now persisted for 8–9 years, so I don't suppose that will go away again. The pain can be maddening at times, but I haven't had a bad attack for ages."

CHAPTER TWENTY-NINE

Moving Along
1933–1934

i

Age, and the economic crisis, had begun to establish themselves as unpleasant companions from which Douglas was unlikely to escape in the future. Added to these, political menaces were building up – first, Fascism in Italy, and later, the much greater menace of Hitler's Germany. Douglas, like others who had grown up in an age in which gentlemen had been able to ignore politics, defiantly tried to continue to do so. He succeeded, as will be seen, only in so far as not taking sides was concerned. He refused to become involved; but several of his friends were deeply committed, while the reverberations of Nazism and Fascism were to affect Douglas personally in his everyday life. Yet to "meddle" or intervene was unthinkable. Basically, perhaps, he was too cynical to believe that the human race could be redeemed from foolishness and insanity. If it wished to commit suicide who was he to try and stop it, when he had not even tried to stop an individual from doing so?[110] Also, supposing he had committed himself in public statements as an anti-Fascist and anti-Nazi, what, he might well have asked himself, would have been the positive benefit to mankind compared with the possibly disastrous consequences for himself and Orioli and other friends? And if one committed oneself in this fashion, might one not be identified as a sympathiser with socialists, communists and half a dozen other types of absurd world-reformers who were all, from his point of view, as mad as each other? As one of the champion non-joiners of his age, he could only say, when challenged: "*Not on your life, dearie!*"

ii

Douglas had gone to Paris again in January 1933 to see his dentist, but was once more unlucky: the dentist had influenza. Douglas hung on in Paris as long as he could afford to, saw a number of old friends, and had his portrait painted by Desmond Harmsworth. By early February he was at the Hotel Comte, Vevey, to which he had probably been invited by the

Macphersons after all. He had one tooth taken out; but he was also expecting crocodile trouble in Florence, yet returned there in the middle of the month. In March he was again back at the Hotel Comte ("Here we are – in the usual luxury!") because, so he wrote to Archie, "things were slightly threatening in Florence", and he didn't want to take any risks. He busied himself while at Vevey by compiling a catalogue of the Macphersons' library. The Florentine threat evaporated, and he returned again in April.

Meanwhile, Bryher had decided to go to Vienna, where her friend H.D. (Hilda Doolittle, who had been married to Richard Aldington) was beginning a course of psycho-analysis with Sigmund Freud. It looks as though an interview had been arranged for Bryher, and possibly also for Douglas, who went with her to Vienna, and who certainly met and talked with Freud. Douglas' interest may have been aroused or encouraged by Bryher, who had had him sent a book by Freud some time in February. In his thanking letter Douglas remarked of the frontispiece portrait that Freud had "a very good head", presumably because Freud's head, like his own, was dolicocepahlic rather than brachycephalic, which he apparently regarded as a retrogressive or at least an undesirable characteristic.

The meeting with Freud took place on 3rd April: there do not appear to be any indications of what was said, or how long the visit lasted. Douglas had a copy of *How about Europe?* sent to Freud very soon afterwards, and Freud, writing to him on 10th April, thanked him for three of his books: "I would like to return the compliment and send you some of my books. You would only have to express the wish; but I fear that my books do not please readers – they annoy or frighten them. I submit to my fate in this respect, but not without envy." A day later, Freud wrote again, a longer letter, saying that he was enjoying *Old Calabria*, which was the book he had chosen to read first. At the beginning of Chapter Six, though, he read that Frederick Barbarossa stayed in Venosa more often than in Sicily, and kept the planetarium there which had been given him by a sultan. "This," he wrote, "brings out my pedantry. I cannot reconcile it with my knowledge of Rotbart. I cannot believe that he was in Southern Italy or Sicily or that he was the friend of a Mohammedan." All the indications were that Barbarossa's grandson Frederick II was the man, especially as he had been confused more than once with his grandfather[111]: originally it had been he who, according to popular legend, was to be kept prisoner in the Kyffhäuser until the liberation of Germany and the creation of a new German Reich. Consequently Adolf Hitler could be regarded as a caricature-like reincarnation – "so the past always glimmers through the very latest moment in time. It is the Messiah-belief of the Germans. May these lines show you how much interest I am finding in your work."

Douglas admired Freud. He liked his scientific approach to the mysteries of psychology; and after meeting him he was impressed by Freud's stoical attitude to the cancer of the jaw which had already troubled him for several years. As to psycho-analysis, perhaps it was useful for those who were desperate; but he did not like it. Not many people of his generation did.

"The Messiah-belief of the Germans . . ." Perhaps this phrase in Freud's letter, or a letter that Douglas received a few weeks later from Oscar Levy[112] made Douglas think, as Levy did, about the implications of Old Testament teaching in Germany. Levy and Douglas wrote to each other about it, and Levy's views were later expressed in a letter he sent to the *New English Weekly.* That journal had published a number of views concerning the behaviour of the Germans, and a good many people had expressed astonishment that a highly civilised people should have sunk to such depths as were demonstrated by persecution of the Jews.

"The explanation," wrote Levy, "is that the modern Germans are less a civilised, than a religious people":

> Their religion comes, strange to say, right out of the Old Testament. The Chosen Race idea which is at the root of the German mentality, springs from the soil of Israel. Israel likewise produced, long before Hitler and Goebbels, its *Ahnenprüfer* (ancestor examiners) in the historical figures of Ezra and Nehemiah. They forbade all intercourse with foreign women and even had already existing marriages nullified (Ezra x). They, too, were all for purity of race, for pride of race, for power of race. The Germans, following their footsteps, do not know how reactionary they are and how akin spiritually to those whom they most detest. Neither do the Jews suspect that it is their own message which now turns against them and that there is no outward difference between the shield of David and the *Swastika* of Hitler. This Hitlerism is nothing but a Jewish heresy.

Levy went on to show that Bolshevism, the other powerful creed threatening Europe, also derived from the Bible, in this case from the New Testament. He wished English politicians could see these movements for what they were, but

> these politicians are either too religious themselves to take an independent view of religion, or they are too irreligious to have any knowledge of religion. Yet this knowledge is important for all of us, if only to understand that there is a gulf between religion and civilisation and that, to a certain extent, they exclude each other.

Douglas wrote to congratulate Levy on his letter, and said he ought to write on the subject at greater length. "No use fighting a disease without a proper diagnosis and yours is the proper diagnosis. Go right ahead. If you have no publisher, I shall see that your MS goes into print." Eventually, after further prompting from Douglas, Levy embarked on this project. But that was not until three years later.

iii

In the spring Douglas went with Pino, Charles Prentice and Ian Parsons, Prentice's junior partner at Chattos, to Calabria. Orioli kept a diary of this holiday, which was afterwards written up, together with memories of other Calabrian visits (and a visit later in 1933 to Scanno and the Sabine hills) and became the book called *Moving Along* (1934). The Scanno diary survives, but the Calabrian one seems to have disappeared; it was probably dismembered either by Orioli himself as he wrote it up, or by Douglas when he took Orioli's manuscript in hand to render it in English that would be acceptable to a publisher. The book was written in order to bring in some money; Orioli had given up his bookshop two or three years earlier and had been forced out of limited-edition publishing by the economic crisis; Douglas felt fairly sure that he had shut up shop as a writer with the completion of *Looking Back*; both men, therefore, hoped to make what they could out of Orioli's diaries. The Calabrian diary which became *Moving Along*, published by Chatto and Windus, was to be a trial run.

Although this is a pleasant enough book, and comes up to the average leisurely conversational type of travel book of the period, it lacks bite and character. Little is left of the vivaciousness and vividness of the descriptions and comments that are typical of Orioli in his extant diaries: they have been deadened into a kind of Douglioli pasta which lacks the character of either contributor. Sometimes the result is positively stilted, as in the conversation on page 35, to which Aldington justifiably took exception. The book is full of Douglasian aphorisms and ejaculations, as Aldington also points out, and the beginning ("We have been moving along; we shall be moving along for some little time . . .") and end ("so much I remember distinctly. And also this: that our way home was all in the dark. The lights of Genazzano had been extinguished") are typically Douglasian. Douglas almost certainly saved himself trouble by following Orioli's sequence of events and allowing the printable comments to stand. The descriptions and comments are of a kind that would have been treated differently by Douglas himself, since the interests of the two men were different; therefore, in trying to do justice to Pino in this respect, Douglas effectively cuts out his own typical flavour; and in cleaning up Orioli's English, he tends to nullify what would otherwise be lively. "If only," as Aldington wrote, "he had tried to preserve the naive and pungent imperfections of Pino's text!"

In spite of these criticisms, *Moving Along* contains much of interest to the student of Douglas. Here we learn, if we did not know it already, of his stoical acceptance of discomfort, as on the occasion when the four travellers arrived, soaked to the skin, at Albidona:

> There was one chair in this room, no light of any kind, a small brazier of lighted charcoal on the floor, and a few wooden boxes to sit on. An old man bent nearly in two was the owner of this establishment. He lit a feeble oil lamp . . . We sat on the wooden boxes, warmed our soaked legs as best we could, and drank some wine . . . I asked the old man whether there was a chance of finding any rooms to sleep in. "I don't think so," he said . . .
>
> Norman said he felt quite at home here. He was really in Old Calabria now, and I could see he was enjoying it. We could sit round the brazier all night, he said, getting our clothes dry gradually, smoking our pipes and drinking wine. What more could anybody want? As to sleeping – damn it, if one cares to sleep, one need only rest one's elbows on one's knees and put one's head into one's hands, and there you are. Delicious!
>
> [They were rescued by the local policeman, who took them to his home.] There was a lovely fire burning in one corner of the room, a real consolation. His wife, who had evidently gone to bed already, was told to dress again and prepare us some boiled eggs and salad and cheese and bread and wine. Neither Charles nor Ian could eat much at first; they were still shivering with cold. I did my best to come up to the occasion, but Norman ate more than the rest of us put together and then regretted that he could eat no more; he said a man could not expect to have a proper appetite at his time of life.
>
> We were just going to bed, when the policeman announced that a native journalist desired to interview Norman . . . A journalist in Albidona! . . . Tired as we were, we felt inclined to send the journalist to Hell. Ian persuaded us to change our minds. He said the journalist was doubtless the policeman's friend, and that it would be impolite not to speak to him after all the kindness we had received from these people . . .
>
> The journalist came in. He was accompanied by a friend; they were both young men of about twenty-four and both of them sickly-looking. We exchanged some elaborate compliments and greetings; then the journalist set to work. He asked questions and his friend wrote down the answers in longhand, while the other was thinking out the next question to ask. Norman gave them a marvellous interview; I only wish some

journalist of real experience had been there. They were both infatuated with him. I never heard him speak like that about Calabria. When he talks to me, he swears at the filthy food and accommodation, the pestilential bugs, and the beastly malaria which he caught there. Now he said that there was no such country on earth, and he named renowned persons and places and products and customs which the journalist had never heard of, and which perhaps never existed . . . Nothing was too good for Calabria! It was a Paradise, and its people the most charming and handsome and cultured in the whole world. What a grand historical tradition, what rivers and mountains, what a climate, what lovely women . . .

Descriptions of the food and sleeping quarters the party encountered on this two weeks' holiday reinforce one's suspicion that Douglas – who after all was sixty-four years old – had a masochistic streak, despite his contemptuous remarks about masochists in other contexts. This raises the question of how greatly, if at all, he loved Calabria; for only love or something nearly as powerful, could have made the sacrifice worth while. He had adopted Calabria, made it his own, and it was of course filled with intimate memories for him – but so were many other places. It seems likely that his love for Calabria did not equal his love for the Vorarlberg, his homeland, or his love for Siren Land, the Sorrentine peninsula, but that it came next in his affections, and that unlike the other two places, there was a certain amount of hate intermingled with the love.

There are interesting glimpses in *Moving Along* of the party on the road, how they formed a pool of money, with equal contributions from each individual, each one in turn being "banker" of the current pool: "All expenses must come out of the pool – food, smoking, journeys, hotels, clothes, love affairs; whoever pays for anything out of his own pocket is a fool." There are also descriptions of their amusements – or at any rate, the printable ones – their teasing and practical jokes and high spirits; and of how Douglas always had a pocket full of sweets for the young and a box of snuff for the old, of his way with eggs (the yolks of which he never ate, but tossed on to the plates of his companions) and with inquisitive natives:

"That photographic machine: what did you pay for it?"
"Five thousand lire" said Norman, without giving me a chance to reply.
"Five thousand lire! That is an enormous sum of money. It must be a very good one."
"It is."
"And what did your watch cost you?"
"I cannot say. It was given me by the Sultan of Turkey."

"I wish he would give me one too. And your walking-stick?"

"My stick," said Norman, "cost eight hundred and fifty lire. It is made of wood which grows in the Island of Zamorgla and nowhere else."

"You must be millionaires."

"We are." Then Norman turned to me: "Never call yourself poor when you talk to these people. Say you are a millionaire, and that you mean to keep every penny of your money and to pay them rather less than what anybody else pays. That will make them respect you. And do you want to make them hate you? Never call them robbers or cut-throats: they like that! Call them rich. Say you know they are rich, and that everybody else knows it too, however poor they may pretend to be. It makes them furious."

So it might, in such a poverty-stricken countryside! If Douglas did much teasing of that kind, he was lucky to survive. But he probably didn't do any of it – despite his advice – unless in an obviously genial manner.

iv

Once back in Florence, Orioli lost no time in getting down to work on the book. And Douglas, about six weeks later, had begun to type it out. It was "uphill work", he wrote to Kenneth Macpherson.

The reminiscences might not have been the only thing brought back to Florence from Calabria, Douglas feared. He wrote, also to Macpherson in Vevey, that he was "a *little* worried about certain symptoms". He wonders whether he could see a specialist at Lausanne, "and whether you could manage me just now" – otherwise he could go to Paris. This carefully worded signal was reinforced a few days later by a letter from Orioli, Douglas having already – on the day Orioli wrote – arrived at Vevey: ". . . I am delighted that Uncle Norman is with you. I have been rather concern [sic] about his health. I don't think he is feeling as well as he pretends to feel. I wish you would persuade him to see a specialist as I don't think Dr Giglioli is any good to N."

The specialist said Douglas' symptoms – which, as ever, he seems to have diagnosed for himself – were "nothing to do with syringomyelia" but were simply signs of a common form of arterio-sclerosis, nothing worth talking about, and that "whoever at my time of life has not got one form or other of it, is a *shit*: a man who has not known how to live. He said I could go to Africa (my test question) as much as I liked. So that's that." Syringomyelia is "dilatation of the central canal of the spinal cord, or formation of abnormal tubular cavities in its substance" (*Shorter OED*).

Why did he think he had got that? Or was the whole business made up or grossly exaggerated, so that he could once again make a strategic retreat from Florence?

After leaving Vevey (10th July) he went to the Vorarlberg, staying, to begin with, with his half-sister Grete Gulbransson, whom he found "frightfully hard up". This visit was followed by two short holidays in Italy with Orioli, working on *Moving Along*. The second of the holidays was taken partly "because my second son turned up in Florence with a *horrible* girl – they made it quite impossible for me to stay there!" To Archie he wrote that Robin seemed to be seriously ill – "heart and stomach, and he has *no money at all*. I sent him £5 . . .". And to Robin he wrote that he found his news "disquieting". He hoped that the adhesions from which Robin was suffering were "not too troublesome", and could not resist adding "You got rid of one of them at all events, in Paris", referring presumably to the "horrible" girl. "Why," he wrote with that complete disregard for the feelings of his correspondents that he some-times affected in his more unlikely suggestions and recommendations, "Why don't you become a Catholic and join some religious order? A very good life in *England*: not here. I have two friends who have done it, and found a solution to all their worries."

When the Calabria book had been revised and sent off to Chatto's, he and Orioli went down to Sant' Agata for a week, towards the end of which they were shown a little flat belonging to a man called Matteo Esposito: "He was a little drunk and we liked him at once." They also liked the flat which they decided to take for the summer. On their last night it was raining; as there was nothing else to do they drank, and continued drinking. Next morning before lunch "Norman shaved, but he was so shaky that he had to held his razor with both hands and would have used three if he had them".

v

All through the years since their meeting, Douglas and René had kept up a regular and frequent correspondence. René had married sometime before August 1925, when he and his wife visited Douglas at Sant' Agata; and latterly had become a schoolmaster at Vence. He had also contracted tuberculosis. For this reason, as soon as René's regular letter failed to arrive in December 1933 and Douglas had no reply after writing four times, he became alarmed, and wrote to his friend "Auntie"[113] to ask if she had seen René lately and whether he was still at Vence: was he ill? Douglas may have arrived at Menton before she could reply, and was soon in no doubt as to René's state of health:

31 Dec 1933

Dear Pino

   Went to see René yesterday. He seems to be at the last gasp; but, as I
could not talk to the doctor who was away, I cannot of course say for
certain. He was in a miserable hole, with a bed too short for him and a
tiny dark window looking due north. I wired to his father to come at
once and take him to some proper place. I shall go to Vence on Wednesday again . . .

René did not improve. Douglas went "nearly every second day" from
Menton to Vence to see him. He could not get up, and Douglas feared it
was a "very bad case"; when he had done what he could and had had
René moved, and called in his father, and stayed as long as he could afford,
he went back to Florence, about the middle of January. Auntie continued
to visit and keep in touch with René and send news of him to Douglas.
   René died on 2nd March, not in the sanatorium to which he had been
moved, but in "a dingy cottage specially hired for that purpose. It is not a
pretty way to treat the dying."
   René's death cannot have been anything but painful for Douglas –
René, whose close friend he had been for more than fifteen years, for
whom he had done so much and had wished to do so much more, a
charming and gifted young man whom everyone liked, the possessor of a
natural athletic ability and a strong bent for things mechanical, whose
life, according to Douglas, was ruined by his parents insisting on his
preparing for the civil service. As he was unable to do what he was best
fitted to do, he became apathetic and indifferent, drifted from job to job,
lost his drive and energy, and cared nothing about his health. "He had
suffered so continuously," wrote Douglas, "for the last six years and so
acutely during the last six months that one cannot be sorry it is now over.
He told me himself he was yearning to be finished with it."

vi

About three weeks after René's death, Grete Gulbransson died, quite
suddenly and unexpectedly of pneumonia, at the age of fifty-one. She
"was the last link between me and my family, as my brother doesn't
count" he wrote to Bryher; and to Archie he grumbled mildly that Grete
"had heaps of things which ought to belong to us, as they were my
father's property and had nothing to do with either my mother or Gretl's
father, but my mother grabbed them when my father was killed and
simply gave them to Gretl. Among them are my father's diaries which
were of no use to her, but which *she would not even let me see.*"

Douglas' health did not improve – nor get noticeably worse. If any treatment existed which could ameliorate his circulatory trouble neither Dr Giglioli nor the Lausanne specialist had provided it. He had a blood test, and began to go to Giglioli daily for injections, but could not notice any difference in his condition. He visited a specialist in Rome in early April, who suggested a slightly different treatment, but Douglas postponed the adoption of this treatment for a few weeks. He wrote to Archie that the trouble had begun "exactly ten years ago" and had got worse in the last one and a half years. He presumably knew; but there is no other evidence – even his own – from 1924 to support this statement. He was fairly, but not unusually, grumpy, and had a go even at Auntie who had done so much for him and René. She was making him a pullover, the first of a good many that followed through the years both for him and for Orioli, and wrote that she proposed sending it to him by some friends who were coming to Florence:

> So frightfully good of you to knit me a sweater! Whatever you do, however, don't send it by the hand of your young and lovely American couple – I really can't see such people just now (had three of them dumped on me the day before yesterday: without warning). And I shall be away at Easter, and on the 8th I have my publisher coming here on his way to Greece and must devote myself entirely to him. So I hope you won't mind if I say that I prefer not to meet them, however exquisite their car may be. I want to live my own life, which won't last much longer, and to Hell with all globe-trotters. What does one get out of such people? A moral stomach-ache – besides having to stand them a lunch or a dinner, for which you get the Devil's thanks. Sheer waste of time! I've had my dose of them.

It must have seemed to Auntie that he was going a little too far, for a couple of weeks later he wrote again on the same subject:

> So glad to get yours of the 4th, but grieved to notice that you seem to be huffy about those Americans. The fact is, I am simply over-run with such people, especially at this season. The day you wrote I had a letter asking me to get rooms for two in a certain pension – why the Hell can't they write to their blasted pensions direct, instead of plaguing me – and not only that, but to order a certain dinner at a certain hour in a certain restaurant for them. So simple! I just have to trot round all day for them. Since your letter came, at least four other people have written to me from Paris and Rome and God knows where, asking me to do this and that for them on their arrival here. It may be different for you. You get these people and may be able to sell them something in

return. I have nothing to sell them, and I find them quite demoralizing, especially those utterly empty Americans, who expect a lunch or dinner as a matter of course. What do you get in return? Not only nothing, but a sensation of disgust with the whole world. They make me spew, and their ridiculous cackle, to which I have to listen, upsets me for the whole day.

The acceptance by Chatto and Windus of Orioli's book had encouraged both him and Douglas to embark on another. Although described by Douglas as "huge" – which it hardly is – this second book was probably Orioli's autobiography, *Adventures of a Bookseller*. They intended to write it at Sant' Agata, where they had reserved a flat the previous autumn. Of the book's profits "I shall get half – about £250 – if it is ever finished," Douglas wrote to Archie.

vii

The visit to Sant' Agata turned out to be disastrous because of the bitchiness of the landlord's wife and the cantankerous drunkenness of the landlord himself. After a few days of it, Douglas and Orioli decided to move to Ischia. On the boat, they got a very good bottle of white Epomeo:

"'Delicious my dear! We are coming to the right place. Such wine. We shall work like hell at Baldino.'

'And drink like fishes,' I said.

'And why not? Can you tell me why not? And what about it?'

And down went another glass of Morgera's white Epomeo."

They got fixed up satisfactorily at Baldino's, and after dinner Douglas made friends with the chef, Ciccio. "We liked him and told him about what he must do in cooking for the future." So that was that.

They made a second beginning on Ischia, on 10th June. They spent the mornings working: "Half past seven, breakfast on the table! N. has started working, I am doing this diary." Usually, the rest of the day was given up to pleasure – walking, idling, sitting in *osterie*, exploring in the mountains, talking to young and old, and looking (most of the time in vain) for privacy in which to carry their casual acquaintanceship with boys and young men a step further.

In this diary we learn much about the informal behaviour of this strange pair: the elderly white-haired magisterial man who liked playing with little boys, and his shorter, stouter, much more volatile and excitable companion who was fifteen years younger.

Douglas was supposed to be on a diet, recommended by a doctor in Rome, which excluded meat (and tobacco) and included very little wine.

The latter recommendation – whether or not the others were observed – can hardly have been adhered to. He and Orioli between them commonly drank three bottles of wine with their evening meal alone, sometimes more, and a good deal during the day as well. They were frequently "squiffy", as Orioli calls it in his diary, at almost any hour in the late afternoon, and nearly always so by the time they went to bed.

Edward Hutton, who said he had never seen Norman drunk, only "tight", might have changed his mind – or his adjectives – if he could have seen Douglas and Orioli staggering along Ischian roads in zig-zag fashion roaring with laughter and smashing a wine bottle on the marble steps of a public monument at Porto, where "N, years and years ago was terribly sick after who knows of how many bottles of Epomeo . . . This night we were not sick, but loughed and loughed and sent to hell all the sits [shits] we have met in our life and the one we shall still meet." Those Ischians who were always "watching and interfering" – deliberate or chance chaperones – and those who failed to come up to expectations or to do as Douglas (especially) and Orioli wished, became shits one by one, finding a place on a list of Authentic Shits, Doubtfuls, and Non-Shits compiled by Douglas and Orioli. To start with there were eighteen Authentic Shits, three Doubtfuls, and twelve Non-Shits. By the end of their visit, some of the last category had been relegated to the first and were joined there by more.

Among the Non-Shits was "Il cane vulcanico, male puppy-spaniel". This was a dog encountered late one night by Douglas and Orioli when they were drunk:

> It was a nice young dog blak and white, what they call here a cane da caccia. N. liked it at once and said he was going to sleep with the dog. "My dear when the devil is hungry eats flies."
>
> It was curiouse how the dog took to N. at once. He followed us home. N. took him in his room and after he told me that the dog was very satisfactory with a real volcanic lust. In the middle of the night N. farted so lowdely that it frighten the dog and he started barking which prevented me to sleep.
>
> "Such a nice young dog, and so volcanic" said N. in the morning.

Quite a number of lines in this diary are very carefully and thoroughly inked out, almost certainly by Douglas, though it seems unlikely that the diary as it stands would have been offered – it would certainly not have been accepted – for publication. Yet passages like the above are allowed to stand. For what reason? Presumably, because Douglas still wished to shock, still wished to convey the impression to whoever might pick up the diary that he indulged in bestiality, still derived satisfaction from Orioli's approving description. It is difficult to know whether such an attitude is more, or less, eccentric than bestiality itself, if it occurred.

Orioli's diary shows Douglas' moodiness, a characteristic which can be deduced from any representative selection of his letters and from the written and spoken reminiscences of friends, but which is seldom if ever mentioned directly and given a name. "I never met a person in my life that have so many moods" wrote Orioli, and proceeds to give examples of some of the moods of one moody day. A mood of frank and sober reminiscence is succeeded by an exploring mood, which is succeeded by a "capricios wine mood":

> Three bottles are brought all different kind of wine . . .
> The bill is very stiff. N. started a nice complaining with the waiter about every item he told them what for. He told them that for a little bit of unitable tough Cow's meet they had the courage to charge us 10 lire. Next time they will charge 20. The son of the proprietor, said that it was not an cow's steak but a piece of Filetto an ordered the waiter to bring the entire joint foe us to inspect. N. goes into an exclamation: Beeeeellooooo, Dovrebbe essere fotografato. We go away without paying. We shall have to pay one day. Anyhow N. managed to reduced the bill.
> After that we went to the Pizzeria. The padrone had promised us to get a good bottle of red wine, he has not done it . . . N. now was in a full quarreling mood. Why not?

On another day he has a "pregnant woman mood" when he cannot stand food that he normally likes. And there were moods of anger, when he would get in a "terrible rage". For instance, after a day of disappointments and a filthy dinner he returned home to find that a table had been taken out of his room by the Baldino girls:

> He replaced the table from the one in the entrance throwing on the floor what was on the table. His rage did not pass even when he was in bed, in trying to put out the light he made his watch drop from the night table, he called me from my room to find it, the glass was smashed, N. said: "Give it to me the bloody watch" and zump he [trough it] against the wall. "It has done its time the bloody fucking watch. I had it since the armistice day."

Orioli bought him a new one.

There are calmer, merrier, more sunlit moments and one impressive pied-piper scene. Douglas had been given a little tin toy by one of the boys he had made friends with. It made the noise of a cicada and Douglas was so enchanted with it that he ordered fifty to be sent over from Naples.

Orioli calls them "little tickytitic toys", and he and Douglas were going to distribute them among the boys of Testaccio:

> At five we started for Testaccio with our fifty tickytitics . . . arrived at Testaccio about six. We are rather disappointed in not seeing boys about. Lucky thing we found Raffaello the ugly shit, who in a few minutes he collected over 40 boys including the village idiot.
> The osteria was now full of boys all very eager to get the tickititic. We arranged all the boys outside one door and let them come in one by one get the toy and then go out by the other door. They got nealry mad with excitement, they nearly push down the door to come in they jump on us every one was crying: "A me, a me signor, uno a me uno a me," some had to go without, two of them were crying we had to give them sweets and money. The noise now was terribly everyone was playing the tickititic. It was quite a concert. In the piazza the parroco and the other people were very surprised at the nois of the tickititics, women came out of the houses . . . men left to work in order to hear the tickytitics. It was like if it had been a festa.

After that, they started singing, and drove away with the cabman and three boys, singing all the time.

Such interludes, when the two chief subjects of the diary seem to be positively enjoying themselves, are exceptional. The prevailing mood is rather sour and liverish. One has the impression of a pair of fairly selfish, rather silly, perhaps rather despairing men, no longer young, who are trying somewhat clumsily and ineffectively to extract love or affection from younger people who seem by inference not only to be indifferent to their charms, but are perhaps secretly half afraid and half derisive. It is a sad picture of two men, who after nearly three months on the island are as lonely, outside their own indissoluble relationship, as when they arrived. The only heartening feature of the diary is its testimony on almost every page to the complete trust and affection for each other which existed between Douglas and Orioli.

In August they were joined by Emilio for a week, and then by Carletto for ten days. Douglas and Orioli left at the end of the month and went to meet John Mavrogordato at Naples where he was seeing his family on to a boat for Spain. They all had dinner together, and Douglas and Orioli took him back to Ischia for a few hours. After two nights in Naples they all set off for Rome and Florence.

Orioli's book *Moving Along* had been published while they were at Sant' Agata. Douglas, going a little too far (as so often), informed Archie that it was "ENTIRELY written by me (entre nous)". It got some good notices. *Venus in the Kitchen*, however, had no success. Douglas refused to let his own name appear in the book when Pinker enquired if it might; and in November he wrote and asked for the manuscript to be sent back. In November, also, was published posthumously Grete Gulbransson's book of family reminiscences, *Geliebte Schatten*. Also, in this month, Douglas and Orioli decided to visit India, or to be more specific, Goa. Apart from a desire to revisit the country, it looks as though Douglas may have thought there was a book in it: "I thought I was able to shut up my own shop [i.e. writing], but it looks as if I were going to be obliged to open it again" he wrote to Robin; and Orioli wrote to Professor Dawkins that he would try to make Douglas write a book about India.

They embarked on the Japanese liner *Terukumi Maru* at Naples on 22nd December. "I hope there will not be too many English passengers: no plum puddings etc, etc," he wrote to Bryher.

CHAPTER THIRTY

India, and Other Travels
1935–1936

i

The visit to India turned out to be mainly a visit to Ceylon, where they spent nearly a month, followed by only seventeen days on the mainland. They were driven out of India by the heat. In spite of this, and a crowded itinerary, Orioli completed a diary recording their visit in about 90,000 words. Most of it is a rather dull and muted chronicle, probably because it was written, as the other diaries were not, for publication. It was offered to Chatto and Windus presumably as a successor to *Moving Along*, but was not accepted. Although the book records nothing disgraceful, Norman is referred to throughout as Lucian.

On reaching Ceylon, they went by car and rail to every district and type of country. Most of Norman's earlier visits (in 1900), described in *Looking Back*, were repeated, with many new ones added, and it is evident that both men enjoyed almost every minute of their stay in the island. In addition to seeing all the recognised sights and landmarks, they climbed Mt. Pedro (8320 feet) and ate as many curries as they could before leaving the island, Norman even being upset on one occasion because he could not have curry for breakfast. Of the ancient buried cities, they carried away nostalgic memories of Mihintale where they sat for hours in the peaceful precincts of the Ambustella dagoba, and Orioli could "see Lucian's face beaming with happiness".

By the time they reached Goa, the heat was such that Lucian was only really comfortable in a cold bath, preferably with a glass of whisky. He stayed in it for a long time, smoking his pipe, as was apparently his habit. Here we also learn that he used, and had always used, a cut-throat razor, and called safety razors "baby's razors". An addition to this slightly aggressive masculinity was made at Trichinopoly, when he was offered a Manila cigar: "Lucian sent them to hell, telling them to offer their manilla to ladies and not to men." They had come with letters of introduction to the Patriarch of Goa, but were afraid of using them as they had heard that they might have to kiss his feet – "What next!"

Goa was the place on which they had fixed their sights from Florence, but its charms do not seem to have appealed, although one might gather that the charms they had looked forward to were human rather than architectural. From Goa they went to Agra, and thence to the Taj Mahal, Fatepur Sikri, and the Fort of Shah Jehan. These were the highlights of their Indian visit. At Bombay they inspected the Towers of Silence and had the simple effects of the place explained to them.

They returned on a P. & O. liner, the *Kaiser-i-Hind*, and distinguished themselves by not dressing for dinner, a conspiracy in which they were joined by James Strachey when he came aboard at Port Said. Their last night on board, before disembarking at Malta, was spent with Strachey. He was very different from his brother Lytton, they decided; the only thing that reminded them of his brother was the peculiar movement of his hands.

They arrived in Florence on 3rd March. Orioli was asked if he was glad to be back. "My answer is," he wrote at the end of *A Glance at the East*, as his account of their journey is called, "that if I could, I would pack up again at once and take the first boat sailing for Colombo or Bombay or the end of the world, if Lucian would come. With such a companion I could go anywhere."

ii

At about the time of their return to Florence Captain Angelo Ravagli arrived in the south of France from New Mexico to collect D. H. Lawrence's remains and take them back to Taos to Frieda Lawrence. But first it was necessary to have Lawrence's body exhumed and then cremated. Douglas, in correspondence again with Auntie, was avid for details:

                                                                25 March 1935

My dear Auntie,

So glad to get your exciting letter about Lawrence. Now do tell me more – about bones and skull etc etc. I love macabre details. And what is the Captain going to do with all this golden hoard, now that he can't get back to Mexico? . . .

I think the idea of writing your memoirs is delicious! You can pay out old scores, and also – don't forget this – invent as much as you please. I am doing my best to stay alive, if only for the pleasure of reading them . . .

Do send those photos of the exhumation, and I shall be delighted to pay for them.

                                                    Your loving
                                                        Uncle N

Auntie appears to have sent him two lots of photographs, presumably of the exhumation.

There was not much to do on his return to Florence, except take up the threads of his fairly complicated private life, and make up, as he told Archie, for lost time in India where making love was very difficult if you don't know the language. He was concerned about a sprained thumb; and his hands and feet were asleep all the time, he wrote; but he was not going to see any more doctors, just wait for the next development.

In July he received an advertisement for Robin's book *Booze-Runner*, and wrote off to him in the hope of getting in touch again:

Florence
1 July 1935

My dear Robin

I received today the circular about your Booze-Runner which I shall of course get (leaving Florence tomorrow for 10 days in the South). So I write your publishers on the chance of your getting this note, and after having vainly written to your former London address several times to ask how you are doing and where you are. The last I heard (from a newspaper) that you were stuck on Ellis Island owing to some passport difficulty . . . And drop me a line if you ever get this note. Best luck to Booze-Runner

Your loving
Dad

With Archie there were no such problems of communication; correspondence was constant and confiding; and now the father had reached a time in life or a state of health which induced him to feel that he should get Archie to come to Florence to discuss his inheritance. Anyway, he was thinking of going to the Vorarlberg, and would Archie like to join him there? But first of all he was going to Chianciano to take a course of carbonic acid baths for his hypertension, as ordered by the doctor. Orioli would go with him and do his liver-cure at the same time, and after that they would be going to Ischia "for certain reasons, in accordance with a promise made last August . . ." He had heard from Robin, in America, that he had had osteomyelitis and nine operations for it, and was working on a farm in Connecticut.

He and Orioli were about ten days at Chianciano. Douglas took only four baths: ". . . the whole thing is a fake. What is the matter with me – tingling of extremities – is the brain, parts of which are no longer nourished, owing to sclerosis of certain blood vessels there. There seems to be nothing to be done."

Late in September, he was in Bludenz, asking Archie if he would like to join him there (£20 enclosed), an invitation that was followed in a day or two by further information: "The state of affairs is this. I left Florence hurriedly (*sap. sat*) and didn't know when I might be returning – *possibly never*. But this morning I have received quite reassuring news from Orioli; I wait for one more letter from him."

The one more necessary letter from Orioli turned into two more, but Douglas returned on 1st October, and five or six days later Archie arrived in Florence by car (". . . one of those ridiculous mousetraps"). Mousetrap or not, Douglas lost no opportunity of being driven by Archie in a series of daily outings all over Tuscany and Emilia. Meanwhile, father and son had looked at and discussed the disposition of Douglas' possessions, and Douglas felt that he was now better equipped than before to make a will.

It was not simply Douglas' age and state of health that turned his thoughts to will-making. The international situation, especially official relations between England and Italy, gave cause for apprehension. It was the time of Mussolini's rape of Abyssinia, of Britain's half-hearted effort to stop it, and the failure of the League of Nations to impose sanctions. The effects of the political situation were felt by all English residents in Italy. Some of them packed up and cleared out: others, like Reggie Turner, took the view that they owed a great deal to the country of their adoption, that it was "brutal" of England to try and stop Italy doing what England itself had done so many times in the past – acquiring a colony by war. "Reggie is doing very well, and becoming very Fascist" wrote Douglas to Edward Hutton on 9th November. "Thinks the English are a pack of fools." To Archie, about a week earlier, he had written:

No news whatever here, except that the atmosphere is becoming decidedly unpleasant, owing to the sanctions. It looks as if it would get worse. If it becomes intolerable I shall go over to Athens, where I have at least three friends – don't like to be in Yugoslavia all alone – and finish Pino's memoirs, which should bring us in £300 each.

He sent Archie his Will. He had put in motion the necessary legal machinery for transferring his flat to Orioli, if the occasion should arise. He was feeling "distinctly low-spirited", and "distinctly grumpy". He expected things to get more and more unpleasant. "Athens? Riviera? India?" He did not know. "I have definitely decided to call myself an old man" he wrote to Bryher, "which is a damned nuisance, but the plain truth. I shall be 68* in a few days, and, anyhow, I have had good fun now and then." Eventually, as usual, he went off to Menton a few days before Christmas.

*He must have meant that he would be entering his 68th year. He used this reckoning on other occasions.

iii

Reggie Turner was a lonely man who, although he received much respect and superficial friendship as one of the sights of Florence and an entertaining survivor from the Nineties, had few close emotional ties. He was devoted to Orioli, and Orioli, with his warmth and vivacity, his human sympathy and kindness, must have seemed to Turner to reciprocate his own feelings. About 1931 Turner let Orioli know that in his will he had left him all his money, which was thought to amount to a good many thousands of pounds.

Orioli therefore had a motive for going to see Turner, quite apart from disinterested kindness, although he often found him boring and exasperating in an old-maidish manner. And Douglas, who half-despised Turner (Lawrence had seen, or guessed, this correctly), now began to regard him with more and more antipathy as a rival for the company of Orioli. He, preferring the more robust and congenial company of Douglas, had nevertheless to go regularly to the Viale Milton lest Reggie indulge in a fit of will-threatening. Douglas would torment Orioli by reciting a particularly delicious menu he had ordered at a restaurant for the evening, and asking Orioli to join him, or sending a friend to pick Orioli up and bring him along. The latter rôle sometimes fell to Aldington:

"Norman wants us to eat *cinghiale* at Betti's tonight," I would say presently. "Will you pick us up about seven?"

At moments of perplexity Pino produced a piece of acting which is hard to describe. He would shrug his shoulders, with his arms and hands lifted in supplication, and at the same time cower or almost cringe, like Shylock deprecating the Doge's wrath.

"I *can* not, I *can* not."

"Why not?"

"*Reggie!* He say I must dine at home with him in Viale Milton tonight, and I bet he give me *lemb chop*."

Words in italics were delivered with an emphasis print cannot convey. The history of the lamb chops and the disgrace attached to them was known to me. Reggie, it seemed, had once given lunch to Pino and Frank Harris at Nice and served lamb chops, whereupon Harris had jeered at this meanness until "Reggie, he blink like mad".

"Oh, well. Surely he can spare you for one evening. When I saw Norman he seemed to be in very good form, but it won't be real fun unless you're there."

Then of course Pino's mind would be the scene of one of those conflicts . . . Pino struggling between fear of compromising his all-important heritage from Reggie and longing to have a merry evening with Norman, instead of hearing what Robbie said to Bosie when Oscar was at Dieppe, for about the hundredth time. At this point Pino would say in abject misery:

"Shall ve have some vine?"

Sometimes the "vine" settled it in our favour, sometimes he might come part way to the restaurant and then he would suddenly think how awful it would be if Reggie left all his money to his servants, and rush off in a taxi to Viale Milton.

"Where's Pino?" Norman would ask when he failed to arrive.

"I'm sorry, but he had engaged to dine with Reggie."

"Umph."

Pino chafed and rebelled against this servitude to Reggie's will as he did from time to time against Norman's domination.

By 1936, life in this respect was even harder for Orioli, as Turner had been afflicted with cancer, and it was therefore twice as difficult for Orioli to refuse his invitations. But Douglas was still displeased with Orioli leaving him to dine alone – which occasionally happened. Pino "is dining with Reggie just now" wrote Douglas to Archie, "as usual (8.10 p.m.) and I shall dine all alone." The last five words constitute a silent rebuke, which on many other occasions was replaced by verbal disapproval or sarcasm. He liked having things his own way – indeed, it was almost a necessary condition of life for him – and it was not his way to dine alone, ever, if he could help it.

No doubt the above rebuke was silent because only a week remained in which Orioli could go to Turner before Douglas and Orioli were to go south together for at least a month to finish Orioli's autobiography. Some of this work was done, in uncomfortable conditions – owing to the effects of the Abyssinian war and sanctions – in Syracuse, where they stayed from mid-January until mid-February.

On his return to Florence, Douglas announced that he was giving up smoking and drinking until the first week in May, as an experiment, to see if it would improve his health. He meant to stick to it. Whether he did or not, he was feeling "pretty groggy" still at the end of March, and complained of having "a sensation of giddiness all the time". In the middle of April Archie arrived on what turned out to be an extended visit. May came, and Douglas wrote to Auntie with wry self-deprecation: "I remain here, and putrefy more and more every day. I am already very *faisandé*" – a joke that was to wear itself threadbare over the next fifteen years; but if putrefaction might be thought to arise from remaining still in one place, no one was in less danger of putrefying; for within ten days he was off with Archie to Capri, thence to Ischia. In June he visited Subiaco and Orvinio with Ian Greenlees;[114] in July went to Vevey and the Vorarlberg with Orioli; in August returned to the Vorarlberg for a month; in October was in Calabria; in November in Monte Carlo; and before the year ended was in the Sabine hills. He was about as likely to rot away with boredom and inanition as a bee or an ant.

iv

By the end of June Orioli's book was finished; the last instalment was sent round to the Giuntina to be set up in type. As soon as that was done the co-authors went off via Vevey (as guests of the Macphersons) to the Vorarlberg.

They put up at the Traube in Thüringen, and got two "very nice rooms. N. got his old one, which he considers a sacred spot. In that room he had many and many moments of happiness and pleasure." They met old friends – and old bores. "Fifo is no more the sweet boy of six years ago, is twenty now, big and lumpy, heavy and empty and rather ugly. He never stops singing and whistling, which irritates both of us." On the whole, though, the diary is in a sunny mood:

> We decided to take a taxi to Thüringen, we sent for one and in a few minutes the car was standing outside the hotel. Talking to the chauffeur there was a young boy, a very pretty creature. N. asked him if he wanted a drive, to which he answered with a lovely smile that he would love it. It was done very quickly and in a second we were driving with the boy on board towards Thüringen.
>
> From Thüringen we walked through the wood to Schnifis with the boy. The chauffeur was sent back. N. was happy and little Louis was delighted to be with such nice people, as he said afterwards to N.
>
> "Not every day one meets such good people . . ."
>
> Darling Louis turned out to be the son of Italians, he understood a little and answered "Shi, Shi". We all got attached to him . . . I thought he was a real darling, and N. in a few hours was in love.

They had another half day with Louis, who joined them at the hotel, where they were staying in Bludenz. They went for a walk all together to the cemetery in which Jakob Jehly and Vanda and Mary Douglass and Grete Gulbransson were buried and back into Bludenz, where they visited Louis' mother, who was:

> A nice, clean woman of about fifty. She received us most cordially and I could see she was pleased that her boy had met us . . . She has another son of 22 or 23 who works at Dalaas, quite far from Bludenz,

he goes there on his bike every morning. He had just arrived from working. She called him, and we had a chat also with him. A very good-looking young man with charming manners, I should not mind at all to become a friend of his. Both the boys have good manners and are dressed properly, clean and well groomed. She has brought them up well, this poor woman . . .

We asked them to let Louis dine with us at the Post. The mother made him wash and put on his best jacket . . . Little Louis had quite good table manners . . .

At half past nine took Louis home after having given him some bananas, cakes, and two packets of cigarettes for his brother and some money for the mother. We went back to the Post and had a good many schnapps, which we found delicious. Had a chat with the young porter, who is as charming as the Fraulein. Gave snuff all round and made all of them sneeze.

Another happy day gone!

Friday, 17 July, 1936.

Got up at half past six. At the station we met darling Louis waiting for us. Pity we had to go, but N. has promised him to come back soon. I would go back too if I had found such a darling friend.

Before saying goodbye we gave him some chocolates and bananas and a few shillings and kissed him goodbye.

And now into the train to be gerostet in Florence.

But not for long. Before the end of the month Douglas had left for Ischia. He had "very good fun" there. Then back to Florence for three days before spending some of Emilio's leave with him in the Italian Tirol. After that Douglas crossed the Alps via Landeck to start his second holiday of the year in the Vorarlberg. Louis, or Alois, as he seems to have signed himself, was the chief attraction. The day after he arrived, Douglas wrote: "Have just dined with him alone here. He is perfect." And he took him away to spend two nights in the Lünersee Hut – the Douglashütte – informing Orioli on a picture postcard of it. "L. flourishing and very happy, but *Bludenz* is not the place. Don't yet know how things can be arranged . . ." (26th August). "Last night we drove to Bürserberg . . . for supper, and walked home by moonlight. All very idyllic, but don't imagine there are no difficulties! We are going away today again, but I don't know where to, nor for how long. To some place, I hope, where the beds don't creak, as they do everywhere except at the Löwen in Bregenz." (2nd September.) "I think I leave on the 12 or 13 probably with L. who wants to come with me as far as the Italian frontier above Malles. Why not? If so, we shall stop a night there. Why not? He has to be back home

here on the 15th ... L is in a golden mood always – day and night"
(8th September). "Credo che arriverò il 14. Partite stamattina da
schruns ..." (10th September).

On 15th September however, Archie, at his cottage in Sussex, received
the following telegram from Bludenz: LAID UP BE PREPARED COME
BLUDENZ WILL WIRE FATHER. On the 19th another telegram came from
Chiasso, but it has not survived. On the 20th, his father wrote him a
letter:

Florence
20 Sept 1936

Dear Archie,
    Hope you got my wire yesterday from Chiasso. It was heart trouble
at Bludenz, and I wasn't allowed to write or do anything. My mother
died of it and it may polish me off one of these days, but the later the
better! Now I am feeling all right. No more mountain-climbing for me,
which is a damned nuisance; have to go slow. I took a car all the way to
Thalwil near Zurich where the Gothard line begins, and got into a
through train to Florence where I arrived this morning at 3.45 – a ghastly
hour.

Heart-trouble? Well, in a sense perhaps. Or perhaps the metaphorical
"heart-trouble" brought on actual palpitations when he fell into the
hands of the gendarmerie. The recorded fact is that he was arrested and
detained in the district court of Bludenz from 3.45 p.m. on 11th September
until 5 p.m. on 18th September. The charge was *Schändung* – rape. He had
walked over from Schruns, where he had been staying with Alois, on the
previous day, and he or they put up at the Burgstaller Gasthof for the
night. Somebody must have complained to the authorities, or his behaviour in public may have been such that the authorities themselves felt
they could no longer ignore it; or possibly Alois or his mother had become
alarmed at the prospect of the boy going, as planned, to the Italian frontier
with Douglas: what guarantee was there that he would not be taken across
it?

Once again, he had gone too far; but this time it looks as though there
was an element involved which had not been present on previous occasions: it looks as though he was ashamed. It looks as though no one, with
the possible exception of Orioli, was told the truth of the affair; as though,
having invented illness as a convenient signal of urgent distress to Archie,
he clung to it as a disguise for a scandal that he was not, in this case, ready
to admit even to friends. Bludenz was his home town; the name of
Douglas was still honoured in the whole province, and Norman was
proud of the fact. To tarnish one's name in distant places was one thing:

to let it happen on the threshold of one's ancestral home was another. The Vorarlbergers are a tolerant and kindly people, not righteous or puritanical, especially where private affairs are concerned; in sixteen years Douglas had only missed an annual visit there on three occasions, and when he came, he was seldom alone: he had come with one or with two companions, and found others locally, and as the years passed and he grew older, the companions seemed to grow younger. And the older he grew, the less did he seem to bother about being discreet. In the end, someone presumably could stand it no longer.

It seems that he was finally released, after a week in custody, "on condition of his leaving the country within twelve hours, three local friends having stood surety for his good behaviour in the meantime",[115] and the whole affair – since the Vorarlbergers honour the name of Douglas – seems to have been hushed up. Did he think, at the time, of his mother, whose "heart-trouble" of the metaphorical kind (which preceded the physical kind by many years) had led her to defy family, neighbours, and public opinion, and which Norman and his brother had apparently warmly approved since it seemed to bring her such fulfilment and happiness? And, remembering it, did the phrase "heart-trouble" – of which Vanda had certainly died – seem to offer a convenient evasion in his letters to Archie and Bryher and possibly to others?

This, at any rate, was for him the end of the Vorarlberg. He never returned; and with his banishment (if that is what it was) the Douglas connection with that part of the world started by his grandfather a little more than a century earlier came to an end. The founder had built, and acquired honour and modest wealth; his son had enjoyed these privileges and earned an even greater respect for the name of Douglas; one grandson had deserted the Vorarlberg, the other, though faithful to it and possessed by it, had proved to be too unorthodox, too eccentric, and had been obliged to leave.

CHAPTER THIRTY-ONE

———— ❖ ————

Interval Between the Acts
September 1936 – May 1937

In October there was a flying visit to Calabria. He told Archie that he wanted to have what might be his last look at it, and Hutton, that he was determined to see the ruined convent of Colorito, which he had never visited. The "last look" does not necessarily refer to his health; it could as easily apply to the political situation. However, he informed Archie, with regard to his heart, he was not going uphill in Calabria: "There are now public motorbuses everywhere and to be quite certain I am taking Emilio with me."

He heard from Robin, and wrote in comment: ". . . very depressing. He wants to give up writing. He also wants to come to Florence. I hope he won't, else I shall have to clear out. The place is not big enough for both of us."

Uncompromising! Robin had started the year in America, where he had been in hospital for two months; and then had managed to get to England, where, during the summer while at Sidmouth, he had met General Waters, who had been Military Attaché at Petersburg when Douglas was there: "Do give my love to Gen¹ Waters. I remember well our life together in the Sergievskaia at Petersburg and am delighted to hear he is flourishing. Perhaps he'll adopt you. Why not?"

Unhelpful! Why not join the Catholic Church? Why not get adopted by General Waters (at the age of thirty-three)? It's a wonder – or a sign of his desperation – that Robin actually contemplated going to Florence. And yet there must have been something faintly reassuring in the knowledge, which surely percolated through to him, that his father, somewhere in the capacious complexity of his relationships, cared or was concerned, always wanted news of Robin, always helped with money when he could afford it. Robin seemed less desperate towards the end of the year than at the beginning, when he had said that he was going to change his name and disappear entirely from the world.

Douglas himself strangely enough – or perhaps it was not strange after the Vorarlberg affair – seemed willing to disappear, to America. He wrote to Bryher that he would be delighted to join her there, but "of course it can't be done, and I must stick it out here". One assumes, from all his previous remarks about America, that he was only too glad it could not be done.

Orioli's book, *The Adventures of a Bookseller*, was being printed, and Douglas was "doing a little index to it". Someone had sent him Frank Harris' *Life and Loves*, which he found "quite disgusting in places and not at all funny". The political attitude to the English in Florence had improved slightly, "but sanctions go on as before, with the consequence that such things as whisky are almot impossible to procure (I have forgotten what it tastes like!) and English tobacco quite impossible . . ."

About ten days before the event he informed Archie that he would have "an absolutely solitary Christmas and New Year. Pino is with Reggie day and night, although Reggie is not dreaming of dying – quite the contrary!" Prentice was coming in January, and Douglas wanted to be in Florence at the time "to see that Pino does not give his book to Chatto's too cheaply". Archie had better not see Robin, he advised: "I'd rather he didn't know I was here. I don't suppose he'll stick at Selfridge's for long. We'll see!" In the New Year Robin wrote that he was giving up writing and going in for advertising, and trying to get back to America.

Orioli's book was ready for distribution in February 1937; it had cost about £800 to produce, and Douglas thought they would get rid of all 300 in the end, but meanwhile it was going off very slowly, "dribbling along".

"Here everything is just the same," wrote Douglas to Bryher at the end of February, without much justification. "There has been a terrific homosexual scandal, but it did not come my way. Thundering sentences, and two or three foreigners, they say, have had to hop it." That was not *quite* the same; nor was the fact that he was now entertaining a little girl in his flat. "I am . . . taking to girls again, as you will see when you come here," he informed Archie rather cryptically, and wrote later on that he had gone "to Impruneta with my new girl (aged 10½)". This little girl was called Renata, and according to "Auntie", she had at one time been left alone all day in a cold, empty house by her parents while they were at work. Douglas had suggested to the father that she should come and keep him company in his flat. If this is the truth, and it very likely is, it was an invitation that was much more generous than wise in the circumstances. The circumstances included the suspicion of foreigners, especially English people, under the Fascist régime, and the increasingly puritanical atmosphere under that régime; and the famous Italian vice of envy. It was not wise of Douglas; but it should by now be obvious that Douglas was by nature more impetuous than prudent – especially where children were concerned.

He was not particularly happy – or unhappy: his thumb had gone wrong again, and he was having daily treatment for it, which after about three months brought it back more or less to normal; but his giddiness was bad: he felt it whenever he stood up or walked, and decided to cut himself off wine and toscano cigars for a couple of months. Did he do it? The trouble with these heroic attempts at abstemiousness was, that once the period was over, or for any special occasion during them – such as a birthday – he felt he had to make up for lost time.

He was keeping in touch with Auntie, who from time to time sent him a pullover she had knitted; and whose memoirs he was reading and encouraging her to continue with. She was involved at this time with Emma Goldman, one of the best known (and best loved) Anarchists of the time, and naturally enough Douglas could not resist teasing her about "world reformers" and "do-gooders"; nor could he resist the occasional thrust at Christianity: "This is another of those blasted feast-days – Easter. Jesus Christ will have a good deal to answer for on the Day of Judgment."

As usual, there were various short trips about Italy with one or another companion. He was in Florence on 28th May: "Scanno was all right," he wrote to Archie the next day, "Now I stay here for a while, at least, to see if and when you are coming." Three days later Archie received a telegram AM AT VENCE NORMAN; and Orioli received a hastily pencilled note posted in Menton on the same evening: "All right so far. Tell Emilio and *take care of him*. Got through! N."

Once again (at the age of sixty-eight) he had had to "hop it" – so quickly on this occasion that he had only been able to take a rucksack with him. It was the fourth country from which he had been obliged to flee knowing that he might never be able to return.

PART VIII

Old Age
1937–1952

CHAPTER THIRTY-TWO

South of France
1937–1941

i

The affair concerned Renata, the little girl who had been in the habit of coming to his flat, and accounts of it are various but unverifiable. The commonest account implies that when Douglas took the little girl back to her parents she did not want to return to that less friendly and comfortable house, and resisted. There was a scene, presumably observed or overheard by neighbours who had, of course, been aware of the girl's visits to Douglas' flat. This resistance – the girl apparently clung to Douglas – was interpreted as an effort by Douglas to keep a hold on her, or to abduct her. Envy of the family favoured by this grand gentleman, coupled with the fact that he was English at this particular period of Italian history, was enough. Letters were written, or statements made to the police. Douglas was apparently warned of the danger he was in by Renata's elder brother. He escaped, according to his own account, with only an hour and a half to spare. Hutton said: ". . . however, the girl was found to be *virgo intacta*." Compton Mackenzie said: "They always turn to little girls in the end" – *they* being sexual deviants of almost any kind. But however impersonal final judgments may have been, Douglas commanded a good deal of sympathy at the time. Bryher and Kenneth Macpherson, Reggie Turner, and of course Orioli – all of whom knew the truth or most of it – stood solidly by him. "Stood" is hardly the word to use of Orioli, who for the next ten weeks devoted himself almost ceaselessly to Douglas' interests; nor is it true of Archie, who came out to Italy as soon as he was able to, and did what he could: nor of "Auntie" in Vence, who saw Douglas through his crisis, fed him, did for him, and protected him against nuisances. He lost no friends over this affair in 1937 as he had done over that other business twenty years earlier. On the contrary. Reggie Turner wrote with slightly sardonic humour that Douglas' friends were "agreeably surprised" that this particular crisis involved a member of the opposite sex. And concern was shown, and help offered, in an unexpected quarter. Lytton Strachey's elder sister Dorothy

429

Bussy, the well-known translator of Gide and other French authors (and, later, the author, herself, of *Olivia*, by "Olivia"), wrote to Sylvia Beach, the bookseller and publisher of *Ulysses*:

51 Gordon Square
London W.C.1.
17 June 1937

Dear Miss Beach,

I have heard recently that Norman Douglas, the author of *South Wind*, is in all sorts of difficulties, financial and other, and I feel that people who have enjoyed his work as much as I have should try to do something, if not to relieve him, at any rate to give him some satisfaction.

His publishers have told me that *South Wind* has never been translated into French. Considering that in England it may be said to have become a classic and has gone into innumerable editions, don't you think it is time it should be? I have been looking at it again recently and still think it extraordinarily brilliant and the kind of book that would probably appeal enormously to the French and lose very little in translation. Could you advise me as to what publishers might take it and how best to approach them? I have several friends at the N.R.F., but am rather inclined to shun them as publishers, as they are often so excessively dilatory. My idea is Plon or Stock, both of whom, I believe, go in for English translation and have good translators. I would at once send off a copy of the book to anyone who you think might consider it, but I feel that a recommendation is necessary and I should be so very grateful if you would advise me how to get it.

I feel sure you will forgive me for troubling you.

Yours sincerely
Dorothy Bussy

Sylvia Beach duly played her part as intermediary with possible publishers for a translation, but nothing came of the project.

Douglas fled from Florence in such a hurry that he and Orioli broke open one of Douglas' locked cupboards (he was a great locker-up) for which he couldn't find the key, so that he could take some necessities from it. He got across the border without being stopped and went, for that one night, to the Hotel Masséna at Menton. One may guess his feelings by the fact that on the following day, when he had gone up to Vence and been received by Auntie, he asked her at once if she knew whether there was a treaty of extradition between Italy and France, and asked her to find out. She packed him into the flat of a friend who was away; and according to her "he was very frightened".

His first thoughts were for Emilio, who all through the years had been so faithful. He had a regular job as well as working in Douglas' flat, but needed the extra money he earned as Douglas' indispensable general factotum now that he had a wife and child to support, and Douglas was perplexed about how to get money to him. Reggie Turner seemed to be the only answer; he was an appalling gossip but it could not be helped – one would have just to ask him to keep quiet and hope for the best:

Dear Reggie,

If I sent you a cheque for £100 could you get it changed . . . and hand the money personally to Emilio? Just say yes or no! Pino can't cash such cheques, as you know.

I should be very glad if you say nothing about this to *anybody*, not on account of Pino, but on account of somebody who sooner or later might (would, I may say) hear about it from Pino, and this would do Emilio harm. I am sure you don't want to be the cause, even indirect, of doing harm to poor Emilio.

This went off to Reggie on 31st May, the day of Douglas' flight, and Reggie of course agreed, and four days later Douglas sent him the cheque with detailed instructions of how to find Emilio, adding: "Drop me a card when you've done it, and tell me what he looks like. He's been ill, you know." And in most of the letters – almost daily letters – that he wrote to Orioli during the next two months, he begged him to "look after Emilio". To Archie he wrote: ". . . But Emilio? That is what hurts *me*."

When he had got over the first shock, and had learned that he could not be extradited, and had re-discovered how kind and affectionate Auntie was, and had met his friend Oscar Levy, he began to feel happier (apart from that "infernal giddiness", which was as bad as ever, if not worse) and wrote with a hint of insouciance to Archie: "All forgotten in a month or so!" If anyone were to talk to Archie about the affair, he was to say "it has a political background, and that otherwise there is nothing in it whatever". That was what Archie was to *say*; but about six days earlier Douglas had written his son an explanation of the whole affair. The envelope of this letter exists, and upon it Archie has written: "Contents destroyed 10/6/37". The destruction of this letter leaves room for an element of doubt as to how Douglas may have conducted himself in this affair. The doubt cannot be lightly dismissed. Douglas felt passionately and tenderly and sensuously for the very young. Being genuinely in love with life, he may have thought that one who loved it as deeply and sympathetically as he did could not go wrong if he gave himself to life in whatever way a true impulse of love seemed to demand. Naturally, one would take no account whatever of conventional morality, for the morality of the Seventies and Eighties, in which he had grown up, was beneath contempt. So one adopted the morality of *warum nicht*, of experimentation, empiricism; if one was normally kind and considerate and averse from cruelty, it was unlikely that any real harm could come of any cheerful or tender intimacy. So – why not? If there was physical intimacy of any kind with Renata, it seems likely that it was harmless. She apparently stated that Douglas had "taken some advantage of her", which could mean anything, including very little; however we are also told that the Examining Magistrate refused to bring a charge against Douglas on this evidence, which suggests that he was not convinced by it.

ii

Within a few days Douglas had begun to settle down and organise his life with that same astonishing aplomb and that same admirable determination not to recriminate or indulge in self-pity ("no use howling") which had always followed any of the innumerable crises, mostly small but occasionally large, which he had left behind him in his life like milestones. First and foremost, he must be as fit as possible and try to defeat that damned giddiness; therefore, hardly any alcohol, no cigars, and as few pipes a day as possible. Secondly he must help Orioli and Carrozza (Douglas' friendly and able lawyer) to organise his defence. Thirdly, he must get Archie to come out, and he had better bring Douglas' will and other documents. Fourthly, money must be raised, though he had enough, thank God, to go on with. Fifthly, Orioli must come and see him and bring him news that it might be wiser not to write, and necessities he had had to leave behind.

Orioli came over on 10th June for about five days. He had been looking after Douglas' flat, keeping in touch with Emilio, and consulting with Carrozza. He continued to run innumerable errands and fulfil all kinds of commissions for Douglas, who was fully conscious of and extremely grateful for this invaluable help. "How quickly you managed it," he wrote about an unspecified but obviously important commission he had given Orioli, "and how relieved I am. You are *wonderful*."

Archie stayed in Florence a week and then went to the south of France for a day to see his father on his way back to England. He went off with a complete set of keys to Douglas' flat in Florence.

This misfortune happened just at a time when Douglas had remembered the ivy on his balcony in Florence and had become very concerned about it, asking Orioli to be sure to get Emilio to help him water it. How was that to be done now? It was a typical Douglas situation, a mess that called for letters right and left – two or three a day to the same person if necessary – to sort the business out (and in the sorting, make it as like as not more complicated). Energy is everywhere apparent; serenity has fled:

"That was damnable of Archie running away with all the keys! . . . Do give the Consul copies of any books of mine, as many as you like. But how get at them if Archie has keys! I am in such a *hell of a rage* about this that I can't write any more . . . I'll write you as soon as I'm calmer!" Next day, more action, a way round the problem, and a more cheerful frame of mind:

Vence

6 July 1937

Dearest Pino

Wrote you yesterday.

That ivy – it is not only ornamental, but symbolical, and I don't want all the neighbours to see it dead.

Therefore will you please go on to Miniati's (or the Colonel's) terrace to see if it is still alive. If it is, put yourself into communication with Emilio, to whom I have just written about it, and get him to water it with a ladder from Miniati's terrace. I am sure Miniati would not object. Will you please do this?

I am giving Archie 5 days to send those keys. If they don't come I'll send you a letter for Ceccherelli to change all the locks.

Just off to Antibes!

Endless love

As to the symbolism of the ivy, perhaps there was a superstition attached to it as there was in the case of the little tree described by Aldington:

> On the verge of the Arno and visible from Pino's front windows was a miserable little tree which somehow managed to retain a few withered leaves until late in December. Norman's belief was that if a few leaves or even one leaf remained on the tree at midnight of December 31st that would be a good omen for the coming year; but it would be a very bad omen if all were blown away.

If the ivy were to die, perhaps that would be a bad omen for Douglas or Orioli or Emilio; but it is also true that just as Douglas cared very much about his appearance in public, and would frequently urge Orioli to "try to look like a gentleman", so he may have cared that no sign of disrepair or neglect should be seen outside the flat. His property, at least, must not be allowed to suggest any kind of decay that might be transferred, by association, to his health or his morals.

By this time, however, it seems likely that he had started to accept the idea that he might never see his flat again: "The affair is not dangerous," he wrote to Bryher, "because they can't get me – at least I think they can't – but it is very doubtful whether I shall ever be able to get into Italy again. That is bad enough, especially at my age, when one cannot strike fresh roots easily." Bad enough, perhaps, but no real deterrent to a spirited and resourceful man who was now becoming rather busy, both socially and in other ways: "Come as soon as you can," he wrote to Orioli in the middle of July:

> We can go to Corsica from Nice. Bring quinine. Said to be malarious in places. Vence is becoming impossible. Firstly, the man who owns this flat has come back and wants it. Secondly, Archie has arrived with his girl whom he calls his wife, and her child, and has taken a flat. That would be nothing, but his *real* wife, Maud, is also in the neighbourhood, and comes here very frequently, nearly every day. We have told Archie, but he is risking it. Thirdly, Auntie wants to get rid of her pottery and set up a shop with books and prints. She wants to talk to you about it. There may be money to be made for both of you.
>
> Don't come without giving me time to write to you what to bring. (No! I enclose a list) . . .

There was a great deal more in this brisk and characteristic letter, with its typical Douglasian asterisks, its arrows pointing to important sentences, its afterthoughts, its underlinings, and its final injunction in large capitals: READ THROUGH AGAIN. He was back in form. Auntie, in fact, wrote to Orioli that Douglas looked "ten years younger" and said he had told her that he had not felt so well for two years: "All the ladies adore him and try their fascination on him – inutile I'm afraid, & I continue to air his linen & dry his tears – as much as he will allow. . . ."

Douglas was not only back in form, but back in business in a small way. He had been asked to write an introduction to a new American edition of *Old Calabria*, and as preparation for this work wrote to Orioli for the three previous editions of the book. He was also arranging to sell fourteen of his manuscripts, making out descriptive slips for them, which he sent to Orioli, asking him to put a reserve price on each item and try to get the manuscripts off to Sotheby's before he came to Vence. This Orioli managed to do, as he had managed so much else so successfully already. A letter from him at this time concerning Renata's father will give some idea – a mere shadowy intimation – of what he had been doing for Douglas in Florence during the ten weeks after 31st May. It will also give a hint of some of the emotions that were at work in one of the parties most nearly concerned in the affair:

Monday 19–7–37

My dearest Norman,

At last I have been able to see F and have a good long talk with him. I went to O last night and made an appointment with him. We met at midnight and went to my place. F is just what I always thought. Absolutely with you and no one in the family is against you and all of them refuse to believe of what they have accused you and the girl. First he went into a fit, he cried, well you know the kind of scene an Italian can make. After I calmed him I got to know more. He is disgusted with his avvocato, who has got from him 150 lire and done nothing. I told him that he has got 850 from Carrozza under pretext of helping the family. F said he never got a penny, but that R is always asking for more money. Pretty state of affair! He told me that Renata is quite well and in a good place, all the family are alowed to visit her, but they cannot go too often as it costs about ten lire to go there, also he told me what agony they when [sic] through on that moment. He only wants the end of the affair and Renata to come out innocent . . . Well, the important thing is that I have made an appointment with F to come to Carrozza with me tomorrow (Tuesday at three o'clock). We have arrange that we shall liquidate R and that Carrozza will look after everything. Your and his interest. He went away very happy and kissed me and told me to tell you "quanto stima hanno di te e come gli vogliamo bene tutti in famiglia" quite happy to have met me . . . He is still frighten of Comissario Barone and more frighten for you than for himself. Barone seems a kind of Capolozzi. I shall get more out of F tomorrow, he was so very agitated last night that I could not get much from him about the family.

As is so often the case, it looks as though the threat to Douglas came mainly from the law or its representatives rather than from the man who might have been considered to be the injured party, or its proxy. A few days later Douglas wrote to Orioli, in reply to another letter, that he was "rather disquieted about that questore going to the Consul! I hope they won't unearth some old story and ruin everything at the last minute? . . . Archie talks of staying here for good . . . I am *frightfully* sick of Vence. Endless love! N"

Orioli arrived in the south of France about 13th August to go to Corsica with Douglas. A few days later they landed at Calvi and drove by car to Bastia. Just before their departure Douglas wrote to Bryher: "My affair is over apparently . . ."

iii

On their second day, they went to Corte, from which centre they made radial trips up valleys and over mountain passes to all parts of the island, often staying overnight in the more remote places. They had difficulty in getting decent accommodation in Corte, and outside the two or three larger towns food was filthy, "worse, and less, than Calabria" – which was saying a good deal. The coastal plains on the east side of the island, which they once drove through, were eighty per cent malarious; and apart from the main roads, driving was "no fun". In spite of these drawbacks, Douglas enjoyed himself sufficiently, and Orioli said he loved the island, though what both probably liked most was each other's company. Douglas wrote that neither of them liked Corsica "*very much*. I am glad I went there, and the devil himself won't get me there again. We had a good dose of it." His giddiness was "quite bloody, unless I am sitting down", and he was still going very carefully with regard to drink and tobacco.

As soon as they had decided to go to Corsica, Douglas had got in touch with René's brother in the south of France, and learned that the parents had retired to Corsica to the family's native village, Moltifao. His eagerness to be associated once again with any place so closely connected with René may be guessed from the fact that he and Orioli went out there to see René's parents as soon as they had secured beds at Corte.

They stayed in Corsica just over a month, Orioli returning directly to Italy, and Douglas separately to Nice, where he had his "last wine and last Toscano". He had now dropped "*all* smoke and *all* drink, and shall keep it up till 23 November. Then we'll see." November 23rd was Emilio's birthday, and Douglas intended, as usual, to drink his health. This celebration was probably not so much a matter of sentiment as of superstitious ritual. To have omitted this annual salutation might – just might – have endangered Emilio's life, and that chance, naturally, must not be allowed to occur.

iv

It was actually on Emilio's birthday that Douglas wrote to Archie with "very bad news from Florence". The case, after being "definitely closed, is to be re-opened again. I know no details save this . . . An expensive lawsuit ending, inevitably, against me with a stiff sentence, which will probably get into Italian and English papers. That, at least, is the *prognosis*, but Carrozza writes that he is not 'without hopes'." Orioli, however, was pessimistic, as the re-opening of the case was against all precedent. Douglas, always ready to escape, thought he might go to "India or some such place" till the storm blew over. "Nobody here," he added to Archie, "knows anything, and Auntie, of course, must never be told." Must never be told what? The truth? Or the fact that the case had been re-opened? More room, alas, for an element of doubt to creep in. (Later, Douglas also wrote twice to Orioli imploring him never to mention "that last *verbale*" to anyone, including Archie.) A few days later, there was slightly better news from Orioli. There was "some hanky-panky going on" in Florence, evidently.

By the end of January 1938, he received assurances from Carrozza that the Florentine affair had at last come to an end. The case was definitely closed. Douglas found it hard to believe and wrote to Archie: ". . . of course, I shan't go there – not likely!" He couldn't understand *why* the case had been dropped after it had been re-opened. *Who* had stopped it, and *how*? Neither Orioli nor Carrozza seem to have informed him on this point: perhaps they did not know. The whole business had cost him £400 – "an expensive prank". Three months later he heard from Carrozza that he could return to any place in Italy other than Florence and need have nothing to fear. But though he may have been tempted, he decided against returning. The political situation had made life not only unpleasant but very uncertain from day to day. Italy was coming more and more under the influence of her ally Germany, and Germany was becoming ever more arrogant and aggressive. In this intensified Fascist atmosphere Orioli was finding it difficult to renew his passport, and it did not look as though he would get it done in time to go with Douglas to Tunisia, which they had tentatively planned to do in the spring. He had also been ill; and Douglas wrote to him that he would have to be "damned careful" of his liver, which had always given trouble.

The Corsican diary had to be typed out, like all the other diaries that Orioli had kept. Douglas had promised to do this, and tried to start on it as soon as he returned to Vence from Corsica, but after trouble with a hired typewriter, he sent the manuscript to Orioli to type. "Stick to diet! Stick to diary!" is the burden of his advice all through February. On the 21st of that month he rushed off to Paris to see Nancy Cunard, who had written that she was ill.

"Nancy NOT particularly well," he reported to Auntie. She had never paid any attention to her health when some cause had to be served, and had driven herself hard in Spain during the winter. And when she returned to France, she never rested, but spent herself utterly on drumming up aid for Spain and engaging wholeheartedly in anti-Fascist propaganda. No wonder that she collapsed from time to time when she asked more of her slender physique than even it could support, well-trained though it had been to live on mere scraps of food and to make do without relaxation or recreation. Douglas, for all his scornful talk of "meddlers" and "the goodness germ" and "world-reformers", admired and had a deep affection for Nancy, and although she could not remember who suggested that they should go to Tunisia together, it was almost certainly he. The wish to return there had been in his mind for months, but since Pino was unable to get his passport, and Nancy would obviously benefit enormously from getting right away from her frenetic political activities, it seems likely enough that the suggestion and the persuading came from him. She arrived in Vence early in April "feeling battered and greatly worried by the state of everything – so clearly heading for war – my heart and mind full of the things of Spain". She could not and did not want to talk to Douglas about this, but simply accepted with gratitude the fact that the two of them, with their entirely different attitudes, could get on so well and look forward with pleasant anticipation to a holiday of several weeks together.

v

They left Marseille on 11th April in a storm. The boat was tossed about like an empty crate, so much so that a grand piano broke loose from its moorings and Nancy Cunard suddenly discovered that she had "flown" across the bar-room and back again, fortunately without injury. Douglas, firmly planted on a chair, remained seated, but was convulsed with laughter

There does not seem to have been much more laughter during this three-week holiday. Nancy put up a vigorous and sensible opposition to Douglas' plan – routine for him – to pool expenses, and he eventually gave in, grumpily. She loathed the squalor of Gafsa and the pestilential Arab boys who followed them everywhere like a cloud of flies; and their journey across the Chott Djerid nearly ended in disaster.

These chotts are partly dried-up salt lakes, full of morasses; but if the driver follows the tracks across them, which are marked by posts, he is safe enough under normal conditions. Unfortunately, after they had driven about fifteen miles, the wind piled up the water so that it covered their route. The car slipped off the track and one wheel stuck in the muddy ooze. The passengers stepped out into a foot of water while the driver and his mate set about trying to get the car up on to the track again. Douglas asserted that the car would never have been got back on the road without his and Nancy Cunard's help, but couldn't think how it had been done. According to her, their offer of help was refused. He produced a large and unexpected flask from an inner pocket and announced his intention of having a drink of whisky every half hour, in which she gladly joined him. They were there altogether for an hour and a half, while the water rose slightly, and the temperature fell and the sun began to go down. She was optimistic, suggesting that if they couldn't drive they could at least walk in the shallow water. He was pessimistic: the wind might drive half the sea in until it was up to their necks! Later, she remembered that on the map the Chott Djerid was not connected to the sea, and reassuringly passed this happy memory on – only to be told brusquely that maps "are often wrong!

You can't map a country like this properly. Just try!" But eventually they were mobile, and were driven to Gafsa, in the dark.

Douglas thought they had been saved from the Chott by the intervention of "the old god Triton, who long ago rendered a similar service to Jason of the Golden Fleece, when his ship became entangled in that very same ooze".

They reached Marseille on 4th May, and there took trains in different directions, without much time for saying good-bye. He waved his stick: "ta-ta, my dear, ta-ta . . ."

vi

Douglas spent the early part of the summer first in the south of France and then in Switzerland. From Vevey he wrote Archie a series of cryptic letters signed "Richard", with the sort of veiled instructions he always sent to a friend he could trust who was still living in a town from which Douglas had fled for fear of arrest. Archie was to keep his eyes and ears open and try to get as much information as possible. This, together with a letter from Archie to Pino, suggests very strongly that Douglas, now within a few months of his seventieth birthday, had added one more indiscretion to the enormous number he had carelessly engaged in all through his life: "Auntie came to a solitary supper with me tonight. She is very worried lest N. should return to this part & then do some 'bétise' in the usual line. She thinks that his entire dossier is in the hands of the local authorities. Well, Well! He must 'gang his ain gait' as they say in the North, & take what comes."

The comment of the son was an absolute mirror-image of what the father's comment would have been if the circumstances had been reversed.

From Vevey Douglas went to Paris for two or three days, until Oscar Levy was ready to go to Étretat, and then they travelled there together. Douglas remained at Étretat all through July and August, apart from one or two short trips. At first, as usual, he seemed to quite like it; then it became "rather a tiresome little place"; but before it could become "a rotten hole", he seems to have forgotten all about it because of the numerous friends who came there to see him. There were many goings and comings even of the same people: it was as though the licence to live in comparative freedom suddenly looked like expiring, and people who were fond of each other wanted to meet again for what might be the last time. Faith Mackenzie was one of those who came to see him after Orioli had joined him at Étretat. Returning to England after a motor tour in France, she made a detour to meet them at Rouen. They spent the evening together; and the next morning the two men said goodbye: "You will

probably never see me again," said Douglas, as he always did. "I can't last
for ever. And why you insist on going back when you might live in France
I can't understand. It's the only civilised country left in Europe, and
don't you forget that next time you want to move."

About a week before the meeting with Faith Mackenzie, Douglas had
spent two or three days at Nancy Cunard's place at Réanville. She had
acquired a Spanish refugee whose husband had disappeared in the civil
war – Narcia, and her son of fourteen, Gervasito, whom Douglas nick-
named Chico.

At the beginning of September, when he had arranged to meet Nancy
Cunard in Paris (she had been to Barcelona for two or three weeks) he took
Chico with him. Days passed and Nancy failed to arrive. Meanwhile, living in Paris was expensive, especially with Chico, for whom he felt
responsible and whom he wished to help. Nancy Cunard arrived on the
25th and, according to her own account, felt ill from "the sudden change
back to proper food". She was also penniless and scantily clothed, "having
felt I must leave everything possible to bombed-out people in Barcelona";
Douglas thought she looked very fit. Meanwhile, the Hotel Montana was
so full of her friends that she could not get in there herself. The Munich
crisis was in full swing, with English and French statesmen flying to and
from Hitler, and time looked short. Douglas did not much want to go
back to the Riviera, but at least the climate was preferable to that of
Normandy, and he could not afford Paris. He stayed two days after Nancy's
arrival and went down to Vence on the 27th, two days before Chamberlain
and Daladier sold the Czechs to Hitler for what the Prime Minister called
"Peace in our time" on 29th September.

According to Nancy Cunard, who seems to have had access to Auntie's
diary, Douglas was one of many who felt the disgrace of this Agreement:
Auntie apparently wrote:

> Norman is here . . . The Peace is not altogether to his liking. Peace
> with dishonour, he calls it. Norman wants Mussolini to be exterminated:
> "Those two gangsters" as he calls Mussolini and Hitler, "to be put on
> the spot". We argued long and with much heat on this subject. How can
> anyone contemplate another war, I demanded, realising, as we must,
> just a little of what it will mean to the world, the unthinkable horror of
> it? N. is 70. At the best, he has only a few years of unsatisfactory
> existence to contemplate. "I don't care about war," he shouted; "you
> talk about bloodshed and maiming. Do you realise how many are being
> done to death and mutilated in prison-camps in Germany and Italy?
> Their prisons won't hold the thousands they cram into them. New ones
> have to be built all the time."

vii

Reggie Turner died on 7th December 1938. In the room of this innerly lonely man when he died were two priests and the author of the *Well of Loneliness*. All his friends and acquaintances – a large circle – were sad at losing him, but glad his suffering had at last come to an end. Orioli sent telegrams to several people, Aldington and Douglas among them. Aldington wrote with some truth that Reggie "deserved well of the Republic of Letters" for his courage in standing by Oscar Wilde when others had deserted him. Douglas, who had received handsome presents from Reggie and had recently, at the moment of his escape from Italy, been deeply indebted to an already sick man for helping him to get money to Emilio – Douglas wrote to Archie: "No letter from Pino: just a wire announcing that shit's death." It is not a pretty epitaph, and its inhumanity is not mitigated by ascribing it to momentary petulance or anger (that Orioli should have had to suffer too) or jealousy (that Orioli had spent so much time with Turner and might soon be rich); yet the comment is in a way characteristic and revealing. Douglas, one can see, was damned if he was going to pay lip service to Turner simply because he had died; and now that he was dead, all the feelings of horror connected with Turner's (and Orioli's) suffering – one's impotence in the face of *anyone's* suffering of that kind – and perhaps also his own fear of irremediable illness and death, found vent in that ugly brevity.

Douglas spent October and most of November at Vence, then moved to the Hotel du Siècle at Monaco where he stayed until the spring of 1939. Archie made a short visit to England, and then returned to his house in Vence. Auntie was still there. Eric, on leave with his family, spent the last four months of it at Vence; they liked it so much that they decided to make a return visit when they could. They were to leave Marseille for Africa on 30th December. Chico and his mother, so Douglas heard, had become "great friends of Picasso, whom I pointed out to them in a Paris café, so that boy may get some better job for the winter than selling chestnuts . . ." Antisemitism was at its height in Italy; Jews were proscribed by law and many were forced to emigrate: Orioli came under suspicion because of his association with Irving Davis, his partner in London. Nancy Cunard had resumed her strenuous activity on behalf of Spain. Robin had settled in America.

Douglas celebrated his seventieth birthday quietly, merely lunching with Eric at Vence. He was now living more quietly altogether, drinking little (for him) and rationing his smoking, in an attempt to relieve the giddiness which had been chronic since the spring of 1937. There was no improvement, but at least no deterioration.

On 26th January 1939, Barcelona fell to Franco, and refugees began to pour over the frontier into France. Douglas told Nancy Cunard, who was organising help for them, that he was "perfectly ready to adopt a Spanish refugee child"; it would have suited him, for he needed a constant companion with whom he could travel; he was afraid to go far afield, especially in sparsely-populated districts, in case his giddiness should involve him in an accident. Nancy Cunard took some time to suggest that Douglas might like to visit a refugee boy in the Dordogne, and he did not manage to get there until May. He had several talks with Gustavo, this Basque boy, but found him "too dull", too depressed: "He doesn't want to come with me. He doesn't *want to* be cheered up." So that was that.

viii

Refugees were also escaping, albeit in smaller numbers, from Italy. "At Castellar they catch refugees every day who have come over the mountains without clothes or money" wrote Douglas to Hutton in March 1939; and by this time Orioli, who had gone to London in January with Carlo to see the solicitors about Turner's legacy, was virtually in the same category. He never returned to Italy. He remained in England most of the time, although there was a brief visit to Paris in April, during which he wrote asking Douglas to visit him there. According to Douglas, Orioli said he couldn't come to the south of France, and "I'm damned" wrote Douglas, "if I'm going to Paris". That was certainly an attitude that would not have prevailed say six months previously. Douglas, who was ready to go to Paris at the drop of a hat if Nancy Cunard were ill, would undoubtedly then have gone there to meet Orioli. It is true that this truculent refusal to meet his old friend was written while Douglas was laid up with 'flu – indeed, he excused himself on this ground more than once to Orioli – but it is out of character that he should have written "I'm damned if I'm going . . ." if he really meant "I can't go". Relations between Douglas and Orioli had shown signs of strain ever since the death of Turner or earlier. Douglas complained in March that he had had no news of Orioli for two months or so, in spite of having written to him eight times, and he probably felt hurt that Orioli had not travelled to England via the south of France so that they could meet. His remarks about Turner also suggest that he may have felt, or may have been prepared to feel, somewhat alienated by the legacy. If only he *had* gone to Paris at the end of March, all might have been well: his refusal or inability to go, coupled perhaps with feelings of guilt on Orioli's part, inevitably increased, though it were ever so slightly, the disharmony in their relationship which had become perceptible since Turner's last illness in the previous autumn. So that when Douglas did eventually get to Paris on the last day of July – there had been nothing to prevent him going before then – and asked Orioli to meet him there, it was Pino's turn to be recalcitrant. Douglas wrote to him twelve times in three weeks trying to arrange a meeting, but it never came off, and eventually Douglas left Paris in what looks like a bad temper, and returned to the south of France – this time to Antibes, where he had taken a room before going to Paris.

ix

His room was at 1 Place Macé, and he liked the place. His landlady, a dressmaker, was *"really nice"*, and they got on well together. His friend of many years, Basil Leng, had bought himself a house about forty minutes' walk away, and there were "a good many other English and Americans whom I know and can meet at the Café Glacier, about 30 yards from my door, whenever I want to . . . My landlady's little boy of $9\frac{1}{2}$ keeps me company whenever he is free and is very useful as a guide in the evenings . . ." Useful, that is, as a guide in the blackout, France and Britain having gone to war with Germany about a week after his arrival in Antibes.

He offered his services to the British Consulate at Cannes, saying that he was "ready to do anything for the Cause. Thank God, they have not even acknowledged receipt of my letter. I hate doing work of any kind, nowadays." His days were quite pleasant. He usually had lunch at the Glacier and was often there for dinner, or afterwards for a drink, though he sometimes went to a cheap Italian restaurant near the harbour. "You say," he wrote to Dawkins, "it is a great thing to be occupied. I do nothing all day long, and find it suits me down to the ground. A question of age? The only drawback is that I am getting *damnably fat*. Why not? There will be five people to carry my coffin instead of four: that's all the difference, and I shan't have to pay for them."

He read a good deal more than he had used to do when there were other things and people to occupy more of his time, mainly the classics, but he also kept fairly well abreast of books by some of his contemporaries, especially those he knew: "Have you read Huxley's last book? Somebody sent it me. Very good on the whole, and yet he will insist on dragging in by the ears a wholly unnecessary character, in order to give the reader tiresome lumps of philosophy (?) which have nothing to do with the story, and hinder its movement. I am afraid he likes preaching. That Mexican travel-book of his was also ruined – for me, at least – by the same stupid trick."

Every evening he would drink a whisky or two "to the damnation of Hitler", but not too much, because of his giddiness. He did not doubt the outcome of the war: "As to Hitler – we shall crack him, but I fear Hitler-*ism* has existed since the beginning of History; like lunacy – a disgusting state of affairs." But of Freud, who had died three weeks after the beginning of the war, he wrote with less nicety of distinction that he was sorry "he did not live to see the smash-up of Hitlerism; it would have done him good".

He had to have a *permis de circulation* to go to or from Nice, Cannes, or Vence, but visited Archie fairly regularly. Archie was still in his house in Vence, as he had been all the year, and was now particularly interested in an American girl. Auntie had moved down to Juan-les-Pins into an apartment. Robin, who had joined the General American Transportation Corporation, seemed at last to be prospering and leading a steady life. He had invited his father to America in February, but received an oblique refusal: "I can't ever manage to get to America – many thanks for inviting me, all the same. I shall always go East or South, if I move at all."

Emilio continued to write with unfailing regularity – as he had done for the last two years – about twice a week; and Douglas, with unfailing regularity, continued to send him money and write to him at least once a week.

In the middle of November he heard from Charles Prentice that Orioli, who had gone to Holland in September, had left for Portugal. Towards the end of the year, he heard from him: "Orioli wrote me – the first LETTER this year – from Lisbon, where he went from Amsterdam. He seems to like it, and has not *yet* got his money from the bank, which is something of a scandal, seeing that R.T. died more than a year ago. He says he may get it in February, and that he is living meanwhile on borrowed money on which he has to pay interest."

At the end of the year he began a new treatment for his giddiness "which has been pretty bad lately – namely, no alcohol of any kind, and a peculiar pill made of methylene, which has the drawback of turning one's urine to a bright blue colour. I shall keep it up till the 20 January and then see."

x

During the first quiet months of 1940 – the period of the phoney war – life in the south of France was little different from that in peacetime. There were soldiers about – a good many up at Vence – and expatriates on the Riviera continued to trickle away slowly to England and America. The place was emptier, yes, but not much different in other ways:

I was at Menton the other day and had a drink at the old place on the esplanade which we used to visit before lunch. It was rather deserted! Then I drove to Castellar and walked down by the path on the other side of the valley, which you will remember. Nothing changed – except myself, who seem to have grown 50 years older.

People went. Basil Leng had gone off in February for a term of six months with the Anglo-American Red Cross; and Archie, who had decided to marry Marion, the American girl, had applied for work at Marseille, in a branch of the Admiralty. He went to live there in May, and was joined by Marion later. They had intended, when they got an apartment, to get Douglas to join them there; but they did not get an apartment before they were obliged, or persuaded, to evacuate to England at the end of June.

Auntie, too, had gone. War had deprived her of a living, and she was said to be very near the end of her money. She went off early in June, to Bordeaux, hoping to get a boat to the USA. She had been warned that if she stayed, she might be one of the first people to be sent to a concentration camp, because of her association with revolutionaries and anti-Fascists.

Two hours before I left I had lunch with Norman. Stockingless, hatless, I had only a small bag and bundle. Having tried in vain to dissuade me from going, he filled my bag with small bottles of brandy, saying "You will need them before you escape from France." He was right, I did . . .

When the moment came for parting he kissed me and again begged me with tears in his eyes not to go, saying "In America you will surely die of pneumonia or be poisoned by bad whisky."

At Bordeaux, before sailing, she received from him a carefully composed letter of introduction to friends of his in the USA which he hoped would be of use to her.

After the fall of France, it was difficult to get news of him. He tried two different channels of communication – via Lisbon, and via Switzerland; but even to reply by wire to or from England took six days; letters sometimes took a month. Archie heard from a friend who came to England from the Riviera, that his father had been given an opportunity to leave the south of France with a boatload of refugees from Cannes. It seems that he agreed to do so, but then changed his mind. "On the whole," wrote Archie, reporting this news to Hutton, "I do not see that any harm can come to him & he is perhaps already Gauleiter for the Côte d'Azur, or Duce of the Balilla." As a comment from a youngish man who had reached the comparative safety of England upon an old and infirm man who was known to hate Fascism and Nazism, and might be exposed to their tyranny at any moment, nothing could have been much more inept or fatuous. That chance to leave, if it had really existed, would have been in June or July; Douglas probably turned it down because he was afraid he would end up in England (where he was uncertain of his position in law) or in the USA, which he regarded as a "perambulating lunatic asylum" and had sworn he would never go to, however politely or evasively he may have replied to invitations.

By October life was becoming increasingly difficult. Food was getting short, for one thing; and money was rationed by the Consulate to £10 per person per month. As far as the English government was concerned, with regard to the export of money, France was technically enemy territory and no one living there could receive money from England. By this time Douglas was trying to get to Portugal, having written to friends there to see if they could have him. By the end of December he had obtained his Spanish and Portuguese visas, but had not yet quite made up his mind to go to Portugal, though he had been sending the address he would go to there to several people. In the middle of January he had still not been granted the French exit visa for which he had applied on 15th October.

Archie had no reliable news of his father until 6th March, when he received a letter from Neil Hogg, Second Secretary of the British Embassy in Lisbon. It had been written on 21st February, and announced that Douglas had reached the Portuguese capital, and had gone to stay with his friend Peter Pitt-Millward, in the north of the country.

CHAPTER THIRTY-THREE

Portugal
1941

i

He reached Lisbon on 18th February after "an incredible, nightmarish journey of a week" (Antibes – Narbonne – Port Bou – Barcelona – Madrid – Lisbon). According to Nancy Cunard, this journey, which Douglas had been dreading ever since he had foreseen the possibility of having to make it, was made more endurable for him by the assistance of "an American film-man" who looked after him.

He stayed two or three days in Lisbon, and made himself known to Neil Hogg, to whom he had been given an introduction by Hogg's cousin, Elizabeth David,[116] and with whom he had already exchanged letters about the possibility of coming to Portugal. Pitt-Millward's place, Douglas' destination, was about 230 miles north of Lisbon; Hogg, seeing that Douglas had had enough of public transport to last him ten years, showed his quality at once by having him driven the whole way in his car, breaking the journey at a hotel at Oporto.

His host's house – Gloria, Ponte do Lima – was palatial, and contained every comfort. Douglas began slowly to recover from the starvation and discomforts of Antibes, "which, all the same, I was sorry to leave, for various other reasons"; but the outlook was bad there, owing to increasing restrictions, and he was afraid for the friends he had left behind. "Here, I have everything I want, cows and pigs and olives and wine," and the two chief servants were Italians from Capri "whom I have known *since they were born*; that helps. So that I am slowly finding myself again. But I have aged horribly of late, and am suffering from most painful rheumatism in my arm." There was even a private chapel in the house (which had been built by a Cardinal), he told Hutton, "in case you ever come this way", and he asked for news of Mavrogordato, Prentice, and other friends. Communication with Portugal was a good deal easier than with the south of France, and by the end of March he had heard from Bryher, Oscar Levy, Prentice, Greenless, Hutton, and others, besides Archie, who was now married and living in Scotland.

Gloria was situated in the wettest corner of Europe, he wrote, and they had only had three and a half fine days in a month, but although he was alone in the enormous house with his host (apart from the servants) there were huge wood fires everywhere. "I shall stay till I am kicked out, or failing that, till the war ends, or failing that, and supposing the war to last longer than I do – then, presumably, for ever . . . I do nothing but eat and sleep which fills up the 24 hours very nicely . . . As to books, there is a good collection of them in this house, but I can't even read with any pleasure just now", though a few days later he admitted to having glanced into "a huge edition of H. Walpole's letters: what a different kind of atmosphere to ours, and how much more pleasant!" He was "very grumpy at not knowing a word of Portuguese", but there was no teacher for miles.

He had heard from Emilio. "He writes pretty cheerfully, but I daresay he is having no good time of it; no better, at least, than others in Florence in his position, which cannot be satisfactory, as there is so little work at his printer's shop." He had had a card from Orioli. "I have not seen Pino," he wrote to Professor Dawkins, "but had a line from him saying nothing whatever. What did he tell you? What is he doing? Has he got his money? And what about his place in Florence? Answer – if you can! I answered his note but he obviously means not to reply."

In April, when the weather was a little warmer, he caught two snakes – "the first I have ever seen in this country, which shows that spring is at last coming in. They were mere babies, and could not be induced to bite, not even when I opened their mouths for them. I left them in the woods where I found them." He complained that transplantation into a strange environment did not agree with him, but he seemed to be making the best of it – as he was nearly always capable of doing – and converting it into familiar terms. If he had been able to stay, it is at least possible that he would have settled down and found a place for himself in this new environment until the war ended. But he was not able to stay; Pitt-Millward wanted to get out of Europe (and, in fact, eventually went to the USA), and talked of leaving. "I should have to leave too, unless I want to starve" wrote Douglas, who, apart from £10 a month, was entirely dependent upon hospitality.

Besides, the police refuse to renew my passport . . . I have written about it to my friend at the Embassy, who may be able to do something. It is damnable, being hunted about like this at my time of life. I left Florence with what I considered the barest necessities. Well, nearly all of them had to be left at Antibes. Now I shall have to leave nearly all that remains to me in this place, because if I come by air, I am only allowed 15 ounces of luggage – or was it pounds? – so that I shall arrive in England as naked as a new-born child, though perhaps a little more attractive, and with about 4/6 in my pocket, if I am lucky.

On 8th May, he went down to Lisbon to try to clarify his legal and financial position in Portugal, and see if anything could be done to improve it. Or perhaps, as he afterwards put it, he was "dumped" in Lisbon by Pitt-Millward. At any rate, he did not return to Gloria.

ii

He was a fortnight in Lisbon in hotels and a pension, and must have been worried during this period about how long his money would last with the new expenses of board and lodgings. Neil Hogg then came to the rescue: he had a spare room in his flat. He said afterwards that he found the spare room an affliction: there were so many people coming and going through Lisbon at the time, and, asking at the Embassy for accommodation, that he felt obliged to offer the room continually to anyone in need of it. He was therefore glad, he said, to be able to offer it to a more permanent guest: it suited him; and it solved an otherwise insoluble problem for Douglas.

The next problems to solve were the passport and financial ones. Renewal of his permit to stay in Portugal seems to have been overlooked; he had outstayed his permit by six months, he wrote in September; but presumably some kind of renewal was given later. As to money, he eventually succeeded in obtaining £20 a month (the maximum) instead of £10, on the grounds of age, infirmity, and consequent inability to travel immediately. His air passage had been booked and paid for before he left Antibes, as a necessary means of obtaining permission to leave France and enter Spain and Portugal; but there were apparently eighty people ahead of him on the waiting list, planes were irregular, of small capacity and crowded with priority passengers; and there were apparently seven to eight hundred on the waiting list behind him. But it must be admitted that as he did not *want* to go to England, he probably did not try very hard to get there. His attitude was ambivalent, partly because he was not sure of his position in law in England, but also because he had become thoroughly Mediterraneanised. He dreaded not only the exterior climate of England, but the interior climate – the climate of thought and morality and behaviour as well. As to English food and drink, in wartime, he must have heard enough about them in Lisbon to know that it would be like going to prison, whereas in Lisbon there was plenty of everything. And if he were to go to England, he wondered if he would "ever get out of the country again, at my age. If I thought that was likely, I should not mind so much. But I don't like the prospect of never seeing olive-trees *etc etc.* again. That is a thought which makes me feel sick at heart." On the other hand, he felt that he could not go on "abusing Hogg's hospitality for ever".

This ambivalent attitude accounts for the fact that he wrote off energetically at first, after his arrival in Lisbon, to friends in England who might be able to pull strings there to get him on an aeroplane as soon as possible; but after he had been in Lisbon about a month, and had obtained an authorisation from the head of the English hospital to say that he was not fit to travel, and had applied for an increase in his allowance of £10 a month because he was obliged to stay, he began to write to his friends that he would not leave Portugal unless he was "kicked out".

He would certainly not go to America, in spite of repeated invitations from Robin, who had been trying to get him to go there ever since he had heard of his father's safe arrival in Portugal. Robin had even written to Richard Aldington (who was living in the USA) about it, but Aldington had written back quite a long letter full of commonsense, concluding: "I'll do anything I can to help to get him over here if you really and truly believe he'd be happier and more comfortable here than in Portugal. Personally, I don't believe he would, though I'd give a great deal to see him again." How right he was! Douglas, no doubt grateful for the interest his more recalcitrant son was now taking in his welfare, replied to Robin – repeatedly – with polite and plausible evasion, but to Archie he wrote: "The only way to get me to America would be to handcuff and chloroform me, and to keep me in an iron cage all the way across. Even then I should escape as soon as possible, and walk all the way to Europe on foot, if necessary . . . Nothing will get me to America – not if they send a war-ship for me, with a pressing autograph invitation from the President. I would sooner die of starvation than of home sickness." He was, he wrote, "hopelessly Europeanised". His host, as well as others, was mystified: ". . . your Father is well, active and bored," he wrote to Robin, who had tried to enlist Hogg's help in getting Douglas to America, "but not so bored as to forget his prejudice against crossing the Atlantic. I do not quite understand on what the prejudice is based – perhaps, as I am half American he does not like to go into details – but I can see clearly that it is deep-rooted." Robin, once roused and in receipt of sympathetic appreciation from his father for his efforts on his behalf, redoubled them. He even wrote to Churchill in an attempt to get his father's allowance of money increased.

Hogg, wrote Douglas, "goes out of his way to make me comfortable in every possible respect (and I should like this to be put on record, if not by the Recording Angel then by some more terrestrial authority)": the problem was, how to pay him back, or, failing that, show his gratitude?

He hit on the idea of the Almanac – a selection of aphorisms from his books, one for every day of the year. According to Hogg, Douglas began work on this not long after he became Hogg's guest.

Once he had conceived the idea, it must have pleased him to be at work again. He apparently had with him many of his own books, possibly a reading copy of each. Once he had got to work, the days must have begun to arrange themselves more satisfactorily around this activity than they had done at Gloria. Hogg was out all day at the Embassy; Douglas no doubt worked in the mornings and walked about Lisbon in the after-noons, having lunched, perhaps, with Orioli and Carlo, whom he met "nearly every day" also at 5 p.m. in a certain café. When Hogg was free in the evening, he and Douglas would "visit the cafés of the town, which we enliven with rather rowdy conversation and the composition of quite incredibly lewd verses. It doesn't seem to do him any harm and it does me a great deal of good." So, as long as he was a guest, and as long as his permit to stay in Portugal lasted, the days must have been quite pleasant. Sometimes he and Orioli and Carlo were able to get into the country for a day: he made excursions to Coimbra for a night, and once or twice to Cintra. His giddiness, he wrote, was much the same as ever.

Until about the middle of the summer, he thought that leaving Antibes was the greatest mistake of his life. He had only left because he had been told that he could get from Lisbon to England whenever he felt like it, and that he would be starved in Antibes; yet he heard from there at the end of May that they were no worse off than when he had left. By the middle of July, however, Leng wrote that he had already learned not to eat, and was now learning how to get on without wine or tobacco. In October Douglas started sending food parcels to his former landlady and her little boy. During the next three months, he sent twenty-three of these parcels.

As usual, his communications with Archie were regular and fairly frequent. Archie had been rejected for service as soon as they heard he had been gassed in the First War; and he had gone through the same sort of experience, while trying to get a job, as his father describes in the intro-duction to *Alone*. Eventually, he and his wife had gone to Scotland.

His wife was expecting a baby, and he consulted his father about names for a boy. His father replied that he had no idea about such things: "What about Marmaduke, or Algernon?", but had to explain in a later letter that they were "meant for a joke". However, "Peter" wouldn't do at all: "I have hardly ever met a Peter that wasn't a shit, or something worse . . . nine-tenths of the Peters I have known were downright shits (like the original). David I prefer to either of the other two, and Andrew to Alexander, which is sure to be contracted to Alec – another shit-producing name." The name difficulty was resolved early in November, when

Victoria Penuel Douglas was born. Her grandfather hoped she would "turn out to be a witch. We have had no witches *in our family* (none that I know of, at least, though we have had a good many bitches) since the Puritan days, when a brace of them were burnt near Edinburgh. Anyhow, you have done your best, and if she was not born on the 31st October – that is obviously the fault of the hospital people."

On 8th December, Douglas was seventy-three. "My birthday was a quiet affair – nothing at all, in fact! I told nobody about it, but some people remembered all the same." Two days later he was sending off some of the fifty or so copies of *An Almanac*; a few had gone earlier. On the 16th, Hogg was informed that he was to be transferred to the Foreign Office at the end of the month. Douglas said that he would try his best to go with Hogg, as he could not survive, even with £20 a month, on his own. He dreaded the thought of his "coming life in England, where I am practically a stranger, and an old and shaky one. There is no help for it! I fear I shall leave my bones in some dreadful suburban cemetery, where the graves are five on the top of each other. Anyhow, I must be near friends of some kind or another, as I don't trust myself alone any more." He was also afraid that he would not be able to correspond easily from England with Emilio; or send any more food parcels to Antibes.

Orioli and Carlo had arrived in Lisbon in November 1939. They could not go to England (and if they could have, would have been interned) and refused to return to Italy. "They have nothing whatever to do," wrote Douglas at the end of November 1941, "and are rather grumpy; the only things that cheers them up is a Fascist defeat, such as yesterday (Gondar). I see them nearly every day . . ." All the same, Orioli was "flourishing" – until early in December. He then became "pretty damned ill . . . with heart-trouble and other complications. I don't like the look of the thing." A week later, the same: "He suffers a good deal. Luckily he has his servant Carlo with him. I go to see him every day, but yesterday he was too bad for my visit." On the 21st, he seemed to be "on the mend"; but after another week was described as "very bad still". On 2nd January, at 8 a.m., he died. Douglas had seen him the previous evening, and Carlo told him afterwards that Orioli had only a few seconds of pain before dying. The funeral, which Douglas attended, was on the 3rd. If Orioli had lived another five weeks he would have been fifty-eight.

What Pino's death meant to Norman can only be imagined, but it can be imagined without difficulty. For fifteen years he and Pino had been almost inseparable companions. They had been deeply and fully intimate in the unlimited freedom of a friendship, rare for Douglas, that was without reservations of any kind.

One of the most unpleasant suggestions ever made in print about

Douglas – and also one of the most reckless and silliest, since it can so easily be disproved – was made by Aldington: ". . . I have heard it said that, although Norman was in Lisbon at the time, his hedonistic self-protection kept from him ever going to see his best friend, Pino, when he was dying in Lisbon during the war; but I don't even know that the facts are as reported, and prefer to think the tale a calumny." He prefers to think the tale a calumny, and let everyone else suspect that it is true. If Douglas was not actually holding Orioli's hand at the last moment, it was not for want of feeling, but for an excess of it. Of that one may be sure, though he would never have admitted it. It is not to be forgotten, either, that Carlo – almost an adopted son – was there too, with Orioli at the end; and Douglas, even if he had felt a strong desire to be with his old friend, would never have intruded upon that relationship. For a man who actively hated the very thought of death, his record with regard to departed friends was not a bad one. He had sat with several who were close to him, at their bedsides, when they might have died at any moment. He well knew his and their helplessness, and faced it: "Every other antagonist can be ignored or bribed or circumvented or crushed outright. But here is a damnable spectre who knocks at the door and does not wait to hear you say 'Come in'. Hateful!"

Hogg, as it turned out, did not leave for London until 5th January, by which time Orioli had died, and been buried. Douglas could not go with Hogg, and had no idea where or how he was going to live. He must have felt exceedingly melancholy for a few days; but then had a stroke of luck: he was able to get a seat in a plane to London on 11th January.

CHAPTER THIRTY-FOUR

England
1942–1946

i

According to Nancy Cunard, he looked well – "strong, rosy, well-fed, ready for everything!" – but even so he had already felt the cold (first of all in the aeroplane) that he was to go on feeling all through that hard wartime winter. Even with a thick vest and three pullovers on, it got through, in the absence of adequate heating and, as he was soon to realise, of sufficiently sustaining food and drink.

After a few days at Faith Mackenzie's, he went to stay in the Palmers' flat in St John's Wood, and remained there nearly a month. Arnold Palmer has described the kind of impression of London which Douglas must have received:

> The friends who might have gathered in celebration of his return were too busy to gather; they greeted him and hurried back to their treadmills . . . Black-out, gas masks, sorry no cigarettes, sirens, identity cards, no sir only the cod . . . coupons – with none of the gradual breaking-in that we had had, it all descended in a lump on this man of 74. There were many days, naturally, when he didn't feel very well . . . and it is not surprising that, always a slightly unaccountable man, he became rather difficult and prickly. He stayed with us for several weeks, but when, eventually, I had to tell him that his bed was "wanted", he took it hard and made little attempt to hide his annoyance. Perhaps he didn't believe me; perhaps he had (to use his own word) been kicked out too often. I can see that now, but at the time he wasn't the only one to feel ruffled. But we both got over it, of course.

After his stay at the Palmers' he went to Nancy Cunard for four or five days, staying in her warm flat in Cliffords Inn. He announced that he must find a place to live in and then some work that would bring him in enough money to live on. (His bank account in London was still immobilised, and would remain so until the Controller of Enemy Property made an order to release it.)

It occurred to Nancy Cunard that he might "do rather well by consenting to write a few articles" – about France after the Occupation, about Lisbon, and about his impressions of England after twenty-five years. Knowing that he could never be persuaded to write for the papers himself, she thought she might interview him for a literary periodical. She decided to put her questions on paper, which, if he liked, he could throw away. The questions poured out like a torrent, and she left the paper on the table for him one day before going out. When she returned, *he* had gone out, but there was an answer waiting for her:

Darling Nancy,

You ask me more than twenty questions and I believe I can answer three or four, and none of them adequately.

What strikes me most in England is that you cannot get a copy of The Times nowadays. Also that the inhabitants of London are more solemn and preoccupied than they used to be.

Who isn't?

I know nothing about the modern buildings. At first sight they don't strike me as ugly, and I hope they are more comfortable than the old ones. They couldn't be less.

As to the young writers and poets – I have not yet read a single one of them. I don't even know their names, having been cut off from English books and papers for so long.

In South France I paid no attention to the reaction of the natives in regard to the German occupation. Politics bore me. The food-crisis was much nearer my heart. When it became acute, I cleared out.

I noticed no Nazi agents in Lisbon, though there may have been thousands of them. The few Germans I met were refugees. And the few Portuguese avoided politics like the plague. And the few newspapers were censored, and therefore no guide to the country's political feelings.

I have no plans, except to try and live in peace henceforward – which will be difficult, if this sort of infernal catechising is going to continue. United States and Germany and Russia and India and all the rest of them: let other people do the thinking and cackling and writing! It seems to amuse them, and does me no harm.

All very unsatisfactory, eh?
Yours ever,
Norman

Yes! It was unsatisfactory! Myopic, almost ostrich-like; self-centred, but curiously impersonal – not self-revealing. "How could anyone who had been through the collapse of France not have a good deal to say?" wondered Nancy Cunard. Even on the subject of food, when pressed for details, he could only produce a comment about the *ersatz* coffee: "It got so bad in the end that I used to pay a little boy to pick the few real coffee beans out of all the rest. And *that* was enough for only *one* good cup at a time!"

About London, though, there was one thing he had noticed during the month he had been there – an increase in "the industrial eye". This eye was quite different from the agricultural one, which was broader, used to looking at larger spaces, instead of focusing on something relatively small: "I have noticed a *great* increase in the industrial eye, with its lesser field of vision." As to humanity, he had no hope for it, none whatever: "There will always be people to make wars . . ."

ii

From Cliffords Inn, he went to Symonds House Hotel in Brook Street, Mayfair. He had last stayed in this hotel about 1892, and had certainly stayed there three years before that, after leaving the Gymnasium at Karlsruhe. Fifty years since his previous visit! – one can imagine that the knowledge of this interesting fact would have given him enormous quiet pleasure; it was just the sort of personal link with the past that he loved, and it could be enjoyed just as much – perhaps even more – if no one else knew about it, or at any rate, knew what it really meant to him.

At this address he soon began to give language lessons, and to do a little reading of manuscripts for a publisher. He evolved a daily routine, as usual, often meeting Nancy Cunard for lunch, and spending part of the afternoon in The Ladder Club, just round the corner. He regularly saw his friends, even those – like Charles Prentice, Mavrogordato, Dawkins and Hutton – who lived far from London; for they appeared in town from time to time, and meetings were arranged.

Symonds Hotel lasted about three and a half months, and then, in June, he had to clear out in order to economise. But once again, he did not move to a less expensive district, but to Half Moon Street. It was as though the whole of his middle life in London, when he had lived cheaply, had dropped out of his mind, and he was thinking himself back to the Walsingham House period. He thought the rent of his new rooms – four and a half guineas a week – "quite absurd, but if I let myself sink, I shall never get up again". He could do, he said, with giving three lessons a day, but couldn't find the pupils; they were all busy doing something else. Susan Palmer was his only constant pupil at that time.

Whether it was lack of money, or unappetising food, or both, he lost his "rosy, well-fed" appearance. "I have got so thin" he wrote to Archie, "that there is room for two people inside my trousers." He had made sporadic attempts to get useful work – his friend Leng had landed a job in the cipher department of the Foreign Office – but did not succeed, and in the end decided that he was better off without one, since he didn't have to pay tax on his earnings as a language teacher.

One thing he never lacked, however unsatisfactory in other ways his environment might be, was friends. He was always effortlessly making new ones. "I found that from the moment of meeting him we got on together like a house on fire," wrote Charles Duff. He added that he was slightly surprised, as people had told him that Douglas was a bit difficult, whereas he found him genial and warm-hearted. With some people, of course, Douglas could be difficult, and not always with those whom one might nominate for that rôle: but for Charles Duff he had had a great respect and admiration since 1927 when Duff had published what is certainly one of the finest examples of subversive irony since Swift, namely, his *Handbook on Hanging*. That was a good start; and the fact that Duff liked a drink, knew where to get good beer in wartime, had sound humane values, and was excellent company, was a good follow-up.

Not long after moving to Half Moon Street, Douglas met Viva King at a dinner party. "I liked him so much that I called on him the next morning in Half Moon St. He was anxious to find an American edition of South Wind to re-read the preface. I ran round to Heywood Hill's & was back in 10 minutes with the very copy . . . My husband was working at decoding & had to have good Italian & I had the idea that he shd have lessons from N.D. They met every week & became very great friends." They became great friends, and so remained until Douglas' death. Willie King, witty, erudite, eccentric, and an authoritative scholar, became Douglas' literary executor. To his conscientiousness and scrupulous attention to detail, and to the fact that he won and kept the absolute confidence of Douglas, a great debt is owed. He went through most, if not all, of Douglas' books with him, page by page, and line by line, asking questions and noting down the answers. A good deal of biographical information was thus revealed that would never have come to light otherwise; and since Douglas imposed quite heavily on his literary executor in the matter of bringing out or preparing new editions of his books, and since Willie King was an indefatigable hunter-down of misprints, checker of facts, and pointer-out of possible errors or mis-statements – in other words, a meticulous editor – much is owed to him in textual improvement and accuracy.

Douglas spent a lot of time with the Kings and had a stimulating and liberating influence which Viva King remembers with gratitude: "His forthright no humbug attitude swept away all my old shibboleths and cobwebs left from convent days. His repeated 'Why not, my dear?' made one wonder 'Why not? indeed!' He was so gay and amusing and

Rabelaisian, I used to think of him as old Silenus – sometimes I used to look under the table for his goat's feet."

It was at the Kings', at a luncheon-party, that Douglas re-met Rebecca West. He seemed to have forgotten her, she wrote, and not to recall that they had known each other quite well: "Someone mentioned his novel They Went and he said 'Nobody read that book except the people who were sent after it by a review in The New Statesman,' and to my delight he began to recall a review I had written when I was fiction reviewer for that periodical. He then added 'It was written by Rose Macaulay, God bless her.'"

iii

Nancy Cunard now lived less than a hundred yards from his own rooms and they were together a great deal, sharing *The Times*, making coffee on a gas ring, eating in or out, and visiting the pubs at night. Not only in London: they went out to Epping Forest to look, in vain, for the first signs of spring; and down to Alresford and Selborne to see if they could find any 'Early Britons'. A few were said to exist there; you could tell them by the shape of the head . . . But no Early Britons, definitely identifiable as such, were discovered.

In August he went up to Banchory, Aberdeen and Edinburgh. The weather "behaved uncommonly well", but otherwise the trip does not seem to have been very enjoyable: "I went some of the old walks and saw some of the old people. By dint of living always in the same place they seemed to me to have become spiritually atrophied, or rather *mineralised*."

It was no use his going to live in the country, he wrote to Archie; he would have nothing whatever to do there, and anyway he hated it; nor did he think he would ever get used to the English climate. It was now made all the worse by the war's added horrors: "Everything is grim and grey, and all the circumstances in which we are obliged to live have a most *demoralising* effect – on me, at all events. My outlook and character are slowly changing under the stress, and not for the better." The demoralisation and the change in character were not evident to those who met him in these years, although it was obvious that he was unhappy in England. Those who knew him would never have expected him to be anything else but that, even in peacetime, in the land of eternal moisture, frightful cold, licensing hours, inedible food, grundyism, and cruelty to children. However, "I can't come to America" he wrote to Robin, "and if I could, I wouldn't," and by the end of the year his mood was more cheerful: ". . . I am doing quite well, and letting the future do what *it* likes. I can squeeze through, easily, for another 2–3 years; and my health is distinctly better, which makes me think that rheumatism is perhaps not a matter of climate after all."

Half Moon Street proved too expensive, and he migrated to the Gloucester Road area, having been invited by his friend Nigel Richards to live in his house at 2 Hereford Square. He was installed there before the end of March. He begged both Archie and Robin not to "give my new address to any one *under any conditions*. I am overrun with a pack of shits of both sexes and all nationalities and ages. *Not to anyone*; not even if it's a question of life and death." He had been in London more than a year, and as he was always ready to please his close friends like Nancy Cunard he was often carried off to other people's houses, or found that new acquaintances dropped into the pubs or clubs he went to and that inevitably a proportion of them were of a superficial, sycophantic or otherwise unpleasing kind; and from time to time, as here, his patience would become exhausted. He had found the winter sufficiently tiring, had a bad cold, which when it went, left him "very groggy. I don't feel at all up to the scratch; always tired, and ready to go to bed again as soon as I have dressed", and he was "grumpy beyond belief" he told Hutton, laying happily into Cicero in the same letter, perhaps as an illustration of the fact:

> . . . he was a typical Roman prig. The "divine Tully" fitted well in with Addison & Co., who were a generation of prigs. He got that future life nonsense at Eleusis, I suppose.

iv

In February 1943, the *Bookseller*, taking up the vexed question of copyright protection for British books in the USA used the case of *South Wind*, which it called "one of the most famous books of the present century", as an example.

In December of the previous year, a new impression of the second English edition of *South Wind* had been published, with a four-page Introductory Note by Douglas, in which he described how the book had been affected by the limitations of the then existing copyright laws. The relevant part of Douglas' Note was reprinted, occupying a page in the *Bookseller*.

As a result of this publicity, Bennett Cerf, of the Modern Library, replied indignantly to what he called "an insult to the American book-publishing world in general, and to my own firm, among several others, in particular". He alleged that Douglas had engaged in double-dealing over a proposed limited edition of *Summer Islands* to be published by Cerf in the USA, by arranging for a cheap edition in England. As soon as Cerf had found this out, he wrote, he had cancelled the American edition, written off the payment for it, and ceased to pay any further (courtesy) royalties on *South Wind*. Douglas, at the time, had written to Cerf that he "had not understood that he was hurting our edition in any way by arranging for this cheap English reprint, and that he frankly did not believe it was any of our business as to whether or not he sold the English rights to the property"...

The editor of the *Bookseller*, justifying his publication of the article, referred to Bennett Cerf's accusations as "silly", and supported Douglas. There was a good deal of confidential evidence that the Modern Library was known for piracy and also for suddenly ceasing to pay courtesy royalties with or without an excuse that was as feeble as the one used in this instance.

In the 1944 and 1945 re-impressions of *South Wind* containing the Introductory Note, as above, Douglas apologised to Hughes, Massie and Co for his implication – though he had not named them – that they had apparently been guilty of neglect in failing to get the book copyrighted in America. He had heard from them that they had done their best at the time.

v

Nancy Cunard, like Douglas, had moved, but to Marylebone, in the opposite direction from himself, and he saw little of her; he had three language pupils a week; he had heard from his people in Antibes that they were all right. In March, in a grumpy and impatient letter to Robin he had written: "My brother is always in Aberdeen, but whether alive or buried I don't know!" Exactly a month later his brother died. As a result of this (going to the funeral was out of the question for him, he wrote) he got in touch with his nephew, John Sholto, whom he had not seen since he was five years old – "Of course I wrote at once to Sholto, whom I addressed as 'Colonel' though he may be only a private for all I know." Douglas reported that he had "a nice dinner" with him (at Sholto's club in London). A report from the other party would have differed: Major J. S. Douglas had been brought up by religiously-minded parents to regard his wicked uncle with a certain amount of distaste; but he much admired his uncle's books, and tried to put all prejudice out of his mind when he asked him to dinner. He was not allowed to get away with such liberal sentiments: he was given the full Douglas treatment, and tested to the limit with strings of obscenities and vilifications. Naturally enough, being the host, and the younger man, he was in a vulnerable position, and did not enjoy the meeting. But the strange thing is that his uncle liked him. He had an odd way of showing it.[117]

His nephew would undoubtedly have stood a better chance of enjoying and appreciating his uncle's company if, like Michael Mavrogordato, he had been a dozen years younger and the son of an old friend. Dr Mavrogordato remembers meeting Douglas quite frequently during the second half of Douglas' years in London. He would often accompany Douglas through the blackout to or from his rooms, glad, as so many people were, to be in his company and at the same time, as few were, to be of use as guide and companion in the darkened streets. The most interesting reminiscence of Douglas recounted by Dr Mavrogordato concerns certain possessions which "always accompanied him" from lodging to lodging. These were "a bronze head of himself . . . by George Thomas, an Edward Lear water-colour of Antibes, given him by Nancy Cunard, and finally the extensive Mardrus and Mather version of the Arabian Nights". A book, a painting, and a sculpture, carefully chosen Lares and Penates that could furnish even a wartime room with memories of wider horizons.

For more than eleven months of the year he was in London, without much joy of any kind: there had been no news of Eric for two years, and of Emilio he knew nothing and feared the worst; Leng was in Persia, and Hogg about to go to Baghdad. Nigel Richards, in whose house he was living, was away on operations with the RAF, so that Douglas, apart from the housekeeper, was the only person in the house: "In the evenings I am nearly always alone in here, eating a *filthy* sandwich at a pub for dinner." Lunches were all right, often with friends; but he didn't much like going out in the evening, in the blackout, with little hope of getting a taxi, sirens sounding, bombing, often fog in the winter, his own dizziness and rheumatism adding to the hazards. Rheumatism kept him awake at night, "so that I am always half asleep by day. In the summer I shall *have to* take a cure somewhere"; and he never felt really warm "having lost all my fat. I weigh 3 lbs less now than I did at 15!" Nevertheless, it seems that he may have enjoyed Christmas, which he shared with Nancy Cunard. She had tender memories of it:

We sat for hours, I know, our arms linked, talking of the things we would do, later . . . later . . . At present we were playing at being in the *Wagons Lits* – the very sofa could be said to resemble one. We were crossing France towards Italy, and as romantic about it as could be! *And why not?*

Maybe this was one of the times you told me (the same sentiment was addressed to one or two others as well, on various occasions) that, when the time came, you would like to think of yourself as "putrefying gracefully in your arms, my dear . . ." – a winning, if at first somewhat startling, remark! It makes me horribly nostalgic to think of that evening now. I cannot tell what kind of charm you had as a young man – nor yet at the age of forty. But, damn it, the charm you had then in 1943, at the age of seventy-five . . .

vi

Air-raids on London had been renewed and were now regular and intense; but Douglas, who had often said that he had "no nerves to speak of", seems to have proved this true. "As to that raid," he replied to Archie's enquiry about a particularly heavy one, "– it made a noise, and I turned round in bed. Quite fatalistic! . . . I had a ceiling on my head the other evening, *not here*, and all the windows in the house were smashed or blown in. No great fun." He would stay in London, he told Nancy Cunard, until towards the end of April, and might then go for a tour of the south-west looking for a place to spend several months in. He was determined to be quite comfortable: "I want bath, breakfast in bed, etc., my reason being that I am going to do myself as well as possible, death being so near."

The raids got even livelier with the arrival of the first of Hitler's secret weapons – the doodle-bug, buzz-bomb, or VI. In June 1944 these began falling all over London and around it through all the twenty-four hours of the day. "One gets damned little sleep nowadays," wrote Douglas towards the end of June; but his preparations for a two- or three-month holiday from London had been made, and on the last day of the month he went down to Oxford, where he stayed for a month – with Oscar Levy and his daughter – and then moved to Chester on 3rd August.

By the 11th, the whole of Florence was in Allied hands, and he was concerned to get in touch with anyone there who could give him information about Emilio, and his flat. Through Nancy Cunard he sent a letter for Emilio to John Gawsworth, a young poet and literary editor who was with the RAF in Italy and had offered to make enquiries on Douglas' behalf. Douglas' own plans were uncertain after the end of the month; he did not know what he would do, except that he would not go to London if he could help it:

> Mrs [Viva] King had just written that they had "119 bombs (official) in one night" and that never a night passes without her house shaking. I wish we could *both* go to Crowley's village and *stay there*. Could we? I might be able to help you with some work.
>
> Love to Aleister

Nancy Cunard, to whom the letter was written, replied that she was there to see Crowley, that he told her he was working against Hitler on the astral plane, that he was most interesting to talk to, and that he had left his "hoolie-goolie period" a long way behind. She had first met him in

1933: Douglas, when? Meanwhile, Douglas wrote that he'd had "one or two nice letters from Crowley who seems to be as wizardish as ever", and he assured Nancy Cunard that Crowley was *nothing* to what he had been: "He was hot stuff, and no mistake, my dear. They can stand a good deal in Italy, but in the end he was too much for them, and he had to go!" It seems unlikely that we shall ever know what kind of friendship existed between these two expatriate Scotsmen who had a little, but not much, in common. Douglas' thin vein of superstition, his love of the macabre and of sexual experiment, must have enabled him to find common ground with Crowley, and he would have been robust enough to not be afraid of him, but perhaps to find him a rich source of interest and amusement.

Instead of going to "Crowley's village", Aston Clinton, Douglas went from Chester to Somerset, and stayed in a farmhouse near Faith Mackenzie where he at least ate well: "meat etc every day, cartloads of eggs, mountains of butter and lakes of cream." He went over every evening to supper with Mrs Mackenzie, and made one or two expeditions. One of these was to Downside, the Catholic public school, at which his friend Desmond Ryan had been a pupil, and where he was now staying. He liked the Abbot, Douglas told Hutton, whom he arranged to meet about this time. He also went to meet a Mrs E. and her son. She was an old friend of Robin's, and he had asked his father especially to meet her. She, however, told Douglas nothing. ". . . and I can't imagine why Robin was so anxious for me to meet her. I guessed she might have been some former friend of his, and that the child might possibly be my grandson. But I learned nothing, and of course did not ask any questions. Anyhow, I tried to be as nice as I could to them."

After a brief visit to Cornwall in bad weather, it seemed to be time to return to London. By this time he had heard so much from his friends there about the aerial onslaught on the city – the V2s had begun – that he made a will before leaving Cornwall.

In London there were alerts every night, and a good many during the day. "But where else to go? I have been hunted up and down the country for 4 months, or nearly . . . Hereford Square and neighbourhood badly knocked about. Another bomb in Harrington Road made an awful mess. Another beside S. Ken. Museum . . . Will is now at bank 161 New Bond Str and I have their receipt for it." He agreed with Archie that it was silly to live in London, but "I could not live in some beastly country pub".

vii

He had been trying for a month or more to get to France, and longed to get to Italy, or at least to get news of Emilio and his flat. Even if he had been considered to be qualified to go to one of these countries in some official capacity – the only way of getting there at all at that time – he would have been found to be too old, so he had little hope, but went on trying. His rheumatism was "simply bloody" and he had difficulty in getting out of his bath.

News from Antibes came through: his former landlady, Mme Mercier, and her son were both "flourishing"; but the little boy could not understand why Douglas didn't return now that he could. "Je languis après vous . . ." he wrote on his mother's letters to Douglas.

That, at any rate, was good news; and the news from Florence which eventually came through from three different sources, was not as bad as it might have been. Emilio, of whom he had heard nothing for more than two years, was all right:

> . . . my flat has been knocked about and it looks as if some of my more valuable belongings had been looted (by the fascists): but something is left. My servant Emilio had a very bad time of it. He was imprisoned for ten months by the fascists; then let out; then put in a concentration camp, where it seems the Allies found him. His flat was also knocked about, but he is living there with wife and child, and has now got a job with Amgot in some printing Department (how lucky I taught him English ages ago) so that I am no longer anxious about him.

That was something to go on with; but when would he ever get out there, if at all? He even wrote to Robin in America underlining the longing he had to get to Italy, just in case Robin knew anyone, or could do anything. Perhaps he was remembering the letter his son had written to Churchill.

viii

Archie, still in Scotland, was teaching now in a preparatory school. His wife was expecting her second child, and Archie wrote, as he had done before, asking his father for advice about names. The reply was mild enough: "I don't much care about Norman, which may yet end in not being a very creditable one . . . I don't care about John, reminds me of my shit brother, and there are thousands of Sholto D's . . . An old Douglas name is James; and if you like something very Scotch why not Gavin?"

Archie had helped him with corrections and alterations to an edition of the *Almanac* that he was preparing for publication in England. It was sent off to Chatto and Windus before Christmas. He was still trying to get his *Late Harvest* published, but the paper famine made this difficult. Nancy Cunard introduced him to the publisher Lindsay Drummond about this time, and he it was who eventually brought the book out.

The bombardment of London by V1s and V2s at this time was so persistent that he felt obliged to do anything which could contribute to "setting his house in order" and wrote to Archie to say that they ought to meet so that they could look at "those Florentine documents" together. These must surely have been papers relating to his flat or to his possessions in it.

Douglas had thought of meeting Archie half way, at Chester, but as Marion had already gone into hospital for the birth of her second child, Archie could not get away, and his father went up to Perthshire and stayed at Comrie for a couple of nights. Gavin was born on 11th January, but his grandfather was unable to see the mother. He doubted, he wrote from London, whether he would come north again at Easter, because "I *may be* trying to write another book, in which to incorporate those *Comments*".[118] By the end of April he was hard at work, and hoped to have the book finished in a few weeks; and, in fact, the typescript was ready by 25th June. He would get the Society of Authors to handle it, he wrote, as neither Secker nor Chatto's had paper to spare, and he could not afford to wait.

Archie, meanwhile, had been seriously ill with cervical adenitis. "Sounds very important," wrote Douglas, "but not nearly as good as what I have: acroparaesthesia."

ix

He was unable to put the idea of getting to France or Italy as soon as possible out of his head. An attempt had been made to interest the British Council in sending him abroad to describe the situation there; but it came to nothing. Nancy Cunard had gone off with journalistic accreditations from the *Burlington Magazine, Horizon*, and *Our Time*. Some such arrangement was a necessity, since the English government would release only £10 a month for private individuals. What she found when she returned to Réanville, her house in Normandy – the wanton vandalism and spiteful desecration of the place – she has described in *Grand Man* and elsewhere. She wondered what had happened to Douglas' things in Florence. So did he:

I am terribly sorry, alas, to hear such bad accounts of your place. I suppose we ought to be grateful to be allowed to live! The funny thing is I can get no answer from Emilio to my letters, which he evidently does not receive, since he wired me the other day, "Attendo sue notizie". Some confusion here. And what do *our* authorities mean by putting an Italian fascist into *my* flat? Of course he will clear out such loot as the fascists have left. My idea was to get to Italy as soon as possible and sell that flat so as to have some money in hand. For all I know, our people have given him a long lease, and, in every case, I shall have difficulty in getting him out. I shall write to my lawyer in Florence about this, and also to a friend at our Embassy at Rome. Do get hold of more news if you can. If only somebody could manage to see Emilio personally and ask him what pieces of property the fascists took away and what is still in his, Emilio's, hands. Not much difficulty, as he works for PWB. *Of course* I want to get to Italy which is much more important for me than Antibes. And I am ready to start tonight . . . I want to get to Florence as soon as possible, although Antibes would be better than not going anywhere: Florence is infinitely preferable.

About ten days later he heard again from Emilio, who had still not had Douglas' letters: there was nothing about the flat, except that Carlo's mother was still living in Orioli's flat beneath, though Emilio had not seen her for a long time. Douglas, in London, was told that his room would be required in August, but solved that problem with time to spare, finding one at 46 Thurloe Square.

Archie came down on a visit just at the time Douglas was moving into his new room; and there was conflicting news about the Florence flat – it was not clear whether, if he returned, he would be able to get the occupants out. Meanwhile the Merciers in Antibes had kept a room for him ever since his departure, and asked why he did not return now the war was over. He explained . . . at length; but heard not long afterwards from Basil Leng that prices were such that he certainly could not have afforded to live there. As to food, in England it seemed to have become "less and worse" he told Nancy Cunard: "I live in a state of chronic semi-starvation. That would be quite endurable, if I could see any prospect of getting away. It is now 3 and half years since I arrived from Lisbon, and they have been among the most melancholy of my life – which I feel is slipping away so quickly (as regards strength, etc) that soon I may not be physically able to manage the journey. I miss you so much!"

x

In the middle of October, Eric (with his wife) suddenly arrived by air for medical treatment. Douglas said he looked very bad, and had jaundice, among other things. He went into the Ross Hospital for Tropical Diseases in the East End, and Douglas went down to see him and wrote to him nearly twice a week during the six weeks he was there. He made a good recovery, and he and his wife left in December. "I don't suppose I shall ever see him again" wrote Douglas.

Also in October *Late Harvest* had been accepted by Lindsay Drummond, and an advance (£150) was paid in November, for publication, it was hoped, in about nine months' time. Five years after the publication of *An Almanac*, and twelve years after *Looking Back*, he was once again in business.

xi

Douglas decided he would attack the problem of getting to Italy on 1st March, by applying for a renewal of his passport and asking for an interview with the "cultural relations man at the Italian Embassy. After that, visas for France and Italy . . . When all is ready, I propose to go to Paris for 2–3 days . . . then to Antibes to pick up some valuable books and papers of mine, and so to *Naples* where I have two people who will put me up while I look in the neighbourhood for some convenient hole in which to die when the time comes."

Towards the end of January he had a long letter from Emilio, with news, none too good, of his books, which had been stored in a villa on the outskirts of Florence. The cases had been broken open by German soldiers, and the contents scattered; the gardener had told Emilio that many of the books had been used as lavatory paper; but on the whole Emilio thought Douglas had been luckier than many English people, some of whom had lost everything. Emilio had rescued many of Douglas' possessions by taking them to his own place.

Meanwhile, before tackling the business of emigration, there were several things to be done. In the first place, he was involved with Mrs E. and her son, and exchanged several letters about them with Robin in America. In February he went to visit them again, gave them as much moral and practical support as he could, and encouraged Robin to do likewise. After the boy and his mother had gone to London, Douglas found accommodation for them at his own address in Thurloe Square.

Secondly, there was the business of the Obelisk Press to try to sort out, with Nancy Cunard's help. He had made arrangements with the Press just before the war, for them to bring out an edition of the *Limericks*. This edition had been published and had sold out, but Douglas had not received any of the 25 per cent of the proceeds which he said he was entitled to. Meanwhile, the business had changed hands; and then it was discovered that both parties had lost their contracts, and Douglas realised that he would have to write the debt off. Meanwhile a good deal of correspondence was necessary.

Thirdly, he was waiting to finish his part in the production of *Late Harvest*, by correcting the proofs. He had them done by the middle of April.

Towards the end of March he went along to the Italian Embassy in person, and succeeded in getting permission to enter and stay in the country. According to legend, his interviewer said to him– "So you want to go back to live in Italy?" and Douglas replied: "No – I want to go back to die there." This is said to have so moved the Embassy official that permission was granted forthwith.

He began to make arrangements as quickly as he could, with an energy (in writing the necessary letters and seeing the people concerned) which had not been evident for several years. He thought first of all that he would be going by sea to Naples, that the overland journey would be too ghastly. Paris and Antibes were scrapped because transport seemed exceedingly difficult, and might be altogether too tiring and delaying. ("Bryher," he reported to Archie, as an illustration of the lengths to which some people were prepared to go in order to avoid the horrors of post-war public transport, "has gone to Switzerland *in a taxi*.") Then the sea voyage was found to be impossible, and residence on Capri equally impossible, because of the enormous rise in the cost of living there. Finally, by the end of May, his plans were completed: he would not stay in Paris more than a few hours; and from Paris he would get into a through train to Rome where he would stay with his friend Ian Greenlees, who was at that time Second Secretary at the British Embassy; then on to Naples.

All through the first fortnight in June his excitement may be read between the lines of his letters: "Up to the neck! Fussed to death! etc." Finally, on 21st June, four years and five months after his arrival from Portugal, he left England for good for the second time in his life. This time he went via Dover and Calais, and was seen off at Victoria by Viva King, John Davenport and several others. Everyone, it was said, was near to tears.

CHAPTER THIRTY-FIVE

Italy
1946–1952

i

He stayed five or six days with Greenlees in Rome. They went out to Olevano and Genazzano, two favoured places they had both visited, together, in former days. He sounded happy: "Have been ¾ drunk ever since my arrival. Everything in abundance here ... Wine in torrents.' Greenlees had him driven to Naples in his car, where he would have stayed with his friend David Jeffreys, who was Vice Consul, but Jeffreys was away, ill, and Douglas had himself driven on to his old refuge, Sant' Agata.

> Food here excellent, and such a lot of it, that I can't get through it. A litre of wine 80 lire, eggs 16 lire (900 to the £). They talk utter rubbish in England about food-conditions here, which are ten times as good as any in London. Coffee (supposed to be unprocurable) is cheaper here than in England, and so on with everything. Figs, apricots, plums, cherries, peaches – about a penny a pound.

> Very warm. I have been for some of the old walks, all alone and rather wistful. The old coachman has died and left no successor ... so that one has to walk. I don't know whether I shall manage some of the longer distances ...

> I shall go to prospect in Capri in a week or two. Horribly expensive, they say.

Sant' Agata had always been a perennial tonic and restorative, and still was; but it had two disadvantages. In the first place, it was crowded with Italians on holiday, and full of their noisy and war-spoiled children. In the second place, it was too full of ghosts. That was the trouble with an especially favoured place, to which one had brought all those whom one had loved most dearly in the vigour of one's youth or the sturdiness of middle age; to come back alone as an old man gave rise to too many melancholy comparisons between then and now, and too many evocations of blissful hours with certain people one would never see again. He confessed to Hutton that he was, "as a matter of fact, rather sad ... I find that the older I get, the more I dislike my own society". He hung on at Sant' Agata all through July, knowing that he could not bear to stay any longer than necessary, but not knowing where to go next.

David Jeffreys had a small place at Positano which he used for his weekends; and Douglas spent two weekends there with him during July; and managed to fix up with a café there to take a room which he kept all through August and September. He was waiting until Capri, which was crammed with people, should be less crowded in October or thereabouts, when accommodation there would be less expensive.

A visitor to Positano in August was Emilio, whom Douglas had seen earlier for half an hour by arrangement when his train stopped at Florence. He came down for ten days of his fortnight's holiday "which he fully deserves, having had none for 5 years". Douglas understood that he would be able to get his flat back in November.

In September he visited Capri for five days, and in October migrated there from Positano. He hoped that he would be able to find somewhere of his own to live: he had already suggested to Kenneth Macpherson, with whom he was again in regular correspondence, that they might share a place on the island. "I have been kicked about Europe long enough," he wrote, and he was determined to end his days on Capri. The trouble was, of course, that he could not afford to buy anything until he had sold his flat in Florence; and he could not sell the flat until it had been repaired and redecorated; and it could not be repaired and redecorated until the tenants had been got out; and now they were actually refusing to get out, and so far Carrozza had been unable to find any way round the problem. "It may and probably will entail a lawsuit lasting over several months, owing to some mistake on the part of the English in drafting the Official Decree." He even went up to Rome at the end of October to see if the Embassy could help; but they couldn't.

It was Edwin Cerio who came to his rescue. He lent him one of his properties, a tiny house in Unghia Marina, looking out over the Certosa towards Monte Solaro. It was through Edwin Cerio, also, in his capacity as *sindaco*, that a signal honour was conferred on Douglas: he was made an honorary citizen of Capri – the only Englishman ever to have been elected to this brotherhood, and a distinction which he shared at the time with a world-famous Italian, Benedetto Croce. Douglas first occupied No. 7 Unghia Marina on 14th November. "The Piazza is about 10 minutes away, and I have the same cook I had 43 years ago, in 1903, and . . . shall be having a little Neapolitan boy of 10 to help and run messages." He was settling in, and seemed happy. And no doubt he was happy – in some respects. It was satisfying to have attained one's objective at last: to be settled in a place on Capri on one's own, even if not *of* one's own, and to have been so honoured by the Capresi. But how long could he afford to stay on the island? How was he, with his tiny fixed income, to overcome the post-war inflation of prices?:

> Food is preposterously dear, all black market, and people in Naples are literally starving. This makes me think that I should like to get in touch with an American firm which can send me monthly parcels here, but on a *business* basis. I could not pay in dollars, but I could let them have a cheque on my London bank. I don't want any jam or honey or marmalade or sweets or chocolates or fish, but such things as bacon, ham, smoked sausages, potted and tinned meat, ox tongues, coffee, sugar, butter. All these things are either unobtainable here or pre-posterously dear, and the situation gets worse every day . . .
>
> It is damnable, having to take such account of money at my time of life . . . I wonder why some US millionaire, or a collection of them, do not send me a small contribution of, say, £1500, to ease the burden of my last years, and this not as an act of charity, but as a sign of appreci-ation for what I have done in the way of increasing the gaiety of nations in America by *South Wind*; in fact, something ought to be done on the lines of what I write on p. 62–64 of *Late Harvest*, which I hope you have received by now. The right kind of millionaires are not as common as they ought to be, and yet they must be there, if one could put one's hand on them. Anyhow, I am living above my income, and that can't go on for ever! Quite damnable – a grey prospect.

This was written to Robin who – it was at any rate possible – might just be in a position to help, one way or another; and was, as a matter of fact, trying to help at this very moment by getting *An Almanac* accepted for publication in the USA. (This project did not succeed.) He also kept Robin informed – as formerly he had only done with Archie – about his affairs: gave him Emilio's address, and the addresses of his London bank, his accountant, and details concerning his flat in Florence. He had had lately he wrote, "several reminders that I am mortal", and wanted to keep in closer touch with Robin since Archie was no longer immediately available – he had seen his wife and children off to America, and then he had flown to Kenya, whether actually to take up some prearranged job, or to look for work, Douglas did not know.

ii

Financially, his position was precarious. That was nothing new, of course: but since he was no longer as tough and energetic as he had been, it was disturbing and unsatisfactory. Also unsatisfactory was *Late Harvest*. It had been published in October, and Douglas did not like its appearance, describing it as a "miserable-looking thing, with tiny print and filthy paper". Typically, he made no allowance for the "authorised economy standard" laid down by the government for the duration of the paper shortage caused by the war. As such, it was a good deal handsomer than most of its kind, the print was perfectly legible, and the paper of rather better than average quality for the time. The chief reason for disappointment, no doubt was the gap between intention and result. *Late Harvest* had been envisaged as an anthology of extracts from his books, with comments. The comments first appeared in two numbers of *Life and Letters Today*, where under the title of each book may be seen an enumeration of the extracts proposed – 133 in all. This version has no introduction, and the comments on the seventeen books are shorter than in the published version. The original typescript is almost identical with this, and the extracts are not arranged "book by book, but in a carefully studied confusion, without headings of any kind; you slide from one topic to another as in the rarest and best kind of conversation. That is all, apart from the Index. No Appendixes."

Paper restrictions, uncertainty of production conditions and of sales, together with the fact that Douglas would rather have had the book out in some form than in none, resulted in a different kind of book. The comments on the books were enlarged, *Retrospective* was written as an introduction, and the appendixes – book reviews and *Summer Islands* – were included to make weight. *Late Harvest* would have been sufficiently fascinating without the appendixes, simply by contributing another series of chapters to an interrupted autobiography, made all the more absorbing by dealing in some detail with seventeen of his books.

Retrospective is a happy illustration of his ability to start anywhere and reach a desired subject in a charmingly discursive and apparently haphazard manner, as in conversation. Twenty years earlier to the day on which he sat down to write it, he had been in Syracuse, to write the Magnus pamphlet. Syracuse leads to the subject of Platen, who stayed (and died) there, and Platen, Douglas remembers, wrote the line "Alas, how have you spent your days!" which Douglas turns into a question and uses as a text: "*How* have you spent your days?" It is a variation of the question at the end of the introduction to *Alone*: "What did you do in the Great War, Grandpapa?" and of the statement of intention at the beginning of *Looking Back*: "The winter of my days has come . . . Now, if ever, is the time to take that promenade into the past and into regions which I shall never see again . . ." Re-visiting places is always, for him, a re-visiting of his own past; and here, while doing this vicariously through his own books, he concerns himself especially, if he feels like it, with each book's genesis and production, with its physical existence as an object. He takes the opportunity of correcting mistakes – information that he has subsequently discovered to be wrong, or literal mistakes of punctuation, and misprinted words. And, if he feels like it, he adds notes to help bring some of the information in his books up to date. He has a paternal concern for all his work and for its accuracy and presentation which, unlike most authors, he reveals quite openly to the reader. This is very engaging.

In the course of reminiscence, much more is added. The genesis or the writing of the books calls to mind people associated with them, and many fond moments with former close friends are re-lived – the Amitrano boy, Enrichetta, Prince Caracciolo, René, Havard Thomas. The book is filled with other characteristic and delightful digressions. One of these is the synopsis of a monograph on London's geology as observed largely in its artefacts – buildings, pavings, roadways, etc – which he thought he might have called "The Stones of London"; it is a subject so peculiarly Douglas' own that it is difficult to imagine anyone else succeeding in the project as Douglas probably would have. Other pleasures include a short diatribe against the word "but", a comparison between the act of writing and the act of bodily evacuation, an explanation of why boys in Italian cities were kept in short trousers as long as possible, and examples of the sort of letters – happy inventions, these – that authors ought to receive.

Written before the end of the war, the book is shot through with that particularly Douglasian brand of nostalgia for place and thing. It gives the book an extra dimension: published after the war, but still in its deep shadow the book appeared just at the right moment; it was an appetising reminder that life, which had seemed extinct, was full of its ancient promise and satisfactions, and was waiting, just waiting, to be lived again as it should be lived.

iii

This winter, in which he celebrated his seventy-eighth birthday, was an exceptionally cold one. It brought snow to Capri and the coldest winter Douglas had ever known there. The rooms in Unghia Marina were fitted with central heating; but solid fuel for the furnace was almost unobtainable, though he had been promised some. And as far as electric fires were concerned, the supply of electricity always failed when most needed. He therefore had to make do with "a prehistoric charcoal brazier; and would now be sitting on it, if I were not afraid of burning my trowsers". His rheumatism was constant, and, at its worst, crippling, so that he had to get himself shaved, and could not brush his hair without considerable pain and extreme difficulty.

He was living as quietly as possible – sitting tight, he would have called it – waiting not very hopefully for some solution to the business of living beyond his means. He could only afford to eat meat once a week, he wrote, and even living rent free, could not help spending at least thirty shillings a day. The Bank of England, he complained, had made him change his money – presumably the original lump sum he took with him, and possibly subsequent cheques drawn abroad on his London bank – at 900 lire to the pound. In March the official rate was 1200, and he could get 2000, he boasted, on the black market. So he both amused himself and at the same time recouped some of his losses by asking friends in England to send him pound notes, one or two at a time, in exchange for a cheque of ten or twenty pounds. It was a game he had always enjoyed, and one which now was more profitable than it had ever been. He did the same thing with Robin in America, though whether, or how, he made payment, is not clear. The dollar – or perhaps two or five-dollar – bills were referred to in Douglas' letters as "snapshots" ("snapshot No. 5 has just arrived"), a type of conspiratorial subterfuge from which he had always derived as much enjoyment as a schoolboy does from the use of code words and secret signs.

He was living as quietly as possible in another sense: avoiding the tiresome consequences of his fame, and particularly of the publicity which surrounded his return to Capri and his honorary citizenship:

> I live as quietly as possible. An Austrian Baron is giving a recital of Goethe – would I, as the only Englishman in Italy who understands Goethe – say a few words? Not likely! Buy a ticket at least? No fear! The local Dante society has a meeting, would I – as the only Englishman in Italy who understands Dante – say a few words? Declined with thanks. An ex-mayor of Capri is giving a lecture on my Italian books: would I mind saying a few words, or at least putting in an appearance? So sorry – can't be managed. And so on. Peace with or without honour, that's my ideal.

iv

Peace (not without honour) was, as a matter of fact, on the way, in spite of appearances to the contrary: for instance, no progress had been made, even as late as July, in obtaining vacant possession of the Florentine flat although the help of the Embassy had once again been sought, and a question had been asked by the Labour MP, Tom Driberg, in the House of Commons. But in April Kenneth Macpherson had arrived on Capri, determined to buy a villa in which Douglas as well as himself would be able to live. Furthermore, he had decided to take on Emilio (whom he had brought down from Florence for a visit to Douglas) as his personal servant; and by the middle of June had done so. By this time, also, he had found a suitable villa.

Meanwhile, the heat of midsummer was as unbearable in his two small rooms as the cold of midwinter, and towards the end of July, when his friend David Jeffreys was on holiday from the Consulate, the two went off together to Scanno for a week in Jeffreys' car. Douglas described Scanno as "perfectly awful in every way". No doubt it too, like Sant' Agata, had been ruined for Douglas by the advent of tourism in the ten years since he had last seen it – by tourism and the inevitable repercussions of fascism and war. So he was pleased enough to scuttle back to Capri (after a couple of days in Rome) with the prospect of getting into Kenneth Macpherson's villa within a week or two.

Moving in was a slow and tiresome business, but seems to have been accomplished by the end of August, though they were not really settled until the autumn. The Villa Tuoro – it had been called Olivella before Macpherson took it over – is situated higher up on Tuoro or Telegrafo hill. It too looked out over the Certosa, and embraced an even wider and more magnificent panorama than that of the little house in Unghia Marina. The Villa Tuoro was described by Nancy Cunard as

> elaborately beautiful as the result of perfect taste and lavish develop-
> ment of natural resources, its terraces embowered, its rooms ideally
> coloured and furnished, spacious and comfortable . . . An invisible spell
> might have been laid around it like a guard. I saw you there alone the
> first time, in the ravishing four rooms or so you had on the lower floor,
> quite separate from, yet part of the delectable villa. An ideal arrange-
> ment! Your own cook, your own establishment entirely; the enchant-
> ing company of Kenneth . . . above when so disposed. Long low rooms,
> shaded or light at will. Book-filled, everything in perfect order.

It was by any standards ideal, and for Douglas it was also a practical and supremely comfortable retreat from "the wearisome actualities of life", from having to cope, at the age of almost seventy-nine, with the exigencies of living beyond his income and trying, unaided, to stave off the invasive depredations of age. In his lifetime, Douglas had enjoyed many favours, and received many gifts; but no greater act of imaginative kindness and practical generosity had ever been conceived for him or bestowed upon him, so tactfully and graciously, as this one. He was not allowed to know, and was tacitly given every encouragement to smother any suspicion he may have had, that this villa had been bought for him rather than for anyone else. The playful and utopian benefits which he envisages for himself in *Late Harvest* (pp. 62–64) as a just reward for the pleasures he has given his readers, are mere pinchbeck beside the solid gold of Macpherson's actual gift.

Shortly before Douglas had started to live in the little house in Unghia Marina in the previous November, he had discovered in Naples a little urchin of ten whom he had set his heart upon seeing again. This he was able to arrange, and Ettore came to Unghia Marina to help Maria Grazia, Douglas' cook, and to run messages and make himself generally useful.

> When I found him in Naples he was a mere skeleton, and so pale that he seemed to be transparent, or at least translucent. I think three more months of that life would have done for him. The mother was in an air-raid shelter with him and the two smaller boys when their house was blitzed and they lost everything they possessed on earth. No compensation, of course! The father was then a prisoner in Germany and his job in Naples – electro-technician – had been given to some one else. He has now got a small one on the railway; not his line at all, but better than nothing. I have got Ettore into some kind of shape physically, but morally he is still rather dislocated and restless after two years' starvation on the streets of Naples. He goes to school now – for the first month or so he couldn't; in fact, I had some difficulty in making him eat – but he has a great deal to catch up.

Ettore, of whom much more was to be heard, moved with Douglas into the Villa Tuoro.

v

Not long after Douglas had moved into the Tuoro, he was visited by Robin, who flew over from the States and stayed on Capri for about a fortnight in September. They had not seen each other for fourteen years. The visit seems to have been successful from every point of view, and could be regarded as the culminating point of a reconciliation which had perhaps begun when Robin had made such efforts on his father's behalf when he was in Portugal. Douglas himself may have considered that Robin's wild oats had been sown and long left behind, that he had at last settled down to a responsible job, that he had apparently shown the best of his nature in his concern for Mrs E. and her son – they undoubtedly helped to bring Robin and his father closer together – and that he, Douglas, had been rather harder on Robin in the past than he need had been.

At about this time the flat in Florence at last became vacant, and Emilio went straight off to see about having it repaired and set in order so that it could be sold as soon as possible. Faith Mackenzie came on a short visit; also Willie and Viva King. In October Douglas set off with David Jeffreys in his car for a fortnight in Calabria. The mode of travel, apart from anything else, seems to have been too much for Douglas. "Calabria was a fearful hustle" he wrote, "up to 1500 *metres* and down to the sea all the time – food vile – two or three punctures every day." He complained that they had never slept twice at the same place and had covered too much ground too quickly.

Soon after their return, sixteen cases of books arrived, sent down from Florence by Emilio. Douglas had been unpacking books and tearing up *thousands* of letters, he told Robin, for the last week, and there was utter confusion everywhere. It was a good thing Kenneth Macpherson was away for a fortnight, and he was alone there with Ettore. But there was bad news too: "All my more valuable books about Italy have been stolen . . . Hundreds of English ones too! Also, the manuscripts which I left with Orioli for cataloguing (to be sold at Sotheby's) have disappeared: a loss of at least £400. Bloody." However, he still had a few manuscripts; should he send Robin a list of them, in case he could dispose of them? "Ten per cent for you." He also had twenty-six large boxes full of photographs – "family, Vorarlberg, Italy, etc." Would Robin like any?

Other treasures came back, if not in these cases, then with Emilio. One of these was a plaster cast of George Thomas' bust of Douglas, who was having a bronze made of it for Robin, and would send it to the USA when it was ready. The large yellow marble tortoise which Douglas had bought in 1902 from the antiquary at Pozzuoli; the lapis-lazuli dagger-hilt from Persia; and a good many other mementoes – had survived, largely owing to Emilio's care.

On 8th December he completed his seventy-ninth year, and entered his eightieth. The household celebrated with nine bottles of champagne. "I am slowly recovering," wrote Douglas two days later.

vi

Repairs and redecorations to the flat in Florence had cost over a million lire (about £850) and only one prospective purchaser had replied to the advertisements which Douglas had inserted in various papers; but she decided not to buy it. Douglas was afraid that the authorities would allocate it to a homeless family which he would never be able to dislodge, he wrote to Archie. He kept both Archie and Robin informed, as usual, of all such matters in which they would have an interest if he were to die suddenly, although, unlike many parents, he hardly ever explicitly mentioned this contingency. It may not have been much in his own mind; he

had always, all his life, liked to keep his house in order from day to day and
to let Archie, at least, know of his every move: that was all he was doing
now.

In February, Emilio, who had made himself responsible for delivering
Douglas' possessions from Florence and for seeing to any business there
connected with the flat, went up to Florence. Wanting to get back quickly,
and never having been in an aeroplane, he announced his intention of
flying back. Kenneth Macpherson advised him strongly against doing so
as there was apparently a high accident rate amongst the old war-torn
machines then in use . . . but when it came to the point, Emilio could not
resist the temptation. The plane crashed. Immediate survivors were taken
to hospital at Livorno, seriously injured. Within a day or two, it seemed
that Emilio had passed a crisis, and was out of danger; but two or three
days after that he died, quite suddenly, having been in a coma most of the
time.

Douglas supposed that Emilio's death had been due to shock and burns.
He referred to six days of "intense suffering" on Emilio's part. Nella and
Elena, his wife and daughter, had been at the hospital with him; Douglas
and Macpherson had planned to visit him there also, as soon as he had
sufficiently recovered. Kenneth Macpherson went to his funeral; Douglas
said he could not face "the journey". His emotions, as usual, were conveyed, if at all, obliquely: "Kenneth," he wrote three weeks later, "is
terribly upset – not to speak of myself, who brought him up"; but he went
so far as to admit that he missed Emilio dreadfully, and that there would
never be anybody who could replace him.

Douglas lent Nella and Elena his flat in Florence for three years, so that
they would not have to face the appalling emptiness of their own apartment. He felt it was the least he could do; and he would have been the first
to admit that it also suited him: if there were any danger of his being
obliged to have a tenant, at least his tenants would be friends, and utterly
reliable. But chiefly, it was, as he wrote to Archie, *unavoidable* – meaning,
most probably, that it was the only adequate gesture that could express the
depth of his feelings.

It was a bad time. Earlier in February, Ettore's mother had reclaimed her
son and "is putting him into some school. This is, for me, the most
severe blow I have had for ages." These words were written after Emilio's
death; but sometimes it is easier to accept an irreversible catastrophe than
one which can still, with improbable luck, a great deal of hard work, or the
expenditure of much nervous energy, be eventually opposed and neutral-
ised. Ettore was his only effective remedy against age and infirmity –
through him he could hold on to life – and he had no idea whether he
would ever see him again.

Not long after these misfortunes had occurred, Douglas made a new will. It was extremely simple:

> I leave all I possess to my two sons Archibald and Robin in equal parts, in the hope that they will be able to divide it equally amongst themselves in a friendly agreement.
> Each of these sons will receive from me a list, identical in every detail, of several of my friends and I request my sons to consign to these friends the things indicated in the above-mentioned list.

That was all. In this way, the reconciliation with Robin that had been taking place quietly during the past few years, was given legal recognition. Twenty years earlier, apparently, Archie had been the sole heir; and whatever the nature of the will Douglas made in 1944 the existence of which he was so careful to inform Archie about, he had not mentioned it at all to Robin, although writing to him on the same day as to Archie.

Work is as good a cure as any for bereavement, and Douglas fortunately had a project in hand. He had decided to enlarge his article on Milton and Salandra.[119] He had settled to this work during the winter, and by the beginning of May had a 13,000-word article ready. He decided to send it in the first instance to Harvard for possible inclusion in their Library Bulletin. In 1926 Harvard College Library had bought Orioli's copy of Salandra's *Adamo Caduto*, thought by Douglas and Orioli to be only the second copy in existence; and as Douglas had negotiated the sale on Orioli's behalf and there was a particular interest in the subject at Harvard, and the appeal of his article was largely an academic one, it seemed a good choice. The article was politely refused, for substantially sound reasons. It was then sent off to *Life and Letters*, whose editor was keen to print it (or anything else by Douglas) and appeared in the August number. But this last attempt by Douglas to call attention to Milton's indebtedness to Salandra – "as flagrant a case of plagiarism as can be found in the annals of literature" – was once again received without comment by the academic world.

Robin had planned a second visit to Capri soon after the conclusion of the first one, and in September he arrived. His friend Mrs E. and her son were still on Capri at the time, having arrived earlier. Robin had been apprehensive, in letters to his father, about such a meeting; but had been assured that it need never occur unless Robin wished. Mrs E., however, seems to have been reluctant to leave the island before seeing Robin – according to Douglas; but Douglas may have contrived the whole thing, in his or Robin's interests. He gave the impression later that all had gone well. Certainly, the boy and his mother left in a hurry, partly because Douglas himself, incorrigible as ever, had been unwise enough to show excessive affection for the boy.

Robin stayed about ten days. When he had returned to Chicago, there was a small traffic in photographs between him and his father. The series of forty-three that Kenneth Macpherson had commissioned, of Norman Douglas at all ages from infancy onwards, was sent to Robin (it was also sent to Archie and to a number of friends); and Robin sent his father copies of snapshots he had taken while on Capri. "Islay and Kenneth," wrote his father, "both want the one of David, and of me with the little boy. This last they *must not have*, as such things get shown around here and may well do me harm. Therefore will you please write to ME that you have mislaid that particular negative, but are looking for it. Meanwhile they will forget about it. Anyway, they must not have that photo."

But what possessed Douglas, in his continuation of this letter two days later, to write under the added date "Nov. 13th" – "Elsa's birthday"? In March, Robin had sent him a photograph of his mother, for which he had been thanked: "Many thanks for the photo of Elsa. Takes me into another world"; and a week after Elsa's birthday, he was writing to Archie

I have troubles of my own about which nobody knows anything, and beside which all other matters melt into *nothing*. My books, save one, are out of print, and there is no paper in England for reprinting – to the great loss of the publisher and myself. This year I have earned £40 (not yet paid) of which the Govt takes 50%. If I had stuck to the Dipl. Service I should certainly have become an Ambassador and be now living on a pension of at least £5000 a year.

And if you had stuck to any of your jobs in Freudenstadt or Paris or Rome or Prague or Red Sea, you would certainly be much better off than you are.

And if my aunt had wheels, she would *probably* be a motor-bus.

As to black thoughts – to Hell with them.

What these troubles were, as to which everything else was as nothing can only be imagined, and can not be imagined with much hope of accuracy since there are so many possibilities to choose from; but an interesting light is cast on this problem by the unprecedented references to Elsa and by an incident that occurred at the end of this year or the beginning of the next. Constantine FitzGibbon and his wife had arrived from Bermuda to stay on Capri, and presently FitzGibbon began his daily talks with Douglas as preparation for writing a biography. One day FitzGibbon asked him if he had a photograph of Elsa. "No!" snapped Douglas instantly, "I destroyed them all – naturally!" But a few days later he produced one –

Robin's? – which he said he had found "quite by accident". This year, incidentally, was the fiftieth anniversary of his marriage; in November and December he had been settling with his young bride in the Villa Maya, in preparation for the birth of Archie. At that time, also, he was still *en disponibilité* and had the option of returning to the Diplomatic Service in an active capacity.

viii

Physically, as he knew, he was very slowly deteriorating, and was determined to make the pace even slower if he could manage to do so without unbearable deprivations. He was under constant treatment: medicines, injections, dieting, various daily timetables, were all tried out willingly by Douglas. He gave them what was probably a fair trial, although his expectations of success were never high, and he enjoyed an occasional and perhaps rather too frequent truancy from his régimes. "*Culatello's* verboten but I'll filch a slice of yours" he said at table to Harold Acton; and his *Dottoressa*[120] having on one occasion made a list of forbidden drinks which she thought was exhaustive, discovered at a later visit that he had been indulging mildly but more than was good for him in rum, which she had forgotten to put on the list. As ever, he enjoyed little teases of this kind, and if, fundamentally, he was teasing himself rather than his doctor, it was because he was ninety per cent certain he was past curing and might as well enjoy himself. He seems to have struck a happy bargain between too much self-denial and too much self-indulgence. His giddiness, which had accompanied him for thirteen years almost constantly except when he was sitting or lying down, persisted; his rheumatism persisted more or less unchanged; his hands became very slowly more troublesome, due to lack of blood in a relevant part of the brain, according to a Neapolitan nerve specialist; and his legs now intermittently felt weak. But he still walked out regularly at his own pace to the Piazza, where he would sit at regular hours of the day at the Café Vittoria, looking over the Bay of Naples – walking always with a stick, and leaning sometimes on some obliging child; and "crawled", as he put it, up to Pepinella's cavern near the Arco Naturale.

If he had no illusions about his health, he had none either – at any rate at this time – about his companions: "I am surrounded by dear friends," he wrote to Archie, "and, from that point of view, could not be better off. I hope you will thank Kenneth, in the event of my evaporating. Try not to forget this."

Archie and his family, in Bermuda, were not so happily situated. Apart from being dogged by ill-health, they were beset by money troubles.

Douglas heard indirectly, through FitzGibbon and a correspondent of his
in Bermuda, that Archie and his family were almost on the verge of starvation. He immediately wired his bank to send them £100; and later in the
year, supplied them with more money. Archie had been put in a difficult
position by the devaluation of the pound and by troubles of a bureaucratic
nature concerned with getting permission to stay on and work in Bermuda.
Douglas enlisted the help of friends, who wrote to people of influence.
Archie succeeded in getting another job. He hoped he might get further
help from his father, for a passage to Europe. His father wrote that he
could do no more. It was probably true, for he said he had sent Archie a
total of £350 that year, and Robin £150; and his income, he said, was £512
"So you can calculate how much is left for me". He had, as a matter of
fact, a few other resources, but very small ones.

The money for Robin was probably sent partly as a contribution towards
the cost of his flying over again for a visit. As in the previous year, this
visit took place in September, but was a double one, as Robin was joined by
his daughter Heather from South Africa, who at this time was about
twenty-five. Rooms were found for them in the same hotel and they saw a
good deal of each other; but they did not see much of Norman Douglas,
who afterwards apologised:

> I was very sorry to have seen so little of you two, but I am not myself
> any more; never feel *well* at any moment of the day, and your doctor will
> tell you all about cerebral arteriosclerosis, which is slowly but surely
> polishing me off.

Lots of love N

Robin appears to have been upset on another account, so that his father
felt constrained to excuse himself on a second occasion, about a fortnight
after the first: "I am very sorry about Ettore, who could easily have come
at any other time. He was anxious to see you as he said you had been so
nice to him in Naples. I also thought you would like to meet him again.
You wrote not long ago . . . as if you cared about him. Well, that's
that."

As to Robin's further plans, they were a matter of choice: "A good idea,
to have Heather as housekeeper, if you like that sort of thing. For my part,
I could not endure it for long; I have had my dose of being cared for and
mothered; I would sooner die like a rat in my hole."

Given a "hole" such as he had at that time, even Robin might have
agreed with him . . .

Ettore was doing well. His people had come over to Capri in January
and told Douglas that he had grown tall and put on flesh, that now he was
never ill, and liked his school very much. In April he came over himself

during the Easter holiday; and in July, Douglas persuaded his mother to take her annual seaside holiday with Ettore and the two younger boys on Ischia while he was there himself.

ix

At the beginning of the year there were already three film companies at work on Capri which, as Douglas wrote, was "in danger of developing into a second Hollywood". One of these companies – the Italian Lux Films – was intending to film *South Wind*, and Douglas had already signed a preliminary contract with them. Graham Greene was to write the script, and for convenience came over to the island and bought Rosaio, that charming little house in Anacapri which Cerio, Compton Mackenzie and Francis Brett-Young had all lived and worked in. Douglas sometimes went up there for consultations, grumbling that the visit to Graham Greene "ruins my whole morning" and that this "damned film business is going to give me lots of trouble". Towards the end of February he said he had heard that they had actually begun filming; but by May there was a hitch in the proceedings, "and I may not get my money after all"; by November the film was "off".

Towards the end of January he wrote that he had finished his *Footnote on Capri*, an essay of about 10,000 words outlining the history of the island. "Not long ago I thought to have closed my little writing-shop for good and all. A glance at these admirable photographs has made me change my mind." The photographs, about three score of them (of which forty-eight appeared in the book when it was eventually published) had been taken by Islay Lyons. They illustrate the whole visible face of Capri in every aspect and at every focal range that the eye would naturally accommodate to, and are a true *revelation* of the island, serenely balanced between the wildly romantic and the solidly actual, between the baroque and the organically functional. The main subject is the island as an environment of human beings; and as with all photographs of this type that arrest the attention they add much to one's own experience. Sights that one has seen a hundred times are suddenly seen once and for all better than ever before. They are guaranteed to make anyone who has been to Capri, long to return.

Douglas' essay is an editorial feat that would have done credit to someone twenty years younger. It is a condensation of the historical parts of his *Capri Materials*, in which, if there is nothing new, there is at least no loss of clarity, incisiveness, and urbanity. There is, in fact, something new as well – the Postscript:

> At this moment Capri is in danger of developing into a second Hollywood, and that, it seems, is precisely what it aspires to become.

The island is too small to endure all these outrages without loss of dignity – the pest of so-called musicians who deafen one's ears in every restaurant, roads blocked up by lorries and cars, steamers and motorboats disgorging a rabble of flashy trippers at every hour of the day.

A final word as to these "latest arrivals". The men will pass; they are a less vulgar crowd than their English representatives in North Wales. In regard to the women, one must be prepared for surprises, since they often clothe themselves in costumes, or in lack of costumes, which leave little to the imagination. Is it not the general experience of mankind that the less one sees, the more one desires to see; in other words, that curiosity in matters of sex is a characteristic of normal humanity? Such curiosity can easily be satisfied hereabouts. There is small scope for what Goethe called "the seeing hand and the feeling eye", inasmuch as these mysteries of the flesh are presented to us, so to speak, on a plate.

Juan-les-Pins must look to its laurels.

Now Capri is not the place for moralising, and even old-fashioned folk like myself will sooner or later be driven to confess that living human thighs and arms and breasts and backs, not to mention certain voluptuous posteriors which would do credit to a Hottentot Venus, are a surprising and delectable sight and one that may presently – who knows? – eclipse the fame of mere terrestrial objects like the Blue Grotto.

This is interesting: the last paragraph seems to be more like an afterthought, a concession to what might be expected of him, rather than his own convinced opinion, which would seem to be better represented by the second paragraph. This whole Postscript suggests that Douglas, who has been called a forerunner of the permissive society, would not have thought that society preferable to those in which he himself had lived.

Footnote on Capri was not published until May 1952. Douglas was too ill to correct the proofs, and never saw the book itself. Perhaps it was just as well. The splendid photographs, which ought never to have been reproduced in a size smaller than quarto became nearly, as Kenneth Macpherson complained, "some wretched glossy smears which invalidated the very *raison d'être* of a delightful essay".

x

Early in March Archie announced his intention of bringing his family over to Capri in May with the idea, apparently untested against the practical possibilities, of getting a job in Italy.

This, alas, is just what his aged parent did not want. He had nothing against Archie – on the contrary – and nothing against Archie's family; in fact, even in his present state of fairly advanced physical decay, he would probably have enjoyed his grandchildren; but he did not want – never in his life had wanted – to live permanently too close to anybody, especially family. With Kenneth Macpherson and Islay Lyons it was all right, because they were uncommonly sensitive and tactful and he was under no pressure from them; they anticipated his needs and moods and an atmosphere of independence was preserved on both sides. Archie was different. If he were to come he would try to stay for at least the rest of his father's life, and perhaps try to stay for the rest of Kenneth Macpherson's; and it would be extremely difficult to make clear to a man with a dependent family whom in addition one loved and felt responsible for to at least some extent, that he must clear out. Furthermore, Kenneth could not stand children. Finally, there was absolutely no means of Archie's earning a living on the island (and not much likelihood of his getting a job in Italy at all) and he had no money to live on even for a short time. His father could not afford to support him, and was unwilling to be placed in a situation in which Kenneth, who had done so much for him, might feel that he should offer to help Archie as well. There was only one thing for it: he must put Archie off as firmly as possible:

Capri

11 Mar 1950

My dear Archie

Got yours of 1st and 4th.

Enclosed notes from Kenneth and David [Jeffreys]. The latter says it would be hopeless for you to try to get any kind of job in Italy. He says Canada or Jamaica or England.

Prices are very high here. Capri is considered the dearest place in Italy; and almost double charges for almost everything on account of "Holy Year".

With the £st at 1650 instead of 2200 you will see that it is now impossible for me to give or lend money, however little.

I am a *guest* here. Robin was grieved last year that "he did not see enough of me", but I cannot ask people to come to Kenneth's house unless they come at *his* invitation. And I myself am too ill to run after them; injections *etc* every day, and I can't make appointments with anybody because I never know how I may be feeling. Among other things, I have been expressly forbidden by the Dr to bother about anything. I have to be left undisturbed.

Things would have been very different a year or so ago.

Can't write more. I should hesitate about coming to Italy, *if* you expect to get a job there. David was most emphatic.

Much love to Marion and the children

always

Fa

If, in spite of this, Archie should decide to come over with his family, they would "have to fend ENTIRELY for themselves" his father wrote. "I am not going to move a finger, and for more than one reason, the simplest being that I CAN'T, being far too ill. He seems to think I am about 50."

The letter to Archie, though not very strongly worded, turned out to be a real stopper; his father did not hear from him again for more than six months.

xi

He had two holidays this year. One was a quick tour through Siren Land, staying one night at Sant' Agata and two at Amalfi. The second little trip was to Ischia, in the middle of June, for three weeks. The pretext was to take the baths; but it was undoubtedly partly in order to share the holiday with Ettore and his mother. His passion for Ettore was not shared by many – if any – of his friends, some of whom were becoming increasingly embarrassed by what they often thought was the foolishness with which he seemed to allow himself to be exploited by both mother and son. One close friend of Douglas' said later quite frankly and spontaneously when the boy's name was mentioned: "Ettore was a little tart", and whether or not the judgment is fair, it is one that several shared, and for which there seemed to be good evidence. Douglas became more and more dependent upon the boy's affection and presence; and in order to persuade him to come over, apparently had to send him more and more money, or provide him with increasingly expensive gifts. One of Ettore's parents, or perhaps both, may have exploited the situation, even to danger point. Blackmail was mentioned by several of Douglas' friends. One, who was in a position to intervene with the police on Douglas' behalf, asserted that Douglas was in danger of arrest by the local police, who were quite ready to believe whatever charges may have been made. Out of his limited income, Douglas lavished a good deal on Ettore and his family – sums, for instance, that would have made Archie's life very much more comfortable than it was at that time. When other forms of self-indulgence had had to be drastically curtailed, this affair with Ettore seems to have been an outlet that was pursued *à la folie*, as occasionally happens when the old are ensnared in a late skirmish with love. Their friends can only stand aghast, or amazed. The fact usually forgotten by the onlookers is that the so-called victims do not mind whether they are being exploited or not; they only wish to go on feeling the compulsion of love, whether it be physical, or sentimental. In the three years between March 1948 and March 1951 Douglas sent more than £400 by post to Ettore's mother, quite apart from money he may have given her when they met.

xii

At the beginning of September he wrote to Robin that Kenneth Macpherson and Islay Lyons would be going to England on the 12th for "two weeks" which he thought would turn into a month. They were going to shut up the house, and he would have to move out of it which would be "*a great hardship*" for him.

He was right about the length of time they were away. He stayed in the Hotel Manfredi Pagano, and during this period enjoyed a visit from Mrs E. and her son which he had partly subsidised.

Macpherson shutting up the house, and Douglas moving out! It didn't take Capri long to fit these facts together. Macpherson and Douglas had quarrelled – obviously! Those two had got tired of the old man, sick to death of him and his little friend . . . within a week the problem was being discussed in England and, apparently, in America, since Douglas heard about the business in a letter from Robin. A week after Macpherson had returned, and Douglas was once again installed in the Villa Tuoro, he replied to Robin: "Kenneth had told me yesterday about that ridiculous nonsense. You may not want to tell me who started it, but I hope you will have the grit to send him, or her, the enclosed *billet doux* from Kenneth & myself. Enough!"

The *billet doux*, written on Villa Tuoro letterheaded paper, and dated 23rd October 1950, was signed by both Kenneth Macpherson and Norman Douglas. It was brief and businesslike:

Dear Sir (or Madam)
    We would be much obliged if, on future occasions, you would be kind enough to stuff your incorrect information up your fucking arse.

Robin apparently had photostats made, and perhaps distributed them to suspected sources of gossip.

In November Douglas contracted erysipelas to add to the list of maladies from which he was already suffering. The Dottoressa came to lunch every Friday now, inventing "a new treatment every week. Like a positive sports' committee, my de-aw. Doesn't believe them any more than I do. What's more, she knows that I know, do you see. Full of invention, I must say. Thinks up more cures than a pharmaceutical encyclopaedia. Can't think where she finds 'em." He enjoyed what he called "their little game" with the Dottoressa, and loved the opportunity it gave him to talk German.

He was now definitely an invalid, he wrote in February, but was "still crawling about". He kept on offering money to Robin who had had some kind of accident, and pressed £100 on him whether he needed it or not, since he felt that he would soon have no more use for money. He seems to have written mostly to Robin because Robin wrote to him, and because Robin visited him and was familiar with the people and some of the details of his daily life. He thought perhaps Archie was not quite as badly off as he made out; but he begged Robin in several successive letters to "keep up with Archie, who is probably not having a good time of it". Helping him was now beyond Douglas' ability, he complained: he was too damned ill and the rate of exchange was against him helping financially, and altogether he was "getting decidedly sick of everything". He liked, he wrote, to think of Robin keeping up some kind of correspondence with Archie.

Eric and his wife came to Capri for nearly three weeks in July; also Elizabeth David; and Ettore, for longer or shorter stays. Robin, who had not come the previous year, came in September, after Douglas had spent three days at Sant' Agata. Robin had been instructed to bring with him – on no account to send through the post, or Douglas would never get it – a drug, a pain-killer, which he had managed to obtain from his dentist. "If you can't get 50 grains, get 30"; but "it must be reliable, in *my* sense of the word" and Robin must be quite sure that it was "the real thing".

Robin was not allowed to come without a score of instructions and preparations being made or laid out for him: where he had better stay in Rome, how he would find a telegram there already written and ready to send to Ettore, who would meet him at Naples station, where he had better dine in Rome, how he was to be sure to lock his baggage and if he hired a porter, how he was to make sure that the man walked *in front of him* so that he could not suddenly disappear with Robin's suitcase, etc. etc. The cornucopia of concern for every stage and every detail of Robin's journey once he had alighted from his plane was poured out to the last drop. Yet every line Douglas wrote cost him infinite trouble now owing to his recalcitrant hand, and owing to the effort of will needed to bother at all about writing, about anything. His letters to all other correspondents – Ettore and his mother excepted – became fewer and fewer and shorter and shorter, although all his older-established friends received something from him in these latter years: Auntie, who had returned to Vence; Hutton; Dawkins, who was himself, like Auntie, intermittently ill; Mavrogordato; Faith Mackenzie; Nancy Cunard; Bryher.

Those who could, came to see him, as Eric had done – Eric, whom he had known for more than forty-two years and who, when all was said and done, had been the most successful of his adopted children; and Harold Acton, in whose life Douglas had played a decisive rôle by advising him at a moment of doubt when he was young, to go to the East, where he had found himself and had consequently been evermore grateful to Douglas:

> Laboriously we set off together from the Villa Tuoro, Norman, Ettore and I; and Norman's step became lighter when we reached La Pica's restaurant. His exuberance returned as soon as we were seated: he offered the traditional pinches of snuff and cracked salty jokes with the waiter. . . . The meal was punctuated with bursts of laughter and arteriosclerosis was sent to blazes. By the time we reached the funicular Norman was almost buoyant. In the mouldy café facing Naples he off-ered me another drink "for the road" – in this case the sea, which he dis-liked. Ettore pressed on me a shiny tin cigarette-case "come ricordo dell'amico di Signor Duglass". As I hesitated to accept a gift more valuable to him than to me, Norman said: "Don't refuse it. Ettore likes nothing better than giving presents." Not to be outdone by his junior, he slipped into my pocket the reprint of an article he had written ages ago about the blue Faraglione lizard. I invited him to visit me on the mainland, to sustain the illusion that he was neither old nor infirm. "My travelling days are over," he repeated. "I shall not leave Capri again."
> This was my last sight of the rugged old stalwart, bidding us farewell from the top of the funicular. It was as if he had turned into a statue of one of the immortals. Standing there in his loose overcoat and shabby beret, he had the elegance of a Scottish Jacobite in exile. He was the most sanguine of the octogenarians I knew: his physique, like his intellect, belonged to the eighteenth rather than to the twentieth century.[121]

In that same month of September "the rugged old stalwart" was, surprisingly, once more at work. On the 8th, he sent off a signed contract to Heinemann for the publication of *Venus in the Kitchen*. As a manuscript it had had a long and chequered career. Now, thanks to the agency of Graham Greene, who wrote the introduction for it, it was at last going to be published, and there was a job to be done, if it was only one of assembly:

> One remembers him . . . handling the typescript of this book, re-sorting the loose carbon pages: there wasn't enough room on the café table what with the drinks, the old blue beret, the snuff-box, the fair copy; the wind would keep on picking up a flimsy carbon leaf and shift-ing it out of place, but the old ruler was back at the old game of ruling

. . . With a certain fuss of pleasure and a great tacit pride he was handling a new book of his own again.

In November he developed erysipelas again. This was cured; but then he got what the Dottoressa described as "a sort of consumption of the skin". He "became very emaciated, and felt the cold terribly. He had from the consumption of the skin a terrible itching. He was a marvellous patient, never bad-tempered with others, only with the disease. His last three months were very painful and miserable. He wanted to die."

I am in a pretty damned bad way. Ettore still here. The others came back 2–3 days ago. Will try to write again. Love, and thinking of you.
I am in a bad way. Your dentist consoles me.
Things are *no better*, and I don't know about holding on much longer. Enclosed from Ettore. Don't forget him.

Such were the bulletins – each almost a complete letter – which he sent to Robin in the month between 9th December and 9th January. On 10th January, with typical conscientiousness, he reported a change: "Dr reports slight improvement (My letter of 2 days ago)" and on January 23rd he wrote to both sons: "My letter of two days ago. Dr reports good progress. Lots of love." This was in sharp contrast to a note he had written to Archie two days previously, on January 21st: "I am in a bad way, and don't expect to live much longer. Thinking of you! Love to all. Fa." The reason for this discrepancy will become apparent.

He was bedridden at the end; and there were three versions of his last words. One asserted that the last person he spoke to was his laundry-woman; she had charged him for eight instead of nine shirts, and he told her she must correct the mistake as he might die in the night – and that night he did die. The other versions were more intimate: "His last coherent words to me before the end" wrote Kenneth Macpherson, "were in his room, after dinner, which he had eaten in bed – 'Well, ta-ta, dearie. God be with you. *You* take him. *I* don't want him'." He was said also to have murmured the word "Love" three times.

Such were the accounts of his death published or told by word of mouth at the time, versions that faithfully observed Douglas' request that the truth be withheld "for the sake of the reputation of Capri". As a quarter of a century has now passed since that request was made, and not even the most ardent Christian on the island will wish to deprive the author of it of his honorary citizenship or his true worth as a human being because he sought to take his own life after a good many weeks of considerable suffering, the truth may be told surely without offence to anyone and, at this late date, surely without betrayal of Douglas himself.

On 21st January, while Kenneth Macpherson and Islay Lyons were away for a few days in Anticoli, Douglas wrote the following note:

Monday
21 Jan 1952

Dearest K

Can't stand this damned nonsense any longer.
Can't even wait for you!
Suffering day and night and a trouble to others.
50 grains of luminal should do the trick.
Please make sure that I am definitely dead, and if possible make out heart-trouble as the cause, for the sake of the reputation of Capri.
Ettore has my keys

Vale!
N

"As I recall," writes Islay Lyons, "but neither Kenneth's nor my sketchy diaries relate, we returned to Capri on Jan. 21st, thereby presumably causing Norman to postpone his decision." (The note announcing this decision was not found until after Douglas' death, lying on his desk.) Once his friends were back, Douglas seems to have found the strength of will, with the reassurance of their companionship, to put up with his bodily condition for two more weeks. "On the night of Feb. 5th," continues Islay Lyons,

after Kenneth and I had gone downstairs to say goodnight to him (the usual formula: "God be with you, my dears. You keep the old bugger. I shan't need him!"), Norman called me back and asked me to bring to his bedside the locked suitcase he kept under the spare bed in his adjoining sitting-room. I knew it also contained his pills and my offer to unlock it for him and take out whatever he wanted was dismissed with a robust chuckle. The next morning he was in coma, there were two more or less empty glass pill-bottles on the bed-table and a great number of small white pills scattered on the carpet. The Dottoressa and the German Sisters attempted resuscitation all that day and the following night. Norman winced and groaned but it was impossible to decipher what he was trying to say. "Get those fucking nuns away from me," seemed a fair guess. Medication was suspended on the Thursday morning and he died that night.

As to Kenneth Macpherson's interpretation of Douglas's last words as being "love, love, love", there may have been a quite natural tendency on such an occasion to hear what one wanted to hear. As written, the phrase sounds a shade too deliberate; perhaps it is best elucidated by Islay Lyons:

"I can only say that those last sounds, the morning before he died, did seem to be a repeated attempt to formulate the word 'love', perhaps as in the phrase 'love to so-and-so'."

He died in fact about 11 p.m. on Thursday 7th February, but to have recorded this officially would have meant having the funeral on Saturday. In order to gain a day, death was registered as having taken place shortly after midnight, early on Friday 8th February. Thus he made his exit, as he had made his entrance – and as he had conducted much of his life – in defiance of law, slipping into and out of life in the hours between the days as slyly and deftly as he ever "evaporated" around a street corner or away from stuffiness and pomposity, solemnity, humbug, or the sheer boredom of doing something he did not wholeheartedly approve of or enjoy.

Don Bernardo = Don Mauro Iguanez; Salonia = Walter Salomone; Gabriel
Mazzaiba = Michael Borg; Pancrazio Melenga = Pancrazio Cipolla.

90 See letters to Archie of 19th and 25th May; 7th and 27th June; 21st July;
14th August; 6th and 27th September; 7th, 10th, 22nd and 30th October;
4th November (Yale).

91 "Elegy" (on D. H. Lawrence), an eleven-page memoir in *The New Adelphi*
III (June-August 1930).

92 Bryher (b. 1894) married Robert McAlmon 1921, marriage dissolved 1926;
and secondly, Kenneth Macpherson 1927, marriage dissolved 1947. See her
autobiography, *The Heart to Artemis* (London, 1963).

93 Malwida von Meysenbug (1816–1903), German-French metaphysical
idealist and revolutionary fellow-traveller, friend of Herzen, Mazzini,
Wagner, and others. See E. H. Carr's *Romantic Exiles* (London, 1933), pp.
144–53; 186–8; 200; 248–51; 271–4. See also Herzen's *Memoirs*; her own
memoirs; and *Alone*, pp. 124–129.

94 Mr P. G. (*Alone*, pp. 138–140) was Perceval Gibbon. See Note to p. 61.

95 "That Worcester affair": Robert had been accused of stealing.

96 Nancy Clara Cunard (1896–1965), daughter of Sir Bache and Lady Maud
Cunard. Her mother, known in her circle as Emerald, was an intimate
friend of George Moore and a patroness of Sir Thomas Beecham. Nancy
was a rebel against outmoded discipline and social conventions, but also,
after briefly kicking up a dust among "The Bright Young Things" of the
Twenties, found these pleasures unrewarding. She was in need of a Cause,
and found two: the Blacks, and the Spanish people. Poet, journalist, publisher and propagandist, she became an advocate of the Negro, producing
a vast anthology of that name in 1934. Her book *Grand Man* (London,
1954), is a glowing tribute to her friendship with Douglas. During and
after the Spanish Civil War she worked tirelessly as both a reporter
(*Manchester Guardian*) and organiser of aid for the Republican Government
and Spanish refugees. See Hugh Ford (ed), *Nancy Cunard: Brave Poet,
Indomitable Rebel* (1968); Daphne Fielding's *Emerald and Nancy* (London,
1968).

97 EMF to ND, 6th November 1923 (Yale). About half a dozen letters from
Forster to Douglas have survived. The earliest of these (10th November
1917) contains a typically gentle but firm criticism of the hedonistic aspects
of *South Wind*.

98 W. H. D. Rouse (1863–1950), apart from being a founding editor of the
Loeb Classics, editor of *The Classical Reveiw*, occasional editor of the Temple
Classics, and an authority on folklore, will always be remembered by
educationists as headmaster of The Perse School, Cambridge, where he
taught ancient languages by the direct method, and in other ways made the
school justly famous. ND, who knew and corresponded with him over a
long period of years, was fond of him.

99 Henry Major Tomlinson (1873–1958). Writer of travel books, novelist and
professional journalist. *The Sea and The Jungle* (1912), a description of a
journey up the Amazon, made his name, and *Mars his Idiot* (1935) summed

up his hatred of war. Wrote a short book on Douglas (1931) which was improved by the addition of a prefatorial word-portrait (1952).

100 "No intervening medium, no mirage, hovered between Lawrence and what his eyes beheld. These things lay before him clear-cut, in their primordial candour, devoid of any suggestion or association." *Looking Back*, p. 350.

101 Letters to Walter Lowenfels discussing this project, and covering the period May to December, 1927, will be found at Dartmouth College and the University of California at Los Angeles.

102 In spite of Virginia Woolf's favourable (but anonymous) review of *South Wind* in *The Times Literary Supplement*, Bloomsbury as a whole thought Douglas' work unworthy of serious consideration, although Carrington, Lytton Strachey's friend, was "a passionate admirer" of ND's work; she aroused his interest and persuaded him to write to ND. Strachey's sister, Dorothy Bussy, was also an admirer (see p. 430). For the development of the Strachey–Douglas friendship see Michael Holroyd's *Lytton Strachey, A Critical Biography*, vol. ii, pp. 561–565.

103 In an interview published in *Paris Review* 23, Spring 1960, p. 76. Nevertheless Huxley helped Douglas, as several other friends did, by sending him limericks.

104 There is an account of the circumstances following the publication of *The Last of the Medici* in Orioli's *Adventures of a Bookseller* (London, 1938), pp. 236–238. The English Government tried to get the former book suppressed, in Italy, but did not succeed.

105 Constantine FitzGibbon's *Norman Douglas, A Pictorial Record* (London, 1953), p. 33.

106 Kenneth Macpherson, among others, wrote that ND was a superstitious man who seemed to know and dread the supernatural, "and perhaps in his heart of hearts mightily feared God. On the nights of full moon, not only did he shutter the windows and pull the curtains, but kept a night-light burning; and, more than that, pronounced ominous warnings that one must *never* sleep with the full moon shining into one's room." (A revised but unpublished typescript, untitled, evoking ND's opinions from scattered book reviews and articles – p. 7; at Yale).

107 Harold Acton's *The Memoirs of an Aesthete* (London, 1948), p. 226.

108 Kenneth Macpherson, who died in 1971, succeeded William King as ND's literary executor. He contributed a sparkling word-portrait of ND in old age to Nancy Cunard's *Grand Man*, wrote a longer memoir *Omnes Eodem Cogimur* (1953), and also other articles and books.

109 This presumably refers to *Paneros* and the limited edition of *Summer Islands*, although the latter was published by Desmond Harmsworth; but it could refer to *Paneros* and *Capri Materials*. The limited edition and collector's market had been affected, like everything else, by the great economic depression of 1929–1930.

110 ND regarded suicide as a man's "inalienable right" (*How about Europe?*, 1941, p. 163) and there are several examples of his respecting that right. Edward Hutton, for instance, has told how Richard Aldington wrote to

him for aid towards the end of the First World War: if Hutton could not
help him to get out of the army, he wrote, he feared he would go mad or
put a revolver to his head. Douglas, told about this, said, "You write back
and tell him to get a decent *Colt* revolver. I don't trust those rotten little
pistols. Tell him that."

111 ND acknowledged this correction (without identifying it) in *Late Harvest*,
p. 49.

112 Oscar Levy (1867–1946) translator of Nietzsche. He and ND met at about
this time, and remained friends for life. The book that ND encouraged him
to write was the ineptly-titled *The Idiocy of Idealism* (London, 1940).

113 "Auntie" was the name by which Mrs Martha Harriet Gordon Crotch
(1879–1967) was known to her friends. She had a pottery-and-antiques
shop in Vence, above Nice, and was a well-known character on the Riviera
in the Twenties and Thirties. She was a friend of Frieda Lawrence, the
Ravaglis, of ND and Orioli, and Nancy Cunard, and others in literary,
expatriate, and bohemian circles. She was also a Christian pacifist and
friend of Emma Goldman, Alexander Berkman, Fenner Brockway and
Ethel Mannin. See *Some Letters of Pino Orioli to Mrs Gordon Crotch* (Edinburgh, Tragara Press, 1974). ND's letters to Auntie are at the University of
California at Los Angeles.

114 Ian Gordon Greenlees, OBE (b. 1913). Director of the British Institute in
Florence since 1968. Author of *Norman Douglas* in the "Writers and their
Work" series for the British Council (1957). Accompanied ND on a number
of walking tours.

115 Monypenny (see note 8) managed somehow to obtain information of this
affair, in spite of official secrecy, and these words from his manuscript
describe the conditions, as he heard of them, attached to Douglas' release.

116 Elizabeth David has subsequently become famous as the author of a select
collection of cookery books.

117 Alan Searle, Maugham's secretary, complained of similar cavalier treatment
on first meeting ND; and Maurice Richardson, who invited ND to lunch
in 1943 found that "by the end of the lunch N was enthusing about the smell
of children's armpits and I got faintly embarrassed".

118 *Some Comments on My Books*. These notes, the basis of what became *Late
Harvest*, were published in two succeeding numbers of *Life and Letters
Today*, December 1943, and January 1944.

119 See page 160, and note 45 to that page.

120 Dottoressa Moor, about seventeen years younger than Douglas, was one
of the first women to qualify as a doctor in Austria. She settled on Capri
after the First World War, and was much loved by the poor amongst
whom she chiefly worked. She was ND's doctor for the last two years of
his life. See her memoirs (ed. Graham Greene), *An Impossible Woman*
(London, 1975).

121 Harold Acton's *More Memoirs of an Aesthete* (London, 1970), pp. 331–3.

INDEX